DR JOHN FAHEY worked at Defence Signals Directorate (1988–1996) and served in a number of regimental and intelligence postings during his service in the British and Australian armies between 1975 and 2014. He is currently an Honorary Fellow of the Department of Security Studies and Criminology at Macquarie University, and managing director of Cynergex Group, a medical education and services company.

* * *

'The remarkable story of how, beginning at Federation, Australia developed its own foreign intelligence institutions. Based on thorough research, it is a comprehensive account that draws on the author's own deep understanding of how intelligence organisations should be run. It is also a warning tale that emphasises that Australia needs to put its own interests first, and that intelligence work requires hard-headed professionals, backed by an informed and responsible government. It fills a major gap in the history of Australian intelligence organisations.'

Professor David Horner, author of *The Spy Catchers:*
The Official History of ASIO 1949–1963

'Great intelligence is often shared by great story telling, and John Fahey shares a great story in *Australia's First Spies*. This book should be a foundational reference for every Indo-Pacific intelligence professional and historian. Just as great intelligence provides value by adding context to raw information, John Fahey adds context to events and brings to life many Australian trailblazers whose fiercely independent all-source intelligence operations established a culture of excellence that carries on today. I've benefitted from Australian intelligence in peace, crisis and combat . . . I now have a better understanding of the foundation that makes it so good.'

Rear Admiral Paul Becker, USN (Retired), Former Director for
Intelligence of the US Pacific Command and Joint Chiefs of Staff

A photograph of the first Japanese air raid on Australian-controlled territory, taken at lunchtime on 9 December 1941, the day after the attack on Pearl Harbor. The photograph was taken by Bridget Tothill from her home on Nauru.

JOHN FAHEY

AUSTRALIA'S FIRST SPIES

The remarkable story of Australia's
intelligence operations, 1901–45

ALLEN&UNWIN
SYDNEY•MELBOURNE•AUCKLAND•LONDON

First published in 2018

Copyright © John Fahey 2018

Allen & Unwin
83 Alexander Street
Crows Nest NSW 2065
Australia
Phone: (61 2) 8425 0100
Email: info@allenandunwin.com
Web: www.allenandunwin.com

A catalogue record for this
book is available from the
National Library of Australia

ISBN 978 1 76063 120 8

Maps by Keith Mitchell
Photograph on p. ii: Diary of Bridget Tothill, National Archives of Australia,
MP 1174/1, 1122.
Index by Garry Cousins
Set in 11/15 pt Minion by Midland Typesetters, Australia
Printed and bound in Australia by Griffin Press

10 9 8 7 6 5 4 3 2 1

The paper in this book is FSC® certified.
FSC® promotes environmentally responsible,
socially beneficial and economically viable
management of the world's forests.

'Never let any government imagine that it can choose perfectly safe courses; rather let it expect to have to take very doubtful ones, because it is found in ordinary affairs that one never seeks to avoid one trouble without running into another; but prudence consists in knowing how to distinguish the character of troubles; and for choice to take the lesser evil.'

Niccolò Machiavelli, *The Prince* (trans. 1908)

CONTENTS

LIST OF FIGURES

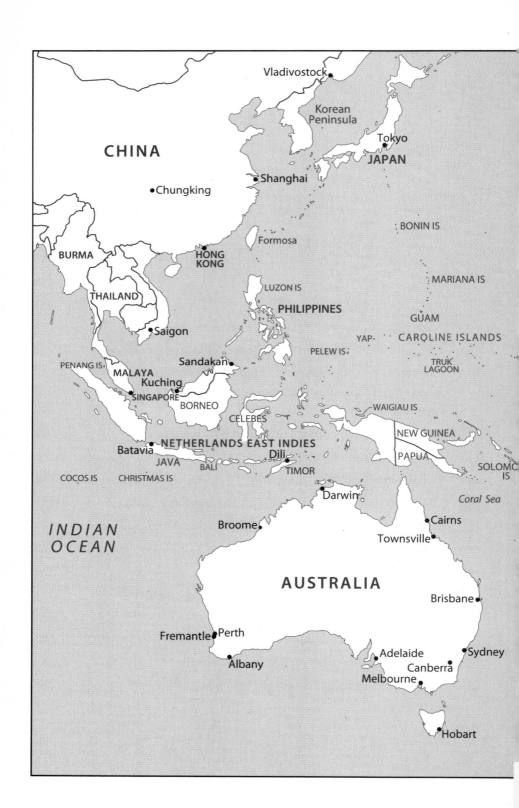

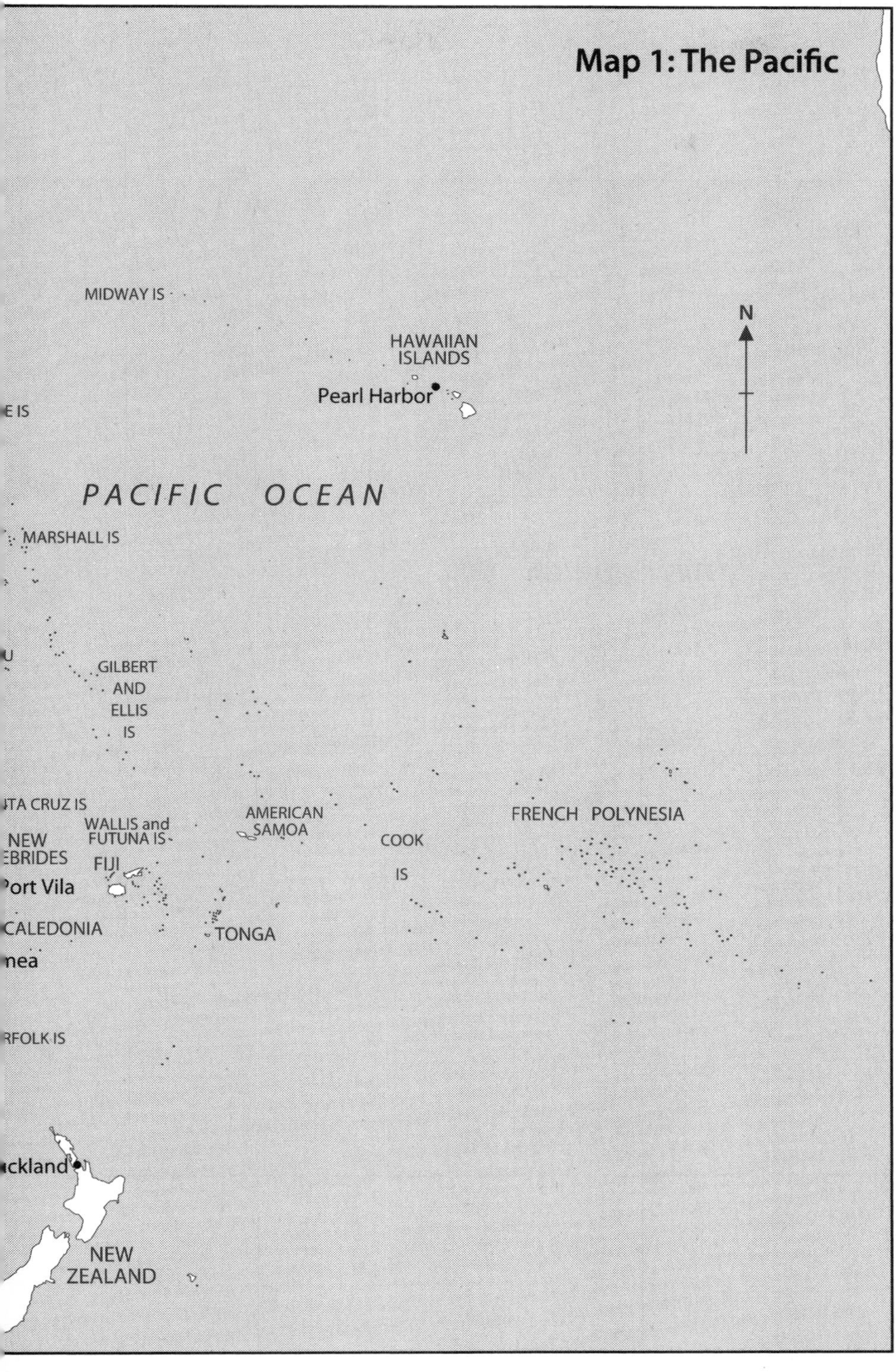

Map 1: The Pacific

N

MIDWAY IS

HAWAIIAN
ISLANDS

Pearl Harbor

E IS

PACIFIC OCEAN

MARSHALL IS

GILBERT
AND
ELLIS
IS

TA CRUZ IS

WALLIS and
FUTUNA IS

AMERICAN
SAMOA

FRENCH POLYNESIA

NEW
EBRIDES

FIJI

COOK
IS

ort Vila

CALEDONIA

nea

TONGA

RFOLK IS

ckland

NEW
ZEALAND

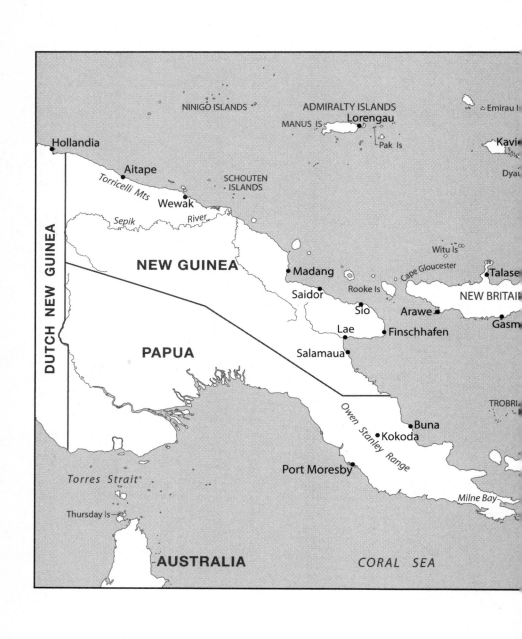

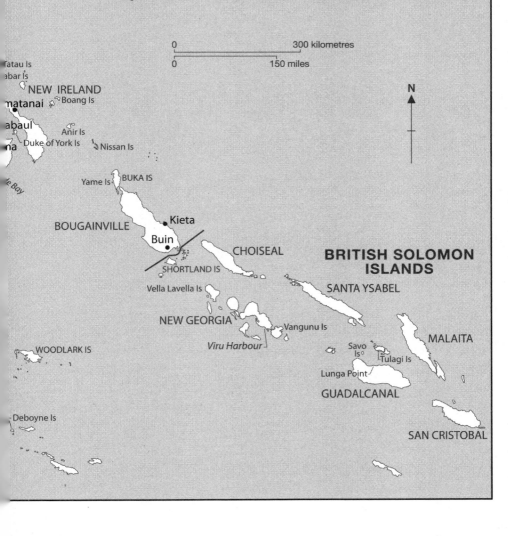

Map 2: New Guinea and the Solomon Islands

0   300 kilometres

0   150 miles

N

Tatau Is
abar Is
NEW IRELAND
matanai   Boang Is
abaul   Anir Is
na   Duke of York Is   Nissan Is
le Bay
Yame Is   BUKA IS

BOUGAINVILLE   Kieta
Buin
SHORTLAND IS   CHOISEAL   **BRITISH SOLOMON ISLANDS**
Vella Lavella Is   SANTA YSABEL

NEW GEORGIA   Vangunu Is   MALAITA
WOODLARK IS   *Viru Harbour*
Savo Is   Tulagi Is
Lunga Point
Deboyne Is   GUADALCANAL

SAN CRISTOBAL

PREFACE

The idea for this book arose out of a conversation with an old colleague, Captain Fred Smith, US Navy (retired), about the lack of good research on Australia's intelligence operations prior to the end of World War II. A British colleague who was present quipped that the proposed book would be the world's shortest. This challenge could not be overlooked, and so *Australia's First Spies* was born.

Australia's First Spies is the history of the practical steps Australia took to exercise control over its national interests immediately the nation was formed on 1 January 1901 until the end of 1945. The starting point of our story, 1 January 1901, is obvious because Australia was declared a unified nation on that day. What is not so well known is that the creation of the Commonwealth of Australia entailed the first ever transfer of responsibility for the management of foreign relationships from the Parliament of Westminster to another parliament of the Empire. Within a few months, Australia's government would take action to protect the country's interests by launching Australia's first ever clandestine intelligence operation against France and Britain in the New Hebrides.

There are four reasons for ending *Australia's First Spies* in 1945. The first is that the defeat of Japan in August 1945 marked the end of the first fundamental threat Australia had to fight off, and intelligence operations contributed to that victory. The second is that 1945 marked both a highpoint in Australia's intelligence capability and, with the onset of peace, the very real risk that Australian government complacency would lead to the destruction of the whole intelligence apparatus that had been so carefully nurtured since 1901. The third reason is that 1945 saw our enemy's enemy return to being our enemy and we now had to defend the nation from the machinations of the Soviet Union's hostile intelligence services. The final reason is more prosaic, in that in 1946 the first moves were made to create the Defence Signals Bureau, the predecessor of my old employer, Defence Signals Directorate, and the Australian Security Intelligence Organisation to protect it. My subsequent career in government allowed me a little access to some of this story and, as I promised never to reveal anything to which I had access, *Australia's First Spies* needs to end in 1945.

The purposes of this book are straightforward. The first purpose is to provide the specialist reader with a well-researched history of Australia's early intelligence operations and to, hopefully, provide the general reader with a readable book that tells the story of our nation's early intelligence operations. The second purpose is to show how the secret history of a country is a far more dependable indicator of what actually happened than all of the public pronouncements and posturing of politicians and appointed officials. *Australia's First Spies* is a book that pays less attention to what was said in favour of closely examining and describing what was done.

As such, *Australia's First Spies* challenges the idea that Australia's early governments sacrificed Australian self-interest in favour of Britain. As the reader will see below, the evidence clearly shows that Australia's governments looked first to protect Australia's national interests and only supported British self-interest when it coincided with Australia's self-interest. When Australia's self-interest was put at risk by British self-interest, as it was in the New Hebrides in 1901, Australia's leaders were Machiavellian enough to launch a clandestine spying operation on Britain and France. This operation clearly shows that Australia's leaders were self-interested men who instinctively understood the primacy of self-interest in all foreign relationships as articulated by Lord Palmerston in his famous description: 'We have no eternal allies, and we have no perpetual enemies. Our interests are eternal and perpetual, and those interests it is our duty to follow.'[1]

With regard to terminology, I have attempted to keep the technical language to a minimum, but sometimes intelligence jargon slips through. In relation to Japanese names, I have followed the Japanese practice of putting the family name first. With placenames, I have made every effort to use modern spelling practice.

Finally, this book is dedicated to the men and women who served in Australia's intelligence services from 1901 to 1945, and to those today quietly working in their job of promoting the self-interest of our nation.

John Fahey

INTRODUCTION

Looking Out for Number One

On 14 September 1853, with no warning, French troops and officials were landed at Balade in New Caledonia from the steam corvette *Le Phoque*.[1] Once ashore, the French admiral Auguste Febvrier-Despointes formally took possession of the islands in the name of Napoleon III. Following this, Despointes chartered the American barque SS *John H. Millay* to take despatches to the French consul in Sydney and to purchase large amounts of stores and supplies there for the garrison, which was to arrive in three other French warships. It was not welcome news in any of the Australian colonies and the suddenness of the French action upset colonial authorities, who had been advocating Britain seize the islands herself.

Faced with the hard reality that France now possessed New Caledonia, the only course of action left to the Australian colonies was to warn London to keep a close eye on the 'scheming Napoleon III' and recommend the Royal Navy increase its strength in the Pacific to counter French expansionism.[2]

Other commentators, such as the letter writer 'P', made clear a deeper frustration over the inability of the Australian colonies to deal with the depredations of European powers in the Pacific. As far as P was concerned, 'If Australia were a nation, there can be no doubt how she would act in the matter; the French occupation would be resisted as an aggression'. P's keenness for war over a few islands well away from Australia is a thoughtless reaction, but his complaint that the Cabinet in London 'will probably take three years to dream over it ... and perhaps come to the conclusion that it does not concern the British Empire' had substance and was widely shared among Australia's political and commercial elites.[3]

Australia's colonies were well aware of the reality of power politics and understood Britain was not going to argue with Napoleon III over New Caledonia because London needed Paris to support her against Russian ambitions in the Ottoman Empire. British national interests were in the Mediterranean and India, not in the Pacific.[4]

The Australian colonies grudgingly accepted France's actions in New Caledonia, but their concerns about further French expansion into the islands of New Guinea and the New Hebrides became acute, as the control of these islands was seen as vital to Australian security and commercial interests. Despite this, the Australian colonies left the matter alone as Britain and France fought the Crimean War and then worked together to limit the expansion of Germany.

The arrival of the new German Empire as a major world power was confirmed in 1871 when German armies comprehensively destroyed French military power in Europe. The rise of Germany now led to problems in the Pacific, specifically in Samoa and, more importantly for Australia, in New Guinea, where German commercial interests and missionaries had established themselves, much to the concern of Australia's governments. By 1883, the Australian colonies, particularly Queensland, were provoked into action by reports in the German press that Germany was moving to annex New Guinea. This led the premier of Queensland, Thomas McIlwraith, to order Mr Henry Chester, the magistrate on Thursday Island, to go to Port Moresby and take possession of all of New Guinea east of the border with the Netherlands East Indies.[5]

Henry Chester carried out his instructions on 4 April 1883 at Port Moresby in front of around two hundred Papuans. Unfortunately, the action had no standing without approval from the British government and they were having none of it. The response from Lord Derby, the Secretary of State for the Colonies, was 'cold, curt, and unsympathetic'. Derby made it clear that the Australian colonies had not considered the 'tremendous responsibility attaching to the annexation of so many islands, inhabited by savages, and situated at so great a distance from Australian and New Zealand'.[6]

Queensland's action did not go unnoticed in Germany and an article by Dr Gerhard Rohife, the German African explorer, appeared in the *Allegemeine Zeitung* of 22 April suggesting Germany had no real interest in the colonisation of New Guinea, which was, according to Rohife, less important than colonies in Africa.[7]

Lord Derby's abrupt dismissal of Australian concerns was not well received in the colonies concerned. The reaction came in the form of a call for a Monroe Doctrine for Australia in a letter dated 11 July 1883 sent to the editor of the *Sydney Morning Herald* from someone using the pen name L' Amour Des Peuples.[8] Australians wanted the region to be exclusively British or, more accurately, Australian.

The problem for London lay in the extent of its imperial interests. As the Empire had expanded so had the need to influence and control those areas adjacent to British colonies and territories. In turn, this led to annexation of these adjacent areas, which now resulted in a need to influence and control the new neighbours as well. In the period 1883 to 1884, Britain occupied Egypt, invaded Sudan, took over one third of Zululand and now, in response to Germany's annexation of northern New Guinea, had to negotiate with Germany and Holland the annexation of the southern part of New Guinea, an outcome widely seen in Australia as having arisen from British trading away of Australian interests.

By the beginning of 1885, the Australian colonies had watched as London had allowed France to take over New Caledonia, and Germany to take over part of New Guinea. Within another two years, on 1 June 1886, the French had moved troops into the New Hebrides, ostensibly, according to the Foreign Office in London, to protect the lives of French subjects there.[9] The claim from London that this was not a French occupation now fell on increasingly distrustful Australian ears and the colonial governments ramped up their pressure on London to take firm action to limit French influence in the islands. This pressure would result in the negotiation of the condominium, which, with great slowness, London and Paris now sought to implement. The issue of the New Hebrides began to assume a significant role in the breakdown of trust between Australia's leaders and the British government.

In 1887, at the Colonial Conference held in London during the Diamond Jubilee of Queen Victoria, the relationship between the British and colonial governments worsened. The representatives of the various Australian colonies were unimpressed with British prevarication over the New Hebrides and they were even less impressed when the prime minister, Lord Salisbury, forcefully rejected Australian concerns. As the meeting was not minuted, it is unclear what Salisbury said, but it was made abundantly clear Britain would not damage its relationship with France to placate Australian demands.[10]

The final step in the breakdown of trust between Australia's colonies and the British government occurred in 1889 at the Samoan Conference held in Berlin between representatives of Britain, Germany and the United States. The Foreign Office had rejected an attempt by the Australian colonies to send their own representatives, arguing the interests of the Australian colonies would be well represented by Foreign Office officials. These officials were, as the *South Australian Register* put it, 'the British Ambassador at Berlin and two other gentlemen equally unacquainted with colonial affairs.'[11]

The resulting Treaty of Berlin (1889) was seen as a defeat for Australian interests, with even the British press commenting that 'the attitude of the British delegates has compromised the Australian colonies'.[12] In Australia, the reaction was one of muted outrage at Australia's marginalisation by 'a patronising Imperium'.[13] British actions made it clear she could not be trusted to protect Australian national interests in the Pacific and, by 1889, Australia's leadership groups understood this all too well.[14]

As the Australian colonies became a nation, there can be no doubt Australia's political leaders were not going to allow Britain to control Australia's external affairs. The evidence for this claim is not just that the new constitution gave the Australian Parliament powers over external affairs in Section 51 (xxix); it lies in the way in which Australia's first government conducted a clandestine intelligence collection operation against France and Britain in the New Hebrides.

This operation, the first secret spying operation in the history of Australia, stands out as a particularly hard-nosed decision because it targeted Britain. The secret agent was tasked to collect intelligence that Edmund Barton's government could use to undermine Britain and force her to deal with French expansion in the New Hebrides. The importance of this operation is that it shows how far the first Australian government was willing to go to protect Australian interests and that from its very foundation as a nation, Australian policy was to look out for number one.

CHAPTER 1

Wilson Le Couteur's Pacific Mission, 1901

On 1 January 1901, Lord Hopetoun, the newly appointed Governor-General of the Commonwealth of Australia, formally declared the founding of the new nation at Sydney's Centennial Park and then, after a little confusion, appointed Edmund Barton as Australia's first, interim, prime minister. As interim prime minister Barton's first task was to call an election for March 1901, to allow the people of Australia to elect a government. Barton won the election and formed the first popularly elected Australian government.

The first elected government of Australia included Alfred Deakin as Attorney-General, Sir George Turner as Treasurer, Sir William Lyne as Minister for Home Affairs, Charles Kingston as Minister for Trade and Customs, and Sir James Dickson as Defence Minister. If we take our lead from the newspapers of the time, it was all about Australia being an independent but loyal white dominion of the British Empire. Of course, this was a necessity given Australia had inherited a war from her colonial governments whose military forces formed part of the British army fighting the Boers of South Africa. Yet when it came to launching a clandestine intelligence operation, the target was not the Boer enemy, nor their German or European supporters, it was closer to home in the New Hebrides (now Vanuatu), where Australia's leaders

1

were concerned that Britain would sacrifice Australia's interests in order to retain French support against Germany in Europe.

When Wilson Le Couteur wrote to Edmund Barton on 8 February 1901 offering his services as an agent willing to undertake an enquiry into the state of affairs in the New Hebrides, he was not put off. Rather, his letter was put on hold and then reviewed over the next four months, until Barton decided a clandestine intelligence operation should be launched using Le Couteur.[1]

In February 1901, as Le Couteur's letter was being considered by senior members of the new Commonwealth government, the nation's Department of Defence had been constituted, but its military establishment remained unconstituted until 1 March, when under Section 51 (vi) and (xxxii) of the Constitution Act, the Commonwealth took control of naval and military defence matters from the states. Given this, and other pressing demands on its time, the new government finally gave the go ahead for Le Couteur's mission sometime in May 1901. Australian forces may have been fighting in South Africa, but, as the Le Couteur mission makes clear, Australia's vested interests took precedence over Britain's imperial ambitions.

It is not surprising Australia sought to protect its interests in the New Hebrides. The territories were right on its doorstep and the French were encroaching into the affairs of the islands in a way that alienated many Australian and British vested interests there. Not least among these were the trading houses of Burns Philp and Le Couteur's former employer, the Australian United Steam Navigation Company, as well as the various missionary groups operating within the islands of the New Hebrides. Then there was the subject of land ownership, which, given the lack of settled agreements between Britain and France, was open to exploitation and a major cause of conflict among settlers and local inhabitants.

The problems in the New Hebrides that were exercising Australian minds were not important in London, and every Australian politician understood this. They also understood that if Britain had to decide whether to keep Paris or Melbourne happy, the growing tension with Germany and Britain's difficulties in South Africa dictated that Paris would be favoured in any decisions about the New Hebrides. This was not something Barton or his government could accept. Wilson Le Couteur's offer of service was manna from heaven.

Wilson Le Couteur was born on Jersey in 1853, making him 48 years old when he offered to become a secret agent. As a Channel Islander, he spoke both English and French and had found himself a position as the agent for the Australian United Steamship Company in the New Hebrides as well as, at some point, being the representative there for Burns Philp.[2] He had close connections with the French in New Caledonia and with the British in the Solomon Islands, and he had excellent access to Australian businessmen, missionaries and settlers. He also had a thorough local knowledge of the islands, their populations and the trading connections operating between them.[3]

This operation was no renegade activity conducted by low-level bureaucrats; it was organised by the highest officials in the Australian government and run by Barton's Private Secretary, Atlee Hunt, who was also the Secretary of the Department of External Affairs and head of the Prime Minister's Department. Hunt personally handled Le Couteur's offer of service as a secret agent to investigate the 'existing condition of affairs' in the New Hebrides, and oversaw all of the administrative arrangements for the operation, including its financing.

The budget for the operation included a wage of £7 15s[4] and expenses of £7[5] a week, a sum equivalent to around $15,268 per week in 2017.[6] Given the mission was planned for twelve weeks, the total budget amounted to £177, $183,200 in 2017 prices, and this did not include the cost of tickets or the time and effort of others, including an ex-police detective, a Mr Lyons,[7] who was used by Barton to secretly investigate the background of Le Couteur before his engagement. Managing this secret payment would not have been difficult, but it would have required care. One thing, however, was the same as today: even in 1901 spying was expensive. It is clear why Le Couteur was an eager volunteer.

The problem facing Australia in the New Hebrides was that France was claiming sovereignty over the archipelago based upon its proximity to New Caledonia. This, plus the violent conflict between indigenous inhabitants and white settlers from Australia, Britain and France, was causing concern to Burns Philp and other large Australian firms, which controlled much of the trade in the archipelago and feared the French would exclude them as they had in New Caledonia.[8] Other Australian commercial interests also strongly opposed any increase in French influence, particularly the buying up of land.

According to Le Couteur, he was prompted to write after listening to Barton's speech at the Sydney Town Hall on 7 February, in which Barton told his listeners the Commonwealth Cabinet was considering the problems arising from French actions in the New Hebrides. It was the first signal that the new government was putting Australia's interests first.[9] This appealed to Le Couteur because he needed a job and he had extensive experience of the New Hebrides.

One of the issues with the New Hebrides was that the archipelago was under the jurisdiction of the High Commissioner for the Western Pacific, a post held by the Governor of Fiji. This put the matter firmly under the auspices of the imperial government in London. Barton's government had no control, and now it needed to influence London to act in Australia's rather than France's interests.[10]

The approach of the Barton government would not have surprised London. Australians had already proven themselves quite capable of putting their own interests before those of Britain. In 1887, following the First Colonial Conference in London, the British prime minister, Lord Salisbury, wrote to the Secretary of State for the Colonies, Henry Holland, in exasperation with the Australians, who were:

the most unreasonable people I have ever heard or dreamt of. They want us to incur all the bloodshed and the danger, and the stupendous cost of a war with France, of which almost the exclusive burden will fall on us, for a group of islands which are as useless as the South Pole—and to which they are only attached by a debating club sentiment.[11]

Whatever one thinks of Lord Salisbury's complaint, the fact was Australia's national interests were no longer those of Britain, and Britain and Australia both had to face up to this. In 1901, Edmund Barton and Atlee Hunt were in a position to ensure Australian interests came first. The trick was to do so without letting London know, and without causing a political outcry from the many advocates of Australia as part of a British Empire.

This was no laughing matter given Australia was undermining Britain's imperial power in the Pacific at the very same time Australian soldiers were fighting for the British in South Africa. Even now, one has to admire the ruthlessness of Barton's actions. We can now see why he directed Le Couteur to 'take every possible care that the object of your visit is not made public in any way'.[12]

Barton passed the responsibility of managing the proposed mission to Hunt, and they arranged for Mr Lyons to undertake a secret investigation into Le Couteur, just in case. Lyons' report was sent to Barton on 23 July.[13] It indicated Wilson Le Couteur was lily white.

On 1 August, acting on the directions of the prime minister, Atlee Hunt formally instructed Le Couteur to visit the New Hebrides and to report to the Commonwealth government on the general state of affairs in those islands.[14] He was to report the actions and utterances of the French Governor of New Caledonia when the governor visited the New Hebrides in September 1901. And he was to visit the northern islands of the New Hebrides and report on French activity there, particularly the way French settlers were obtaining land. He was also to find out the numbers of French and British residents, and report on how they saw the future of the islands.

Other tasks included general reporting on public opinion in the islands on the issue of crime there, and the adequacy of the dual control exercised by the French and British in dealing with it. He was also to investigate reported murders and what action the French and British authorities were taking in response. Le Couteur was to report all of this information to Prime Minister Barton in strict secrecy and as frequently as possible.[15]

Le Couteur departed Sydney aboard SS *Mambare* on 7 August and arrived at Aneityum Island on 16 August. Over the next thirteen days he visited 26 of the islands on his way into and then out of the New Hebrides.[16] Not a bad effort for an amateur spy.

From 7 September to 15 October, Le Couteur stayed in Vila, the principal settlement in the archipelago and the headquarters (HQ) of both the British and French administrations. It appears by this time Le Couteur had already provided Barton with three reports: one sent on 9 September, a letter of 3 October and another on 20 October.[17] The French governor of New Caledonia did not visit during Le Couteur's mission, sending Monsieur G. Aubry-Lecomte, the Chief of the Department of Native Affairs, to act as his representative on board the warship FS *Meurthe*.[18] Apparently, Aubry-Lecomte did not speak in public or attend public events. The main impact of Aubry-Lecomte's arrival in the New Hebrides was a demand among the British residents for a British official of equivalent rank to be sent as a counterbalance as soon as possible.[19]

In relation to the crimes committed by the indigenous inhabitants against British and French settlers, Le Couteur reported that the locals feared the French colonists more than the British because the French took a much more aggressive approach in punishing those involved in criminal activity. Yet the main complaint all of the European settlers had was the absence of British and French men-of-war during cyclone season, a period of four months when they felt completely unprotected.[20] Le Couteur also reported the French were moving more settlers into the New Hebrides and that the French population of Sandwich (Efate), Epi, Malakula and (Espiritu) Santo islands had more than tripled from 92 in 1899 to 299 in 1901.[21] Of particular concern to Le Couteur was the increase in the number of Catholic missionaries, who had come to the region to counteract the influence of the Presbyterian missionaries.[22] As Le Couteur reported it, all of the colonist groups—French, British and Australian—were of the view that the Presbyterian missionaries were causing the biggest problem by stirring up the locals and preventing their employment by planters and other settlers.[23]

Le Couteur was also able to confirm the truth of the rumours of murders and violence that Edmund Barton and Atlee Hunt had mentioned in their instructions. He recounted an incident that occurred the day before his arrival at White Sands, Tanna Island, where there had been a violent confrontation between a boat's crew and local inhabitants that left six of the locals dead. The violence in the New Hebrides appeared to arise from disputes over land ownership between the indigenous owners and the newly arrived European planters and farmers. This situation was aggravated by bad behaviour by Europeans, such as one Frank Whitford, an Englishman who worked for the French recruiting local labour. In fact, Le Couteur's description of Whitford's kidnapping of locals accords more with the blackbirding activities of the 1860s than with labour recruitment, even in the early 1900s. Whitford, Le Couteur reported, did 'not enjoy an enviable reputation in the islands'.[24]

The report provides a detailed social and economic survey of the New Hebrides and discusses drunkenness among the local population due to alcohol supplied by, according to Le Couteur, the French. It also describes, however, the European settlers in the New Hebrides as uniformly hostile to all government, and their zeal in pushing for London and Paris to come to an agreement as more practical than patriotic, because they considered it necessary for them to exploit the islands more effectively. The real issue was the trading of land between the local population and European settlers. The former viewed the transfer of title as temporary, while the latter saw it as permanent. The lack of any centralised system for the registration of title deeds and transfer of land was a major cause of confusion, and this was responsible for most of the violent disputes between Europeans and the indigenous population.[25]

All in all, Australia's first civilian secret agent had done a good job for the price. His mission provides evidence of how quickly a fledgling Australian nation moved to secure its national interests at the expense of Britain and France. Australia's colonies had experienced the subordination of their interests to those of Britain and this reinforced a desire that the new nation of Australia should protect her own interests herself. In 1853, they had seen London strip Queensland of New Guinea and then allow the Germans to establish a colony there. They had watched as Britain allowed France to increase its influence in the New Hebrides at their expense. They had suffered the humiliations of being excluded from the Samoa Conference and of being lectured by British officials and prime ministers over their pursuit of their own national interests. The creation of Australia with a constitution that provided its parliament with power over external affairs was a rejection of the idea that Britain would compeletely control Australian foreign policy. The launching of Le Couteur to spy on Britain and France in the New Hebrides was more than a rejection of British oversight; it was an emphatic exercise of sovereign power by a nation protecting its own interests first.

The Le Couteur mission was also a remarkably professional and well-organised operation and, at a cost of $283,200 in 2016 prices, a serious undertaking. It was not a jolly jape by a bored gentleman. Le Couteur may have been a gentleman, but in 1901 gentlemen were the most effective spies available. There were no satellites, no imagery, no means of harnessing the electromagnetic spectrum and very little technical intelligence to get hold of. This left human intelligence (HUMINT) as the only method, and it was the preserve of educated upper-middle-class males because only they could access the corridors of power where the secrets were kept. The cleaner and the handyman had limited access and female spies, such as the unfortunate

Margaretha Geertruida Zelle, more famous under her Indonesian name Mata Hari, had to wait until the demands of total war made employing women as spies socially acceptable.

All of this challenges the idea Australia's early governments took a subservient position within the Empire. It also demonstrates one of the contentions of this book: that a nation's clandestine intelligence activity tells us more about its real ambitions than any public pronouncements.

CHAPTER 2

Atlee Hunt: Public Servant, Spy Master, 1901–23

The Le Couteur mission was not the only intelligence activity the Australian government launched against Britain and France in the New Hebrides. In fact, it formed part of a coordinated multi-source intelligence operation, which included the secret and confidential reporting from John Haggard, the British Consul on Noumea, and from the agents and contacts of Burns Philp and other trading firms in the region.[1] Other Australian intelligence activity of the time included the formation of the Admiralty's Reporting Officer network, which was controlled by the Australian Commonwealth Naval Board (ACNB). Australia's military was also sending officers abroad to collect intelligence, including Major William Thorsby Bridges.[2] Behind much of this activity, we find one man playing varying roles, most of them central to the operation of the early Australia intelligence system. This man was Atlee Hunt, Edmund Barton's private secretary and, concurrently, Secretary of the Department of External Affairs. He was also Australia's first and most successful spymaster.

Atlee Hunt was educated at Sydney Grammar School and from there took a position in the NSW Lands Department in 1879. While working within the department, Hunt studied for the bar, to which he gained admission on 21 March 1892.[3]

In his new career as a barrister, Hunt slowly began to build a reputation, acting on behalf of the creditors of August Richard Lichberg, a general store-keeper. Hunt won an injunction in this case, his first court victory.[4] The win would have been nice for the new barrister, who was still supplementing his income by tutoring.[5]

As time went by, Hunt expanded his reputation and his circle of friends, among whom was Edmund Barton. Barton had sat as the arbitrator in the McSharry case, in which Hunt acted as junior counsel under Arthur Smith, representing the NSW government.[6] Barton found for McSharry, but awarded only £13,408, a judgment that left McSharry £46,592 out of pocket.[7]

As a leading activist for Federation, Hunt worked closely with Barton, organising the NSW Federal Association and Federal League to promote the yes vote in the NSW referendum on Federation. In 1901, Hunt was appointed as Barton's private secretary and Secretary and Permanent Head of the Department of External Affairs, later Home Affairs.[8] Hunt won the External Affairs position over George Charles Stewart, who had left the Tasmanian civil service on being promised it. Hunt's success was not simply due to his association with Barton. The deciding voice had been that of Alfred Deakin, who may have been swayed by Hunt's capacity for getting along with people, something at which Stewart did not excel.[9]

Hunt's tenure as private secretary to Australia's prime ministers ended with the election of Andrew Fisher's Australian Labour Party (ALP) govern-ment on 13 April 1910.[10] His close association with the preceding conservative prime ministers could not be overlooked, and he was removed as head of the Prime Minister's Department. He was, however, a professional public servant with an excellent reputation, particularly for managing and enforc-ing the *Immigration Restriction Act 1901*, and the Fisher Government kept him in the role of Secretary of the Home Affairs Department. From there, he continued to set up Australia's nascent intelligence organisation. Hunt would serve as Secretary at Home Affairs until William (Billy) Hughes moved him to the position of Public Service Arbitrator in 1921.

As Barton and Hunt settled into the job of establishing Australia's first government, the priorities were, as we have seen above, mixed and demanding. There was a war still being fought in South Africa, and there were demands from those who had sacrificed position in order to bring about the new Commonwealth. One of the most pressing priorities was the implementation and enforcement of the Immigration Restriction Act, the foundation of the White Australia policy.[11]

Effective enforcement of the immigration laws required good intelligence allowing Atlee Hunt and his department to identify individuals who were excluded under the provisions of the Act. Given the level of resources available to the Commonwealth at the time, Hunt embarked on establishing an extensive intelligence reporting system drawing on state government departments, including police forces, and harbour and various other officials. He also drew upon the services of customs officers and worthy people all over Australia. In short, he established an ad hoc intelligence system using the unpaid services of individuals and governments to provide information on immigration matters and suspicious individuals. He even extended this network overseas, using the good offices of state trade representatives in Asia and around the world.

One of the main reasons Hunt opened up channels to the state trade representatives in Asia was that they were the officials who put the arguments for the admission of Asian businessmen into Australia. This upset politicians intent on keeping Australia white, and it also upset the protectionist politicians led by Barton and Deakin. Hunt used his position to influence the decisions of the trade representatives and slowly began to expand their reporting into economic and commercial spheres until state governments began to close their trade offices.

Before 1901, the states of Victoria, New South Wales and Queensland appointed trade representatives to collect commercial intelligence in the United States, South Africa, Singapore, China (Shanghai) and Japan. The Victorian government, led at the time by Alfred Deakin, under pressure from the Victorian Chamber of Manufacturers, appointed its first trade representative, James McInnes Sinclair, during the economic slump of the mid-1890s. Sinclair, a close friend of Deakin, was based in North America, with responsibility for both the United States and Canada.[12] In 1902, New South Wales decided to go three better, appointing trade representatives in Cape Town, San Francisco and, importantly for our story, Kobe, Japan, in 1902. The first appointee as NSW Commercial Commissioner in Kobe, A.P. Whitely, died shortly after arriving there and was replaced by the long-serving resident engineer of the NSW railways, John Bligh Suttor.[13] It was an inspired choice. John Suttor went on to learn Japanese and became so well known and respected in Kobe that when he died, the local merchants commissioned a statue in his memory.[14]

John Suttor's job was to observe and report to Sydney on the conduct of trade in what was then called the Far East (now South-East Asia), and particularly on Japanese trade.[15] James M. Sinclair, the Victorian government's agent in Singapore, also reported on trade matters in the Far East,[16] as did the Victorian representative in Kobe and later Shanghai, R.B. Levien.[17] Queensland appointed Frederick Jones as its trade commissioner in Hong Kong. By the end of 1906, there were four Australian trade commissioners or agents operating in Asia reporting commercial intelligence.

As already noted, Atlee Hunt was well aware of the activities of these trade commissioners, particularly their efforts in assisting Asian businessmen to meet the requirement of the Commonwealth's Immigration Restriction Act. Although today we see the Act as particularly racist, it was not as racist as many Australians of the period wanted it to be. The less racist version of the Act that Barton and Deakin had got through Parliament enabled the Commonwealth to ease the bureaucratic restrictions on Asian visitors by authorising state trade commissioners to provide a simple letter of introduction for Chinese and Japanese business travellers.[18]

The reality was, however, that after Federation the states had little real interest in keeping their trade representatives abroad. In April 1906, Queensland closed its Hong Kong office,[19] while Victoria closed its Shanghai office in 1909 and the Singapore office in 1912.[20] The Victorian representative in Singapore, James Sinclair, did not return to Australia but remained in Asia. He had been a long-term friend of the Australian Dr George Ernest Morrison, now a senior political advisor to the Chinese government and the Beijing correspondent for *The Times* of London.[21] It seems that in addition to his duties for the Victorian government, Sinclair worked for the Department of External Affairs in a capacity he would not reveal.[22] By 1912, there was only John Suttor in Kobe.[23]

Suttor was a strong advocate of Australia developing its trade with Asia, and specifically with Japan. He reflected the NSW government's more open approach towards Japan, and it is no surprise that New South Wales was almost alone in providing Japanese-language classes in selected high schools and at the University of Sydney. This attitude of the NSW government had grown from the influence of free traders such as Sir Henry Parkes and William Henry Suttor, John Suttor's uncle.[24]

Atlee Hunt saw John Suttor as a useful source of low-cost independent information on Japan and the Far East. Suttor's reports arrived untouched by the Imperial Government in London and provided a crosscheck against other intelligence coming out of London.[25] By June 1916, with World War I increasing in intensity and Edmund Piesse in Military Intelligence raising the focus on Japan's ambitions in the Pacific, John Suttor found himself being given clandestine tasks for the first time.

Suttor was instructed to obtain intelligence on Japanese shipbuilding and the organisation of Japan's merchant marine for the ACNB. For the first time, he was instructed to keep his work strictly secret.[26] With this, Suttor crossed the threshold that divides the trade representative and diplomat from the spy.

John Suttor carried out these tasks, but the NSW government noted that his mission had crept from supplying open-source information and reporting political perspectives to obtaining sensitive military intelligence.[27] In late 1916, the NSW government raised concerns Suttor was being put at risk.[28] The Japanese treatment of suspect spies could be savagely brutal, and the NSW government was right in raising its concerns. After all, he was the representative of New South Wales and not Australia. Suttor's military reporting seems to have tapered off after New South Wales made its views clear.

Dr George Ernest Morrison (popularly known as 'Morrison of Peking') was an Australian expat known to the Australian government. Morrison had gained entrée to the highest levels of the Chinese government by virtue of being the *Times* correspondent, and had become a senior policy advisor. The question was whether Morrison was working for the Chinese government, *The Times* or the British government. Anything he found out would have to be reported to his editors and to the British government. Although there is little evidence in the files of Morrison playing a double or triple game, his motivation would always be in question. He was not a safe bet, and Australia does not seem to have placed much faith in him as a prospective secret agent.

Following his arrival in Beijing in 1911, Morrison provided advice to various Chinese officials and political leaders, and in 1912 was appointed political advisor to the Chinese Government of President Yuan Shi Kai.[29] In this role, Morrison worked to promote China's interests. Although he was seen by some as being in favour of Japanese influence in China, his support of

Japan seems to have been an attempt to counter Russian influence in China. This reflected official British policy of the time, which further suggests that Morrison was working for the Foreign Office in London.[30]

Morrison's early views on Japanese involvement in China changed as the aggressive nature of Japan's ambitions became more apparent. In January 1915, Japan's attempt to impose its Twenty-One Demands severely damaged its standing in China, and Morrison came to see Japan as just another predatory imperial power seeking to tear off its own piece of China. His 1916 correspondence with his friend, the Victorian Trade Commissioner James Sinclair, shows Morrison starting to describe the Japanese as just another colonial power, and developing a growing sensitivity towards Japan's ambitions.[31]

Whatever the case with Morrison, there is no doubt Suttor and Sinclair collected secret intelligence for the Australian government. Government archives contain secret reports provided by Suttor to the Commonwealth via the NSW Government, and J.M. Sinclair later admitted in a letter to Senator George Pearce that he had worked for the Commonwealth Department of External Affairs when he had been the trade delegate for Victoria.[32] These men were not, however, intelligence officers, and this reduced their usefulness as there was no way government officials or commercial agents could involve themselves in darker intelligence activities such as blackmail, bribery, seduction and theft.

The intelligence model created by Atlee Hunt in the early years of the Commonwealth relied on the coopting of patriotic Australians who filled official and business posts into an informal intelligence network. Commonwealth customs officers, military officers, state police officers and trade commissioners all fitted the bill. They were already engaged on official duties, and Hunt's requirements simply added a few additional tasks to their daily work. It was a cheap and easy way to build an intelligence system quickly, and, as we have seen, it generated a reasonable level of intelligence. What it did not do was allow penetration of foreign governments and the theft of their deeper secrets. This was a job for a secret intelligence service, not for a network of informal sources.

CHAPTER 3

Enlightened Princes and Wise Generals: Military Intelligence in Early Australia

Sometime around 500 BC, a Chinese soldier or official, given the name Sun Tzu, wrote a book called *The Art of War* that today is regarded in many places as a masterpiece of advice for generals on how to conduct war and warlike operations. In *The Art of War*, the author is at pains to detail the way intelligence contributes to victory, stating that: 'the reason the enlightened prince and the wise general conquer the enemy . . . is foreknowledge. What is called foreknowledge . . . must be obtained from men who know the enemy situation'.[1]

Australia's new army, ably led by Major General Sir Edward Hutton, who had previously commanded the NSW Military Forces, now instituted its own intelligence-collection operations in line with the advice provided so long ago in China. The target of the Australian Army's first intelligence-collection operation was France and its Pacific colony of New Caledonia.[2]

Major William Bridges was sent to New Caledonia at the request of the War Office in London. The mission was clandestine, with Bridges operating under the cover of being a Dalgety commercial agent.[3] His task was to spy out and map the military defences of New Caledonia, a job Major General Hutton described as 'secret and somewhat dangerous'.[4] The reports, field sketches and photographs compiled by Bridges were kept in Australia and shared with the War Office in London.[5] This history makes it clear that the Australia Army was born with intelligence collection as part of its functions. Unfortunately, as we will soon see, men who begrudged 'rank, honours and a few hundred pieces of gold' soon challenged the importance that Australia's enlightened princes and wise generals placed on obtaining intelligence.

The initial interest of Australia's military commanders in France, Germany and other European nations was reasonable in the circumstances that existed in 1901 and 1902. Events further afield soon changed Australian perspectives, as Russia and the newly risen Asian power of Japan went to war in 1904.

The Japanese attack on the Imperial Russian Navy's Far East Fleet based at Port Arthur, on the Liaodong Peninsula of Manchuria, occurred suddenly during negotiations between the two powers over the division of spoils in northern China and Manchuria. The Imperial Japanese Navy (IJN) quickly bottled up the Russian fleet at Port Arthur while conducting a landing of the Imperial Japanese Army (IJA) in Korea at Inchon. Within two months, Russia had lost the initiative. Its fleet had been seriously depleted, its admiral killed and the remainder trapped at Port Arthur, while the IJA, under General Kuroki Tamemoto, was poised on the Yalu River for an invasion of Manchuria. The opportunity to observe the fighting led Australia to send its first military observer to a foreign war, albeit as part of the British contingent.

The situation the world faced in February 1904 was startling. First, Japan, a newly modernised Asian state, had declared war on one of the largest European powers. Secondly, to the shock of many Europeans, Japan was proving itself a highly competent military power and had taken the initiative away from Russia. If Japan's actions were a shock to Europe, they were even more concerning for Australia, New Zealand and the United States, the nations sharing the Pacific with Japan.

Hostilities began on 8 February 1904, when, three hours ahead of the declaration of war, Japan launched a surprise amphibious attack on Port Arthur. The Japanese decision to launch this attack was clever, as was their justifying it by comparing it with Russia's surprise attack on Sweden in 1808. It presaged what would become a standard Japanese practice of launching military strikes immediately on or just before the formal declaration of war.

The Japanese attack on Port Arthur successfully disrupted Russia's response and neutralised the Russian Fleet by trapping it inside Port Arthur. Significantly, the Russian Commander-in-Chief (C-in-C), Vice Admiral Stephan Markov, who had been sent to lead the fleet, was killed on HIRMS *Petropavlovsk* when it hit a Japanese mine on 13 April 1904. This initial naval success did little to win the war, which now settled into a siege, and Western military attachés flocked to the front in order to observe modern warfare and how the Japanese conducted it.

Australian interest in the war was intense. The Cabinet quickly agreed to send Australian military observers to join the British Military Mission, and in early March 1904, Prime Minister Deakin wrote to the Governor-General asking that London arrange for two Australian officers to be attached to the Japanese Army in the field. Atlee Hunt managed the details, later writing to tell the Governor-General that the Commonwealth was keen to have news as soon as possible.[6]

On 24 March 1904, the Secretary of State for the Colonies notified the Governor-General that the Imperial Japanese Government would be 'pleased to allow one Australian Officer to be attached to the Field Army'.[7] On 26 March, the Australian government notified the Governor-General that the officer selected was Colonel John Charles Hoad, CMG, who left Sydney on the SS *Empire* on 30 March.[8]

The speed with which Hoad was despatched to Japan is a clear indication of the Australian government's desire to obtain as much information as possible on Japan and its military. The fact that Hoad was also directed by Cabinet to report directly to the Minister for Defence was highly unusual.[9] What was more unusual was Hoad was not the choice of Major General Hutton, who fought Hoad's appointment on the grounds that he was an officer 'of limited capacity and military knowledge'.[10] However incompetent Hoad might have been as an officer, he was, unfortunately for Hutton, well connected, and he had the support of the Governor-General, Lord Hopetoun, to whom he was aide-de-camp.

Colonel Hoad went as a member of the British military mission commanded by Lieutenant General W. Nicholson.[11] Supporting Japan in its war with Russia was important to Britain, and she expended considerable effort in building up the Japanese as a counter to Russia in the Far East, China and Afghanistan. The war promised to limit St Petersburg's expansionist policies in the Pacific, and Britain was keen for a Japanese victory.

Hutton's judgement of Hoad proved correct. The reports Hoad produced were bad, consisting of publicly available information and some details of the equipment issued to Japanese soldiers. He drew all of his information from Japanese government gazettes, newspapers and the published estimates. General Nicholson described them as 'very meagre'.[12] Later in his career, when he was continuing his war with Hutton by attacking Hutton's protégé William Bridges, Hoad would advise Senator George Pearce that these details were all a 'trained officer' needed to make a decision.[13] General Nicholson described Hoad best as an officer 'of inferior education and small military capacity', but 'personally pleasant, good tempered and obliging'. Hoad was the perfect courtier, and he won over his fellow attachés. He even obtained an audience with the Empress of Japan.

Austin Chapman, the Defence Minister who had sent Hoad, did not last long and was replaced by the alcoholic Andrew Dawson in April 1904. Dawson had a real antipathy towards Hutton, and this led to a bitter fight to reduce Hutton's standing by creating a military board headed by the Defence Minister. The rationale for this is not outlined in the documentary record, but most likely it was the desire of the politicians to influence military decisions in order to ensure their electorates benefited as much as possible.

The argument over the creation of a military board became public when Dawson released a minute criticising Hutton to the press. Hutton, rightly seeing this as an underhanded attack on his professionalism, responded. The subsequent conduct of the argument in public amply demonstrated the dysfunction at the top of Australia's army.[14]

A contributing factor to this dysfunction was the prestige and pay attached to positions in the socially sensitive militia. Officers vied for position and promotion, and Hutton's insistence on making the army more professional threatened the status of many important men. Hutton's support was restricted to the small cadre of professional officers, such as William Bridges, Brudenell White and Harry Chauvel. In August 1904, James W. McCay, a federal member and a militia officer, replaced Dawson as minister—something of a record; Australia had ten ministers of defence in its first ten years. McCay lasted just over two years, with the others averaging around eleven months each in the position.

This instability led to a breakdown in the relationship between the professional soldiers led by Major General Hutton and the politicians and their social contacts in the militia. The attacks on Hutton are often portrayed as an exercise in Australian nationalism because Australians were trying to replace a British general with an Australian one.[15] This is a superficial reading of the situation. In fact, it was a tawdry brawl between personalities and factions within the military, made worse by politicians ensuring that their parish retained its small and isolated bands of badly trained militia.

Major General Edward Hutton did not need to retain his position in Australia. He was a British officer and he resigned his commission on 10 November 1904, the same day Colonel Hoad stepped off the train from Sydney, having returned abruptly and without authority from his appointment as an attaché to the Japanese Army.[16] Hoad had returned without clear permission because he knew if he stayed overseas he would be passed over in the annual promotions.[17] He was not going to let that happen, and so he returned and won his promotion.[18]

The whole affair is odd, and the file has clearly been tampered with, as it contains only one document, which is obviously from another file and sounds like a retrospective justification of Hoad's actions:

> It is not understood that, unless events in the East should make it desirable to prolong his stay, he should be absent for a longer period than six months, i.e., he would have the full benefit of the season in which military operations are likely to be active, and to return to Australia before the winter.[19]

Whoever pushed this line in Cabinet appears to have had little or no understanding of military affairs and the necessity of observing the operation of the IJA in all circumstances, including winter quarters. Colonel Hoad's arrival in Melbourne on 10 November 1904 was a surprise to nearly everyone. Bridges, Chauvel and Brudenell White seem to have run a campaign to undermine Hoad, but, despite their best efforts, Hoad was promoted and appointed as Hutton's replacement. Now he controlled all senior promotions within the Australian Army, and revenge was on the agenda.[20]

None of this sits well with the eagerness the government had initially displayed to obtain information on the fighting, and it is clear that Hoad had spent little or no time at the front. Indeed, he was with the Japanese Field Army at Liaoyang from 13 June to 24 September 1904, arriving sixteen days after the battle of Liaoyang had finished.[21] The shortness of Hoad's mission drew the attention of the papers and members of Parliament, no doubt prompted by Hutton's supporters within the military.

Reading Hoad's report today—a list of the personal equipment carried by Japanese soldiers, a description of the Japanese recruitment system and the syllabi of courses in the IJA—it is clear Hoad just threw whatever information he had to hand into a badly written document.[22] It has not one jot of information on how the IJA thought, planned, organised or operated. As an exercise in intelligence collection it was a dismal failure, and one for which the blame can be laid squarely at the feet of Australia's Cabinet.

The following year, 1905, provided a jolt of monumental proportions to Australia and the nations of the Pacific when on 27 and 28 May, Admiral Togo Heihachiro destroyed Russia's naval power at the Battle of Tsushima, often described as the most decisive naval battle since Trafalgar in 1805.[23] After Tsushima, Australian interest in Japan's military prowess morphed into fear.

In Britain, Russia's defeat was welcome news, although it was tinged with the growing realisation that Britain's control of the seas was being challenged by more than just German rearmament. The IJN's victory added to growing Admiralty concerns of decreasing British naval strength across the globe, although the main concern was and remained Germany. The Dreadnought program that was now planned to counter German naval ambition also needed to meet the growing power of the United States and Japan, and that would be expensive.

In Australia, Prime Minister Alfred Deakin, Senator George Pearce and William Watt, a member of the Victorian Parliament, were increasingly concerned about Japan. Having proven itself capable against a major European power, Japan was likely to grow in confidence and become the Asian threat Australia feared. This was not racism; it was a realistic appraisal that an Asian nation had become a modern power, stronger than Australia. For Australia, the challenge was to discover what Japan wanted, and the extent of its capabilities and willingness to take that by force of arms. The need for better intelligence was now apparent to government.

In 1905, the identified threat was a naval one. Given Australia is an island, any attempt to attack it relied, as it does today, on an enemy with a high naval capability. Defence against this threat was also naval, and although the Australian Squadron of the Royal Navy (RN) was small, it was part of the world's largest navy and one that operated a worldwide intelligence system. For the army, the situation was different, as there was no intelligence organisation to support its commanders or its HQ staff. Meeting this shortfall in capability took time, and it was not until 6 December 1907 that Colonel William Bridges, in the position of Chief of the General Staff (CGS), created the Intelligence Corps to meet the needs of Australia's military commanders.[24]

The work required of the Intelligence Corps was, as is typical of most intelligence work, rather mundane. One of the major gaps identified by the General Staff was the lack of reliable maps of the Australian landmass. This was not easy to remedy, because it would entail years of work involving constant resurveying to include the latest changes. This was the most important task given to Colonel James Whiteside McCay, the former politician and now Australia's first Director of Military Intelligence (DMI). The tasking was one thing; the problem of resources was the real issue.

Colonel McCay looked to his social network and prevailed upon John Monash, an old school friend, to join the Intelligence Corps and organise the surveying and mapping of Australia. Monash was promoted to Lieutenant Colonel and appointed Commandant of the Victorian Section of the Corps.[25] Even with Monash leading the mapping effort, the sheer scale of the work involved was well beyond anything the resources of the Corps could manage.[26]

By 1909, when the first Intelligence School of Instruction was held, the new Corps numbered 85, including 53 officers, all part-time militia. Thirty-five of the officers attended the School of Instruction, not a bad effort given the part-time nature of the Corps at the time.[27]

By May 1909, the fighting among the military officers had reached a point where the Australian government tried to bring the warring factions under some sort of control. The two main factions consisted of senior militia officers led by Major General Hoad and a cadre of regular officers led by William Bridges, who were supporters of General Hutton and his ideas. Hutton had decided that Bridges was the man best suited to serve as the CGS, but Bridges was a colonel and junior to the well-connected Hoad.

The appointment of Bridges as CGS was never going to work, and the government eventually had to give way when Hoad returned to Australia from Britain in early 1909. The stratagem used to get around the problem of Bridges was clumsy. George Pearce and others in the government convinced Bridges to step down as CGS in order to represent Australia at the

1909 Imperial Conference. He agreed after he was given a written assurance he would be reinstated as CGS on his return, and Hoad became the CGS on 26 May.[28] When Bridges returned, the written assurance proved worthless, and Senator Pearce expended considerable energy in convincing Bridges to stay in the army.

Hoad's hostility towards Bridges is made crystal clear in the documentary evidence. One only has to read items such as the minute Bridges submitted to Pearce on 12 July 1909 on the reform of the army[29] or the comments of Colonel Ernest Wallack and Major General Hoad on Bridges' recommendations. Hoad demanded to know who had authorised Bridges to write the minute in the first place and railed against junior officers or the past occupants of posts being asked to provide advice on subjects for which they were no longer responsible.[30] Bridges lost this battle, and would remain on the outer until after 6 October 1911, the day Major General Hoad died from a heart attack.[31]

This did not mean all was well in Bridges' Intelligence Corps. For the army, the blowout in the cost of running the Corps, from AU£6973 for the 1909/10 financial year to AU£14,592 in 1911/12, an increase of 109 per cent, was unsustainable.[32] This increase caused dissent among those parts of the army whose budgets were being raided to pay the increasing cost of the intelligence experiment. The new Corps was winning a lot of enemies, and so Major General G.M. Kirkpatrick, the Inspector-General of the Commonwealth Military Forces, was asked to investigate. He found there was no justification for the increased expenditure.[33]

Kirkpatrick's investigation concluded that the recruitment of substantial numbers of militia officers by the Corps resulted in substantial training costs. Yet despite the increased size of the Corps, it could not meet the day-to-day needs of the General Staff or military commanders. This was because the work the Corps was undertaking arose from a process of self-generated tasking, most of which, Kirkpatrick found, was not relevant to the needs of the General Staff.[34]

Damningly, Kirkpatrick also found that the one task everyone agreed was essential, the mapping of Australia, had not progressed. Kirkpatrick identified the sheer size of the task as the issue, and that it required 'a settled plan of operation for some time ahead'. As far as Kirkpatrick could find, no such plan existed.[35] Colonel McCay attempted to mollify Kirkpatrick by pointing out he was looking to obtain the services of twelve Royal Engineers or Royal

Australian Engineers to map 10,000 square miles (26,000 square kilometres) of Australia per annum.[36] McCay's approach was patently inadequate.

Kirkpatrick also found that the Intelligence Corps had failed to establish the required companies of trained and experienced guides that the army would need to undertake reconnaissance and guiding duties in the remoter parts of Australia. In a defence emergency on Australian soil, Australia's field commanders were rightly concerned they had no capability to operate in the more remote regions. The failure to raise and train the companies was a substantial one, as it alienated the Intelligence Corps' most important customers—its own commanders.

As to whether the Corps should collect information on foreign countries in the Pacific, Kirkpatrick was emphatically opposed. He wrote that if the Corps could not provide basic support to army units, it should not be undertaking other work that lay outside the normal purview of Military Intelligence.[37] Foreign political and economic intelligence was not the army's job. This information should be obtained from the usual sources: the War Office and the Chief of the Imperial General Staff in London.[38]

Kirkpatrick preferred a focus on counterespionage and internal security operations. In his view, foreign diplomatic and consular officials were little better than spies, and he recommended that Military Intelligence keep a close eye on these officials and other aliens. For this reason, Kirkpatrick felt that Military Intelligence should involve itself in internal security operations against civilians.

Counterintelligence and internal security operations offer a cheap and apparently easy strategy for governments looking to establish an intelligence capability. First, they are easy to conduct because existing agencies such as police, customs and the military can be used to provide the manpower. Secondly, they are cheap, in that they are conducted on home soil. Thirdly, they are more morally acceptable because they defend the people and nation against the duplicitous spies of other nations. Fourthly, they are short, sharp and sweet because operatives do not need to be trained in languages or cultural sensitivities, or in how to stay undetected in a hostile environment. Security intelligence is easy work compared to the hard and expensive work of collecting foreign intelligence.

However, security intelligence presents the greatest danger to the body politic it purports to defend and although in 1911 Major General Kirkpatrick was in no position to know, by 1945 Australia's Military Intelligence Branch would be complicit in some of the most egregious abuses of civil liberties in Australian history. Kirkpatrick laid the foundation for this abuse in 1911 when he recommended the Intelligence Corps focus on domestic intelligence matters.[39]

The army's Intelligence Corps did not survive for long. In 1914, it was disbanded and its personnel posted to the newly formed 1st Division of the AIF raised specifically for service overseas.

Meanwhile, Atlee Hunt continued his work in organising an informal intelligence system (see Figure 3.1). He also persisted with his efforts to create an external foreign intelligence service utilising his own assets, including John Suttor, and later, those of the army, through the good offices of Edmund

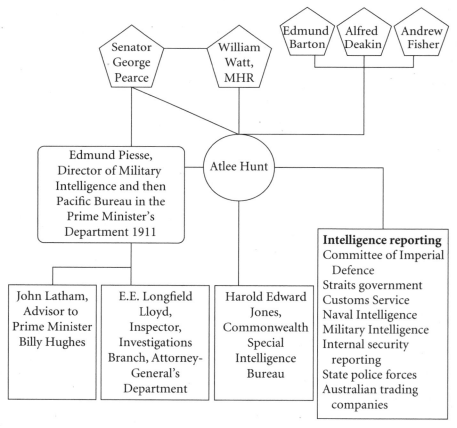

Figure 3.1: Atlee Hunt's informal intelligence network, 1901–23

Piesse. Throughout the period, Hunt worked most closely with the ACNB's Naval Intelligence Service to collect intelligence in the Netherlands East Indies, Malaya, New Guinea and the islands of the Pacific.

When the war finally broke out in August 1914, it would be the Royal Australian Navy (RAN) that was best situated to conduct intelligence collection operations in Australia's region, while the army struggled to recruit, train and equip the Australian Imperial Force (AIF) for service overseas. This left the ACNB as Australia's main intelligence organisation, which remained firmly focused on the region because of its role as the Admiralty's reporting centre for the Pacific and South-East Asia. The solid foundations of the peacetime intelligence reporting system would enable the RAN to carry out the first intelligence coup of the war—the seizure of Germany's naval codes— and conduct the first effective military operation by British forces in World War I with the capture of Rabaul in September 1914.

CHAPTER 4

A Prescient Letter: Suspecting Japanese Spies

On 17 May 1909, John Gillet Fearnley, a lieutenant of the RAN Volunteer Reserve (RANVR), wrote a five-page letter to the Australian Minister for Defence, Senator George Pearce, providing evidence in support of his concerns about suspicious Japanese activity in and around northern Australia.[1] Fearnley was in a good position to comment on such matters, as he had just arrived in Sydney from Cairns, where he had been a leading member of the community and the owner of one of the largest lighterage and steve-doring companies in the town. In his letter to Pearce, Fearnley admitted that he did not know what the Japanese were up to or why. He believed, however, that the activity was not 'disinterested curiosity' and that it was not neces-sary 'for commercial purposes'.[2] Fearnley informed Pearce that the only way Australia could understand Japan's interest was if it operated its own profes-sional secret intelligence service. This advice makes John Fearnley the first official to formally recommend to a minister of the Australian government that the country should create its own professional spy organisation.

John Gillett Fearnley was an Australian, but like many Australians of his time he was not Australian born. He was the son of a Lancashire mill manager who arrived in Australia in 1880 and made for Cairns in the new colony of Queensland, as far north as he could go. Once in Cairns, he began work as the agent for Messrs Thomas and Madden, a shipping agency and general goods importer.[3] By 1887, Fearnley was well enough off to marry Margaret Mary Smith, the daughter of James Thorneloe Smith, a civil engineer and member of the Queensland Legislative Council.[4] Two years later, Fearnley became a partner of William Charles Smith (James's brother) in a general merchant, shipping and insurance agency called Smith and Fearnley.[5] By 1893, he bought a home at Balaclava Estate, on the Mulgrave Road a few miles from Cairns.[6]

Smith and Fearnley became one of the biggest stevedoring and light-erage companies in northern Queensland. In addition to stevedoring,[7] it operated lighters, including the steamer *Vigilant*, and acted as the agent for the Adelaide Steamship Company.[8] With this background, John Fearnley was well placed to spot odd characters and strange behaviour among the sailors, crews and ships plying the waters of northern Australia. He also fitted the profile of the patriotic Australian official that Atlee Hunt typically recruited for his informal intelligence network.

Fearnley had not just made himself rich; he had made himself respected. As well as his business interests, he collected the necessary appointments of any prosperous Queenslander. He was commissioned as a lieutenant in the Queensland Maritime Defence Force[9] and admitted as a justice of the peace. He was elected an alderman of Cairns,[10] and appointed as a commissioner of audit as well as a licensing commissioner. He may have been the son of a Lancashire mill manager, but by the age of 32 he was a full member of the Queensland establishment.

It was during this time in Cairns that John Fearnley had the opportunity to observe the activities of Japanese seafarers and fishermen at close quarters. Most of what he saw, as he frankly admitted, was the usual day-to-day work of any seafarer and fisherman. There were occasions, however, when he noted odd things about the crews and activities of some Japanese vessels. Of particular interest to Fearnley were the careful mapping and soundings the Japanese appeared to be making. His concern was that, by the standards of the time, the Japanese were going well beyond the normal measuring that seafarers and fishermen would undertake in their work.

Of course, Fearnley's concerns can be dismissed as the standard racist responses to the Japanese that afflicted many Australians of the period, yet in his naval reporting and his behaviour as a leading resident of Cairns, he did not display the usual racist attitudes that would bring his judgements into question.

Cairns in the late-nineteenth and early twentieth centuries was as multi-cultural a place as you could find anywhere. Europeans from all backgrounds lived and worked alongside Chinese, Japanese and other Asian merchants, sailors and fishermen. Throughout the period, there is no evidence in the Cairns public record of John Fearnley expressing anti-Asian views or opposing the presence of Japanese residents in the town. In this, he was not alone, and the documentary evidence shows that the good burghers of Cairns were tolerant of Asian residents.

A good example of this tolerance was the response of the Cairns Council and mayor to a petition raised in July and August of 1897 demanding that the Japanese prostitutes in Cairns be removed. The petition got short shrift from the aldermen and the mayor, who publicly defended the Japanese women for their discretion by arguing that they did 'nothing to offend the eyes of passers-by'. By comparison, the mayor described the demoralising effect of 'drunken, degraded and brutal white women', who appeared 'stripped to the waist in public' and 'used such language as would make a bullock driver shudder'.[11] The Japanese prostitutes stayed; neither John Fearnley nor his wife signed the petition.[12]

Further evidence of Fearnley's even-handedness is obvious in his reporting as a naval officer. In one report on the activities of Japanese bêche-de-mer, or sea cucumber, fishermen accused of spying, he clearly exonerates them and finds that disgruntled white fishermen were spreading the allegations to harm their competitors.[13] This report was one of many generated by the unfounded allegations of Japanese espionage operations in North Queensland and around northern Australia.[14] Even the Anglican bishop of North Queensland raised questions about their activities.[15] The conclusion of Fearnley and fellow RANVR officers who investigated these matters were that the allegations were untrue.

Despite his findings on the bêche-de-mer fishermen, John Fearnley was concerned about some Japanese activity. As noted above, he was well placed to identify odd behaviour among the Japanese visiting northern waters. Things like expensive clothing worn by a deckhand or, rather amusingly, a Japanese hotel cook reading Thomas Carlyle in English. The question was, who were these odd characters?

In other cases, Fearnley recognised the skill with which Japanese masters and sailors took soundings, and plotted and charted the coast and its waters, as well above that expected of simple fishermen in pursuit of quarry.[16] When Fearnley wrote to Pearce that there was 'abundant evidence' of Japanese espionage being carried out against Australia, he was gilding the lily a little. The visit of a Japanese officer, Major Asada Ryoitsu, did, however, add weight to Fearnley's warnings.

The letter John Fearnley wrote to Senator Pearce arose from a conversation between the two as they walked home from the Naval Drill Shed at Rushcutters Bay on 24 April 1909.[17] There is no doubt that Senator Pearce was interested in what he was being told, because he forwarded the letter to the CGS, Major General Charles Hoad, for comment.

What is striking about Fearnley's letter is his realpolitik assessment of the potential issue for Australia should Britain become distracted by a major war in Europe and should a major Asian power—read Japan—take advantage of this. Great Britain, Fearnley wrote, will look to her own security first because she 'could not despatch an effective force to our assistance whilst the German menace exists. She dare not imperil her own safety to save Australia.'[18]

Added to this concern was the reality of the distances the IJN and RN needed to cross in the event of a confrontation. The IJN's battle fleet was six to seven days' steaming from Australia, while the Home Fleet was six to twelve weeks away. This fact alone justified the creation of the secret civilian intelligence service Fearnley was recommending. Australia and Britain needed forewarning of possible Japanese aggression, and this required spies on the ground in Japan.

The men recruited for this work, Fearnley advised, needed to be carefully and secretly selected from 'responsible officers from either naval or military forces'. These men should be experienced in Japanese manners and society, but, oddly, not necessarily proficient in the Japanese language, 'since this might excite suspicion'.[19]

John Gillet Fearnley is one of the first Australian military officers to write to an Australian Minister of Defence that Australia could not rely on Britain in the event of Japan attacking Australia. Yet Fearnley went further, critiquing Britain's intelligence-collection capabilities by highlighting its failures in Germany:

Hitherto we have relied upon the British Department for Intelligence, but I would respectfully submit that Australia's interests in Japan's movements is greater and more vital than that of Great Britain, and that, in view of the recent disclosures as to the inaccuracy of British knowledge of Germany's naval preparations, we may be pardoned if we seek information first hand in the case of Japan.[20]

What is surprising is that George Pearce, an Australian minister of the Crown, accepted this without demur, and not only did he listen to Fearnley's views, he passed them on to the CGS, Major General Hoad. Within three days, a memorandum from the CGS dismissed all concerns of Japanese spying in Queensland and insisted that 'any trained officer' who reads the newspapers, government gazettes and publicly available financial estimates was able to perform an intelligence role.[21] There can be little doubt that this response was written by Hoad and not William Bridges. Intelligence had been the responsibility of William Bridges for some time, and he had played an instrumental role in creating the Intelligence Corps.[22] The association of Bridges with the new Corps made it a target for Hoad.

The suspicious activity Fearnley outlined for the minister did not mean that he believed Japan was planning an attack on Australia. What he was clearly saying was that no one in Australia knew what motivated the Japanese activity. All he could say was that it was 'not merely disinterested curiosity'.[23] What it was Fearnley could not say, and neither could any Australian official or government. Australia, therefore, needed to spy on the Japanese in order to ascertain 'the true significance of our ally's interest in our coast', because their activities might or might not be espionage.[24] This was sound advice.

Not only was Fearnley correct in his claim that Japan was collecting intelligence on Australia, but his description of the suspicious activity accurately portrays the way Japanese staff officers from the operations branches of the IJN and the IJA conducted personal reconnaissance missions—disguised as tourists, seafarers and commercial travellers.[25] What he did not know was that this activity was ad hoc and very badly coordinated.

A striking example of this sort of intelligence operation is that conducted by Major Asada in March 1912. Australian officials had been notified of his visit, but the substance and reasons for it had not been explained. These officials asked state police forces and the Military Intelligence Branch to conduct surveillance of Asada as he travelled around Australia. This surveillance was obvious and amateurish, and Asada appears to have played to the gallery, to the extent of behaving quite rudely.

Instead of explaining his presence and engaging with local observers, Asada chose to amuse himself by playing cat and mouse with them and by using Japanese for his speeches and conversations, which he knew the Australian observers could not understand. The result was a souring of relations and, as the visit was well organised, it led the Western Australian section of the Intelligence Corps to suspect that Asada's visit was prearranged by a network of Japanese agents in Australia.[26]

The only evidence for this suspicion were the elaborate arrangements made to get Asada to places where Japanese residents were numerous, and the show made of greeting him. The result was that the Commonwealth began to investigate legislation to protect the nation from espionage, culminating in the passing of the *Crimes Act 1914*.[27] Ironically, Major Asada was not a spy or even an intelligence officer; he was from the operations branch of the Imperial General Staff, in Australia to have a look for himself.[28]

Asada had no concern about the impact of his visit on Australians, and he had even less for the damage he did to the relationship between Australia and Japan. Having Mr Ichikawa of the Mitsui Bussan Kaisha company post to him a package of maps and plans of Australian fortifications on his return to Japan caused further damage to an already ruptured relationship. The crudity of Asada's activity is indicative of an amateur playing a game rather than a professional conducting intelligence collection.

Later examples of this approach include the 1941 visit to Australia of Major Hashida Sei, an officer of the Japanese Department of Supply;[29] and the description of the IJA's HUMINT collection activity before the invasion of Malaya in Tsuji Masanobu's book *Singapore: The Japanese Version*.[30]

Tsuji, who served as an operations staff officer in the plans section of the 25th Army, IJA, was based in Saigon while he planned the invasion of Malaya.[31] He describes how staff officers, majors Asaeda Y. and Hayashi Tadahiko, conducted reconnaissance of Thailand and Malaya disguised as civilian tourists.[32] The way these operations were conducted in 1941 was identical to John Fearnley's description of Japanese intelligence-collection through reconnaissance in Northern Australia before 1914.

In August 1914, all of Australia's attention would be drawn away from Japan and the Pacific to Europe, and specifically to Germany and Austria. The Great War had started, and there were real enemies that needed to be dealt with, while Japan had become an important ally of Britain. It was the IJN that would secure the Pacific and Indian oceans for Britain, thus releasing Royal Navy ships for service in home waters and the Atlantic. One of the operational roles that the IJN took over was escorting the first troopships from New Zealand to Albany in Western Australia and then forming part of the escort of the ANZACs from Albany to the Middle East.[33]

Despite this, Australian officials and politicians kept a close eye on the Pacific and on Japan and, although the Australian government's advisors would correctly assess in 1918 that there was little hard evidence of Japanese espionage in Australia, suspicions remained deeply ingrained.[34] Japan might be Britain's ally, but she was the most obvious threat to Austalia's position in Asia.

CHAPTER 5

Join the Navy and Spy on the World

No nation with a navy is bereft of a spy. Where a sailor goes, a sailor sees and a sailor hears. They are the epitome of Sun Tzu's living agents, those who are 'clever, talented, wise and able to gain access', and who return with intelligence.[1] By its very nature, a navy constantly has to collect, analyse and assess intelligence to accurately chart the currents, winds and other characteristics of the water it sails upon. This makes every sailor an intelligence collector, and having them report their sightings and observations ashore in foreign lands is a simple extension of their everyday tasks at sea.

Navies need to do this, not from any malign intent, although the intelligence can always be put to malign purpose, but because ships at sea need to identify those places where they can victual, obtain fresh water and access repair facilities. In turn, this requires negotiation with the government controlling that place, and an evaluation of its friendliness and attitudes. Intelligence is thus part of the genetic coding of the sailor, and history is replete with examples.

The RAN was created on 10 July 1911 from the small vessels comprising the Auxiliary Squadron that supported the Admiralty's Australian Naval Station based in Sydney, to which were added the newly arrived destroyers, HMAS *Yarra* and HMAS *Parramatta*.[2] The third destroyer, HMAS *Warrego*, was shipped to Sydney in parts and assembled at Cockatoo Island, the NSW Government dockyard, where it was launched on 4 April 1911. Control of the Commonwealth's naval forces remained vested in the ACNB, which had been formed under the Defence Council in 1905.[3] The development of Australia's naval force is important to our story because not only did it provide Australia with sailors who would bring back intelligence, but it also integrated Australia into the Admiralty's existing intelligence-collection systems, including the Reporting Officer system.

The immediate result of this was that the two terminal ports in Australia, Fremantle in the west and Sydney in the east, became intelligence-reporting centres responsible for managing and analysing intelligence coming in from reporting officers throughout the region. By 1913, the Admiralty had sent out an intelligence expert, Major Percy Molloy of the Royal Marine Light Infantry, who worked as the District Naval Officer at Fremantle before being posted to Melbourne where he was to assist the RAN establish an Intelligence Department within Navy Office.[4]

On 8 September 1913, the Admiralty instructed that the Intelligence Centre at Sydney was to be handed over to the ACNB, and that this centre was to be the contact point for the processing and transmission of naval intelligence between the ACNB and the Admiralty in London.[5] The Admiralty also made it clear that the ACNB was to carry the cost of these operations by having an Australian naval officer understudy Major Molloy with a view to taking over his duties at the end of twelve months.[6]

These arrangements began the process of the Admiralty passing off the financial cost and responsibility for intelligence collection in the Asia–Pacific region to Australia, while keeping the Australian system in immediate contact with the Admiralty. Both Fremantle and Sydney were to remain in direct communication with the Admiralty in London, and reports on the arrival and departure of foreign ships of war and, during wartime, of enemy merchant ships, were to be immediate and complete.[7] This was the world's first broad-ocean surveillance system, and it was designed to keep the Admiralty in London abreast of all notable events at sea and of the dispositions of foreign naval forces.

The ACNB had also received the Admiralty's blessing to create its own intelligence organisation within Navy Office in Melbourne. The duties of this organisation, the Intelligence Branch, were to be much more clearly defined than those of the Army's Intelligence Corps. For the navy, the problem in war was quite simply one of ramping up the existing peacetime intelligence organisation to meet the increased demands and tempo imposed by wartime conditions. The very first paragraph of the *RAN Instructions for the Naval Intelligence Service* clearly stated this principle:

> The collection and distribution of Naval Intelligence will be conducted by the same organization in peace as in war, except that in war there will be certain extensions and modifications of the system.[8]

Like all bluewater navies, the RAN needed active collection of information on all shipping movements into and out of Australia's region, as well as knowledge of the victualling and replenishment services available in the ports and countries within that region. There was also a need to keep abreast of the internal political situation within countries in the region and between them. All of this was a necessity if the ships of the RAN and the RN were to operate effectively within the region.

This need led to the development of close ties between the ACNB's Australian Station and the RN's newly formed stations in China, the East Indies, Cape Town and the West Indies.[9] These titles denoted the regions into which the Admiralty divided the world, so that comprehensive and timely intelligence on the world's maritime affairs could be maintained in London. Reporting by each of these stations to the Admiralty in London was copied to all of the other stations, ensuring the relevant commanders-in-chief were as well informed as possible on events worldwide.[10]

Responsibility for managing Australia's participation in this worldwide system lay with Navy Office, where the Intelligence Branch received information directly from and reported intelligence directly to the Admiralty. Navy Office also directly communicated with the neighbouring China, East Indies and Cape stations and, via the Intelligence Branch, supplied the fleet with information, although this was capable of being supplemented by local naval intelligence officers and district naval officers (DNOs) who could transmit intelligence directly to fleet units when time was of the essence.

One stroke of luck for the ACNB was the appointment of Captain Walter H.S.C. Thring to the Australian Naval Staff in 1913. Captain Thring had served in the RN since 1893 and had enjoyed a career that saw him promoted to Commander in 1908. Thring's progress had come to a halt after he fell from grace with his Admiral, Lord Charles Beresford, who had become embroiled in a bitter fight with the First Sea Lord, Admiral of the Fleet Jackie Fisher. Because of this and his own bouts of ill health, Thring was passed over while seven officers were promoted to captain over his head. Believing his career in the RN was finished, Thring resigned his commission in February 1911.[11] Nineteen months later, in August 1912, the ACNB approached the Admiralty to find a senior gunnery or torpedo lieutenant who could be appointed as an assistant to Rear Admiral William R. Creswell, the First Naval Member of the ACNB. The ACNB regarded this appointment as urgent, as the new ships making up Australia's Fleet Unit were due to be delivered over the next year or so, and the C-in-C, Australia Station, Admiral Sir George King-Hall, RN, believed that Creswell was 'able, but antiquated' and would need the help of a more up-to-date officer to manage the RAN.[12]

As luck would have it, the old-boy network came through for Australia, and Captain Francis Fitzgerald Haworth-Booth, the Australian Naval Representative in London, was given Thring's name by Captain Edward Phillpotts, the Naval Assistant to the Second Sea Lord. Haworth-Booth described Thring as 'a brilliant Officer' who had been awarded 'five First-Class Certificates' and been 'promoted Lieutenant for meritorious examinations'. He also detailed Thring's career as Flag Commander (Chief Intelligence Officer) to Lord Charles Beresford, and explained that he had completed the Naval 'War' College Course but had resigned because of the 'dissension between Lord Charles Beresford and the Admiralty'.[13]

On 17 December 1912, Walter Thring accepted a two-year appointment as a Lieutenant Commander in the RAN with a salary of £600 per annum. Thring quickly took on responsibility for Australia's naval defence, naval intelligence and censorship. In quick order, he also replaced Creswell on the Federal Munitions Committee and took over the administration of the Australian Mercantile Marine. Creswell describes the impact Thring had—'Immediately on his appointment, Captain Thring prepared the *War Book* comprehending all that would be necessary to be done in the event of war', adding that this work had 'enabled the immediate taking up by the Fleet of the War Stations requested by the Admiralty'.[14] Thring's energy and professionalism ensured that when war broke out in 1914, the RAN was able to immediately contribute to the Imperial war effort.

In his recommendations after the war, Creswell took the trouble to point out that Thring had 'directed the Intelligence Service which he organised with careful and continuous attention and with such success as to elicit praise from the highest Naval Authorities, the Lords Commissioners of the Admiralty themselves'.[15] This was high praise indeed, and indicated the impact of Australian intelligence successes between 1914 and 1918. These included the first capture and exploitation of German wireless telegraphy codes during the war, a significant cryptological coup, which was managed with extreme professionalism; and the running of one of the most audacious and prolonged HUMINT operations of World War I.

In looking at Australia in August 1914, it is difficult not to admire the level of professionalism displayed by the RAN and the Australian government as a whole. The preparedness and the resulting capacity to move to full war readiness were markedly different from 1939. In 1914, the RAN was the dominant service and the first to undertake military operations, whereas in 1939, the RAN had lost its position as the mainstay of Australia's defence. This loss was partially due to government parsimony and partially due to the increased status of the army following its sacrifices between 1915 and 1918.

In the field of intelligence, the RAN, or more accurately the ACNB, was the first Australian government organisation to be permitted direct liaison on a day-to-day basis with its imperial counterpart. The army and all other organs of state communicated with their UK counterparts via the Governor-General's Office, where all of the British codes and ciphers used by the Dominions Office in London were secured. Because of the need for the rapid communication of maritime intelligence on a day-to-day basis, the ACNB and the RAN had separate Admiralty codes, and the Lords of the Admiralty did not defer to the Secretary of State for the Dominions.

The purposes of the Naval Intelligence System were twofold. First, it was to fully inform the Admiralty in London, Navy Office in Melbourne and the officers commanding His Majesty's Ships and shore stations of the distribution and movements of all ships of war and merchant shipping in their region. It was also required to keep them abreast of all relevant matters that could potentially affect the operations of the fleet. Lastly, it provided warnings to all British merchant ships of the threats posed by enemy ships of war on trade routes, so they could avoid capture or molestation.[16]

The fundamental strength of the peacetime Naval Intelligence System was that it required only minor changes, some extensions and modifications to fulfil its wartime role. The receipt of the 'warning telegram' from the Admiralty triggered these extensions and modifications, including the change in the system of encoding communications and the imposition of censorship on radiotelegraphy (SIGINT collection).

The warning telegram also authorised DNOs to become transmitting radio stations, sending the latest intelligence to the fleet and detached units, and broadcasting trade-route warnings to British merchant shipping. In Australia, the terminal trade ports, Sydney and Fremantle, became the chief stations for the broadcasting of the trade-route warnings to merchant vessels in the Indian and South Pacific oceans and adjoining seas.[17]

The peacetime organisation centred on the Admiralty as the world-wide coordination centre for all maritime intelligence, with Navy Office in Melbourne as the coordination centre for Australia's designated area of interest. Within Australia, each state had its own DNO, who acted as the chief naval intelligence officer for the state and held responsibility for the littoral areas off that state's coast. Under the DNOs were Sub-DNOs based at each port. Except in emergencies, the Sub-DNO passed all reports on the first of each month to the DNO, who, in turn, passed them on, along with his own report, to Navy Office. Navy Office then passed these reports to the Admiralty, with copies going to the neighbouring stations.[18]

In 1914, this reporting covered the movements of all ships of war, important merchant vessels, suspicious vessels and any suspicious activity involving coal, fuel oil, ammunition or warlike stores. It also covered political and economic activity in surrounding nations. In wartime, the reporting extended to cover the movements of enemy merchant vessels or suspicious craft, all aircraft activity, the sounds of gunfire or other indications of the presence of ships of war and mines, and the time and content of any intercepted radio message.[19]

All reporting formats were standardised, as was the mechanism for communication. The movement of foreign ships of war was always to be reported by telegram or the fastest possible means, while other reporting was via post, unless considered urgent. As the *Instructions* made clear, 'the value of most intelligence lies in the rapidity with which it can be communicated to the officer concerned'.[20] The RAN was very flexible when it came to getting information to commanders in a timely way. Radio and telegraphy were used readily, and the ACNB appears to have been less concerned with the cost than many other government departments of the time.

The Naval Intelligence System drew upon manifold sources of information, and DNOs and intelligence officers were told to 'gradually develop a system' to make the most of them.[21] This brought numerous officials into the system, including local collectors of customs, police, postmasters, newspapermen, shipping officials, masters of vessels, and people returning from abroad. Even the army's resources were tapped, and DNOs were encouraged to establish close relations with their Military Intelligence counterparts with a view to developing mutually beneficial cooperation.[22]

In Australia in 1914, the Naval Intelligence System also drew upon the Customs Department's 115 signal stations spread along the coast, and the customs officers in Adelaide, Albany, Brisbane, Fremantle, Hobart, Melbourne, Newcastle, Port Darwin, Port Pirie, Sydney, Thursday Island and Townsville. The Administrator of Norfolk Island was appointed as a reporting officer, as were the customs officers in New Guinea at Port Moresby and on Samarai, and, following the capture of Rabaul, the Administrator of Rabaul. In New Zealand, the customs officers at Auckland, Dunedin, Invercargill, Lyttelton, Napier and Wellington were participants in the Australian Naval Intelligence System, as was the customs officer at Suva in Fiji.[23]

In addition, the masters of all British vessels were required to report sightings of foreign men-of-war and, during wartime, enemy merchant vessels and other suspicious craft to the naval reporting officer at their next port. The content of these forms was coded and, in wartime, telegraphed to the intelligence centres at Sydney or Fremantle. In peacetime, to save money, they were posted. All reports were forwarded as soon as practicable to Navy Office in Melbourne and to the Admiralty in London.[24]

This visual surveillance system, which in 1914, ended at the horizon or at the distance a human could see, was supported by a new surveillance system that listened to the messages carried by wireless telegraphy. It was the birth of signals intelligence (SIGINT).

By 1914, the Admiralty was well aware of the importance of SIGINT, and the hard evidence for this lies in the intricate planning for the seizing of German codebooks in Australia on the outbreak of war, which is the subject of our next chapter. This aside, the ACNB also had its own new part-time

SIGINT organisation—the 30 Royal Australian Navy Wireless Telegraphy Service (RAN W/T Service) stations, which were entirely manned by naval personnel and therefore able to conduct the sensitive work of intercepting and reporting enemy and other wireless messages to Naval Intelligence. The RAN W/T Service was a distinct entity, and was never associated with the wartime RAN Radio Service, which consisted of commercial stations taken over by the ACNB at the beginning of the war.

The RAN W/T Service stations were kept inland, to avoid the risk of raiding parties, as they acted as communication centres for the distribution of intelligence and, in their own right, as SIGINT collectors in accordance with the Admiralty instructions of 1910.[25]

The sensitive nature of the RAN's W/T stations' wireless-intercept activity is made clear in the secret Volume III of Admiral of the Fleet Lord Jellicoe's 1919 report, which described their role as collecting 'all W/T messages made by the enemy for the information of the Intelligence Department'.[26] This was work of a 'very secret nature' and therefore 'should be entirely under the control and administration of the Intelligence Department'. To ensure that the ACNB understood the sensitivity of the information being conveyed by these stations, Jellicoe advised that all information must be transmitted back to the ACNB and the intelligence centres by cable.[27] Jellicoe's personal experience of wireless intercept, or SIGINT, supplied by the Admiralty's Room 40, NID25, had convinced him of its value, and had alerted him to the compromises that poor operating procedures presented to a navy.

The focus of all of this effort was purely naval, but because of the need for naval vessels to enter foreign waters and ports, and for the ACNB to formulate and advise the government, Naval Intelligence was required to supply information about the countries bordering the Pacific.[28] This meant that the ACNB and the Naval Intelligence centres had to collect intelligence on foreign countries, which risked the RAN becoming the de facto Australian intelligence agency, something the ACNB did not want to happen.

The ACNB's reticence was understandable. First, its intelligence role was to collect information on the operational activities and capabilities of the navies operating in the Pacific. If RAN officers were also to collect strategic and other foreign intelligence, it would divert them from meeting the ACNB's tasking. The second issue was the usual one of who was going to pay for the collection of national intelligence. The ACNB would not have been keen for its budget to be diverted to meet the needs of other departments. These sorts of reservations are legitimate, and the Australian government had to face the reality that if it wanted intelligence information on strategic economic and political matters, it needed to establish a dedicated body for that work.

In 1914, Navy Office, like its army equivalent, operated a counterespionage system in ports and harbours around Australia. Members of the RANVR and the DNOs at state and local level undertook the majority of this work. Unlike the army, the RAN had enough work on its plate managing the demands of maritime intelligence, and in tracking enemy activity in the islands to Australia's north and in the waters of the western Pacific. As a result, its counterespionage effort did not expand beyond its ports and bases into the wider community. The ACNB and the RAN remained firmly focused on international activity and the control of the seas.

As the cataclysm broke across the horizon in August 1914, no one in Australia dreamt that the ensuing fighting would scar the country the way it did. The small nation almost at the end of the earth suffered 59,342 killed and 166,819 wounded, and these casualties left an indelible mark on the nation's psyche, one that remains to this day, more than 100 years later.[29] The unleashing of industrial warfare shocked all nations. Never before in human history had destruction on such a scale and at such intensity been possible. At the end of the war in 1918, people around the world expressed their relief that it was over by calling it the 'Great War' and by turning towards the chimera of peaceful coexistence through international cooperation. What few realised was that it was just round one in a conflict that would last until 1945. During this entire period, Australia's intelligence effort prospered and dwindled before slowly coming back to health and wealth in the second round of fighting between 1939 and 1945. This is the rest of our story, and its beginnings are the great successes of Australian intelligence in 1914 and 1916–19.

CHAPTER 6

Australian Intelligence Success, 1914

As Australia entered the war in August 1914, the first naval action taken was the conversion of the peacetime surveillance system to a war footing. The second was the initiation of a plan for the RAN to seize all German vessels operating within Australian waters. This plan was predicated on the expectation that German vessels in Australian waters could be seized before their masters became aware that Britain and Germany were at war. More importantly, their codebooks and ciphers could be captured. This is the story of that plan and its outcome.

In August 1914, all doubt was removed as Germany and Austria were now clearly identified as the immediate threat to Britain and, by extension, Australia. As always, one of the first actions to be taken was to find and arrest all those who could present a threat to the nation. In this case, measures were implemented to detain Germans and Austrians who may have been spies or who were military reservists present in Australia when war was declared.[1] This action required little in the way of intelligence collection and was left to the usual civil authorities. Indeed, despite the general, and sometimes intense, suspicion of Germans and Austrians, it appeared no actual spies were caught in Australia.

Did this mean there were no German spies active in Australia in the first twenty years of the country's history? The answer is that there were possibly two. The first suspect was Dr Walter de Haas, the German Trade Commissioner in Australia.[2] At the beginning of the war, de Haas was interned as an enemy alien and, much to the outrage of the press, was allowed to return to Germany in late 1915.[3] Walter de Haas was a businessman working for Messrs Weber, Lohmann and Co., the agents for North German Lloyd,[4] and he may be the 'Walter de Hass' who arrived in Sydney aboard the RMS *Oceania* on Wednesday 22 November 1893,[5] and who later lived at Perry Street in Sydney until November 1902, when the premises were put up for sale.[6] In early 1903, he was appointed to the position of German Trade Commissioner to the acclaim of many Sydney businessmen.[7]

The sole basis for claiming de Haas was a spy was that he undertook a trip around Australia between September and December 1911 that caused concern within the Department of Defence and the Department of External Affairs.[8] The truth of the matter is that his activities during his trip betrayed no intelligence activity beyond the collection of information expected of a trade commissioner as part of his regular duties.[9] It was not even his first trip north; he had conducted a similar journey in 1904.[10]

The organisation that undertook the 1911 investigation of Dr de Haas's tour of northern Australia was Atlee Hunt's, and although it can be argued that Hunt was not running an organisation, this is true only in the formal sense. The fact was that from the moment de Haas left Sydney until the moment he returned and was cleared by Hunt, he was watched and reported on by government officials from a variety of state and Commonwealth departments and agencies. It may not have been a formal intelligence organisation, but it was effective.

The second possible spy, Paul Gustav Hentschel, a German teacher, was the only identified German spy in Australia during this period, and was visiting from the United Kingdom, where he had been a long-term resident. He arrived in Australia on 13 January 1911 on the SS *Gneisenau* and departed in June 1913.[11] What he did in Australia is unknown, but it seems unlikely that he was here to escape the British, given that, realistically, Germany was a closer and a safer haven. The reality is either that he was spying or, more mundanely, trying to save his marriage.

Hentschel's work as a German spy had got him and his wife, Patricia, involved in a seamy affair involving a ménage-à-trois with an RN gunnery instructor, Warrant Officer George Parrott. It appears that Mrs Hentschel seduced Parrott into stealing 23 classified manuals from HMS *Agamemnon*, which were then passed to the German Navy's intelligence branch (Nachrichten Abteilung) by the Hentschels.[12]

This activity appears to have strained the Hentschel marriage, and he sailed to Australia, where he subsequently applied for naturalisation.[13] While he was doing this, he was also writing to his wife. Britain's new Counter Espionage Bureau, led by Vernon Kell, intercepted his letters and discovered the details of the Parrott affair.[14]

For some reason, Hentschel returned to Britain in June 1913. He later claimed it was to bring his family out to Australia, but given his marital difficulties, this explanation is hard to accept. Indeed, it may have been the case that his German employers were unhappy and had somehow communicated that to him. His subsequent action in making a very public confession of his spying strongly suggests he was trying to extricate himself from the role of spy.

Whatever the case, Hentschel had come to Australia and started the process of applying for residency. This makes him the first foreign spy to be identified beyond any doubt in Australia. Unfortunately for Hentschel, back in Britain, Vernon Kell was waiting for him.

Once Hentschel returned to the United Kingdom, Kell's bureau attempted to turn him into a double agent with a payment of £100.[15] In a clever move, Hentschel countered by surrendering himself to the police as a spy. Once he was arrested and brought before the court, Hentschel exposed Kell's offer, and the matter was quietly hushed up and Hentschel threatened into silence.[16] Hentschel never returned to Australia.[17]

When war broke out in 1914, Military Intelligence took upon itself the job of finding other Paul Hentschels in Australia, while the RAN initiated one of the great intelligence coups of 1914–18. This involved the pre-planned seizure of German merchant ships and the capture of their secret codebooks for exploitation by the Admiralty. The RAN was to mount this operation as soon as the Naval Staff and the ACNB received the warning telegram from the Admiralty in London. At the same time, the already operational Naval Intelligence System underwent the required modifications and extensions, the new codebooks were brought from their safes, the DNOs and Sub-DNOs became receiving/transmitting stations, and SIGINT collection began in earnest.

As Australia went to war in 1914, there was no national intelligence effort. Military Intelligence was undertaking counterespionage activity, and the

RAN was preparing to mount aggressive SIGINT and HUMINT operations against the enemy. These operations would be conducted in accordance with the Admiralty's plan for the outbreak of war, and although the state of the RAN's intelligence system was impressive for the time, there was no centralised oversight mechanism and no assessment system outside of the military and naval staffs. This led to unnecessary disputes and turf wars, and it meant that there were as many opinions about what a piece of intelligence meant as there were people reading it. That said, in the 1914–18 period, the level of cooperation between the RAN and the army was good, especially when compared to what would happen between 1939 and 1945.

For Australia, the opening months of the war in 1914 included one of the first SIGINT coups in naval history. In the first two days of August 1914, Germany's Pacific Squadron was detected by SIGINT operating in the area of the Bismarck Archipelago and not, as the Admiralty had expected, in the China Sea.[18] In what can only be described as slovenly operational security by the Germans, SMS *Scharnhorst* was detected signalling Yap and Nauru in an attempt to contact the *Nurnberg*. This lax use of radio then exposed SMS *Geier* and the survey ship SMS *Planet*, and their rough positions were plotted from direction finding (DF) bearings.

The successful detection of the German squadron's position shows the power of SIGINT even in 1914. DF and traffic analysis of German radio messages provided the RAN and the Admiralty with good tactical and operational intelligence on the composition and movements of the German Pacific Squadron. The intelligence picture being built up through this process was complemented on 3 August when a message ordering the *Scharnhorst* to proceed to the Mariana Islands was intercepted and broken out on 13 August. Unfortunately, the information it revealed was ignored because it had been so easily obtained.[19]

The result was that the Australian task force, consisting of HMAS *Australia*, HMAS *Sydney*, HMAS *Yarra* and escorting destroyers, steamed north to look for the Germans off New Britain. If this proved unsuccessful, as it did, the cruiser HMAS *Sydney*, accompanied by the destroyers HMAS *Warrego*, HMAS *Parramatta* and HMAS *Yarra*, was to land troops at Rabaul in order to destroy the German radio transmitter there and capture German New Guinea.[20] This mission was completed in September 1914, when Rabaul, and thus the whole of German New Guinea, was captured by Australia.

The detection and reporting of the German Cruiser Squadron was a

SIGINT success, even though naval commanders ignored the information. Later analysis would show that the SIGINT had been good, and that had the Australian Squadron responded to it, the RAN would have fought the first major naval engagement of 1914–18. Yet this success was not the biggest coup of 1914. This happened much further south, in Australia itself.

On 2 August, two days before the formal British declaration of war, but the day after Germany's declaration of war with Russia, the Admiralty in London activated the Examination Service. Now all vessels entering or leaving Australian ports were subjected to search and seizure operations by naval and customs officers. By 8 August 1914, RAN intelligence had identified the German ships *Greifswald*, *Neumünster* and *Thüringen* in dock at Fremantle, the *Prinz Sigismund*, *Signal* and *Cannstatt* in Brisbane and the *Berlin* in Sydney. Preparations were now made to seize these ships and take their codebooks.

The plan worked so well that by 10 August a copy of the *Handelsschiffs-verkehrsbuch* (HVB, literally merchant ships' transport book), the German maritime codebook, were in the hands of the RAN when the local naval authorities at Fremantle boarded and searched the *Greifswald*.[21] The news was telegraphed the same day to the ACNB, which then ordered the DNO at Fremantle, Captain C.J. Clare, RAN, to begin SIGINT-interception operations from the *Greifswald* and use the captured codebooks to break the intercepted traffic. In addition, all other RAN stations were ordered to send intercepted German traffic to Fremantle for decoding.[22]

This action ensured that the ACNB and the Admiralty were able to read German maritime traffic within a week of the war starting. While the immediate needs of the ACNB and the Admiralty were being met, in Fremantle Captain Clare engaged George A. Pfizer, the Senior Master of Modern Languages at the Perth Modern School, to translate and make copies of the captured books. On 15 August, copies of Germany's codebooks were forwarded to the ACNB in Melbourne and the Admiralty in London via the hand of a master of a British ship.[23]

A second set of HVB codebooks were also seized from the German merchant ship SS *Hobart* on the morning of 12 August by Captain J.T. Richardson, RAN, who, being a better storyteller than Clare in Fremantle, made this the tale everyone came to know.[24]

The *Hobart*, en route from Fremantle to Adelaide and Melbourne, had compromised herself when she routinely signalled her position to the signal station at Esperance. This enabled Richardson to prepare to seize and search her as she negotiated the difficult transit of Port Phillip heads.[25] Richardson, accompanied by a party of disguised sailors, boarded and took command of the SS *Oonah* as she departed Melbourne for Burnie and Devonport in order to intercept the *Hobart*, which they did just inside Port Phillip heads. All of this was seen by the *Oonah*'s passengers and quickly reported in the Tasmanian press.[26]

The original plan had been to board the *Hobart* quickly and seize control of her before the captain or crew had time to throw their codebooks overboard.[27] The boarding and seizure of the *Hobart* went to plan, although the boarding only occurred after the *Oonah* signalled the *Hobart* to stop and Richardson and his party had been transferred by boat across to her. Surprisingly, despite all of the *Oonah*'s passengers being aware of the outbreak of war, the captain of the *Hobart*, Jürgen Paulsen, did not throw his codebooks overboard but left them in a hidden compartment.[28]

Working on the assumption that the captain would have hidden the books in his cabin, Richardson bedded down in the captain's bunk and pretended to sleep. A little later, just like in a Richard Hannay story, the German captain and a crewman entered the cabin and attempted to retrieve the codebooks from the secret compartment in the footrest of the captain's desk. According to Richardson's tale, he rather theatrically jumped up and seized the books at gunpoint.[29] Theatrical or not, the documentary evidence supports Richardson's account, with a signal reporting the books captured received at the ACNB at 1015 hours on 12 August.[30]

By 3 September, the RAN had captured four sets of the HVB—off the *Greifswald*, *Hobart*, *Prinz Sigismund* and *Neumünster*—and a variety of other codebooks, including the *Signalbuch der Kaiserlichen Marine* (SKM, literally signal book of the Imperial Navy), and technical data off many other ships. Within a month of hostilities opening, Germany's entire naval communications system was completely compromised.

The surprising thing in all of this was not the size of the RAN's successes, it was the complacency of the Imperial German Navy (IGN), which, despite knowing that a large number of its ships had been quickly captured, continued to use the HVB and SKM codes until early 1916, when they changed to the *Allgemeinefunkspruchbuch* (AFB, or general radio communications book).[31] This would not be the last time that military commanders failed to display a realistic appraisal of enemy codebreaking capabilities.

Yet the seizing of the codebooks was not the real intelligence success. It was what was *done* with the captured books that was the real triumph.

The most important part of the whole exercise was the speed with which active decoding was begun at Fremantle, and the speed with which the lessons learned there and in Port Phillip Bay were passed throughout the RAN and to the Admiralty.[32] Within 24 hours, on 13 August, the DNO and Sub-District DNOs (SDNOs) on Thursday Island and at Newcastle were receiving directions on what to do to restrain the crews, officers and masters of any further ships detained.[33] Concurrently, in Melbourne, further copying, decoding and reporting was begun using the services of Mr Lyng, a Danish citizen employed as a German interpreter at the Naval Works Department, and other personnel.[34] Mr Lyng appears to have been tasked with taking the books to HMAS *Sydney*, where he would begin the work of translating them.

As the ACNB was exploiting the captured German codes, it was also considering how to deal with German diplomatic communications being passed via civilian telegraphic cables. The ACNB team looked at the problem and formed a view that the German diplomatic traffic was most likely encoded using a German edition of the International ABC Code that Naval Intelligence could not yet read. Atlee Hunt at External Affairs was approached and asked if his department could assist the ACNB in obtaining a copy of this publication.[35] Unfortunately, External Affairs did not have a copy but Hunt advised that the German edition might just be a simple translation of the English one, making it irrelevant to the work being carried out. Hunt also advised the ACNB 'that it is not desired to make a formal search under the extreme powers conferred on the Minister of Defence in cases of war'. The implication was clear. Any such action would tip the Germans off, and this would result in serious consequences. Hunt further recommended that the matter be left to him, and he would have 'two or three agents' obtain a copy of the book.[36]

In 1914, Australia, a nation less than fifteen years old, had naval and civilian HUMINT collectors operating in support of the SIGINT collection effort, who effectively destroyed the integrity of Germany's communications security within six weeks of war being declared.[37] Few Australians are aware of this significant victory.

Of course, life is never simple, and even in wartime the lawyers can intrude and make it even less simple. This is exactly what happened.

The seizure of Germany's naval codes might appear to the modern reader to be a simple matter of national security. Alas, it was anything but. The difficulty was that, as the codebooks formed part of the furniture and fittings of the seized vessels, they came under the control of the Prize Court, which in Australia came under the jurisdiction of the state Supreme Courts acting on behalf of the Court of Admiralty, and as far as such courts were formally concerned, the demands of war were irrelevant to the droit of Admiralty.[38]

On 3 September, the Secretary of the Department of Trade and Customs began asking the ACNB to return the codebooks, so that they could be brought into the registry of the relevant courts until the distribution of prize money and the fate of the seized vessels were decided.[39] Luckily, despite the legal constraints, the various courts appreciated the impact of the law on what was a successful naval operation and worked to speed up the process. The NSW Supreme Court, however, required the Crown Solicitor for the Commonwealth, Gordon Castle, to apply formally for the codebooks of the *Berlin* to be subjected to a formal 'handing out of court to the Proper Officer of the Crown'. To do this, Castle had to file an undertaking in the Registry of the Court 'to keep the books in good order and condition and to return the books to the Registrar of the court in the same condition as received'.[40] Castle was told the books were to be kept available in case the court required their urgent return. It was as good as putting it all in the newspaper but, luckily, there were no German spies in Australia to report the matter.

This provides a clear explanation as to why the various codebooks and documentation had to be copied out. The courts required the return of the original documents in their original condition, but there was nothing to stop the ACNB from copying the originals as many times as they liked, and they did. Eighty-five copies were made and 50 of these were sent to the Admiralty in London, along with five copies to the East India, Mediterranean, Cape of Good Hope and China stations, as well as to the Australian Squadron. Three copies were sent to Hong Kong, three to New Zealand and single copies to HMS *Pyramus*, HMAS *Melbourne* and HMS *Minotaur*, and one to the Captain in Charge of Naval Establishments in Sydney.[41]

Distribution of the duplicated codebooks was accomplished by placing them in weighted bags in the charge of the masters of RMS *Maloja*, SS *Aldenham* and RMS *Otway*.[42] These masters were ordered to throw the bags and cases over the side if they faced capture by any warship. All of the packages arrived safely at their respective destinations and helped establish Britain's highly successful exploitation of German maritime, zeppelin and U-boat communications throughout the war.[43]

What is not as well appreciated about this whole affair is that as the RAN was breaking the German codes in Fremantle, Melbourne and Sydney, the Admiralty in London had not yet obtained copies of these codes. This led to all German naval traffic intercepted in Britain being transmitted to Melbourne for decryption, placing the ACNB and its codebreakers, Mr Lyng and, later on, Senior Master Wheatley, Head of the Senior Masters at the Naval College, at the centre of Britain's codebreaking establishment.[44]

The work undertaken by the ACNB's codebreakers comprised decryption of old messages, including a message dated 16 July 1914 from the SS *Main* to the chief of the German Cruiser Squadron at Tsingtao (Qingdao), detailing the movement of four British armoured cruisers through the Formosa (Taiwan) Strait. This message had been relayed by the British-controlled Fukkikaku (Fuguijao) Signal Station and was most likely intercepted there by British officials. Other messages included traffic sent to the *Scharnhorst*, and messages announcing the arrival of the *Main* at Wusung Roads, off Shanghai, on 28 May.[45] More recent messages were also worked on, including traffic from the German warships steaming off the South American coast after the Battle of Coronel on 1 November. The technical notes in the files indicate that these units had changed their working by altering the cipher key used with the codebooks. This key had been broken in Melbourne and the results sent to the Admiralty for use in Room 40.

The action of the RAN in seizing the codes of the German merchant fleet and IGN was a major coup, but the sophistication of the exploitation and the way the work in Australia provided intelligence in Europe was the real intelligence success. In fact, it was one of the most significant successes in SIGINT between 1914 and 1918, as the information obtained from these early codebooks not only compromised German communications, it compromised how German codes were put together. This enabled Britain to stay ahead of the German cryptographers, because the latter made the error of not acting on the possibility of compromise, and simply redesigned their new codes using the same algorithms as the earlier codes. This made it easy for British cryptanalysts to break the new systems implemented in 1916. In 1914, Australia was, for a while, a world leader in SIGINT.

CHAPTER 7

The Wanetta Organisation, 1902-20

The war had started well for Australia's Naval Intelligence Section and the ACNB. They had secured Germany's codes and, despite the interference of the Courts of Admiralty around the country, managed to keep this information secret. The operations at the beginning of the war had also shown that the best intelligence operations combine HUMINT and SIGINT in support of one another. The successes and speed with which the captured documentation and codebooks were exploited demonstrates a level of sophistication in the Navy Office of 1914 that was not replicated in 1939. In the intervening 25 years, the ACNB and RAN would suffer a significant degradation in capabilities, starting around 1919 when the Australian government began a process of cutting defence spending that continued right up until 1937.

The successes in Australian intelligence collection in 1914 arose from a combined effort, in which HUMINT operations were used to obtain secret intelligence from the enemy that enabled a much more powerful SIGINT attack to be implemented and maintained. This series of operations shows the importance of a mixed approach. The only rub was that the HUMINT effort involved was limited to Australia's own shores, and to the small number of officers and men working for the RAN in the ports of Australia. What

Australia lacked was a HUMINT capability that could obtain intelligence abroad.

Good HUMINT requires good humans. This is such an obvious truism that it is often overlooked until it is too late. In 1914, the ACNB would find that its capability to conduct HUMINT operations in Asia was to be stymied by the lack of suitable personnel to carry out the work. Asian languages and familiarity with Asia and Asians was a significant shortfall in Australia's capabilities of the period. Of course, Australia could access the intelligence being sent to Britain by her network of consular officials, supplemented by the routine reporting of British shipping agents. In terms of broad-ocean surveillance, this system worked well, but not in dealing with the clandestine activities of German intelligence agents operating against the British Empire internationally.

The problem of this German intelligence activity came to a head in Australia's region in early 1915, when it became obvious the Germans were attempting to support nationalist rebels in India by supplying arms via the neutral Netherlands East Indies (NEI, now Indonesia).[1] The schemes being implemented involved German agents in the still neutral United States purchasing weapons and ammunition and shipping them from American ports in American ships to the also neutral NEI. From the NEI, the German agents could then arrange meetings with India's nationalists and send the arms as required. In theory, this was a workable plan. The only flaw was the ineptitude of German intelligence in avoiding detection by US authorities.

The German espionage operation in the United States involved sabotage rather than intelligence, and this resulted in a series of attacks that either failed or were devastating, particularly the blasts that destroyed the rail wharves on Black Tom Island in New York Harbor. These operations were appalling because, rather than making Germany safer, they severely damaged its reputation and made all of its espionage activities the focus of US government attention. The final straw was the Zimmermann Telegram debacle of 1917, which the much more sophisticated British intelligence operation in America ruthlessly exploited to drive the United States into the war against Germany. Germany's espionage operations in the United States are probably the best example of the dangers associated with direct action.

With the US government and people increasingly angry at the behaviour of the Germans and suspicious of the intentions and activities of the British and their allies, it was difficult for the British to take serious steps against the German gun-running operations, particularly when the shipments were being sent to the NEI. The answer was an intelligence capability within the NEI and South-East Asia, something Britain did not yet have in place.

The ease with which German speakers could operate within the NEI was a matter of substantial concern to British colonial administrations in India, Singapore and surrounding colonies. This became even more acute following the mutiny in Singapore of the 5th Indian Light Infantry Regiment and the Malay States Guides Mountain Battery in February 1915.[2] The causes of the mutiny appear to have been poor discipline, an unpopular commanding officer and the fact that the men were concerned about being sent to the Middle East to fight fellow Muslims.[3] It was also thought that a German prisoner, August Diehn, a suspected intelligence officer, had played a part in stirring up the men.

This mutiny underscored the concerns about German intelligence activity in the NEI. It was around this period that the ACNB happened across Reginald (Reg) Hockings of Thursday Island, a man whose background and knowledge made him eminently suitable for the role of intelligence officer operating in the NEI.

Hockings was born in South Brisbane in 1868 and educated at Kangaroo Point Public School before taking up a position with the merchant houses of Samuel Hodgson and Co. of Brisbane, and, later, Parbury, Lamb and Co., also of Brisbane. In March 1888, Hockings went north and joined James Clark[4] to form the Wanetta Pearling Company, based on Thursday Island. Pearling proved profitable for Hockings and he became wealthy enough to buy plantations on Boeton (Buton) Island in the south-east Celebes. He even became Vice-Consul for the Netherlands at Thursday Island.[5] This background made him a prime candidate for work as an intelligence agent in the NEI and South-East Asia.

Exactly how Reg Hockings was recruited into foreign intelligence work is unknown, but it is more than likely that Atlee Hunt at External Affairs recommended him to the ACNB. The grounds for this belief are that Hockings and Hunt had a relationship going back a number of years, and the circumstantial evidence suggests that Hockings and his company were part of Atlee Hunt's informal intelligence system.

The relationship between Hunt and Hockings appears to have started in November 1903, when Hunt approved the Wanetta Pearling Company's application to bring in groups of 25 to 30 Asian pearlers to work in the Torres Strait pearling industry.[6] Two years later, Atlee Hunt visited Thursday Island as part of an inspection tour of New Guinea.[7] It is highly likely that the two men met and reinforced what appears until then to have been a long-distance relationship via correspondence.

Further evidence that Hockings was a source for Atlee Hunt can be seen in the Commonwealth Parliamentary Hansard of 21 September 1905, which reports that in answering F.F. Bamford's question on Thursday Island pearling, Prime Minister Deakin relied on information that, Deakin stated, Atlee Hunt had just obtained from pearlers on Thursday Island.[8]

Other signs that Reg Hockings and the Wanetta Pearling Company enjoyed a special relationship with the Australian government was Atlee Hunt's role in obtaining permission for the company to operate its own wireless network. Hockings wanted to build a wireless base station on Thursday Island and to equip his luggers with transmitting and receiving equipment. Hunt ensured that the necessary permissions were granted and that Wanetta Pearling became the first pearling company to be so equipped. The increase in capability that this brought was immense. Wanetta Pearling could now send situation reports back to Thursday Island, from where, if they were of interest to Hunt or the government, including the ACNB, they could be telegraphed, so that a sighting in the Indonesian Archipelago could be on the desk of Naval Intelligence within hours.

From a commercial perspective, the equipping of the luggers allowed Wanetta to deploy its vessels more astutely and to avoid sending follow-up vessels to areas where the fishing was proving uncompetitive. This made the company much more flexible in the way its luggers operated, and it provided a constant stream of intelligence back to Australia. All of this put the Wanetta Pearling Company at the forefront of radio communications in northern Australia.

Wanetta was also one of the very few Australian companies to gain the approval of the Papuan administration to fish in Papuan and New Guinea waters. Again, Atlee Hunt controlled the activities of the Papuan administration, and most likely ensured that Hockings' company obtained this approval. The return for Hunt would have been the intelligence that Wanetta's skippers were collecting and sending back to Australia.

All of this suggests that Reg Hockings and his company were undertaking intelligence-collection missions for Atlee Hunt and External Affairs well before he made himself available to the ACNB in 1915. When Hockings wrote his letter offering his services as a secret agent, he was not just offering himself, but a small fleet of radio-equipped pearling luggers supported by a long-range radio transmitter and receiver station and company wharves and facilities on Thursday Island.

The organisation that Reg Hockings was offering for service was highly capable, and not just because of its sophisticated radio network, but because the crews of Wanetta's luggers were multicultural and included Malay and Indonesian seafarers and fishermen who were well known throughout the NEI. It was an entire espionage organisation and it fell right into the lap of the ACNB just as the need for such an outfit became critical.

Reg Hocking and the Wanetta Pearling Company became secret agents of the ACNB and Admiralty in February 1916, when Admiralty Signal 269 arrived approving his employment as a secret agent.[9] This approval from the Admiralty did not mark the initiation of the Wanetta network, as by the time it was received by Navy Office, Hockings' two trusted Malay assistants, Thomas Loban and Batcho Mingo, to whom Hockings referred as No. 1 and No. 2 respectively, were already active in the islands to Australia's north. It appears from the evidence that the ACNB had already tasked the Wanetta network but had now also offered its services to the Admiralty.

The organisation that Hockings ran embarked on a program of general surveillance and intelligence collection throughout the NEI, Portuguese Timor and the islands of the Celebes (now Sulawesi). The organisation consisted of a hard core of Hockings on the lugger *Wanetta*, accompanied by Loban, Mingo and a crew, and his nephew and partner, Norman Hockings, who managed the company's facilities on Thursday Island and manned the radio link with the *Wanetta*. The two assistants, Loban and Mingo, were most likely from Borneo, and had worked for Hockings for thirteen and fifteen years respectively. It seems that once he had volunteered his services as a spy, they joined him.[10]

Batcho Mingo and Thomas Loban departed Australia aboard the French warship *Kersaint* to join the Australian Destroyer Flotilla at Dili, in Portuguese Timor, in October 1915.[11] From there, Loban accompanied Hockings to Humboldt Baai (now Yos Sudarso Bay, Jayapura), where he went ashore to make contact with local police and the domestic servants working for senior Dutch officials.[12] Mingo was placed aboard an Australian destroyer and acted as an intelligence gatherer and translator during the patrols around Sandakan and Singapore. Later, he went to Djambea (Emden) where he was betrayed to the NEI authorities. Despite the NEI authorities issuing a warrant for his arrest, Mingo continued his espionage work unperturbed.[13]

At this stage, the main tasks given to the Wanetta organisation were to travel throughout the archipelago and try to identify and track vessels, their cargoes and their intended destinations. The organisation was well equipped for this task, as its lugger was well known in the archipelago as a legitimate pearler and did not stand out. Neither did Hockings, with his plantation interests in the Celebes and his standing in the NEI.

As well as identifying and reporting shipping movements to the ACNB, the organisation was also tasked with identifying the presence of German agents within the NEI and to report the attitudes of the local NEI officials and population to the war and towards Britain and Australia. As part of this task, the organisation expended considerable effort in the dangerous work of developing sources among local police and officials and the domestic servants of senior Dutch officials. Loban took the lead in this work after he accompanied Hockings to Humboldt Baai.

During 1915, the organisation was also tasked with identifying those German intelligence officers operating in the NEI who were involved with the attempts to ship arms to India. The arms themselves were to be investigated, as were the ships carrying them. One of the individuals they were specifically asked to find was August Diehn, the German businessman who was thought to be a spy and had escaped British captivity in Singapore.[14]

Although the British authorities had no hard evidence, it was suspected that, along with the Helfferich brothers, Diehn was a member of one of the more effective German espionage and intelligence operations working in South-East Asia, channelling money and arms to the nascent nationalists in India and other British colonies, and sending information back to Germany. He was also suspected of being the mastermind behind the exploits of the German commerce raider SMS *Emden*.

The objective of these operations was to draw British forces away from Europe by fomenting rebellion within British colonies, particularly India, where there was already a large and well-organised anti-British political organisation. This made Diehn and the Helfferich brothers important targets for British intelligence and thus for the Wanetta organisation.

The Wanetta organisation was successful in tracking Diehn to Bali, and Loban was sent to follow up his activities there and look for a secret German radio transmitter believed to be on the island. While carrying out this task, he and an assistant were attacked by a tiger and barely escaped with their lives.[15] He did not find much to report other than that Diehn was trying to buy an oil mill. He did discover, however, that the Dutch Resident on Bali was pro-Allies and kept a very close watch on the activities of all Germans on the island, including Deihn.[16]

With Diehn identified as being on Bali buying his oil mill, Loban returned to the *Wanetta* and accompanied Hockings on visits to ports in the NEI in an effort to identify and inspect the American vessels there. Two high-interest US vessels they were seeking were the SS *Annie Larsen* and the SS *Maverick*, which the British suspected were running the guns destined for the Indian nationalists.[17] It appears that this suspicion was well founded, but the German plan failed because of the incompetence of the German operatives in the United States. At the time, however, this operation was accorded an extremely high priority and was of great interest in London.

In fact, the priority of the operation was so high that an interdepartmental committee in London comprising representatives from the Foreign Office, Colonial Office, India Office, Admiralty and War Office had been established to coordinate it.[18] The importance attached to this task explains the attention the Wanetta organisation gave to finding these vessels and the risks Hockings and his men took to board them. One good example of these risks is the way Loban finally got information on the *Maverick* in late 1917.

Having just arrived in Tanjoeng (Tanjung) Priok, Hockings and Loban found that the *Maverick* was also berthed there. In order to get to her, Loban demonstrated considerable chutzpah by 'borrowing' a motorcycle from the post office in Batavia (now Jakarta) and riding it out to Tanjoeng Priok for an entire week, during which he cajoled information about her cargo and true destination out of the *Maverick*'s American mate and captain's boy.[19]

In addition, Loban, assisted by W.G. Beckett, the British Consul-General at Batavia, worked to identify the activities and cargoes of suspicious vessels operating out of Batavia. The relationship between Hockings and Beckett was close, and Beckett was an important part of the organisation. When Beckett suddenly died at Weltevreden, Batavia, on 19 September 1917,[20] Hockings described it as an event that was 'very serious at the present time'.[21]

Another high-priority task given to the Wanetta organisation was locating the missing Australian vessel SS *Matunga*, operated by Burns Philp. All that was known in Melbourne was that the *Matunga* had disappeared between her departure from Sydney and nearing Rabaul, and it was feared that the German raider SMS *Wolf* had taken her. This fear was well founded.

Although on the face of it the *Matunga* appeared to be just another of the Burns Philp trading vessels, she had an interesting history. In 1913, she had been fitted out on the orders of Atlee Hunt, and at Commonwealth expense, with a powerful radio transceiver station.[22] This activity was covered by a formal agreement between the Department of External Affairs and Burns Philp, even though radio communications on maritime vessels was not the province of External Affairs.

Why External Affairs financed this activity is unknown, but it was secret, and Atlee Hunt acted to keep it that way. Whatever the radio work being conducted on the *Matunga*, it was sensitive enough that in August 1914 Hunt sent a coded telegram to the Lieutenant-Governor of Papua ordering him to impress upon all passengers and crew, 'but most especially the wireless operators, the need for the strictest secrecy in relation to all matters heard on board or on arrival in Australia'.[23] This suggests the *Matunga*'s radio operators were probably involved in SIGINT collection against German New Guinea.

On 7 August 1917, *Wolf* intercepted the *Matunga* off Rabaul, captured her and later looted and sunk her after taking the crew and passengers off. The popular explanation for the taking of the *Matunga* was that she had compromised herself by radioing her departure from Sydney and the details of her cargo. The *Wolf*, operating in northern waters, somehow then picked up this transmission and laid in wait on *Matunga*'s approach to Rabaul. According to some versions, it was detected on approach to Rabaul by the aircraft from the *Wolf*. Another version is that *Matunga* radioed her imminent arrival in Rabaul and the *Wolf* pounced.[24]

Although plausible, the idea that the *Matunga*'s wireless operators, who appear to have been involved in SIGINT collection themselves, compromised her position by carelessly transmitting messages is hard to believe. If they had done this on departure from Sydney, it would have resulted in a rebuke from the Naval signal station, and this would have been logged. No such log entry appears to have been found at the time, as no mention is made in the files of the *Matunga* breaking radio silence or security. Given the effort that was put into the ACNB's investigation into the loss of the *Matunga*, the absence of this evidence is important, as it indicates that poor radio security did not cause the loss of the vessel as most of the sources suggest. As for the *Matunga* transmitting her arrival at Rabaul, again, it is plausible, but knowing the *Wolf* was in the area, why would she do this? Some care has to be taken with the stories of how the *Matunga* was captured because they come from the British captives held aboard the *Wolf*, and it is unlikely that the Germans told civilian captives they intended to release later how they had really detected the *Matunga*. It has the feel of a cover story.

It is more likely the Germans noted something odd about the *Matunga*. It might have been that the *Wolf* detected *Matunga* using naval or other non-commercial codes or they had heard something about her from their contacts ashore. After all, there were German citizens throughout the archipelago, passing intelligence of this sort to the *Wolf*. This latter explanation seems more convincing, because the ACNB did not simply chalk the *Matunga* up to experience; it ordered an extensive investigation and search for both her and the *Wolf*.

Reg Hockings and the Wanetta organisation were among those tasked with finding both ships. The organisation conducted searches all over the archipelago and its men even walked across islands to inspect inlets hidden from the open sea. It was during this activity that Mingo was captured on Waigiau (Waigeo) Island, tortured and interrogated by the Dutch authorities. In 1919, Reg Hockings put Mingo's capture down to insecurity in Australia: 'someone in Sydney spoke too freely of my mission and it got to a certain neutral quarter'.[25] He may have been right, but it could also have been that the constant flow of communications and the resulting work carried out by the organisation was now attracting attention.

One of the major problems experienced by the Wanetta organisation was the complicated way its instructions were sent. The actual acceptance of the tasks appears to have been left to the ACNB and Naval Intelligence at Navy Office in Melbourne. These tasks were conducted on behalf of the Admiralty and the Colonial, Foreign and War offices in London, the Australian government and ACNB and Naval commanders in Singapore, Hong Kong and Shanghai. Far too many people knew about the Wanetta organisation and far too much was being asked of it. Other British government agencies in China, India and Malaya also appear to have been aware of the Wanetta organisation and Hockings' role in it.[26] It did not stop there.

One example of how the Wanetta organisation's work was being passed around government occurred in late 1918, when a British diplomat turned up without warning at Hockings' estate on Boeton (Buton) Island. This individual asked him to supply information, but Hockings wrote that he only revealed information a normal planter or resident would have known. The 'diplomat' thanked him and left, but as Hockings reported, 'the look he gave me on parting led me to believe he knew more about me than we discussed'.[27]

After this episode, he had to deal with yet another visit, this time from an American who 'presented himself with papers from Singapore and Macassar referring him to me for assistance'. In this case, Hockings observed his American visitor for three days before deciding he 'passed muster', then sat down and wrote an extensive report for the use of the US government. During this time he told the American how the British had intercepted cash transfers of around 5 million Guilders from American sources to the Germans in the NEI and how it had all been 'spent' on British operations.[28] The American was, Hockings reported, somewhat surprised at this revelation.[29]

Given the way the Wanetta organisation's exploits were being passed around in official circles, it was no wonder Mingo was captured while crossing Waigiau Island to look for the *Matunga*. The record does not divulge how the Dutch identified him, but it is unlikely they were overly interested in him. Their real target was Hockings, the white man for whom they knew Mingo and the others worked. In his reports, Hockings detailed how Mingo was passed up the chain of the NEI administration, being interrogated at each level in turn, until the Governor of the NEI personally interrogated him. Mingo kept the identity of Hockings and his other comrades secret, and his health suffered accordingly. Hockings describes his physical state on his release from hospital as being that of a skeleton.[30] In order to get Mingo out of the NEI, Hockings and the British Consul-General at Macassar, Lazarus Sarkies Arathoon, pledged their word to the Governor of the NEI that they would keep him available.[31] They left the NEI with Mingo in December 1919 and were back in Australia on New Year's Day 1920.

Reg Hockings did not leave Batcho Mingo to die in the NEI and he did not abandon Tommy Loban either. In fact, during their service in the war,

Hockings seems to have persuaded the Australian government to issue both men with 'alien registration certificates', Mingo getting his, no. 509, on 5 February 1917, and Loban no. 516 on 7 February 1917. This was something of a feat, because the conditions for this status forbade the holders from changing their abode without notifying police.[32] After the war, Hockings would fight to have both men granted permanent residency, or, as he put it, the 'common right to live in Australia if they desire', free of the threat of expulsion at the hands of Australian officials. He got that too.

Despite the White Australia policy, the authorities also agreed to let the Armenian, Lazarus Arathoon, settle in Australia. The ACNB accepted Hockings' arguments on behalf of Arathoon and recommended that Prime Minister Hughes duly approach the British government to allow Arathoon to live in Australia. The Governor-General sent Hughes's request to the Secretary of State for the Colonies on 15 October 1920, but bureaucracy, a force much greater than racism, now intruded to stop Arathoon being given residency. In London, the Foreign Secretary decided Arathoon could not get a certificate of British naturalisation until he had completed the regulation five years of service. This decision was probably made on advice against setting a dangerous precedent. Arathoon's service as the acting Vice-Consul at Macassar did not count towards this period of service and neither did his work for the Wanetta organisation. Arathoon was told he should resubmit his application in April 1922.[33] Lazarus Sarkies Arathoon, MBE, died at Macassar on 10 April 1932 and was buried on 17 April 1932 in Batavia.[34]

In support of his appeals for his assistants to be allowed to remain in Australia as free men and for Lazarus Arathoon to be admitted, Reg Hockings called Mingo and Loban his 'trusted servants', who had been vital in 'reaching places it was impossible for me to go and for visiting ground one person alone could not cover'.[35] He called Arathoon a man upon whose secrecy 'my life depended'.[36] As far as Hockings was concerned, 'The secret of my mission, my safety and liberty remained in their loyalty . . . They did their job well.'[37] All of these men and the nameless others who manned and sailed the *Wanetta*, are part of Australia's intelligence history.

With the end of the war, it appears Reg Hockings did not give up his role as a secret intelligence officer, and his services were simply transferred from Navy Office in Melbourne to the C-in-C, China Station, to whom he was still reporting in September 1920.[38] In the covering memorandum to a report dated 23 September 1920, Hockings informed the C-in-C that the Dutch were still actively hunting the 'Britisher' and an inspector had been visiting Ternate and its surrounding regions. Hockings remained confident his identity had still not been compromised, and this strongly suggests he continued to collect intelligence, most likely on the Indian and other nationalist groups operating within the NEI.

Hockings arrived back on Thursday Island around 15 September 1920, and sent his reports and memos through to the ACNB on 23 September, telling the Secretary of that body he would be arriving in Melbourne on 20 October.[39] Atlee Hunt, still at External Affairs, stayed abreast of developments and arranged for the First Naval Member, Rear Admiral Sir Percy Grant, to meet Hockings aboard HMAS *Australia* before he left Sydney on the evening of Thursday, 7 December 1920.[40] Hunt was to act as Reg Hockings' chaperone.[41] Unfortunately, due to delays in inspecting ships, the Admiral was late getting back to HMAS *Australia* and Hockings had had to leave. It was then arranged for the First Naval Member to meet with Hockings on his return to Sydney on 19 December, although the record does not disclose whether this happened. This writer hopes it did.[42]

It appears life returned to normal for Reg Hockings and the Wanetta Pearling Company, and that Atlee Hunt was no longer playing any role in the management of Australia's foreign interests. Like all good spies, Reg Hockings, Tommy Loban, Batcho Mingo, Lazarus Arathoon and Norman Hockings simply returned to their public lives, leaving little trace of their exploits other than in the dark and dry recesses of the official archive.

CHAPTER 8

Almost Had It: National Intelligence, 1901–20

In the first two decades of Australia's history, official interest in intelligence collection was not confined to the armed services. Civilian departments of the new Commonwealth government were also keen to develop intelligence systems and, as we saw in the case of Wilson Le Couteur, they were not backward in conducting clandestine intelligence collection if they believed it was required. Indeed, the Le Couteur mission was an entirely civilian affair, run by civilian officials led and organised by Atlee Hunt of the departments of External Affairs and Prime Minister on behalf of Edmund Barton.

Atlee Hunt seems to have had quite a knack for intelligence at a time in history when few people understood intelligence or had any experience in running intelligence operations. Yet Hunt crops up in the Le Couteur mission, as a functionary in some of the military intelligence missions of this period and most certainly as a significant player in the work of the Wanetta organisation. All of this suggests Atlee Hunt was a significant force in the organisation and conduct of early Australian intelligence operations.

It is no surprise that the man heading the External Affairs Department should take an interest in intelligence. Hunt's department was responsible for the enforcement of the Immigration Restriction Act and in ensuring that all aliens were registered and tracked in Australia. He was also responsible for ensuring anyone who was forbidden to enter Australia was detected and deported. To this end, Hunt created a network of intelligence collectors ranging across members of the armed services, customs and state police forces and agencies (see Figure 8.1). This was most likely the reason he recruited Reginald Hockings.

Atlee Hunt's requirements for intelligence extended beyond Australia, and he obtained it from two main sources. The first was the imperial government in London and its various colonial governments in Asia, including reporting

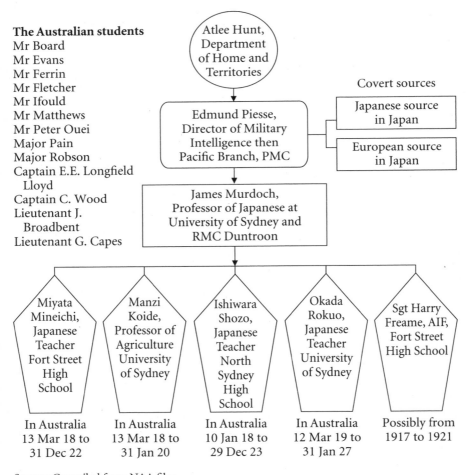

Source: Compiled from NAA files.

Figure 8.1: Australia's first organised intelligence-collection operation

from the governments of India and the Malay Straits to Australia's Governor-General. The fact remained, however, that the reporting received in Australia was only what those governments wished to share, and Hunt never knew if they were sharing it all.

The second source was entirely Australian, and was made up of the agents of trading companies, such as Burns Philp, and the various states officials and trade representatives posted overseas, whose activities we looked at earlier. This system worked, but in the way a Heath Robinson machine might work, and the demands of war had placed great strains upon it. Atlee Hunt, along with many others including George Pearce, William Watt and Edmund Piesse, understood this. They shared a concern over how much leeway Britain would give Japan in the Pacific and Asia in return for her assistance in Europe, and they shared the concern that Britain would act in her own interests first.

This group of government officials and politicians was keen to put an intelligence system in place to keep an eye not only on Japan, but also on Britain and any other countries involving themselves in the region. Other than Atlee Hunt, the most influential of these officials on intelligence developments in Australia over the next few years was Edmund Piesse, a lawyer and militia officer who had joined the Intelligence Corps in 1909 and completed the intelligence course of that year.

When war came in 1914, Edmund Piesse made a startling career choice. Rather than rushing off with the 1st AIF, he chose to remain in Australia and direct the national intelligence effort in the Pacific and the countries around it, particularly Japan. Piesse, like John Fearnley among others, was concerned about Japan and its ultimate intentions. They all understood how powerful Japan had become and how capable it was in waging war. They also suspected that it was overly interested in Australia, but, as we have already explored, they did not know why.

In focusing Australia's attention on Japan and Asia, the biggest issue Piesse and everyone else had was a simple one: no white Australians spoke Japanese, and few whites spoke any other Asian languages. The result was that while Australia might fret about Japan and its intentions, they could not even read the public statements in the Japanese press. The only source of Japanese-language skills was the NSW Trade Commissioner John Suttor in Kobe, and he could only supply so much.

This lack of language capability was not just a problem in Australia. Even in Britain, where the relationship with Japan was seen as a strategic necessity, few could communicate with Britain's main Asian ally. With the increased intensity of the fighting in Europe and the need to engage more closely with the Japanese, Britain had created a language course for military officers, and by 1917 British officers were being removed from active service and sent to Tokyo to learn the language and customs, and to network.[1]

In Australia, in 1909, John Fearnley had recommended that men should be selected to spy on Japan. In 1911, he again raised this suggestion with George Pearce, but this time he recommended that these men be familiar with Japanese customs and attitudes. In 1916, Edmund Piesse, now the Director of Military Intelligence, and Captain Walter Thring, Head of Naval Intelligence, agreed that action was essential, and that selected officers be selected and trained in Japanese. As it happened, the NSW government had already created a rudimentary program of Japanese-language education at Fort Street High School, and a commercial provider was operating as the Berlitz Schools of Languages of Australia, out of Ocean House, Moore Street (now Martin Place), Sydney.[2] This made Sydney the logical place to start.

In April 1916, the acting prime minister, none other than Senator George Pearce, started the ball rolling on Japanese-language training for military officers. This action was taken while Billy Hughes was overseas visiting Britain, and it is likely that Pearce and William Watt, among others, colluded behind Hughes's back to authorise this program. Pearce exploited Hughes's absence and involved the CGS in a minute recommending the Military Board appoint a Japanese-language instructor at Duntroon Military College.[3] By May 1916, the subject was raised at the Conference of Premiers in Adelaide where they noted a 'necessity of greatly increased attention to the teaching of modern languages in the various public schools'.[4] Even the Associated Chambers of Commerce for the Commonwealth were now calling for the establishment of a 'Chair of Eastern Languages in the respective universities of the various states'. Of course, it all came down to who was to pay, but all this activity meant that people with real political pull were creating the conditions for Japanese-language training to be implemented.

In June and July 1916, the ACNB began to grapple with the Japanese-language issue as well. Captain Thring had proposed that a chair in Oriental Studies be established at a university and that the ACNB order the RAN

College to begin teaching Japanese and other languages to selected midshipmen.[5] This initiative fitted well with the plans of George Pearce and Military Intelligence, and with the ambitions of General J.W. Parnell, the Commandant of Duntroon, to establish a lectureship in Japanese at the University of Sydney at Commonwealth cost. The idea was that the Commonwealth would provide the University of Sydney with the necessary funding to establish the chair, providing the University made the professor available to teach Japanese at Duntroon and the Naval College.[6]

At this point it all looked good, but now the petty politics of middle managers stopped the introduction of the training at the Naval College. The college council was opposed to introducing Japanese, and mounted a campaign of passive resistance that the best efforts of the Naval Staff and the ACNB could not overcome.[7] The council wanted the college to teach French, an idea the Naval Staff 'deprecated', but the council, particularly the teaching staff, insisted upon this, and the ACNB dropped the matter, choosing instead to encourage those officers who wished to learn Japanese to find their own training.[8] This was the mechanism by which RAN paymaster officers such as Eric Nave would be trained.

Now a search had to be made for a suitable teacher of Japanese. The first stop in this search was London, where Billy Hughes asked the British government for help in finding a suitable Japanese scholar. There was not much the British could do to help, as they faced the same problem. The next stop was the British ambassador in Tokyo and, as luck would have it, he was able to nominate two possible candidates, A.M. Cardew of Cox and Company of Calcutta and James Murdoch, a 60-year-old Scottish journalist now teaching in Japan.[9]

The ambassador's recommendations were qualified, particularly in the case of Cardew, who turned out to be a former army officer 'believed to be on special service for the government of India'.[10] The ambassador felt that given this, 'he may not be available'.[11] The ambassador was correct. A.M. Cardew, a captain in the Royal Engineers and a noted Asian scholar proficient in Japanese and Chinese, was heavily engaged in counterintelligence activities against Japanese penetration of India and China.[12]

Optimistically, on 10 July 1916, the Australian government formally approached the Viceroy of India asking for Cardew's services and asking 'under what conditions' he might be made available. The reply on 17 July 1916 greatly regretted that the services of Captain Cardew 'cannot be spared at present'.[13]

As for James Murdoch, he was a journalist well acquainted with Australia and deeply imbued with a knowledge and understanding of the Japanese language and culture. The ambassador felt that £600 per annum would be a fair salary,[14] an amount that in 2016 figures equates to around $345,800 (labour value) based on average weekly earnings.[15] On 29 July 1916, the Australian government authorised the British ambassador to offer James Murdoch this salary, a three-year engagement and first-class tickets to Australia, on the understanding that he was to be attached to the University of Melbourne or the University of Sydney and would be required to visit Duntroon periodically.[16] By 11 November 1916, Murdoch had agreed and all of the arrangements were in place for him to travel to Melbourne as soon as possible. These arrangements were vague and it would later turn out that Murdoch had negotiated the entry into Australia of his Japanese wife and her brother, Okada Rokuo, who was included in the group of Japanese language teachers admitted under the program.

James Murdoch was no stranger to Australia, as he had lived and worked as a teacher in Brisbane before becoming a journalist for William Lane's radical magazine *Boomerang*. In 1889, Murdoch had moved to Tokyo to take up a position at the prestigious First Higher School, which acted as a feeder for Tokyo Imperial University. Murdoch was introduced to the highest levels of Japanese society and seemed to prosper, which, given he had written egregiously racist material about East Asians in the *Boomerang*, was ironic. More comical though was that Murdoch had a very broad Scottish accent that made it difficult for his Japanese students to understand what he was saying.

In September 1893, Murdoch had left Japan to join his old friend William Lane at New Australia, outside of Asuncion in Paraguay. It was not a happy or rewarding experience, as the disaffected members of Australian society soon became disaffected with their new society, as well as with William Lane. In 1894, Lane and 63 loyalists moved south to try for utopia again in a colony they called Cosme. James Murdoch lasted only three days at New Australia before he left for London. He returned to Japan in 1894 and worked in various educational institutions until 1908, when his teaching contract at the Seventh Higher School in Kagoshima was not renewed. He then moved into journalism, contributing to the *Kobe Chronicle*, and, presumably because journalism in Japan did not pay, became a citron farmer. The call to return to Australia in 1917 was probably very welcome.

On his arrival in Australia, James Murdoch learned that he was to be appointed Chair of Oriental Languages at the University of Sydney. It was closer to Duntroon than Melbourne and it was more interested in having such a chair.[17]

The cover story for Murdoch's appointment was that the University of Sydney was moving to meet the growing demand created by increased commercial and cultural links between New South Wales and Japan. The Japanese Consul-General in Sydney, however, was fully aware that Murdoch and Murdoch's brother-in-law, Okada Rokuo, were going to be teaching Japanese to military officers at Duntroon, and that there was more to the initiative than cultural and commercial links.[18] The only people who seem to have been confused by the cover story were the authorities at the Naval College, where the Commandant, Captain C.H. Morgan, had to write to Captain Thring to find out who Murdoch was.[19]

In October 1917, Professor Murdoch returned to Japan to recruit further teachers of Japanese for the NSW Department of Education and lecturers for the University of Sydney. While in Japan, Murdoch maintained a correspondence with Edmund Piesse using a cover name, H. McRae of 39 Broadway, Camberwell, Victoria, to get past the ubiquitous Japanese surveillance system.[20] The tradecraft was basic, as the address was Piesse's private residence and McRae was his wife's maiden name.

By 20 December 1917, Murdoch had recruited Miyata Mineichi, described as a teacher of Japanese, and Manzi Koide, described as a Professor of Agriculture, to come to Sydney to work as Japanese-language teachers. The two men were to arrive on the *Aki Maru* on 13 March 1918.[21] Professor Miyata would move on to Fort Street High School and later provide private tuition to RAN students, including Eric Nave and Eric Kingsford-Smith (see Chapter 10).[22]

Oddly, James Murdoch had left his wife, Takeko, in Japan. Mrs Murdoch, accompanied by her brother, Okada Rokuo, finally arrived in Australia aboard the *Kamakura Maru* on 19 March 1919. The entry of Murdoch's wife and brother-in-law was managed quietly, and Mrs Murdoch's admission into Australia was approved with a note that no further action under the Immigration Act was required.[23] It is almost as if someone had told James Murdoch that attempting to bring in a Japanese wife might prevent him taking up the post. There is some evidence of this in the response of Atlee

Hunt to the arrival of Murdoch's family. Hunt appeared a little perplexed by the arrival of two Japanese and quickly directed the Collector of Customs in Sydney to 'ascertain and advise' him on just how many Japanese were helping Professor Murdoch and what their names were.[24]

Despite concerns that the Okada clan was invading Australia, the matter soon died off. Marginal notes in the file provided informal guidance to officials that they need not worry about annual extensions for the three men concerned, but that yearly reports were required to ensure they did not change employment.[25]

In September 1919, Professor Murdoch was bringing in yet another Japanese, Ishiwara Shozo, to teach at Fort Street High School in Sydney. Permission for Ishiwara's admission was given to the Collector of Customs in Sydney on 27 September 1919, five days after the NSW Director of Education made the request.[26]

All of this activity would gladden the heart of any intelligence professional. The Australian and NSW governments were actively undermining their own White Australia policies by bringing Japanese teachers into the country so that Australian students could learn Japanese in order to increase trade and commercial relationships and to spy. The work of Piesse, Murdoch and Thring, and their backers in Cabinet and the armed services, started to bring results. Two young officers, lieutenants John Broadbent and George Capes of the army's staff corps, had become proficient enough in Japanese to accompany James Murdoch to Tokyo to undertake the Japanese-language course run through the British Embassy there.[27] In addition, other young officers, including E.E. Longfield Lloyd and Eric Nave, had started to learn Japanese.

By 1921, Piesse and Murdoch had created one of the foundations of an intelligence system: language-training courses for military officers and future spies. There was a central bureau within the Prime Minister's Department, and there was a Japanese-language program staffed by six Japanese teachers: Professor Miyata Mineichi, Okada Rokuo, Ishiwara Shozo, Isamitsu Kitakoji and the Australians James Murdoch and his deputy, Arthur Lindsay Sadler. It provided perfect cover for bringing individual Japanese to Australia in order to turn them into Australian agents. Whether this crossed anyone's mind at the time is not recorded. If no one thought of it, then it was a big mistake. There is no better spy than an insider.

Although there is no clear record of Piesse having tasked anyone to undertake secret missions inside Japan, there are hints he may have placed two secret agents there. In his paper 'The Far Eastern question: recent developments and their significance for Australia', Piesse refers to two sources 'with exceptional qualifications, one a European and one an Asiatic' who had been supplying him with the information upon which he based his reports to the government.[28] Who the European was is anyone's guess, but the Asiatic may well have been Professor Manzi Koide, who accompanied Murdoch to Australia in March 1918. Koide had returned to Japan at the end of January 1920, and there is every possibility that he was providing intelligence to Australia.[29] If so, then he may indeed be Australia's first clandestine foreign agent.

All of this good work came to a shuddering stop in 1921, when the newly created system was hit with three massive losses. The first was the implosion of the relationship between William Watt and Billy Hughes. Watt and Hughes had been at loggerheads for a while, but when Hughes went behind Watt's back during wool clip negotiations in London in April 1920, Watt was finally forced out of government and later resigned. Piesse and Murdoch had now lost their most ardent supporter and, although Senator George Pearce was still an ally, he appears to have been unwilling to fight Hughes.

The next to go was Atlee Hunt, who was moved from his position as Secretary of External Affairs to the newly created position of Arbitrator for the Commonwealth Public Service under the *Arbitration (Public Service) Act 1920* in February 1921.[30] It does not appear that Hunt wanted this job, but he held this position until he retired in 1931. His main preoccupation in the years following his appointment seems to have been to make himself as unpopular as he could with successive governments until he retired.[31] The final blow for the language program came on 30 October 1921, when Professor Murdoch died at his home in Baulkham Hills.[32] Edmund Piesse was now devoid of supporters, and he was left to run the Japanese-language program and the Pacific Branch without assistance and in the face of growing hostility from Hughes and those around Hughes.

Hughes was no fool when it came to political manoeuvrings. Watt was part of a group that included politicians such as George Pearce and Littleton Groom, and officials such as Atlee Hunt and Edmund Piesse. In fact, Edmund Piesse was a close friend of Watt's. With the nomination of Piesse as the Head of the Pacific Branch during his absence overseas in 1919, Hughes would have become immediately hostile to both Piesse and his new intelligence organisation.[33]

This new branch, the Pacific Branch, was the first truly strategic civilian intelligence organisation created in Australia. Its objectives were outlined as being a 'part of the intelligence arrangements for the Commonwealth', with no administrative duties, but solely tasked to 'study the affairs of the countries of the Far East and of the Pacific (including the US)'.[34] The Australian government had created the specialist language-training courses for spies and now the organisation to run them. Their intended targets were everyone in the region, including the Americans.

The first moves in establishing this organisation took place at a Cabinet meeting chaired by Watt on 8 May 1919, when approval was given for the appointment of an officer to take charge of Far Eastern questions. This officer was to build up Australia's understanding of Asia and the Pacific, and to oversee the collection of intelligence and information on the nations and their relationships. The official had no executive role and was not responsible for the conduct of Australia's external relations.[35]

The survival of the newly created intelligence branch depended on Watt maintaining a modus vivendi with Hughes. With Watt's sudden resignation, it was incumbent on Piesse to make himself and his organisation as useful to Hughes and his supporters in the government as he could. Unfortunately, Piesse did not do this; in fact, he did the exact opposite. The fight between Watt and Hughes continued after Watt resigned from the government, and the ground upon which Watt chose to fight was Australia's attitude—that is Hughes's attitude—towards Japan. Watt embarrassed Hughes by issuing a public statement expressing admiration for the work of Japan as Britain's ally in the fighting of 1914–18. This was a very public denigration of Hughes's position at Versailles and would have rankled anyone, let alone a man as self-important as Hughes.

Even now, Piesse and his Pacific Branch could have survived, but Piesse rashly entered the fray by writing reports supportive of Japan, such as 'Japanese Expansion as it Affects Australia'. Historian Neville Meaney believes that Piesse's reports represented a mellowing of his attitudes towards Japan and this got him into trouble with Hughes.[36] What got Piesse into trouble, though, was aligning himself with William Watt. Hughes was not the sort of man to see them in any light other than that of immediate political necessity. Watt had gone, and Piesse would follow. Piesse now chose to visit Japan and Asia, removing himself from Australia between September 1919 and March 1920, just when the Pacific Branch needed him in Melbourne to protect it.

The next stage of Hughes's attack was simplicity itself. He gave Piesse his head and allowed him to develop his pro-Japanese arguments to such an extent that Piesse eventually argued to exempt the Japanese from the provisions of the Immigration Restriction Act. This left Piesse completely isolated, and now that Hughes had paid out the rope, he pulled it tight by cutting Piesse's access to secret intelligence reporting from Britain, India and the other British colonies in Asia.[37] Piesse had been obtaining these from the Governor-General's office, an arrangement George Pearce had put in place.[38] The reason this reporting had to come via the Governor-General was simply that the Governor-General controlled British codes and cipher keys in Australia and these reports had to be decoded before being handed over to the Australian government.[39]

The reports Piesse was obtaining were 'Extracts from newspapers' and the 'Intelligence summaries' prepared by the Indian Army General Staff, as well as reports and summaries from other departments of the Indian government concerning the 'activities of the Japanese'.[40] The Indian government had also agreed to release 'highly secret' information, including 'The Indian Brief Against Japan' and the 'Weekly report of the Director Central Intelligence'.[41] Hughes arranged for all of these to be sent to him from 14 May 1920,[42] and by July he had cut off Piesse's access.

Hughes cut Piesse off to stop him having access to intelligence that Hughes saw as irrelevant but as useful to his opponents. The fact that Hughes stopped the flow of reports in July 1920 underlines the political imperatives behind his action. When Lord Forster, the new Governor-General, was informed that the reports were no longer required, he demanded a reason.[43] The reply was that 'these reports have not been found to contain information of relevance to the Commonwealth Government'.[44] So Lord Forster ended the flow of reporting, leaving government ministers isolated and ill informed.[45]

On 9 February 1923, Billy Hughes was forced to resign as prime minister following the Country Party's refusal to serve under him. Stanley Melbourne Bruce became the new prime minister, but as Piesse was soon to learn, Bruce had little interest in international affairs, foreign policy or intelligence. This was the final straw, and Piesse tendered his resignation in August 1923, taking a position in the Melbourne law firm Davies and Campbell.[46]

Tellingly, the resignation of Edmund Piesse was discussed in Cabinet on 20 November 1923 and Earle Page, as the acting prime minister, was delegated to speak to Watt about the arrangements to be made with Piesse following his departure from the public service. This was no ordinary resignation, and it appears that the Cabinet felt Piesse deserved much more than just a final pay cheque.[47] That said, by getting involved in the political infighting of parliamentarians, Piesse destroyed the Pacific Branch and deprived Australia of an effective Australian foreign intelligence organisation until May 1952. The nation would have benefited far more if Piesse had played a better political game and given Hughes what he wanted.

CHAPTER 9

The First Coastwatcher

With the demise of the Pacific Branch and the Japanese-language program, Australia lost its fledgling intelligence agency, leaving the armed services as the only active intelligence collectors for the nation. And even there, the scaling down of the Japanese-language program saw the military trainees enrolled in it diverted into other roles within the military or, in the case of the RAN, being sent off to work for the RN's China Station in Hong Kong. Although, from an Australian national perspective, the loss of RAN personnel to the RN was less than optimal, it did ensure that the ACNB and the RAN remained involved in the collection of foreign intelligence, and that it retained a level of expertise in this work that the Australian Army and the new Royal Australian Air Force (RAAF) could not.

At the time that the battle between William Watt and Billy Hughes was hotting up, the ACNB and RAN were facing dramatic cuts in budgets and operational capability. As part of a strategy to limit the impact of these cuts and to ensure that the RAN remained a viable part of the Admiralty's Pacific force, the ACNB and the Admiralty managed to inveigle the Australian government into inviting Admiral of the Fleet and hero of the Battle of Jutland, Viscount Jellicoe of Scapa, to conduct an enquiry into the defence of the Commonwealth. This enquiry was charged to determine two things for the Australian government:

first, what was needed to ensure Australia's defence; and secondly, what would it cost to have the RN maintain a large fleet in Australia's region.[1]

Volume III of Jellicoe's report is dedicated to intelligence collection, reporting and management, and is important in our story. In this volume, Admiral Jellicoe identified the need for an independent intelligence branch within the Australian Naval Staff, and for the ACNB to complement this with a coastguard or, failing that, a coastwatching organisation. Jellicoe's enthusiasm for a naval intelligence organisation came from his personal experience of the support Room 40 provided the Home Fleet when, under his command, it interdicted and engaged the German High Seas Fleet at Jutland. In his report, Jellicoe wrote:

> The war has shown the exceeding value of a first-rate Naval Intelligence Organisation. It is no exaggeration to say that the great majority of the information obtained for Great Britain during the war, apart from actual military intelligence, was the work of the Naval Intelligence Division at the Admiralty.[2]

At the time Jellicoe was writing his report, there was a section of the Australian Naval Staff that handled intelligence activity, but it sat within and was subordinate to the operations department. It also needs to be said that, between 1914 and 1918, Naval Intelligence, under the leadership of Thring and others, had done an excellent job. What Jellicoe was after, however, was the duplication of the Admiralty's intelligence system in Australia. This would provide the RAN, the ACNB and the Admiralty with the flow of timely and accurate intelligence that they required to conduct their operations.

To increase the intelligence-collection capability of the Australian Naval Staff, Jellicoe also recommended that in wartime his suggested coastguard should operate the high-power and medium-power signal stations used to communicate with the fleets and with His Majesty's (HM) ships operating closer to shore. As part of this activity, they would detect and fix the positions of all aircraft and surface vessels using 'Y' Procedure and fix the positions of RN and RAN Ships using 'B' and 'X' procedures (see Chapter 10). These stations would also have 'special' SIGINT duties, intercepting and reporting radio traffic, including the communications of neutral countries. Jellicoe was recommending an Australian SIGINT service of some complexity and sophistication.

Jellicoe submitted his report to the Governor-General in August 1919, but the Australian government had no appetite for maintaining naval expenditure at its present levels, let alone increasing it. Armed with Jellicoe's report, however, the ACNB strove to convince the government that it should fund the RAN to better provide for Australia's defence. Optimistically, it even tried to get the army to support the formation of the coastwatching organisation.[3] Unsurprisingly, the army was not interested.

With the failure of the government to adopt Jellicoe's recommendations, the ACNB had no choice but to fall back on the pre-1914 system that had been formalised in the Admiralty Instructions of October 1915.[4] These ensured that the ACNB and RAN retained access to Admiralty intelligence, including the latest techniques and technology for collecting it, by supplying intelligence and weather information to RN ships deployed to the Indian and Pacific oceans and in the areas around Australia.[5]

The Australian region was subdivided into districts in accordance with Admiralty instructions. These districts were defined by the waters off each state and territory, and around Christmas and Cocos islands, New Guinea and the other islands to the north. Responsibility for reporting intelligence matters was delegated to the senior naval officer (SNO) resident there; New South Wales was the only district with a dedicated intelligence officer, in Sydney.[6]

Each SNO was required to run a small intelligence centre and to manage a network of reporting officers. These were recruited from among local officials and government officers, including postmasters, harbourmasters and other functionaries, who were posted in remote locations. They were to provide intelligence reporting of maritime activity, including ship movements and suspicious activity, in exactly the same way as the DNOs and Sub-DNOs. The difference was the reporting officers were not naval personnel and they were not a cost for the ACNB.[7]

Seagoing intelligence officers were also employed, but their intelligence role was supplementary to their job on board. Thus, deck, gunnery or supply officers could find themselves with intelligence-collection and reporting duties for which they had only the most basic guidance. In line with Admiralty practice, however, the paymaster officers steadily came to dominate the intelligence role. Only on flagships was an officer appointed to manage intelligence, and even there, the officer's intelligence role was on top of other duties.

The three missions of the RAN intelligence system were the collection, collation and circulation of general intelligence regarding the Australian Station; the collection of the information required to answer the Naval General Questionnaire; and the establishment of a coastwatching organisation to meet the ACNB's need to conduct surveillance of coastal areas.[8]

The only development in the system was an increased interest in the creation of a voluntary and, most importantly, unpaid coastwatching service. The idea of a coastwatching service was nothing new in 1919 when Jellicoe conducted his enquiry. In fact, it can be argued that the story of Australia's coastwatchers really began on 21 February 1912, when the 32-year-old harbourmaster at Broome, the colourful and energetic Welshman Captain Ancell Clement Gregory, applied for a commission in the RANVR. In the documentary evidence, Ancell Gregory comes across as what Australians call 'a bit of a chancer', a man on the make. His letter to Captain Frederick Tickell, the Director of Naval Reserves, leaves the reader with a strong impression that Ancell Gregory was a man who made his own luck.[9]

Gregory appears to have struck up an acquaintance with Tickell on board HMAS *Parramatta* during the time it stayed in Broome on its maiden voyage to Australia. The basis for Gregory's application was that there was a need for a commissioned naval officer in Broome because there were now twelve 'white divers' coming to Broome to work as pearlers and as many as another 40 expected for the next pearling season.[10] This large contingent of white divers included, according to Gregory, many ex-RN divers, who could be a considerable asset if they were formed into a RANVR unit, which a newly commissioned Gregory could command. As pitches go, it was a good effort.

The influx of white divers into Broome was a result of the Australian government's requirement that white men replace Asian divers in the pearling industry before the end of 1913.[11] The impact of the Immigration Restriction Act had caused an enormous degree of dislocation within pearling that saw almost the entire Australian pearling fleet, including James Clark and Reg Hockings' Wanetta Pearling Company, depart Australia for the NEI rather than comply with the Act. Because of this, the Commonwealth encouraged the replacement of Japanese and Asian divers with white divers. This was the basis for Gregory's assessment.

So far, so good! It was now, however, that Gregory gilded the lily just a little too much in claiming that he had been appointed a sub-lieutenant in the Imperial Reserve because he had been a master in sail and a chief officer in the Blue Funnel Line. He then underlined his qualifications by emphasising that, as a pearler and harbourmaster at Broome, he was very familiar with the northern and western coasts of Australia.[12] On 5 March 1912, the Secretary, Naval Reserves, replied telling Gregory his name had been added to a list of men who, if the need for a seagoing reserve arose, would be approached to serve. Other than that, commissions in the RANVR were reserved for members of the Citizen Naval Forces (Universal Training). It was not a warm welcome.

Navy Office's reply to Gregory may have been cool, but it was not a rejection. The idea of using Gregory appealed to someone, who wrote on the file that such an appointment would be 'a good one, meeting present requirements'.[13] The problem doesn't appear to have been Gregory himself, but a concern that the divers and divers' attendants Gregory was proposing to recruit would most likely still be members of the Royal Fleet Reserve and thus unavailable for service in the RAN.[14] Gregory had overplayed his hand.

Navy Office's interest was piqued, however, and the naval representative in London was instructed to find out if the divers could be made available to the RAN and to enquire what rank Gregory had held while in the RN. Now it all came unstuck.[15] Admiralty informed the ACNB that it was quite happy to let it recruit the ex-RN divers, who would have been automatically struck off the reserve list when they left the United Kingdom, but that as far as the Admiralty was aware, no divers or divers' assistants had done so.[16] The Admiralty could also find no evidence of Gregory having ever served in the Royal Naval Reserve.[17] This news killed off any enthusiasm to appoint Gregory, and the matter was dropped.

If Navy Office had known Gregory as well as the residents of Broome did, they would have understood that he was not a man who let a fish go once he had decided to land it. Seven years later, on 18 May 1919, Gregory wrote to the Honourable H. Gregory, MHR (no relation), asking for his assistance in obtaining a commission in the Naval Reserve. The Honourable H. Gregory wrote to the Honourable A. Poynton, Acting Minister for the Navy, who placed the matter before the ACNB. The board again declined the offer of service, but by 29 March 1920, a telegram ordering Captain Gregory to attend

Navy Office and report to the secretary for his orders was sent following his appointment as an honorary lieutenant in the RANVR on 26 March 1920.[18]

Around Broome, Ancell Gregory was seen as quick, ruthless and as a man with strange friends, including the local Japanese. Gregory had quickly worked out that if you needed to borrow money in Broome, you could get it from the Japanese because they were prohibited from owning luggers and so were keen to arrange partnerships with white businessmen prepared to act as frontmen. Ancell Gregory was more than happy to act as a frontman for his Japanese partner, Murakami Yasukichi, a local merchant and photographer.

The relationship between these two men blossomed to a degree that it caused considerable disquiet among the white population of Broome. Gregory not only ignored this, but in 1912, while in Britain overseeing the fit-out of two Western Australian government vessels, caused even more consternation by letting Murakami's family live in the Gregory home, which just happened to be located in the most prestigious white suburb of Broome. This act, as well as many more, created an outcry that Gregory ignored.

Whatever Gregory's posturing about his naval background and his suitability for a commission in the RANVR, he appears to have been a loyal and freethinking friend.

Gregory and Murakami seem to have been successful and by 1909, Gregory was able to give up going to sea himself. Gregory and Murakami retained control of their large pearling fleet and other interests through the artifice of a company called Gregory and Co., nominally owned by Gregory's brother F.C. 'Clem' Gregory.[19] All of this was exposed in January 1911, when one of Gregory and Co.'s indentured workers, Tommy Kitchie, was charged with wilful disobedience and turned up in the Broome Police Court with a lawyer to represent him. It is thought that Gregory's enemies put up the money for Kitchie's lawyer. Kitchie won the case when the lawyer argued that although Ancell Gregory had transferred the ownership of his luggers to Gregory and Co., he had not transferred the permits for indentured workers and thus, as Gregory and Co. was not Tommy Kitchie's master, he could not have been wilfully disobedient. The Broome establishment got some of their own back.

It was soon after this that Murakami began to experience financial difficulties, which culminated in 1915 in the collapse of his Japanese banking business. Again, Gregory stepped in and hired Murakami to manage the

Dampier Hotel, paying him half the profits. When Murakami was declared bankrupt in 1918, his marriage fell apart but Gregory continued their joint business ventures, including the first commercial production of cultivated pearls in Australia. The support provided by Gregory allowed Murakami to get back on his feet and once again get married and raise a family.[20] In 1936, Gregory was paying for Murakami and his wife to travel to Darwin and set up a new photography business there.[21] The loyalty of Gregory cannot just be written off as self-interest. Even from this distance in time, there is a touching aspect to this relationship between two migrants to Australia, one Japanese and the other Welsh, who worked together to build something in the face of bureaucracy and pomposity.

As to his commission in the RAN, Gregory's blend of non-conformist showman, adventurer and ruthless businessman finally worked, and on 26 March 1920 he was appointed to an honorary commission in the RANVR.[22] The secret orders issued to Honorary Lieutenant A.C. Gregory on 29 March 1920 required him to forward 'certain information' from the coast between North West Cape in the south and Cape Londonderry in the north, to meet the requirements of Naval Intelligence.

The secret orders issued to the unpaid Honorary Lieutenant specified that he was to report all information on 'aliens', especially Japanese, reports of any unauthorised landings, information on fuel coal and reliable men with specialist qualifications, and information on unsurveyed harbours, anchorages and approaches along the coast.[23] Gregory was required to report once a month by registered post to the Secretary, Department of the Navy, in Melbourne. He was to number his reports consecutively from 01 and to send them double-enveloped, the inner envelope being marked 'Confidential', and the outer envelope bearing only the address. They were to be sent by British ships only. It was also made clear to Gregory that he was not to incur any expense on behalf of the Commonwealth without the prior sanction of the ACNB. Gregory dutifully acknowledged his instructions and began work as Australia's first coastwatcher, a group that would share his entrepreneurial aspirations.[24]

The evidence for Ancell Gregory's claim to be Australia's first true coastwatcher lies in a letter from Captain Henry Cochrane, RAN, the Second Naval Member of the ACNB, to Rear Admiral William R. Creswell, RAN, the First Naval Member, on 15 March 1920. In this letter Cochrane recommends to Creswell that the ACNB create a coastwatching network comprised of volunteer 'gentlemen with approved credentials' who would be appointed honorary lieutenants in the RANVR and could then be tasked with providing the ACNB with intelligence from their areas of responsibility. The marginal notes on this letter mention Ancell Gregory as the first such appointment.[25]

The role to which Gregory was appointed was, although honorary, still official. All this meant was that it did not cost the ACNB money, not that it was seen as unimportant. An indication of the significance the ACNB attached to the role was the orders given to the DNO at Fremantle to meet Lieutenant Gregory on the SS *Wandilla* when it called at Fremantle en route to Broome and provide Gregory with a copy of the Australian 'Disc' Code and instructions for its use in sending secret telegrams. The DNO was also ordered to supply Gregory with the stationery, forms, envelopes and stamps necessary for his duties. Again, the ACNB emphasised that Gregory was to be made very aware of the 'system for accounting for the expenditure of "O.S." [Official Service] stamps'.[26] It seems that in 1920 these stamps caused a great deal of concern.

The instructions covering foreigners, especially Japanese, were quite extensive. Gregory was to report on the numbers employed in the territories within his observation and on the seagoing craft he became aware of. The number of each nationality or race was to be reported as well as the reasons for any change in these numbers. He was also required to report on any suspicious characters and on the behaviour of foreigners towards local citizens. All incidents of unrest between races and groups were to be reported, as were intermarriages.[27]

For a man with close business links to Japanese businessmen and particularly to Murakami, these requirements must have been either amusing or disconcerting. Given Gregory's approach to life, I suspect he found them amusing. It appears from the file that the First Naval Member may have suspected this, as he expressed concern about Gregory reporting on individuals he knew, asked that the extent of this reporting be minimised, and stressed the need for strict confidentiality and discretion be impressed on Gregory.[28]

Although the idea of forming a coastwatcher organisation has been credited to Captain C.J. Clare, RAN, the officer serving as the Director of Naval Reserves in 1912,[29] the reality is that Ancell Gregory initiated the idea, and the documentary evidence shows that the naval officer who pushed the employment of Gregory and of other gentlemen who could become 'the nucleus of a body of war "Coast Watchers", to assist the Naval Board' was Captain Henry Cochrane.[30]

In this case, the ACNB was intent on winning part of the battle with the government over Jellicoe's recommendations—a voluntary coastwatcher service was the next best thing to paid coastguards. Admiral Creswell made it clear that 'as this Intelligence system is now being started I suggest Capt. Thring should be written to and asked to obtain from the Naval Intelligence Department 25 copies of any "questionnaires" issued by that dept.'.[31]

Gregory quickly set to work. His Report No. 1 was sent on 2 May 1920 and Report No. 2 on 28 May. These reports covered many of the subjects he had been directed by the ACNB to address.[32] Captain Cochrane found Gregory's reporting 'very interesting', as did Joseph Cook, the Minister for the Navy.[33] By 1 July, Captain Cochrane was writing to the new First Naval Member, Rear Admiral Sir Percy Grant, that the 'appointment of this officer [Gregory] has already justified itself'.[34]

The reasons for this praise to Admiral Percy were that he was newly appointed and Cochrane was attempting to counter a negative minute from Joseph Cook, who was doubtful about extending the system because he feared 'it may create another sub-department at Headquarters'.[35] Cochrane argued that Gregory's reporting showed an unpaid coastwatcher system could work and that, as the men appointed would be unpaid, it imposed no new cost. He even addressed Minister Cook's concerns about new departments at HQ by pointing out that the coastwatchers would be reporting to the already existing Naval Intelligence Section.[36]

Cochrane's defence of the proposed system appears to have worked. Later, sometime around 1931 or 1932, an undated report with the title 'The RAN and Australian naval policy' detailed that Navy Office was a 'Naval Intelligence Centre in the world wide Admiralty Intelligence Organisation' and that the Australian part of this organisation 'extends, mainly on a voluntary (unpaid) basis, throughout Australia and the mandated and certain other territories'.[37]

Ancell Gregory's application to be appointed a commissioned officer in the RAN had that most necessary of recommendations: it had come at the right time. The ACNB now needed to find men of Gregory's stature and position to create an organisation somewhat along the lines of that recommended by Jellicoe. They sought to supplement his appointment with a 'gentleman who has just gone to Fiji to take up a govt. appointment . . . if the members of the Naval Board desired'.[38]

By 1939, this small beginning would result in more than 700 coastwatchers around the Australian coast and in the islands to the north and north-east of the continent.[39] In August 1939, it would fall to Lieutenant Commander Eric Feldt to take the peacetime coastwatcher organisation to war. Preparing it for war would take more effort than anyone realised in 1920. He would have to deal with the issues that arose from the original voluntary structure of the organisation, but that is a story for later (see Chapter 13). In 1939, Ancell Gregory was still in Broome, still successful and still eager to serve.[40]

The coastwatcher system that Eric Feldt would later re-energise would prove to be one of the most effective and reliable HUMINT systems that operated on any side between 1939 and 1945. It would also be one of the most highly decorated military units in Australian history, even though it was mainly comprised of dislocated 'chancers' living in remote places.

CHAPTER 10

Australian Signals Intelligence, 1914–29

By 1914, Britain was well versed in the utility of SIGINT, and, as we have seen, the RAN, as part of the Admiralty's worldwide intelligence system, played a significant role in the SIGINT successes in 1914. Following on from this were the successes of the Admiralty's Room 40, Old Building, and the other groups exploiting transmissions by radio or cable. These groups, and particularly Room 40, quickly grew from adjuncts to naval or Military Intelligence to centres of strategic and political intelligence serving the highest policymakers in Britain and the Empire.

Suddenly, civilian politicians and officials could see inside the thinking of their opposite numbers in other governments. Government realised how useful SIGINT could be in dealing with international affairs. On 1 November 1919, the British government established the Government Code and Cypher School (GC&CS), the first national SIGINT organisation in world history. The decision to establish GC&CS is significant because it was not made to meet the dire and immediate necessity of war, but to meet the day-to-day needs of peacetime government. The age of the spy had arrived.

Despite its national role, GC&CS remained an Admiralty responsibility in which Room 40 personnel, such as Commander Alexander (Alastair) Denniston, RN, Alfred (Dilly) Knox, William (Nobby) Clarke, Frank Adcock and Walter Horace Bruford, held important posts. In April 1922, though, the Foreign Office finally took administrative control of GC&CS. The change did not result from any reappraisal of GC&CS's role, but from the embarrassment of the Foreign Secretary, Lord Curzon, whose indiscreet comments to the French Ambassador criticising his Cabinet colleagues were intercepted, decrypted and circulated by GC&CS to those colleagues.[1] Curzon was not going to let that happen again, and brought GC&CS under the Foreign Office and thus under the sway, if not control, of the Secret Intelligence Service, also known as MI6.

In the case of Australia, Jellicoe saw the ACNB and its Naval Intelligence Department as the future centre for all intelligence collection in the Far East. This fitted in with his brief, but what did not was his recommendation that Australia be encouraged to create its own intelligence organisations, particularly a SIGINT organisation. Jellicoe had justified this recommendation by pointing out that Australia, being physically in Asia, would be a very keen collector of intelligence on Asia and would provide Britain with material that she could not otherwise obtain. This raised some complaint within the Admiralty that Jellicoe was going beyond his brief,[2] but the real threat to Jellicoe's recommendations would come from the Australian government's antipathy to paying for a national intelligence system on this scale.

The idea of Australia as a major centre for the collection of intelligence for the Admiralty was not new, but SIGINT had now changed the face of intelligence, and intelligence organisations had to deal with a flow of reporting on a scale far beyond anything a HUMINT system could generate. This was a problem because, to be effective, SIGINT had to be kept extremely secret and yet produced huge amounts of material that had to be transmitted by telegraphic or other means that also had to be kept secret. All of this meant a secret communications infrastructure on a scale never before contemplated by government. This was the beginning of what we today call the internet.

There is no point collecting intelligence if it cannot be provided to the decision-maker who needs to see it. In the early 1920s, as Jellicoe was writing, it could take an important telegram up to seven days to get from Australia to Britain, and this was without any additional reporting of SIGINT. The problem was a lack of bandwidth, the curse of all SIGINT, and, in the early 1920s, having to compete with everyday telegraphic traffic on the commercially operated network of transoceanic telegraphic cables. The only logical answer to this was to build a long-range wireless system or lay more and larger cables. Both of these projects were subject to serious commercial and international blocks, due to the need to negotiate with the United States, Canada and other interested parties.[3]

Not only would Australia and Britain have to build a suitable communications system covering the earth, but they would also need to recruit and train specialist operators to conduct intercept operations. This was not going to be easy, because these operators needed to work at higher speeds than ordinary telegraphists and had to be conversant with Asian signalling and languages. All of this was expensive.

The modest program put in place to teach Japanese could not meet these needs. The Japanese did not even use standard international Morse, because this could not carry the pictographs and syllables that make up the Japanese language. Japanese communications used Japanese Morse, also known as KANA or, more correctly, Wabun code. Telegraphists working as intercept operators had to be trained to listen to and take this down, but to do so they needed to speak some Japanese. Professor Murdoch's program could only train a few officers, not the large numbers of intercept operators, clerks and traffic analysts that would be required.

None of this really mattered, because with the death of James Murdoch, the last vestiges of the Japanese-language program were brushed out of existence. The only Japanese-language training available was that provided commercially by Japanese teachers living in Sydney.

In the meantime, the ACNB looked to its existing capabilities as a means of collecting SIGINT. Foremost among these were the yeomen telegraphists aboard ships and working the coastal signal stations, which controlled signal traffic between ships at sea, ports and other authorities. The signal stations had become part of the wartime censorship system, charged with ensuring no sensitive information was passed by ship's radio. During the war, this role had expanded to include the active interception and reporting of enemy communications during the periods of radio silence between schedules. This was relatively simple work as the enemy used standard Morse. It may not have been seen as such at the time, but this was SIGINT.

All of this activity was centrally controlled, with each station's attached censor reporting directly to the Naval Intelligence Section at Navy Office while also reporting information of immediate and local tactical importance to the relevant DNO. This centralisation of control at a national level gave the signal station system one of the characteristics of a SIGINT system, even though censorship did not include cryptography, traffic analysis (TA) or cryptanalysis. The 'system in force in peace' was, to paraphrase the Admiralty, simply modified and extended for war. It demonstrated a very real interest in obtaining intelligence from enemy and other radio transmissions, while preventing the leakage of intelligence from friendly radio networks.[4] It was SIGINT and it met the Admiralty's demand for 'prompt and accurate operational intelligence'.[5]

The fact that the Australian system did not include extensive cryptanalysis or codebreaking has fooled many historians into thinking that there was no SIGINT effort in Australia when in fact there was an extensive system operating throughout the 1914–19 period. The issue appears to be the modern habit of equating SIGINT solely with cryptanalysis, when, in fact, cryptanalysis is only one part of the SIGINT system.

The most important intelligence in SIGINT, especially at the tactical level where time is of the essence, is geolocation through DF and tactical information derived from TA. DF is vital for telling commanders the rough location of enemy forces, while TA provides information on who is communicating at what times and frequencies, what level of organisation they are and how active they are. In fact, TA can provide an enormous amount of intelligence without a single word of a message being understood.

TA not only provides the date and time of the message and the frequency it was sent on, but also the call signs that are communicating, allowing identification of the units involved. It also provides the number of messages in the series, allowing accurate collation of the traffic, and can provide insights into standard preambles and sign-offs that serve to identify the sender. Added to this, TA tells you just what grade of message you are dealing with, while the level of urgency and activity can be deduced from the speed of reply and total numbers of messages being sent compared to other equivalent periods. TA also tells you if the activity is routine or special. In a lot of instances, the only thing TA does not tell you is what the target is saying inside the message.

The value of TA is greatest at the tactical and operational levels, not at the high policy level, where the actual communication contains the gold. TA provides the foundation from which all cryptanalytical attacks are launched on a cipher or code.

Another misconception that has been incorporated into the history of British intelligence in Asia during this period is that it was of limited scope and value. The truth is that Britain was making full use of its technical capacity to spy on all the countries in Asia that used British telegraphic cables. This activity was compromised in 1925 when Vice Admiral William R. (Blinker) Hall, the Director of Naval Intelligence (DNI) between 1914 and 1918, handed 10,000 Room 40 decrypts to the American lawyer Amos Peaslee, so that Peaslee could prosecute a case against the German government for acts of sabotage in the United States.[6] Why Hall did what he did and how he had secreted away so many of Room 40's messages is unknown, but a National Security Agency (NSA) report into this event credits Hall with providing Germany with the evidence needed to develop ENIGMA.[7] It also makes Hall the forerunner to Edward Snowden.

British cable companies in all British-controlled areas, including China, copied messages sent by any government or organisation of interest, including those of the United States, China, USSR and Japan, and passed them to Room 40 for further distribution to the Foreign Office, Ministry of Munitions the Board of Trade, and, it should be remembered, to the Indian government in New Delhi, which shared Australian concerns. This type of activity is the bread and butter of SIGINT. It is dry, boring and mundane, except to the economists, trade commissioners and those charged with running a wartime economy. It is not known how many messages from Asia were intercepted and passed along, but there is little doubt many were.

Following Jellicoe's report, in January 1920 the Admiralty announced that a conference would be held in Singapore for the flag officers commanding the East Indies Squadron at Trincomalee in Ceylon (now Sri Lanka), the China Station at Hong Kong and the Australian Fleet at Sydney. The aim of the conference was to develop the strategic advice the Admiralty would provide to the 1921 Imperial Conference in London. Part of this advice would concern the arrangements for the future coordination of intelligence collection and wireless communications between the stations in the Far East and the Admiralty in London.[8]

The conference was finally held at Penang, Malaya, in March 1921. Australia accepted the majority of the recommendations arising from the conference, but refused to endorse the automatic subordination of the Australian Squadron to Imperial Command at the outbreak of war. Instead,

Australia would retain control and only consider this sort of transfer if a crisis arose.

On the subject of intelligence, Australia agreed to contribute to the development of the wireless telegraphy network in the Pacific and to the tweaking of the Admiralty's intelligence system. The importance of this to Australia lay in the need to keep Britain committed to Asia and to ensure she maintained a fleet and all of the support systems that fleet needed, including intelligence systems.[9] The price was Australia's commitment to building part of the necessary infrastructure, including the high-capacity, high-power beam radio stations.

The threat posed by Japan was now being seen as more serious. Not only was the IJN becoming increasingly capable, but the RN was becoming increasingly less so. The assessment of the conference was that good intelligence was essential for the success of any future operations against Japan. Early intelligence, it was hoped, could provide sufficient warning of Japanese aggression against Britain or her imperial holdings in Asia, to provide a 'defensive period' of around 38 days, the time it would take the Home Fleet to sail to the East.[10] In order to achieve this, the conference agreed a Pacific Naval Intelligence Centre (PNIC) should be co-located with the fleet HQ at Singapore. This PNIC would provide intelligence to the Admiralty in London and the governments of Australia and New Zealand, as well as the administrations in India, Burma, Malaya and the NEI.[11]

The intended PNIC was seen as a combined entity, with representation from all of the services as well as, one supposes, from the SIS and the Security Service (MI5). This latter inclusion is implied by the agreement that one requirement of the PNIC was that it would conduct both HUMINT and SIGINT collection operations. The PNIC would be responsible for the establishment and running of agents in Asia, particularly in security intelligence matters, and for the study of wireless telegraphy, cable and telephone networks.[12] In addition, the conference proposed two high-frequency direction-finding (HFDF) networks be established, one covering the Indonesian Archipelago from stations at Seletar on Singapore, Kuching in Sarawak and a station in North Borneo, and the second covering the south-west Pacific and the archipelago from stations located at Nauru, Rabaul on New Britain and one in New Guinea.[13] These shore-based networks would be complemented by shipboard HFDF capabilities on all HM ships in the squadrons.

As events would prove, the Penang conference was highly optimistic. Britain and her Empire just did not have the resources in place. The HFDF system had to be built, as did the intercept sites, and this would be a costly exercise for governments in Britain, Australia and everywhere else who were now battling to bring military spending down from the massive highs of the war. Both the existing and future budgets were under strain, as Britain owed enormous sums of money to the United States and other lenders, money she had borrowed to fund the war.

The other problem was manpower. Like Australia, Britain had no Asian-language capability of any size. The existing program could send a few commissioned officers to Tokyo from Britain, India and Australia every year, but no soldiers, sailors or airmen.[14] The issue was not as acute in relation to Chinese, because many British soldiers and service personnel learned Chinese while stationed in China as garrison troops. In an emergency, the population of Hong Kong could also be drawn upon to provide the linguists needed. Japanese was a problem of a completely different order.

Still, a sailor has to make do with what is available, and this is what the ACNB did. In June 1921, it ordered all ships and stations to ensure telegraphists practised taking Japanese Morse in a secret program called the 'B Telegraphic Code'.[15] Japanese Morse Code manuals were distributed to all RAN telegraphic stations and major units, and commanding officers warned that neither the activity nor the fact that the RAN had access to this code were to be discussed. This training of RAN operators in KANA was to be supervised by warrant officer telegraphists and, in an effort to ensure the Japanese did not intercept the RAN using KANA, practice was restricted to internal buzzer sets.[16]

The idea behind this program was to make use of suitably trained telegraphists to intercept Japanese Morse during quiet periods on their shifts while they maintained guard, a listening watch, on their assigned frequencies. Now, rather than listening to the universe's background radiation or their favourite music, RAN telegraphists would scan the spectrum and report what they heard.[17]

This activity was reported monthly to Navy Office, which also detailed the progress being made by the trainees and the level of proficiency being attained.[18] The ACNB also ordered that all recruit telegraphists be trained in both international and Japanese Morse.[19] This was a step too far. The average telegraphist rating under training was not up to the task of learning International Morse, the technical aspects of telegraphy *and* Japanese Morse in the time allocated to training them, and the idea had to be dropped.[20]

By 1 July 1921, 47 blueprints containing copies of Japanese Morse systems and other SIGINT information had been distributed to ships and shore stations for the training program.[21] All of this activity was in accordance with the decisions of the Penang Conference, but by October 1921 the Admiralty had concerns about the training impost on its own wireless ratings.[22] Similar issues were arising in Australia, and by March 1922 the scheme had run into real trouble. At the end of that month, following a letter from the Rear Admiral Commanding HMA Fleet, the program was abandoned.[23]

The abandonment of the listening watch and local training program did not end the ACNB's attempts to develop the RAN's SIGINT capability. As 1922 progressed, SIGINT in the RAN increased slowly through the artifice of using telegraphists aboard HMA ships to conduct intercept activity during the long quiet periods as they transited the region. The rationale for this lay in the practical experience of the telegraphists in intercepting radio transmissions from around the world at particular times of the day. The official view, though, was that ships needed to be in close proximity to a target to collect SIGINT.

In June 1922, HMAS *Sydney* proved that intercept operators afloat could conduct SIGINT operations against Japanese high-frequency (HF) transmissions in the Mandated Territories during her visit to Noumea.[24] It was a small advance, but it was an advance all the same.

In 1922, another step forward in the creation of an effective SIGINT attack on the Japanese was taken when Paymaster Lieutenant Eric Nave, RAN, went to Tokyo for formal Japanese-language training. At the time, it was unlikely that anyone understood the contribution Eric Nave would make to the Admiralty's SIGINT operations in Asia, but he was destined to become one of the RN's leading Japanese cryptologists.[25]

Eric Nave was born in Adelaide in 1899 and gained employment as a clerk with the South Australian Railways in 1915, most likely due to the good offices of his father, a senior official there.[26] Nave remained with the railway until February 1917, when he left to join the RAN as a Paymaster Clerk on 1 March 1917. Exactly three years later, Nave was promoted to Paymaster Sub-Lieutenant, backdated to 1 September 1919, and it was during this time that he found himself a Japanese teacher in Sydney and developed the skills that would see him 'loaned' to the RN and posted to Tokyo on 16 February 1921.[27]

The teacher of Japanese that Eric Nave found had been 'brought out from Japan especially to teach the language in schools here'.[28] The teacher was Miyata Mineichi, one of James Murdoch's recruits. This action directly connects Nave with James Murdoch, Edmund Piesse and, at a bit of a remove, Atlee Hunt. Later, Professor Murdoch tutored Nave and told him about his plans to take captains J.R. Broadbent and G.H. Capes to Tokyo in September 1920 for further training.[29] Nave was keen to be sent to Japan as part of this group, but the wheels of Navy Office turned slowly, particularly as Professor Murdoch was difficult to communicate with, and Nave had to wait.

As Nave waited to find out if he would be sent to Japan, he arranged to take lessons from Professor Miyata. The cost of educating Nave was carefully managed, and Miyata's fee of £4 5s ($AU1986.00 labour value in 2017)[30] was paid for two students, Nave and Paymaster Lieutenant Eric Kingsford-Smith (the brother of the famous aviator Charles Kingsford-Smith).[31] The aptitude of both men was such that, on 20 March 1919, Miyata reported to Navy Office that they had made 'remarkable progress and that they can speak, write and read short fundamental sentences with considerable fluency'.[32]

Nave's further education in Japan was approved by the ACNB on 31 December 1920, and the naval attaché at the British Embassy was informed via the RAN representative in London.[33] Eric Nave departed Australia aboard the SS *Eastern* on 28 February 1921. Now Australia had three students in Tokyo: Nave, Broadbent and Capes.[34] In Tokyo, Nave met another language student, Lieutenant R. Chichester, RN, who may have passed on his interest in cryptography to Nave.[35] Eric Nave soon came to the attention of the Admiralty and his posting to HMS *Hawkins*, on the China Station, was arranged while he was still on the course in Japan.[36]

While Nave was in Japan, the RAN continued to develop its capabilities using the opportunities afforded by routine cruises in the islands to Australia's north. In 1923, the Winter Cruise saw the first combined intelligence operation involving concurrent SIGINT and HUMINT operations when two RAAF officers, E.A. Mustard, DFC, and A.E. Hempel, joined HMAS *Adelaide* and *Brisbane* respectively to survey the islands for suitable airfield locations.[37] They paid particular attention to the Deboyne and Admiralty islands, and to the area around Aitape on the north coast of New Guinea. In 1932, another operation using a RAAF A9-2 aircraft for aerial reconnaissance and photography was conducted from HMAS *Australia*, while her specialist SIGINT team conducted intercept operations below deck.[38] These operations display a surprising level of sophistication and commitment by the RAN and RAAF, particularly given the financial stringency that existed at the time.

By 1924, the pace picked up as the Admiralty increased pressure on the China and Australian stations to send more SIGINT intercept to the newly formed Japanese Naval Section at GC&CS. This new section had been created because of tension between the Foreign Office and the services over restrictions imposed on the type of intelligence GC&CS was to produce. The Admiralty finally buckled in 1924, and financed and staffed the Naval Section under the leadership of Paymaster Commander E.P. Jones. Experienced Japanese linguists and intelligence officers from the China Station were then posted to this section.[39] This meant Admiralty had a dedicated team looking at IJN traffic. All it needed was the raw material of SIGINT to work on, and this required the China and Australian stations to start aggressively collecting SIGINT.

The Admiralty instructed the C-in-C, China Station, to establish the first of the 'Y' Stations in the Far East at Hong Kong—'Y' Procedure was the early covername for SIGINT operations. The Hong Kong station was to collect and conduct TA and low-level decrypts of IJN traffic for local analysis while forwarding all encrypted IJN traffic to GC&CS.[40] The result was a slow and painful increase in capability through 1924 until 1925, when Hong Kong began to produce better results. Part of this increase in capability may have been due to the arrival of Eric Nave there on 12 June 1925 to take up 'specialist duties (W/T Procedure 'Y')' and as interpreter in Japanese under the direct supervision of the C-in-C China Station.[41] Within a short period, the flow of intercept increased to a point where the Naval Section at GC&CS was unable to cope.[42]

In Australia, in July 1924, the army intruded into SIGINT by suggesting that a voluntary civilian radio intelligence bureau be established to conduct radio interception activity. The main proponent of this idea was a Major H.A. Corbet in Perth. His idea was odd, and not because he thought a voluntary organisation could conduct SIGINT. The odd bit was that he thought that wireless specialists working for Amalgamated Wireless Australasia Ltd (AWA) would be allowed to spend their 'down-time' intercepting and reporting foreign communications.[43] The more experienced ACNB replied to this proposal by pointing out that AWA staff had plenty to do even when they were not taking messages. Undoubtedly, the ACNB knew from direct experience that AWA did nothing for free, and moved to kill off Major Corbet's idea as quickly as they could by proposing no further action be taken.

It was not the end of the matter. It seems others, maybe even politicians, took up the idea. On 2 December 1924, Commander Frank G. Cresswell had to reinforce the initial rejection of Corbet's idea by pointedly informing the head of Naval Branch that the ACNB's preferred option was the provision of modern recording receivers at certain shore stations.[44] Cresswell also made it clear that this issue was strictly a naval matter, and that the army and others should stay out of it. Cresswell and the ACNB were not interested in using amateur radio enthusiasts; they were looking to build an organisation of professionals equipped with modern high-speed recorders like the Dictaphone.[45]

And this brings us to technology, an important part of the Australian SIGINT story and one of the least considered factors in much of the history of SIGINT during this period. One of the most difficult areas for the radio operators and specialists of the time was propagation, particularly in the tropics, the area of most interest to Australia.[46] It has to be remembered that Professor Edward Appleton's proof of the Kennelly–Heaviside layer's ability to reflect radio waves was only confirmed in 1924.[47] Until this happened, the Admiralty and everyone else thought that SIGINT interception of radio messages could only be done on a ship passing close to an enemy coast.

Even simple tasks like getting accurate recordings of the actual message were an issue. The usual method at the time was for the intercept operator to write down the message as he heard or misheard it. This left the analysts at a loss, because they could not identify what was operator error or actual message content. The answer lay in the invention of devices that recorded the actual sound of the message as it was intercepted: the Dictaphone Company's electronic recording equipment.

In 1924, the ACNB acquired two Creed Relay high-speed wireless telegraphic recorders from the Admiralty to record Japanese Morse for the small group of expert telegraphists and linguists capable of working on them.[48] These recorders were found to be highly suitable for radio signals emanating from close to Australia. For the much more distant and very faint IJN traffic, however, the Creed Relay was too crude to pick up the signals, and the audio recorders were not sensitive enough.[49] The answer was the new US Dictaphone, which had been developed to record music, specifically symphony orchestras for later broadcast by commercial radio stations.

The Dictaphone was a high-speed electric recorder and was one of the most important advances ever made in capturing sound electrically. Western Electric designed and built the first such recorder, which comprised a Bell microphone connected to a valve that supplied the amplified signal to a Bell electromagnetic cutting head. This new technology extended the frequency spectrum that could be recorded from 200 Hertz at the bottom to 6000 Hertz at the top, which was 3600 Hertz higher than any mechanical recording system.[50] This was the technology now sought by the ACNB. The value of this technology lay in its capacity to record the actual sounds so they could be replayed repeatedly to cryptologists and other operators. This was a major advance in SIGINT capability.

By 1925, Dictaphone had developed a similar device designed specifically for capturing telephone messages. The ACNB's interest in this technology most likely explains why the Dictaphone Company opened its first office in Australia in 1926, the same year the Dictaphone was enhanced by the addition of piezoelectric featherweight styli, and the company sought an Australian patent for these 'improvements in phonographic machines'.[51] The success of the Dictaphone in the ACNB's SIGINT operations may also be the reason the company took out further patents relating to 'improvements in shaving and resurfacing of phonograph records' in 1928, something the RAN needed to do during ship deployments.[52]

These developments improved SIGINT collection in three ways. First, it enabled raw signals to be sent back for further technical analysis; secondly, it meant that the number of intercept operators required for tasks could be reduced; and thirdly, it meant that intercept operators did not have to be as highly trained as first thought.

The addition of this technology paid dividends as RAN intercept operators began to realise that they could hear IJN traffic emanating from the Home Islands of Japan. The experience of these operators was confirmed with Professor Appleton's proof at the end of 1924 that radio beams bounced off the ionosphere to land at great distances from their origin.[53] This propensity of radio waves made Australia a very important part of the SIGINT system, when it was realised the nation was perfectly situated for intercepting HF transmissions originating in Europe and the Americas (see Figure 10.1).[54]

The significance of Appleton's discovery and of the experience being gained in Australia and Asia meant that long-range interception could be systematically exploited from the safety of Australia and other British territories. 'Y' Procedure had become even more attractive as an intelligence technique, and the Admiralty's insistence on only using ships for 'Y' Procedure was no longer as significant as once thought.[55]

The importance of this work should not be underestimated. At the time these developments were being achieved, neither the Admiralty nor the

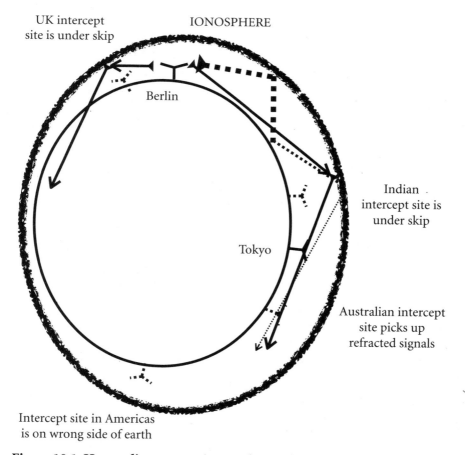

Figure 10.1: How radio propagation made Australia important in intercepting long-range Japanese diplomatic high-frequency transmissions

ACNB knew how the IJN operated. They did not even know if it was using International Morse or a special syllabic Morse.[56] The new technology and the active program of listening and recording began adding slowly to the intelligence picture of Japan's wireless communications. The contribution made by the American entertainment and electronic industries and academic research into the behaviour of radio waves had produced greater advances in SIGINT than codebreaking. These developments, along with the recruitment and training of specialist SIGINT intercept operators, crystallise a truth that is often overlooked in the story of SIGINT: it is an industrial activity in which intelligence is only produced by large, well-run organisations made up of numerous specialities and work groups of which the cryptanalysts are only one part. A factory is required to produce good SIGINT.

In October 1924, cryptanalysis of IJN messages was lagging behind the advances in technology, and Lieutenant Nave was now starting to insist on getting better access to the raw materials. One example is his insistence on being given the updated copy of the Japanese Naval Telegraph Code that Captain Broadbent had brought back from Tokyo. This appears to have been the first time an Australian cryptologist demanded to see the raw material himself in order to form his own judgements as to its value. The fact that Nave was given the copy he demanded indicates that the RAN and Navy Office were more sophisticated than is sometimes assumed.

Nave's plan of attack on the IJN's codes appears to have been to obtain an intercept of their plain-language messages to learn their operating procedures. This was an important first step, because the idiographic nature of Japanese made abbreviation difficult. Once he had mastered this, Nave then proposed attacking the Japanese Economic Code in preparation for the attack on more heavily enciphered traffic. This is where the other specialists came in, because Nave needed experienced wireless ratings skilled in reading Japanese messages. It seems that the ACNB and the RAN were looking at concentrating this capability on the flagship, HMAS *Australia*.[57]

These plans changed because the Admiralty needed to find qualified personnel to work on the China Station so that the newly created Naval Section at GC&CS could be kept supplied with intercept. Eric Nave was an obvious candidate, and in late 1924 the Admiralty requested that he be made available for service on the China Station. In early 1925 the ACNB agreed.[58]

As Eric Nave was being sent to the China Station, the ACNB was obtaining four portable Marconi medium-frequency direction-finding (MFDF) kits from the Admiralty. These kits were positioned at RANVR bases—in Port Melbourne, Edgecliff in Sydney, Fremantle in Western Australia, and Brisbane—under the command of the DNO in each port. The primary objective was to train the RANVR in DF operations, thus providing the RAN with a portable DF capability that could be quickly assembled and deployed.[59]

The year 1926 would prove a good one for SIGINT on the China Station and in Australia. At the end of 1925, Eric Nave had doubts there would be enough intercept taken to keep him fully employed.[60] He feared that the difficulties of dealing with Japanese traffic might result in the whole program being wound down. This did not happen and instead more resources, although of a limited nature, were committed to the work, and Nave was posted to HMS *Titania*, the Submarine Depot Ship, where SIGINT operations were being extended and new equipment, including Dictaphones, was being installed.[61]

The problems in training enough specialist operators that had eroded confidence in the ability of the China Station to cover the IJN effectively had been resolved by the Dictaphone, and the concerns about the unbreakability of the IJN codes were also put aside.[62] Instead, the Admiralty informed the C-in-C, China Station, and the ACNB that SIGINT was 'a subject to which the Admiralty attached the greatest importance'.[63] The C-in-C, China Station, was instructed to increase the urgency and effort being put into the SIGINT attack on the IJN.[64] These orders, along with the arrival of Dictaphones and other equipment seemed to have worked, and by July 1926, the Naval Intelligence Division (NID) was reporting to the Admiralty that considerable progress had been made.

The Admiralty added to the attack on the IJN's codes by posting Lieutenant Commander Stephen Lushington to HMS *Ambrose*. Lushington was a SIGINT specialist with close ties to GC&CS, and appears to have been its man in the East.[65] To provide Lushington and GC&CS with material, the C-in-C, China Station, was instructed to ensure that any HM ships venturing into waters near Japanese locations were manned and equipped to undertake SIGINT. This approach had just been proven in the Mediterranean, where a single destroyer with a dedicated SIGINT team aboard had collected more material in a few weeks than the entire Mediterranean Fleet had in six months.[66]

This telegram appears to have been what prompted Commander Cresswell to continue the schedule of small SIGINT operations by the RAN.[67] The sending of a single destroyer with a small group of specialists on board was well within the RAN's capability, as Cresswell knew. He also knew his operators were intercepting IJN traffic from Funabashi and Tokyo at the Navy Office's own communications centre in Melbourne. This was long-range interception indeed, and Cresswell reported that the Admiralty-supplied receivers had been highly effective in picking up these transmissions.[68]

China Station had also passed a report from Nave on Japanese communications that identified the call sign 'AB' as Imperial HQ. AB carried all IJN Admiralty traffic and broadcast routinely on even hours, while the Major Stations, the next level down, broadcast on the odd hours to all ships and minor stations within their geographic area of responsibility.

The work on AB also provided a major crib into the IJN's codes, the realisation that the hierarchical IJN forced subordinate call signs to pass messages intended for one another via their higher control station. This meant that two different operators were sending the same message twice in quick succession, and this dramatically increased operator error. This duplication enabled the rapid identification of call signs and their relationships to one another. More importantly, the errors stood out when the recording of each version of the message was compared. This sort of crib seriously undermined the security of the IJN's codes.

Another important characteristic of IJN wireless procedure was also identified: the IJN's telegraphists were not very good. Their lack of uniformity, frequent duplication and mixing of code with clear transmissions enabled the British to quickly build up their net diagrams, the paper charts of call signs, their frequencies, opertating times and other technical data. Net diagrams are the first output of traffic analysis and provide an indexed file of all activity noted on a network.

Even AB, Tokyo, was guilty of coupling international call signs with secret ones. The result was that the British 'Y' Organisation, although small, quickly identified the secret call signs of eleven of the seventeen major shore stations, as well as those for the battleships HIJMS *Mutsu*, *Nagato*, *Yamashiro* and *Kirishima*; the cruisers *Nagara*, *Tone*, *Yubari*, *Iwate*, *Kasuga*, *Komahashi*, *Kamakaze* and *Tanikase*; and ten destroyers and six fleet tankers.[69]

By June 1926, the SIGINT attack on the IJN was going so well that the

Admiralty expressed its pleasure at the great progress made by the China Station. It had good reason to be pleased, as in December 1926 alone, China Station intercepted and recorded more than 1000 Japanese messages.[70] The difficulties had been overcome 'by great zeal and ability on the part of those concerned'.[71] One officer singled out for individual praise by their lordships was Paymaster Lieutenant T.E. Nave, RAN.[72] One of Atlee Hunt and Edmund Piesse's tyros was beginning to make an impact.

In Australia, the loss of Eric Nave to the RN did not mean the end of the ACNB's efforts in cryptanalysis, as the work started by Nave was taken over by a civilian employee, R.A. Ball,[73] who had just completed the Japanese-language course in Tokyo.[74] On his return to the ACNB, Ball's contribution to SIGINT was just as important as the one Nave was making in Hong Kong at the time.

Australia's SIGINT effort was now benefiting from the newly improved Dictaphone equipment and the arrival of better recorders that now meant small vessels could undertake quite extensive SIGINT operations to supplement the listening watches kept at the RAN W/T Service shore stations. Electrical Commander Cresswell, the staff officer responsible for communications, now argued for a SIGINT mission to Rabaul, where transmissions from the IJN stations at Funabashi, Yap, Truk (Chuuk), Jaluit and the Bonin (Ogasawara) Islands were being picked up.[75] The mission would last three months and would be conducted under the cover of the regular goodwill mission by an Australian destroyer to the Mandated Territories.[76]

Ball supported Cresswell's suggestions, arguing that as he was now available to fill the role of Japanese linguist at Navy Office, the other Japanese linguists could be released to take part in SIGINT operations. Ball believed that the RAN could provide different intelligence to that obtained on the China Station because the RAN would be operating against the Japanese in the Mandated Territories. He also believed that giving the telegraphists practical experience would result in more cribs being detected in Japanese operating procedures.[77]

All of these ideas were contained in a report Ball wrote expanding on some of Nave's suggestions. Among Ball's recommendations was that all intercept be recorded using Dictaphone to ensure that no loss of syllabic groups occurred during 'Y' operations. His procedure placed a heavy emphasis on Dictaphone recordings, with manual cover only being used when the Dictaphone records were being changed over. Ball's procedure also provided a bi-graph system for noting Japanese syllabic groups corresponding to English letters and a table into which this information could be entered. Another of Ball's improvements was ensuring messages were numbered consecutively according to the order in which they were intercepted, rather than relying on the less dependable original message externals (the message numbers and other operating information attached by the original Japanese telegraphist).

Other issues, such as atmospheric breaks in transmissions and losses due to technical reasons, were to be marked by '?' to enable linguists and cryptanalysts to understand the reasons for gaps. All of this would make it easier for the linguist to read the intercept. It removed obvious errors and suggested possible groups for identified gaps. This initial analysis would then be compared with the Dictaphone record if necessary. During this activity, the linguist would identify and exclude plain-language private messages and messages of no intelligence value. The final intercept, or 'take' as it is called, of encrypted messages and plain-language official messages would then be forwarded to the DNI.

Ball was also a keen advocate of linguists working closely with intercept operators to establish station identities and construct net diagrams, forming the basis for further exploitation through TA. Ball 'earnestly' submitted that this routine be put in place and allowed to run for a period to establish whether it worked.[78] For the time, this was quite a sophisticated state of affairs, and the resulting improvement in the RAN's SIGINT capability was noted in the Admiralty.

Commander Cresswell's proposal for a SIGINT mission was now agreed, and the Assistant Chief of the Naval Staff (CNS), Commander H.T. Baillie-Grohman, took responsibility for it. Baillie-Grohman informed the CNS, Rear Admiral William Napier, RN, that not only did he accept the importance placed on 'Y' Procedure by the Admiralty, but he had already approached General E.A. Wisdom, the Administrator of New Guinea, to request the use of his steam yacht SY *Franklin* in a 'Y' Procedure mission.[79]

The *Franklin* was selected because, as the Administrator's official yacht, she was a known entity in the waters near the Japanese Mandate. She was also big enough, the ACNB hoped, to house the SIGINT team and its equipment. *Franklin* would prove problematic, however, because no one had realised that the wind would create vibrations within her rigging that would cause background noise and electrical interference from static. Her electrical system also turned out to be a major source of unwanted interference. All of this was unknown when the mission was put in place.

Using the cover story that she was to undertake transmission and reception trials in the seas around and to the north of New Britain and New Ireland, the *Franklin* was fitted out in Sydney in early 1927. The mission lasted from April until July 1927. Warrant Telegraphist B. Harding led the team of four telegraphists, which included Leading Telegraphist H.J. Barnes, of whom we will read more later.[80]

This mission was not a local or spur-of-the-moment operation. The support that Navy Office and the intercept team received not only included Eric Naves' intelligence, but also British HUMINT, most likely from SIS, as serendipity cannot explain how the detailed report on Japanese wireless developments from W. Turner, the General Manager of Reuters in the Far East, arrived in Australia just before the *Franklin* mission.[81]

This report, passed from the highest levels of the British government to Australia for use on the mission,[82] described Japan's telegraphy system in detail. It also outlined how the Japanese Communications Department operated a dozen home stations and an overseas network including Fukkikaku (Fuguijao) on Formosa (Taiwan), Dairen in Kwantung, Seoul in Korea, Otomari (Korsakov) in Sakhalin and Paramushiro (Paramushir) in the Kuril Islands during the fishing season.[83] Turner's report provided information that the IJA and IJN operated their own networks independent of the Communications Department and one another. Further, it described the dockyard network of three private stations that coordinated berthing and repairs of vessels.[84] The only information Turner had on the Japanese Mandated Territories was that there were seven stations, but he had no details on them.[85]

The intercept team on *Franklin* were setting out well prepared and provided with excellent intelligence. It was only when they were at sea that they discovered the *Franklin*'s unsuitability.

The team installed improvised short-wave transmitting gear and Navy Office receiving gear, selected by Harding. Two-way simplex working was established and maintained with Navy Office on two frequencies, 33.5 and 35 metres, from the date of departure until *Franklin* reached a point 700 nautical miles north of Sydney. From there, she continued north to New Guinea, while her intercept team installed and tested their intercept equipment and initiated the interminable and only partially successful routine of fault-finding, noise reduction and vibration abatement.[86]

In the areas around New Britain and New Ireland, two-way communication was maintained between 1730 and 0830 hours (K and L time zones). The intercept operators encountered a number of serious technical problems caused by the swaying of the yacht, and noise and vibration caused by the wind passing through the rigging. The vibration was serious enough to make reception very difficult, and the team had to use a smaller antenna condenser to reduce oscillation and lessen these problems. They even had to begin screening all the electrical wiring on board in an effort to reduce induction issues.[87]

On top of these issues, the team also had to contend with the failure of the motor in the Dictaphone, which, luckily, they were able to replace in Port Moresby. Then, on arrival in Rabaul, they found out that the Administrator had been forced to surrender his copy of the naval cipher to the Defence Department when the Prime Minister's Department had taken responsibility for Papua New Guinea. This meant they could not communicate with Navy Office on 'Y' Procedure matters or with the intercept operators who had left the now immobilised *Franklin* to conduct operations ashore.[88]

Navy Office was not amused and signalled 'The seriousness of this failure is being represented in the right quarters', particularly as the Secretary of the Department of Defence had not replied to Navy Office's original request for action.[89] Baillie-Grohman also ordered the wireless telegraphic group not to conduct 'Y' Procedure operations from Government House in Rabaul for security reasons.[90]

The SIGINT operation conducted by the *Franklin* team was well thought out and well organised. Security was maintained at the highest level, with good cover being provided by the vessel itself, and when matters slipped, by senior officers in Melbourne. Despite all the setbacks, the mission was not only a procedural and technical success, but also an intelligence success. Harding's team had identified the call signs of HIJMS *Tone* (call sign JLF), *Katata* (call sign JWH), *Minekaze*, *Nagato*, *Kongo*, the submarine tender *Chogei*, submarines *i52*, *i53*, and two other submarine call signs unattributed to vessels. Effectively, the *Franklin* mission identified the IJN's 1927 submarine net, as described in Figure 10.2.

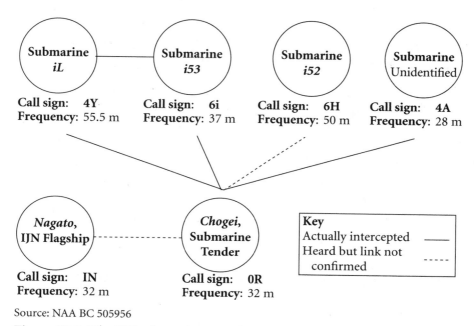

Source: NAA BC 505956

Figure 10.2: The IJN submarine net identified by SY *Franklin*, 1927

Another significant success of the mission was that the Dictaphone worked very well and 100 recordings were made, 97 of which were of Japanese transmissions.[91] This data allowed the identification of 99 call signs as well as their frequencies and schedules. This was all the information needed to begin the job of constructing net diagrams and developing an order of battle.[92]

The mission also identified a number of new procedure signs and their meanings, and the secret call signs used by a number of IJN stations and vessels, such as the submarine flotilla. The success of the mission was due to the cribs provided by the numerous errors committed by Japanese operators, and by the intercept operators aboard *Franklin* identifying operator and equipment idiosyncrasies in messages from the international call sign and the secret call sign of the targeted transmission.[93]

The *Franklin*'s Dictaphone records were received at Navy Office on 3 August 1927 and copies of these, plus 424 message transcripts taken by hand, along with Warrant Officer Harding's report, were immediately forwarded to the Admiralty. The originals were forwarded to Ball, and Petty Officer Telegraphist L.G. Porter, who was expert in reading Japanese Morse.[94]

The only fly in the ointment was provided by the Acting Secretary of the Department of Defence, who complained that it was 'quite impossible, without lamentably disorganising the current work of the office, to make Mr Ball available for full time on this work, at any rate while the temporary arrangements in the Secretariat continue'.[95]

His superior released Ball for two hours every afternoon to look at the material, and it was hoped that the return of Paymaster Lieutenant Nave in September 1927 would enable the latter to take the material to London with him.[96] It appears that the Acting Secretary of the Department of Defence did not really understand what was being done.

Further planning on 'Y' Procedure activity was undertaken in September 1927, to see if the inaugural voyage of the newly acquired cruisers HMAS *Australia* and HMAS *Canberra* back to Australia could be used as a collection opportunity. This voyage provided excellent cover while the two ships crossed the Pacific. It was also recommended that Nave be asked to assist in these arrangements.[97]

On 21 February 1928, the Admiralty wrote to the ACNB expressing appreciation of the 'effort at interception on board Steam Yacht *Franklin* and ashore at Rabaul', but advising that the lack of live cryptographic traffic made the activity 'unremunerative'.[98] The bulk of the traffic was plain-language commercial and civilian messages, with almost no operational coded traffic. This was a gloomy assessment given the operation proved the concept of mobile SIGINT collection by a small team. However, the China Sea and Pacific Ocean operations were not producing enough encrypted traffic for the Naval Section at GC&CS to make an effective attack on the IJN's ciphers.

Australia faced its own resourcing problems, not least of which was a lack of qualified and experienced personnel for SIGINT operations, made worse by the loss of experienced staff as their period of engagement came to an end. In July 1928, the RAN lost Petty Officer Porter and two of the leading telegraphists who had served with him on *Franklin*. This was a quarter of the RAN's specialist SIGINT operators and three-quarters of their most experienced team. The last man in this team, Leading Telegraphist Barnes, was posted to HMAS *Canberra*. This loss was so serious that Commander Cresswell informed the CNS, and the ACNB even considered passing this information to the Admiralty.[99] It was a serious blow to the Navy's nascent SIGINT organisation.

Yet 1928 saw its breakthroughs. Technology was now available that enabled a lot more to be done by fewer people, and the senior officers of Australia's navy were strong advocates of the importance of good foreign intelligence collection, especially SIGINT. Despite the limitations imposed by falling budgets and the lack of linguists and other specialists, enough intelligence was being collected to deduce the IJN's order of battle from TA and the creation of the first net diagrams. In addition, Eric Nave broke the IJN's nine-letter general-purpose '43' code, and although the exploitation of this breakthrough was limited by the lack of linguists, it represented a real step forward in the attack on the IJN.[100] The RN certainly thought so. In his annual officer's appraisal, Nave was described as a 'diligent and efficient' officer of 'exceptional' zeal and energy, who was 'an exceptionally able Japanese interpreter according to Japanese Naval Officers, with whom he is very popular'.[101] He was also an excellent spy.

CHAPTER 11

Hand to Mouth: Australian Signals Intelligence in the 1930s

In September 1930, Captain H.J. Freakes, RAN, the commanding officer of HMAS *Albatross*, informed the Commodore Commanding the Australian Squadron of the success of *Albatross*'s SIGINT in targeting IJN radio communications in the Mandated Territories. This operation was mounted under the cover of the RAN's routine Winter Cruise, and Freakes reported that his team had identified the call signs, frequencies and schedules of twelve Japanese wireless stations, and assembled data on operator and equipment characteristics. They had also collected intercept.[1] This work was not being done full time. In fact, the ship's telegraphists were undertaking the SIGINT during their quiet periods on watch, when they were not busy processing, taking and sending ship's traffic. The telegraphists on HMAS *Australia* and *Anzac* were also doing this work, although they do not seem to have been as successful as *Albatross*'s team.[2]

The Commodore, Rear Admiral W.S. Chalmers, may have been happy with the work of *Albatross* and the other ships conducting the Winter Cruise, but when he put in his report on the activity he complained, as only operations officers can complain, that the Admiralty's insistence on classifying SIGINT as 'Most Secret' prevented him and his staff from ever using it.[3] The ACNB and Admiralty quietly ignored Chalmers.

The RAN's SIGINT operations continued and, in May 1931, Chalmers issued another report on the work. *Australia*, *Canberra* and *Albatross* were all using documentation, including that classified as most secret, supplied by the C-in-C, China Station, while *Anzac* was not. Chalmers believed she was not capable of conducting SIGINT, except when she was cruising through the islands to Australia's north. By this time, it appears the RAN could find enough personnel for three four-man SIGINT teams on *Australia*, *Canberra* and *Albatross*. The RAN was only gradually moving away from the practice of using ordinary ships' telegraphists for SIGINT work during quiet periods.

The training program that had been implemented for SIGINT operators included lectures by officers, particularly by the Japanese linguist Paymaster Lieutenant W.E. McLaughlin, RAN, of *Australia*. McLaughlin, whose career was blighted by alcoholism,[4] instructed students on the Japanese language, Japanese Morse and the 'system of "transportation" used in converting the [Japanese] language into the Morse code'.[5]

As well as mounting mobile operations, the ACNB was having the RAN conduct SIGINT intercept from fixed wireless stations, such as Garden Island in Sydney. Again, telegraphists conducted the SIGINT activity during quiet periods, particularly overnight, between 6 p.m. and 8 a.m., when the ionosphere was in its best position to reflect HF signals from the area around Japan to Sydney and other parts of Australia.

The frequencies covered ranged from 5000 to 20,000 kilohertz, with particular attention being given to 5000 to 6600 kilohertz, where the greater portion of the IJN traffic was to be heard.[6] The take was forwarded in accordance with China Station's ' "Most Secret" Memorandum No. 02508, pages 22 (i, A, B) revised July 1931', to the Admiralty; ACNB; C-in-C, China Station; and Commodore Commanding HMA Squadron.

At this time, one of the telegraphists aboard *Albatross* was Leading Telegraphist H.J. Barnes, an important contributor to these early days of semi-independent RAN SIGINT operations.[7] Barnes was a career sailor who had transferred from the RN to the RAN on 31 December 1924.[8] He had served on the 1927 *Franklin* SIGINT mission and been intimately involved with the creation of the RAN's SIGINT capability throughout the period we are currently examining. As such, he was a scarce commodity and very good at his job, which led to Rear Admiral Alfred Evans personally requesting that Barnes be assigned to oversee the SIGINT activity on *Albatross* during the forthcoming Winter Cruise.[9] The job given to Barnes was important. He was not only overseeing the 'Y' collection operation, he was training four telegraphists—Albert Herman, Allan Oswald, William Ralston and Gordon Davis—in Japanese Morse and SIGINT operations.

The need of the RAN and the Admiralty to get across the IJN's radio communications meant that Barnes was now being deployed as much as possible, and this was interfering with his career, as he could not be released for normal promotional courses. As Barnes was retained on *Albatross* for the forthcoming Winter Cruise, he would yet again miss the scheduled promotional course.[10]

The ACNB issued a direction to the captain superintendent of Naval Training that Barnes was not to be adversely affected by his inability to attend the course. Despite the ACNB's pleas, however, the bureaucratic rules were enforced and Barnes was not promoted until 31 December 1933, after he had attended the required courses.[11]

As Barnes was carrying out his duty aboard *Albatross*, the financial situation for the ACNB was worsening significantly, and this affected the whole of the RAN, including SIGINT. Throughout 1931 and into 1932, SIGINT was conducted on a casual basis at selected shore stations and aboard *Albatross* during the Summer Cruise.[12] The savage budget cuts implemented by the Australian government as the Great Depression took hold were now impacting everything, including 'Y' procedure. Financial stringency destroyed the nation's naval power between 1929 and 1932, when funding fell by just over half to reach its lowest point in history. This ensured the RAN was in no position to replicate its successes of 1914 in 1939.[13]

It was during this period that Japan began to move in pursuit of its strategic objectives in China. The Japanese actions were in accord with the assessment of the British chiefs of staff that it would only move when Britain, America and the European powers were distracted by events in Europe. In January 1932, with the Great Depression biting hard across the world, Japan took the opportunity to attack China at Shanghai.

The first indication anyone had of Japan's intentions was the undetected arrival of the IJN fleet at the mouth of Shanghai's Huangpu River where the Japanese had suddenly bottled up the international naval forces in an exceptionally well-executed *coup de main*. On top of this, the IJN used carrier-borne aircraft to attack civilian centres and military concentrations for the first time in history. Even more exceptional, the Japanese conducted a successful opposed landing involving 3000 troops, which they rapidly increased to around 100,000 within a month. They then flanked the Chinese defenders by landing the 11th Infantry Division at Liuhe, behind the Chinese front line, and effectively won the limited war they had unofficially conducted. Any capable commander looking at this series of operations would have felt a shiver up the spine. It was an operation of great skill and forethought. The IJN had arrived unannounced and unexpected and neutralised foreign naval power in the Huangpu; they conducted an opposed amphibious landing and the terror bombing of a city. It was ruthless warfare.

The Japanese action at Shanghai caused consternation in London, Washington and Melbourne. On 3 February, the ACNB issued orders that SIGINT and HFDF operations were to be ramped up as much as the essential communications of HMA ships and stations allowed, and that signals from China were to be targeted exclusively.[14] On 4 February, Commodore L.S. Holbrook, the commander of the Australian Squadron, reported to the CNS that all ships and submarines had been placed on intercept duties and the intercept on red forms (the Admiralty's special SIGINT reporting form) was to be passed to Melbourne with the ACNB's approval.[15] By 15 February, the excitement died down as it became clear that the Japanese were not going to attack the international naval forces or cantonments in Shanghai. Navy Office now ordered the cessation of SIGINT work at Garden Island, although HMA ships and submarines were kept on guard.[16]

In February and March, Garden Island and *Albatross* intercepted and logged numerous undecipherable messages to and from diplomatic authorities, which were forwarded to Navy Office via mail.[17] All of this traffic was subsequently forwarded to the Admiralty in London.[18]

The special interception operation was terminated on 29 March following the successful negotiation of the ceasefire between China and Japan.[19] With the end of the crisis at Shanghai, the RAN's SIGINT capability was re-tasked with a new IJN target, its Training Squadron, commanded by Admiral Imamura Nobujiro and consisting of the cruisers HIJMS *Asama*, his flagship, and HIJMS *Iwate*, which was touring Australia in April and May 1932 as part of its annual training cruise.[20]

This operation allowed Paymaster Lieutenant W.E. McLaughlin, the RAN Liaison Officer aboard *Asama*, to gain access to and copy the frequencies and schedule used by the squadron. McLaughlin passed these back to the RAN for the SIGINT teams on the guard ships to use.[21] McLaughlin's information helped target the RAN's SIGINT effort, and the IJN's traffic on the frequencies 5720 and 5640 kilohertz was quickly identified and taken.[22] How McLaughlin obtained this information and the risks he took are not described, but it must have been an extremely foolhardy action, even though it was successful.

This operation gleaned considerable technical information, which suggests that McLaughlin got hold of more than just the frequencies and schedules. The ACNB was able to ascertain that each IJN vessel was using two different transmitters, one for each frequency, and that a single call sign, NU, associated with *Asama*, was used for all messages broadcast for call sign AB, now believed to be Tokyo and for another unidentified call sign, BK, also believed to be in the Home Islands, probably Tokyo. The actual SIGINT operation, shown in Figure 11.1, noted that call sign AB gave 'receipts' for all messages sent by NU during the 0400 hour schedules, with NU sending repeats as necessary. Call sign BK did not reply to NU, nor did NU send any repeats to this call sign, which remained silent on the intercepted frequencies.[23]

This procedure fitted with what the RAN already knew of IJN habits in managing wireless telegraphy. The IJN appears to have kept communications between ship and shore to the senior ship in any group while restricting ship-to-ship communications to signal lamps and flags.

Other useful information gleaned included the use of the prefix 'For Exercise' on all messages sent by the squadron, possibly indicating that the

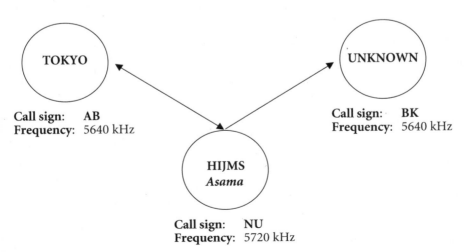

Figure 11.1: IJN training squadron net, 1932

IJN telegraphists were under training, or that the squadron was a training establishment or that IJN was avoiding using encrypted traffic while in Australian waters.[24]

A more important finding, though, was that most of the IJN traffic between Tokyo and the squadron dealt with the technical details of propagation, including the quality of reception in the Home Islands and aboard the squadron.[25] It would appear the IJN was mapping radio propagation around Australia and the southern seas.

The IJN's interest in radio propagation in the waters around Australia is unsurprising. All navies conduct this type of research even today. The problem was, as John Fearnley had said back in 1909, 'we ought to know' the 'true significance of our ally's interest in our coast'.[26] By the end of 1932, Australia still did not understand Japan's intentions, and neither did Britain.

Intelligence about Japan's intentions was hard to obtain. Japanese society was hierarchical, strictly regimented and hostile towards outsiders. Yet at the end of 1932, HUMINT was obtained from a source inside Japan that convinced the First Sea Lord, Admiral Sir Ernle Chatfield, that Japan had developed plans to attack Singapore. The source of this intelligence is unknown, but it was either an SIS agent or, more likely, an agent of the Indian Government operating against Japan.

The intelligence indicated that Japan planned to capture Singapore by landing an infantry division on the island supported by light artillery, naval gunfire and carrier-borne aircraft. Effectively, she would use the techniques she had perfected at Shanghai. In fact, the intelligence suggested this plan was readied at the time of the Shanghai Crisis in case Britain should take action against Japan.[27]

The details of the plan were informative. The IJN would transport the invasion force in eighteen transport ships, escorted by a carrier task force. They would proceed to the Pelew Islands (Palau) for assembly before proceeding to Singapore. The estimated steaming was eight days, not including the time required at Palau to reorganise the loading of stores and troops, war gaming and finalisation of orders.[28] As a foretaste of what would occur in 1941, it was accurate, although in 1941 the direct attack on Singapore was discarded in favour of an advance down Malaya.

General William Bartholomew, the Director of Military Operations at the War Office, quite rightly questioned the real meaning of the intelligence.

Although Bartholomew accepted it was genuine, he believed that the planning was just contingency planning of a type undertaken by all militaries the world over. The First Sea Lord did not dispute this, but he emphasised that the Japanese plan was identical to the Admiralty's own thinking on how best to neutralise Singapore as a base. At this point, the interest of the chiefs of staff returned to the issues of maintaining capability in financially straitened times.

It was no different in Australia. Shanghai had caused concern, but it had blown over without any real consequences outside China. In Australia, the ACNB continued its role as the major intelligence collector. Despite losing funding, it managed to maintain its existing capabilities and even considered how to increase them in the future.

Among the capabilities under consideration was the imperial HFDF network, which had still not been progressed. The ACNB needed to look to how it could meet the Admiralty's plans for the Pacific and Indian oceans. This HFDF saga would persist throughout the 1930s and 1940s. The cost of the stations, the technical difficulties and the obtuseness of Australia's political and official classes would all serve to ensure that when the Japanese did attack, Australia would have no capacity for effective DF.

Even in Britain, there were arguments against the DF system. One of these was that as soon as Japan decided on war, the IJN would impose strict radio silence for all Japanese shipping and IJN units, making them impossible to locate. What the naysayers were overlooking was that neutral shipping would report the presence of the Japanese ships, particularly their men-of-war. Allied ships that were attacked by Japanese ships would send out distress signals. DF would pick up these neutral and friendly transmissions, and thus the general location of the Japanese ships as well.

With the introduction of MFDF capability at Melbourne, Sydney, Brisbane and Fremantle, the ACNB attempted to increase the RAN's DF capabilities by expanding research. Luckily, this was a period of substantial technical advancement in radio reception, and with the development of the Adcock aerial, which reduced errors in MFDF and allowed DF to be conducted against HF signals as well, the capability of the RAN's DF sites was dramatically improved.

Of course, technological development was a two-edged sword, and the RAN felt this, as by 1933 its existing Marconi equipment was virtually obsolete. To re-equip Darwin and Rabaul with modern technology, prefer-ably that designed and built for the Admiralty, the ACNB had to approach the Admiralty and negotiate its supply.[29]

Australia needed the modern Marconi receivers and recording equipment, the Adcock aerials and peripheral equipment that the Admiralty had ordered. The Admiralty appeared keen to provide the ACNB with this equipment, as it lowered its unit cost. It also increased the interoperability of Australia's DF sites with UK and Empire stations, and it allowed a faster construction, with the planned HFDF station at Darwin being operational by early 1934.

Unfortunately, Australia's government was not as keen, because defence was the last thing upon which they wanted to spend scarce funds. Because of this, the ACNB attempted to pitch a value-add by suggesting that the naval DF role be combined with a civilian DF role, the provision of navigational infor-mation for the proposed airmail service between Australia and Singapore.[30] As for Rabaul, here the ACNB had to deal with the monopoly activity of AWA, which ran the civil radio services in New Guinea on contract from the Commonwealth.[31] The ACNB had little option but to seek permission for AWA to conduct DF operations.

This intermixing of civilian and naval resources in what the Admiralty saw as secret 'Y' Procedure work caused the Admiralty to refuse the ACNB access to the Marconi equipment and the Adcock aerial. The Admiralty would not authorise the supply of the equipment if civilian agencies, including the Royal Mail and Department of Aviation, were involved.[32] The difficulty was the Admiralty did not control access to SIGINT, the Co-ordination of Wireless Telegraphy Interception Committee did, and they were never going to allow uncleared access to the techniques and technology of SIGINT.

Their lordships' reply was, as always, polite. Their excuse for refusing was that civilian staff would be inexperienced with the equipment and they would have difficulty in obtaining replacement parts.[33] The Admiralty told the ACNB to purchase Marconi's commercially available equipment that worked between 90 and 750 kilohertz and from 300 to 30,000 kilohertz.[34] This was the Admiralty's last communication on this subject until February 1935, although the Singapore Naval Conference of January 1934 endorsed the building of the Darwin station as soon as possible.[35]

Still, it was not all bad news. Despite the difficulties of poor funding and low resourcing, the Admiralty's SIGINT activity in Asia continued to grow.

An example of this is found in the Admiralty publication *Amendment No. 2*, a routine amendment dealing with the changes to secret SIGINT documentation and its distribution list. *Amendment No. 2* shows that by June 1934, interest in Japanese SIGINT had developed to a point where not only were RN stations around the world getting a copy, but so was Australia and, for the first time, the DNI in Ottawa.[36] Another important feature of *Amendment No. 2* was that it explicitly nominated the IJN as the target of a highly secret and systematic SIGINT campaign. It even warned recipients that they were to exercise extreme care when in company with IJN ships not to compromise the SIGINT-collection campaign through 'indiscriminate' searching of frequencies.[37]

In this simple routine amendment, we find hard evidence that the Admiralty was not sitting on its hands waiting for the Japanese to make a move. Rather, under the auspices of the Admiralty, the ACNB and other dominions' naval authorities, the British Empire was conducting a sustained and aggressive SIGINT attack on IJN communications.[38]

The January 1934 Singapore Naval Conference made it clear that Britain now regarded the IJN as its principal threat in Asia. The attendees included representatives from the British and Indian armies, the Royal Air Force (RAF), the flag officers of the China and East Indies stations, the Admiral Commanding HMA Squadron and the Commander of the Royal New Zealand Navy (RNZN), as well as senior staff officers from the Admiralty.[39] Significantly, it did not include representatives from the Australian General Staff or the RAAF, a sign of the dysfunction bedevilling high-level Australian strategic thinking.[40] The official aim of the conference was to discuss war plans in the Far East.[41]

The assessment of the conference was that the existing appraisal of the chiefs of staff was still correct. The first indication of Japanese aggression would be the recall of the Japanese merchant fleet and the imposition of radio silence. The IJN would then move its units from their prearranged positions and strike at vital targets. This appraisal reflected the experience gained in Europe in August 1914, and it reflected Japan's behaviour at Port Arthur in 1904 and Shanghai in 1932, although the latter incident did not involve the recall of the merchant fleet. It also predicted what Japan would do in December 1941.

The other decisions made at the conference that affected Australia were a recommendation that the ACNB build and operate two medium- to high-power wireless telegraphy stations, one at Canberra and the other co-located with the DF and intercept station at Darwin. The Singapore conference re-emphasised the importance of the proposed HFDF station at Darwin by recommending its rapid construction.[42]

The need for more SIGINT capability was also making itself felt, as the amount of any intelligence coming out of Japan was rapidly declining, and what was being obtained via diplomatic and other open channels amounted to lies and disinformation, particularly when it came to matters concerning Manchukuo, Japan's puppet state created in north-eastern China in 1932.[43] To overcome this increasing lack of information, it was announced at the conference that the Admiralty proposed to establish a Naval Intelligence Centre in the Far East. The commander of this new centre was to be a senior officer of the Naval Intelligence Division, and Captain W.E.C. Tait, RN, was currently on the China Station arranging this. Given the importance of the RAN in the plans, it suggested Australia provide an officer of commander rank to serve on the staff of this new organisation.[44]

Later in 1934, the head of SIS, Admiral Sir Hugh Sinclair, RN, called a meeting of the Co-ordination of Wireless Telegraphy Interception Committee to discuss the expansion of SIGINT services in the Far East.[45] The meeting, held in November, was attended by Sinclair, SIS representatives including GC&CS, the Admiralty, War Office and Air Ministry—and, possibly, Paymaster Lieutenant Eric Nave, who recalled being present at such a meeting at the time.[46] It was this gathering that most likely agreed to the establishment of the Far Eastern Combined Bureau (FECB) in response to the Admiralty's recommendations for such an organisation.

At around the same time as the Wireless Telegraphy Interception Committee was making its recommendations, the Foreign Office, Dominions Office and government of India persuaded the UK Treasury to fund an increase in the establishment of the SIGINT station at Hong Kong. Mobile collection operations also continued, one of which, conducted by a SIGINT team of eight personnel aboard HMS *Medway*, collected Japanese communications in the Mandated Territories. What made the *Medway* operation notable was the size of the SIGINT team, and the fact that it was a dedicated team with no other roles aboard *Medway*.[47]

Unfortunately, the results were again disappointing, and the eight sailors aboard *Medway* were moved ashore to provide the SIGINT element for the new combined organisation. The result of this was that deployed teams were not used in this way again until war broke out in 1939.[48]

Other contributors to the SIGINT picture included the British Army at Shanghai, and the British telegraphic companies, which were copying messages and forwarding them back to China Station and GC&CS for analysis via SIS and other channels. All of this provided the raw material for the intelligence picture the Singapore strategy relied on. This reliance made it somewhat easier to persuade Treasury to fund an increased intelligence effort, as it was a substantially cheaper alternative to increasing the size of the fleet in the Far East or the building of the promised naval bases.

The new FECB increased SIGINT capability at Hong Kong with the approval of the construction of the HFDF stations at Stonecutters Island, Shanghai, Sandakan, Kuching and Singapore.[49] Not all of this expenditure came from the UK Treasury. The colonies, especially India, the Straits Settlement and Hong Kong, bore a substantial part of the cost. As always, Australia did not allocate any funds for the work. The excuse was that the expected construction and operation of the DF stations at Darwin and Rabaul was a sizeable enough contribution. The Japanese captured Rabaul before the first sod was turned on either of the two stations.[50]

The FECB was set up in Hong Kong, despite the British Army recommending it went to their facility at Shanghai. This was not taken up, as the weakness of the British garrison and the tendency of the IJN to arrive unannounced made Shanghai too exposed. More importantly, the telegraphic cables running to and from Shanghai were easy to tap and represented a serious security risk.[51]

The FECB began operating in April 1935 from a building inside the HMS *Tamar* Naval Dockyard in Hong Kong. Importantly, the SIGINT intercept site was built at Stonecutters Island to support the operations of the FECB. This was a significant step in creating a modern intelligence capability at the time.

In London, Australian stocks were falling with the Committee of Imperial Defence (CID) and the Chiefs of Staff Committee. The documentary evidence, although nowhere explicitly saying so, gives a feeling of frustration that Australia was not prepared to pull its weight. In CID Paper 418-C, the CID is adamant that Darwin was not just important from a naval perspective, but also for the control of the air space over northern Australia. The CID was

disconcerted at what it saw as a failure of Australia to appreciate the importance of rapid communication when dealing with the threat of fast-moving
aircraft. If northern Australia was to be effectively defended, then a station at
Darwin capable of medium- and high-frequency communications and DF
was essential.[52] The Japanese aircrew that arrived over Darwin at 9.58 a.m. on
19 February 1942 were grateful that the CID's concerns carried no weight in
Australia. The general alarm for the raid was only given at 10.00 a.m.

It is at this point we return to the RAN and its SIGINT story. By 1934, the
experienced and efficient SIGINT operator, now Petty Officer Harold John
Barnes, was frustrated with the slowness of his promotion in the RAN and
was looking at a career outside the RAN. Even with his CV, leaving the RAN
in mid-1934 was a bit of a risk, but luck smiled on Barnes and he was offered
and accepted a job as the manager of the British Phosphate Commission's
telegraphy station on Nauru.[53]

Despite his decision to leave the RAN, Harold Barnes stayed on with the
RANVR and, with the connivance of the now promoted Captain Cresswell
and other officers, agreed to carry out SIGINT collection from Nauru. Here
he and Cresswell ran into the roadblock of bureaucracy, as the Financial
Section at Navy Office struggled to deal with the idea that Barnes would not
be parading at a naval depot in Australia and argued that he could not be
paid as a RANVR member. Cresswell argued that Barnes would be rendering
as much as 182 hours of service per year as against the 48 hours required of
other RANVR members, and that this met the requirements for his continued
retention and payment. The ACNB, in true naval style, overcame the problem
by paying Barnes a special annual allowance of £5, equivalent to $2810 in
2018, from its own funds.[54] Harold Barnes was now Australia's only RANVR
member parading outside Australia and being paid from a navy slush fund.

This little story is not an amusing insight into the way bureaucracy works,
for that is a subject that rarely amuses. What it tells us is that the ACNB
found a way around the bureaucracy to establish a clandestine SIGINT intercept site on a Pacific island manned by Barnes, one of its most experienced
SIGINT intercept operators. The operation also involved the Administrator
of the island, who was also a RANVR officer. Barnes produced intercept for
Navy Office in Melbourne and for the FECB and GC&CS. The involvement
of the British in this activity is clearly shown in the files, where they express
their concerns about the risk posed by having such an experienced SIGINT

operator working alone in such an exposed location.[55] China Station, however, was supportive of the operation and explained that the take from Barnes was being carried in British vessels by the hand of the master.[56] The operation lasted more than four years until 1938 and perhaps even longer, as Harold Barnes was still forwarding intelligence to the ACNB in December 1940, when he provided photography and other intelligence on the German raiders SMS *Komet* and *Orion* during their attack on the phosphate-loading facilities on 27 December.[57]

In July 1934, SIGINT again proved its worth when it provided hard evidence that a Japanese spy had penetrated the Singapore Naval Conference and passed the entire proceedings to Tokyo. This intelligence had been derived from the diplomatic traffic from the Japanese Consul-General in Singapore.

The intelligence obtained from the Consul-General's messages showed that there were two spies, both white British officials, who had been spying for money. The two agents had provided Tokyo with the plans for the expansion of the Singapore naval base and, most alarmingly, a verbatim record of the points made by the C-in-C, China Station, Admiral Frederic Dreyer, at the conference aboard HMS *Kent*. This meant the spy had been in the room.

The spies also passed on details of the secret submarine facilities, the outcome of RAF tests on the landing capabilities of the island's airbases and the details of the army's new fortress.[58] One of the spies turned out to be a cartographer from the Singapore Public Works Department. He had been easy to identify because of the accuracy of the maps and plans he provided. He could not, however, have been the source of the intelligence from the conference.

A quick check of those present soon identified a female shorthand typist from the Civil Government of Singapore. The Japanese Consul-General had sent messages to Tokyo relating to the spies because their intelligence was so good as to be suspicious. He had then insisted on meeting the shorthand typist to check the validity of her story.[59] The Consul-General also betrayed that this shorthand typist had been passing information for some time, and that it had all been accurate. The result was that by January 1934, the Admiralty and the ACNB were informing their respective governments that Japan had detailed knowledge of Britain's weaknesses in the Far East and that Singapore was nowhere near ready as a naval base.[60]

The identification of the two Japanese sources at Singapore was a small victory. In Australia in 1935, austerity ruled the day and nothing much changed in the way SIGINT operations were being conducted. The ACNB continued to train ratings and petty officers to undertake SIGINT work, but was constrained by the continuing lack of funds and resources.

Regardless of these restraints, the work of plotting the IJN's vessels and networks continued, as did the cryptanalytical attack on IJN and other Japanese codes. By 1938, the cryptanalysts at FECB were working on six IJN codes, including those used by the IJN dockyards, intelligence system, operations department, fleet code and ship-to-shore systems. The work was no doubt well assisted by poor Japanese discipline and numerous errors enabling significant cribs to be obtained. Another major contribution to the SIGINT effort was Japan's own aggressiveness, as her military adventures in China led to a massive increase in the volume and tempo of coded traffic. This ensured that by 1937, even though they had not yet broken the IJA or IJN main systems, the codebreakers of the FECB and GC&CS had enough material to enable a blunt-force attack to be launched.

Japan's introduction of new codes between 1937 and 1939 improved their security, but not as much as some suggest. Sloppy procedure and unnecessary duplication, and the mixing of clear and encrypted traffic, continued to undermine the security of the IJN's communications, and the RAN's collection effort continued to benefit. Another crib that was now identified was the impact of excessive Japanese formality in communications. This insistence on formality may not appear significant, but when the cryptanalysts knew that immediately following a message's externals, the message number, date and time and call sign, there would be stock phrases such as 'I have the honour to report to your excellency that . . .', the number of combinations they needed to examine was massively reduced.[61] This made it much easier to break out the formal greetings, and this provided the entrée into the code itself. This crib, among many others, allowed Eric Nave and John Tiltman, Britain's leading cryptanalyst, to break the IJN's codes with so few resources.[62]

F.H. Hinsley, the official historian of British intelligence in World War II, does say that throughout this period 'some Japanese SIGINT continued to be available because of the familiarity with Japan's communications systems that had been built up over the years'.[63] Effectively, traffic analysis, DF and the cribs derived from these sources were now paying dividends.

Still, the changes in the IJN's codes rendered a substantial part of their communications beyond the reach of FECB and GC&CS until September 1939, when the IJN's fleet code fell to GC&CS's attack.[64]

As the 1930s progressed, the prospect of war increased. The ACNB maintained its small SIGINT capability and planned to train RANVR telegraphists to man DF stations in the coming war.[65] The ACNB even reviewed the establishment for SIGINT operators, and looked to increase the number of positions from ten to fifteen.[66] The board even increased the Special Duty Allowance paid to the ratings of the Shore Wireless Service, who were volunteers for and employed on this form of special duty.[67]

On the outbreak of war in 1939, the RAN found itself desperately short of telegraphist trainees, qualified telegraphists and 'Y' Procedure specialists. It lacked shipboard equipment and even the high-powered wireless station, HMAS *Harman* in Canberra, was not ready, as the Department of Works needed a further £25,256 to complete it.[68] At Darwin and Rabaul, there was nothing. In 1939, Australia was in a much worse position than she had been in 1914. Even the decisions the government would make were unpredictable. The Menzies government, cowed by the opposition's hostility and their own fears as to involvement in foreign wars, hoped to avoid too early or too heavy a commitment of Australian forces to the coming fight in Europe when they had growing concerns over Japan in the Pacific.[69]

The crowd at Centennial Park, Sydney, at the Federation celebrations for the new nation of Australia, 1 January 1901. This was the first time the Parliament of Westminster transferred constitutional responsibility for external affairs to a dominion. With that transfer, Australia launched its first intelligence operation in March 1901—against Britain and France.
National Library of Australia (NLA)

The managers of the new nation's affairs. *Standing, left to right*: Muirhead Collins, of Defence; Atlee Hunt, of External Affairs; David Miller, of Home Affairs. *Sitting, left to right*: Robert Garran, of Attorney-General's; Harry Wollaston, of Trade and Customs; Robert Scott, of Post-Master General's; George Allen, of Treasury. National Archives of Australia (NAA)

Sir Edmund Barton, Australia's first prime minister and the authority for the first Australian clandestine spying mission against France and Britain in 1901, spearheaded by William Le Couteur. State Library of NSW

The first post office in the New Hebrides, built by the British and French Condominium. This was the post office that Le Couteur used to receive and send correspondence with Atlee Hunt during his mission. Courtesy of Martin Treadwell

Walter de Haas, the German businessman who arrived in Sydney on 22 November 1893 and who was appointed German Trade Commissioner in 1903, photographed in 1915 during his internment at Liverpool Camp. Despite the confected outrage of Australian newspapers, de Haas was repatriated to Germany in late 1915. NAA

The Scottish linguist and scholar Professor James Murdoch, who set up the first Japanese language program for the Australian government and who participated in the collection of political intelligence in Japan. State Library of Queensland (SLQ)

Captain Myer and members of the crew of the SS *Greifswald* en route to Fremantle, where the ship was apprehended on the outbreak of war. Captain Myer failed to destroy his secret code books, which were seized by Australian Naval authorities who immediately began decoding intercepted signals forwarded by the Admiralty in London. NLA

A rare photograph of Reg Hockings, owner of the Wanetta Pearling Company, who avoided publicity by never marrying and living on his plantation on Boeton Island, Celebes. *Brisbane Courier*, 24 June 1934

Reg Hocking's lugger, the radio-equipped *Wanetta*, at Thursday Island in 1919. Last known to be operating in the Maldives in the 1970s. University of Queensland Library

Thursday Island, c. 1917–1920, with some luggers of the fleet and views of Prince of Wales Island on the left horizon and Friday Island on the right. NLA

SS *Matunga*, the Burns Philp trader sought by Reg Hockings and the Admiralty. SLQ

Australia's first official, although unpaid, coastwatcher, Ancell
Clement Gregory, and his wife, Kate, in 1921. Courtesy of Kate Lance

Lugger of the Torres Strait type used by Ancell Gregory at Broome. Courtesy of Kate Lance

Ancell Gregory's close friend and business partner Murakami Yasukichi and his wife, Theresa Shingeno, photographed in the late 1930s.
State Library of Western Australia

Flagship of the Australian Fleet, HMAS *Australia*.

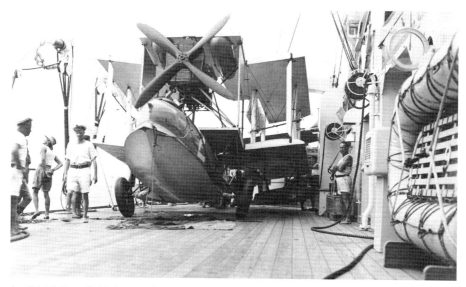

An RAAF Seagull A9-2 stowed on HMAS *Australia* during the Islands Cruise of 1932. This was the second combined intelligence collection operation integrating RAAF HUMINT with RAN SIGINT. NAA

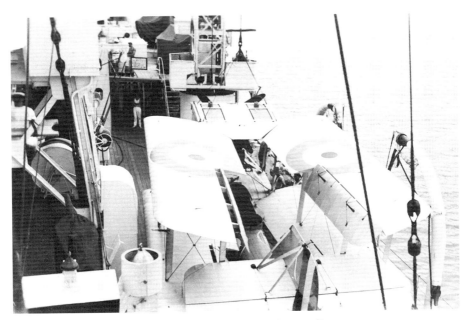

Islands Cruise, 1932: Stowage of Seagull A9-2 on HMAS *Australia*. NAA

Islands Cruise, 1932: Photograph of a mission station on Darnley Island, taken from Seagull A9-2 on HMAS *Australia*. NAA

CHAPTER 12

Harry Freame's
Japanese Mission, 1941

On 30 December 1963, Mrs Harriett E. Freame sent a letter to the prime minister of Australia, Sir Robert Menzies.[1] Mrs Freame was looking to Menzies to assist her in some way in erecting a gravestone for her husband, Wykeham Henry (Harry) Freame,[2] one of the original heroes of Gallipoli and, Mrs Freame claimed, an Australian spy who died from injuries he sustained while spying for Australia in Tokyo.[3]

Mrs Freame also sought compensation for Harry Freame's death, and supported her claim that he had died in the service of his country by detailing what he had reported on his deathbed in front of her and other witnesses. The truth of her assertions could easily be rejected, and they were. The government had a death certificate discounting Harry Freame's claims, and they had paid her some small compensation. Yet the Australian government's rejection of Harriet Freame's requests seems too rushed to be complacent. This leads to a conclusion that perhaps there is substance to Harriett Freame's story, as Harry Freame's history takes us back to the Japanese-language program of James Murdoch and Edmund Piesse, and to the machinations of the peacetime Military Intelligence Branch at Eastern Command and the Commonwealth Investigative Branch. Harry Freame's career seems to link to many of the players in Australia's interwar intelligence.

Wykeham Henry (Harry) Freame was born in Osaka, Japan, in about 1880, to William Henry Freame, an English sailor, and Kitagawa Sei, the daughter of Kitagawa Yasuaki, a local samurai [shizoku] from Shiga Prefecture. This marriage was a historical event in its own right, because Kitagawa Yasuaki was the first Japanese head of a family to officially initiate a marriage to a foreigner in Japan. On 29 April 1873, when he petitioned the Shiga Prefectural Office for permission for Sei to marry William Freame, it led to a great deal of documentation, as prefecture and Ministry of Finance officials tried to deal with the unique event. Finally, on 7 June 1873, the Main Office of the Great Council of State approved the marriage.[4]

What the Japanese authorities did not know was that William Freame had married Ellen Coker on 20 June 1867 in Melbourne, and had a six-year-old son, William Henry George Freame.[5] Ellen Freame finally addressed William's bigamy in 1877 when she sought and was granted a divorce in New South Wales with no co-respondent mentioned.[6]

In Japan, William Freame appears to have made a living teaching English at a kyoritsu gakko (a common school) and working for a steamship company in Nagasaki.[7] In the Japanese sources, William is described as 'anything but a refined gentleman', as he had the manners of a sailor.[8] He did not impress Miyake Setsurei, a journalist, who rudely described him as looking like he had kuronbo (black) blood in his veins, and rated Freame's grammar and pronunciation as poor. Miyake also mentions that Freame called his wife 'Misesu' [Missus].[9] The marriage produced two children, Harry and his sister Grace. In marrying Freame, Sei lost her Japanese nationality and William Freame did not have her made a British citizen, most likely because this would have uncovered his bigamy.[10]

It is difficult to work out when Harry Freame was born because he consistently lied about his date of birth. This started in August 1914, when he enlisted in the Australian Army claiming to be 29 when it was more likely he was 32.[11] From here, his age slid downwards as he sought to win or keep government positions. We do know he was born before the end of 1881, the year his father died.[12] He also persistently lied about who his father was, possibly because of the challenges of navigating the world as a 'half-caste'. Harriett Freame, Harry's second wife, was just as bamboozled as everyone else, and she still believed in 1963 that her husband's father had been dean of Oxford University, a position that has never existed.

Although the record is hazy, it appears that Harry was educated at Osaka until the age of fifteen or sixteen, when he left for England and entered the merchant marine, most likely as a ship's boy. We can discount the early newspaper accounts that he served in the IJN. Navies of the early twentieth century did not enlist boy sailors and then just let them go at the age of fifteen or sixteen to further their education.

What is certain is Harry Freame served as a British merchant seaman on 22 voyages between May 1902 and November 1909, which are all recorded on his seaman's discharge book. During this period, in 1906 Harry met and married Edith May Soppitt of Middlesbrough, but remained at sea, undertaking nine voyages between 1909 and 1912. One thing about Harry Freame is that he would prove a better husband and father than William had ever been.[13] His wages as a sailor and, later on, as a soldier, were paid to his wife, and when he decided to return to Australia, he brought his family with him. He would later nurse an ailing Edith, who may have been suffering from psychiatric problems, on the family farm at Kentucky, New South Wales.

After his arrival in Australia, Freame seems to have worked as a horse breaker at Glen Innes in New South Wales before he joined the Australian Army in 1914, receiving the regimental number 764 and being posted to the 1st Infantry Battalion. In late October 1914, Freame and the other men of the 1st Infantry Battalion departed Australia for the Middle East and eventually Gallipoli, where he found fame if not fortune.

At Gallipoli, Freame served as a scout. Why is unclear, but maybe it was because of the tall stories that circulated about his previous adventures as a scout in the Mexican Army and in German East Africa. These stories, many of which appeared in newspapers and other popular publications of the time, appear fanciful and it has been impossible to substantiate Freame's service in the Mexican Army of Porfirio Diaz or identify a Major Ziegler with whom Freame claimed to have served under in Mexico and German East Africa. No Major Ziegler is listed as part of Diaz's small 25,000-man Mexican Army, and the two gaps in Freame's seaman's papers, 1906–07 and 1912–14, do not coincide with the Maji Maji Rebellion in German East Africa in 1905 or the presidency of President Diaz, which ended on 31 May 1911.[14] It is likely that Freame simply jumped ship on both occasions.

At Gallipoli, Harry Freame displayed initiative and courage and, if he was a fantasist, he was either brave or reckless. The evidence suggests he was most likely reckless. The fact Freame dressed up as a Wild West scout wearing a bandana and two pistols (one on each hip), sporting a shoulder holster and carrying a Bowie knife, betrays a 'look at me' element in his character that would make him a dangerous man to be around on a battlefield.

Still, it has to be said, Harry Freame was not your average soldier.[15] He was half Japanese in an all-white army who landed at Gallipoli already a lance corporal and, a few months later, was a sergeant. It tells us he was both good at what he did and at impressing senior officers, including E.E. Longfield Lloyd, a man who would later play a significant role in Freame's life. Freame's antics even impressed Charles Bean, who would later describe Freame as 'probably the most trusted scout at Anzac'.[16] This description needs to be taken with a pinch of salt as Charles Bean and the AIF that landed at Gallipoli in 1915 were barely trained and had no experience of warfighting.

A good example of the amateurism of the AIF is provided by Bean's own reporting of a failed trench raid carried out by Australian troops, led by Lieutenant G.A. Street on the night of 4 June 1915. Freame apparently reconnoitred the route the party took.[17] This raid, which was intended to knock out a machine gun post, failed when Street's party unexpectedly ran into Turkish troops in a trench. The alarmed Turks began machine gunning the Australian trenches and it was decided that the 1st Battalion would mount another raid on the same target at 0255 hours on 5 June. This second raid was undertaken by 50 men led by Captain Lloyd. It was a debacle. The Turkish line was at full alert and waiting to repel any further attacks. No experienced troops would have even considered crossing the ground. As if this was not bad enough, even if they reached the Turkish machine gun they could not destroy it, as the engineers previously assigned to destroy it had gone to bed following the failure of Street's raid. As Bean tells it, Lloyd's party crossed no-man's-land under heavy Turkish fire and attempted to disable the gun by shooting it with a rifle.[18] The gun survived unscathed while five Australians died and 28 were wounded.[19]

Freame lasted five months at Gallipoli until 14 August, when he was badly wounded in a Turkish attack and evacuated from the peninsula. He was repatriated to Australia ten months later, which gives some indication of the seriousness of his wounds.[20] In his time at Gallipoli, Harry Freame won Australia's first Distinguished Conduct Medal (DCM) and earned a mention in despatches.[21] These were serious awards and, putting aside the inexperience of the AIF and its commanders, they were very significant awards for a sergeant.

The importance of Bean's account is that it shows that Harry Freame served alongside Lloyd, who was also repatriated to Australia in 1916. Lloyd was posted to the Intelligence Section of the General Staff in Sydney, where he worked for Edmund Piesse. Given his close association with Harry Freame, it is no surprise that he was soon a student in Professor Murdoch's Japanese-language program.[22] From here, Lloyd would go on to serve in the Commonwealth Investigations Branch from 1921 and to fill senior roles in Australia's security intelligence system, including the Director of the Security Service, until his retirement following the establishment of the Australian Security Intelligence Organisation (ASIO) in 1949.[23]

The first mention of Harry Freame's heroism at Gallipoli was in the pages of the *Farmer and Settler* of 26 May 1916, almost two months before he disembarked back in Sydney on 22 July 1916.[24] The story was picked up by papers throughout New South Wales, and differing versions would appear at regular intervals in 1916, 1922 and 1931.[25] Harry Freame's colourful exploits at Gallipoli would make him a hero long before Bean's *The Story of Anzac* was published in 1924.[26]

Freame arrived back in Australia after Lloyd, but it is likely that the two maintained their relationship of officer and soldier. It is also likely that, given the emphasis of Military Intelligence on Japan and the Japanese, Lloyd introduced Freame to Military Intelligence. We can be sure Harry Freame was working for someone, as he was able to set himself up at 2 Bondi Road, Bondi, where he was living on 20 November 1916, the day he was officially discharged from the army.[27] Harry Freame is most likely the Japanese-speaking returned soldier working under James Murdoch at Fort Street School.[28] Given his connections with Lloyd and Military Intelligence, however, there is every possibility that he worked as a translator and an agent, keeping tabs on Japanese consular staff, visitors and members of the Japanese business community in Sydney and New South Wales.

Harry Freame's next move occurred on 6 January 1920, when he took up an orchard block at Kentucky, on the New England Tablelands, which he acquired in a grant from the NSW Soldier Settlement Loan Scheme.[29] His presence in Kentucky is corroborated by newspaper reports, including one about a short conversation Freame had with General Birdwood during the latter's visit to the Kentucky settlement on 29 April 1920.[30] There is no evidence of Freame having a continuing relationship with Military Intelligence and Lloyd and it is likely the association ceased.

Like many returned soldiers who, despite having no experience or training, were set up as farmers on relatively poor land, the Freames found the going hard. The Freames had it harder because Edith Freame became ill and was in and out of hospital for twelve years until her death in 1939. Harry Freame was declared bankrupt and his 40 acres at Kentucky stripped from him.[31] According to his second wife, Harriett, it was at this time that he was employed as an agent by Military Intelligence.[32] Her claim is corroborated in a minute dated 9 October 1940 confirming that Harry Freame had been employed in defence work of a 'highly secret nature' since 4 December 1939.[33] It seems he had left intelligence work only to find himself back in it after the outbreak of World War II.

Harry Freame was a rare commodity in 1939. He was a returned soldier who was not an officer and he could speak fluent Japanese. It is no surprise that Military Intelligence snapped him up and began using him as a field agent spying on the Japanese community in New South Wales. Given the small size of this community and the abysmal tradecraft employed by Military Intelligence agents, it is likely Freame was quickly identified as a spy. The level of Australian tradecraft at this time was so bad that the Japanese diplomats at the Consulate-General in Sydney publicly teased Longfield Lloyd about the surveillance operation mounted against Major Hashida in 1941.

From the documentary evidence it appears that Freame's handler was a Major Scott, a militia officer who had served in France in 1916 and 1917 and suffered severe shell shock.[34] Between the wars, he served as a militia officer and owned an insurance brokerage, and was heavily involved in right-wing politics throughout the interwar period, though not with the mythical Old Guard.[35] Major Scott was also involved in the Australia–Japan Society, either as an agent provocateur, or because he really supported its objective of closer relations.

Scott's management of Freame as an agent was poor. Despite Freame's work being described as 'highly secret' and known only to Scott, Lieutenant Colonel Hodgson, the Secretary of the External Affairs Department, was aware of Freame by 30 August 1940.[36] Scott impressed on Hodgson the need for absolute secrecy in relation to Freame and his work but, stunningly, passed

Freame's private telephone number and address to Hodgson.[37] Nothing in the file suggests that Freame was asked about this, or that any effort was made to ascertain why Hodgson wanted to talk to an agent whose existence was supposedly a closely guarded secret.

By this time Freame was not just working for Scott as a secret agent, but had begun working for the Military Censor as a Japanese linguist, a post he took up at the end of August 1940 without Major Scott's knowledge. Hodgson most likely found out about Freame through his connection with the Military Censor.[38] This suggests that Freame's name was being bandied around government without any concern for his safety and that his putative handler was completely unaware of his holding at least two different positions, one in counterintelligence and one with the Censor. Now a third was in the offing, with Hodgson offering Freame the position of translator on the staff of Australia's first mission to Japan, led by Sir John Latham as first minister.

This extraordinary situation was now made enormously worse on Friday, 13 September 1940, when Freame's details, including his 'special defence work' and his appointment as the interpreter to the Australian Legation in Tokyo, were published in the press.[39] Someone somewhere had background briefed the press, and the *Daily Telegraph* in Sydney, *The Sun* and *The Argus* in Melbourne, *The Mercury* in Hobart, the *West Australian* in Perth and *The Advertiser* in Adelaide published all of the details. Only three newspapers, the *Sydney Morning Herald*, *The Examiner* in Launceston and the *Cootamundra Herald*, omitted the reference to special defence work.[40]

On 17 September, Major Scott responded to the breach of security by asking Section 1C of Military Intelligence to ask *The Sun* 'what the special defence work is and who supplied this information'.[41] The whole affair now spiralled out of control as the Minister for the Army, P.A. McBride, wrote to the Minister for External Affairs, John (Black Jack) McEwen, raising the army's 'considerable embarrassment' and stating that 'the possibility cannot be overlooked that this appointment may now be viewed with suspicion in Tokyo'.[42] McBride clearly laid the blame for this on Hodgson and, in a remarkable example of shutting a stable door too late, asked for McEwen's 'assurance that suitable action' was taken 'to ensure that no breach of security is possible in future'.[43]

McEwen was not called 'Black Jack' for nothing. His reply of 2 October 1940 firmly put McBride in his place. McEwen accepted Hodgson's assurances that there had been 'no disclosure of any confidential information to the press about the activities of Mr Freame'.[44] Having defended Hodgson and the department, McEwen went on the offensive, pointing out to McBride that Freame's activities were 'well known to the Japanese authorities here, including the Consul-General'.[45] Rubbing it in, McEwen tells McBride that Freame's controller, Major Scott, had only become aware of Freame's employment by the Military Censor on 1 October.[46]

As if this were not bad enough, McEwen also told McBride that Hodgson had 'specially raised the question of his [Freame's] appointment to the staff of the Tokyo [Australian] Legation with the Consul-General of Japan, with a view to ascertaining his attitude towards the appointment'.[47] The response of the Consul-General was that the appointment 'was an excellent one, as Mr Freame had created a very favourable impression'.[48]

The naivety on display here stuns, even today. The idea that Japanese diplomats could provide any assurance of Freame's safety in Japan, where he would fall under the authority of the Kempeitai, was something that, even in 1940, anyone able to read the press reports from Japan knew could not be relied upon. Australian government ministers, military officers and officials had openly disclosed Freame was a secret agent being sent to Tokyo at the same time Japan's Minister for War, Lieutenant General Tojo Hideki, had just publicly announced that the IJA would 'not hesitate to take drastic measures against Japanese who assisted foreign secret agents and those who were pro-British'.[49] Harry Freame was half Japanese, and no one in Australia seemed to understand what this entailed.

The country that Harry Freame was going to in 1941 was not a democracy or even a well-run monarchy or autocracy. In 1941, Japan was a nation in chaos as military factions struggled to impose their policy on the country via the Emperor. Assassination of opponents was frequent and, as General Tojo made perfectly clear, murdering Japanese or foreigners, with the exception of Americans, was seen as perfectly acceptable.

All of this was known in Australia. In 1935, British diplomatic reporting made available to Australia described the travails of a 75-year-old Australian citizen, the Reverend J.N. Mackenzie, at the hands of the Japanese military police, the Kempeitai.[50] Mackenzie had worked for 25 years as a missionary caring for lepers in Korea. His work was highly regarded by both the Japanese government and the Government-General of Korea. All of this was meaningless when the Kempeitai arrested Mackenzie for taking photographs of some children. Mackenzie's crime was not photographing children, it was having a camera.

Mackenzie was interrogated for more than two days and it was not gentle. G.H. Phipps, the British Consul-General in Korea reported that the interrogation only stopped at actual physical injury, behaviour that Mr Phipps reported 'reflects little credit on the force'.[51]

Mackenzie was lucky his arrest embarrassed the Japanese government enough for a face-saving plan to be implemented where he agreed to the charge of being an 'international spy'. This meant he could be brought before the civil authorities, who treated him with courtesy, while convicting him and fining him a petty 25 yen. Mr Phipps' warned both the British and Australian governments that the 'gendarmerie [the other title of the Kempeitai] is unfortunately independent of the civil government and is . . . very much a law unto itself'.[52] Anyone willing to read the file on Mackenzie should have realised that it did not matter what Japan's Consul-General said—the Kempeitai would do as it pleased.

The Mackenzie affair was not even the worst. In 1940, the Japanese authorities cracked down on anyone thought to be a spy, particularly a British spy. British spies were now targeted because Foreign Minister Matsuoka Yosuke had stopped the Kempeitai chasing American spies, and the Soviet spies were too hard to catch. The Kempeitai immediately arrested eleven British citizens who had attracted their attention. One of those arrested was James Melville Cox, the Reuters correspondent in Tokyo and an SIS agent. Cox had initially been compromised in 1936 when he posted classified information on the refitting of HIJMS *Nagato* in a letter signed 'Jimmy' from a favourite haunt, the Teikoku Hotel in Tokyo.[53] The Kempeitai had intercepted the letter but could not identify 'Jimmy'. The importance of Jimmy lay in the loss of face it caused the IJN to have the Kempeitai discover a British spy operating successfully against its dockyards. The matter was important enough that the Kempeitai now employed the most important tool in intelligence work: they recorded everything and began a systematic investigation of the matter.

Cox's letter provided the Kempeitai with three major insights. First, the name 'Jimmy' indicated a European, as did posting it from the Teikoku Hotel. Secondly, they knew the spy was interested in shipbuilding and the IJN. Thirdly, and most importantly, they knew the spy existed.

As the investigation proceeded, suspicion fell on Cox. The Kempeitai knew the name 'Jimmy' was the diminutive of James, and Cox did frequent the Teikoku Hotel. More incriminatingly, Cox's handwriting was similar to that on the original letter and he used similar stationery. Despite this, there was little the Kempeitai could do until 1937 when the Military Secrets Act was revised to cover civilians and foreigners. In 1940, with the Americans out of bounds and amid growing tension, the Military Service Bureau ordered the Kempeitai to clamp down on foreign suspects and the gloves came off.[54] James Cox was immediately picked up and taken to Kempeitai HQ in Tokyo.

Cox was interrogated, supposedly in an attempt to get him to incriminate the British Ambassador, Sir Robert Craigie, in espionage activities. How it happened no one really knows, but Cox ended up dead in the courtyard of Kempeitai HQ. The explanation provided was that he had thrown himself from the fourth-floor window.[55]

While the British government officially accepted suicide as the cause of Cox's death, the subsequent British investigation by Patrick Dean of the Foreign Office strongly suggested Cox had been tortured and murdered. The difficulties with the Japanese version were that the window in question 'was a yard [90 centimetres] square' and was protected by a large sill 90 centimetres above the floor, from which an already weakened and injured Cox would have had to launch himself. He would have had to negotiate this while eluding the two guards who always escorted prisoners.[56] Dean also found Cox's body had travelled 6 metres out from the wall of the building. The British investigation, while publicly accepting the suicide claim, privately thought Cox was either thrown through the window or that his body was placed in the courtyard after he had died in another place.[57]

Further evidence that Cox had been murdered was provided by a British resident of Nagasaki, and probable SIS agent, Vanya Ringer, who was arrested at the same time as Cox. On 29 July, the day Cox died, Ringer reported that he was told of Cox's death and threatened with the same if he did not tell the truth. Ringer had no doubt Cox had been murdered, as throughout his own detention he was always accompanied by at least two Kempeitai guards.[58] Ringer's unpublished memoirs are the source of much of the information available on Cox's death, and he obtained a large part of his information from Cox's widow, who sailed home with him on the SS *Nankin*. She told Ringer she saw more than twenty needle marks on her husband's body.[59]

The British responded with a carefully choreographed rounding-up of suspected Japanese spies in India and Singapore, which included Shinozaki Mamoru, the press attaché at the Japanese Consulate-General in Singapore. The way this was done suggests Cox was indeed an SIS officer. The evidence used in court against Shinozaki included his assistance to Colonel Tanikawa Kazuo and Captain Kunitake Teruhito of the IJA's Imperial General Staff, and his running of two agents, Gunner Frank Gardener of the Royal Artillery and Corporal Compton of the RAF, who had passed him information on troop movements in and out of Malaya.[60]

More substantive, though, is the fact that James Cox's widow was paid £5000 by the British government, a significant sum of money in 1940. This strongly suggests that James Cox was either an SIS agent or an SIS officer working under the cover of journalism in Japan.[61]

The details of Cox's death had been reported in the Australian press, and it is impossible that the Australian authorities planning to send Harry Freame to Tokyo did not know about the crackdown in Japan.[62] Yet despite all the press reporting of July 1940, Harry Freame boarded the SS *Tanda* on 11 October 1940 and set sail for Tokyo, where suspected spies were thrown out of fourth-floor windows.[63]

The outcome was entirely predictable. Freame arrived in Japan and started his duties as an interpreter and odd job man around the legation. Sometime during this period it would appear that the Kempeitai decided to take action against him. In their eyes, Freame was more than a British spy; he was a traitor working from the legation of a British colony. Given the evidence of the Kempeitai's aggressive and violent response to British spying, the claims of the Freame family that Harry was attacked and garrotted on a Tokyo street on 27 January 1941 are most likely true.[64]

The first formal claim that Harry Freame had died as a result of being garrotted by the Japanese security forces was raised in a letter written by Harriett Freame to Harry's old comrade, now Colonel Lloyd, the Director of the new Commonwealth Security Service, on 16 June 1941. In this letter, Harriett detailed how worried Harry and she had been by the press reporting of his posting to Tokyo and that Harry had told her he was being 'shadowed here and there after those silly people of the *Sun* Office' printed their story.[65] If Freame was being clandestinely shadowed around Sydney prior to his departure for Tokyo, he should have never been sent. The fact that he was allowed to proceed is an indictment of the amateurism surrounding Australia's security intelligence establishment of the time. It also explains why Lloyd took such a deep interest in the subsequent investigations and why, despite all of her efforts, Harriett Freame failed to get any support from subsequent Australian governments.

The tone of Harriett Freame's letters indicates that she was well aware of a security angle to Harry's work in Tokyo. In her letter, Harriett thanks Lloyd for his 'lovely letter and tribute to Harry' while adding 'I cannot write it but I would welcome an interview at anytime' and 'I would love to tell you about it. I know it was as you say, but I don't know if Sir John Latham is even aware . . .' It is a strong indication that Freame had been involved in something more than providing his services as an interpreter to the Australian Legation and that Lloyd was directly involved.

Despite the insistence of Freame's family that he died of injuries some four months after his garrotting in Tokyo, the official position was he died of cancer of the gall bladder, and his death certificate, which lists carcinoma of the gall bladder, supports this. Cancer of the gall bladder is, however, uncommon and it does not accord with the clinical findings of Dr Ikeda, the Japanese doctor who examined Freame at St Luke's International Medical Centre in Tokyo shortly after the attack.[66] Dr Ikeda found that Freame had suddenly lost his voice and suffered difficulty in swallowing. A laryngoscopy was conducted, and a complete paralysis of the left nervus laryngeus recurrens diagnosed, a finding consistent with a failed garrotting, not gall bladder cancer. Freame's blood count was normal, as were his stools and urine, and the X-rays of his lungs and lower oesophagus showed no abnormality, although Dr Ikeda lists 'a certain pathology in the mediastinum [the area between the lungs]'.[67]

To the lay reader, much of the medical information above is meaningless. The test results, however, showing normal stools and blood count and that there was no evidence of pancreatic, liver or stomach cancer on X-ray, is close to being impossible in gall bladder cancer. Freame's signs and symptoms were not those of a man with terminal cancer in his liver, pancreas or gall bladder.[68] The cause of death given in the official death certificate is not sustainable on the clinical evidence.

Freame returned to Australia after the attack and then died. A further complication is that the medical practitioner who issued the death certificate, Dr M.O. Stormon, was found by Military Intelligence to have been in close contact with the 'Secretary to the Minister for External Affairs', Fredrick Stewart.[69] At face value this suggests that two Commonwealth ministers, the Minister for External Affairs and the Minister for Health, were taking a direct interest in the medical condition of a temporary clerk.[70] This is not easily explained unless there was significant sensitivity about Freame's death in government circles.

Further evidence of governmental concern is seen in the telegram sent to Sir John Latham in Tokyo telling him that the department was 'confronted with question as to whether contributing factor in death was his service in Japan' and, if this was so, then there was a 'moral obligation to offer some compensation' to his destitute widow. Latham abruptly dismissed the department's concerns.[71]

In 1947, Latham would again reject compensation for Harriett Freame, writing, 'I can see no reason which would afford a sufficient ground for an application for further payment to Mr Freame's widow upon any other than compassionate grounds'.[72] Apparently, the ex gratia payment of £50 paid in October 1941, reduced by Treasury from the £100 recommended by the minister, was good enough.[73] Harry Freame's grateful nation had provided his widow with approximately six weeks' worth of his annual £400 salary.[74] The payout left his family destitute and Harriett was forced to bury Harry in an unmarked grave in the Church of England section of the Northern Suburbs Cemetery in Sydney. The grave is still there and still unmarked.

There is no doubt that Harry Freame's death caused a great deal of interest in official circles, but most of officialdom was keen to bury him and move on. Even his old comrade Lloyd did little for him or his family other than advising the Department of External Affairs that the 'possibility of Mr Freame having received [his] injury in Japan is not a remote one'.[75] All of this strongly suggests that Harry Freame, who was a security intelligence agent working clandestinely against the Japanese in Australia, was sent on an intelligence mission to Japan where he was attacked by the Kempeitai and subsequently died of his injuries after returning to Australia. If this is so, then Wykeham Henry Freame was the first Australian clandestine intelligence operative to be killed while serving his country. If so, as an ex-soldier, decorated war hero and Australian spy, it is wrong that he should be lying in an unmarked grave in Sydney, unacknowledged and unwanted by his country. Still, this is the fate of many a good spy.

CHAPTER 13

The Coastwatchers Go to War, 1939-42

Less than a week after Australia declared itself at war, on 8 September 1939 the ex-permanent RAN officer Lieutenant Commander Eric Feldt was appointed as Staff Officer (Intelligence) (SO (I)) at Port Moresby. His old classmate at the Naval College, Commander Rupert Long, who was now the DNI, instigated this action. Feldt's instructions were simple: he was 'to develop an organisation by which intelligence could be obtained' in Papua, New Guinea, the Solomon Islands and the New Hebrides, and their surrounding littoral areas.[1] The resources allocated for Feldt to carry out this task consisted of £200 in travelling expenses.[2] No staff, no organisation, just travel expenses.

Eric Augustus Feldt was born in 1899 at Ingham, Queensland, into a large Swedish family of cane farmers.[3] He attended Brisbane Grammar for one year, 1912, before he was accepted as a cadet midshipman in the class of 1913 at the Royal Australian Naval College. Here he met Rupert Long, the man who, as Australia's DNI between 1939 and 1945, would be Feldt's boss throughout the war.

Feldt had done well at the naval college, becoming the Chief Cadet Captain and winning colours for rugby and athletics. He graduated as a midshipman in January 1917 and was posted to the RN. He returned to

Australia aboard HMS *Swordsman* in 1919 and was promoted to lieutenant in February 1920.[4]

Despite his orthodox career as a RAN officer, life in a rundown navy had no allure for Eric Feldt. In April 1923 he left the permanent RAN and took up a position as a clerk in the administration of the New Guinea Mandate.[5] From there, he made his way to patrol officer before becoming a district officer. He later held appointments as the Mining Warden, Morobe Goldfields, before rising to the position of Chief Mining Warden, New Guinea.[6]

As far as his naval career was concerned, Feldt, like many ex-regular officers of the time, remained on the RAN Emergency List, being promoted to Lieutenant Commander and granted the war service rank of Commander in 1928.[7] As war approached, the ACNB, advised by the office of the DNI, looked to revitalise the Admiralty's Reporting Officer system and coast-watcher organisation. In late 1939, Rupert Long asked Eric Feldt to take on the job of organising the reporting officers in the islands.

Feldt had all of the qualities needed. First, as a classmate of Long's and an ex-permanent officer of the RAN, he was a known quantity. Secondly, as a long-time resident of New Guinea and a former patrol and district officer, he knew the local populations of New Guinea very well. Thirdly, as the Chief Mining Warden for New Guinea, he was closely networked into all levels of the European community throughout the territory. Fourthly, the fact that he held such a senior position showed that he was no slouch, working hard and effectively. For the ACNB, Eric Feldt was manna from heaven.

With no support staff, Feldt had to rely on the network of honorary (unpaid) civilian reporting officers and, with some qualifications, the assis-tance of the New Guinea administration and the friendly support of No. 11 Squadron, RAAF, based at Port Moresby.[8]

In September 1939, in accordance with the plans drawn up by the Admiralty in late 1938 for a worldwide intelligence organisation, the ACNB activated the wartime provisions for collecting intelligence and commu-nicating it to the Admiralty.[9] In Feldt's area of responsibility, the reporting officers consisted of two Australian officials, the Treasurer of the New Guinea administration in Rabaul and the District Officer at Madang; and two British Colonial officials, the Resident Commissioner of the British Solomon Islands in Tulagi and the Resident Commissioner at Port Vila.[10] These British officials were not answerable to the Australian government but to the Colonial Office in London via the British Commissioner for the Western Pacific, a dual role held by the Governor of Fiji. For practical purposes, however, the Admiralty had placed them, in their roles as reporting officers, under the auspices of the ACNB and, thus, Rupert Long as the Australian DNI.

Each reporting officer held the Admiralty's confidential books, codes and other documentation and, upon the receipt of the Admiralty's Warning Signal of 3 September 1939, began reporting all shipping movements in accordance with their instructions. In addition to these reporting officers, a number of district officers and assistant district officers were appointed coastwatchers. In all areas other than Papua, these men began reporting shipping activity to the relevant reporting officer using locally created codes and their government supplied tele-radios. These tele-radios operated in three networks run by AWA base stations, at Rabaul, Port Moresby and Samarai Island just south of Milne Bay. Each of these base stations could communicate with Sydney.[11]

In the Mandated Territory, the AWA network consisted of the base station at Rabaul working schedules with AWA stations at Salamaua, Madang, Wewak, Lorengau, Kavieng and Kieta. Each of these stations then serviced a local net of tele-radio stations.[12]

In the British Solomon Islands, the British administration controlled a single network with a base station at Tulagi. This station maintained contact with the outside world via Rabaul or Suva in Fiji.[13]

In the New Hebrides, also a British territory, the radio network consisted entirely of tele-radios, with the control station at Port Vila.[14] All of these networks, but particularly the low-powered tele-radio networks, suffered from the atmospherics of the area, and this resulted in them having to communicate at precise times of the day in order to get the right angle of refraction off the ionosphere for their sky wave.[15]

From a strategic perspective, the positioning of the individual tele-radios and their control stations would prove both fortuitous and unfortunate. Fortuitous because they were well situated to observe the invading Japanese, if they came; unfortunate because they were in all of the places the Japanese would invade.

Feldt arrived in Port Moresby on 21 September 1939 and addressed a couple of immediate problems. The first was the need to have the coastwatchers use the same code, PLAYFAIR, copies of which Feldt had brought with him. Feldt met and briefed the Naval Officer-in-Command, who undertook to distribute PLAYFAIR to the reporting officers and coastwatchers of Papua. Feldt then headed off to Rabaul to ask the Administrator of New Guinea, Sir Walter McNicoll, to do the same there.[16]

Feldt's initial assessment of the situation showed that large tracts of his area were uncovered, and he moved to begin a program of confirming the willingness and ability of existing coastwatchers to continue their voluntary duties, and to recruit more coastwatchers to cover the gaps.[17]

Like all good commanders, Feldt went and looked for himself. He toured the east coast of New Ireland by car, bicycle and foot. He visited Pak Island, Lorengau on Manus Island, Dyaul Island and Sicacui on Latangai Island by schooner. He appointed 26 honorary coastwatchers in these areas. He then proceeded to Bougainville and the Solomon Islands, appointing a further 38 coastwatchers in those territories.[18] He continued on to Salamaua in New Guinea and was flown by flying boat around the coast, appointing even more coastwatchers and providing the pilot of the flying boat with navigational and geographical assistance.[19]

This grand tour of the area of operations allowed Feldt to fill the gaps in the existing coastwatcher network and to identify that the strategically important pinch point at Buka Passage and the area between Buka and Latangai islands were unobserved. He also realised that messages from coastwatchers at other important passages through the islands took too long to get to Naval Intelligence.[20]

From his personal reconnaissance, Feldt was able to put a comprehensive plan to Long for the organisation of the coastwatcher organisation in the islands. This addressed the need for a special frequency, 'X', to be made available for all coastwatchers, which required the manufacture and distribution of 33 radio crystals for coastwatcher tele-radios. For coastwatchers in strategically important locations, particularly those overlooking pinch points, the ACNB distributed a further sixteen X frequency tele-radios at their own cost and distributed these to the relevant coastwatchers. In one location, Anir Island, a Chief Yeoman of Signals, S. Lamont, RAN, had to be sent because there was no European to undertake the work.

From the number of crystals and tele-radios handed out, at the end of November 1939 the coastwatcher network in Feldt's area of operations had been expanded to 50 stations, and AWA had been contracted to maintain a 24-hour listening watch of the X frequency the network now used.[21] It would take from June to November 1940 for all of this equipment to be manufac-tured, freighted to Port Moresby and then distributed by RAAF flying boats to the coastwatch posts.[22]

The scheme was then expanded to include Thursday Island and Torres Strait, North Queensland and the Northern Territory. Six more tele-radios were lent by the ACNB to the New Hebrides administration for use in their area. Feldt then conducted visits along the south coast of Papua, then Tulagi Island, Buka Passage, and the Trobriand and Woodlark islands in January 1940. Finally, in early 1940, two service personnel joined Feldt in the area, Flight Lieutenant Thompson, RAAF, at Tulagi and S. Lamont at Port Moresby. Lamont would later deploy to Anir Island.[23] Feldt was to accompany Lamont to Anir in HMAS *Manoora* on 10 May 1940, but the cruise was cancelled, so Feldt and Lamont borrowed a launch from the administration to get there and establish the post.[24]

By January 1940, Feldt's coastwatchers were providing the DNI with reporting on everything nautical. One report of this period, provided by the local police, two Catholic missionaries and a visiting patrol officer, detailed the arrival of HMAS *Kanimbla* at Wanimo Harbour on 28 December 1939. Another report, from the Schouten Islands, detailed the arrival of the govern-ment vessel *Thetis* on 3 January 1940 and described another darkened vessel, thought to be *Kanimbla*, that steamed around the island on 4 January, showing chinks of light through her blackout. There was even a report of an explosion heard over an area of more than 80 kilometres that Feldt put down to a meteorite.[25] Although these reports are the minutiae of small isolated locations, they proved the system was working and that information was being forwarded in a timely fashion.

Feldt had done an enormous amount in setting up the coastwatch system by himself. He had established at least 50 stations across the outer arc of the eastern archipelago and another extensive arc of stations on the southern coast of Papua. It was no mean feat. On 3 November 1940, Lieutenant H.A. Mackenzie, RAN, along with an Able Seaman Writer, was posted as the Assistant SO (I) Port Moresby to help Feldt.[26]

Feldt now had two people to assist him with the load of administering a large organisation spread across a massive area. This now led him to consider his worst-case scenario, the loss of Port Moresby. The plan in this instance was for the organisation to take to the jungle, and preparations for this eventuality were undertaken by establishing supply caches at Koitaki and at Rouna in the high ranges.[27]

In Melbourne, Commander Long was working hard trying to build up an effective intelligence system, and prevent Military Intelligence from causing mayhem with the one the ACNB had already established. As Long described to Feldt in a letter of 13 January 1940, the declaration of war had caught the army on the hop, and it was now playing catch-up and trying to build its own reporting system in a mad rush.[28]

The problem for Long was that the army was trying to recruit the navy's coastwatchers and, when unable to, adding army tasks to the work the coast-watchers were doing for the navy. In New Guinea, this had alienated the Administrator, who felt his patrol and district officers were being distracted from their real jobs.[29]

In January 1940, the situation threatened to get out of control, as the military bureaucrats of the General Staff in Melbourne issued instructions to the coastwatchers, whom they now regarded as military reporting officers, to use the army's highly redundant and very ponderous signal procedures, including nil returns every day.[30] Effectively, they wanted a daily signal saying 'nothing to report'.

This instruction was presumptuous, as the coastwatchers concerned were working for the ACNB. Far worse, it was lunacy. Signal procedures in the RAN of 1939 differed from army signalling because the RAN operated in a more sophisticated electronic environment in which radio messages that were too long or too frequent gave away the position and direction of a ship. HFDF could not locate ships that remained radio silent and so the RAN kept messages extremely brief and never sent nil returns. For coastwatchers, the threat posed by enemy warships and raiders, to say nothing of the IJN's SIGINT capabil-ities, was very real. The signal sent out by the General Staff shows a marked lack of understanding of the problems involved in clandestine coastwatching.

Long's approach was to recommend the establishment of a combined operations HQ manned by the three services at Port Moresby. He was using this as the thin edge of a wedge to get such combined organisations estab-lished in Australia, and particularly in Melbourne, where the RAN, army and RAAF commands were located.[31]

The difficulties continued as Military Intelligence began increasing its efforts to find out more about the RAN's coastwatching activities and organisation. This was not the usual inter-service rivalry; it was a takeover bid. The particular officer who was causing Long concern was a civilian ex-subordinate of his in Naval Intelligence. This man was Robert Frederick Bird Wake, who had left his position as clerk in Naval Intelligence and joined the Commonwealth Investigation Branch (CIB), where he had risen to the rank of inspector-in-charge, Queensland. Rupert Long later gave evidence at a judicial investigation of Wake that while he respected Wake's ability to find things out, he believed that Wake lacked the ethical and moral standards required of a man delving into other people's private lives.[32]

In July 1940, when Lieutenant Colonel Wake began nosing around Feldt's organisation, he held the concurrent appointments of Head of Military Intelligence in Queensland, State Director of the Security Service in Queensland and, his actual job, Inspector-in-Charge for the CIB in Queensland.[33] In effect, he had centralised all security and intelligence roles in Queensland in his own hands, and no one in the Australian government appears to have seen the dangers in allowing this. It is likely Wake was moving against Feldt's organisation with the support of Military Intelligence, who wanted it brought under army control.

Initially, Feldt got along quite well with Robert Wake, but this changed when Long alerted Feldt to Wake's active criticism of the coastwatcher organisation at meetings in Melbourne.[34] Wake had alleged that Feldt had not recruited enough people and that the duties of those he had recruited were so limited that they were unable to meet the army's needs.[35] It was typical Military Intelligence, and it was typical Robert Wake. By October 1940, Eric Feldt's view of Wake had hardened, and he wrote to Long that 'Hereward the Wake . . . is the worst double-crossing bastard I have ever had dealings with.'[36]

The year 1940 brought another difficulty over which no one had any control: the price of copra fell drastically, and coastwatchers were either losing their jobs or watching their incomes fall substantially. The result was that the men Feldt had recruited were leaving the islands or couldn't pay AWA the rental for their tele-radios. The ACNB raised the issue with the Commonwealth-controlled AWA, and it was agreed that the rental payments would be suspended as long as the tele-radios were used only for coastwatch traffic.[37]

Originally, the concept of operations for the coastwatch system was that all reports would be sent directly to Melbourne. With the advent of Long's Area Combined Headquarters (ACHQ), however, it was decided that reports should go to the local ACHQ, which in this case was Port Moresby.[38] Further changes occurred as Australian defensive preparations, such as the RAAF aerodromes at Rabaul, Gavutu and Vila, were put in place. To enable the aircraft based at these locations to respond quickly to coastwatcher reports, naval liaison officers were posted to the airfields.[39] A naval liaison officer was also placed at Tulagi, and Lieutenant Mackenzie was sent as the Naval Intelligence Officer (NIO) to Rabaul. Each liaison officer had an assistant and a small group of signallers and coders to assist them. In addition, the RAAF staff at these airfields kept a listening watch on X frequency at all times, and duplicated the warnings being sent to the forward commands.[40]

It was at this juncture, May 1941, that the ACHQ was relocated to Townsville, and so Feldt and his small party moved to the new location, leaving an NIO at Port Moresby. In Townsville, Feldt's title was changed to Supervising Officer (Intelligence) (SO (I)), and his staff was increased by the appointment of K.L. Murray as his civil assistant.[41] It was also at this time that Long's idea of the Combined Operations and Intelligence Centre (COIC) was adopted, and COICs were established at Townsville, Port Moresby and Rabaul, among other locations.

New coastwatcher posts were also created, one at Toma, in the hinterland of Rabaul, and one in the mountains of Guadalcanal. The general idea was that, following invasion, the civilian coastwatchers would cease operations due to the risk of being shot as spies. It was intended, however, that military coastwatchers would continue reporting from behind enemy lines using these inland posts.[42] This plan for continued military coastwatching suffered from a significant flaw, in that there was no system in place to support them, and no equipment, supply caches or any of the other essentials necessary to enable them to carry out their duties.[43]

Thus, as war with Japan came closer, Feldt had an operational HQ at Townsville, and local NIOs at Thursday Island, Port Moresby, Rabaul, Tulagi and Vila, each controlling their local coastwatcher networks. The radio reporting system had a dedicated, constantly monitored frequency, X, and its own code, PLAYFAIR, and each NIO could communicate reports directly to Melbourne for the ACNB, the chiefs of staff and the COIC now established at Victoria Barracks in St Kilda Road, Melbourne.[44]

The first blood for the coastwatcher system was drawn because of the wide knowledge that it existed. In June 1940, an Italian ship, the SS *Romolo*, was caught out by Italy's declaration of war, and her captain attempted to escape by steaming eastward of San Cristobal Island in the Solomons to avoid detection by coastwatchers. The pursuing Australian warships guessed he would know of the existence of the coastwatch network and would steam eastward. *Romolo* was caught by HMAS *Manoora* and the captain scuttled his ship rather than surrender.[45]

The next brush with the war was more immediate. On 24 December 1940, the coastwatch station at Kavieng on New Ireland reported that German commerce raiders had landed survivors of merchant ships on Emirau Island. Lieutenant Mackenzie travelled from Rabaul to Emirau and interviewed the survivors, sending selected ships' officers to Port Moresby for interrogation. From the information gleaned, a comprehensive picture of the voyages, activities and capabilities of the raiders in question was compiled. Other than this, the main business was handling the many odd and false reports, and the occasional valid one.[46]

The system Feldt put in place was intelligence at its best. It produced a lot of material through which intelligence officers sifted, looking for the occasional speck of gold. In the period before the Japanese entered the war, Australia's intelligence system did find some specks, including the area of operations of the *Takaichiho Maru*, a suspected spy ship. Other specks were Japanese flights over Kavieng, the Admiralty Islands and the Solomons. The lack of a proper system for evaluating and assessing intelligence into a broad picture meant, however, that not much use was made of any of these reports.[47]

As tension in Asia continued to grow, the ACNB also authorised the reorganisation of the coastwatcher organisation, with the creation of an additional layer of control and coordination. Until June 1941, the supervision of coastwatch personnel had been left to the local civilian administration on the spot. By mid-1941, however, the DNI moved to appoint dedicated RAN intelligence officers to key points.[48] Lieutenant H.A. Mackenzie, RAN, was appointed as the NIO at Rabaul; Sub-Lieutenant J.C.H. Gill, RANVR, at Port Moresby; Lieutenant Commander H.A.G. Crawford, RANVR, at Thursday Island; Sub-Lieutenant D.S. Macfarlane, RANVR, at Tulagi; and Lieutenant H.W. Bullock, RANVR, at Vila.[49]

On 8 December 1941, the whole coastwatch system was alerted that war was imminent, and the stations on Anir, Rooke (Umboi), Duke of York, Nissau (Nissan) islands and at Toimonapu Bay on Bougainville Island were placed on 24-hour operations.[50] At Rabaul, the Assistant SO (I) had become unwell, and Sub-Lieutenant Gill was sent to relieve him. Gill was sent because it was expected that the Japanese would attack Rabaul, and that the NIO there, Lieutenant Mackenzie, would need the help.[51] Pay Lieutenant J.H. Paterson, RANVR, was appointed NIO at Port Moresby, while pay lieutenants Macfarlane, RANVR, and Bullock, RANVR, remained at Tulagi and Port Vila respectively.[52]

The success of Feldt's work in preparing the coastwatchers for the coming Japanese war was clearly demonstrated when only one coastwatcher left his station at the outbreak of war.[53]

The first sign that the Japanese were on the way was an aerial reconnaissance of Nauru on 8 December, followed by aerial reconnaissance of Rabaul and Tabar Island on 9 December. These were the first sightings of the Japanese made by Con L. Page (later Sub-Lieutenant, RANVR), a planter on Tabar Island, which sat on the most direct air route from the Japanese airbase on Truk to Rabaul.[54] Page's warnings arrived at Rabaul 40 minutes before the Japanese aircraft. The first Japanese attack, the bombing of Nauru just outside Feldt's area of operations, took place on 9 December. After this, nothing happened until the Japanese undertook aerial reconnaissance missions over Salamaua, Lae and Madang on 28 December. Coastwatchers reported all of this activity, except that at Nauru.[55]

On 4 January, the war heated up, with two Japanese bombing attacks on Rabaul for which Page again provided 40 minutes' warning. This was enough time for the RAAF to get its outmatched Wirraway fighters airborne so the Japanese could shoot them down rather than destroy them on the ground.

On the same day, the coastwatchers at Tulagi, Tabar and Kieta reported Japanese aircraft. On 10 December, Percy Good at Kissa reported six aircraft flying south. On 11, 12 and 13 December, Page on Tabar reported aircraft. On 12 December, the Rev. A.P.H. Freund on Rooke Island also reported aircraft, as did A.F. Kyle at Namatanai. On 13 and 14 December, J.K. McCarthy entered the war by reporting aircraft at Talasea.[56]

The Japanese continued aerial reconnaissance of Rabaul and the surrounding islands and waters until 21 January, when they launched bombing attacks against Kavieng, Lorengau, Madang and Salamaua. That night in Rabaul, Mackenzie burnt the codebooks and confidential papers, and the last

Hudson bomber flew away, leaving the RAAF ground staff to set out for Wide Bay to be evacuated.[57]

The Japanese attack, when it came, was quick and efficient, with the garrison's defence turning into a shambles, of which the defining moment was the premature demolition of the RAAF bomb dump. The resulting shockwave destroyed every radio valve in Rabaul, cutting it off from the outside world. The only working tele-radio left was with the coastwatchers at Toma, 6 kilometres south-east of Vunakanau Airfield, where the entire garrison now retreated. To the outside world, the only indication that Rabaul and Kavieng had fallen was the sudden loss of all communications. Eric Feldt was very unimpressed, and he made this clear when he wrote to Long on 31 March:

> The whole Rabaul business smells badly and I hope there will be a thorough check up on the stories told ... Having seen the result of indiscipline in the AIF I told all the Subs and under here that in future everything will be done Whale Island style.[58]

A cascade of retreating troops and vehicles tumbled down to Toma, and this attracted the Japanese. Mackenzie decided to destroy the tele-radio and lead his nine men out of New Britain by walking down the coast and picking up a boat. As they were preparing for the trek they were joined by Lieutenant Colonel H.H. Carr, the Commanding Officer of 2/22nd Battalion; Lieutenant Figgis, the Intelligence Officer; and Superintendent W.B. Ball of the Rabaul Police.[59] This extended party then took to the jungle.[60]

At Kavieng on New Ireland, the Japanese had an anticlimactic experience, with Major J. Edmunds-Wilson's 1st Independent Rifle Company choosing discretion and departing, apparently in accordance with their orders. If Edmunds-Wilson was trying to save the lives of his men, it was in vain. The Japanese captured the bulk of the company and most of them were killed when the ship taking them to Hainan Island, off the coast of China, the *Montevideo Maru*, was torpedoed by the US submarine *Sturgeon* in the South China Sea.

The withdrawal of Australian defenders from Rabaul and Kavieng was complemented by a significant loss of coastwatchers. The coastwatchers at Kavieng on New Ireland and Waterfall Bay on New Britain were evacuated, and those on the islands of Nissan, Anir, Duke of York, Dyaul and Pak disappeared. Only the stations at Lorengau and Namatanai remained.[61]

Once they had taken Rabaul and Kavieng, the Japanese spread out across New Britain and New Ireland and the littoral areas around them, and conducted clearing operations that were complete by 28 January.[62] By this time, Feldt had also lost Rabaul, Gasmata, Tabar, Namatanai, and Kavieng. At the end of January 1942, all the stations in the western Solomon Islands were gone, and by 18 February, Japanese troops occupied the Admiralty Islands and Duke of York Island.[63]

The coastwatchers on the ground now had to deal with the threat posed by bad security back in Australia. This was in fact so bad that at the end of January the Australian Broadcasting Commission (ABC) aired in its news that Port Moresby was receiving advanced warning of Japanese air raids from a radio station at Gasmata.[64] Someone in the Australian government seems to have thought that broadcasting this to the people of Australia would help raise morale.[65] It is not known if the Australian public derived any benefit, but we know the Japanese did. On 8 February they landed a party of troops and captured the coastwatchers, Assistant District Officer J.E. Daymond, R.T. Squires and Sub-Lieutenant E.H.F. Mitchell, RANVR. Surprisingly, Daymond and Squires were taken into custody and not killed out of hand.[66] Mitchell, who had hidden in the jungle, reported the capture of his colleagues and tried to cross New Britain from south to north. He was also captured. All three men subsequently died on the *Montevideo Maru*.[67]

The loss of the Gasmata station caused problems for Feldt in Townsville.[68] He already knew that the explosion in Rabaul had destroyed the radios there, but he couldn't account for why Mackenzie's radio, 16 kilometres away in Toma, was not operating.[69] It was decided that someone had to go and find out what had happened. That someone was a civilian, J.K. McCarthy.[70]

McCarthy, who was at the western end of New Britain, now had to cross the whole island from west to east. This was a 520-kilometre trek through jungle and enemy-occupied territory around Toma. The trip was expected to take at least ten days and more likely two weeks.[71]

The incident at Gasmata had also caused Feldt to become more insistent with Long that his coastwatchers needed to be looked after more effectively. If McCarthy, a civilian official, were to be captured on his reconnaissance mission, it would make him a spy liable to be executed and, worse, his family would have no right to death benefits. While Feldt raised these issues with

Long, McCarthy was back in his district at the town of Talasea preparing for the expedition.[72] As Feldt told Long on 4 February:

> I do not want to see them [McCarthy's party] picked up by sending information now which will only be used for a Minister to make a statement, for a headline in a newspaper or a sentence in a B.B.C. announcement. So . . . look to you not to give the word 'GO' until the news will be of real use. We will only get one chance—a bloke will last about a week to a fortnight if they [the Japanese] start after him.[73]

McCarthy got together a team of three coastwatchers, himself and two local planters, Flight Lieutenant G.H.R. Marsland, RAAF, and Lieutenant K.C. Douglas, RANVR.[74] The Toma party consisted of McCarthy, Marsland, local radio operator Nelson Tokidoro, and a small number of local police.[75] Douglas and a larger party of local police remained and manned the station at Talasea, keeping an eye on the local villages in case Japanese patrols entered the area.

McCarthy's party travelled along the coast by launch, travelling at night and hiding up under the jungle canopy by day. They also maintained radio silence for two weeks to avoid the possibility of detection by Japanese HFDF stations and shipboard teams.[76] As the party moved towards Toma and Rabaul, Major G.W.L. Townsend of the Australian New Guinea Administrative Unit (ANGAU)[77] began collecting small motor launches that could undertake the evacuation of survivors from New Britain to New Guinea.[78] At Finschhafen in New Guinea, the coastwatch organisation was growing under its newly appointed commander, Captain G.C. Harris, ANGAU. This group now included W.A. Money, a planter, and the three lay missionaries, A.P.H. Freund, A. Obst and V. Neumann, who had taken up the sword against the Japanese.[79]

At Madang in New Guinea, another coastwatch group was formed consisting of A. Kirkwall-Smith, planters B.G. Hall and R. Emery, and medical practitioner Dr R.A. Chugg. All were appointed to ANGAU then moved to Rooke Island, where they joined up with the Finschhafen group and began the process of planning the evacuation of survivors from Rabaul and New Britain to Port Moresby.[80]

By this time, McCarthy's party had reached Pondo Plantation, around 80 kilometres south-west of Rabaul. At Pondo, three local men, R. Olander,

L. Bell and F. Holland, joined McCarthy's group.[81] The group avoided detection by patrolling Japanese destroyers, and made contact with Captain A.G. Cameron and a small party of eleven soldiers who had managed to keep together as a functioning subunit. On 14 February, McCarthy signalled Townsville to have the groups evacuated.

Feldt immediately spoke to Major General B.M. Morris, the General Officer Commanding (GOC), Port Moresby, and it was agreed that Cameron would use McCarthy's launch to take his men to Talasea for evacuation.[82] Cameron took the launch but sailed to Salamaua and led his men to Port Moresby from there, leaving McCarthy's party stranded in enemy territory. It was an enormously selfish action that led to all military personnel on New Britain being put under McCarthy's command by an undoubtedly horrified and embarrassed GOC.[83]

McCarthy had successfully completed his intelligence mission. He had obtained the entire story of Rabaul from Cameron and the other survivors which he then sent back to Port Moresby and Townsville on 14 February.[84] On 18 February, Major General Morris gave the civilian McCarthy authority over all Australian military officers on New Britain irrespective of rank when he approved McCarthy's plans to rescue stragglers.[85]

At Pondo, McCarthy's party collected information from the local population using their local police personnel and it soon became clear that numerous small parties of Australian soldiers, possibly totalling around 600, were spread all over the area.[86] In order to cover the ground, the party split into two search groups, one led by Holland and the other by McCarthy. A third group under Marsland and Bell remained at Pondo to repair a damaged launch they had found on a plantation.[87]

Holland's group made its way westward along the southern coast of New Britain, looking to pick up groups of AIF stragglers following the coast. McCarthy's party searched local plantations to find soldiers who may have remained there. This activity was now becoming urgent because the Japanese were losing patience with Australian stragglers who ignored advice to surrender.

It is also likely that the frontline Japanese units were now being reinforced by depot elements, including Kempeitai, who were less well disposed to anyone causing difficulty. The evidence for this is that the initial easygoing Japanese attitude became more ruthless and ferocious. This change led to the massacre of 160 Australian soldiers at Tol in Wide Bay, and an increasingly brutal treatment of any civilians suspected of having assisted Australians.[88]

Within a few weeks, McCarthy's party had located and concentrated 200 survivors of Rabaul at Pondo. Among these were the Commanding Officer of the 2/22nd Battalion, Lieutenant Mackenzie, Sub-Lieutenant Gill and Chief Yeoman Lamont, Signalman C.C. Francis, Yeoman J.T. Knight and Writer T.J. Douglas.[89] This was not the end of their travails. Francis died on the track at Ril plantation on 24 February, and Knight and Douglas had to be left at a mission station at Wide Bay with Lamont, who stayed to nurse them.[90] All three were never seen again. These four deaths were among the first suffered by the coastwatch organisation.

McCarthy's plan was to load the sick and wounded on the *Aussi* and the *Malahuka* and have Holland take them back by sea. McCarthy would lead the rest of the party on the 320-kilometre trek westward to the coast of New Britain nearest to New Guinea.[91] As Holland approached Talasea on 14 March, he forwarded a signal from Mackenzie giving the location of more survivors at Waterfall Bay, 160 kilometres east north-east of Gasmata. Because of this, the coastwatchers on Rooke Island moved forward in the four launches *Gnair*, *Bavaria*, *Unboi* and *Totol* to pick up and ferry the survivors across to Witu Island. At Witu, the survivors were placed on board the motor schooner *Lakatoi* and evacuated.[92]

In all, McCarthy and his helpers rescued 397 survivors and crossed hundreds of kilometres of jungle and enemy territory. They had searched for and found isolated groups of survivors in the jungles, villages and plantations of New Britain, brought them all to assembly areas and then arranged their safe evacuation. It was a remarkable set of achievements.

While coastwatchers on New Britain were rescuing survivors from Rabaul, the action moved eastwards towards New Ireland, Bougainville and the Solomon Islands as the Japanese secured the approaches to Rabaul and Truk. On 30 March, IJN vessels arrived off Buin and Buka, and occupied Buka and the Shortland Islands.[93] The Japanese were seizing ground to build a line of airfields from which aircraft could provide air cover to naval forces operating southwards from Rabaul. This had made both Rabaul and Kavieng objectives, and now Bougainville and the Solomons as well. A little later, they would make an attempt on Milne Bay for the same reason, and begin work on what would become Henderson Field on Guadalcanal. If these airfields were built, they would close off the whole of the Solomon Sea and northern Coral Sea to Allied naval forces.

On 7 March 1942, almost twelve weeks after the attack on Pearl Harbor, convoy ZK.7, carrying Major General Alexander Patch's Americal Division, was the first US convoy to sail from Melbourne to New Caledonia. The same day, aerial reconnaissance sighted a Japanese convoy 90 kilometres north-east of Buna on the New Guinea coast.[94] The Japanese convoy was heading for Salamaua and Lae to establish operational bases and airfields there.

The only Allied personnel at any of these places were small detachments of coastwatchers and members of ANGAU. At Buka, the planter Percy Good had remained behind. Good had been an AWA radio operator before becoming a planter and coastwatcher. At the outbreak of the Japanese war, he was 50 years old and somewhat infirm, which prevented him from taking to the jungle, so he passed his tele-radio to four soldiers, privates J.H. Wigley, E.D. Otton, W.A. Ross and B. Swanson, who had been part of the 1st Independent Company at Kieta.[95] It turned out to be a waste of time because they did not know how to operate a tele-radio.[96]

When the Japanese arrived at Buka, they reconnoitred the island, took soundings of Queen Carola Harbour and placed buoys. They also interviewed the locals, including Percy Good. The Japanese placed Good on parole and he quite rightly did not report the arrival of the Japanese vessels. F.P. Archer on Yame Island had, however, sighted the Japanese, and he sent a note by local runner to W.J. Read at Aravia on northern Bougainville.[97] Read promptly informed Port Moresby and Townsville, and from there it was passed to the Australian government, then the ABC and its avid listeners, the Japanese.[98]

Armed with the ABC's information, the Japanese immediately returned to Queen Carol Harbour and brutally killed Percy Good.[99] They also arrested Father James Hennessy, who survived to die aboard the *Montevideo Maru*.[100] By June 1942, the ABC had contributed to the capture and eventual death in custody of three coastwatchers and one Catholic priest, as well as the torture and execution of Percy Good.[101]

Percy Good's death finally brought the status of the civilian coastwatchers into 'sharp focus' in Melbourne.[102] It was used by Feldt to force the ACNB to remove the petty bureaucratic blocks to the appointment of civilian coastwatchers to military ranks in the RANVR.[103] Eric Feldt played hard when he signalled:

As Good Was Coastwatcher Performing His Duty What Is Position Of Mrs Good And Others Regarding Pension Rights. Is Any Progress Being Made To Appoint Read Mason And Page To Naval Forces Or Are They Expected To Give Their Lives As Good Has Done Without Recompense Or Protection.[104]

By 2 May 1942, Read was appointed a Lieutenant, Page and Mitchell Sub-Lieutenants, and Mason a Petty Officer in the RANVR.[105] All of the other civilian coastwatchers were given similar appointments.[106]

At this time Eric Feldt was controlling Lieutenant J.H. Mackie's unit, his detachment of four soldiers at Kieta, Assistant District Officer W.J. (Jack) Read, Department of Agriculture field officer Eric Guthrie, and government field officer and medical assistant Frank Green at Aravia. He was also controlling A. Drummond Thompson and another four soldiers at Numa Numa, Sergeant Yauwika and Corporal Sali of the local police at Kieta, and now Paul Edward Mason at Inus on Bougainville Island.[107]

The Japanese were now becoming more aggressive and more accurate, which suggests they were employing HFDF to geolocate the position of coastwatcher tele-radios. On 30 March 1942, Feldt signalled all coastwatchers warning them to prepare for more Japanese activity.[108] A decision was made to withdraw the remaining civilians, leaving Read at Aravia, Mason at a point on a ridge above Kieta and the four soldiers, Wigley, Otton, Ross and Swanson, in the town of Kieta.[109] Lieutenant Mackie and his remaining men were to conduct patrols across the island, collecting information.

On Bougainville, coastwatch operations benefited from the fact the Japanese largely ignored the island and the population remained largely neutral if restless. This restlessness showed itself at Kieta, where, with the departure of the Europeans, the local population rioted and looted until order was restored by Brother Henry, a New Zealand missionary, and Dr Kröning, a planter who had previously been the senior German official at Kieta.[110] It also should be said that many locals were scared by Percy Good's execution.[111] Any residual doubts the locals had about the Japanese were soon removed when they cut the throat of the Chief of Lemankoa at Kieta in front of a crowd because he had refused to come down to receive his Japanese armband. Every local now knew the new 'big men' were very dangerous.[112]

Whole villages now disappeared into the jungle on the approach of Japanese parties, and opportunists, including many of the local police, flocked to serve the new big men. At Kieta, the Japanese enjoyed considerable support from the locals and were even able to form a gang called the 'Black Dogs'. Experienced coastwatchers like P.E. Mason really feared the Black Dogs because, as he told Lieutenant Commander Mackenzie: 'I have a poor opinion of the Nips but a great respect for a local pack when quarry is on the run and there is women and loot and blood in the air.'[113]

The local population formed the gravest threat to the safety of the coastwatchers because they had the bushcraft to track them. Only other locals could avoid detection by their countrymen.

The early experience on Bougainville demonstrated the two cardinal requirements for successful coastwatcher activity. First, a supportive or at least neutral local population willing to provide manpower, local knowledge and early warning of an enemy approach; and secondly, and almost as importantly, a quiescent enemy. In the early part of the campaign on Bougainville these conditions allowed Read, Mason, Mackie and the others in the coastwatching organisation to maintain themselves for eighteen months after the arrival of the Japanese. As Japanese interest in Bougainville intensified, however, this would change.

On Tabar Island, Con Page, the first coastwatcher to report Japanese aircraft flying towards Rabaul, stayed at his post. His continued activity drew the attention of the Japanese, who began aggressively searching for him. Despite the danger, and despite numerous instructions from Feldt in Townsville to stop sending messages, Page continued.[114] The circumstances under which Page was operating were difficult. In March, atmospheric conditions made communicating with him almost impossible. He was lucky that his signal bounced into Rockhampton and was picked up there. This signal reported that Page was having trouble with a German and that he was thinking of 'packing up and heading for the nearest port'.[115] Page left it too late and was captured on 16 June 1942.

The Japanese troops who had hunted Page had apparently been reinforced by professionals, probably Kempeitai or Tokkeitai (IJN secret police). Evidence of this is shown by the way they conscripted locals to lead their patrols, and their use of tracker dogs on the island. On 13 June, remarkably and foolhardily, Page had signalled Feldt about the chase and that the

Japanese were re-embarking onto a ship. Feldt requested the RAAF to attack this vessel.[116] At the same time, Feldt was organising for a US submarine to pick up Page on the night of 17–18 June, which was the earliest this could be done. It was too late for Page.

On the day Page was captured Feldt was informed that Commander Task Force (COMTASKFOR) could not supply the submarine and so he organised an RAAF Catalina to attempt a dusk pick-up. On 17 June, FERDINAND, the covername now being used by Feldt's coastwatchers,[117] listed Con Page as a casualty. He had not been heard on air since 13 June.[118] Around this time, Con Page and John Talmage, who had been captured on Tatau Island, were taken to Nago Island off Kavieng and beheaded.[119]

New Ireland was another place where coastwatchers paid a heavy price. At Namatanai, the coastwatchers were the assistant district officers Alan (Bill) Kyle and Gregory Benham. They had stayed on to oversee the administration of the district, and to secure the safety and loyalty of the local population. With the capture of Rabaul, both men decided to withdraw down the eastern coast of New Ireland, picking up European stragglers for evacuation to Port Moresby. By early February, they made Metlik. There, Kyle signalled Townsville and Port Moresby that he had a boat and ten evacuees and needed further instructions as to what he should do. Port Moresby ordered Kyle to remain on New Ireland without talking to Feldt in Townsville.

In his later book, Eric Feldt thought this decision was wrong, and he believed that Kyle only obeyed because he thought the order had come from Feldt himself. Kyle and Benham remained on New Ireland and withdrew into the high country leaving Rayman, their assistant, to take the evacuees to Tulagi for evacuation. The issue for Kyle's party was that there were still a large number of refugees on the island, and the local inhabitants put them in touch with Kyle. Within a short period, the party had picked up ten new military refugees escaping from Rabaul. They did not have the food or other supplies for these numbers, and so Kyle signalled for a supply drop, a new receiver and other equipment. On 28 May, Kyle sent another signal requesting urgent assistance.

Six weeks later, Kyle's party was at Muliama, where it had joined up with district officer Major J.H. McDonald's party of civilians from Kavieng. They reported that they had retrieved some dropped supplies, but the Japanese were now driving them hard using the services of locals. Feldt ordered Kyle and his party to withdraw into the mountains, carrying as much as possible, and to avoid all contact with anyone, including escaping Australian soldiers.[120] The problem for the coastwatchers was that their rescue role was overwhelming their intelligence role, and Kyle's party was a good example. They had already got one group off to Tulagi for evacuation, and now they had accumulated 21 refugees, all of whom were later successfully evacuated.

This activity, while humane, was not intelligence collection, and that was the core responsibility of the coastwatchers. Once free of their refugees, Kyle and Benham returned to their intelligence-collection role and prepared posts from which they could obtain intelligence in the lead-up to what would become the Battle of the Coral Sea. Their reports added to the intelligence picture that enabled Admiral Chester Nimitz's task force to engage and drive off the IJN attack force heading for Port Moresby in the Battle of the Coral Sea.

Their activity did not escape detection. The IJN was well aware that these parties were supplying Allied commands with substantial intelligence ranging from weather reports to sightings of IJN ships, aircraft and ground forces. There can be little doubt that the IJN was also using SIGINT and DF against these parties, and that the low-grade cipher, PLAYFAIR, was compromised. There is also no doubt that either Kempeitai or Tokkeitai personnel were involved, as by 28 May 1942 Kyle's party was being aggressively chased by Japanese patrols using local police personnel as trackers. These moved quickly down to Matakan and Matankuk, and down both coasts to encircle Kyle and Benham's party, whose difficulties were multiplied by the growing neutrality of the now terrified locals, caught between the coastwatchers and the increasingly brutal Japanese. Kyle and Benham had little choice but to radio for extraction. There was no way they could survive without assistance from the locals and they could not avoid their own police trackers now working for the Japanese.[121] Feldt organised a submarine to pick up the two men on 30 May but this was unsuccessful.

A further attempt was then arranged using a local planter, now Pilot Officer Cecil Mason, RAAF, who was to land from a US submarine, *S-38*, to help extract Kyle, Benham and their party. Mason went ashore at Cape Sena near Muliama on New Ireland on 19 July, and made contact with three locals. While he waited for them to get the village bossman, Mason noted that some of the locals were wearing Rising Sun armbands, and when the bossman arrived, he was not friendly. This unsettled Mason and he returned to the *S-38* on 20 July.

On 21 July, Mason went ashore on the west coast of Large Feni Island (Ambitle) and re-embarked on 22 July. While ashore, Mason had made contact with a local boy who reported no Japanese were on the island but the coastwatcher Petty Officer Woodroffe was. Mason had given the boy a note for Woodroffe, asking him to light a signal fire at a point a little south of where Mason had originally landed.[122] The signal fire was subsequently sighted and the commanding officer of *S-38* suggested Mason go and get Woodroffe. Three landings and no sleep for 36 hours had, however, exhausted Mason and he decided to go ashore the following night, 23 July, at 1930 hrs.

While they waited for Mason's return, the *S-38* crew observed an IJN patrol boat making 10 knots on a south-easterly course to the general area where Mason had been landed, and this craft lingered in the area for four days before departing.[123] There could be no doubt they had been compromised and Mason lured ashore, most likely by the Kempeitai. Cecil Mason was never seen again.

The casualties did not stop there. After sending a signal on 30 May, Kyle and Benham went silent.[124] Feldt had now lost four more coastwatchers—Bill Kyle, Gregory Benham, Roy Woodroffe and Cecil Mason—the last trying to rescue the first three. The fate of Kyle and Benham now fitted the more brutal pattern of Japanese behaviour. They were interrogated, most likely by the Kempeitai, and then beheaded at Nago Island on 1 September 1942.[125] The price paid by the local population was even higher, and many lost their lives or were raped, brutalised and robbed by the Japanese and their collaborators. It would get worse.

CHAPTER 14

The Lions in the Den: Japanese Counterintelligence

As the Japanese moved southward capturing more and more territory, no one was more surprised at the speed and extent of Japanese success than the Japanese themselves. The rapid military triumphs were both welcome and problematic. Now the Japanese were suddenly faced with the need to occupy and control much larger areas of South-East Asia than they had planned for. This entailed taking control on the ground and then establishing defensive systems to hold the newly captured territories and defend them from Allied counterattacks. Implicit in this was the need to establish effective internal security to meet the threats posed by civil unrest, insurgency and, importantly for our story, espionage by Allied intelligence organisations.

As Japan prepared itself for war with the West in the late 1930s, its intelligence system was little changed from the reforms introduced in 1907 following the end of the Russo-Japanese War. This war had shown Japanese commanders and government officials that the flow of intelligence had relied on opportunity and had been far too ad hoc to provide much benefit. The IJA therefore restructured its staff operations, combining responsibility for all foreign intelligence collection and assessment within the Second Department of the General Staff.[1]

As Figure 14.1 shows, the Second Department of the General Staff was now organised into four sections, 5th covering the USSR, 6th Europe and the USA, 7th China and 8th being responsible for the conduct of conspiracy and propaganda operations. IJA SIGINT operations remained outside of Second Department as a stand-alone entity reporting directly to the General Staff. The outcome of this was that intelligence remained a tactical activity with little relevance for strategic planning or thinking. This was in line with the philosophy that the IJA had inherited, along with its staff system, from the Prussian model they had selected for the structure of their army.[2]

The biggest problem the modern historian has in identifying the effectiveness of the Japanese intelligence effort is that very little of the documentary evidence exists, as the Japanese burned all of their intelligence records before the occupation and, understandably, few ex-Japanese intelligence officers have spoken or written about their service between 1941 and 1945.[3] This leaves the field empty, with the exceptions of Ken Kotani's book *Japanese Intelligence in World War II*, and snippets of information in intelligence debriefings of IJA and IJN personnel conducted by war crimes investigators and intelligence agencies, particularly the US Strategic Services Unit, after 1945.

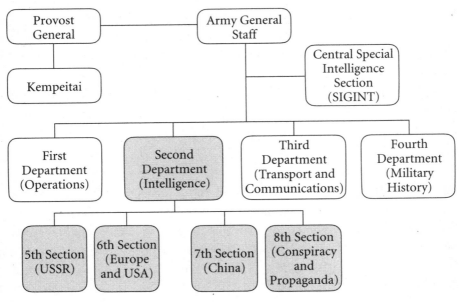

Figure 14.1: The IJA intelligence organisation

Like the IJA, the IJN had identified the same issues with its intelligence, and it too moved to centralise intelligence in the Third Department of the Naval Staff.[4]

The greater problem that was created by this approach was that intelligence remained strictly within its service silo and, even worse, within the silos that would be created within each service. Effectively, the IJN only conducted intelligence activity of importance to the IJN while the IJA did the same for itself, while individual generals only conducted intelligence of relevance to their own command. It would even transpire that individual commanders would withhold and use intelligence as a card during the interminable debates that led to decisions.

Alongside the reorganisation of the armed services' intelligence collection and assessment systems, the Japanese also reorganised its HUMINT and SIGINT organisations: the Toku-Jo-Han (Special Intelligence Section), which was responsible for conducting SIGINT; and the Special Duty Agencies (SDA), charged with conducting overseas espionage. Those parts of the Japanese intelligence system that most concern our story—the internal security organisations, the IJA's secret military police the Kempeitai, and the IJN's equivalent Tokubetsu Keisatsutai (Tokkeitai)—remained unchanged.[5]

The Kempeitai was not strictly part of the IJA, as it was directly controlled by the War Department in Tokyo, just as the Tokkeitai was controlled by the Navy Department.[6] The real difference between the Kempeitai and Tokkeitai was that the latter restricted itself to IJN bases, ships and areas under its direct control. The Kempeitai was left responsible for conducting counterespionage and internal security operations everywhere else.

In this role, the Kempeitai had the authority to conduct any investigations, apprehensions and examinations they deemed necessary. They were even able to extend their control over Japanese civilians, nominally the concern of the Japanese Consular Police, as this organisation was effectively subordinated to the local Kempeitai HQ.[7] In China, away from the front line and areas where IJA formations were based, the Kempeitai was responsible for all counter-espionage work, particularly in the major cities.[8]

The specific tasks of the Kempeitai were clearly laid out and were, in order of importance: first, the collection of information on the local community and for preserving peace and order; secondly, the investigation of foreign intelligence agents and the identification of their activities; and thirdly, the collection of other intelligence as directed.[9]

The Kempeitai was different from the IJA's intelligence department because it was not subordinate to the IJA or even Imperial HQ, but to the War Ministry and the Provost Marshal General of the IJA.[10] This gave the Kempeitai its secret police character and made it a fearsome organisation, even for members of the IJA.[11] That said, the control of the Kempeitai was delegated to the commanding general for a theatre, and Tokyo did not issue instructions directly to Kempeitai units within that theatre.[12] This was left to the commanding general.

The structure of the Kempeitai was highly flexible, and was changed within various theatres and commands to suit the needs of that command at the time. Its basic organisation is, however, set out in Figure 14.2.

The Kempeitai was not easy to join. Potential recruits had to be proven soldiers who had demonstrated consistent loyalty and dedication to the ideas of Bushido (the samurai code) and the superiority of the Japanese race. Oddly, there was a long waiting list of volunteers from other branches of the IJA wanting to transfer across. This suggests that service in the Kempeitai held significant attractions, because the training was even more brutal than that ordinary soldiers had to go through.

The training given to Kempeitai soldiers included judo, mob control, Shinto mental conditioning, indoctrination in the superiority of the Japanese race, clandestine tradecraft, espionage, running of agent networks and interrogation techniques. All of this was done within a very brutal, rough and tumble regime that tested the potential Kempeitai soldier to the maximum.[13] The various schools—approximately four may have existed—produced around 300 graduates each per year, providing 1200 new soldiers annually.[14]

The Kempeitai—and on New Ireland and Bougainville, the Tokkeitai— were thus the main opponents the operatives of the Services Reconnaissance Department (SRD) and the coastwatch organisation faced when they operated behind Japanese lines. These elite counterespionage troops would demonstrate determination and aggression in hunting the Allied operatives on the ground, and their ferocious brutality severely limited the willingness of local populations to protect or support Allied operatives.

The effectiveness of these organisations can be gauged from the way the Japanese response to the activities of SRD and coastwatch parties changed

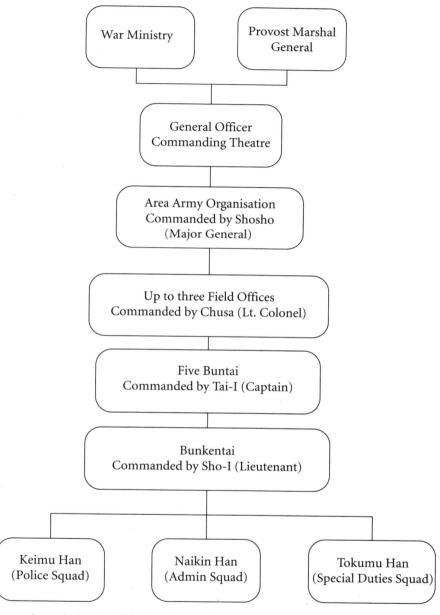

Source: Strategic Services Unit, *Japanese Intelligence Service*, Section II, Japanese Military Intelligence in China, Section 6.a., CIA, www.cia.gov/library/readingroom/docs/JAPANESE%20INTELLIGENCE%20ORGANIZATIONS%20IN%20CHINA%20%20%20(WWII)_0001.pdf

Figure 14.2: Organisation of the Kempeitai (Japanese military police)

from a more live-and-let-live approach, with Japanese patrols lacking aggression and determination, to the patrols chasing Allied operatives for long periods and using locals in tracking and attacking coastwatchers and SRD personnel.

The enlistment of locals as guides and trackers was probably the single most effective strategy in making occupied areas unsustainable for Allied personnel.[15] More than once, Eric Feldt, in his book *The Coastwatchers*, relates the concerns of experienced coastwatchers about the increasing use of locals to track them. These worries can also be found in the official record.[16] As we will see below, once the Japanese were using local guides and carriers, whole areas became too dangerous for any Allied operatives to enter.

One of the other changes in the way the IJA operated was that they reined in the use of terror, which was proving counterproductive. Killing locals and stealing their food and animals, as well as raping and kidnapping their women, led to significant hostility among locals and a marked unwillingness to work for the Japanese. The fact that whole villages could simply lift up everything they owned and walk off into the jungle made this a significant problem in New Guinea, New Ireland and the Solomons, where the jungle afforded real protection to the locals. On Timor and the western end of the archipelago this was not the case.

In New Guinea, the way the Japanese operated made a marked impact on the Allied Intelligence Bureau (AIB), and particularly on SRD and ANGAU parties. At one time, in the Buna area, the Orokaiva tribe was being described in AIB intelligence reports as 'extremely treacherous' and having provided the Japanese with large parties of warriors.[17] These warriors had attacked neutral villages that had refused to assist either the Australians or the Japanese in the Adjora, Serapi and Bofu areas. The reward must have been rapine, money and goods. At the same time, the Japanese were still executing anyone who offered resistance, beheading a villager from Lokanu, Kavieng, at Salamaua.[18]

The AIB was advised by the Far Eastern Liaison Office (FELO) that the local inhabitants would support whoever treated them better, but it was not that simple. The Japanese mixed bribery with harsh treatment of any dissent or failure to collaborate. One example of this is the bayonetting to death of eleven Biagi tribesmen at Deniki in September and the raping of women at Kokoda, Wairope and Buna, acts that alienated many locals in that area.[19] The kidnapping of women to serve as comfort women in Japanese brothels further alienated local villagers.[20] This was made worse by the wanton destruction of villagers' gardens and the ill treatment of any locals conscripted by the Japanese for work. Unsupervised indigenous police working for the Japanese also indulged in rape, theft and mistreatment of locals. By 11 May 1943, however, the Japanese were trying to retrieve the situation by ordering that chiefs be treated with respect.[21]

The brutality of the Japanese meant that a local headman had little choice. If he did not supply manpower and material as demanded, he faced execution or other punishments for himself, his family and his village. It was therefore much safer to provide the support demanded by the Japanese.

On the other hand, the provision of support to transient AIB operatives presented the entire village with the certainty of severe punishment once the Japanese found out—and they would find out because, while their handling of intelligence processing and assessment was extremely poor at the higher level, their handling of tactical intelligence and, particularly their handling of security intelligence, was, as a result of a long history of surveillance operations in Japan, Korea and China, extremely good.

The system used by the Japanese was described in July 1945 by Corporal Koram bin Anduat of the British North Borneo Police. Corporal bin Anduat described how the Kempeitai operated in Borneo, and his testimony provides a rare insight into their counterintelligence efforts against Australian and Allied intelligence operations in occupied areas.

Anduat described how in Borneo the Japanese took over and completely disarmed the civil police, even taking their knives off them, and set them to work digging trenches, guarding facilities and even fishing.[22] In time, some of the police were integrated into the Kempeitai's network and carried out counterespionage duties and other support functions. At Lahad Datu, the head of the Kempeitai was an officer named Djumi, and, from Anduat's description, this man was most likely a warrant officer.

Very quickly after their arrival, the Kempeitai established an extensive network of clandestine agents throughout the area, consisting of men, women and children, the latter both boys and girls aged between twelve and fifteen.[23] The clandestine male agents were distributed one to each village, regardless of whatever other agents were already in place. The Japanese would call a meeting of all the village headmen in an area and force them to provide lists of their male villagers. The list was then supplied by the Japanese military authorities to the Kempeitai, who would select a name and offer the individual paid work of an unspecified nature. If the selected villager agreed, then they became the secret Kempeitai agent in the village. If not, then another name was selected.[24]

Each clandestine agent was then tasked by his handler and told that under no circumstances were they to divulge to anyone the work they were to do, under threat of death or other punishment. A second clandestine network operated by a Japanese company, which, in the case described, was the Usira Company, provided the Kempeitai with a check on these agents and on how well they were protecting their status.[25]

The description provided by Corporal bin Anduat shows that in the Lahad Datu area of Borneo, the Japanese were sticking to the systems and organisations they used in China and other places. In these areas, Japanese companies provided logistical and intelligence support to the IJA. The company had two roles: to obtain resources, including food and other supplies, and local labour for the IJA; and to maintain an extensive internal espionage organisation throughout the area. This espionage system was completely independent of the Kempeitai's agent networks, although the company worked extremely closely with the Kempeitai.[26] If the company agents became aware of the identity of the Kempeitai's agent in a village, that agent was brought in to Kempeitai HQ and imprisoned or executed.

At Lahad Datu, a Kempeitai warrant officer acted as the liaison officer between Kempeitai HQ and the village agents. Like most Kempeitai, he only wore his uniform in his office, going about the area he worked dressed in local clothing. This did not fool anyone, according to Anduat, as everyone in the entire district knew at one look that he was a Japanese dressed in Malay clothing. The poorly disguised warrant officer nevertheless conducted his rounds of the villages twice a week to collect intelligence from his agents. He hid the identity of the agents by visiting a number of houses, including the agents'. It was during these rounds that agents were paid, but on a results basis. If they had nothing, they got nothing. The pressure was therefore always on the agent to find something to report.

The unfortunate women recruited as agents were taken from their villages to work as comfort women in brothels, exclusively for the use of Japanese Kempeitai personnel. After a period serving as comfort women, some were selected and trained as clandestine agents. These women were used on surveillance operations and as field agents in their own right, with the job of recruiting networks of other women in an extended spying system reaching into all areas of village life.[27]

The Kempeitai also worked closely with the Kenchiji, the local Japanese district administrator, as well as the local Japanese companies. The result was a duplicated and overlapping surveillance and intelligence system that not only reported extensively on everything happening, but also double-checked itself. This system was highly effective in heavily populated areas, such as Timor and Java. It was particularly effective in Java because the Javanese had no love for their Dutch overlords and did not intend to support their return by assisting any white agents. The effectiveness of the Kempeitai's system and the hostility of the Javanese and other populations towards the Dutch help explain the failure of the AIB's operations in those areas.

In the east of the archipelago, the Kempeitai enjoyed similar success around the populated centres such as Lae and Rabaul, but not so much within the jungle-covered and sparsely populated hinterland. They did, however, make the local populations wary, and they did win converts who made it difficult for AIB and coastwatchers personnel to conduct operations.

The threat to AIB and coastwatcher operations did not just come from the Kempeitai and their local assistants, but also from the SIGINT operations conducted by the IJN and IJA right across the Pacific, and from the SIGINT listening posts established by the Kempeitai across the islands, including on Tabar, Lihir, Tanga and Feni islands.[28] In addition to these listening posts, each military post and larger IJN vessel had the capability to intercept and conduct DF on radio transmissions. The increased risk of compromise from SIGINT was well recognised within the coastwatch organisation as early as 1943.[29]

The IJN's Toku-Jo-Han had initiated its SIGINT operations as soon as it was formed, and it is claimed that by the 1920s they had broken the diplomatic codes of the United States, the United Kingdom and China. Given the access that the Toku-Jo-Han had to the telegraphic traffic carried on the mainline cables traversing China, it is completely unsurprising that they broke these systems.[30] Despite these successes, Toku-Jo-Han faced considerable problems in dealing with Allied communications and codes during the war. This does not mean they were not dangerous.

The organisation of Japanese intelligence within a given area of operations varied according to the perceived needs of the commanders responsible for it. SIGINT was an integral part of its activities.[31] Indeed, we know from the Strategic Services Unit report that the Kempeitai in China had an integral SIGINT capability within its organisations and that this conducted detection activity similar to that of the Radio Security Service (RSS) operating in Britain, India and, later on, Australia.

Before the end of the war, the information the Allies had on Japanese SIGINT capability was limited, and they found it difficult to tell how useful SIGINT was to the Japanese conduct of the war. Postwar investigations and analysis clearly showed that while the Japanese intelligence effort completely failed to influence the strategic direction of the war, it did contribute significantly to Japan's conduct of tactical operations. In SIGINT, this was as true as it was for HUMINT.

The reality was that both the IJA and IJN had significant successes in intercepting, if not breaking, Allied communications. In a postwar report by the Strategic Services Unit, it was found that the IJN had been intercepting US naval communications from call sign VHM located at Darwin. The traffic from this intercept was passed to Tokyo, and one source indicated that it was only in Tokyo that it could be broken.[32]

Despite the dismissive tone of the source, the fact is that the IJN could have conducted traffic analysis and DF on the intercepted signals—and obviously did so, as the source knew the call sign of the station and its location of Darwin.[33] Later in his debriefing, this source disclosed that he and his Filipino colleagues believed they had identified the arrival of General MacArthur at Leyte when, on 18 October 1944, a station called 'Tacloban Field' requested a jeep be provided at the jetty for HALIFAX HIMSELF. They had already associated the codeword HALIFAX with MacArthur or his HQ and postulated that HALIFAX HIMSELF was MacArthur. The source then went on to describe in considerable detail the Leyte Gulf landings, including orders from HALIFAX for stricter radio discipline.

The source of this information appears to have been an English-speaking Filipino, either recruited or conscripted as one of a number of Filipino intercept operators working for the Japanese.[34] What is interesting about him is that he admits to the US interrogators that he was 'greatly intrigued by the possibilities of long-skip VHF signals' and he wanted 'to know just how the sporadic E-Layer behaved in tropical regions'. This clearly indicates that he was much more than just a basic-level intercept operator, and that he was very conversant with the propagation of radio signals and the equipment he was using—a simple super-regenerative VHF receiver he had built and a Packard Bell disc recorder.[35]

The evidence provided to the Strategic Services Unit by this source indicates that he worked for the Japanese in both Manila and, after being evacuated on 29 December 1944, Shanghai.[36] This suggests that with the fall of Singapore and the occupation of the Philippines, the IJN and the IJA were able to access a very large and competent pool of English-speaking personnel. There can be little doubt that the individuals recruited functioned as intercept operators, traffic analysts and interpreters, thus providing the Japanese with a considerable boost in their effectiveness against Allied communications.

The importance of this lies in the fact that as Allied units and personnel were overrun, their communications became highly vulnerable to the Japanese SIGINT effort. It also brings into question the effectiveness of the very low-level codes and ciphers used by the SRD and coastwatch organisations, and it helps explain the ease with which Japanese forces were able to interdict SRD and coastwatch parties later in the war. The Japanese were competent in identifying radio traffic from such parties and were quite capable of identifying the radio reporting coming from islands far away from their immediate operating areas. Using a radio to communicate from Japanese-occupied areas was a dangerous undertaking, and the only advantage was that the terrain made it difficult for the Japanese to get to locations quickly, so coastwatchers and other AIB operators could get clear before they arrived.

Of course, this advantage could be countered, and it was. The answer was in fact simple. The IJA quickly realised that sending a single patrol, or even two, on a direct trek towards the area from which a signal came allowed sufficient time for the Allied party to make good its escape. The change in tactics was to insert a large number of smaller patrols, led by local guides, along the coastline of the island from which a signal was detected. These patrols would then sweep inland, cutting off the retreating Allied party or forcing it deeper into the jungles and mountains to make good an escape. The issue now facing the party was that the long line of sweeping Japanese patrols meant it had to cover long distances very quickly and this led to it spending most of its time on the run. The outcome of this was that even if they weren't caught, they were prevented from observing activity along the coast and, even if they did observe activity, they could not afford to stop or set up the radio to send the intelligence.

The Japanese had yet another extremely important source of intelligence they could exploit in their battle against the AIB and its parties in Japanese-controlled territory. This source was the captured AIB operatives, whose rudimentary training did not prepare them to resist the sophisticated interrogation techniques of experienced Kempeitai officers. Interrogation would prove to be the most bountiful source of detailed intelligence the Japanese developed on the AIB, its various organisations, and their functions, personalities and resources. In fact, by 1945, the Kempeitai had completely mapped the entire AIB organisation, its operations, plans, personalities and techniques.[37]

All of the intelligence obtained on Allied espionage operations in the Southern Army area was passed back to its HQ at Saigon, where a dedicated section collated and studied it to build the picture of Allied intelligence in South-East Asia. The intelligence derived also appears to have been communicated to Imperial HQ in Tokyo.[38]

All this meant that by the end of 1942, following the capture of the LIZARD II party, it is likely that the Kempeitai on Timor began putting together a very good picture of the way AIB parties operated. They would also have obtained good information on how the AIB parties were being prepared and despatched. All of this intelligence would have been collated and analysed in Singapore and Saigon, and appropriate countermeasures put in place. The history of the AIB's operations in Timor and Java clearly shows, as we will see later, that the AIB operatives being inserted into these areas were doomed from the very beginning. The AIB failed to develop a proper appreciation of the enemy they faced. Had it done so, it might have realised the impossibility of its ambitions for setting South-East Asia ablaze and it would have saved the lives of many good men and countless locals. That, however, is a later part of this story. Now we need to look at the AIB, its founding, and its hopes and ambitions.

CHAPTER 15

Herding Cats: The Allied Intelligence Bureau

As Australia's SIGINT effort was forming and receiving reinforcements from the US Navy's CAST cryptanalytical unit in the Philippines, and British and Dutch SIGINT refugees, another intelligence initiative was being finalised in the creation of what was expected to be Australia's first HUMINT organisation. As we have just seen, Australian efforts in HUMINT had met both abject failure and, although it was as yet unclear, resounding success. The Harry Freame operation had clearly demonstrated to anyone involved that HUMINT operations conducted within a foreign nation, particularly one as hostile as Japan was at the time, demanded great sophistication and subtlety, and highly professional tradecraft. Even Britain's SIS, perhaps one of the oldest and most professional intelligence organisations of the time, suffered losses at the hands of the Kempeitai, which demonstrated its ruthlessness by murdering the SIS officer James Cox. The likelihood of Australia being able to create an effective HUMINT system as Japanese forces swept ever further southward was unlikely, and to make things worse, the arriving Americans were equally lacking in real experience of such operations.

In early 1942, as the war situation appeared to become more and more critical, Australia's government agreed to the establishment of an organisation, the Inter-Allied Services Department (ISD) which later became

Special Operations Australia (SOA) and, in 1943, was yet again retitled as the Services Reconnaisance Department (SRD) of the Allied Intelligence Bureau (AIB), the latter formed by MacArthur's General Headquarters, South West Pacific Area (GHQ, SWPA). Given the multiple titles given to the organisation between 1941 and 1944 we will use the title SRD throughout to reduce confusion.

SRD's brief was to conduct HUMINT operations behind enemy lines as well as sabotage and other direct action.[1] This decision mixed two types of activity that do not mix. The first was the collection of intelligence, an undertaking that requires a quiescent target and sits uneasily with the second, the conduct of sabotage, disruption and propaganda operations to harass and annoy the very same target. These two activities cannot be run at the same time, as the experience of the SRD amply demonstrates.

A significant difficulty facing the Australian government and its military advisors in early 1942 was that they had no experience of foreign intelligence operations and thus had to rely on the experience and advice of the security intelligence organisations and officials that dominated Australia's military intelligence system. The problem was that these officials and organisations were mostly inept. As the Harry Freame operation clearly demonstrated, there is a significant difference between conducting a security intelligence operation at home and doing so in a foreign country. The foreign intelligence operative is at risk every minute of every day, and a small error, such as sending a letter from a favourite hotel, can result in death.

The other issue Australia faced in creating its HUMINT capability was that far too many people wanted to be involved. The idea of spying attracts people in search of escape and adventure, and it beguiles others with its appeal of making them initiates of the most profound of secrets. The hard truth is that good intelligence, be it SIGINT or HUMINT, is about the everyday, the mundane, and the conscientiously careful recording and consideration of the information gleaned by one's activities. This is not what people looking to blow things up are going to tolerate.

On top of all this, the Australian government and its military advisors now had to contend with the arrival on 17 March 1942 of US General Douglas MacArthur, fresh from the Philippines and now looking to take command of US forces in Australia and the SWPA. They were overjoyed at the arrival of someone promoted as a real American hero, and MacArthur was given a hero's welcome as he arrived at Spencer Street Railway Station in Melbourne on 21 March 1942.[2]

On 26 March, General MacArthur, accompanied by his Chief of Staff, Major General Richard K. Sutherland and his Deputy Chief of Staff, Brigadier General Richard K. Marshall, attended a meeting of Australia's Advisory War Council, the all-party grouping that provided advice to the government on the conduct of the war. This was a unique honour, and MacArthur made the most of it by putting forward his view that the Western Allies should concentrate on beating Japan first.[3] It was what the council wanted to hear, but it would not garner meaningful support in Washington and none at all in London.

As MacArthur expounded his Pacific-first views and egged the Australian government on to put pressure on Washington, he was dealing with the reality that in mid-1942 he had to take up the defensive until his forces were strong enough to engage with the now entrenching Japanese. Part of this defensive strategy was the establishment of effective intelligence and irregular warfare units, and this merged well with developments in Australia.

The first worry for any intelligence organisation is money, and the SRD was no different. Australia had already established a secret fund on 21 February 1940 with £500 ($148,900 in 2017 prices).[4] By 16 January 1946, the cost of the AIB was £180,000, of which Australia contributed one-third, with the NEI and the United States paying a third each.[5]

The size and cost of the whole HUMINT, propaganda and sabotage organisation was well beyond anything Australia wanted to or could service. The final arrangement was finally formalised as a subordinate organisation of General MacArthur's GHQ, SWPA on 6 July 1942.[6] This was not a simple matter.

The reason for much of the complexity and confusion surrounding the HUMINT organisation in Australia during the war arose from the fact that Australia, Britain, the NEI and the United States were manipulating it in their own national interests. On top of this, military commanders like Blamey, MacArthur and, later, Lord Mountbatten were trying to gain greater control while, in the background, Britain's SIS and Special Operations Executive (SOE) were fighting one another for control of the organisation, and General Donovan's Office of Strategic Services (OSS) in Washington was trying to penetrate MacArthur's command against his express wishes.

As we have already noted, the SRD began life as the ISD before becoming SOA, an organisation intended to operate under General Thomas Blamey's direct control. On 6 July 1942, SOA became the SRD, part of the AIB under the command of General MacArthur's GHQ, SWPA. Section B, Secret Intelligence Australia (SIA), headed by Captain Roy Kendall, RNR, Britain's SIS station chief in Australia, was not really controlled by GHQ, SWPA nor by Australia and never would be. In fact, B Section was controlled and tasked by the head of Britain's SIS, Major General Stewart Menzies, and Australia, the United States and the NEI were paying for this.[7]

Section A, commanded by Lieutenant Colonel Grey Egerton Mott of the British SOE was not entirely under MacArthur's command or even control, as it worked for SOE in London and Land HQ (LHQ) in Australia. In fact, the whole AIB organisation was a bringing together of diverse organisations that saw themselves as distinctly different and as working for different masters. This situation would never be resolved.

All of these issues aside, General MacArthur's Chief of Staff, General Sutherland, specified the mission of the AIB as:

> To obtain and report information on the enemy in the South West Pacific Area, exclusive of the continent of Australia and Tasmania, and in addition, where practicable, to weaken the enemy by sabotage and destruction of morale and lend aid and assistance to local efforts to the same end in enemy occupied territories.[8]

AIB was to be organised with an HQ element commanded by Australia's DMI, Colonel C.G. Roberts, whose title was Controller, with Colonel Allison W. Ind, US Army, as his deputy.[9] While Mott was in charge of Section A, SRD, and Kendall of Section B, SIA, Section C was left empty at present, and an Australian, Commander J.C.R. Proud, RANVR, was placed in charge of Section D, Military Propaganda. Each commander of land, air and naval forces in SWPA, as well as Admiral F.W. Coster of the Netherlands, was required to appoint a liaison officer to serve on the coordinating staff that was to be established to serve and advise the controller AIB. The controller was to be responsible to GHQ, SWPA for the efficient functioning of AIB, and for the execution of all missions that GHQ, SWPA directed the AIB to undertake from time to time. The Deputy Controller, Colonel Ind, was to be the financial controller of the AIB and directly responsible to MacArthur, not GHQ, SWPA.[10] This little arrangement was in fact significant, as it effectively gave Ind direct access to MacArthur, something the Australian, Colonel Roberts, did not have.

A Section, SRD, or SOA, was charged with obtaining information on the enemy and with conducting sabotage operations against it. B Section, SIA, was charged with the collection of information on the enemy and its activities 'through certain special means and channels'. C Section was charged with obtaining all possible information on the enemy through agencies such as 'coast watchers, native agents and civilian operatives'.[11] D Section, which would later incorporate FELO, was charged with the preparation of propaganda materials useful to the other sections until GHQ expanded its activities. Colonel Roberts was ordered to avoid 'excessive staff and complex organisation' and to report to GHQ as required.

The directive was circulated by Major General Sutherland to Brigadier General C.A. Willoughby, MacArthur's G2 (Chief of Intelligence), the prime minister of Australia, John Curtin; and all of the various commanders and officers mentioned above.[12] It appears that the Australian prime minister did not rate any special consideration.

The arrangements agreed in July 1942 did not last very long, as the various sections of the AIB attempted to go their own way and some, particularly Captain Kendall's SIS operation, Section B, SIA, continued their own activities without any reference to General MacArthur, GHQ, SWPA or the Australian authorities. By 16 April 1943, a new memorandum was issued by Major General Sutherland outlining administrative adjustments to the AIB that were intended to simplify the organisation and ensure an economy of manpower, increased efficiency and better coordination.[13] Effectively, this was an attempt by MacArthur and his HQ to ensure control of those areas and activities of high interest to the United States—that is, to keep the British out of the Philippines and the wider Pacific theatre.

Just before these new arrangements were put together and promulgated, a small disturbance occurred within the closed shop of MacArthur's staff and close associates. One of these associates, an intimate of MacArthur's from the Philippines, was Gerald H. Wilkinson, a British businessman who had been the manager of the Theo H. Davies Company in Manila. Gerald Wilkinson was the SIS resident in the Philippines, and the conduit through which the British were passing intelligence on Japan to the United States.[14] It was through this activity, and his standing as a businessman, that Wilkinson became an associate of MacArthur, although it must be said that he was not a welcome one, as MacArthur's Senior Intelligence Officer, Brigadier Charles Willoughby was very hostile towards him.

By 1942, Wilkinson was a Lieutenant Colonel in the British Army and seems to have maintained his relationship with MacArthur after the two of them arrived in Australia by keeping MacArthur informed of what was going on within Australia's official and military. MacArthur appears to have been happy to maintain contact with Wilkinson, despite knowing that he was sending information to London via British communication links. By the end of 1942, however, Wilkinson was on the outer, MacArthur telling John Curtin that Wilkinson was not a member of his staff and that he did not even have any connection with GHQ.[15] By April 1943, despite the direct intervention of Churchill, Wilkinson was back in London having been informally declared persona non grata.[16] It is likely that MacArthur discovered there was some truth in Brigadier Willoughby's evaluation of Wilkinson as being a member of a 'net of potential spies' who are 'loyal to no one, but themselves and the Empire'.[17]

In fact, Gerald Wilkinson was a good member of SIS and was carrying out his instructions to spy on MacArthur. Wilkinson kept a diary of his exploits and detailed his work in reporting on MacArthur's presidential ambitions, which, given Franklin Roosevelt's fears, was pure gold to London in 1942. Indeed, Wilkinson described MacArthur as 'ruthless, vain, unscrupulous and self-conscious . . . but . . . a man of real calibre, with a vivid imagination, a capacity to learn rapidly from the past, a leader of men'.[18]

It appears that Lieutenant Colonel Gerald Wilkinson continued his career spying on the United States after being transferred to William Stephenson's British Security Co-ordination (BSC) organisation in New York. BSC was the entity registered by the US State Department to represent British interests and so it did, although the interests were those of SIS and SOE.

Wilkinson's brief was much wider than simply conducting liaison activities with the Americans. As William Stephenson explained, Wilkinson's work was 'somewhat outside the charter of British Security Coordination activities'.[19] Essentially, Wilkinson was focusing on collecting economic, commercial and political intelligence vital to Britain's long-term postwar interests, the true job of all national intelligence activity.

Given all of this, there can be little doubt that if Gerald Wilkinson was targeting General MacArthur and the United States in Asia, Roy Kendall and his team were likewise collecting intelligence on the US as well. The joke is that the US was paying one-third of the cost, as were Australia and the NEI.

The US was not blind to British machinations, and there is no doubt that many US officials, including military officers, saw Australia as part of British plotting. If we look at the reorganisation of AIB that was put in place in April 1943, we can get some idea of the reasons MacArthur and the US military moved to exclude Britain and Australia from involvement in the Philippines, which was now allocated to Colonel Ind as Chief of Philippine Section.[20]

Essentially, MacArthur had divided the SWPA up among the Allied nations, with Australia having control of the North East Area, comprising Papua, New Guinea, the Solomons and so on, via Eric Feldt's FERDINAND organisation of coastwatchers. The NEI was left to the Dutch, with Commander J.J. Quéré in charge of activity in Indonesia and the islands previously under Dutch control, while Borneo, Sarawak and Portuguese Timor were left to the AIB.[21]

Within this new arrangement, the AIB was still charged with passing all information it obtained to GHQ, SWPA and not to transmit such information to other entities unless authorised by GHQ, SWPA. This instruction had serious repercussions, and the Australian military authorities now mounted a campaign to have it rescinded on the quite legitimate grounds that it transgressed upon Australia's sovereign rights as a nation. The order to stop providing information to anyone outside SWPA without GHQ approval also caused serious ructions in London, as the British reacted to the possibility that the combined US and Australian Central Bureau (see Chapter 19) would be prevented from sharing its technical information and intelligence product with GC&CS and other British SIGINT agencies and units throughout the world. It was not, as we will see, a decision welcomed in Australia or Britain, and it was widely ignored by Central Bureau and Kendall's SIA organisation, both of which had a very close relationship.

SIA HQ was located in an old house, Craigroyston, on Bowen Terrace, in the Brisbane suburb of New Farm. It had a training facility and communications centre, commanded by Major Gustavus (George) Sears, including an antenna farm, at Newman House, Caboolture, just north of Brisbane. It was from Craigroyston that Kendall and the SIS controlled operations in South-East Asia, and kept an eye on the Americans and Australians.

The SIS organisation at Craigroyston included at least three people: Kendall as what would now be called the head of station, Third Officer Eve Walker, Women's Royal Naval Service (WRNS), as his deputy and Gustavus Sears as his communications specialist. Paymaster Lieutenant Commander Alan E.N. Merry may also have been part of Kendall's station, but then again, he may have been operating independently in the same way as Gerald Wilkinson.

The documentary evidence shows that Kendall was not just involved in HUMINT collection, but also in assisting Lieutenant Colonel Alastair Sandford and the Australian Army in keeping Central Bureau independent of GHQ, SWPA and free of total US control. Kendall was intimately involved in the decision-making process that led to the RSS being placed under Sandford's control and in assisting Group Captain F.W. Winterbotham in bringing MacArthur and his command under the control of the ULTRA security system (the codename for the intelligence product derived from high-level German cipher communications sent via ENIGMA). That is a story for later on.

At SIA, it is clear that the most important official after Kendall was Third Officer Eve Walker, WRNS. Third officer was a rank equivalent to sub-lieutenant in the navy or lieutenant in the army—a junior officer. Despite this, Eve Walker had a reputation within SIA for being the person who got things done. This included finding scarce stores, aircraft and even submarines for operations.[22] One Australian historian, Alan Powell, has said that Eve Walker 'clearly had an influential role at SIA HQ', and the evidence suggests he was not wrong.[23]

Eve Walker was a woman of background. Writing under the by-line, Eve Fayne, she had been a journalist on the *Daily Mail* when it was uncommon to find a woman in such a position. She had gained some notoriety as an advocate for women wearing trousers instead of skirts as a means of saving on cloth during the war.[24] Now she was a junior WRNS officer working for SIS in Brisbane.

A good example of Eve Walker's capabilities is that when an important Security Service (MI5) officer, Lieutenant Colonel E.A. (Tim) Airy, the Security Liaison Officer in Ceylon, visited the SIS station in Brisbane during Kendall's absence in 1944, it was Third Officer Walker who met with him and provided the briefings. Airy's visit was a serious venture, as the Security Service in London had failed in its previous efforts to get the Australian government to form an effective security organisation to protect British and

American secrets shared with Australia. The first attempt at this, Military Mission 104, led by an Australian, Lieutenant Colonel John Mawhood, had ended in disaster. Unfortunately, Mawhood had allowed himself to get caught up in the fight between Australia's General Staff and the Attorney-General's Department over who should control internal security intelligence operations. Mawhood had sided with Sir George Knowles, the Secretary of the Attorney-General's Department, and Knowles had lost the battle. Airy was now on a similar mission, but one that aimed at avoiding entanglements and gently guiding Australia towards creating a new and more effective security organisation.

As part of his tour of inspection, Airy had arranged to meet with Kendall, but Kendall was out of Australia when he arrived and the meeting was held with Eve Walker. The meeting between Walker and Airy was held clandestinely in Brisbane, and Airy reported to the Security Service that she had insisted that Airy be 'extremely careful' in meeting her.[25] The fact that the meeting was left to Eve Walker and not to Major Gustavus Sears[26] or another British officer, supports Alan Powell's contention that Eve Walker was more than the usual Third Officer, WRNS. Airy described Walker as 'slightly of the "cloak and dagger" type', intelligent and, he believed, responsible for all of the counterintelligence work in Australia that SIS had been reporting on.[27] Unfortunately for this story, the tenor and content of this reporting is not available, even if it still exists.

Further evidence of her significance is provided by the fact that she was stationed in New Guinea for three months at the end of 1945. She was the only WREN known to have served there. Later, after her visit to Australia with the BOAC delegation, Eve Walker shows up working as a journalist in Japan.[28]

The rationale for the clandestine meeting was that Walker and Kendall were 'very distrustful of the Australian Security Service, particularly its Deputy Director in Queensland, Lieutenant Colonel Wake'.[29] The relationship between the SIS station run by Kendall and the Australian Security Service was, according to Airy, non-existent. There was no cooperation of any kind, and Kendall's station treated the Australian Security Service almost as a hostile service.[30] From the documentary evidence, it appears that there was some justification to SIS's attitude, particularly in relation to Robert Wake.[31] Whatever the difficulties were with Wake, Airy also reported that the Australian Director-General of Security, Brigadier W. Simpson, did 'not understand what Captain Kendall does' and that Simpson was 'somewhat suspicious and jealous of him'.[32] Although there is no evidence for Simpson having ordered Wake to conduct collection operations against the SIS in Brisbane, given the history of Wake and Simpson, it is highly likely that such operations occurred.[33]

What we can surmise from the SIS operation in Brisbane is that it was a very important station for the SIS.[34] Among its duties was maintaining oversight of Central Bureau on behalf of the head of SIS, codenamed 'C', who was also director of GC&CS. It also enabled Kendall and SIS to ensure that when the RSS was established in Australia to monitor possible enemy transmissions and their own communications, it was placed under the control of Alastair Sandford at Central Bureau.[35] This decision kept Australia's Security Service away from any involvement in SIGINT while leaving the SIS with direct access to Australian RSS intercept and findings. It also ensured that the RSS in Australia reflected the arrangements in Britain, where the RSS had been removed from the Security Service and brought under GC&CS in May 1940.[36]

Kendall's operations were not all about Australia. The station in Brisbane also controlled the activities of SIA, which although part of the AIB, functioned as an independent organisation barely under the control of MacArthur's GHQ or any other entity other than Kendall and his team. One operation that does appear to have been run out of Brisbane by Kendall was the recruitment of Muslims from Asia as SIS agents. The way these agents were recruited was simple and the idea was probably formulated by the Rajah of Sarawak, Sir Charles Vyner de Windt Brooke. The operation required British authorities in Saudi Arabia to identify Asian pilgrims visiting Mecca, particularly itinerant mullahs, who had run out of money. The SIS then recruited some of these pilgrims as agents and brought them back to India or, if they were Indonesian, to Australia to train them, before inserting them back in their home locations armed with a low-power transceiver for contacting their controller, most often members of the M Special Unit.[37]

Despite the work Kendall's SIA was doing in support of MacArthur and the SWPA, there can be little doubt that SIA was not a fully functional part of MacArthur's command. It is a prime example of just how convoluted things can get in the world of intelligence.

If the situation with the SIA was unresolved, things were only slightly better in A Section, or SRD. The problem with SRD was that it did not see itself as an intelligence-collection organisation. It had been created in the image of the SOE, the sabotage and irregular warfare organisation established by Winston Churchill and placed under the Minister for Economic Warfare, Hugh Dalton, with instructions to set Europe ablaze. The people in SRD did not want to collect intelligence, they wanted to blow things up.

The SRD, led initially by Lieutenant Colonel Mott and later by Lieutenant Colonel Ambrose E.B. Trappes-Lomax, had established the infrastructure needed to train special forces soldiers and irregulars. Mott also oversaw the establishment of the essential communications network, with stations at Craigieburn, just north of Melbourne, Darwin and, shared with Kendall's SIA, Cairns. The issue for the military commanders was that Mott and SRD wanted to get on with the job of setting Asia ablaze, but the orders for such operations were not forthcoming from either the Australian commanders or MacArthur's GHQ. The result was that Mott began planning operations without reference to MacArthur or his staff and, as Alan Powell put it, 'the seeds of future problems remained', as MacArthur's GHQ and General Blamey now vied to control SRD while SRD saw itself as working for London.[38]

As for FELO, it appears no one cared. The staff consisted of Lieutenant Commander Proud as its Director, Major V.V.W. Purcell, formerly Director-General of Information and Publicity in Malaya, and three other ranks. FELO's office in Melbourne was in Proud's quarters.[39]

The last section, Section C, Combined Field Intelligence Service, which had been left without a director was essentially the coastwatch organisation established by the ACNB and now led by Eric Feldt. The ACNB was not keen on handing this organisation over, and Rupert Long and Eric Feldt were even less keen. In 1942 and early 1943, however, they had enough to think about just keeping their coastwatchers alive and out of enemy hands to become too involved in the inter-service fight to control air, ground and coastal observation organisations. This battle, led by Colonel Roberts at AIB, would eventually result in Feldt's organisation being absorbed into the AIB, but the ACNB and the RAN were quite successful in keeping their coastwatchers away from the sort of operations that SRD and other elements of AIB wanted to undertake. Eventually, as we will see below, the ACNB withdrew all of its personnel from the AIB after they were put at risk in New Guinea in ill-thought-out operations that resulted in unnecessary casualties.

With such a diverse set of organisations and personalities all under the same controlling organisation, it was soon obvious that there were major problems of command and control, and that none of these could be easily resolved. The GHQ, SWPA Administrative Directive of 6 July 1942 attempted to put the AIB back on track, at least as far as MacArthur's GHQ was concerned.[40] The real issue, keeping the British from interfering in the Philippines and other areas of American interest, had been settled with the division of the SWPA into regions in April 1943.[41] All that was left was tweaking of the administrative and support organisations.

The training organisation had now been moved north to Cairns, after it was realised that training personnel in the windy and mainly frigid environment of Wilsons Promontory did not adequately prepare them for operations in the tropical jungles of the islands to Australia's north. Each section was responsible for training its own personnel, and SIA and SOA could also, 'within reasonable limits', use the Cairns establishment for training. The establishment remained strictly under the control of AIB, however.[42]

Another organisation that stayed the same was the Lugger Maintenance Section in Darwin. This organisation maintained the small craft used by the various sections and got them ready for sea. It also acted as a staging point for parties deploying to enemy areas, and managed communications with the small craft while they were en route to their objectives and drop-off and pick-up points. Other than this, the Lugger Section did not play an active role in actual operations.

Despite all of this, and the hard work and dedicated efforts of the personnel within AIB, the outcomes were not what were expected. The first issue was that, with all operations in the Philippines now controlled by MacArthur, GHQ, SWPA had begun to lose interest in those areas not central to the recovery of the Philippines. On top of this, as we will see, SRD operations in Indonesia and Timor would be disasters. SIA, under the control of SIS, would continue whatever it was that SIS wanted done, and it is virtually impossible for anyone outside of SIS to know how successful it was. From a strictly Australian perspective, however, the activities of SIA would be of little value in the battle to remove the Japanese from the islands. Before we turn, though, to the HUMINT operations conducted by the SRD and the coastwatchers, we need to return to the story of SIGINT in the defence of Australia, and the role it played in the seven months of sea battles that decided the war in the Pacific.

CHAPTER 16

Australia's First National Signals Intelligence Effort

On 3 September 1939, Australia's armed forces were in no position to fight a modern war against an advanced enemy like Germany. The best they could do was support British forces in Europe, the Middle East and the Mediterranean. In Australia, the small cadre of professional sailors, soldiers and airmen struggled to put the war plans into operation and oversee the mobilisation of the volunteer forces that would serve overseas while bringing the conscripted militia onto a war footing, albeit one restricted to the home front. The administrative overhead associated with this was significant and demanding. To make matters worse, there was no central defence organisation, no supply system, no instructional schools beyond those used for training local militia, no command and control system that could take charge of both the field forces and the national defence, no communications system worth speaking of and no intelligence system, just small intelligence organisations within the forces.

As we have seen, Naval Intelligence Section was the most sophisticated of the service intelligence organisations but it lacked manpower everywhere, with the exception of its honorary coastwatcher and reporting officer systems. The army's Military Intelligence Branch had lost itself in internal security intelligence matters that it had neither the legal right nor aptitude to manage. Other than this, it was scrambling to fill the positions in the 2nd AIF and its wartime establishment at home. The RAAF intelligence capability was minute, inexperienced and much less developed than the intelligence entities of the other two services.

All this meant that the three service intelligence branches were disconnected from each other and served their respective services, not the broader strategic needs of the nation. There were no mechanisms for coordinating intelligence collection, analysis assessment or distribution at an inter-service level, let alone at a whole-of-government level. There was no vetting and, as we have seen, there was precious little security for HUMINT activity or any other secret activity of government in Australia. In fact, Australia's intelligence system was closer in character to that of Japan than to that of Britain.

SIGINT was different. First, Australia did not control 'Y' Procedure, as SIGINT was then called. 'Y' Procedure was controlled by the 'Y' Committee in London and by a number of specialist subcommittees. The foundation for the centralisation of cryptanalysis and SIGINT operations under GC&CS was laid in 1922, when the British armed services agreed to second their cryptanalytical staff to GC&CS and put them under the control of the Foreign Office.[1] In 1923, the head of SIS was renamed the chief of the secret service and the director of GC&CS. While GC&CS remained separate from SIS, this put the same official in charge of both foreign intelligence organisations. Because of this administrative arrangement and, more importantly, the financial constraints imposed by the economic circumstances of the inter-war years, the British armed services were forced into pooling resources and agreeing to a more sensible division of responsibilities under the direction of the 'Y' Committee. Thereafter, the influence of the Foreign Office and SIS over British SIGINT became more pervasive, if not more active.

The establishment of the Joint Intelligence Committee (JIC) on 7 July 1936 reduced even further the authority of single services over SIGINT collection.[2] According to F.H. Hinsley, the British official historian, the JIC was established to provide support to the new Joint Planning Staff by coordinating all of the inter-departmental reports and intelligence appreciations, and to coordinate the tasking of the intelligence services on behalf of a growing number of government departments that were now required to run an economy and government preparing for total war. This whole new structure provided support to the Cabinet, the Committee of Imperial Defence, the Chiefs of Staff Committee and all of the other organs of state involved in planning for or managing defence.

The other factor that influenced the willingness of Britain to allow Australian or any other Commonwealth country to involve itself in high-level SIGINT was the extreme sensitivity of SIGINT to compromise. This sensitivity had always existed, but it was seriously exacerbated by the Hall–Peaslee compromise of August 1925. As we saw earlier, this involved Vice Admiral William Hall, the wartime head of Room 40, handing more than 10,000 highly secret Room 40 decrypts to an American lawyer, Amos Peaslee, acting on behalf of American companies seeking damages for their losses to German saboteurs during World War I. Hall appears to have taken a substantial number of Room 40's highly secret files home with him after the end of the war, and it was from these that he provided Peaslee with the decrypts. By March 1925, the decrypts were in the hands of the German government, the defendants in Peaslee's lawsuit, and, according to a National Security Appreciation conducted of the incident sometime after 1955, the Germans responded immediately by introducing one-time pads and purchasing and modifying the stickered ENIGMA machine.[3]

It is easy to see why Admiral Ragnar M. Colvin, RN, may have been less than keen on an Australian national SIGINT effort, and why the authorities in London were less than enthusiastic in supporting any such action.

The sensitivities in London were not germane to the concerns held by Australian officers and civilians in government about the poor state of Australian intelligence in 1939. One of those most concerned was, as we now know, the DNI, Commander Rupert Long. With the declaration of war by the Menzies government, some impetus was given to dealing with these concerns, even if the government did not back its rhetoric with the money the services needed to develop an effective intelligence system. In late November 1939, as the RAN struggled to find enough sailors to man its routine communications, Long laid the problem of SIGINT before the Naval Staff, particularly Rear Admiral Colvin.[4] Long, an advocate of the joint approach the British had implemented, had been pushing for combined operational and intelligence structures.

The initiative for a joint operations and planning organisation in Australia came from the RAN, specifically from Long, but it was brought to the Defence Committee on 26 January 1939 by Admiral Colvin.[5] Colvin then ensured the idea was delayed by agreeing to have it considered by a Joint Planning Committee (JPC), which would report to the chiefs of staff on the issues surrounding the proposal.

On 6 August 1940, the JPC recommended that a Central War Room be established in H Block of Victoria Barracks in Melbourne, and that the COIC be placed next door. The Central War Room was to be the joint HQ from which the three service chiefs and senior ministers could run the strategic direction of the war. It would be continually manned, although the attached COIC would not.

The recommendations made by the JPC were sensible enough, but did not address the needs of civilian organisations or the political leadership. Nowhere was it mentioned that the prime minister and Cabinet ministers might need to be involved in decision-making if the feared attack on Australia took place. There was also a complete lack of consideration as to how the military authorities would manage the impact of operations on the civilian population, and how military and civilian agencies and departments would cooperate.

Despite the Defence Committee endorsement and discussion in Cabinet in January 1941, the recommendations for a Central War Room and a supporting COIC went nowhere. The Central War Room was made unworkable by the very restricted space it was given at Victoria Barracks and because it was given no equipment. It was also made redundant because the chiefs of staff chose to meet elsewhere.[6] Even as Malaya was falling to the Japanese, Australia still had no effective coordination between the three services.[7] As to intelligence, on 27 January 1942 the Chief of the Air Staff (CAS), Air Vice Marshal S.J. Goble, was writing to the Secretary of the Defence Committee complaining that there was no effective COIC, and 'there still appears to be a disinclination on the part of the intelligence sections of the three services to use this combined organisation'.[8]

SIGINT was a different matter than joint intelligence or operational control centres, as the Australian armed services in the first years of the war regarded SIGINT as a single-service matter. The question that needed to be answered on the approach of war in 1939 was how SIGINT was to be managed in Australia and who was to be responsible for strategic SIGINT collection.

The subject had been brought before the chiefs of staff on 12 December 1939, when Admiral Colvin dutifully tabled his DNI's minute on the need for an Australian cryptanalytical organisation to deal with traffic from enemy raiders that might operate in Australian waters. Having tabled Long's minute, Colvin then spoke against his own DNI's proposal.[9]

Long's minute is unremarkable. He was recommending that Australia approach the relevant British authorities for advice on whether Australia should establish its own cryptanalytical organisation. If the British authorities supported this, Long suggested they be asked to supply some of the specialist personnel and equipment that Australia lacked. It may have been this recommendation that put Colvin off. As an RN officer, Colvin would have been well aware that the philosophy at GC&CS was for cryptanalysis to be concentrated in one location, GC&CS, and that any request for cryptanalysts and specialised equipment to be sent to Australia would fall on deaf ears in London.

In his own minute, Colvin carefully undermines Long's suggestion. He uses Long's own words to recommend to the chiefs that no action be taken to establish any Australian cryptanalytical organisation without first obtaining the advice and assistance of GC&CS.[10] He even uses Long's observations that there was a dearth of qualified personnel in Australia, that Australia was too far from the action in the Atlantic and Europe, and that the creation of an Australian cryptanalytical organisation risked duplication.[11] Australia's CNS was arguing for Australia not to develop its own SIGINT capability.

Rear Admiral Colvin makes it abundantly clear that he was not initiating the discussion, but attempting to counter suggestions that Australia should create its own cryptanalytical agency. Colvin expressed a very Eurocentric view:

> It would seem that most of the enemy messages intercepted is Atlantic traffic and the reception of such traffic in Australia is certain for only about 12 hours per diem. Only a very few messages are received each week which would not (or may not) have been intercepted by UK authorities and dealt with by the Imperial Cryptographic Organization. Thus it is improbable that there would be obtainable in Australia sufficient material upon which cryptographers could work, without merely duplicating the work being done in the UK, with much less prospect of success owing to obvious limitations.[12]

Colvin was completely wrong: simple physics meant that signals intercepted in Australia could not be intercepted in Britain or the entire western hemisphere. This is one reason Australia eventually became an important part of the worldwide Allied SIGINT system.

As time would tell, the high-power, high-frequency transmissions out of Germany and Italy could not be picked up in Britain, as the distance was too far for the ground wave, and the sky wave bounced off the ionosphere too far above Britain and Europe to be intercepted there. As for Canada and the United States, along with the entire western hemisphere, they were on the other side of the earth, and most of the signals of interest were whizzing by into the vacuum of space.

The sky waves from directional antennae in Germany and Italy directed towards the east could, however, be easily picked up at Australian sites, and in order to capture this traffic, Australian intercept sites would need to be built and operated. This single chip enabled Australia to get into the ULTRA game.

The challenge that remained, the one that Long was raising, was that Australia needed to create its own capability to decrypt intercept, so that signals of importance to the security and interests of Australia were readily available for the Australian government. It was a reasonable argument, although asking Britain to supply the necessary specialists and equipment was not.

The truth may be that Long annoyed Colvin by sending a copy of his 28 November minute directly to the CGS, Lieutenant General Ernest Ker Squires, without first letting Colvin know. This may have been a deliberate attempt by Long to get around Colvin. If it was, he was playing a dangerous game. First, Admiral Colvin was his chief, not Squires. Secondly, Colvin and Squires were British officers brought in to serve as chiefs of staff of their respective services, but this does not mean they were friends and, in fact, they had already butted heads over resources.

By December 1938, the ACNB's operational budget had risen 16 per cent from AU£2.55 million in 1937 to £2.96 million, while the funding of new naval construction had fallen almost 80 per cent from 1936 to 1938. In the context of such severe cuts to the navy budget, Squires, as the newly appointed CGS, had put a plan to the Lyons government recommending the reorganisation of the Australian Army include a permanent force of 7500 regular soldiers and a program to re-equip and upgrade the militia.[13] In response, Colvin had threatened to resign.[14] So there was little love lost between Colvin and Squires or their respective services. For Long to approach Squires directly was, to put it mildly, very courageous. It worked, though, because Squires championed Long's suggestion in his subsequent reply to Colvin:

> I consider that we should at least have a nucleus organization in Australia against the contingencies of operations in and about Australia and her territories. The work is clearly of a highly skilled nature and much practice is necessary, and the sooner a commencement can be made the better.[15]

This is a significant turnaround in the history of Australian intelligence. Until this discussion, the great champions of intelligence, especially of SIGINT, had been the ACNB and the RAN. In 1939, the ACNB was surrendering the lead in this area to the CGS, General Squires, a British Army officer.

This did not mean that the RAN led by Colvin was not trying to build up its SIGINT capabilities, because it was. The difference lay in the scope of the SIGINT operation. The ACNB, led by Admiral Colvin, appears to have wanted to keep Australian SIGINT focused on tactical intelligence of immediate use to the military and naval forces of the Commonwealth. What Squires and Long were looking for was an Australian national SIGINT effort, something that, as we will later see, was not supported in London. Colvin's lack of enthusiasm may have been due to the attitude of the British authorities, one that was adamantly opposed to having anyone other than GC&CS deal with diplomatic and other non-tactical SIGINT. As we will see below, the British feared that any Australian attempt to conduct SIGINT operations against Japanese diplomatic traffic would put critically important sources of SIGINT at risk in Europe.

In light of Colvin's concerns, Squires conceded that Australia did need to approach Britain and ask advice on the matter. He made clear, however, that he was not recommending that Australia seek British permission to establish an Australian cryptanalytical organisation, but that the British authorities be asked for advice on how best to do this and on how to integrate it into the existing British system.

The other major point of difference was that Squires was focused on the Japanese and their operations in China. The Japanese had now been fighting on the Chinese mainland since July 1937, and this was producing a flood of intercept of which only a small portion was being decrypted by FECB and GC&CS. The activity of the IJA in China and the IJN in support of these operations was of great importance for Australia, and General Squires understood this. Squires did not want Australia's new cryptanalytical organisation to target Germany or her European allies, he wanted it to target Japan:

> So far as the Army is concerned the type of material mainly required for practice is that transmitted by the Japanese in the course of their operations in China. Whilst some of this may be intercepted direct (thus giving practice to signal personnel as well) a considerable quantity would have to come from the British organization in the Far East.[16]

Colvin, however, with the support of the CAS, Air Vice Marshal Goble, countered Squires by the simple expedient of having his fellow chiefs agree to refer the matter to the Defence Committee.[17] This, as Colvin probably intended, delayed further action on Long's suggestions for more than a year.

The question of whether Australia should establish its own version of GC&CS went before the Defence Committee on 15 February 1940. Unfortunately, by this time Lieutenant General Squires was absent, as he was dying from cancer. Major General John Northcott, the Acting CGS, represented Squires on the committee. Northcott, who did not understand intelligence, fell into line with Colvin's recommendation that no further action be taken until advice had been obtained from Britain.[18] On 11 April 1940, the prime minister, Robert Menzies, wrote to the Secretary of State for Dominion Affairs for advice.[19]

London only replied to Menzies' letter six months later, on 15 October 1940, a sure sign of serious discussion around Whitehall. Eleven months had passed since Long had first raised the question of Australia creating its own cryptanalysis organisation. Lord Cranborne, the Secretary of State for Dominion Affairs advised that the British authorities felt it was inadvisable, 'for the present', to envisage any large-scale cryptanalytical organisation in Australia.[20] Cranborne did recommend, however, that Australia should contribute to the combined SIGINT effort, now centred on GC&CS, by forming a small-scale cryptanalytical organisation from the existing SIGINT organisations operating in Australia.[21] Cranborne advised that this new organisation should continue to work on IJN codes in cooperation with FECB in Singapore and GC&CS in Britain and, importantly, expand its operations to cover fixed commercial wireless station traffic throughout the world.[22] These were fair and reasonable suggestions.

Despite the clear recommendation from Cranborne, the Defence Committee continued to prevaricate. At its normal meeting on 5 December 1940, the committee deferred consideration of the matter until it had been discussed with the Admiralty's Chief of the Naval Intelligence Staff, Captain F.J. Wylie, RN, who was due to visit Australia later that month. In the interim, the CNS would discuss the matter with the CGS and CAS, and raise the question of training army and RAAF personnel in this type of work. Effectively, Australia's own military advisors had postponed taking action on any aspect of SIGINT for a full fifteen months since the country had entered the war in Europe.[23]

While all this was happening, the army had taken the initiative and established a small cryptographic group in Sydney. This group comprised academics from the University of Sydney, including Professor A.P. Treweek (also a major in the Sydney University Regiment), professors A.D. Trendall and T.G. Room, R.J. Lyons and Lieutenant I.H. Longfield Lloyd, Australian Military Forces (AMF) (the son of Colonel E.E. Longfield Lloyd of the Security Service), who worked part-time on Japan's codes. Administrative responsibility was vested in the GOC, Eastern Command, and Major Reginald Powell of the Military Intelligence Branch oversaw its operations.

The Sydney cryptographic group was not particularly effective, and the claims by Major Powell that they were making considerable progress in breaking Japan's diplomatic codes can be discounted because the resources being dedicated to the problem were minuscule.[24] None of the academics involved, with the exception of Treweek who was a militia officer, was being paid, and they appear to have been working on Japanese codes in their spare time on an honorary basis. There is no documentation for the payment of salaries to them, and the Senate of the University of Sydney had not released them from their responsibilities. The idea that six or seven academics could make advances that large and well-resourced US and British agencies could not is hard to believe.

Through no fault of their own, the group lacked the necessary equipment and supporting services, and the amount of raw intercept they could obtain was small and partial. The number of messages crossing their desks could not have provided the statistical data necessary for decryption. Likewise, they had no secure contact with the intercept operators, and no ability to apply TA to cribs and those cribs to their cryptanalysis. In short, they were operating without any of the infrastructure necessary for making headway against Japan's codes.

Finally, as far as this analysis is concerned, there is no evidence of any such advances in the archives. There are no files of broken-out messages or reports derived from them. There are no files showing exchanges of intelligence between the army and any other body. All we have is Major Powell's unsubstantiated claims and a single decryption he forwarded in his report. Australia was now paying the price of its own failure to adequately fund its own defence between 1918 and 1939 and for the destruction of Edmund Piesse's Pacific Branch.

The one decrypt Powell did forward is telling. It was not a decrypt of any Japanese coded message, but of a love letter between a named British official in Hong Kong and a married Australian woman, who is also named in the files. These two people appear to have shared a shipboard romance en route to their destinations in Asia. Even today, this letter is disconcerting, as the woman was the wife of a senior Australian officer and no attempt has been made to disguise either identity.[25]

Over at Navy Office, things had changed. The initiative on SIGINT had been lost in the deliberations of the Defence Committee, and the army had its own program. In an effort to meet the needs of the RAN, in September 1940 Navy Office established the Special Intelligence Bureau, a small cryptanalytical section within the NID. But they could not find suitable people any more than the army could.[26]

The biggest skill gap was the lack of Japanese linguists. The old language program had qualified a few officers, but most of those had been lost to the services and only a few, like Nave, remained available. The Australian authorities also made things even harder for themselves by refusing to consider recruiting Japanese Australians for the work. Harry Freame was the exception, and he was only involved because he was a highly decorated and well known-returned serviceman and had served with E.E. Longfield Lloyd, who was now the Director of the Commonwealth Security Service.

In all of this gloom, a little serendipity now intervened and Eric Nave was back in Australia convalescing from tropical sprue, a serious digestive condition that afflicted many serving in tropical climes. Nave was now a commander in the RN and would normally have been repatriated to Britain, but FECB did not want to risk losing him to GC&CS if he returned to Britain. It was arranged for him to go to Melbourne before the Admiralty could stop it.[27] This turned out to be a mistake.

The truth appears to have been that the newly married Nave had had enough of Singapore and did not want to return. As he was an RN officer, the ACNB had no authority to allow him to stay in Australia, but Nave had a friend in Australia, Admiral Colvin, who had been the British Naval Attaché in Tokyo when Nave undertook language training there. Added to this, Colvin was an old China hand who knew of Nave's good work and who understood the plight of someone suffering from tropical sprue. It is also likely that Colvin was influenced by his DNI, Commander Long, and his Communications Staff Officer, Commander Jack Newman, who were both keen to keep Nave for cryptanalytical and SIGINT work in Australia. Whatever reservations Colvin had about Australian plans for a national SIGINT effort, he was supportive of keeping an experienced Japanese linguist and cryptologist like Nave in Australia. The evidence for this is that in the tussle that now developed between the Admiralty and the ACNB for Nave's services, the ACNB was able to hold on to the RN's man.[28] Only Colvin, with the help of the RAN's doctors, could have accomplished that.

As the Admiralty wanted Nave back in Singapore, the ACNB used its medical board to argue that he was not fit enough to be posted back there. The Admiralty then insisted that Nave return to the United Kingdom. The Australian riposte was that Nave was so ill he could not even travel through the tropics to get back to Britain.[29] This gambit worked, and the Red Book recorded that in July 1940 Nave was posted to the Melbourne Communications Intelligence Unit (CIU; Special Intelligence Bureau).[30]

At the Melbourne CIU, Nave's job was to lead the establishment of the Special Intelligence Bureau. Records suggest that he was the sole commissioned officer until November 1940, when Paymaster Lieutenant Keith Stafford Miller was posted in to join him.[31] Miller had resigned his commission on 5 November 1927, but was brought back onto the RAN Emergency List on 21 October 1940, most likely at Nave's insistence.

There is no documentary proof that Miller was a Japanese linguist, but he remained in the Melbourne CIU until September 1945.[32] He then stayed with the RAN until January 1949, when he was appointed to the Commonwealth Public Service as an officer of the Joint Intelligence Organisation.[33] This shows that by the end of the war Miller was a hardened intelligence professional.

In January 1941, Captain Wylie, RN, the head of FECB in Singapore, visited Australia to provide the RAN with advice on the conduct and management of its SIGINT effort, and to discuss proposals for the division of labour on SIGINT operations against the IJN. The meeting in the Conference Room at Navy Office consisted of Wylie; the Second Naval Member, Commodore J.W. Durnford; Captain J. Burnett; and commanders Long, Newman and R.F. Nichols. The discussion ranged over the RAN's plans and the potential difficulties they foresaw with the other services, especially with the army's 'horror' of any form of joint operation, and its inability to differentiate between operational and strategic intelligence activity.[34] The other matter discussed was the liaison arrangements between the C-in-C, Singapore and the C-in-C of the Dutch forces in the NEI.

Also discussed was the Admiralty's request that the ACNB provide three additional HFDF stations collocated alongside existing stations. The Admiralty wanted the ACNB to contribute to the DF network in Asia, even though the Australian government had wriggled out of this commitment in the mid-1930s. Raising it now, Wylie admitted, was 'rather tall', but it was essential if the British and Allied forces in Asia were to deal with a Japanese attack. Duplication of the HFDF stations had arisen from the experience in the Atlantic, where having just one DF station at a site caused too many errors in fixes and prevented multiple simultaneous fixes being made.[35]

Captain Burnett, RAN, challenged the effectiveness of this more complex and expensive system, and put the view that the operations staff did not see much value in the intelligence being provided. Burnett was making the usual complaint of all operations officers—that they had no use for messages saying there was no change in the disposition of target vessels.[36] What Burnett did not appreciate was that a 'no change' message had value, in that it confirmed that the target vessels had remained in position. This intelligence was not a guess, but the product of a lot of work.[37] Each 'no change' message required 300–400 bearings a day and around 2000 bearings a week, all of which required coordination and plotting in order for the SIGINT system to categorically report that no IJN vessels had moved.[38] Wylie explained this to the meeting, for the benefit of Burnett.

Wylie also emphasised the importance of combined intelligence operations, including analysis and assessment processes. While each service element collected, collated and distributed its own intelligence product to its respective service, Wylie said they should also distribute it into a central pool from which the other services and governmental agencies could self-select intelligence product. This important point was not lost on the RAN officers present, as someone noted 'Very Good. We should remember this' in the margin of the minutes of the meeting.[39]

The discussions between Wylie and the RAN also covered the suggested Australian cryptanalytical organisation. It is highly likely that this subject was raised with Wylie by Long and, later, by Nave. Wylie followed the official line already outlined by Lord Cranborne: that Australia should not contemplate a large organisation but look to expanding the existing organisation now being led by Nave.

As for the RAAF, it had no operational SIGINT capability and the RAN had fewer than twenty naval ratings qualified to undertake SIGINT intercept operations. The other factor was the lack of intercept sites. The RAN was only now preparing HMAS *Coonawarra* at Darwin and HMAS *Harman* at Canberra to provide cover of the IJN nets, and the army's intercept site at Park Orchards, in the outer suburbs of eastern Melbourne, was being used to intercept Japanese diplomatic and international commercial traffic. A fourth intercept site, Jandakot in Western Australia, was being commissioned with one receiver to listen for German surface raiders. The Jandakot site would shortly be supplied with a second receiver so that the intercept operators there could work Japanese Morse.[40] The advice to keep any new organisation small was sensible, and the obvious way forward for Australia was to merge the army's cryptographic group in Sydney with Nave's Special Intelligence Bureau in Melbourne.

On 2 May 1941, a conference was held in Melbourne to settle the issue of Australia's SIGINT effort. This conference was important because it involved everyone: Long from the RAN; Lieutenant Colonel Edwards, Major J.C.W O'Connor and Captain E.H. Fleiter from the army; and Professor Room from the cryptographic group in Sydney.[41] At this meeting, Long 'intimated' that the ACNB had established a SIGINT section, before he and Colonel K.A. McKenzie left the meeting to allow the SIGINT specialists to discuss the technical details of the work being done by the cryptographic group in Sydney.[42]

This conference was also significant because it was not about service SIGINT at all—the focus was on breaking Japan's diplomatic codes. This was about an Australia strategic SIGINT effort directed towards meeting Australian self-interest. The first order of business was to see if they all agreed that breaking the Japanese diplomatic codes was a feasible objective for the new organisation. They agreed it was. The second order of business was whether Australia should do this, and they argued that as the FECB 'may not always be available', it was essential for Australia to have its own independent capability.[43] The new organisation's manpower was to be four officers and three clerks, on top of the existing naval organisation in Melbourne, and it would be a joint organisation along similar lines to FECB.[44]

All of this was passed to FECB in Singapore, and the army agreed to ensure that Eastern Command would continue to provide the unofficial Sydney group with support and that all of their activities would still be covered by the strictest security measures as detailed by the RAN.[45]

On 15 May 1941, Australia's naval and military authorities tasked the Sydney group with conducting a cryptanalytic attack on Japanese consular and diplomatic messages. The minute from the CNS to the CGS made it clear that the intercepted traffic was to be attacked in Australia by the cryptographic group and that Commander Nave now believed some of the members of the Sydney group would be 'most useful' in dealing with Japanese diplomatic traffic.[46] This is the first time Australian chiefs of staff clearly state a position of Australian independence in SIGINT matters.

Professor Arthur Sadler, who had worked as James Murdoch's assistant and whom Nave had identified as the most competent Japanese linguist, now fell under the malign eye of the Military Police Intelligence Bureau operating in New South Wales. The problem was that Sadler, a Japanese linguist and expert, had a Japanese wife. This made him unacceptable to the dysfunctional security apparatus and, acting on their advice, the GOC Eastern Command would not recommend Sadler because he was 'inclined to be indiscreet'.[47]

From May 1941, things began to speed up as the ACNB requested the CGS to consider posting one of the Sydney academics and a clerk to Melbourne as soon as possible, to be followed by the remaining members, plus three clerical staff, immediately afterwards.[48] The army actioned this request on 27 May.[49]

All of this may appear to a modern reader to be simple, but, as anyone who has served in the military knows, even in wartime the military is a vast and slow-moving bureaucracy. And there are other slow-moving bureaucracies too.

In June 1941, the CGS, General Vernon Sturdee, wrote to the Minister for the Army, Percy Spender, requesting permission to call up the professors in Sydney for military service in the rank of major.[50] Sturdee emphasised that the work of these men would be 'of the greatest importance' in both collecting intelligence and training military personnel to work on Japanese signals and codes. The best the army could do was to make all four academics temporary majors on special duty, with Treweek, Lyons and Room going to Melbourne and Professor Trendall staying in Sydney.[51]

The Senate of the University of Sydney released Room, Lyons and Treweek for service on 4 June, and while the Senate was happy with Treweek and Lyons being appointed majors, it wanted Professor Room to be made a full colonel, to keep him on a pay level equivalent to his university salary.[52] The university also wanted the army to pay for all the costs of moving the men to Melbourne.

Now the two bureaucracies engaged in mortal combat. Professor Sir Robert Wallace, the Vice-Chancellor of the university, took the matter to Percy Spender, who appears to have been bemused by the fuss. Spender wanted to know from Sturdee what he should tell Professor Wallace, given there was little likelihood of the military establishment agreeing to make Professor Room a full colonel and pay £5000 a year for his services.[53] The army suggested employing Professor Room as a civilian under the ACNB, which, luckily, agreed.[54] Finally, on 25 July, Professor Wallace was informed that Room and Lyons could be employed to undertake the special work in a civilian capacity and at salaries equivalent to those they had been paid at the university.

With the administrative nightmare of employing the four academics overcome, it was the turn of Frank Sinclair, the Secretary of the Department of the Army, to interfere. This took the form of an objection to the interception and reading of Japanese diplomatic traffic because it could contravene international agreements giving 'diplomatic messages immunity from interference'.[55] Sinclair was Australia's version of Henry Stimson, the US Secretary of State who withdrew funding from the first US SIGINT operation led by Herbert Yardley because, as he later wrote in his memoirs, 'Gentlemen do not read each other's mail.'[56]

It was left to the Deputy CGS, Colonel John Chapman, to write to Sinclair telling him that the diplomatic telegrams involved were sighted in the cable companies' offices and copies made, and that everyone was doing it. Chapman also noted that diplomatic telegrams and radio messages were not subject to privilege and thus fair game.[57] It was a big boys' game played with big boys' rules.

On 14 November 1941, the Defence Committee agenda included an item on Australia's small special intelligence organisation and, on 28 November, the three chiefs of staff, sitting as the Defence Committee, formally approved the organisation, its establishment and its mission.[58] They even recommended that the chiefs of staff be given authority to increase the size of the organisation, as and when it became necessary.[59]

By December 1941, Australia's national SIGINT organisation, the Special Intelligence Bureau, consisted of Professor Room; Eric Nave, RN; Paymaster Lieutenant Commander A.E.N. Merry, RN; a Japanese linguist from FECB and paid for by the Admiralty; Paymaster Lieutenant Commander W.E. McLaughlin, RAN; Paymaster Lieutenant Miller; A.B. Jamison; and three secretaries, Misses Robertson, Eldridge and Shearer. The ACNB was paying for all of these, with the exception of Merry. The army paid for Major Treweek, A.A. Mason, R.J. Lyons and Lieutenant Longfield Lloyd.[60]

The whole process of creating the Special Intelligence Bureau had taken two years, from 28 November 1939 to 28 November 1941, and its creation only preceded General Yamashita's landing in Malaya by two weeks.

During February and March 1942, reinforcements for the bureau were hastily sent out from the Admiralty and Foreign Office in London. They included the Japanese linguists Lieutenant Commander E. Colegrave, RN, and Hubert Graves, Henry Archer and A.R.V. Cooper of the Consular Service.[61] Archer had served as the British Consul-General in Harbin, China, and was a competent Japanese linguist. Hubert Graves had served as Consul-General at Kobe in Japan and was a very competent linguist.[62] The posting of these British personnel clearly shows that despite Australia having initiated the development of the Special Intelligence Bureau, GC&CS was heavily involved every step of the way.

CHAPTER 17

Battle in Asia and the Pacific, 1941–42

As the Japanese swept south, US personnel and resources were starting to arrive in Australia, with the first 4600 US soldiers landing in Brisbane on 22 December 1941. In early 1942, as the situation turned from bad to worse, the Australian government began to panic and even considered evacuation of Canberra to Wagga Wagga. Military 'refugees' began to pour in from Singapore, the NEI and the Philippines, and among those refugees were the men from the SIGINT intercept sites in Singapore and Corregidor, in the Philippines.

On 20 January, the prime ministers of Australia, Canada and New Zealand received a telegram from the Secretary of State for Dominion Affairs in London, Lord Cranborne, informing them that the entire Naval Intelligence Staff, SIGINT organisation and supporting elements at Singapore had been moved to Colombo in Ceylon.[1] Admiral Sir Geoffrey Layton, RN, the C-in-C, Eastern Fleet had ordered this action on 1 January in what was a clear signal of impending defeat in Malaya.

On the same day as the news of FECB's evacuation from Singapore was communicated, news arrived from the Australian naval attaché at the Legation in Washington concerning another evacuation. This was the US Navy's CAST unit, which had been evacuated to Java in the NEI. For Australia, this was bad news with a silver lining. The US Navy was looking for a secure base in Australia or New Zealand from which CAST could continue to operate.

The ACNB jumped at the chance and immediately invited CAST to establish operations in Australia. It did not pass the offer on to New Zealand as requested by the naval attaché, but kept the news secret, ensuring CAST would come to Australia.

The US Navy's offer had come about as the alternative positions for the CAST unit rapidly became untenable. First the Philippines and then Malaya, Singapore and now the NEI all became insecure. Even Colombo would soon be judged too insecure for FECB and its SIGINT elements, and it would be relocated to Kilindini in East Africa, from where it would operate for most of the next four years.

The final act in the movement of CAST to Australia came about as the unit was attempting to establish operations in support of the US Navy in Java. Vice Admiral William Glassford, the US Navy Commander in Java, did not believe the NEI could be held, and advised the Navy Department in Washington to remove CAST to the greater security of Australia.[2] The advice from Glassford, and the rapid destruction of the NEI defences in the string of naval battles over January and February 1942, convinced the Navy Department to open discussions with both the British and the Australian naval attachés. In due course, Australia's attaché informed Australia and CAST's new home was decided.

The impact of CAST on Australian SIGINT cannot be understated. This single US unit had eight officers and 68 other ranks, comprising Japanese linguists, cryptographers and experienced intercept operators trained in Japanese Morse, along with their equipment.[3] In early 1942, it was larger than all of Australia's SIGINT organisations combined. On 23 February, the CNS quickly cabled the attaché that the US personnel 'would be a valuable addition to W/T intelligence and the Special Intelligence Organisation that now exists in Australia'.[4] This was fast work for Australia.

Although it would not be immediately apparent, CAST was not coming to Australia to supplement Australian SIGINT but to serve the needs of the US Navy and OP-20-G in the Office of Chief of Naval Operations in Washington. Neither was it joining in with the RAN's existing SIGINT organisation; it was in fact going to launch a hostile takeover, one so complete that it very soon became clear that the ACNB was left with little control over the new entity, called Fleet Radio Unit Melbourne (FRUMEL).[5]

FRUMEL made use of many RAN personnel, but at the lowest possible levels, and they worked for OP-20-G, not the ACNB. In some ways, it is difficult to say that FRUMEL was an Australian operation; it was Australian only in that it was located in Melbourne and used Australian personnel for much of its grunt work. Admiral Joseph R. Redman at OP-20-G in Washington exercised almost complete control over policy decisions, unit procedures, and all command and control, even down to deciding whether the SIGINT produced by FRUMEL should be shown to anyone outside the US Navy. At best, Australia was FRUMEL's landlord, but its operations did involve Australians, particularly in the first part of 1942, so it is part of our story.

One of the major mistakes made in historical accounts of the war in the Pacific is to overlook the US response and focus on the losses suffered in Malaya, the Philippines and in South-East Asia more generally. In fact, when it is examined carefully, the US response was extraordinary. It was certainly beyond anything the Japanese thought possible.[6] It is somewhat sobering to consider that on 10 May 1942, the very same day General J.M. Wainwright and General W.F. Sharp finalised the surrender of all Filipino and American troops in the Philippines, the US Navy permanently wrested the strategic initiative from Japan in the Battle of the Coral Sea. Within five months, the US Navy had put the Japanese permanently onto the defensive. In less than another month, by the end of 7 June 1942, the US Navy would destroy the strategic reach of the IJN at the Battle of Midway. This was a startling turnaround and one that is too often neglected.

As CAST arrived in Melbourne over March and April 1942, the military situation was critical. Singapore had fallen, the British were in full retreat through Burma to India, and Rear Admiral Karel Doorman's English, Dutch and American fleet was being systematically destroyed. The extent of the IJN's victory is shown by the losses inflicted on the Allied navies between 27 February and 1 March 1942—ten ships, including two heavy cruisers, three light cruisers and five destroyers—in the two battles of the Java Sea and the Battle of Sunda Strait.

The CAST advance party led by Lieutenant Rudolph (Rudy) Fabian quickly established operations in Melbourne.[7] Intercept operations were commenced immediately and IJN messages were soon being couriered by motorcycle every two hours to the cryptanalytical section based at the Monterey Apartments, in Queens Road, South Melbourne, which the Americans had taken over rather than try to squeeze into Victoria Barracks.[8]

The Americans were not impressed by the state of the facilities at the RAN's Moorabbin intercept site, which was slowly being built by Australian workers.[9] The pace of work annoyed the Americans so much they built the antenna farm and accommodation facilities themselves.[10] They also quickly took control of the inexperienced sailors and members of the Women's Royal Australian Naval Service (WRANS), who constituted the bulk of the workforce at Moorabbin, and began training them in the use of the American equipment, particularly the KANA typewriters, and in US Navy processing techniques.

The contrast between the attitude of the Australians in Melbourne and the aggressive impatience of Lieutenant Fabian and his unit must have been stark, but polite American pushiness got things moving without ruining relationships. Given their extensive experience of working Japanese naval codes and their recent exploits in the Philippines and Java, the Americans held the upper hand and were easily able to impress the less experienced Australians.

The equipment suite salvaged from Corregidor was, by Australian standards, quite extensive, and included portable DF equipment and the valuable KANA typewriters. They had no IBM card-punching equipment, however, and the PURPLE machine that OP-20-G had sent them needed multiple faults fixed before it could be made to operate with any reliability.[11] The CAST unit was lucky to have procured the services of Ralph E. Cook, an electrical engineer and officer in the US Navy Reserve. Cook had been a field engineer for IBM until he was called up for duty in April 1941, and he played a significant role in getting the equipment operational.

Cook began automating as much of the cryptanalytic process as he could, and he kept the IBM equipment running. His main problem was obtaining more IBM equipment, and it would be late 1942 before any more arrived from Washington. Even then, it was missing the card feeder and the printing mechanism for the tabulator. The tabulating section at FRUMEL had to hand-punch cards for three months until the missing equipment arrived.[12]

Despite all the political, organisational and logistical difficulties affecting FRUMEL at its creation, the men and women, American, British and Australian, continued to carry out their duties and to learn the art and science of SIGINT. It was during these first four months of FRUMEL's life that it made its most significant contribution to the war effort by providing SIGINT on the IJN's Indian Ocean raid of March, the Battle of the Coral Sea in May and then the Battle of Midway in June.

As soon as it had arrived in Melbourne, FRUMEL began receiving intercept from the site at Moorabbin and sites at HMAS *Coonawarra* outside Darwin, Adelaide River, Exmouth in Western Australia and HMAS *Harman* in Canberra, as well as from SIGINT teams afloat on both US and RAN ships. All of this was supplemented by SIGINT flowing in from US and British sites around the world.[13]

One of the first SIGINT wins FRUMEL and other SIGINT sites achieved was the preservation of Admiral James Somerville's Eastern Fleet in April 1942. SIGINT enabled Somerville's unpractised and unready fleet to avoid Admiral Nagumo's force, sparing them the destruction that befell Karel Doorman's fleet.[14]

Initial indications of the IJN's intentions to extend operations into the Indian Ocean came from intercepted IJN signals on 3 March, which were orders for setting up a submarine base at Penang in Malaya. On 7 March, further IJN traffic referred to a timetable for an operation against a location identified by the digraph ZL. The British cryptanalysts at Colombo had tentatively identified ZL as the Andaman Islands, as it had been used in IJN traffic relating to setting up a seaplane base there. This indicated the IJN was planning a move into the Indian Ocean. The reasons for the IJN's move west were not known, but the traffic analysis showed a build-up was occurring. Further evidence was slowly collected as IJN units moved to Malaya, Singapore and the archipelago, and traffic analysis at FRUMEL, the Fleet Radio Unit, Pacific (FRUPAC) in Hawaii and Colombo produced a picture of a substantial concentration of IJN forces.

On 21 March, FECB at Colombo informed Somerville that the IJN was planning a major attack on 'DG'. By 26 March, Admiral Nimitz, C-in-C, Pacific Fleet (CINCPACFLT) at Pearl Harbor, believed the IJN was going to break out into the Indian Ocean, and he warned Somerville, confirming the intelligence Somerville had been given by FECB. Nagumo's target, DG, was finally identified from a crib from a confused IJN radio operator who identified DG as KO-RO-N-BO when he spelled it out in KANA.[15] Somerville ordered Allied merchant ships to run to India for safety and withdrew his own fleet to Port T, a secret base established at Addu Atoll in the Maldives. This action left the whole Bay of Bengal and Colombo unprotected, but the Admiralty had ordered Somerville to keep his fleet intact, even if it meant the loss of Ceylon.[16]

The IJN's Indian Ocean raid resulted in unfortunate losses, including the aircraft carrier HMS *Hermes*; the two cruisers HMS *Cornwall* and HMS *Derbyshire*; and HMAS *Vampire*, HMS *Tenedos* and 26 merchant ships. Some of these losses were unnecessary. The *Hermes, Cornwall, Derbyshire* and *Vampire* were lost because Somerville thought the SIGINT was wrong when Nagumo's force did not appear precisely on 1 April as predicted.[17] Despite this error, Allied SIGINT now had a firm grip on IJN communications, and this allowed commanders and governments to act on the basis of reliable information. One of the actions that SIGINT made possible was the Doolittle Raid on Tokyo.

This attack has often been described as having been carried out by sixteen B-25 (Mitchell) medium bombers of the US Army's 17th Bomb Group launched from the aircraft carrier USS *Hornet*. Although it is true that the actual attacks on Tokyo, Yokohama, Nagoya, Kobe and Osaka were to be carried out by the heavy land-based aircraft launched from *Hornet*, the attack was made by Task Force 16 (TF16), commanded by Admiral Halsey. TF16 comprised the carriers *Hornet* and *Enterprise*, the two heavy cruisers *Northampton* and *Salt Lake City*, four destroyers and a re-fuelling tanker.[18] An IJN picket boat, the 90-foot long fishing junk, *Nitta Maru*, sighted and reported the presence of TF16 at approximately 0744 hrs on 18 April and Halsey decided to launch the B-25s immediately. They launched approximately 650 nautical miles from the Japanese coast, around 150 nautical miles further out than planned.

The B-25s reached Japan and took the Japanese government and military by surprise. A Japanese aircraft carrying General Tojo was forced to take evasive action when one of the B-25s passed so close the occupants saw that the pilot was Caucasian. After completing their mission, the B-25s flew on to crash-land in China, or in one case, Russia. The *Nitta Maru* did not go down without a fight, shooting down one US aircraft that attacked her and exchanging fire with the destroyer USS *Nashville*. It took 928 6-inch rounds and 1200 rounds of .50-calibre machine gun ammunition to sink her.[19]

This operation was only possible because the SIGINT flowing into Washington from FRUPAC, FRUMEL and the other SIGINT sites provided the US Navy and President Roosevelt with accurate positional information for the IJN's fleet units. The Americans knew that neither Nagumo nor the Combined Fleet could intercept the *Hornet*, and this made the operation feasible.

The military destruction caused by the Doolittle Raid was minuscule, but its political and psychological impact on Japan's military and government was massive. Admiral Yamamoto vomited when he was told Tokyo had just been bombed.[20] It was a stroke of genius. Lieutenant Colonel James (Jimmy) Doolittle's raid of 18 April 1942 completely negated Japan's strategy and shattered the confidence of Japan's senior military leadership that they could hold the Americans at bay.

Doolittle's raid made it imperative that the IJN regain face by inflicting a serious loss on the Allies. The RN had refused battle in the Indian Ocean; seizing Port Moresby was the next best thing. As the IJN's plans progressed, FRUMEL in Melbourne and FRUPAC in Hawaii were busy intercepting and breaking out the IJN's communications. The product from FECB had fallen away due to its withdrawal from Colombo to Kilindini, but FRUMEL and FRUPAC, supported by other SIGINT entities, kept the IJN well covered, and the Japanese plans to seize Port Moresby and to reach further into the Pacific to prevent more Doolittle-type raids were being unwrapped.

Indications of the IJN's intentions towards Port Moresby began to accumulate as the work of revictualling, rearming and repairing the ships assigned to the task force created more and more traffic. Even the target of the intended operation was easily identified from the intercept of weather messages for the Coral Sea and the area around Papua, New Guinea. In early March, a message in JN25 (the main IJN code), directing the carriers HIJMS *Soryu* and HIJMS *Hiryu* to move from the Indian Ocean back to Truk to take part in Operation MO, was intercepted and broken out.[21] On 3 April, FRUPAC broke out traffic indicating the IJN planned to launch an operation from Rabaul, and OP-20-G in Washington added an assessment that the IJN had increased reconnaissance of the Coral Sea.[22]

On the Japanese side, they had no idea what they were up against.[23] They were expecting 200 combat aircraft operating from airfields between Townsville and Darwin and the remnants of Somerville's Fleet, possibly a battleship and up to three cruisers, with some submarines as a screen and maybe even a carrier.[24] Their assessment of ground forces was more accurate;

Port Moresby was defended by a small garrison made up of the militia of the Australian 30th Brigade, and an artillery regiment armed with field guns last used in 1918. At the time of the Doolittle Raid, the IJN's Combined Fleet Staff thought the Americans had only two carriers left in the Pacific. Their appreciation of American naval strength was consistently poor and they were having great difficulty identifying US naval strength and locations.[25]

There were, however, 225 land-based combat aircraft concentrated around the Coral Sea, and the US carriers *Lexington* and *Yorktown* in Admiral Frank Fletcher's Task Force 17, would prove capable of bringing more. In addition, there were strong US submarine forces operating within the intended area of operations, as well as an RAN force.[26] In the face of these forces, conducting a successful transit to and amphibious assault on Port Moresby would not be easy. Again, the IJN and IJA were implementing plans that made little use of the limited intelligence that they had available and the IJN was about to pay the price.

On 9 April 1942, FRUMEL intercepted IJN traffic indicating that a major Japanese task force was moving to capture Port Moresby. The evidence for this assessment was found in a JN25 message from Admiral Yamamoto Isoroku requesting a report on the progress of repairs to the carrier HIJMS *Kaga*. FRUMEL believed *Kaga* had been damaged off Lombok and was now in dock for repairs. This message also compromised the Port Moresby operation when Yamamoto wanted to know *Kaga*'s status because she was needed for the attack on RZP,[27] which FRUMEL had already identified as Port Moresby.[28] The analysts at FRUMEL now increased the intensity of their operations and began identifying the other IJN elements assigned to the RZP campaign, including the new light carrier *Shoho*, and the 5th Cruiser Division consisting of *Nachi*, *Huguro* and *Myko*.[29]

On 20 April, FRUMEL and other sites showed the 5th Carrier Division, consisting of *Shokaku*, *Zuikaku* and possibly *Shoho*, en route to Truk carrying approximately 357 combat aircraft.[30] By 27 April, FRUMEL was reporting that the 5th Carrier Division, plus *Shoho*, the 5th Cruiser Division less *Nachi*, the 29th Destroyer Division and half the 8th Submarine Squadron were all now at Truk, and that two Occupation (assault) Forces, RZP, Moresby and RXB, Tulagi had been formed and allocated call signs in the Truk Area Network. FRUMEL also established that the 5th Carrier Division was now passing messages across the operational net for New Britain Command while apparently sailing to operations in the waters around the Solomon Islands.[31]

The next day, 28 April, FRUMEL was reporting that the 5th Air Attack Force was conducting offensive air patrols between 80 and 120 degrees up to 700 miles (1200 kilometres) from Rabaul. By 30 April, the existence of the Port Moresby Occupation Force aboard the *Fumi Maru* and another merchant ship had been confirmed, and their orders to depart Rabaul and rendezvous with the Saipan Base Force off Deboyne Island on 'X-minus 5' were reported by FRUMEL.[32]

If there is a single element in SIGINT more important than the others it is cribs. On the eve of the Battle of the Coral Sea, FRUMEL, FRUPAC and the other sites working against the IJN benefited enormously from the IJN's inability to distribute new codebook and additive tables in time for their introduction on 1 May 1942. These delays led to the new additive tables being used with the old JN25B codebook, and meant Allied SIGINT could read IJN traffic until the table expired on 25 May. It allowed FRUPAC, FRUMEL and FECB to verify the IJN's preparations for the assault on Port Moresby and, even more importantly, to decrypt the IJN's battle plans for the capture of Midway Island.[33]

The Battle of the Coral Sea occurred over five days, from 4 to 8 May, and its twists and turns are clearly shown in FRUMEL's records from 0640 hours on 4 May onwards. The first Japanese contact with the opposing naval force was relayed to the IJN Task Force by a Japanese aircraft that reported one Allied battleship, two cruisers, one carrier and seven destroyers. At 1250 hours, the Japanese reporting mentions one enemy battleship being sunk. Further intercepts of air–ground networks on New Britain on 6 May show Chichijima Air Group sighting an enemy task force of one battleship, three carriers and five destroyers 195 degrees and 200 miles (300 kilometres) from Tulagi. A large volume of operational traffic was subsequently intercepted over 7 May, and the battle report on the same day from the 5th Carrier Division's flag officer described the failure of one attack by dive bombers and fifteen bombers because they ran low on fuel.

The following day, FRUMEL's record shows the Japanese reporting the sinking of the *Saratoga* and the striking of *Yorktown* with three torpedoes and eight bombs over the two days. They also reported that *Shokaku* had been set on fire but that this was being managed, and that her aircraft had flown over to *Zuikaku*.[34] Most importantly, FRUMEL was able to report that Rabaul had sent a broadcast ordering that the attack on Port Moresby be postponed.[35]

The battle assessment from FRUMEL on 10 May indicated that Yamamoto had postponed the seizure of Port Moresby by five months and had ordered the 5th Carrier Division back to home waters because of the damage it had suffered. FRUMEL also provided comment on intercept to underline the fact that the *Shoho* had not been intercepted sending traffic and that her captain was now having his messages routed via *Iro*, a fleet oiler. This intelligence indicated to the traffic analysts and cryptanalysts that *Shoho* had been sunk. They had derived this assessment from the previous habit of the Japanese, first seen during the Battle of the Java Sea, to continue sending official messages to the captains of sunken warships using the original ship's call sign but routed to the ship the surviving captain was now on.[36]

FRUMEL was also able to report that 22 of *Shoho*'s aircraft had crash-landed, and that *Shokaku* had been hit by three torpedoes and eight bombs, and was listing and restricted in speed to alternating between 12 and 16 knots.[37]

Records show that the combined US and Australian cryptanalytical organisation in Melbourne was contributing its fair share to the intelligence picture of the IJN. It is hard to say how much use the US commanders made of this intelligence, but the fact is they had it at their fingertips.

Despite the indecisive nature of the Battle of the Coral Sea, it provided the Allied SIGINT system with a vast amount of operational traffic that was available for considered analysis and assessment once the battle was over. This provided deep insights into the IJN's procedures and cryptographic systems, as individual operators, working under the stress of combat, made numerous errors that provided cribs. This follow-up analysis led to the recovery of many code values in the five-digit code and provided a vast trove of information for the traffic analysts at FRUPAC, FRUMEL, FECB, OP-20-G and GC&CS. The battle may not have resulted in a decisive victory for the US Navy, but it blew open the IJN's communications.[38]

In the lead-up to and during the Battle of the Coral Sea FRUMEL, FRUPAC and FECB were collecting and reading IJN traffic on another, larger, operation that the IJN intended to launch against US forces in the Pacific. The designator for this target was AF in the Western Pacific. A number of the intercept and cryptanalytical units working the Japanese problem formed the view

Steam yacht *Franklin*, used by RAN for SIGINT high-frequency propagation research and intercept operations against the Imperial Japanese Navy (IJN) in Mandated Territories, 1927.
Royal Australian Navy

HIJMS *Asama* under tow, Port Melbourne, 1932. This vessel conducted propagation trials in Australian waters during which Lieutenant W.E. McLaughlin stole the radio frequencies and schedules. State Library of Victoria (SLV)

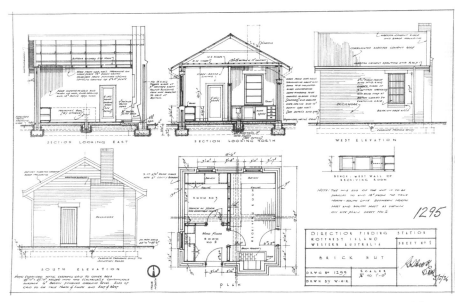

Plan for the HFDF station intended for Rottnest Island in 1936 but later built at Jandakot in Perth. Two further stations were built, one at Darwin and one at Canberra, as part of Australia's belated response to the proposals agreed at the 1921 Penang Conference. NAA

Security poster warning service personnel about loose talk. It would have been more accurate had it portrayed the Director General of the ABC or an Australian newspaper proprietor as the puppet master. SLV

Harry Freame around 1920, when he was a Japanese language teacher working for Professor Murdoch in Sydney. Goodyear Family Collection, courtesy of Sheila Spence

Freame and his daughter Grace on Anzac Day, 1937. This was the Harry Freame sent to Tokyo in October 1940. Goodyear Family Collection, courtesy of Sheila Spence

The lions waiting for Freame in Tokyo: Japanese Military Police (Kempeitai). The Kempeitai would prove a formidable foe of Australian intelligence and special forces personnel.

The headquarters of Fleet Radio Unit, Melbourne (FRUMEL), Monterey, Melbourne, c. 1943. NAA

A photograph of Women's Royal Australian Naval Service (WRANS) personnel outside Monterey. The faces at the windows indicate the excitement of this unique occasion. NAA

FRUMEL's Teleprinter Room showing the highly sophisticated (for the time) electronic, tabulating and card index files used in code breaking in the 1940s. NAA

FRUMEL's Radio Control Room showing wireless telegraphists encrypting signals using punched tape devices and readers. NAA

FRUMEL's Coding Room. WRANS were employed to do the bulk of this type of work. NAA

Victoria Barracks, Melbourne, home of the Special Intelligence Bureau headed by Professor T.G. Room, and also Land HQ and Military Intelligence Branch. NAA

Australia's first line of defence in January 1940. Tom Weeks, radio operator on Thursday Island, dressed to kill in his uniform, First World War webbing equipment and two-tone shoes. NAA

A photograph of Patrol Officer Eric Feldt exploring the Sepik River in 1924. Feldt's experience of the geography, climate and the peoples of the islands was an important factor in the success of the RAN Coastwatch organisation. NAA

A three-part tele-radio, similar to that carried by coastwatchers while eluding their Japanese pursuers. Note the bulky batteries on the back of the rack. NAA

A tele-radio antenna array of the type carried by coastwatchers in New Guinea and the Solomon Islands. NAA

AWA radio station, Rabaul, in 1937, with a worker sweeping volcanic ash off the roof—demonstrating the difficulties of radio communication in the tropics, where thunderstorms were just one cause of bad atmospherics. NAA

German raider photographed on 27 December 1940 by Petty Officer H.J. Barnes, RANR, radio operator on Nauru and clandestine SIGINT operator. He faced capture if the Germans landed, something the Admiralty had warned Australia about. NAA

that AF was most likely Midway Island. Others, particularly OP-20-G in Washington, believed AF was the Aleutian Islands.[39] Others thought it could be Port Moresby and some thought it designated a target for a revenge raid on Hawaii or, even more implausibly, a target on the west coast of the continental United States.[40] At FRUPAC, the analysts continued to believe that the IJN was planning to attack and seize Midway Island.

It was at this point that FRUMEL helped clear up some of the confusion and thus played a role in saving Midway Island.[41] FRUMEL had already provided SIGINT showing that Yamamoto had postponed the attack of Port Moresby until the outcome of another operation had been decided. FRUMEL and other SIGINT sites were also intercepting Japanese traffic that indicated the Japanese were now considering a rapid land assault across the Owen Stanley Range against Port Moresby as the most suitable strategy at this time.[42] With a naval assault on Port Moresby moving out of consideration, this left Midway, Hawaii, the Aleutians and the west coast of the continental United States as the potential objectives.

The main evidence that Midway was the target was the continued use of the place designator AF in IJN traffic. Three messages dated 18 May referred to AF as the target. The first message stated that an IJN unit intended to be 'fifty miles NW of AF' on the day of the attack.[43] The second originated from the Chiba Air Group requesting ammunition for AF to be sent via Imieji.[44] The third message, from Combined Fleet, clearly mentioned Midway as a destination for five torpedo craft taken from Jaluit and Wake aboard an unidentified vessel.[45] All of these messages were obtained and broken out two weeks ahead of the attack on Midway.

On 18 May, FRUMEL was reporting that the 5th Carrier Division—*Shokaku* and *Zuikaku*—were getting replacement aircraft, including four fighters, fifteen bombers and ten torpedo planes in preparation for the campaign.[46] On 21 May, FRUMEL intercepted a message from Naval Intelligence in Tokyo to Yamamoto, reporting that 'AF informed Pearl Harbor that they had only enough water for 2 weeks and asked for immediate resupply'.[47] The Americans at FRUPAC were waiting for this message, which they had generated in the hope the Japanese would report it alongside the designator AF. FRUPAC had called the garrison on Midway using the secure telephone cable and asked them to radio in clear for a water resupply. The IJN swallowed it hook, line and sinker.

The following day, FRUMEL added to the growing picture by intercepting and reporting information that Yamamoto wanted the aircraft transport ship *Hishin Maru* to load twelve or more carrier bombers for the forthcoming campaign, indicating that it might be starting before *Zuikaku* had completed her refit. On 23 May, FRUMEL reported the IJN had changed its geographic designators for phase one of the intended operation, and in so doing avoided the designators YU, FU, MA and MI.[48] They probably thought MI was too obvious and retained AF as the designator for Midway.

By 24 May, 14th Air Group orders to move to Midway Island following its capture were reported by FRUMEL, as were orders to the 2nd Combined Landing Party and 7th Cruiser Division to concentrate at Saipan with 2nd Destroyer Division, one carrier division, and the 6th and 7th Air Squadrons, plus additional 4th Fleet units that were now joining the escorting force.[49]

The volume of intelligence traffic originated by Jaluit was also noted by FRUMEL as was the fact that, on 25 May, the call signs for the C-in-C, Combined Fleet, and the Commander 2nd Fleet were added to the action address list of Jaluit's messages, indicating these commanders were now present within Jaluit's area of responsibility.[50] This was traffic analysis at its best.

On 27 May, FRUMEL reported the IJN attack force would arrive off Midway at 1900 hours on 6 June. This information came from a message sent from Saipan informing Yamamoto of the schedules of the 4th, 1st and 11th Air Fleets. Now the Americans had the place, date and time of the IJN's attack. All they needed was the composition of the attacking force, and this arrived on 29 May, when FRUMEL intercepted and reported that the C-in-C, 2nd Fleet, was at sea in the Truk communications zone and that the Midway invasion force consisting of 1st Carrier Division, *Kaga* and *Akagi*; 2nd Carrier Division, *Soryu* and *Hiryu*; 7th Cruiser Division, *Kumano*, *Suzuya*, *Mikuma* and *Mogami*; 18th Cruiser Division, *Tenryu* and *Tatsuta*; three or four battleships; 2nd Destroyer Division; part of 4th Destroyer Squadron; 6th Destroyer Division and associated transports; and 3rd Submarine Squadron were underway.[51] All of these vessels had put to sea and then gone silent, while a large volume of traffic was being broadcast from shore stations to them, clearly showing they were maintaining radio silence. This silence was noted by FRUMEL on 2 June as the 'calm before the storm'.[52]

The storm broke on 3 June, with each side's aircraft finding the other and launching preliminary air attacks. The battle started in earnest on 4 June and raged until 6 June, with the IJN losing the carriers *Akagi, Kaga, Hiryu* and *Soryu*, as well as the heavy cruiser *Mikuma*. FRUMEL's record of the battle mentions these losses and notes the exceptionally heavy volume of operational traffic using secret call signs in the Midway and Aleutian areas. FRUMEL also noted that Admiral Yamamoto was not at Midway, but located on board a ship near Jaluit, from which he was overseeing the Midway battle. On 7 June, FRUMEL suggested that the carrier *Akagi* had been sunk because messages to the 1st Air Fleet's commander were being passed to another vessel's call sign, indicating he was on board that vessel and not on *Akagi*. FRUMEL also reported that the carrier *Ryujo* might have joined the Midway force.[53]

By 8 June, FRUMEL had DF fixes on *Nagara* and 1st Air Fleet; C-in-C, 2nd Fleet; C-in-C, Combined Fleet; Commander 7th Cruiser Division; the tanker *Genyo Maru*, and five submarines. It was able to say, 'The Midway Occupation Force appears to be retiring to Saipan,' and it was. The losses suffered by the IJN were quickly detected by SIGINT. By 18 June, FRUMEL was emphasising the fact that none of the carriers of the 1st and 2nd carrier divisions had been intercepted since the battle, and that the Chief of Staff, 1st Air Fleet, was now communicating with 3rd and 5th Carrier Divisions. As the FRUMEL report puts it, this 'accentuates the fact that none of the vessels of the 1st and 2nd Carrier divisions have been heard on net' because they are gone.[54]

Administrative traffic from personnel offices to the commanding officers of *Akagi, Kaga, Soryu* and *Hiryu* confirmed their loss on 2 July. All of this was confirmed in message 566 from Commander, First Air Fleet, on 6 June that was eventually broken out and read on 28 September 1942.

Midway was the deathblow for all the IJN's ambitions. It killed the romantic military idea that a large decisive battle could win a war against a major power, and it destroyed any hope of delaying the expected US counter-offensives. After Midway, Japan was on the defensive and war, real war, total war was coming to the Japanese Home Islands.

On 14 June, Yamamoto Isoroku, the C-in-C, Combined Fleet, signalled all IJN units and personnel that the carriers *Kaga* and *Soryu* and the cruiser *Mikuma* had been badly damaged. Fittingly, the epitaph for Combined Fleet was written by a cryptanalyst at FRUMEL:[55] 'C-in-C, Combined Fleet is apparently feeding false information to his own subordinates, presumably for purposes of morale and propaganda.'[56]

With the defeat of the IJN at Midway, the defensive phase of the naval war in the Pacific and Indian oceans was now over and the offensive phase began in earnest. Within two months of Midway, the US Navy forced the pace of the war in the Pacific by launching Operation WATCHTOWER, the US Navy invasion of Tulagi, Gavutu-Tanambogo and Guadalcanal.

Guadalcanal would see the integration of HUMINT from FERDINAND, SIGINT from FRUMEL and FRUPAC, and imagery from aerial photo-reconnaissance missions pioneered by Vice Admiral Robert L. Ghormley of the US Navy. Ghormley, having seen how the British were using aerial recon-naissance in their operations against German-occupied Europe,[57] believed that the integration of aerial reconnaissance with SIGINT provided a more comprehensive picture, and he was right.

On the Japanese side, the intelligence picture being built was good. On 5 August, the Special Duty Group (Radio Intelligence) (SPD) at Imperial HQ in Tokyo issued a warning to the IJA's 8th Fleet that there was a marked increase in enemy communications in the South Seas Area. The Japanese were using DF and traffic analysis to produce this intelligence and, to be frank, it was good tactical intelligence. Fortunately for the Allies, the operations staff of 8th Fleet chose to ignore the possibility of an attack on Guadalcanal or any of the islands, preferring to assign the increase to the overland advance on Port Moresby.[58] A further piece of luck occurred on 6 August, when Imperial HQ ignored a report from the garrison on Guadalcanal that all of the indigenous workers on the airfield had fled into the jungle on the evening of 5 August. The disappearance of the locals from the airfield was most likely prompted by Lieutenant F.A. Rhodes's party passing warnings to the locals working on the airfield.[59]

All of this intelligence was relayed to Vice Admiral Mikawa Gunichi's 8th Fleet Command at Rabaul. Mikawa discounted the threat of a US attack on Guadalcanal, and in the early morning of 7 August, Admiral Richmond Kelly Turner began an unopposed landing there of 13,500 marines of General Alexander Vandegrift's 1st Marine Division.

Admiral Turner was not unopposed for long. Mikawa responded aggres-sively and obtained permission from Yamamoto to take the heavy cruiser, HIJMS *Chokai*; four other heavy cruisers of Admiral Goto Aritomo's Cruiser

Division 6; two light cruisers of Division 18; and a single destroyer HIJMS *Yunagi*, south to Savo Island.[60]

The presence of this IJN fleet around Rabaul was known to FRUMEL, FRUPAC, OP-20-G and naval intelligence, and it had been repeatedly reported to US naval commanders. When the IJN changed its code settings on 1 June from JN25B to JN25C, this did not stop the reading of the messages, but it delayed them significantly. This meant that although FRUMEL and FRUPAC eventually broke out Mikawa's concept of operations for Guadalcanal, it took until 23 August, three weeks after the Battle of Savo Island, to report the findings.[61]

Mikawa attacked the Allied warships in the south and, through a mix of superb torpedo technology and superior watch-keeping and night-fighting capabilities, his squadron burst upon the Allies and fatally damaged the cruiser HMAS *Canberra* in the first few minutes. They then took the bow off the USS *Chicago*. The Japanese turned north and sank the US cruisers *Astoria*, *Vincennes* and *Quincy*.[62] The US Navy was lucky that Mikawa's aggressive streak stopped at sinking warships. If he had continued and engaged the undefended US transports lying off Guadalcanal, he would have inflicted a major strategic defeat on the US Navy. Those amphibious landing ships and transports were the only such vessels then available in the Pacific, and their loss would have slowed the US operations considerably.[63]

The Allied defeat at Savo Island should not have happened. The US Task Force under Admiral Turner had ample information from 14th Naval District's Combat Intelligence Unit on the IJN elements in the waters around Rabaul. He and his officers, including Captain Howard Bode of USS *Chicago*, the former head of foreign intelligence at the Office of Naval Intelligence (ONI), were well aware that the Japanese knew the location of the US and Australian vessels because they had been attacking them from the air. On top of this, a reconnaissance report, supposedly from an RAAF aircraft shadowing Mikawa's task force, was received in the US Task Force one hour before Mikawa's attack was launched.[64]

It is at this point in our story that we can dispense with the excuse that Turner was let down by SIGINT. Turner and his command were receiving SIGINT support from FRUMEL and FRUPAC, and we know that SIGINT from FRUMEL indicated a force of eight IJN warships had been detected at 1125 hours on 8 August, 50 miles (80 kilometres) north of the Bougainville

Strait and steering 120 degrees at 15 knots.[65] The official Admiralty report on the Battle of Savo Island attributes the sighting and identification of this force to an RAAF aircraft, but there is no record of an RAAF squadron operating anywhere in the area at the time of the sighting, and the weather was so bad that Rear Admiral John S. McCain's air patrols could not take off, a fact of which Admiral Turner seems to have been unaware.[66] It is likely that the Admiralty was working off a sanitised report that used an RAAF overflight and sighting as plausible cover to disguise the true source, which was probably SIGINT.[67]

Admiral Turner appears to have been adequately warned by FRUMEL and FRUPAC that an IJN Task Force of eight warships was heading his way, and that they appeared intent on engaging his force. Turner also missed the significance of the two IJN aerial reconnaissance missions flown over his task force that evening. Even if he was untrusting of the SIGINT, reconnaissance overflights should have alerted him that his command was being targeted for attack. The idea that a change of codes prevented SIGINT from providing sufficient warning is wrong. SIGINT is not just cryptanalysis, it is also DF, TA and the other technical elements, and all of these were available and being reported to Admiral Turner. The hard truth is he was caught unprepared because he did not take the intelligence picture seriously.[68]

The next phase of operations around Guadalcanal was well covered by SIGINT coming out of FRUMEL, FRUPAC, FECB, India and OP-20-G in Washington. Once again, attempting to force a main fleet action, the IJN assembled another force based on Admiral Goto's Cruiser Division 6 and Admiral Nagumo's carrier *Shokaku*. This force was to sail south and engage the US Navy in yet another encounter battle. This time, SIGINT kept the US commanders informed, or they decided not to ignore it, and by 22 August, Admiral Ghormley and the other US commanders knew there was another fleet action brewing.[69]

To meet this threat the US Navy assembled a task force comprising the carriers *Enterprise* and *Saratoga*; one battleship, *North Carolina*; four cruisers, *Portland*, *New Orleans*, *Minneapolis* and HMAS *Australia*; and eleven destroyers, supported by 101 land-based aircraft. The Allied task force faced an IJN force comprising the fleet carriers *Shokaku* and *Zuikaku*; the light carrier *Ryujo*; the seaplane carrier *Chitose*; the battleships *Hiyei* and *Kirishima*; nine heavy cruisers, *Suzuya*, *Kumano*, *Chikuma*, *Tone*, *Ataga*, *Maya*, *Takao*,

Myoko and *Haguro*; 27 destroyers and five transports, supported by 100 land-based aircraft.[70]

The US Navy commanders understood good SIGINT was essential in these encounter battles, and a four-man mobile SIGINT detachment commanded by Lieutenant Gilvin Slonim was on board the USS *Enterprise* to provide tactical SIGINT directly to Admiral Thomas Kinkaid.[71] Another team was on *Saratoga* providing tactical SIGINT to its commander and air commander. In this encounter, the carrier *Ryujo* was so severely damaged that it later sank, and the Japanese troop convoy coming down the slot off Guadalcanal's west coast was subjected to heavy air attack, resulting in the loss of the reinforcing troops and their equipment. More significantly, the IJN lost another 90 aircraft along with their aircrew.[72]

The IJN was not defeated yet, though. As September arrived and operations continued, IJN submarines began inflicting losses. They severely damaged the carrier *Saratoga* and sank the carrier *Wasp* on 15 September, and seriously damaged USS *North Carolina* and sank the destroyer USS *O'Brien*.[73] The IJN efforts to defeat the US invasion of Guadalcanal continued with a remarkable ferocity culminating in the Battle of Tassafaronga between 30 November and 1 December 1942. During the Guadalcanal campaign, the IJN lost two battleships, *Hiyei* and *Kirishima*, and the light aircraft carrier *Ryujo*; and the fleet carriers *Zuiko* and *Shokaku* and the seaplane carrier *Chitose* were damaged. Other losses included five cruisers sunk and eight damaged, and thirteen destroyers sunk and 39 damaged.[74]

FRUMEL, with its Australian contingent now firmly led by the communicator Commander Newman, continued its work supporting the US Navy in the Pacific. Its relevance was slowly diminishing, however, as the US Navy's island-hopping campaign pushed closer to the Japanese Home Islands. Eventually, the US Navy began removing US personnel and equipment from FRUMEL so that by January 1945, 90 per cent of FRUMEL's SIGINT function was gone. Unfortunately, the tenor of the poor relationship between FRUMEL and Central Bureau transferred to Commander Newman's residual RAN SIGINT operation, which Lieutenant Colonel Alastair Sandford was more than happy to describe as 'a sort of glorified communications channel'.[75] Newman's organisation now had no friends in Australia, and despite the contribution its Australian personnel had made to Allied victories in the Pacific, they were completely sidelined by Central Bureau.

Central Bureau had not adopted FRUMEL's closed approach to SIGINT, but had developed itself along British lines, which emphasised cooperation. The result was that when Rudy Fabian and the US Navy organisation left FRUMEL, Commander Newman was left friendless. Everything he now did was subject to criticism.[76] The animus was so significant that Alastair Sandford, who was not known for narrowness or bitterness, wanted Newman and the remnants of FRUMEL cut out of all SIGINT, and the last Australian cryptanalyst at FRUMEL, Lieutenant Colonel Treweek, removed and posted to Central Bureau.[77] He got both. FRUMEL was now completely isolated from Australia's 'Y' service and, thus, from Britain's. The ACNB had backed the wrong horse.

For Australia, FRUMEL provided a wake-up call. In 1941, Britain may have failed to live up to the expectations created in Australia, but she never let Australia down. Despite the attitude of the Curtin government and despite the failings of the Australian government in protecting the secrets of her allies, the British argued with the United States on behalf of Australia in many of the lower-level policy arenas, particularly SIGINT. FRUMEL provided a stark lesson for Australia as to how a real international relationship worked. The United States did not regard Australia as a member of an extended family. It was, as the ACNB found out, just another player at the card table, and it had better ante up or lose its seat at the table.

CHAPTER 18

Establishing Central Bureau, 1942

On 3 March 1942, Colonel C.G. Roberts, the Australian DMI, raised with Major General Sydney Rowell, the Deputy CGS, the need for the army to have its own SIGINT unit.[1] The issue the army faced was that while the ACNB and RAN were operating a 'Y' organisation, it was focused on Japanese naval and diplomatic traffic and not on Japanese military traffic, that is IJA ground-to-ground and air-to-ground communications. The only SIGINT entity that the Australian Army had been able to raise was the special intelligence section that had just been transplanted from Sydney to Melbourne, and this was dedicated to Japanese diplomatic and international commercial traffic. The army had no dedicated SIGINT capability for gaining intelligence about Japanese ground forces and their activities. The solution was the arrival in Australia of No. 4 Special Wireless Telegraphy Section (SWS), an AIF SIGINT intercept unit trained by the British in the Middle East and now returned as part of the AIF withdrawal home.

No. 4 SWS was quickly renamed No. 4 Australian Special Wireless Section (ASWS), to designate its national allegiance and it arrived at Adelaide on 15 March 1942 looking to provide the Australian Army with its first experienced intercept and analytical organisation capable of supporting operations in the field.[2] It joined an Australian SIGINT system that included the newly formed Special Intelligence Bureau, Commander Newman's RAN communications unit and the small RAAF intercept section at Darwin.[3] The refugees coming in from CAST, FECB and the NEI were supplementing these small units. No. 4 ASWS were not refugees, but they were unskilled in dealing with Japanese Morse, KANA, and IJA ciphers and systems.[4] They were accustomed to German and Italian targets.

As the Japanese rushed into the islands adjacent to Australia and chased down the Allied navies that had survived the initial onslaught, it was well understood by the military authorities that a large-scale SIGINT organisation was required. By 23 April, Australia had obtained two three-figure IJA codebooks captured by US forces in the Philippines and brought to Australia by CAST. Captain Alastair (Mic) Sandford offered copies to the Indian Army in New Delhi.[5] The Australian SIGINT operation was underway.

The returning ASWS units were highly experienced in intercept operations and traffic analysis, but not in higher-level cryptanalysis. The basis for this capability was to be the newly formed Special Intelligence Bureau led by Professor Trendall but currently operating under ACNB auspices. This meant that Australia had no capacity for research and investigation of the ciphered or coded messages that would constitute the bulk of IJA intercept.

The answer was for the US and Australian armies to combine their resources in a single SIGINT organisation answerable to the US Army's General Headquarters (GHQ) in the newly created SWPA assigned to General Douglas MacArthur.[6] The personnel for this would come from the Australian and US armies, the RAAF and, it was hoped, from the RAN. According to the DMI, Colonel C.G. Roberts, the new 'Y' organisation would work with the intelligence personnel of the special 'Type B' W/T sections.[7] These intelligence personnel would be 'directed and advised from the Central Bureau, which will also co-ordinate their work and keep them up to date with latest developments and discoveries'.[8]

The Deputy CGS, Major General Sydney Rowell, approved the recommendations on 3 April 1942. Central Bureau had been created.[9]

Central Bureau would become Australia's leading 'Y' or SIGINT organisation, without enjoying the successes of FRUMEL. There would be no Indian Ocean raids, no major fleet actions like Coral Sea or Midway for Central Bureau; there would be no shoot-downs of the enemy's supreme commander.

Instead, there would be a long, demanding grind to produce intelligence on an industrial scale as only SIGINT can do. Central Bureau took up this challenge and became Australia's first intelligence factory.

Central Bureau was born of necessity and from the training and experience provided to the AIF from working within the British system, which was not as riven by the inter-service and interpersonal rivalries that afflicted US intelligence. Geoffrey Ballard, in his history of the Special Wireless Sections, argues that it was the training provided by the experienced British organisation in the Middle East that enabled No. 4 ASWS, the first Australian Army operational SIGINT unit, to perform its duties so effectively in Greece and Crete.[10] This ensured that Jack W. Ryan and Alastair W. Sandford, men who were to become prominent in SIGINT back in Australia, had an excellent appreciation of the value of cooperation in SIGINT operations.

The contribution that these men made to Australia's SIGINT efforts has been overshadowed by the attention paid to the work of the cryptanalysts in popular films such as *The Imitation Game* and in books like Craig Collie's *Code Breakers*. Without the work and organisational skills of people like Ryan and Sandford, the cryptanalysts would not have achieved as much as they eventually did. Cryptanalysts rely on traffic analysts and they both rely on excellent intercept operators and good communication links. All of this required organising.

On 15 January 1942, the men and officers of 4 ASWS in the Middle East received their notice to move and, on 19 January, they departed Souq-el-Gharb for Australia via Kilo 89, the large Australian camp near Gaza. Here Mic Sandford re-joined the Section from detached service with the British SIGINT organisation in the Western Desert. This experience seems to have been significant enough for Ballard to report that Sandford was keen to introduce the lessons he had learned into 4 ASWS's operations.[11]

As 4 ASWS travelled back to Australia, the future organisation, Central Bureau did not exist. Certainly, the Special Intelligence Bureau was up and running, but this was a home-grown organisation lacking the experience that 4 ASWS had gained working closely with the British. Planning of the new organisation did not take place in Australia, but aboard the SS *Orcades* on the leg from Colombo to Adelaide. The instigation of planning after Colombo suggests that the ASWS officers, captains Ryan, Henry and Sandford, had spoken with the FECB's element in Colombo.

According to Ballard, Jack Ryan asked Brigadier C.H. Simpson, the 1 Corps Chief Signals Officer, and Lieutenant Colonel K.A. Wills, the Deputy DMI, 1 Corps, to define the role of the ASWS when it arrived in Australia. Simpson and Wills advised that the SIGINT organisation in Australia should be greatly expanded. A planning group comprising Ryan, Henry and Sandford began work and designed Australia's SIGINT organisation 'somewhere at sea'.[12]

By the middle of March 1942, No. 4 ASWS had expanded to 70 personnel based at Park Orchards in Melbourne, alongside the Special Intelligence Bureau's intercept component led by Lieutenant J. Jennings. Jennings' unit was tasked with the intercept of Japanese diplomatic traffic for decrypting by Eric Nave and the Bureau, which was housed in the attic of Victoria Barracks in Melbourne. The Bureau had already made an impact by supplying the Australian authorities with the message of 4 December 1941 that instructed the Japanese Consul-General to immediately destroy his codes and ciphers.[13]

In addition to these assets, as we saw in the previous chapter, the parties from the US Navy's station CAST had begun arriving from the Philippines and establishing their own cryptanalytical organisation. There were also British from FECB in Singapore and Dutch refugees from the NEI SIGINT organisation Kamer 14 (Room 14) in Bandung.[14]

The remaining SIGINT capabilities were the RAN SIGINT organisation operating under Commander Nave and Commander Newman, which would become FRUMEL with the arrival of CAST, and a small RAAF intercept site operating in Darwin under the command of Flight Lieutenant H.R. Booth, who had worked at FECB at Singapore.[15] It was a small beginning, but it was one built on the foundations provided by the proven British and US SIGINT systems.

On 3 March, the DMI, Colonel C.G. Roberts, recommended the formation of a central 'Y' staff of cryptographers and linguists to undertake long-term research and investigation of codes and ciphers.[16] This entity would be located close to the new GHQ, SWPA. This was the first time the name Central Bureau was applied to a SIGINT organisation in Australia. This organisation would begin with fourteen personnel: six officers and eight other ranks from the Intelligence Corps.[17] In its support, a new Type B Special Wireless Section with an Intelligence Corps section of two officers and twenty other ranks would be created to work in forward areas under the control of the Central Bureau.[18]

The organisation envisaged would serve the needs of GHQ, SWPA but remain outside its command structure. This was an important distinction, as it was intended as a mechanism to preserve Australian control of Central Bureau activity if faced with US demands for it to be subordinated to MacArthur or the US Army. It would turn out to be a very prescient act. It was not until January 1943 that Central Bureau was formally placed under the direct command of GHQ, SWPA.[19]

This did not mean that the SIGINT needs of GHQ, SWPA and its subordinate formations were ignored. These would be met by providing subsections for attachment to formations as required. These subsections would consist of US Army Radio Intercept Detachments, RAAF Wireless Intercept Sections and 'Type B' Special Wireless Sections, of which No. 4 ASWS was one.[20]

The CGS, Major General Rowell, signed off on the proposal on 3 April 1942, and two days later No. 4 ASWS was transferred from 1 Australian Corps and combined with Lieutenant J. Jennings' diplomatic and commercial section to form No. 5 ASWS, the nucleus for Central Bureau's training and field intercept organisation.

The reality of the new relationship with the US Army now came into play, and Brigadier General Spencer B. Akin, MacArthur's Chief Signal Officer, took command of Central Bureau. His immediate subordinate was Colonel J.R. Sherr, US Army, as Director, with Captain Alastair Sandford appointed as the Australian Deputy and, very importantly, as the Secretary of the 'Y' Committee in Australia. This latter position provided Sandford with a great deal of organisational power, as it moved him outside the direct control of his US Army superiors and gave him a direct link to the 'Y' Committee in London and LHQ in Melbourne, while also giving him control of the meetings and all of the correspondence. In time, Sandford would go on to fill the role of Deputy Director, Central Bureau, and become the functional head of Central Bureau and the Australian officer responsible for Australia's SIGINT system and its relationship with both the United Kingdom and the United States.[21]

The way the coordination of 'Y' intelligence in Australia was arranged ensured that Australia would be able to resist very determined US efforts to prevent it pursuing its own SIGINT operations in its national interests. The Australians very quickly realised that although the British had restricted their activities to operating within the agreed 'Y' system, the US attitude was that Australia should be totally excluded. The decisions that saved Australia's national SIGINT effort were those made at this time. Australia had a direct line to London, and Australia's interests in Japanese SIGINT coincided with Britain's interests in preventing the US Navy and, later on, the US Army from excluding Britain from Japanese SIGINT collection and from playing any role in the defeat of Japan.

In early 1942 it was agreed that Central Bureau would be a combined US, Australian and British unit in Melbourne, close to GHQ, SWPA and the other service commands. Central Bureau personnel would all operate 'under the same roof if possible', and they would maintain the closest relationship with the naval cryptographic bureau.[22] Manning and financing for the organisation would be shared, with the United States providing 50 per cent of the manpower and finance, and the Australian Army and RAAF 25 per cent each.[23]

The Central Bureau would deal with 'all intercepted traffic, which cannot be interpreted by field sections' and deal with captured codes and similar material and 'to make available to all concerned the result of such work and other research'.[24] It would also cooperate closely with Washington, London, India and all other 'Y' research centres, and coordinate tasking, training and responsibilities with the services. From its very beginnings, Central Bureau was a cooperative venture involving Australia, Britain, Canada and the United States and all of the armed services of those nations that needed to be involved. The existing naval organisation, soon to become FRUMEL, was completely opposed to this openness.

The insular nature of FRUMEL ensured that as time progressed, it would become a minor player in the worldwide SIGINT system. By the end of 1943, the situation had become so bad that Sandford was writing to Edward Travis, the Deputy Head of GC&CS, about the behaviour of FRUMEL and its personnel. Sandford's complaint was FRUMEL's complete rejection of any level of cooperation. In evidence of this, he described how Major Treweek had been lent for duty at Central Bureau for a fortnight and during that time had refused to divulge any details of his work at FRUMEL. Sandford's rhetorical question to Travis was 'This is unutterably stupid, is it not?'[25]

Sandford's frustration is understandable. The complaint he had about Treweek's behaviour pales in comparison to the operational impact of the US Navy's approach to SIGINT exchanges vital to the conduct of operations. Figure 18.1 clearly shows how the US Navy kept FRUMEL and FRUPAC

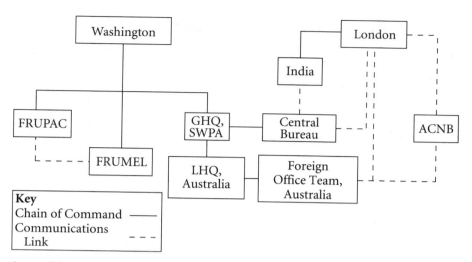

Source: 'Y' Board general notes on SIGINT and W/T intelligence in Australia and New Zealand, National Archives, UK, HW 55/93

Figure 18.1: Signals intelligence in the South West Pacific Area, 1942

isolated from the US Army, Australia and MacArthur. FRUMEL remained an exclusively US Navy organisation controlled directly by OP-20-G. All exchanges of information had to be processed by Washington when Admiral Redman and his brother, Captain John R. Redman, continued the internecine SIGINT warfare between the US Navy and the US Army. The system they operated meant that vital tactical intelligence passed between GHQ, SWPA and the US Navy in the Pacific had to pass across the desks in OP-20-G in Washington. This meant that SIGINT obtained by Central Bureau relating to the situation on Guadalcanal had to be passed to Noumea and then to Pearl Harbor, from which it was passed to OP-20-G or the ONI in Washington. From the ONI it was then passed back along the same circuits to the relevant US Navy commanders on Guadalcanal.

Intelligence passing the other way was passed up the line as already described, then across to the Department of the Army and down to GHQ, SWPA. If the material was being sent to Australia, it was sent to the Australian liaison officer in Washington and then, via the External Affairs circuits, to the army in Melbourne, and from there to the relevant commander or unit.[26]

All of this duplication and delay was required so that Admiral Ernest King and his minions in OP-20-G could ensure that the US Navy did not surrender any influence or authority to the US Army, Britain or Australia. It is a sublime example of the way institutional politics can overwhelm rational practice.

Central Bureau was different. The ethos of the organisation remained inclusive and cooperative, and this enabled personnel from the US Army ground and air elements to work in harmony with one another and with the personnel of the Australian Army and RAAF, as well as with the British, Canadian and New Zealand elements. A great deal of the credit for this harmony has to go to Alastair Sandford and men like Abraham Sinkov, Robert Cahill and Ralph E. Cook, who would later go on to great careers as senior officers of the NSA.

The first meeting of the new Australian 'Y' Committee was held on 7 April 1942 at Victoria Barracks. It established a training subcommittee for intercept operators under Commander Newman, with Flight Lieutenant W.C. Blakeley, RAAF, and Captain Jack Ryan assisting. A technical subcommittee, comprising Commander Newman, Squadron Leader John Hall, RAAF, Ryan and

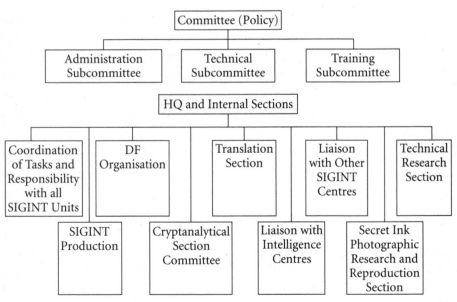

Note: This is the functional diagram prepared for the committee by Captain Sandford in 1942. By this time, Central Bureau had become a substantial organisation.

Source: A6923, SIZ, NAA, BC 302 3504

Figure 18.2: Organisation of Central Bureau

Lieutenant D.G. Egan, US Army, was also established, and charged with overseeing the purchase and development of equipment.

The other matter the committee had to deal with was finding suitable accommodation for Central Bureau. This was not as easy as it sounded, as it had to be within 3 miles (5 kilometres) of Victoria Barracks on St Kilda Road, and close to GHQ, FRUMEL and the chiefs of staff of the three services. This was a big ask, as the area was already heavily populated and there was very little in the way of buildings or facilities left.[27]

On 10 April 1942, the 'Y' Committee held its second meeting. Squadron Leader Hall was appointed Vice Chair, and approval was given for the expenditure of AU£100,000 on purchasing and installing radio and other equipment at Central Bureau.[28] It was also decided that the committee would secure regular air communication between Charters Towers and Melbourne for the transportation of intercept raw material, equipment and personnel to northern Australia.

Local SIGINT units were given direct liaison authority to provide intelligence to the operational formations in their area. This enabled Flight Lieutenant Booth's RAAF SIGINT unit at Townsville to provide urgent tactical intelligence directly to the Townsville Area Fighter Sector HQ.[29] Another decision, an important one, was that all captured documents throughout SWPA were to be passed to Captain Sandford for exploitation. This was the decision that would later lead to the establishment of the American-run and manned Allied Translator and Interpretation Service (ATIS) and its co-location with Central Bureau for the rest of the war.[30]

On 14 April, a Special Intelligence Personnel Section was created for attachment to GHQ, with two officers, of captain or lieutenant rank, and 28 other ranks who would undergo training before being allotted to the Special Wireless/Telegraph Sections Type B being created for service on forward areas.[31] Effectively, the Australian and US authorities were recreating the Middle Eastern theatre's Combined Bureau Middle East (CBME) in Australia. The CBME had been formed at the direction of the British chiefs of staff, with the British Army responsible for its administration but its elements being supplied by army, navy and air force and, with regard to civilian experts, GC&CS. The intention behind the CBME was to ensure commanders had quick access to all SIGINT while ensuring all SIGINT matters, and especially the security of cryptanalytical activity, remained firmly controlled by GC&CS.[32] As an intelligence officer working within the CBME system, Sandford appreciated the difficulties of managing the security arrangements for ULTRA before the establishment of the Special Liaison Units (SLUs), predominantly operated by the RAF, and the Special Communication Units (SCUs) operated by the army.

A lot has been written about ULTRA, its importance to the Allied war effort and the role of various people in creating the breakthroughs in cryptography that enabled Britain to produce ULTRA decrypts. The most important thing about ULTRA was not the mathematical breakthroughs or even the technology that was created to assist in these breakthroughs, but the enormous size and cost of the project and the extent of its ambitions. The investment made in this project was not one that could easily be written off, and neither was the importance of the intelligence it produced. The result was that the security of ULTRA material was a highly sensitive issue and ULTRA was subjected to tight control. ULTRA was, however, simply a codeword used from June 1941 to cover intelligence product derived from high-level German cipher communications sent via ENIGMA. Initially this material was distributed in Britain under the cover BONIFACE, a fictitious SIS agent used to sanitise SIGINT as a source, and, later, under the designator CX.[33] Japanese diplomatic and high-grade cipher traffic was similarly handled under the codewords PURPLE and MAGIC. Because of a number of serious early leaks and compromises, which luckily the Germans ignored, an entire secure communications system was developed for the passing of ULTRA via dedicated SCUs.

The SCUs managed the SIGINT communication system, including the use of hand-operated circuits to carry ULTRA, while the SLU held responsibility for decrypting all ULTRA signals on a link, circulating them within the relevant HQ and supervising the security precautions laid down by the Main Committee, the 'Y' Board, in London.[34] This system allowed a more rapid dissemination of ULTRA, as the respective SLU or SCU, operating within strict guidelines, could modify the security precautions to meet urgent operational demands. They could also conduct the indoctrination of local ULTRA consumers and manage their subsequent access to ULTRA using the need-to-know principle. As we will later see, this was to be an area of great difficulty in Australia and within MacArthur's command.

In May, the 'Y' Committee reconvened and discussed developments. The minutes show that the RAN, RAAF and army were sharing information and

Commander Newman from FRUMEL reported on the deployment of a small naval 'Y' unit to the Townsville area in the near future. Sandford reported that a small army intercept section with three sets and twelve operators was almost ready to send to Darwin. Behind the scenes, though, the relationship between FRUMEL and Central Bureau was deteriorating rapidly, despite the best efforts of the latter, and by July 1942, all contact between FRUMEL and the committee ceased. Some contact was maintained, including the secure direct telephone line between FRUMEL and Central Bureau for passing urgent technical information on IJN air-to-ground links.[35] One example of just how bad it had become, and how quickly, is a letter Commander Newman sent to Captain Sandford in May 1942:

> The following remarks are forwarded with diffidence, but are designed to assist in the provision of maximum reliable intelligence, and to avoid duplication of effort. The remarks and suggestions are based on W/T 'Activity Reports' and other correspondence that has been received from Central Bureau.
>
> The object of Central Bureau's 'Activity Reports' is not clear. The information contained therein ... is incomplete, redundant, and outside the scope of their function ...
>
> To be brutally candid [!], a review of the Central Bureau reports to date reveals <u>no</u> real W/T Intelligence, but shows that effort has been expended on matters which are incidental to Naval 'Y' Intelligence and are not within the province of Central Bureau or within its capabilities which are necessarily limited by shortness of experience.
>
> The advice is given, for what it is worth, that the Central Bureau should concentrate on the original object of that body when inaugurated—viz Radio Intelligence of Japanese Naval and Military air activities (particularly in regard to short-range air attacks); and of the Japanese Army. Any information concerning call identification, methods, movements etc may be original information for this area. Central Bureau is not producing such information.[36]

Newman's memorandum caused a stink, and by 25 July he was writing to apologise for his 'very rude' letter.[37] The cause of the strained relationship between the two organisations was not hard to find. It lay in the animosity that coloured all dealings between the US Navy and the US Army in Washington. The jockeying for resources and status had not stopped when the United States entered the war. In truth, it got somewhat worse, as the US Navy sought to make the Pacific the main US campaign and the US Army followed the strategic lead of President Roosevelt and General George Marshall in making Europe the main campaign.

In Australia, this problematic relationship bedevilled all attempts to bring about a more harmonious relationship. Other examples of the difficulties are shown by small irritations, such as when Vice Admiral Herbert F. Leary, US Navy, Commander of the naval forces in the SWPA, pointedly left Central Bureau off the list of authorities to which FRUMEL could distribute SIGINT.[38]

This forced the Australian 'Y' Committee to ask Sandford to approach Lieutenant Colonel Sherr at GHQ, SWPA to have the decision changed.[39] The relationship was not helped by the attitude of the US Navy in Washington, where all things army, and especially all things MacArthur, were regarded with hostility. To be fair to FRUMEL and its leaders, particularly Lieutenant Rudy Fabian, they worked for Captain Redman, the Director of Naval Communications and OP-20-G. But both the ACNB's willingness to subordinate its SIGINT effort almost entirely to the wishes of the US Navy, and Jack Newman's attack on Central Bureau, helped doom FRUMEL.

Meanwhile, the relationships between the US Army ground and air contingents and the Australian Army and RAAF could not have been better. Alastair Sandford and Hall, Booth and Blakeley of the RAAF made it their business to get on. When the main body of Americans arrived, there was an easy division of labour, with the Australians taking responsibility for traffic analysis and the Americans for the cryptanalytical work.[40]

Braggadocio notwithstanding, it is entirely possible that the effectiveness of the cooperation and close collaboration between the United States, Australian, British, Canadian and New Zealand personnel at Central Bureau paved the way for the UK–US Agreement (UKUSA) and the creation of the postwar five-eyes SIGINT community that still functions so effectively today. This is borne out by a document from the end of the war on postwar SIGINT cooperation entitled 'General Notes on Special and W/T Intelligence in Australia and New Zealand', describing how the United States, Britain, Canada, Australian and New Zealand could cooperate in worldwide SIGINT collection.[41] These notes provide an early framework that seems, from what we know, to have informed the drafting of the UKUSA.

The US Army posted highly experienced officers, including General Akin, Abraham Sinkov and Colonel Sherr to Australia when they could have served effectively in the US Army Signals Intelligence Service based at Arlington Hall, Virginia. This, and the posting of the 837th Detachment to Australia as the US Army component of Central Bureau, demonstrates the willingness of the US Army to invest in Australia's new SIGINT organisation and to supply it with some of the best people available.[42] This contrasts starkly to the closed and uncooperative attitude of the US Navy.

Once established, the main challenge facing Central Bureau in May 1942 was one that Admiralty had tried to get Australia to address in the 1930s. The available DF system was so limited that effective DF of Japanese surface units and especially aircraft was almost impossible. Japanese advances had led to the loss or destruction of many US, UK and NEI DF sites, and this added substantially to the complications created by Australia's pre-war failure to build the required stations. The Australian 'Y' Committee and its subordinated army and RAAF elements were trying hard to rectify the shortfalls, but the work was slow. Understandably, the US Army and US Navy were critical of the delays and the gaps that the lack of DF capability were causing in tactical intelligence.

Even the emergency program to build fixed DF stations in Queensland at Rockhampton, Cloncurry and Mareeba had not moved beyond the planning stage. Despite their best efforts, the problem remained a significant one until DF capabilities were imported from Britain and the US. The 'Y' Committee now moved to create a dedicated DF system controlled by an independent DF organisation.[43]

By the end of May 1942, the DF situation had eased, with eight MFDF sites now operational and mobile low-frequency direction-finding (LFDF) equipment mounted on trucks providing good results. The work on the DF sites at Mareeba, Cloncurry and Rockhampton had been taken over by the Americans, led by Lieutenant Colonel Sherr. It was proceeding quickly because of his orders for the work to continue 24 hours a day, strongly suggesting that the construction had now fallen to US Army units.[44] By 6 July, the Allied Works Council had agreed to provide a further 48 workmen, labourers, cable-jointers and other trades, to further speed up the building and commissioning of the DF stations.[45]

In addition, the US Army Air Force was obtaining ten more LEAR AVIA radio compass combination sets to use as mobile DF units on trucks. Providing both DF coverage of the 150–1500 kilohertz range and coverage of communications in the 1500–6800 kilohertz range, these would be made available for the Special W/T Section, Type B and would be controlled by Central Bureau.

On 3 June, 51 Special W/T Section left Ringwood in Victoria, arriving in Darwin on 11 June.[46] By 2 July, the flow of intercept from 51 Special W/T Section would be described by the 'Y' Committee as 'highly satisfactory' with good inter-service cooperation.[47] The 52 Special W/T Section was reorganised at Ferntree Gully in Melbourne with Lieutenant Litchfield posted in and his recording equipment requested. The unit was to be brought up to operational strength by reinforcement with the remainder of 2 Corps Radio Intelligence Section.[48] Another subunit prepared for deployment was a detachment of 55 Special W/T Section, and it was planned for the rest of 55 ASWS, two officers and 53 men with three lorries, one van and four trucks, to move to Port Moresby after 22 August.[49] The RAAF was also asked to lend 55 ASWS two DF sets, along with four operators, to supplement the existing system in New Guinea.[50]

The need for trained personnel had also led to the recruitment and training of women to serve as intercept operators and support staff at Central Bureau. The RAAF had established the Women's Australian Auxiliary Air Force (WAAAF) at Central Bureau, and the army was organising one B Section of the Australian Women's Army Service (AWAS) as part of the establishment.[51] As Central Bureau grew, it was running out of accommodation in Melbourne. Because of the need to maintain secrecy, however, the 'Y' Committee wanted to sequester all Central Bureau personnel within accommodation isolated from other military personnel.[52] Now they had to contend with separate accommodation for female personnel, which the army found taxing. Despite some officers in Military Intelligence believing that SIGINT personnel of any sex were more likely to disclose SIGINT secrets to their housemates,[53] the issue was fixed by taking a gamble that the female personnel would not discuss their secret work if they were billeted in civilian accommodation. The gamble paid off, and many of the women involved were lodged in rooming houses, with families or together in rented flats and apartments. There were no reported compromises.

The building of the ASWS subunits had resulted in six special wireless sections being created, and this whole organisation was now made the Australian Special Wireless Group (ASWG), based under Major Jack Ryan at Bonegilla in Victoria. By July 1942, 2 Special Intelligence Personnel Section (SIPS) and 5 SIPS had also been raised and trained, after which 3 SIPS and 4 SIPS were to be raised.[54] All of these intelligence sections were to be posted into the existing Army Special W/T Sections.

As Figure 18.3 shows, Central Bureau was destined to become a very large unit, surpassing FRUMEL in size, reach and production. It had also become highly sophisticated as it began producing strategic SIGINT and the Special Intelligence Bureau began to settle down to the work of intercepting and analysing Japanese diplomatic traffic. It also produced the full range of operational and tactical SIGINT. Central Bureau was more than another SIGINT unit; it was, as the NSA's Center for Cryptologic History later described it, 'A Complete Signals Intelligence Agency'.[55]

Central Bureau not only conducted cryptanalysis, traffic analysis and the coordination of DF, it also operated the diplomatic cryptanalytical section under Professor Room, providing linguist, clerical and machine sections,

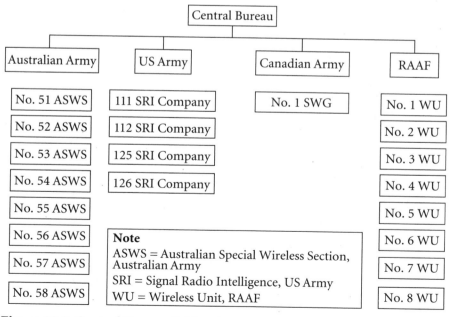

Figure 18.3: Central Bureau field units

communications sections, and financial and managerial sections.[56] By August 1945, FRUMEL was still a small unit of 200–300 personnel while Central Bureau had 4324 personnel posted to it or its subunits.[57]

The size of Central Bureau's workforce was complemented by its budget and equipment holdings, which were much larger than those allocated by the US Navy to FRUMEL. Central Bureau would go on to provide the military commands of the SWPA with the tactical and operational intelligence they needed to defeat the Japanese forces in the Solomons, Papua New Guinea and the Philippines. The contribution was significant and continuous until the end of the war. Central Bureau's contribution to the war was never to be as eye-catching as that made by FRUMEL to the battles of the Java and Coral seas and Midway, and the shooting down of Admiral Yamamoto's plane. But in terms of intercept and intelligence product provided to the Allies in the Pacific, Central Bureau made the greatest contribution, serving not only General MacArthur's command and the needs of the US Navy, but also the strategic requirements of Britain, the United States and other Allied powers, including New Zealand and Nationalist China. It is fitting that Central Bureau provided the foundation for Australia's postwar SIGINT organisation.

CHAPTER 19

Stepping on Toes: Australia's Attack on Japan's Diplomatic Codes

Early in the war, the Australian armed services of their own accord looked at Australia's strategic intelligence capability and realised the country had none. They had then pushed for the creation of an Australian SIGINT capability that would serve Australia's strategic needs by targeting Japanese codes and ciphers, including those of the IJA and IJN and, much more importantly, those of the Japanese Foreign Office and consular service. This decision was supported by the then CGS, Lieutenant General Ernest Squires, who although a British Army officer, as Australia's senior soldier seems to have understood the need for Australia to have its own national capability separate from, but complementary to Britain's. It was for this reason that General Squires had authorised the creation of the Special Intelligence Bureau in Sydney, before he unfortunately died and the whole project fell into a state of abeyance.

With the outbreak of war with Japan at the end of 1941, the organisation started by Squires had only just been authorised and was being brought together. It had moved on from being a part-time arrangement using the academics from the University of Sydney to carry out some cryptanalytical work to one where the bulk of the staff were in Melbourne and working under the control of Eric Nave at Victoria Barracks. The problem that now arose was that they became unwelcome because the US Navy did not want either the academics or the British officers and consular officials involved in the SIGINT work at FRUMEL, and they certainly did not want Australia working on Japanese diplomatic traffic. Washington did not want Australia putting MAGIC at risk, and Britain was equally concerned about the impact on ULTRA. The question that would now need to be answered was how could Australia be safely brought into ULTRA.

British and American sensitivities over ULTRA and MAGIC were substantial, and they were determined to ensure that they were never leaked. ULTRA and MAGIC were strictly limited intelligence only seen by officials and commanders with an absolute need to know. In order to see any ULTRA or MAGIC, the individual had to be indoctrinated—that is, briefed on the sensitivity of the material and the strict need to comply with the security requirements. These included burning ULTRA and MAGIC documents after reading and never immediately acting upon the intelligence they conveyed without having discussed the matter with and gained the approval of the responsible special liaison officer (SLO). Even then, permission to act might be withheld without explanation. Another requirement was never divulging the existence of ULTRA or MAGIC to anyone who was not indoctrinated.

At the beginning of 1942, Australia was not part of this system. It had no Special Liaison Units (SLU) or SLU communications links for carrying ULTRA. There were no SLOs, and no one was indoctrinated, other than certain UK and US officers, which in the latter case did not even include General MacArthur's Intelligence Chief, Brigadier General Charles A. Willoughby.[1] It is also clear that General MacArthur was not provided with all of the ULTRA or MAGIC that the US produced, and that General George Marshall and President Roosevelt kept his access to this material to a minimum.

In Britain, there was substantial concern about Australia compromising ULTRA. If this had happened, it would have been a serious issue for Britain, as Japanese ULTRA was far more important to Britain than may be apparent at first glance. Unlike the Americans, the British understood that neither they nor the US could stop Australia from intercepting Japanese diplomatic traffic if Australia decided to. The pragmatic approach was to accept that keeping the Japanese ignorant of the success of such attacks was the objective and this meant bringing Australia into the ULTRA and MAGIC compartments, because once inside, they could force the Australians into complying with the security requirements.

The importance of Japan's diplomatic traffic to Britain in the 1941–44 period is hard to overstate when it is realised that the only insight the Allied powers had into high-level German political and strategic thinking was obtained from the reports of Japanese diplomats in Berlin and Rome. These secrets were unobtainable through ULTRA or any other intelligence sources and were a unique window into German strategic thinking and plans.[2]

It can be argued that the Japanese constituted Britain's most productive high-level intelligence source across all of Europe between mid-1940 and mid-1945. It was certainly among the ULTRA material that Churchill wanted to see.

Churchill's interest in Japanese diplomatic messages is highlighted in his response to reading a report from the Japanese Ambassador to Germany, General Oshima Hiroshi, on 22 October 1941. This report detailed Oshima's tour of German invasion preparations at Boulogne in France. The Japanese Embassy in Berlin had passed this message on 7 October and GC&CS had broken it out the very same day, but it was not put in front of Churchill for fifteen days. This led to a major explosion during which the head of SIS and all others within hearing were subjected to a severe Churchillian upbraiding.[3] Churchill ordered C to ensure that all Japanese diplomatic cables be immediately moved to the 'Director/'C' Archive', the file maintained by C of all raw 'Y' intercept of immediate and direct interest to Churchill.[4]

The reason for Churchill's explosion was that in October 1941 the accepted view was that the Germans were on the verge of defeating the Soviet Union and would then turn back to the invasion of Britain. Given German troops were on the outskirts of Moscow and Stalin had just ordered the evacuation of the Soviet government from the city, there was some justification for pessimism.

Japan's diplomatic traffic was important in another way; it offered the potential for cribs that could break open Germany's high-level ENIGMA traffic. This possibility existed because there was always the hope that the Japanese might transmit the full-text versions of German reports sent by the as yet unbroken high-level ENIGMA. The resending of a decrypted high-grade message in the readable Japanese cipher would have been a crib of monumental proportions.

The importance of Japanese diplomatic traffic as a source of intelligence to Britain remained high and it proved to be in the long term as well. On 10 July

1943, Japanese diplomatic traffic from the ambassador in Berlin provided useful information on problems affecting Germany's U-boats. Oshima had met with Grand Admiral Dönitz, who had openly discussed with him the concerns of his U-boat commanders about the British successfully diverting their convoys around waiting U-boat picket lines, and about British aircraft detecting surfaced U-boats without triggering the Metox radar receiver the U-boats were using as a warning device. The theories, Dönitz told the ambassador, included that the British had a new 10 cm radar system that did not trigger the Metox, that they had broken ENIGMA, or that there were nests of spies reporting on U-boat departures.[5] The issue was resolved to the erroneous satisfaction of the Germans when they later discovered the Metox emitted its own very small signal.

Later again, in May 1944, the entire text of the Japanese naval attaché's report on his tour of German defences in northern France, including detailed descriptions of the command structure, German expectations of Allied plans and German operational policies, was made available to Churchill and his advisors the morning after it was sent by the attaché.[6] This intelligence on German defences in northern France came a month ahead of the D-Day landings in Normandy.

This was the traffic that Australia's Special Intelligence Bureau had been formed to intercept and analyse, and the importance of this source to Britain explains why GC&CS was less than enthusiastic about this initiative and the United States even less so.

The first sign of US hostility was the way Lieutenant Fabian's CAST unit took over the combined US Navy/ACNB SIGINT unit, now renamed FRUMEL in accordance with US Navy nomenclature. Fabian and OP-20-G made no bones about the work Eric Nave and his team of Australian academics and British consular officials were doing on Japanese diplomatic ciphers. It had no place in the US Navy's plans and Fabian set out to put an end to it. As the British had already guessed, this proved harder to accomplish than Fabian and OP-20-G thought. By October 1942, however, Fabian and the US Navy, supported by Commander Newman, had made life so difficult for Nave and his team that they wanted out of FRUMEL.

In October 1942, the discord among the Australian and British personnel at FRUMEL erupted when Consul C.W. Archer of the Foreign Office wrote to the Deputy DMI, Lieutenant Colonel Robert A. Little, raising concerns over the discussions between FRUMEL and LHQ over the future disposition of the Australian and British group working on Japanese diplomatic traffic.[7] The members of the cipher-breaking group, the Special Intelligence Bureau's title under FRUMEL, were disgruntled at the way they were being treated. This group had been working on Japanese diplomatic and commercial ciphers, and had been co-located with the ACNB's cryptanalytical unit. With the arrival of Lieutenant Fabian's US Navy SIGINT unit from the Philippines and its takeover of the RAN unit, problems soon arose. These included those caused by the inter-service jealousies plaguing the US armed forces but also involved poor Australian security practices and matters of high policy, specifically the involvement of Australia in the intercept and decryption of Japanese diplomatic traffic. The US Navy immediately moved to expel the civilians, particularly the Foreign Office officials and all non-naval personnel, from FRUMEL and all naval SIGINT organisations.

The decision to get rid of the civilians was made way above Lieutenant Fabian's head at the Department of the Navy. In fact, privately, Fabian was positive about the work of the Diplomatic Section, but emphasised that 'since they had left Monterey they have given nothing'.[8] This was not a question of simple jealousy; it was a matter of high policy involving the highest-level decision-makers in Washington and perhaps even President Roosevelt himself. The real issue for Fabian and his superiors was where the Diplomatic Section was obtaining its keys from. Fabian reported that although he had no way of knowing, he suspected they were getting the keys 'from Washington via the Admiralty'.[9] It would appear there were two sides to the story of FRUMEL's unwillingness to cooperate.

For the Australian Army, the question was whether to accept the decision of the ACNB or go it alone and take over the Diplomatic Section in the Australian national interest. The Australian Army rightly chose to protect Australia's national interest by retaining the Diplomatic Section, and it was sensibly decided to co-locate it in Brisbane, where Alastair Sandford could control it. Archer and his Foreign Office colleague, Graves, were against this.[10]

The arguments against the planned move north ranged from weak to strong. The weakest was that moving to Brisbane would entail a loss of continuity in the flow of intelligence. This argument drew on the experience of moving the intercept unit from Melbourne to Bonegilla, which did indeed lead to a loss of cover. The move of the Diplomatic Section to Brisbane would not impact coverage, however, although it would have interrupted the flow of intelligence.

A stronger argument put by Archer was the imminent change in the Japanese ciphers for Greater East Asia scheduled for November. If this occurred during the move of the group, they would lose valuable insights into the new cipher, as they would fail to intercept the usual Japanese mishandling of the changeover. This might lead to the loss of Australia's capability in reading these particular ciphers.[11] Of course, if the intercept sites were working and unaffected by the move, then this would entail delay and not loss.

The strongest argument was that the move would result in the loss of the very experienced and highly capable female workforce based in Melbourne, at least two of whom, Archer believed, had proven themselves good crypt-analysts. Most of the female cryptological workforce would have been lost due to their family commitments in Melbourne and, as we will see later, to the Australian government's antediluvian attitude towards women working outside the confines of a family kitchen. Consul Archer's claim that 'all of us feel most strongly that geographical stability is a "sine qua non" for efficient work' was substantial, and someone reading his letter marked this sentence in the margin.[12]

Archer, also keen to counter the US Navy's efforts to restrict communication on SIGINT matters outside of Australia, argued for a continuation of the current practice of sending the intelligence derived from diplomatic decryption in Melbourne to the Foreign Office and the Ministry of Economic Warfare in London. These telegrams had previously been sent under the auspices of the ACNB to the Admiralty. This would no longer be possible if the group moved under the auspices of LHQ, so a new system for transmission and distribution would need to be set up.

But the crux of Archer's letter comes down to the treatment he and his colleague Graves had experienced at the hands of Lieutenant Commander Fabian, Commander Newman and another, unidentified, RAN commander. It appears that Archer, Graves and the DNI, Commander Long, were overruled by a committee made up of these relatively junior officers. Technically, Archer and Graves were full colonel equivalents and outranked everyone at FRUMEL. This committee, without any apology, summarily dismissed the work of the diplomatic group and the arguments they put.[13] And this was all happening with the tacit approval of Navy Office.

At LHQ, Lieutenant Colonel Little accepted Archer's claims of unfair and overbearing treatment, most likely because he was well briefed by Long, the DNI. In a letter to the DMI, Little made it clear that Archer, Graves and the others, including Commander Nave, were not alone in their concern over the heavy-handed approach of the US Navy at FRUMEL. As Little describes it:

> My feeling is that since the advent of USN [US Navy] Crypto Sec under Lt Cdr Fabian [the Australian] Army have not been treated fairly as although Army provided about ⅓ of the staff and all the intercepts all Army was allowed to have was a précis of the diplomatic material. More recently we have been permitted to read through in the presence of a NO [Naval Officer] some of the diplomatic messages that Commander Nave was good enough to pass to us. These were taken away as soon as read.[14]

Although this reads as if Fabian and FRUMEL were being extremely ungracious towards the Australian Army, the reality was that Fabian had good grounds for his concern. He had found Japanese frequency lists that FRUMEL had supplied to Central Bureau being 'freely passed around Victoria Barracks' and marked as being from the US Navy.[15] Lax security in handling ULTRA was not just a problem in Australia, but also within the US commands in the Pacific, where action was taken by Admiral King to impress upon his commanders the serious consequences for their careers of failing to enforce discipline in the handling of ULTRA.[16]

The reality was that FRUMEL was abiding by the procedure for reading all ULTRA and MAGIC material that applied to British and American commanders in all theatres and he was following the direct orders of the Commander Allied Naval Forces, SWPA, to restrict the distribution of SIGINT to the US Navy, RAN and to General MacArthur and General Sutherland only.[17]

But Little's point is significant. The United States was dictating to Australia how much of the intelligence Australia was paying to produce it would be allowed to see. No nation-state can tolerate this situation and the Australian Army wasn't going to accept this high handedness.

The need to preserve the Special Intelligence Bureau as an Australian operation cooperating with Britain's SIGINT organisation had been identified by

General Squires in 1940, and it was reiterated in 1942 by Little. He was also rightly suspicious of General MacArthur, and felt that if they simply moved Archer's Bureau to Central Bureau it was likely that MacArthur would also move to close it down:

> I am of the opinion that this diplomatic group should be continued for the benefit of the Commonwealth Government and the forces but think it would be better to keep it under the [Australian] Army away from Central Bureau as if under Central Bureau it would again be under GHQ control who might act similarly to USN.[18]

Little was right. Washington would progressively become more and more alarmed at the disregard for the security of ULTRA in Australia and the SWPA, and so too would London—with good reason.

Security within the broader Australian government and its institutions was appalling. Ministers disregarded security measures, with Herbert Evatt, the Minister for External Affairs and concurrently the Attorney-General, the worst of the lot. Even the prime minister, an ex-journalist, was lax with security in providing background briefings to the Canberra Press Gallery that ranged right across policy and operations. At the same time, intelligence was suspected to be leaking out of Australia via Chinese Nationalist reporting and via the Soviet legation in Harbin in China.[19] Then there was the slapdash approach of the Australian military itself. In fact, the only people who were operating an effective security system were the SIGINT organisations themselves and the senior levels of Naval and Military Intelligence.

The alternative to making Australia a member of the club was to leave her to her own devices. GC&CS understood that 'if the Australians wish to have a diplomatic section we cannot prevent them'.[20] Commander Denniston at GC&CS believed, however, that leaving Australia to her own devices would result in 'an inefficient and insecure section' operating against the Japanese, and this risked exposing the success of GC&CS and the United States in defeating the Japanese ciphers and codes.[21]

The answer was pragmatic. Bring Australia into the club via Central Bureau, and force Australia to comply with ULTRA security requirements.[22] This offer was passed to Australia via a Mr Loxley, who spoke to Alfred Stirling at the Australian High Commission to inform him that 'we set the highest store on security and we could only offer collaboration to a section whose security is beyond all doubt, and whose circulation of results is strictly limited'.[23]

By mid-March 1943, Australia's military commanders finally agreed that ULTRA would only be made available to Australian military officials and not to the Australian government, which was now being excluded and 'kept in ignorance of this type of information for security reasons'.[24]

The answer the DMI, Colonel John Rogers, and the Deputy DMI, Little, came up with was to place Archer's Bureau under dual control, with Sandford at Central Bureau being responsible for its technical SIGINT and Little at LHQ being responsible for policy and administration. This protected the Special Intelligence Bureau and now opened a whole range of issues, including to whom it should distribute diplomatic traffic. With this decision, Archer stepped back and Professor Trendall, an Australian, took day-to-day charge of the bureau.

The distribution list for the traffic was restricted to the Australian DMI, DNI and Director of Intelligence RAAF, as well as General MacArthur and his G2, General Willoughby. It was also extended to the DMI, New Zealand, and the New Zealand Naval Board. The only organisation on the list was Central Bureau.[25] ULTRA material from Japanese diplomatic traffic would not be extended to any Australian civil department until July 1943 or, officially, to any Australian ministers even after some civilian officials received it.[26] Even then, the addition of Colonel W.R. Hodgson, the civilian Secretary of the Department of External Affairs to the list in mid-1943 was damage control, following his discovery of the existence of Trendall's bureau and its work.

This decision to exclude Australia's political leadership from access to ULTRA seems extraordinary, but the likelihood is that it was done with the approval of Prime Minister Curtin. There is no doubt that Curtin was briefed on SIGINT activity. The record shows that Curtin received information from the British High Commissioner, Sir Ronald Cross, and that the decision to exclude the Australian Cabinet from access to ULTRA intelligence was done with the tacit if not explicit approval of Australia's prime minister.[27]

Whether Curtin was briefed on the precise details is another matter, but the likelihood is that a decision to exclude his Cabinet colleagues and Australia's political class was made with his approval and that this is why General Richard Dewing, the senior British SLO, advised Britain that the politics in Australia could always change.[28] This was code for the Australian prime ministership being filled by someone other than Curtin, implying the replacement might not continue the arrangement to exclude politicians.

The Australian Army now moved to exploit the capabilities and advantages of Trendall's bureau, and the collection site operated by 52 ASWS at Bonegilla in Victoria, to win friends and influence people. In January 1943, at the request of the Foreign Office in London, Little wrote to the DMI, GHQ, New Zealand, offering access to the 'Weekly ULTRA Diplomatic Summary' produced by the bureau. The offer was not a case of largesse; it was so the Foreign Office could send ULTRA intelligence to Mr Boulter, the ex-British Consul in the Philippines and the Foreign Office's man in New Zealand.[29] This kept ULTRA within the existing military 'Y' communications network, keeping the British High Commission and the civil departments of the New Zealand government out of the ULTRA picture.

At the same time, Little also authorised Lieutenant Colonel W.H. Stratton in New Delhi to offer the DMI GHQ, India, increased cooperation between Trendall's bureau and the Wireless Experimental Centre (WEC) in India.[30] The reply on 15 May from Brigadier B.P.T. O'Brien on behalf of the DMI India, Major General W.J. Cawthorn, was fulsome. The DMI India was not only interested but also 'very anxious to perfect our "Y" liaison with you'.[31] This correspondence also details how the British were still reading all four Japanese diplomatic systems—Machine, Fuji, L.A. and X Cipher—in the United Kingdom and the last three in India. Brigadier O'Brien also informed Little that the intercept of these systems was done at sites in the United Kingdom, Mauritius and India, and went further and proposed that, as the operational tempo increased, an exchange of liaison officers should take place between Central Bureau and India's WEC, and that a division of effort should be agreed, including a deliberate overlap of cover for southern Java, Celebes and the Philippines.[32] Australia was now an active member of the ULTRA club.

The contribution Australia was making to SIGINT production from Japanese diplomatic and commercial traffic was growing due to the increasing technical capability of 52 ASWS at Bonegilla. Although Bonegilla was not a bad location for an intercept site targeting German beam transmissions to the east, it was being increasingly affected by electrical interference from the army base growing up around it, and there was a better location for the intercept of beam transmissions from Europe at Mornington. It was decided to relocate 52 ASWS to Mornington Racecourse.

The importance of the work being done by the bureau and 52 ASWS was now readily acknowledged by GC&CS, which informed Sandford in July 1943 of its appreciation for the Kuibyshev (now Samara) traffic that was now being routinely passed on by Trendall.[33] It was also agreed that the first priority for the Diplomatic Section was the Berlin to Tokyo links followed by IRW (Rome) on 19,520 kilohertz, the main station working from Europe to the Far East, because it could be consistently intercepted at Mornington. The technical reality that Australia was 'ideally situated for receiving our most important and at the same time most difficult services, namely Berlin to the Far East', was not initially well accepted at GC&CS.[34] J.H. Williams, who had earlier advised his superiors that 'every effort should be made to obtain Australian co-operations in the Interception of Berlin-Tokyo traffic', had persisted, however, and the quality of the intercept from Australia, where the sky wave was coming down, was so much better than anything being captured in India or Africa that all doubts were soon removed.[35]

The man upon whom the 'Y' Committee in London and GC&CS now depended to ensure the security and efficiency of the work was Sandford, now a Lieutenant Colonel and the Deputy Director of Central Bureau. The growing importance of Australia's contribution meant that a representative had to attend the 'Y' policy meetings in London and Washington. Sandford was the agreed representative, and when he headed off to London in early 1943, Williams of GC&CS was 'very anxious to meet' him when he came to Bletchley.[36] There can be little doubt that London now regarded Sandford as the de facto head of Australian SIGINT and perhaps even as its founder.[37]

Sandford was next at Bletchley Park on 10 May 1943, as Australia's representative at the Anglo-American Conference on the Japanese 'Y' problem.[38] While there, Sandford met Mr Williams, Hugh Waterfield and Major Carr to discuss Australia's contribution to the intercept cover of Japan's diplomatic traffic. The first item agreed was that Sandford would arrange for Australia to adjust cover on Japanese diplomatic traffic to suit the needs of GC&CS. In return, Australia would receive the diplomatic intelligence derived from this material. This material given to Australia would be restricted to intelligence affecting Greater East Asia, but nothing relating to events in Europe would be provided. It was made clear that the Japanese ULTRA relating to Germany and the war in Europe was not going to be released to Australia.[39]

The Mornington intercept site now had twelve intercept positions operated by personnel who were ex-post office employees. GC&CS wanted at least fifteen intercept positions, but left it up to Sandford as to how he would achieve this, although they believed it would not be difficult.[40] GC&CS then provided Sandford with its tasking in priority order.

First priority was given to the Japanese diplomatic, Japanese military and naval attaché links from Berlin and Rome to Tokyo. The Tokyo to Berlin link operating between 0300Z (0300 hours Zulu time, the equivalent of Greenwich Mean Time) and 1000Z was second priority, and then Japanese diplomatic and attaché traffic on all other links was third priority. German diplomatic traffic, FLORADORA, was also listed as a third-priority task.[41]

With this agreement worked out, Sandford was able to head back to Australia having preserved the country's involvement in SIGINT operations. At this distance in time, it may not look much, but it was. Australia was now a formal player in the worldwide SIGINT system, and although this meant only access to ULTRA affecting the Greater East Asia Co-Prosperity Sphere, it was still access. This was as close as Australia ever got to the upper-level decision-making of the Western Alliance. This relationship set the model used in SIGINT even today.

It was at this conference that the formal set of rules, the *Provisional Notes on Wireless Interception ('Y') Organisation in the Field—1943*, were agreed for the management of 'Y' personnel, units and materials. Sandford's involvement in agreeing this set of rules committed Australia to enforcing compliance. Denniston's plot was developing and it is more than likely that Alastair Sandford was in on it.

The *Provisional Notes* were distributed to all British commanders responsible for units engaged on 'Y' work, and they directed that 'Y' personnel and units were provided to commands for intelligence collection from enemy communications only and were never to be used on other tasks, such as internal communications or security monitoring of own-force communications.[42] Control of all 'Y' personnel and units was vested in the DMI at the relevant GHQ, who was assisted on technical signals proficiency by the GHQ signals officer in charge. The Intelligence Section of GHQ could advise the DMI, but he did not answer to this organisation, making it quite clear that while a GHQ might task a 'Y' organisation, it did not command the unit, which remained under command of the national organisation representing the national strategic interest.[43]

A significant change in the status of 'Y' personnel was that no matter where they were working or for whom, they were to be regarded as GHQ troops attached to a subordinate formation and not as the troops of that formation. In military terms, this is significant because it meant local commanders did not 'own' 'Y' units and could not task them, except in accordance with the tasking provided by the GHQ that owned the 'Y' unit.

Another area of activity detailed in the *Provisional Notes* was the security of SIGINT material. The 'Y' authorities did not insist that the interception of enemy signals be kept secret, but they did insist that the results of those intercept operations must be kept secret. To this end, the *Provisional Notes* banned the use of the word 'intercept' on telephone links or in clear-language communications of any sort. In fact, the view was that the word should not be used in any circumstance at all if it could be avoided.[44] Information obtained from intercept operations was to remain secured within the 'Y' organisation and its units, and it was never to be communicated outside unless it had been 'sanitised'—that is, once all evidence of 'Y' as the source had been removed or disguised.[45] The provision of raw intercept to anyone outside the 'Y' organisation was forbidden.[46] Even then, the only people allowed to see SIGINT were those who were 'indoctrinated'—that is, those formally briefed into the security requirements by an SLO and who had a need to know. The provision of 'Y' material for information only was forbidden.[47]

These instructions were timely, because the army authorities now responsible for ULTRA and 'Y' security in Australia were faced with their first breach of ULTRA security. This came to light when Colonel Hodgson became aware of ULTRA in late May or early June 1943. The breach had occurred in the Dominions Office in London, where someone erroneously showed the liaison officer from External Affairs an ULTRA message detailing a report from the Japanese Minister in Moscow that mentioned William Slater, the Australian Minister in Kuybyshev.[48] As if this was not bad enough, the liaison officer told him the intercept came from Australia.[49] It was a serious breach of security.

Adding to the compromise, this information had now been passed back to Hodgson in Australia on the External Affairs circuit, a non-ULTRA communications system. Hodgson was not happy, and he immediately contacted Little at LHQ to know why the information had not gone to him directly.[50] It was decided that Hodgson should be indoctrinated into ULTRA and that ULTRA from Trendall's bureau would be turned into a précis for Hodgson's eyes only. That was not enough. Hodgson was not prepared to keep his minister, Evatt, ignorant of ULTRA intelligence he felt the minister needed to see. Little insisted that Hodgson had to comply, that they could not have Hodgson go to Evatt and have Evatt raise it in Cabinet. There was no choice really. Army had to compromise and Hodgson got his précis and, if there was anything in it he believed Evatt needed to see, he would call upon the CGS, General Northcott, who would review the intelligence and, if he agreed with Hodgson that Evatt should see it, then it would be 'sanitised' to hide SIGINT as the source and provided to Evatt.[51] Hodgson agreed to this procedure and it remained in place until 1967, when Malcolm Fraser was appointed Minister for the Army and demanded he be indoctrinated.

All this was coordinated with GC&CS. Paymaster Commander Merry, GC&CS's man at FRUMEL, acted as a link between the Australian authorities at LHQ and GC&CS, and he no doubt assisted in the establishment of the system for Hodgson. London took on the responsibility of managing the distribution of ULTRA to Hodgson, leaving Washington to distribute ULTRA to all of the other readers within SWPA.[52] This was a real necessity because, as it turned out, Washington was actively withholding a significant amount of ULTRA from General MacArthur and GHQ, SWPA.

It was now that the fears Lieutenant Colonel Little had expressed about General MacArthur moving to prevent Australia working on Japanese diplomatic ULTRA proved prescient.[53] In early April 1943, while Sandford was absent in the United Kingdom and Washington, Sutherland told Sandford's deputy, Squadron Leader Booth, that no civilians should be employed at Central Bureau. At this time, the only civilian working at Central Bureau was Professor Room, but he was about to be joined by Professor Trendall, R.J. Lyons and Commander Nave.[54] Booth and the Australian officers at Central Bureau objected to this and raised the matter with Little, as they believed it was 'essential that the services of these able men be retained'.[55]

This was the first move against the personnel of Trendall's bureau being involved in Central Bureau. It is most likely that GHQ, SWPA had now been pressured by people in Washington, who had become aware of Australia's increasing role by Sandford's visits to the 'Y' Committee in London, GC&CS and Arlington Hall in Washington. Sutherland's instruction that no civilians be employed makes it clear that it was not Australia's role as an intercept site that was being targeted, but its cryptanalytical attack on Japanese diplomatic traffic, for this was the work undertaken by Trendall's team.[56]

On top of this, Sutherland now ordered Central Bureau to stop all exchanges of information with British SIGINT authorities.[57] This could have been another of MacArthur's attempts to make life harder for people he saw as competitors, but this explanation doesn't fit with the wholesale nature of the interference by Sutherland. The specific area of disagreement was over exchanges of ULTRA intelligence and 'Y' technical information between the Australian elements within Central Bureau and Trendall's bureau and the WEC and other agencies in India.

By the end of 1943, it appears that an effective modus operandi had been negotiated for Australian participation in the interception and cryptanalysis of Japanese diplomatic traffic. The British government had achieved its major requirement for the establishment of this relationship on an even basis: a commitment by Australia's military authorities to ensuring the security of ULTRA.

At the beginning of 1944, the situation had changed so sufficiently that even Washington was willing to share its ULTRA insights with Australia.[58] The Foreign Office had obtained the agreement of the US State Department to send summaries of the highest-grade Japanese diplomatic ULTRA to Sandford for distribution to Colonel Hodgson only. These messages were for Hodgson's eyes only and were not even to be sent to Central Bureau. This was a major change in policy. Now it was the Australian government, although only at an official and not a political level, that was to see a particular line of ULTRA. The reason for the exclusion of Central Bureau was exceptional. The US State Department and other officials in Washington did not want MacArthur to see this form of ULTRA, as they were excluding him deliberately. They also did not want MacArthur or other military authorities to know that Australia was now receiving ULTRA that they were not.[59] Political intrigue was not just an Australian problem.[60]

The agreements and arrangements made between the Foreign Office and the State Department may have legitimised Australia's status at one level, but this did not mean all US authorities were happy. At the same time these arrangements were introduced, MacArthur's HQ renewed its efforts to stop the exchanges between Australia's SIGINT establishment, GC&CS and India. In early January 1944, General Akin and Colonel Sherr, Sandford's bosses, ordered him to cease direct communication with London and Delhi, and to pass all communications on 'Y' matters through Akin. This order led to a meeting between Sandford, Brigadier Rogers and General Blamey on 21 January 1944.[61] The notes from this meeting make it clear that the Australians believed Akin was acting on General Sutherland's orders, and that Blamey saw it as an affront to Australian sovereignty, something he would not tolerate.[62]

Blamey instructed Rogers and Sandford to demand that any such orders be put in writing by Akin or Sutherland and he would then take it up with MacArthur. The notes also confirm the fact that Australia's involvement in ULTRA was a matter of the highest policy, well outside the purview of General MacArthur or any senior commander. During this set of meetings, the files make it crystal clear that Blamey was acting on the orders of the Australian government, most likely Prime Minister John Curtin, to ensure the 'firm undertakings' Australia had given to Sir Ronald Cross, the British High Commissioner to Australia, that Australia would remain committed to the imperial 'Y' system and reject any instructions from US authorities to exclude Britain from SIGINT activity in the Pacific were adhered to.[63]

The most important statement by Blamey during this meeting was that if Akin raised this matter in writing, Blamey as the C-in-C of Australia's military forces would confront Sutherland and if he did not back down, Blamey would inform GHQ, SWPA that they should form their own version of Central Bureau and split away from the Australian organisation, which would continue to work as part of Britain's 'Y' system.[64]

This was the penultimate step in the creation of an independent Australian national SIGINT authority. Australia was willing to go it alone if the choice was between doing this or giving up its right to be part of Britain's 'Y' system or any other system for that matter. It was an unambiguous statement of Australian independence.

CHAPTER 20

Allied Secret Intelligence Compromised, 1944

On 14 December 1944, Alastair Sandford wrote to his friend Lieutenant Colonel R.A. Little, the long-serving Deputy DMI. It was a friendly and personal letter in which Sandford outlined his visit to Melbourne and his intention to take a few days' leave in Adelaide before going to Darwin. Sandford was heading to Darwin to arrange the accommodation for the Canadian Army's Special Wireless Group (SWG), which would soon be arriving to conduct intercept operations. After this long preamble, Sandford got to the point and, as is often the case when the preamble is long, the news was bad.

What Sandford had to tell Little was that the worst thing that could possibly befall a SIGINT agency had happened at Central Bureau. Central Bureau was now intercepting its own intelligence being passed by the IJA in Harbin, China, to the Japanese Imperial HQ in Tokyo.[1] Japan had breached 'Y' security and were reading their own messages being reported in Allied communications. It was exactly what Lieutenant Rudy Fabian, OP-20-G, the US Navy and the US Army, as well as the 'Y' authorities in Britain, had feared. Poor Australian security had shattered the security of 'Y' Procedure.

What was worse, it was not just Sandford and his senior officers who were aware of this breach, so too were the British and Americans. The failure of Australia's security could not be hidden, and, amazingly, Group Captain

F.W. Winterbotham, the Chief Security Officer for ULTRA in the UK government and Squadron Leader S.F. Burley, who was responsible for the distribution of ULTRA to British formations in the east, were in Australia and visiting Little in Melbourne when the news broke.[2] They were in Australia to deal with 'a number of extremely difficult breaches of security', including the fact that the source of the Japanese intelligence was, 'as we suspected . . . the Soviet Ambassador in Australia'.[3] The question was, as Sandford put it, 'how the Japanese obtain the information from the Soviet[s] and secondly, how the Soviet Ambassador himself obtains the information'.[4]

The information in this letter was for Little's 'ears alone' and the only other person who appears to have been aware of this crisis was the CGS, General Northcott, and perhaps, the C-in-C, General Blamey.[5] This was not the first time that 'Y' Procedure had been compromised in Australia, and it most certainly was not the first time that Australian secrets flowed out of Australia.

Problems first appeared in 1940, when Australia was provided with intelligence derived from the communications of the Japanese Consul-General in Sydney. This detailed the Consul-General's intelligence reporting as including the name of a British man-of-war berthed in Sydney Harbour to the Imperial HQ in Tokyo. The Consul-General was also reported as having passed technical intelligence on New South Wales's power transmission line between Sydney and Newcastle, and information on the floating dock in Newcastle.[6] He was even able to report on the reorganisation of the Australian Army's 8th Military District in Port Moresby, accurately listing the islands brought under that HQ.[7]

A month later, another British intelligence report message, classified SECRET, was passed around Melbourne and Canberra. This was obviously derived from SIGINT, as it provided the details of another message from the Japanese Consul-General in Sydney to his government in Tokyo. This dealt with Australia's purchase of training aircraft from Japan in exchange for wool and wheat, and included the Consul-General's recommendation that Tokyo provide an accommodating response, in the hope of splitting Australia from the United States.[8]

It is clear from these reports that GC&CS was reading Japanese diplomatic traffic and sharing the intelligence with Australia. It also shows how poor was Australia's handling of sensitive information.[9] Not only were these reports passed around the service chiefs, they were sent to officials, including committee secretaries and junior staff officers.[10] Among them were the Assistant Secretary of the Defence Committee, Frank Sinclair; the Assistant Secretary of the Department of Defence, Lieutenant Colonel A.J. Wilson, who was also the War Book Officer; and the liaison officers for the three services.[11] There was effectively no compartmentalisation and no control.

Paul Hasluck provides a good example of this state of affairs in his autobiography, *Diplomatic Witness*, where he describes his first day working as a public servant in the Department of External Affairs in Canberra. He found the department housed in ten rooms coming off a single corridor. Each room was full of desks covered in unsecured papers, and in one room the cipher section worked loudly enough for them to be easily overheard in the corridor. The Central Records Room, the most important room in the department, was located just inside the main entrance and, 'from the point of view of security', was 'in the most vulnerable place that could have been chosen'.[12] There were no guards and no restriction on access.[13]

The only security advantage Colonel W.R. Hodgson's department held was that it worked in utter chaos. The chaos was so bad the officers of the department could not find files, making it likely that no spy could either. According to Hasluck, who later wrote the civil volumes of the *Official History of Australia in the War of 1939–1945*, the department's files were 'among the worst organised and the worst kept' of all Australia's archives. External Affairs worked on 'personal memory'.[14]

The issue of Australian insecurity was not confined to officials; it came from the very top. In April 1941, British government officials in London were startled to read in *The Times* information that could only have come from Most Secret cables that had just been tabled in Cabinet. *The Times* had not got a scoop; rather, it had reprinted a report from the *Sydney Morning Herald* of 23 April. Australia's prime minister, Robert Menzies, had sent the contents of the cables to his deputy, Arthur Fadden, without the permission of Churchill or any other British authority. On 26 April, an embarrassed Menzies was urgently cabling Fadden that he was 'amazed at the close relation' between the report in the *Sydney Morning Herald* and the texts of the cables.[15] The subject matter within the cables included the German order of battle in the Balkans, and this could only have come from ULTRA.

Given this incident, it is easy to see why Britain was concerned at allowing Australia to undertake ULTRA work when this subject was raised a little time later. The fact that the British were so pragmatic and so tolerant is something Australian history has been slow to acknowledge. Menzies' behaviour in this case was appalling.

With those in the very top of government prepared to ignore security when it suited them and officials who could not run their departments properly, it is no surprise that Australia's security services were abysmal. They lacked cohesion, resources, training, procedures, protocols and any understanding of what ensuring security meant. They spent their time looking for German and Italian spies who did not exist and in harassing Italian priests, Jehovah's Witnesses and anyone else they deemed a security threat. They completely missed the growing networks of NKGB and GRU (USSR foreign military intelligence) spies and agents that would later compromise ULTRA and the standing of Australia as a country that could be trusted.

The other subject they completely overlooked was education on and enforcement of proper security arrangements in government departments. The armed services had their own arrangements, imported from Britain, and these extended to 'Y' Procedure and its own completely independent security arrangements. Outside of these, however, it was up to every government department and agency to make their own arrangements, and so there was no security anywhere outside of the armed services.

In 1942, in response to growing American and British unease at Australia's insecurity and the establishment of FRUMEL and the Central Bureau, Australia finally formed a new Security Service. It turned out to be just as dysfunctional as its predecessor organisations. London continued to worry about the 'little problems' with the 'new Security Service in Australia'.[16] But hope trumped realism at the Security Service in London when E.E. Longfield Lloyd acted as an intermediary on behalf of the new Australian Director-General of the Security Service, Brigadier William Ballantyne Simpson.[17] This led to the Security Service allowing Lloyd more time to bring some method to the new service. He didn't, and it kept chasing priests and Italian cane growers, and eating in Chinese restaurants to find Japanese spies listening to the conversations of officers. They remained completely unaware that Soviet intelligence had penetrated their own service and many Commonwealth government agencies, particularly External Affairs. These were the agents stealing Australia's secrets for the Soviet Union. These secrets were duly passed from Moscow to the Soviet Legation at Harbin, from where Australia's

DMI, Colonel Rogers, and other Australian officers believed they were in turn obtained by the Japanese.[18]

By early 1943, concern about Australian security had increased in London and Washington because of the growing complaints from FRUMEL and the US Navy. Major General Stewart Menzies, the head of SIS, signalled Major General Dewing, the senior British officer in Australia, to relay that he was now 'greatly concerned about the way in which the Australian military was handling ULTRA Japanese diplomatic material'.[19] C questioned 'whether Australian authorities fully appreciate importance of security concerning this material'. C's main anxieties were the distribution controls in place and just who was seeing the diplomatic cables.[20]

As we have seen, British concerns lay in the importance of Japanese ULTRA to the intelligence window Britain had into high-level German planning.[21] Seen from this perspective, C's approach was reasonable. He wanted Dewing to assure him that Australian security was sufficient for ULTRA and that Australia would put the necessary controls in place in the same way as the other Dominions. If he got this assurance from Dewing, then C would cooperate fully in assisting Australia to develop its capabilities in Japanese diplomatic cryptanalysis.[22]

Luckily for Australia, Dewing was a reasonable man. In his reply to C, he outlined the difficulties between FRUMEL and Central Bureau, and emphasised Fabian's unwillingness to cooperate with anybody. Dewing contrasted this with Sandford's excellent relationships, including with Paymaster Lieutenant Commander Alan Merry, RN, Britain's last representative at FRUMEL, and with other organisations and individuals. Dewing, in a very British way, gently pressed the knife deeply into Fabian and FRUMEL, telling C,

> The information at my disposal indicates that Fabian's [sic] has been consistently overworked and probably as a result of this his general attitude has introduced an unfortunate element into his relationship with British and Australian members of the Special Intelligence Bureau.[23]

Importantly, Dewing informed C that, 'I am satisfied that present security of Sandford party is good.'[24] Effectively, this message saved Australia's efforts to develop its own ULTRA program. On 30 March 1943, Dewing confirmed that Australian security for the proposed ULTRA operations against Japan's diplomatic traffic was sound.[25] The Australian military authorities had agreed to the security regulations regarding ULTRA and SIGINT activities, and to adopting the standardised British nomenclature for identifying the various types of intelligence derived from 'Y' work.[26] They had also agreed to ensure that all people admitted to the compartment would be indoctrinated to understand the risk that any breach of security posed in drying up intelligence all over the world. Lieutenant Colonel Little had also agreed that no Australian politician would be given access to any SIGINT.[27]

The security arrangements for ULTRA were not left to Australia or Major General Dewing. As we have already seen, the SIS had its own station in Australia led by Captain Kendall, and this included Lieutenant Commander Merry, who was at FRUMEL, ostensibly as an analyst on the Four Sign Japanese code. It is clear from the documentary evidence that Merry was reporting to SIS what the US Navy and the RAN were working on, and, more importantly, what they were doing with SIGINT.[28] Merry also reported to Kendall in Brisbane, but he appears to have had his own communications circuit back to SIS, most likely via Major General Dewing's office in Melbourne. It was Merry who alerted GC&CS that the Australian Secretary of the Department of External Affairs, Hodgson, had been made aware of ULTRA information.[29]

All now seemed to be well, but this was not to prove the case for long. On 29 July 1943, Alastair Sandford signalled C that Central Bureau had reports from 'a fairly reliable source', a phrase denoting SIGINT, that indicated Tokyo was obtaining intelligence from inside Australia.[30] Rogers, the Australian DMI, Sandford and Little suspected the Soviet Legation in Canberra was sending the intelligence to Moscow and somehow the Japanese were getting hold of it.[31] The Australians now wanted to launch a cryptanalytical attack on the Soviet codes.[32]

London's response was measured, very measured, as it took more than five weeks for a reply to be sent in September, prompted even then by a number of later signals from Sandford.[33] The reply came from C, as the Chair of the 'Y' Board, and it downplayed the incident, telling Sandford the Soviets used one-time tables for all diplomatic traffic and this made Soviet messages unreadable to both GC&CS and the Japanese. He then muddied the waters by asking if Sandford had considered that the Japanese were reading the messages being sent by other allies or neutrals in Australia. C then asked Sandford to send specimens of these messages for further investigation.[34]

The low-level replies to Sandford's signal and the widening of the potential culprits to cover Allied and neutral nations represented in Australia suggests that London was running an agenda. What that was is impossible to answer, but London was well aware that secret information had been leaking to the Japanese from the Chinese Nationalists, led by the Kuomintang, in China. London was also aware that no one could trust the Soviets.

The problem of Nationalist Chinese insecure communications was long-standing.[35] Nationalist codes and ciphers were low grade and easy to break, and GC&CS had been reading them for a long time, as had the IJA, which had broken them as early as 1936.[36] According to Yamamoto Hayashi of the Harbin Agency of IJA Intelligence, this provided the IJA with a direct line into US and British intentions throughout the Pacific War.[37]

IJA SIGINT intercept operations were directed against Chinese Nationalist traffic between Chungking (Chongqing), London, New Delhi and Ceylon.[38] The IJA was also intercepting communications to and from Washington and even Ankara. The communications of the Nationalist Legations in Melbourne and Sydney were also being intercepted and broken by the IJA.[39] The British regarded the situation with the Nationalist Chinese as so bad that in April 1944, as the preparations for D-Day were culminating, Britain jammed China's diplomatic radio links and stopped all diplomatic bag privileges.[40] This was a serious step to take against an ally, but the needs of the moment overturned the need to be nice.

Following this spate of signals in July 1943, nothing else is seen on this case until December 1944, when investigations by Central Bureau finally uncovered the IJA's sources as being the Nationalist Chinese military liaison officer network (see Figure 20.1).[41] These liaison officers worked back to D8, the Nationalist Chinese Intelligence in Chungking. By this time, though, there was more to worry about than poorly protected Nationalist Chinese communications.

The Nationalist Chinese were not Japan's only source of intelligence on Australia's military activity and intelligence organisation. The Kempeitai were finding a very fruitful source that would quickly compromise the AIB and most of its operations, particularly those conducted by the SRD. This source

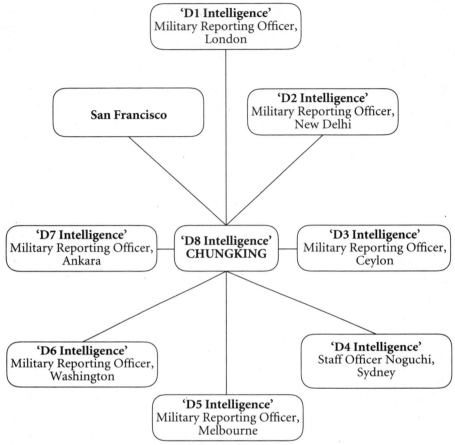

Figure 20.1: The Nationalist Chinese military's reporting officer network, 1940s

would even compromise ULTRA intelligence by sending ULTRA material across insecure radio channels. The source was the SRD itself.

On 29 January 1944, the SRD despatched Operation COBRA to Dari Baai on Timor and into the hands of the waiting Kempeitai. The COBRA operatives were taken and their radio operator coerced into sending false intelligence back to Australia. COBRA's first five messages back to Australia lacked the necessary safe word (authenticator) telling SRD COBRA had not been compromised. This word was 'Slender', and it was only sent in message No. 6, DTG 1005Z/6/3.[42] It was only sent after SRD had alerted the watching Kempeitai to the missing authenticator by inserting the phrases 'this particular girl' and 'she is not the fat rpt fat one'.[43] COBRA's radio operator had broken tradecraft rules by writing the word slender in his notebook, and the Kempeitai realised the COBRA operator was alerting SRD to his compromise by omitting the authenticator.

The SRD replied to message No. 6 on 7 March, committing perhaps the most egregious breach of 'Y' security in Asia during World War II when it told COBRA:

> Your six big relief. Col Maj C and all here sick at heart past week due *intercept of Jap cipher* [Author's italics] naming you personally and apparently claiming your capture Jan 29.[44]

The SRD had just broken every rule in the 'Y' security rulebook, putting SIGINT into a low-level code and transmitting it on a normal communications circuit to a unit behind enemy lines. And they had not cleared this action with anyone.

This breach was massive. It told the Japanese that Australia and the Allies were reading Japanese codes and just how quickly they were doing so. There can be little doubt that the breach was quickly identified, as General Blamey was shown messages No. 6 and No. 8 from COBRA, no doubt trying to ascertain for himself whether the SRD had breached 'Y' security instructions in sending ULTRA to an agent behind enemy lines.[45]

The precise SIGINT the SRD had compromised was a Central Bureau report of a message sent from Davao in the Philippines to Singapore on 18 February 1944, reporting the capture of Lieutenant Cashman, whom the Japanese describe as having been 'a student at MELBOURNE Spy Intelligence HQ'.[46] That the Kempeitai in Dili placed a premium on Cashman's information is shown by the fact that a report of his disclosures was sent to the Vice Minister of War in Tokyo and, by default, to Imperial HQ as well.[47]

It is little wonder that Sandford and Central Bureau were concerned, and it would explain why Group Captain Winterbotham happened to be in Australia later in 1944 dealing with 'a number of extremely difficult breaches of security'.[48]

What saved the Allied SIGINT effort following this extraordinary breach of 'Y' Procedure by the AIB and SRD? The Japanese. Their response was to explain it away and do nothing. The Japanese told Lieutenant Cashman that 'their cipher could not possibly be cracked, and even if it could, Australia would not send such information to the field'.[49] Luckily, for the Allied SIGINT effort, the Japanese did not realise just how inept the AIB and SRD were.

By this stage of the war, mid-1944, the evidence of breaches of SIGINT security was growing, and there can be little doubt that both London and Washington now wanted action taken to protect SIGINT from any further compromise. There is also a suspicion that Captain Kendall and Third Officer Eve Walker of SIS were working with Alastair Sandford on the issue. The fact that the head of the British Special Liaison Service, Group Captain Winterbotham, was in Australia in the months immediately after D-Day suggests he had significant reason to be there.

The suspicion that Sandford was running a counterintelligence operation at Central Bureau directed against the leakage of ULTRA in Australia is only supported by circumstantial evidence. First, there is his close relationship with the SIS Station Chief, Captain Kendall, RN, and his support of Eve Walker's counterintelligence operations against Robert Wake's Security Service in Brisbane. As well as these, the files show that by late November 1944, Sandford had accumulated considerable evidence of IJA reporting of Top Secret intelligence derived from the Harbin Special Intelligence source. This included intelligence from the Soviet Minister in Australia on MacArthur's plans on Leyte Island, Bicol Peninsula and Ragoru Bay, and on the decision of the Australian government not to despatch troops to the Philippines until arrangements for shipping and aircraft were finalised.[50] Other information sent was so specific the analysts at Central Bureau could confirm it was derived from secret Australian reporting. It included the following:

Para. 1: The enemy's appreciation of JAPANESE strength in the PHILIPPINES at the beginning of November (D4 report sent on November the 7th).

Sub-Para. (1) Air strength (as of November the 3rd):

Northern Sector:	281 planes
Central Sector:	107 planes
Southern Sector:	61 planes
TOTAL	449 planes

Sub-Para. (2): Ground Strength (as of November the 1st):

LUZON ISLAND:	161,200 men
Central Sector:	51,900 men
Southern Sector:	60,900 men
TOTAL	274,000 men[51]

This intelligence was assessed in Australia as being identical to intelligence that appeared in the *Australian Military Forces Weekly Intelligence Review* No. 118, issued on 4 November and received at LHQ on 7 November, the date the Japanese believed it was issued.[52] This report was stolen in Australia and provided to the Soviet Legation so quickly that the Japanese were broadcasting it on 11 November. It took the NKGB or GRU less than four days to get this report to their colleagues in Harbin, from where it was either stolen by the Kempeitai or given to the Japanese by the Soviets.[53]

According to Sandford, the signal containing this intelligence, MBJ 30028 of 25 November 1944, 'caused a very considerable stir overseas'.[54] The 'stir' was created by the fact that the information reported in MBJ 30028 was derived directly from an ULTRA and the Japanese had clearly identified the Soviet Ambassador as the original source. The other reason for the 'stir' was that the Japanese were rebroadcasting it only four days after it being released in Australia.

The impact of MBJ 30028 was that Winterbotham postponed his departure for Washington and the United Kingdom to meet with the DMI the following Thursday and he thought, Sandford tells Little, that 'the matter is one of serious insecurity on a global scale'.[55] At the meeting, Winterbotham was asked by the Australian DMI to bring out to Australia a 'Special Section 5 man', and although there is no other mention of a Special Section 5, SIS Section Five dealt with counterespionage and this no doubt referred to a plan to send the SIS officer Lieutenant Colonel C.H. (Dick) Ellis, to deal with the problem.[56] In the meantime, it was 'most imperative . . . that no action whatsoever be taken until his arrival'.[57]

On the same day as Sandford was writing to Little, Christmas Day 1944, Central Bureau issued another message from Tokyo sent on 19 December to Saigon, Rabaul and Singapore. This message provided the divisional dispositions of Australia's military forces on Bougainville and New Britain, and in New Guinea. It was not ULTRA material, but it referenced that source D4 was

Staff Officer Noguchi based in Sydney.[58] Other than this disclosure, the identity of the D group of informants remained unknown until late January, when a message Tokyo had broadcast on 29 August was finally deciphered. It disclosed that the D source were the communications links between Nationalist Chinese attachés and Chungking.[59] This was backed up by GC&CS work on IJN messages. Once the Nationalist Chinese communications were identified as the links, London advised Australia to cut the Nationalist Chinese government off from all access to sensitive information.[60] The Nationalist Chinese as the D source was finally confirmed on 3 February 1945.[61]

But this did not explain Japanese access to ULTRA material. By early 1945, the Australian military authorities were sure enough to inform the Security Service that the Soviet Legation in Canberra was leaking intelligence to the Japanese, although they did not know how.[62]

It stood to reason that the Soviets were responsible for more of the leaks than the Chinese. Australia had already taken steps against the Chinese in April 1943, when all Australian military formations and commands were ordered to 'ensure that no information is given to Chinese Naval or Military Attachés that would be detrimental to the Allied cause'.[63] Despite this, it may be the Nationalist Chinese were still being given access to sensitive information, but why so much? The truth of the matter is that the Chinese were accidently compromising some sensitive information, but the Soviets and their Australian spies were stealing everything they could lay their hands on. The Nationalist Chinese attachés now had to have prior LHQ approval to visit any operational area.[64]

But the Soviet problem continued, while the Japanese and the Soviets in Harbin played games of double- and triplecross with one another. The Soviets knew that the IJA's Ha-Toku-Cho (Harbin Special Information) organisation had penetrated their consulate, and the IJA knew the Soviets knew.[65] The NKGB were using this knowledge to feed false information to the Japanese and, to make it believable, it is highly likely they would have sprinkled some gold in the mud to keep the Japanese confident of the material.[66] This is a standard practice, and the use of intelligence from Australia that did not harm Soviet interests and had the double value of harming US interests in Asia, even slowing the US advance up the Pacific, fitted the bill very nicely. The Japanese, aware that there was a good chance the Soviets were doing this, carefully dissected everything they were given.[67]

Yet this does not explain how Tokyo was broadcasting Australian SIGINT issued on 7 November to its commands on 11 November. This intelligence was not delayed long enough to have gone through a process of careful dissection. It had either been quickly stolen from the Soviets in Harbin, a risky undertaking, or been passed directly to the Japanese by the Soviets in an effort to slow the American advance towards Japan. This was realpolitik of the highest level, and it puts to rest the idea that those communists who passed intelligence to their Soviet masters did no real harm to the war effort.

The difficulty was how to handle this issue. The advice from GC&CS via Winterbotham was clear. Do nothing, the idea being that any change would immediately draw enemy attention and this risked further, if not complete, compromise of ULTRA to the Japanese and their German allies. In his letter of 3 February to the Director-General of Security, Brigadier William Simpson, Little advised that no action be taken, but Simpson was in no mood to cooperate with the army.

On 2 February, Simpson telephoned the CGS informing him that he had received information from London that he wished to pass on to the army and that he would like an officer to be nominated to meet with him. The officer selected was Little. On contacting Simpson by telephone, Little was told that there was no information from London but Simpson wanted to talk about D (Chinese Nationalist) intelligence activity. The ploy used by Simpson, telling an outright lie, was standard practice in the wartime Security Service and among its senior officers. Little put Simpson off by pointing out that such a discussion would be pointless until Lieutenant Colonel Ellis of SIS had arrived in Australia.[68] Little now contacted Sandford and asked him to send an urgent signal to GC&CS requesting Ellis's presence in Australia. It was also agreed that Simpson would have a meeting with Blamey in Canberra on 8 February to clarify matters. Until then, the army asked Simpson to do nothing about D intelligence until he received clearance to do so.[69]

By 2 February, Sandford recommended that Simpson and the Security Service should not be told GC&CS was sending out the raw text of the Chungking traffic, and that he only be told the Japanese were obtaining the information from their own SIGINT operations.[70] Unfortunately, Brigadier Rogers had already given Simpson the raw text from Chunking proving that GC&CS was reading Chinese communications.[71]

Now that Simpson had been told of the GC&CS operation, he had to be indoctrinated by Squadron Leader Burley, now the SLO in the SWPA. Burley visited Canberra to do so.[72] The meeting was not a happy one, although it was not as rough as Burley expected it to be.

Simpson displayed an utter lack of ethics by staying silent during the indoctrination until Burley told him that D intelligence was derived from Nationalist Chinese attachés and not from Soviet spies.[73] At this point Simpson began to argue that he had the right to disseminate ULTRA within his service, before Burley bluntly told him this could not happen. Burley then ordered Simpson, a novel experience for Simpson, to burn ULTRA immediately after reading it.[74] Now, Burley reports, Simpson was 'up on his hind legs'.[75] He complained that if he could not show ULTRA to his people, it was useless. This prompted no response from Burley so Simpson started name-dropping, threatening to speak to the Australian prime minister and Herbert Evatt about 'all of this nonsense'. He even questioned Burley's standing because he was a relatively junior officer.[76]

Simpson did not know how SLOs worked. He had no appreciation of the fact that SLOs were the direct representatives of Prime Minister Churchill, President Roosevelt and the relevant national SIGINT agencies on all ULTRA matters. They were always mid-level officers, so as not to attract attention, but they held the power to cut off any commander they believed could not be trusted with ULTRA. The distribution list on Burley's signal gives the game away. Winterbotham was the only action addressee, while the Australian authorities, including the C-in-C, General Blamey, the CGS, DMI, Deputy DMI and Lieutenant Colonel Sandford, were information addressees only. They were included as a courtesy and had no executive role in the activity.

Burley exercised his powers as SLO and made it emphatically clear to Simpson that he was forbidden to speak to Australia's prime minister on this matter without the clearance of the CGS.[77] It was now that Simpson lost all standing. Not only did he 'bluster and brag', he reverted to his legal training and struck out the references to the British Official Secrets Act and the US legislation covering the indoctrination process before he signed the form.[78] The outcome was predictable. Squadron Leader Burley notified Group Captain Winterbotham that Simpson was not a person 'who should handle or have access to the material', as 'he is obviously one who would not hesitate to act first and ask after'.[79] Simpson and his Security Service were immediately and formally cut off from ULTRA. This meant that Australia was to be completely excluded from access to VENONA, the SIGINT exploitation of NKGB communications from around the world including Canberra, until many years after the formation of ASIO in 1949.

Simpson continued playing games until 19 February, when Blamey instructed him to take no action on the leaks from the Chinese attachés or the Soviet legation until further advice was available. Blamey then cruelly told Simpson, a man he did not like, that he might assist the war effort by running an education campaign on security-mindedness in government departments.[80] Blamey may have been spiteful, but he had made a very valid point.

Blamey's put-down was nothing compared to the blast that came from Winterbotham in London. He informed Australia that the authorities in London and Washington were 'Gravely Concerned' at Simpson's behaviour and Australia's continuing failure to manage ULTRA security. It was not up to the Director-General of Security in Australia to take action on the matters being discussed. This decision would only be made with the full approval of the national SIGINT boards of the United States, Britain and Australia, or there would be serious ramifications. Winterbotham's last sentence, 'the matter of ULTRA security is global', made it very clear what he was saying.[81]

On 17 March, the CGS passed Winterbotham's directions on to Simpson. It was the end of the matter as far as Australia's Security Service was concerned. But it was also the end of the matter as far as Australia being an equal partner in ULTRA was concerned.

Seven months later, Simpson resigned as the Director-General of Security and ascended to the bench of the Supreme Court of the ACT, overseeing the law in what amounted to a local government area. It was not as he hoped the High Court of Australia, but it had to do, and it did allow him to potter around as the Judge Advocate General for the Australian Army and the RAAF, and to chair inquiries into wheat production and air accidents. As Director-General of Security, Simpson was one of those connections of Evatt's who had been promoted well beyond his capacity. He was no loss to intelligence when he returned to the law.

The end of this tale falls outside the purview of this book, as it lies in the story of VENONA, the Petrov Affair and the exposure of Australia's networks of traitors, who used their good intentions to paper over the reality of their spying for Moscow. VENONA and Petrov arose from the breaches of ULTRA security that occurred in Australia between 1943 and 1945, and it is not beyond the bounds of possibility that VENONA started in Australia. While that is not part of our story, ULTRA and 'Y' Procedure SIGINT are, and we now need to look at the winding-down of what was, by any measure, an exceptional wartime achievement.

CHAPTER 21

Saving Australian SIGINT, 1945-47

In December 1943, London asked Central Bureau to provide the raw take of Japanese diplomatic, naval and military attaché and commercial traffic obtained by Australian 'Y' units and organisations.[1] This request was passed to Sandford, who contacted the Deputy DMI, Lieutenant Colonel Little, in Melbourne asking Professor Trendall to provide the necessary details.[2] Trendall replied that the Mornington Intercept Site (52 ASWG) was passing an average of 3000 groups of Japanese diplomatic traffic per day to London. He also detailed that the naval and military attaché traffic amounted to 800–900 messages a month, which were sent to London as microfilm via air mail. This level of activity meant that the Mornington Intercept Site was fully tasked and, according to Trendall, could not take on any more at present.[3]

At around this time, Sandford was also communicating with Trendall via Little on the subject of KANA commercial traffic. Sandford wanted to know the amount of this traffic being intercepted and requested that any such intercept be forwarded to London for cryptanalysis.[4] It turned out that Trendall's section was not collecting KANA commercial traffic.[5] As London wanted this material, the work expanded, with another 15,000 groups per day of Japanese commercial, diplomatic and attaché intercept being added to the current stream.[6] All of this traffic was being sent on the War Office circuit between LHQ in Melbourne and the War Office in London. The circuit had now reached full capacity, and it was impossible to send any more data up this link. In response, GC&CS had now arranged for traffic to be sent via the United States–owned trans-Pacific telegraph cable.[7]

An advantage of the Australia-derived intercept was its high level of accuracy due to Australia's geographic position allowing much better reception of the Japanese long-range radio traffic. This provided the cryptanalysts at GC&CS with take that was not as corrupted by difficult reception conditions. The result was that GC&CS could work on the Japanese 3366 and 4680 code systems more efficiently.[8]

The ability of Central Bureau to contribute more to the Allied SIGINT system was constrained by the lack of capacity in 'Y' communications. The situation was worsened because the telegraphic cables crossing the Indian Ocean were believed to be compromised, as they ran through countries where they could be tapped by German intelligence.

By 1943, the plan for the management of SIGINT communication was laid out in a diagram similar to Figure 21.1. The idea was that the military authorities could pass summaries of paraphrased or sanitised SIGINT across their Most Secret communications circuits. Within this was a much more secure system for carrying ULTRA material to the local SIGINT authorities for distribution as they deemed appropriate, while further in, and even more secret, was the technical chat circuit for exchange of technical SIGINT information on cryptanalysis and traffic analysis matters.

The problem was bandwidth of the existing links, which could not cope with the mass of data being produced. This issue had been foreseen. Before the war, the British Government had tried to interest Australia, New Zealand and the other dominions in creating a high-capacity system to carry large volumes of traffic. No action had been taken and now there was a vital need to increase communication capacity.[9]

After war broke out, the British government proposed a worldwide wireless system dedicated to carrying intercepted enemy traffic. This proposal was put to Prime Minister John Curtin in August 1942.[10] According to the British High Commissioner to Australia, Sir Ronald Cross, plans for this had been developed and authorised in the United Kingdom 'some time ago', and had envisaged dedicated 'Y' communication stations in Egypt, India, East and West Africa, Canada and Australia.[11] The system

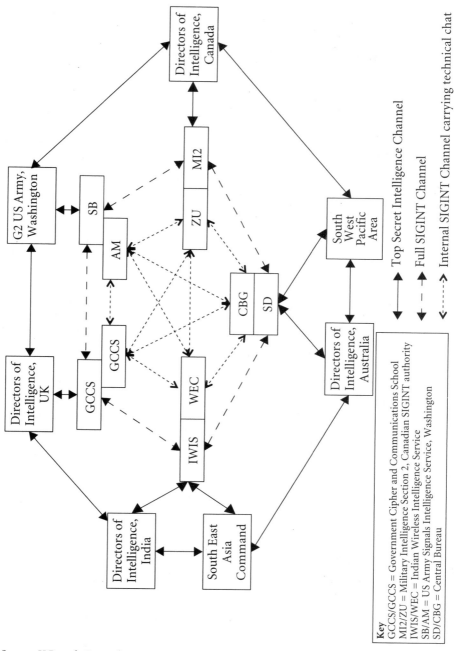

Source: Y Board, General notes on special and W/T intelligence in Australia and New Zealand, National Archives, UK, KW 52/93

Figure 21.1: Secret circuits in 'Y' communications

was to be managed by the Air Ministry in Britain and had proceeded well everywhere but Australia.

The position of the British government, as conveyed by Cross, was that, as Australia would benefit from this system, it would be equitable for the Commonwealth government to bear part of the cost. Someone reading the letter has subsequently marked the part of the sentence about the benefit of the system to Australia.[12] The Air Ministry was hoping to open negotiations on the establishment of the station or stations in Australia, and the ball was firmly in Australia's court. As it was the Air Ministry handling this at the British end, it was decreed in Australia that the Department of Air (DoA) would manage the work, providing the Commonwealth allocated the cash.

The DoA appears not to have really understood the proposal and did not even know which agencies it was for. It continually referred to the 'Combined Bureau' [sic] needing to send intelligence to London and perhaps other centres. After examination, the DoA believed that if the necessary encryption systems were purchased from the United Kingdom, the RAAF could undertake the work. The estimated cost of this approach, AU£4000 was way off the mark, as the antenna array and transmission building had already been costed at £12,000, three times the DoA's estimate for the whole station.[13]

The Department of the Navy and the ACNB did not really care who ran the proposed SIGINT communications system. Whether a service, government department or company, it was immaterial to the navy.[14] On 14 October 1942, the Australian Defence Committee comprising the three service chiefs recommended that the British proposal be adopted, but in principle only. The details were left to the Air Ministry and the DoA.[15]

At around this time, Central Bureau was receiving 2500 intercepted messages per week, 60 operational messages and 2800 DF bearings from just two Type B sections operating in the field, and without the subsection at Port Moresby contributing to the whole.[16] These numbers do not include traffic transmitted. With an increase in operational activity expected from the forthcoming Allied offensives in the SWPA and the increasing size of the 'Y' organisation collecting Japanese communications, data flows would only grow. The need for a massive increase in the capacity of the communications links and signalling organisations was clear.

The details turned out to be rather larger than expected. On 22 October 1942, the Secretary of the Department of Defence Co-ordination put the cost of a station at £72,000. This was broken down into £12,000 for the transmitter station, including power, aerials and building; £10,000 for the receiving station; and £50,000 for the establishment of a full intercept centre, including DF. Staff would be approximately 77 officers and other ranks, at an annual estimated cost of £23,100.[17]

It was now that Fredrick Shedden, Australia's secretary for everything, raised the history of the Imperial Naval Wireless stations at Darwin and HMAS *Harman*.[18] The British government had recommended these stations and the Commonwealth had agreed. The estimated cost was originally £189,000 with a maximum of £200,000, but the final cost was £400,000, a painful experience for the Commonwealth.

Shedden then started wrangling. He argued, with some justification, that Australia's military advisors did not know if the 'Y' communications system was needed and, because of the history of the imperial naval network's cost overruns, Australia needed to consider carefully 'the basis on which any scheme is to be established'.[19] John Curtin repeated Shedden's arguments in their entirety to Sir Ronald Cross on 24 November 1942.[20] This was, however, simple parsimony and a repeat of the indifference that had led to Australia being totally unprepared for war in 1939, a situation for which Fredrick Shedden has never been held accountable despite being the leading defence bureaucrat during the entire period.

On 5 January 1943, Cross informed Curtin that the 'Y' communications system was needed to carry raw intercept from the Australian intercept sites to the United Kingdom at an estimated volume of 100,000 groups per day. This link was to form the Australian part of a system authorised by the UK chiefs of staff, preferably to be located in Melbourne, and it would work direct to GC&CS. The British estimate of the cost was £50,000, substantially below the figures being used by Shedden to sink the proposal.[21]

Now that Shedden had successfully raised the issue of value to Australia, the Defence Communications Committee dutifully handballed the proposal to the Postmaster-General's Department (PMG) for further consideration.[22] By June 1943, the PMG had failed to progress the matter, but informed Shedden that they had 'no knowledge of any factors which, from the point of view of your department, may make the use of submarine cables undesirable'.[23] Five months passed before a decision was made to allow the army and RAAF to transmit 'Y' intercept to the United Kingdom using existing facilities and additional cryptographic systems. The displaced traffic from these circuits would be passed over to the transmitters in Lyndhurst, Victoria.

This proposal ran into some difficulties because the Air Ministry was adamant that only the RAAF should operate the systems. The Air Ministry's counterproposal was to offer to supply the RAAF with the necessary transmitters to establish the circuits as soon as possible, and move the army to the work of ciphering and deciphering the traffic. The Australian response was to agree with the proposals 'in principle' but have the Defence Committee refer the matter back to the Defence Communications Committee.[24] On 4 May 1944, the Defence Committee finally approved the Air Ministry's proposals and nothing continued to happen.

Nothing now happened so effectively that by 15 August 1944, the RAAF was still investigating the installation of transmitters and the Air Ministry had only just despatched two Type ET4750 15-kilowatt transmitters and two Type CRK 100 triple diversity receivers for installation at RAAF Amberley in Queensland and at Zillmere, also in Queensland. The initial cost of this was £7480.[25] By 28 November, it had risen to £16,950. The increase was due to the need to build the necessary infrastructure, including a 33-kilovolt line and antennae to support the transmitters and receivers.

At the end of 1944, more than two years after Sir Ronald Cross had raised the issue, the Commonwealth had still not built the Australian link in the worldwide 'Y' communications system.

All of this was high policy and was occurring at a level well above Central Bureau and well above Alastair Sandford, yet Sandford supported by officers within Military Intelligence would now take the lead in preventing the dissolution of Australia's newly created SIGINT capability.

The story of the 'Y' communications system demonstrates the hurdles Central Bureau had to confront when dealing with government. Despite the limitations imposed, Central Bureau continued its job of supplying the commanders in the field with tactical and operational SIGINT, and in acting as Australia's SIGINT agency in the worldwide system that had evolved from British and American cooperation.

The task facing Central Bureau was immense. The area of operations that needed to be covered was 245,629,636 square kilometres, more than three times the size of the 72,200,000 square kilometres in Europe and the North Atlantic. Even manpower was becoming short as the Australian government rushed to demobilise as many service personnel as they could. The speed with which the Australian government moved to demobilise is understandable, but it continued a system in which the heaviest burden for Australia's defence continued to fall on the soldiers of the AIF, the US National Guard and US conscripts.[26]

If the attitude towards manpower was bad, the attitude towards womanpower was even worse. Women were not even considered as a source of labour until Australia began to realise there would never be enough male volunteers to meet the needs of the three services. Women had been enlisted to make up this shortfall, but only within Australia. The jobs women were temporarily allowed to do included communications, administration and logistics. This employment pattern immediately drew women into SIGINT work at Central Bureau where they were allowed to fill all positions, except those in frontline intercept units.

The result was that as the female personnel took over roles, they learned them and became highly skilled members of both FRUMEL and Central Bureau. Both organisations became dependent upon their female personnel because there were a lot of them and there was no competition for them from field formations. Secondly, they turned out to be exceptionally hardworking and extremely competent. The commanders of the SIGINT units quickly realised this, and found their female members were just as good at cryptanalysis, traffic analysis, and the technical work of intercepting, transcribing and reporting enemy communications as their male counterparts. It was a view that was fully supported by General Northcott, the Chief of the General Staff.[27]

The integration of women into the SIGINT organisations in Melbourne led to the usual difficulties of trying to accommodate them properly in a system that was entirely focused on dealing with men. The WRANS at FRUMEL were accommodated on site at the Moorabbin intercept sites and had to make do with the available accommodation, some of which was less than salubrious. At Central Bureau, the difficulty was solved by allowing women to live in civilian accommodation. As we saw earlier, as far as one can see in the files, not one of these women betrayed SIGINT secrets.

The real threat to Central Bureau's female members did not come from the army or other services, but from the government. The ALP never adjusted its bias against women in the workforce and saw their employment as a temporary wartime measure which would end at the cessation of hostilities, if not before. Women were not going to be allowed to change the male unionist grip on Australia's workplaces. The ALP government was determined they would all return to their kitchens as soon as possible. To be fair, no conservative politicians challenged this position either.

Given Parliament's hostility towards the employment of women generally and the blind adherence to keeping Australian troops at home, the idea of allowing Australian women in the services to serve outside of Australia was anathema.

By 1944, the attitude of Australia's ministers was bizarrely out of date. There seemed to be a wilful ignoring of the numbers of American women serving in Australia and in the islands of the Pacific. They also overlooked the growing number of British servicewomen serving in Australia and the Pacific and the irony that when Australia's women were banned from serving with Central Bureau overseas, the 'Y' Signals Intelligence Board in London ordered British female intercept personnel to Australia.[28] Neither the Curtin nor Chifley governments could get their heads around the reality that highly trained and experienced women were invaluable.

It all came to a head at the end of January 1945, when the decision was made to move Central Bureau to the Philippines in support of GHQ, SWPA. This required Central Bureau to 'rid' itself of personnel who could not serve overseas. Blamey, who had agreed to this move, did not believe there would be any difficulties from the Australian government about the entire unit moving. Based on this, Lieutenant Colonel Sandford reassured Lieutenant Colonel Little that only 'one or two very minor adjustments to our W/E [war establishment]' would be required.[29] Sandford assumed his female personnel would be deployed as part of the move.[30]

Given this assumption, Sandford specifically addressed the need for housekeeping personnel for the women, recommending a war establishment for AWAS housekeeping of one AWAS officer, five NCOs and nineteen AWAS, including clerks, cooks, a tailoress and other support staff.[31]

The response was not long in coming. On 5 February, Little wrote to Sandford telling him that the army was unlikely to get Cabinet approval to move the female personnel beyond New Guinea.[32] He advised Sandford that if he wished further action on this matter, he should submit his requests to the Deputy DMI.

From the tone of the letter, it is obvious that Sandford had most likely discussed the matter with Little, and that he was not going to accept the decision on his female personnel. Sandford's position was difficult because Central Bureau was by now a combined Australian, UK and US unit, and women of all three nations were an integral part of its specialist workforce. When the unit moved forward to Manila, the UK and US female service personnel would go, but the Australian women would be sent home. On paper, this does not seem a big thing, but anyone who has served in a military organisation knows the impact of such a decision. The idea of having to leave your comrades when you have no choice is bad enough, but being forced to leave them because a government decrees it, is devastating. Having that decree based on something as silly as your gender and nationality is obscene in its narrow-mindedness.

The Americans were not too concerned, and it looks like they thought the discussion could not be serious. General Akin was transferring the entire unit, including its 125 Australian women from the army and WAAAF, to Manila, along with its large contingent of US Army Women's Auxiliary Corps (WAC) personnel.[33]

In early May 1945, the Australian Cabinet asked for a report from the CGS on the matter. This was placed before Cabinet on 16 May and explained that the US Army's manning at Central Bureau amounted to 50 per cent of the total, while the Australian Army and the RAAF each provided 25 per cent. The number of women in the unit was 306: comprising 181 US WACs, 60 AWAS and 65 WAAAF, all of them highly trained and experienced specialists in the work of Central Bureau.[34] The CGS even argued that:

> Since an initial training of three months is required before it can be established whether the trainee has the necessary ability and flair for the work, it will be impracticable for Central Bureau to find and train suitable personnel for replacement of the AWAS's (and WAAAF's) employed prior to movement to the Philippine Islands and the efficiency of the unit must suffer in the meantime because the majority of the AWAS's (and WAAAF's) employed have now had two years or more experience of the work in which they are extremely proficient.[35]

The CGS made it clear to Cabinet that the idea of replacing them with male members of the AIF was unworkable.

The CGS strongly endorsed Major General Akin's request for the deployment of the AWAS and WAAAF personnel to Manila, and he emphasised that Akin was acting on behalf of General MacArthur. There is no doubt that the Australian Army's commanders at the highest level wanted the women to go to Manila. They had already had to deal with the narrow-mindedness of Cabinet when it imposed 'severe limitations' on the deployment of women to New Guinea and the islands. They even addressed the ALP's ideological obsession by making it clear that only women who volunteered would be deployed.

Effectively, the government's most senior military advisor was telling Cabinet to send the women to Manila because they were the best available people for the job. He was also advising that if they did not go, it would lead to a serious loss of capability for MacArthur and GHQ, and that 'the flow of vital information will be adversely affected'.[36]

None of this cut any ice with the Australian War Cabinet. On 28 May 1945, the Secretary to the War Cabinet, Fredrick Shedden, issued War Cabinet Minute 4198 stating:

The proposal that members of the Australian Women's Services, at present on the strength of the Allied Central Bureau be transferred to Manila with this establishment was not approved. A definite limit has been laid down by the Government on the number of women to be permitted to serve outside Australia and War Cabinet did not consider that this should be increased.[37]

The decision of Australia's War Cabinet was perverse and it was wrong. It was patronising, sexist, narrow-minded and indicative of the ideological decrepitude of the ALP and the vacuous opposition being led by the Tut-like Billy Hughes.

Now the game turned to the male personnel of Central Bureau and an old foe, Major General Colin (C.H.) Simpson, the Signal Officer-in-Chief (SO in C), re-entered the field in June. Simpson recommended Central Bureau reduce its manning in line with government policy to return service personnel to their civilian occupations as quickly as possible. This policy was a pet of Ben Chifley, who was keen to get Australians back to working on the postwar workers' paradise. Of course, in June 1945, the war was still raging in the Pacific, but the Americans were now doing most of the fighting, so perhaps Chifley had a point.

General Simpson's rationale for reducing Central Bureau's establishment was that the four officers and 29 other ranks assigned to provide him with data were not reporting any to him.[38] Simpson wanted sixteen signals personnel, two officers and fourteen other ranks reassigned from Central Bureau back to his signals organisation because they were 'owned' by it. Brigadier Rogers, the DMI, concurred in the recommendation, provided that the newly promoted Major A.G. Henry was left at Central Bureau along with a small section—one officer and five signallers—to cover certain circuits.[39] At the time of this discussion, the Australian Army strength at Central Bureau was 69 officers and 553 other ranks and, based on the 25 per cent rule, the RAAF would have had a similar number.[40] The US personnel were rapidly moving out to provide support to the fighting troops in the Philippines.

At the same time as Australia was running down its SIGINT commitment to the war against Japan, it was welcoming SIGINT personnel and units from the United Kingdom and Canada. In January 1945, the Canadian Special W/T Group had arrived in Australia and was preparing to take up its designated operational position just outside of Darwin.[41] This unit comprised twelve officers, seventeen warrant officers and NCOs and 268 other ranks, and made a substantial contribution to the SIGINT effort in SWPA.

The deployment of the Canadians and of specialist SIGINT staff to Lord Mountbatten's South East Asia Command and MacArthur's SWPA was part of Britain's push back into the Pacific in the face of high US policy to exclude Britain and other European powers from the region. This policy was resisted by Britain through the re-establishing of a powerful British naval task force supported by an extensive intelligence system.

In March 1944, GC&CS and the British armed services, sitting as the Signals Intelligence Board, issued a 'General Statement of Policy in Regard to Japanese Military and Military/Air Intelligence Preparatory to the Discussions in Washington', which stated:

> The Board cannot readily accept the view that SWPA because it is under an American C-in-C is an exclusively American concern. The example of Eisenhower in Europe is parallel and his Interallied organisation a model for all. Neither can we accept that the Australians are

not British. Judged from the British point of view the suggestion made by Colonel Carter Clarke that the Central Bureau in Brisbane [C.B.B.] should be divided and the Australian side deal only with diplomatic traffic or such other as might be of concern to the Australian Government has no appeal since British Troops are engaged in this theatre and, in the C.B.B., much more than half the staff is British. The British cannot afford to risk a waning interest on the part of General MacArthur in Australian concerns. In the opinion of the War Office, the work of the Australian military Intelligence under Brigadier Rogers is first rate and essential to S.W.P.A. The Board must therefore support the purely British element in Australia.[42]

These minutes also show that Australia was actively supporting the British push and that 'General Blamey is understood to desire that Central Bureau should preserve its inter-Allied complexion or perhaps more accurately stated should not lose its Australian identity.'[43] The board made the decision for the deployment on 17 August 1944 at a meeting attended by C, Major General Menzies, as Director of GC&CS; Commodore E.G.N. Rushbrooke; Major General J.A. Sinclair; Air Vice Marshal F.F. Inglis; and Commander E.W.H. Travis representing GC&CS.[44] By August 1944 SIGINT in the Pacific had become a substantial issue in Anglo-American rivalry as the United States moved to eject GC&CS from any involvement in Japanese SIGINT. The British were having none of it and at a meeting of the Deputy Directors' Committee on Japanese Signals on Saturday 5 August 1944, the US suggestion that all the British Japanese sections move to the United States under the Signals Intelligence Service, US Army, at Arlington Hall was rejected on the grounds that moving British SIGINT personnel to Arlington Hall in Washington would entail them being absorbed into a less well developed organisation which had failed in its attempts to adopt a joint service approach.[45] In addition, the decision to send the Canadians to Australia was ratified providing the Canadians could guarantee 'its removal would not affect the interception of main-line Japanese traffic in Canada'.[46]

As 1944 moved towards a close, the growing British concerns over the disjointed US SIGINT system would become an important influence on the thinking of the US SIGINT establishment, particularly those like Abraham Sinkov who worked within the joint service environment of Central Bureau and would go on to play major roles in the establishment of the National Security Agency and the negotiation of the UKUSA on SIGINT.

Britain was still, at the end of 1944, operating three large SIGINT centres: Colombo, covering IJN traffic; Delhi, covering the IJA; and Brisbane, covering IJA and IJN air and surface traffic. These stations were still producing valuable SIGINT and their importance rose as US commanders began moving their own SIGINT units further north as they advanced on Japan.

By August 1945, the Australians were well aware of the declining interest of the US in SIGINT activities in Australia. Sandford was now reporting to LHQ that US units had now taken over all of the tasking, coverage and discrimination of Japanese circuits north of the Halmahera Islands in the northern Indonesian Archipelago. As a result, Central Bureau was no longer required in the Philippines, and Sandford recommended Central Bureau's forward HQ and operations be ended.[47]

On 25 August, Sandford wrote to Professor T.G. Room, the leader of the Special Intelligence Bureau's attack on Japanese diplomatic and commercial traffic, to inform him there would be no further requirement for cryptanalysis of Japanese diplomatic or commercial traffic. Under the surrender agreement, all such traffic would be sent in clear language and, thus, Room's services were no longer required. It would appear that Sandford was endeavouring to return all of Central Bureau's and the Special Intelligence Bureau's technical staff to their civilian employment.[48] On 13 October, the Signals Intelligence Board in London asked Brigadier A. Lycett at GC&CS to inform the Air Ministry that, as of 0001Z, 15 October 1945, the 'YOKE' link to Central Bureau in Brisbane be discontinued.[49]

The work of Central Bureau was now over, and the only task that remained was to try to keep an Australian SIGINT organisation in existence after the war. There can be little doubt that this was a problem that exercised the minds of Alastair Sandford, Robert Little and perhaps Rupert Long, as well as a number of Australia's senior military commanders. One task that could be used to keep a nucleus working was the writing of Central Bureau's unit history and the history of Australia's wartime SIGINT work, including that of the Special Intelligence Bureau. This work was also vital in ensuring that the technical and organisational experience of the organisations was recorded and available as evidence in justifying the need for a peacetime SIGINT organisation.

The nucleus retained at Central Bureau consisted of ten officers and four other ranks, as well as one US Army Special Wireless Company operating twelve intercept positions and conducting research into all types of Morse and non-Morse communications. The RAAF looked after its own needs and was to advise the army on the organisation it wished to retain. No mention was made of the ACNB's needs or what was intended for the RAN in the postwar period.[50]

This is not the end of the story. The nucleus retained at Central Bureau continued to be led by Alastair Sandford while he oversaw the completion by Eric Nave of Central Bureau's technical histories. What else Sandford was doing is hard to tell, but it is clear that he was working on matters that required a number of trips on 'Special Duty' to the United Kingdom and Europe in March and April 1946.[51] Following his return, he was placed on the Retirement List on 8 August 1946.[52] Sandford was now officially retired from the army, yet, oddly, his army record notes his departure for the United Kingdom aboard the SS *Chitral* on 17 October 1946. On the same day, he was moved from the Retirement List (RSL) to the Retirement List (LWOP) and attached to the Australian Army Staff, London, on 8 November 1946.[53] This suggests Alastair Sandford was travelling to the United Kingdom on official business. This business can have been nothing other than to negotiate with GC&CS and SIS the foundation of the Defence Signals Bureau (DSB) as the postwar Australian National SIGINT authority, thus keeping Australia as a partner in the worldwide SIGINT system that would soon be established under UKUSA.

This idea is not far-fetched. Sandford was known and trusted by the British and, importantly, he had been trained by them and had demonstrated a significant degree of leadership and diplomacy in steering Central Bureau and the Special Intelligence Bureau through the often difficult relationships that existed between Australia, Britain and the US during the war. Negotiating the establishment of DSB in August 1947 and its subsequent integration into UKUSA was something Sandford was well positioned to achieve. All of this means that Sandford holds a far more important place in the history of Australian intelligence than he has ever been given credit for.

A final oddity in Sandford's career is that, contrary to established policy, he was permitted by the minister to take his discharge in London on 31 January 1947.[54] Following this, Sandford remained in London and in the late 1950s, he was living in Italy and serving as the head of British Petroleum in that country, where he was heavily involved with the British Council. His final honour, an OBE in 1968, was for this work. Although there is no evidence for it at all, Sandford's civilian career would appear a very good one for a spy working for SIS.

For his wartime service, Sandford was awarded the US Medal of Freedom with Bronze Palm in 1947.[55] The citation reads:

Lieutenant Colonel A. W. Sandford, SX11231, Australian Imperial Forces. For meritorious service which has aided the US in the prosecution of the war against the enemy in the Southwest Pacific Area, from March 1942 to August 1945. As an Assistant Director, Central Bureau, Office of the Chief Signal Officer, IJA, Southwest Pacific Area, later US Army Forces, Pacific, Colonel Sandford displayed outstanding technical skill in organizing and coordinating activities of the Australian personnel in effectively prosecuting the mission of radio intelligence. Under his distinguished leadership, much valuable information was furnished in Military Intelligence. Through exceptional professional ability, resourcefulness, and unremitting devotion to duty, Colonel Sandford made a most significant contribution to the success of Allied operations in the Southwest Pacific Area.

CHAPTER 22

Coastwatching Behind Enemy Lines

The Japanese assault on Asia and the Pacific had succeeded beyond anything Japanese planners had foreseen. Their successes were so fast and so extensive that they were sure it would take the United States and Britain a long time to regroup and launch the counteroffensives the Japanese were sure would come.[1] What the Japanese did not expect was that those counteroffensives would come within a month of the US surrender at Corregidor, when the US Navy caught the Japanese Combined Fleet off Midway Island and destroyed its strategic capability.[2] Within another month, on 7 August, the US Navy had opened the Guadalcanal campaign that would draw the IJN and IJA into a six-month battle of attrition and drain Japanese strength for the defence of the areas it had already captured.

For Australia, there were losses of territory, as New Britain and New Ireland were occupied and the Japanese swept down the north coast of New Guinea, heading towards Milne Bay and Port Moresby. One of the major advantages for the Allies, however, was that their intelligence system remained intact, and while the SIGINT organisations were being reorganised in Melbourne, they maintained cover of the IJN and IJA nets, and fed intelligence to GHQ, SWPA and the US Navy's Command South Pacific (COMSOUPAC). The other major Allied intelligence system to remain intact and in place was Eric

Feldt's coastwatch network. This was now, however, operating behind enemy lines, something that had never been envisaged when the organisation was established.

With their capture of Rabaul, the Japanese had removed the threat it posed to their base on Truk.[3] In Rabaul, they had also obtained a strategically important port that enabled them to control the waters of the eastern archipelago, and a forward air base from which they could cover any operations to capture Port Moresby, Buna and Guadalcanal in the British Solomons.[4] The importance of these locations lay in airfields, which, once constructed, would allow the IJN to provide the land-based air cover under which its surface fleet could operate to cut the Allied supply lines to the west coast of the United States.

The Japanese threat assessment showed that any major attack on their southern position would come from the British in the Indian Ocean or the Americans in the Pacific. By mid-March, Imperial HQ had ordered that Japanese forces in the islands regroup, consolidate their positions and establish the military administration of the newly conquered areas.[5] By late May, the Japanese believed that peace and order had been restored in the newly occupied areas, and the military administration was progressing smoothly.[6]

While this regrouping and consolidation was going on, the Imperial HQ considered its options, including invading Australia, an idea pushed by the IJN Section. This was quickly discounted for the alternative of seizing Port Moresby, Fiji, Samoa and New Caledonia, as well as areas in the archipelago from which a naval and air campaign against northern Australia and the sea lanes from the west coast of the United States could be launched.[7]

As soon as Rabaul fell, the Japanese mopped up the fleeing Australian garrison and other Europeans on New Britain. On New Ireland, the situation was not as bad, because the Japanese were not particularly interested once they had seized Kavieng. At this point, the focus was on Buna, Buka, Bougainville and the Solomon Islands as jumping off places for their campaigns against Port Moresby, New Caledonia and Fiji.

This was the plan until the Battle of the Coral Sea. On 17 July 1942, Imperial HQ released the 17th Army from the mission of capturing Fiji and New Caledonia, and the following day, the 17th Army ordered the South Seas Detachment at Rabaul to capture Buna and launch an attack on Port Moresby over the Kokoda Track.[8] This was the situation in the islands as Feldt's coastwatchers reorganised themselves to continue their work.

For Eric Feldt and the coastwatcher organisation, this period of the war involved extracting coastwatch parties now encumbered by civilian and military refugees. The situation was unsustainable. First, coastwatchers were being distracted from their primary task of collecting and reporting intelligence; secondly, the refugees were drawing the Japanese onto the coastwatcher parties. On Bougainville, New Britain and New Ireland the situation was bad, while in the British Solomon Islands protectorate things were slightly better, and intelligence was kept flowing despite the problems.

In Australia, Feldt was facing other issues, principally defending the organisation from a takeover by what he termed the army's 'Boy's Own Annual brigade', who had suddenly realised they lacked any intelligence and observer system of their own. For the army, the answer was obvious. The RAN would be forced to hand over coastwatchers across New Guinea, the Torres Straits and northern Australia to the army.

The pressure from army finally led to a meeting at Victoria Barracks, Melbourne, on 16 April 1942 between Colonel Roberts, AMF, and Wing Commander S.G. Brearley, RAAF; supported by Colonel Elliott R. Thorpe, US Army, and commanders Long and Feldt. The RAAF and US Army representatives, who were attempting to create an effective early warning system for air raids, raised the need for a single joint-service observer organisation led by a single commander, who would of course be an RAAF officer.

Long responded by recommending Feldt as the commander of any joint organisation, keeping the proposed organisation under Navy Office.[9] Colonel Roberts half-heartedly proposed that the organisation be placed under General Morris's 8th Military District in Port Moresby. This was immediately rejected by Colonel Thorpe, who made it clear that General MacArthur's GHQ would control this organisation. Colonel Roberts quickly concurred with this decision, as indeed he had most likely always intended.[10] Roberts was no friend of Feldt's coastwatchers, and had been working behind the scenes to bring them under the auspices of Military Intelligence.[11]

What Roberts and Military Intelligence did not appreciate was that the coastwatcher organisation's area of operations straddled not only MacArthur's SWPA and Admiral Chester Nimitz's South Pacific Area, but Australian and British territories, which, in the Solomons, were not under Australian control. The arrangement for control of coastwatching in the Solomons was a government-to-government agreement giving Navy Office the responsibility for the management of the Admiralty's Reporting Officer system. For the Australian Army or the United States to take over this role needed British approval.

The other problem was that Feldt's coastwatchers were on the ground providing intelligence essential to the operations of the US Navy in the Pacific. There was little likelihood that the US Navy, the only force in direct contact with large Japanese forces, would tolerate any disruption to the flow of intelligence from Feldt's coastwatchers.

The result was a compromise with army looking after observer posts in New Guinea and Papua, and Feldt retaining control of the coastwatchers on Bougainville, New Britain, New Ireland and the Solomon Islands. This agreement did not end the infighting and Colonel Roberts would eventually drag Feldt's organisation into his unsuccessful outfit later in the war.

With the agreement made at the meeting between the services, the new division of responsibilities meant the break-up of the coastwatcher group created by District Officer J.K. McCarthy and Captain G.C. Harris in order to evacuate refugees from New Britain. Two members of the group, R. Chugg and R. Emery of the New Guinea Volunteer Rifles, remained with ANGAU, while McCarthy, Harris and the rest became part of the coastwatcher organisation.[12] L. Bell, K.C. Douglas and R. Olander were appointed to the RANVR, Bell and Douglas as lieutenants and Olander as a Sub-Lieutenant. At the same time W.L. Tupling on Ninigo and K.H. McColl at Wuvulu were picked up sending signals from their remote islands. These two were subsequently ordered back and were appointed petty officers in the RANVR, while Morton Johnson, who had been building cocoa dryers on Ninigo, was made a sergeant in ANGAU.[13]

While Long and Feldt were battling the army, the situation in the islands was deteriorating as the Japanese established their military administration and consolidated their hold. This made them the new big men,[14] a reality that augured ill for the coastwatchers. As the Japanese became the distributors of work and wealth, they would win over a portion of the local population, who would assist them in tracking down coastwatch parties. On Bougainville, this is exactly what was about to happen.

Until this time, conditions on Bougainville had allowed the coastwatchers Jack Read and Paul Mason, accompanied by a party of soldiers and locals, to continue reporting intelligence, including advance—in most cases very much so—notice of Japanese air raids flying against various targets in the area of operations. As the tempo of the military operations increased, so did Read and Mason's reporting. But the IJN's SIGINT system, which, contrary to popular belief, was well organised and highly effective in identifying signals and their location, exposed them to danger.

As the coastwatchers transmitted their reports, there is no doubt the Japanese were conducting SIGINT operations against them, most likely using English-speaking Filipino intercept operators. They would have been aware of the relationship between the movements of IJN aircraft within line of sight of Bougainville and the transmission of the coastwatch messages reporting them. This would explain the appearance of more and more Japanese vessels in the anchorages around Bougainville, especially the area between Buin and the Shortland Islands. These vessels would have been fixing the signals and reducing the triangulation error to manageable proportions. The coastwatchers, well aware of the threat, attempted to shield their ground wave to avoid detection.[15]

The only advantage the coastwatchers had in this game was that triangulation, no matter how good, does not pinpoint a location but provides a triangular area within which the targeted transmitter is operating, as Figure 22.1 shows. This triangle can be reduced, but not to a pinpoint. This factor meant that the Japanese search parties had to cover a lot of ground when searching for a detected transmitter, and that is where the skilled local trackers came into their own. This need to search the triangle provided sufficient warning for coastwatcher parties to pack up their portable equipment and move. This was a slow process, however, because in 1942 portable was a relative term.

The portable equipment carried by a coastwatcher party needed a gang of carriers, somewhere between fifteen and 30. The tele-radio used by coastwatchers was, for its time, an excellent fixed-point radio set, and could be split into three components—the receiver, transmitter and speakers—for transportation. Each component weighed 32–45 kilograms, making a total load of up to 120 kilograms, not including the antennae, keys, batteries, charging engine and benzene fuel. It took between twelve and sixteen strong and experienced men to carry it and its accessories, and it was a nightmare to carry across broken ground and through jungle.[16]

Apart from the radio, a coastwatcher party had to carry its own provisions, tents, camp equipment, weapons, ammunition, medical equipment and water. Yet this was not all that needed to be carried. Whatever motivated

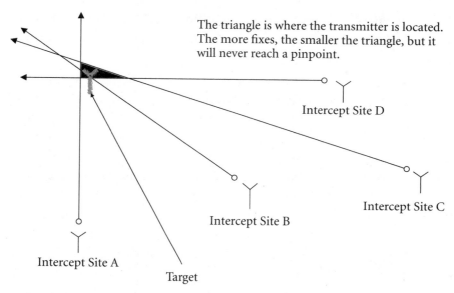

The triangle is where the transmitter is located. The more fixes, the smaller the triangle, but it will never reach a pinpoint.

Intercept Site D

Intercept Site C

Intercept Site B

Intercept Site A

Target

Figure 22.1: Direction-finding fixes on a target transmitter

the locals to assist the coastwatchers, it was not entirely altruistic and most definitely not patriotism. The carriers and support provided by village big men had to be paid for in commodities they wanted rather than cash, which is lighter to carry. The villagers quite rightly wanted things they could not get, like burlap (hessian), cotton cloth and, most of all, twist tobacco. This required a lot of muscle and a lot of food for energy. The image of small groups of coastwatchers stealthily making their way through the jungle is utterly wrong; in reality, it was more like a travelling circus.

As time went by and Japanese plans were more frequently thwarted, it was logical for Japanese commanders to bring in experts from the Kempeitai or the IJN's own Tokkeitai. On Bougainville, the Japanese began inserting many more patrols from the sea, and to establish supply and equipment caches for these patrols to use. They also began employing locals to work for them, which increased their standing as the new big men. This they reinforced by terrorising the locals if there was any hint of opposition or resistance.

As the Japanese reliance on local labour increased, the coastwatchers exploited it by inserting their own loyal police and carriers into the Japanese workforce. This provided the coastwatchers with raw intelligence on what the Japanese were doing, how far they had progressed, and where the most valuable targets such as ammunition and fuel stocks were hidden. All of this was being passed back to Townsville and Port Moresby, adding to the wealth of information the Allies were receiving.

The activities of the coastwatchers on Bougainville and other islands had now really begun to attract attention. This increased Japanese anxiety about them may have come from reading the coastwatch codes, enabling the Japanese to form a picture of just how comprehensive the coastwatch reporting was. The idea that the Japanese were reading coastwatch codes is not far-fetched. They had extensive experience of breaking and reading the Nationalist Chinese codes, and they had captured documentation on low-level British and US codes during their rapid advances of early 1942. It is more than likely that cryptanalytical research was now providing them with considerable insights into the remaining low-level codes used by coast-watchers and others.

By the middle of 1942, with the tempo of operations building in the lead-up to Guadalcanal, the Japanese took action to clear Bougainville of its coastwatchers. They started by sending large patrols across the interior of Bougainville in an effort to catch the coastwatchers. These patrols didn't work.

This activity, and the violence of the Black Dogs, the group of locals formed at Buka, would later be attributed to Tashiro Tsunesuke, a Japanese civilian who had lived in Rabaul and Bougainville since 1917. Tsunesuke left Rabaul just before the outbreak of hostilities and had returned with the Japanese military administration in 1942. The evidence later collected against Tsunesuke doesn't stack up, and it is unlikely that he was anything other than a coopted civilian forced to work for the Japanese administration. The man who does look like the professional counterintelligence operative was Tsunesuke's boss, Petty Officer Harada, of the 1st Base Force.

Petty Officer Harada was fluent in English but could only speak a little pidgin, and this probably resulted in him acquiring Tsunesuke.[17] The fact that a naval NCO could obtain such a scarce asset indicates that Harada was Tokkeitai. Only a Tokkeitai NCO would be left controlling a Japanese civilian with the sort of knowledge and background Tsunesuke had.

Further evidence that Harada was Tokkeitai comes from stories that even today are told on Bougainville. Harada was the head of propaganda and local pacification on the island, and was also responsible for investigating anyone suspected of helping the enemy.[18] He was also widely feared by the local population and by IJN personnel.

The situation was now so bad that Paul Mason and the others could not carry out the plan detailed in the map in Figure 22.2. Mason hurriedly withdrew across the top of the island and just evaded capture.[19] This withdrawal led to collateral damage when a European planter, Tom Ebery, who had been hiding in the area, was found by the Japanese. Ebery was later killed or died crossing the Mailoh River near Bogisago on 4 January 1943. Some reports say he was tortured and then killed.[20]

Mason's party were in a bleak situation. If they stayed in the area, they would most likely be caught, and even if they weren't captured, they would be moving and unable to provide intelligence. Lieutenant Commander Mackenzie, who now controlled the parties on Bougainville as well as in the Solomons, ordered Mason to head north and join Read. En route, Mason came across another European, Frank Roche, a miner who had stayed to protect his valuable mining plant. Mason stayed with Roche for two days while a jungle sore on his foot healed. Roche refused to leave his equipment and was killed by the Japanese tracking Mason's party.[21]

On 27 January 1943, after covering 160 kilometres Mason found Lieutenant J.H. Mackie's camp and the next day they all arrived at Jack Read's location. By this stage, Read had arranged the evacuation of all Europeans on the island and numbers of Chinese men, women and children, who were at risk of being murdered or raped by the Japanese and the Black Dogs. By now, Mason, Read and Lieutenant Mackie's section had been on Bougainville for almost a year. It was time for them to leave. Yet both coastwatchers decided to stay because they believed they owed this to the local inhabitants who had risked so much to help them.[22]

In Townsville, concern continued to grow as the brutality and aggressive nature of the Japanese counterintelligence activity increased. Feldt now believed everyone on Bougainville needed to be extracted.[23] This included nuns and the Chinese, as well as the remnants of 1 Independent Company. The evacuation was timed for the end of December and took place on New Year's Eve when Read led the evacuation of the last Europeans, including the nuns, by the USS *Nautilus*.[24]

Despite this removal of the civilians, the situation continued to get worse. Paul Mason now joined Read, as the southern end of Bougainville became too dangerous. Japanese patrolling became even more aggressive and they found many Chinese civilians and inflicted great suffering on them. They also started pushing back Lieutenant Mackie's outposts.[25]

Mackie's unit, which was part of the AIF and not subordinate to FERDINAND (the coastwatchers), now signalled Army HQ to request permission to withdraw. Colonel Roberts and the AIB used this as an excuse to interfere in FERDINAND's arrangements for the extraction operations by arranging a separate evacuation of Lieutenant Mackie's section.[26] The inclusion of three nuns, eight other women, 27 children, and missionary Usaia Sotutu's wife and family, does not appear to have been contemplated by Roberts.[27] According to Feldt, on 29 March, when Read boarded the submarine USS *Gato*, commanded by Lieutenant Commander Robert J. Foley, US Navy, it was news to Foley that 51 people were in the party.[28] In true US submariner fashion, however, Foley and his crew made it happen, and they squeezed the entire party into the *Gato*.[29]

Before Lieutenant Commander Foley could embark the refugees, he had to disembark Lieutenant Douglas N. Bedkober and another section of Independent Company troops, plus ten more from the AIF, as well as J.H. Keenan from FERDINAND and two locals, one from Buka and one from South Bougainville, who were to return to the local areas to spread the news of Guadalcanal and other Allied victories among their families and friends.[30]

In April 1943, a second evacuation was undertaken. The submarine landed E.D. (Wobby) Robinson and G. Stevenson, and took off Lieutenant Mackie and his last twelve men, Bishop Wade of Bougainville, nine missionaries, a planter, R. Stuart, an unknown European man, eight Chinese, seven other men and one child.[31]

Despite the success of the reliefs conducted by submarine, the situation on Bougainville really began to unravel two days before the arrival of the last submarine. The first disaster was the crashing of the RAAF Catalina conducting the resupply drop, which killed three of the crew and seriously injured four others.[32] To make it even worse, heavy rain and difficult ground prevented the evacuation of the injured, who now needed to be nursed by the FERDINAND team.

The party on Bougainville included five experienced operatives—Wobby Robinson, Stevenson, Mason, Read and Keenan—and 22 new soldiers, seven Chinese men plus the carriers required for such a big group. This was a very large number of people to hide from the Japanese. On top of this, they had four injured airmen. Things were out of control. Despite this, they planned to establish a network of observation posts to cover the island (see Figure 22.2).

The plan they were working to was to cover the whole of Bougainville. Keenan would lead a party in the north, Read and Robinson in the central east, Sergeant G. McPhee on the west coast, and Mason and Stevenson with eight soldiers, Usaia, William McNicol and ten local police in the south. Lieutenant Bedkober and his remaining soldiers would guard the main camp with the injured RAAF crew.[33]

Mason's party set off in May 1943 for the west coast so as to travel by canoe to the south of the island. They found signs of Japanese activity everywhere, including inland when they moved there for safety. A few days later, because of a lack of carriers, they could not carry everything at once. It would appear that fear of the Japanese had frightened the locals sufficiently for them to refuse assistance to FERDINAND parties. Mason's group had to cache its equipment and provisions, leaving a local police officer and some carriers as guards. Within a short time, the Japanese attacked the cache, killed one carrier, captured the police officer and scattered the rest.[34]

Now the inexperience of the AIF troops became a liability, as they did not move through the jungle like the FERDINAND personnel or the carriers. They made noise, lost equipment, wasted supplies and demonstrated a lack of familiarity with jungle living that handicapped the FERDINAND personnel. In an environment where there is no margin for error, this was a bad omen.[35] On Saturday, 26 June 1943, another serious loss occurred when a Japanese patrol attacked Stevenson, Usaia and their small group while they rested in a village. The group had posted sentries on two paths leading to the village, but a local man led the Japanese by a third. The Japanese immediately attacked, killing Stevenson. Usaia led the survivors to Mason's party the next day. They had lost all of their equipment and food, and the Japanese, aided by the local inhabitants, were close behind.

In the north, the Japanese activity was so intense that Keenan's party could not collect intelligence, let alone send messages to Townsville and Port Moresby. At Lunga (Lungga) on Guadalcanal in the Solomons, the Deputy Supervising Intelligence Officer, Lieutenant Commander I. Pryce-Jones, recommended immediate evacuation of all parties on Bougainville, and Commodore J.C. McManus concurred.[36] On 29 June, Mason's party

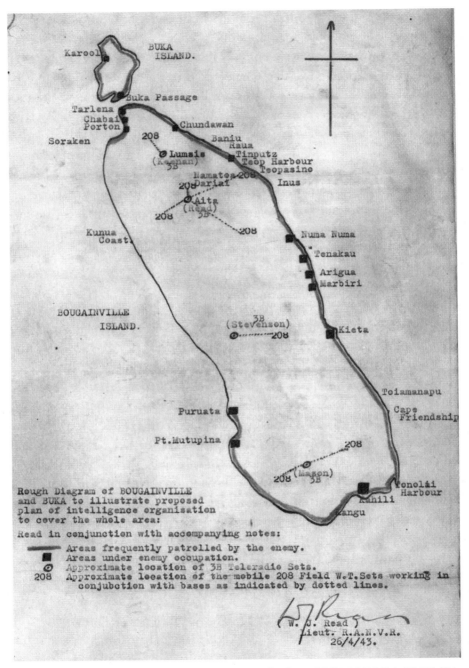

Source: 'Reports from coastwatchers in the Solomon Islands area', BC410664, NAA: B3476, 37A

Figure 22.2: Planned coastwatcher coverage of Bougainville, 1943

was ambushed and in the confusion lost William McNicol, a police officer, and several carriers who bolted into the bush. They also lost all of their equipment, including their packs, which they had to drop in order to run. For seven days, the Japanese chased the remainder of the party until they managed to break clear. On 18 July 1943, Mason's party made contact with Keenan.

Read and Robinson on the east coast were seeing little of interest, but again the aggression of the Japanese patrols was creating a grave risk of contact. In early June, the Japanese fell upon Read and Robinson's camp and destroyed their food and equipment, although they missed the tele-radio hidden in the jungle. In the north, Keenan was attacked twice in succession, forcing him to abandon his tele-radio and move south to join Read and Robinson. Read sent Keenan and his surviving party off to the west coast and moved his own party to the AIF camp with the injured RAAF aircrew in it. What Read didn't know was that Bedkober's party had also been heavily attacked and suffered significant losses on 16 June.

Early that morning, Bedkober had sent Sergeant V.M. Day and three soldiers to prepare a drop site. Around 45 minutes after Day's group had left Bedkober at Sikoriapia Village, they heard heavy firing as a force of 80 Japanese and 40 locals attacked the village. One of the RAAF crew, Flight Officer C.S. Dunn, was shot dead, Bedkober and Corporal J. Fenwick were captured on the spot, and the rest of the party was rounded up later. The situation that FERDINAND faced on Bougainville was that Mason was off the air, Bedkober's party was wiped out, McPhee was running from the Japanese who had attacked Bedkober, and Read and Robinson were barely surviving. Aggressive Japanese patrolling with local assistance had shattered FERDINAND's operations on Bougainville in less than a fortnight.[37]

On 26 June, Read signalled FERDINAND that Bougainville was untenable and all personnel needed to be evacuated immediately.[38] Read's signal led to the US Third Fleet's unit 31 (CTF 31) requesting COMSOUPAC urgently extricate the 130 personnel, as the Japanese were now conducting wide and coordinated efforts to surround them. It was assessed that some parties could be concentrated by 20 July at a point on the mid-west coast between Belua and Cape Moltke, with the remainder ready by 31 July.[39] On 31 July, the last of FERDINAND's personnel were taken off Bougainville and all coastwatching activity ceased.

The operations on Bougainville had proven expensive. FERDINAND had suffered nine killed, wounded or captured, and had listened as aggressive and capable Japanese forces chased three major coastwatch parties so effectively that no intelligence was obtained. For FERDINAND, Bougainville was a failure and a demonstration of how difficult such intelligence operations became when the local population was not entirely supportive.

Yet it was not all doom and gloom for FERDINAND, because further south, in the British Solomons, the coastwatchers were winning the admiration and respect of the US forces fighting the Japanese in and around Guadalcanal. This now takes us back to early 1942, when the Japanese moved south to threaten the Solomons.

In 1942, the Solomon Islands was a British territory controlled by the Resident Commissioner, who at this time was W.S. Marchant. Marchant had decided to stay in the Solomons, but to withdraw his administrators and district officers from the northern parts of the islands and set up his HQ on Tulagi.[40] From here, Marchant administered the islands and kept a firm British hand on what would happen on British territory. To make sure that he and his staff had standing with the military, he commissioned himself as a Lieutenant Colonel and was appointed to the command of the British Solomon Islands Protectorate Defence Force (BSIPDF), into which he then conscripted all his district officers.[41]

As we have already seen, however, the responsibility for coastwatching in the Solomons fell to the ACNB, and Marchant had to cooperate with Eric Feldt in this activity.[42] He even lost some of his officials, men like F.A. Rhodes and K.D. Hay, who were appointed sub-lieutenants in the RANVR, and A.M. Andresen and L. Schroeder, who were appointed petty officers, so they could serve as coastwatchers.[43]

The situation on Tulagi and in the Solomons generally was getting more difficult as the Japanese ramped up their air offensive, particularly against Tulagi itself. Although the effect of the Japanese attacks was reduced by the early warning coming from the coastwatchers on Bougainville, the difficulties of trying to run the government from Tulagi became too difficult for Marchant, so he decided to move his administration to Malaita Island. This caused a conflict with the coastwatch organisation, because Marchant wanted to take Lieutenant Commander D.S. Macfarlane, RANVR, the only qualified

Smoke from the burning oil storage tanks after the German attack on Nauru, December 1940. NAA

The phosphate loader and gantry on Nauru was a major target for the German raiders. Smoke from the burning oil storage tanks can be seen in the background. NAA

Ruby Boye-Jones at her tele-radio on Vanikoro Island, Santa Cruz Group. She sent detailed reports four times a day. Courtesy Boye Family Collection, Sea Power Centre—Australia

British Solomon Islands Protectorate Defence Force soldier, probably Sergeant William Bennett, at Segi station on New Georgia, operating a tele-radio. Australian War Memorial (AWM)

Captain Roy Kendall, RNR, Secret Intelligence Service
(SIS) Head of Station and Secret Intelligence Australia
(SIA), Brisbane, 1942 to 1946. Later he was elected
Senator for Queensland. NAA

A rare photograph of Eve Walker as part of the BOAC delegation in Melbourne, 1946.
From 1943 to1945, Eve Walker, using the cover of a Third Officer WRNS, was Roy Kendall's
deputy in Brisbane and ran the SIS counterintelligence effort against the United States
and Australia. *The Women's Weekly*, 15 June 1946, NLA

Central Bureau headquarters, 21 Henry Street, Ascot, Brisbane. Central Bureau worked for General Douglas MacArthur but was controlled by SIGINT authorities in Washington and London and was closely monitored by Kendall's SIS on London's behalf. AWM

Alastair Sandford, the head of Central Bureau and the unheralded father of Australian SIGINT.

No. 3 Wireless Unit, RAAF, based at Coomalie Creek, NT, 1944—part of Central Bureau's extensive intercept organisation. AWM

Lieutenant W.J. Reid (hand on hip) and DSIO, Lieutenant Commander I. Pryce-Jones
(second from right), with members of the British Solomon Islands Police, probably
late 1943 on Guadalcanal. AWM

Coastwatcher Donald Kennedy's house at Segi, New Georgia. AWM

The Services Reconnaissance Department (SRD) Maintenance Lugger Section's Snake-class junk, HMAS *Tigersnake*, which transported SRD parties and supplies into Japanese-occupied islands. NAA

Photo of Petty Officer Roy Woodroffe when he was a leading telegraphist. He was captured around July 1942 and subsequently executed by the Japanese in late 1942. AWM

Coastwatch communications dugout, Guadalcanal, October 1943, with operator and runner. The radio on the left was used to communicate with higher headquarters and supported military commands, and the AWA tele-radio set on the right was used for monitoring X frequency used by the coastwatcher network. AWM

Sergeant Yauwika of the British Solomon Islands Protectorate Native Police being presented the Loyal Service Medal by Lieutenant Commander I. Pryce-Jones, RANVR, for his work as a coastwatcher at Kieta, 14 October 1943. AWM

Coastwatchers in late 1942. *Front, left to right*: L.E. Ashton, L.C. Noakes, F.A. Rhodes, E. Feldt, H.A. Mackenzie, G.H.R. Marsland, H.R. Koch, A. Campbell. *Back, left to right*: M.H. Wright, R.I. Skinner, K.W.T. Bridge, R.C. Cambridge, L.A. Walker, H.A.F. Robertson, C.W. Seaton, H.L. Williams. All of the men in this photograph survived the war, a tribute to the professionalism of Eric Feldt's organisation. AWM

An appalling truth revealed: the 12 August 1945 signal to the SRD from the Kempeitai on Timor, sarcastically confirming the compromise of all SRD operations on the island. NAA intelligence officer in the Solomons, with him. Macfarlane, however, had been ordered by Feldt to go to Guadalcanal.[44]

Marchant's reasons for moving to Malaita were sound. He needed to establish a radio network that could communicate with Port Moresby, Suva on Fiji and Townsville, as well as with the stations spread throughout the Solomons and the islands of the South Pacific. The mountains inland from Auki on Malaita provided one of the best locations for this, and Marchant established the retransmission station there for the entire FERDINAND network in New Britain, New Ireland and the Solomon Islands. Professional operators, including T.W. Sexton, the Government Wireless Officer, C.N.F. Bengough and H.W. Bullen, operated the station.[45] This team was very experienced in picking up signals from the entire region in the difficult atmospherics of the tropics, and re-encrypting the messages in a higher-grade code for transmission to the NIO at Port Vila; from there they were sent to Admiral W.F. Halsey's South Pacific Area.[46]

An important station in this network was the Vanikoro post on Vanikoro Island in the Santa Cruz group. On this island was a female coastwatcher, 51-year old Mrs Ruby Boye-Jones, supported by her husband, Sydney Boye-Jones, who was the manager of the timber company on Vanikoro. Mrs Boye-Jones provided retransmission services for Marchant's signals to Vila when atmospheric conditions were bad, and she furnished local intelligence reports as well as weather reports, which she sent four times a day.

The IJN was well aware of Mrs Boye-Jones's activities, and in 1942 she was sent threatening messages by the Japanese intercept operators listening to her messages. The threats did not stop her. In line with his policy of appointing all FERDINAND operatives to a military rank, Eric Feldt worked at getting Ruby Boye-Jones appointed to a position as a WRANS. This proved difficult because, as an Australian servicewoman in 1942, she was forbidden by government policy to be where she was, even if it was her home. It took until 27 July 1943, and then she was only appointed as an Honorary Third Officer, WRANS. This was the best Feldt could do.[47]

Eric Feldt held Ruby Boye-Jones in high esteem and commended her to Admiral Halsey, Commander of South Pacific Area. Halsey also held her in high esteem, because he not only accepted Feldt's commendation, but also made a personal flight to the remote island to personally thank her for her work.[48] Later, when Halsey was told Mrs Boye-Jones had become ill on

Vanikoro, he ordered a US Navy aircraft to airlift her to hospital. She was the only European woman to have actively served as a FERDINAND operative in the Pacific.

Mrs Boye-Jones's dedicated reporting of weather conditions and sea states day after day without fail provided vital intelligence for the US Navy. Weather reporting is an often overlooked but important facet of intelligence collection. In the North Atlantic, being on a weather ship was a most dangerous job, as the enemy naval and air forces regarded these ships as high-priority targets and could easily find them through HFDF. Mrs Boye-Jones may have just been sending weather reports, but they were most definitely highly regarded.

Sydney Boye-Jones remained at her side throughout and shared the same risks. He was also an active participant in keeping the tele-radio working and Vanikoro Island secure. He was a highly experienced ships pilot for the Solomon Islands and very eager to serve.[49]

From June 1942, FERDINAND reporting was showing an increasing level of Japanese interest in Guadalcanal where FERDINAND had six posts. K.D. Hay, A.M. Andresen, and Lieutenant Macfarlane, RANVR, manned a post on Gold Ridge in the centre of Guadalcanal. Sub-Lieutenant F.A. Rhodes, RANVR, manned a post in the north.[50] District Officer Martin Clemens manned a post at Aola on Guadalcanal, Leif Schroeder was on Savo Island, and Geoffrey Kruper was at Tunnibulli (Tatamba), at the south-eastern end of Santa Ysabel Island.[51] The final post was on the north-western part of Guadalcanal Island and manned by District Officer D.G. Kennedy, assisted by Assistant Medical Practitioner Hugh Wheatley. This was the most exposed of all the posts.[52]

Kennedy decided, correctly, that his post was too exposed and withdrew his party, first to Segi Plantation on New Georgia Island, and then to Santa Ysabel Island.[53] While Kennedy was at Segi towards the end of March 1942, he decided to send Wheatley, who as half-Solomon Islander could blend in among the local population, to reconnoitre the north-western Solomons. Nothing was ever heard of Wheatley, the schooner or its crew again. It is likely they were either sunk by the advancing Japanese or captured and executed.[54]

As time passed in early 1942, the coastwatch posts passed their sighting and weather information back to Marchant's HQ, where it was re-encrypted and passed to Australia and to the various US naval and military commands throughout the Pacific.[55] This early intelligence reporting provided the stretched Allied commands with reliable sighting information on major Japanese naval and aerial concentrations. Among the intelligence provided was a report of 5 May from Kennedy on Santa Ysabel Island warning of a major IJN force moving towards Tulagi. This report enabled US carriers to get into position and launch the final air attacks that ended the Battle of the Coral Sea.[56]

Schroeder on Savo Island watched this engagement from his vantage point and was able to report the sinking of nine Japanese vessels by the US air attacks. This was the first check suffered by the IJN, and it was made possible by the good intelligence provided by the SIGINT of FRUMEL and the HUMINT provided by FERDINAND.

Despite the setback suffered by the IJN at Coral Sea, Tulagi was occupied on 6 May 1942, and now the Japanese could extend their reconnaissance activities onto Guadalcanal and the other islands of the Solomons. Clemens' party was now in close contact with the Japanese and he quickly exploited this by sending a number of his police and carriers to work for the Japanese. These men reported the precise locations and activities of the Japanese and, on many occasions, assisted Japanese units in getting lost in the jungles of Guadalcanal.[57]

These minor disruptions did not slow the Japanese down and they moved to occupy strategically important positions, not least the grassy area near Lunga where, in June, they started building the airfield that they and the US Marines would spend the rest of the year fighting to control. This airfield, soon to be renamed Henderson Field, was right below Gold Ridge, where Hay, Andresen and Macfarlane watched and reported all they saw, along with the information their carriers and police were gleaning while working as labourers for the Japanese.[58]

This activity continued until late July, when the coastwatch posts were ordered to cease radio transmissions and maintain listening watches only. This instruction only meant one thing—an Allied assault was intended and Guadalcanal was the most likely target. To the north, the coastwatchers on Bougainville were watching the skies for Japanese aircraft, and the choke-points at Buka Passage and the Shortland Islands for signs of the IJN.[59]

On 7 August 1942, at approximately 0900 hours, the first wave of Marines went ashore between Lunga Point and Tagoma. Across the sound, the Marines went ashore on Tulagi led by two FERDINAND guides, Sub-Lieutenant Dick Horton and Sub-Lieutenant Henry Josselyn.[60] As we have already seen, the Japanese responded aggressively at sea and in the air. The landing beaches were soon attacked by waves of Japanese aircraft, but the FERDINAND parties on Bougainville provided early warnings of these at 1027 hours, enabling the fleet to weigh anchor and disperse. Only two ships, USS *Jervis*, hit by a torpedo and sunk the next day, and USS *George F. Elliott*, set alight by what appears to have been a suicide attack by a single aircraft, were lost.[61] It could have been much worse.

Now the coastwatchers on Guadalcanal came into their own by acting as guides for the US forces ashore and afloat, and by collecting HUMINT that no other unit could collect. Macfarlane sent his cook boy, police and carriers to work for the Japanese as labourers from Monday to Friday. Each weekend, the Japanese would give them leave and they would dutifully turn up at Macfarlane's post and provide detailed reporting on the Japanese dispositions and activities, and the locations of their stores and weapons.[62]

With the success of the Marine landings, the coastwatchers had to provide time-sensitive tactical intelligence to the Divisional HQ ashore. This was no easy task. The Marines were under siege and because of the Battle of Savo Island were now without naval support. Knowing what the Japanese were doing was of vital importance to Major General Vandegrift and his staff, and he was heavily reliant on the coastwatchers. In order to improve communication with Vandegrift's HQ, Mackenzie, accompanied by Lieutenant G.H.C. Train, and two other men, R. Eedie and Rayman, landed at Lunga a week after the first landings and established themselves close to Vandegrift's HQ. The Marines found this so useful they provided three operators, privates Page, Adams and Berkstresser, to assist in the work.

This centre began disseminating intelligence, including air-raid warnings from Paul Mason on Bougainville, Jack Read at Buka, F.A. Rhodes and Leif Schroeder on the west coast of Guadalcanal, and Macfarlane overlooking Lunga airfield.[63] These warnings were so timely they turned out to be too timely. The problem lay with the divisional HQ issuing an 'air raid yellow' alert ceasing all work despite the raid aircraft being two hours' flying time away. Vandegrift ordered that 'air raid yellow' warnings not be given until the attack was 30 minutes away and the 'red' warning at ten minutes.[64]

At Segi Plantation on New Georgia, another coastwatcher, New Zealander D.G. Kennedy, was directly under the Japanese flight path to Lunga, which was optimal for reporting. The only complication was that the Japanese forces were now at Viru Harbour, 14 kilometres north of Kennedy's position.[65] Kennedy decided he needed to hold his ground, so he organised an attack on the Japanese at Viru, wiping them out. He wiped out two more barges and their crews, then attacked a 25-man Japanese patrol, although many of them escaped into the jungle.[66] These scuffles with the Japanese did not come cost-free. Kennedy was wounded in the thigh and two of his men were killed.

The wound did not stop Kennedy and he stayed on New Georgia.[67] In all of this action, Kennedy's party had destroyed three barges, killed 54 Japanese and captured twenty more. They also rescued 22 shot-down US aircrew from the jungles of New Georgia or from islands close to it. The rescued aircrew and captured Japanese were flown out from New Georgia shortly after this series of actions.[68]

At this time, the need to provide intelligence of Japanese naval activity in the area of water lying between Santa Ysabel Island in the east and New Georgia, Vangunu and Pavuvu islands to the west, now nicknamed 'the Slot', was vital. The IJN had already displayed its fighting prowess on 9 August, two days after the Marine landings on Guadalcanal, when it inflicted the greatest naval defeat in US history at the Battle of Savo Island. Leif Schroeder, who on Savo Island had the best bird's-eye view of this battle, on the night of 8–9 August reported the action that saw the sinking of HMAS *Canberra*, USS *Chicago*, *Astoria*, *Vincennes* and *Quincy*.[69] Schroeder would also witness and report on the battles of Cape Esperance on 11–12 October, Guadalcanal between 2 and 15 November and Tassafaronga on 30 November, also called the second, third and fourth battles of Savo Island. The waters around Savo are now named Iron Bottom Sound as a result.

As well as attempting to bring the US Navy to a major fleet engagement at Guadalcanal, the IJN also had to reinforce and supply the Japanese forces on the island. The intensity of the fighting in the waters around Savo Island and in the Slot meant that slow-moving transports had no chance of surviving the voyage. The IJN then began using fast-moving destroyers and other vessels to carry supplies and reinforcements to Guadalcanal. This was the 'Tokyo Express', and the intelligence of each IJN attempt to transit these waters was dutifully reported by the coastwatchers on Vella Lavella and Choiseul islands.

In late August 1942, the situation on Guadalcanal was still serious, but this did not stop Walter Brookbank, the most senior public servant working for Navy Office's intelligence section, from visiting Mackenzie on Guadalcanal, and holding meetings with Vandegrift and his intelligence and operations staff. Commander Long had sent Brookbank, a man with extensive experience of the office politics of intelligence, to find out exactly what was going on at Guadalcanal.

Brookbank's visit was no sightseeing tour. He was on Guadalcanal as part of a visit to the US Navy in the Pacific Area, most likely undertaken as a result of a dispute between Chester Nimitz, Commander of the Pacific Operational Area and Vice Admiral Leary, Commander of the South West Pacific Area, officially under Nimitz but part of General MacArthur's command. The argument was, as usual, about who was in charge, part of which included the tasking of coastwatcher posts.

It might seem surprising that a civilian was sent to test these waters but, given the fact that all the senior RAN positions were held by RN admirals, it may have been thought inadvisable to have them try to influence the US Navy led by the stridently anti-British Ernest King. The other advantage of Brookbank was that he could say what needed to be said without causing a big stir because, after all, he was just a civilian.

Brookbank was able to get an agreement from the parties that Feldt's coastwatchers would concentrate on supporting one operational HQ in the Solomons. He could also report back to Navy Office the very flattering praise being heaped upon Feldt's coastwatchers by the US commanders on Guadalcanal.[70]

The task of supporting the US Marines on Guadalcanal was, however, impacting Feldt's ability to place coastwatchers in other areas of operation. The biggest issue was the complaining from GHQ, SWPA, led by Colonel Roberts, that the RAN was cutting the army out of coastwatching operations. Roberts appears to have piggybacked this complaint onto the efforts of COMSOUWESPACFOR to interpose himself into the operations around Guadalcanal.[71] The problem for Feldt was that he did not have the personnel to make up new parties, and Roberts was now offering to put together parties owned and led by army. Given the divergence between Feldt's view of intelligence as not involving any direct action, such as sabotage, and the army's desire to mount raids and blow things up, there was never going to be an easy settlement of the issue.

On 12 October, Long wrote to Feldt informing him that he was going to fight to ensure Feldt's parties being put onto the Solomons were led by naval officers, and he believed that the Americans would not be too keen on parties led by Australian Army or RAAF personnel, of whom they had no prior experience.[72] Feldt, backed by Long, continued efforts to keep the organisation from being turned into a guerrilla or irregular fighting force by ensuring that parties were led by people who understood that the intelligence role was the most important contribution they could make to the war. It was an ongoing battle against some elements in the US Marines as well.

But something had to be done, so FERDINAND inserted two parties using the USS *Grampus* on the night of 6–7 October 1942. One party, led by Josselyn and Keenan, went to Vella Lavella. The other party, led by A.N.A. Waddell and Sergeant C.W. Seaton, AIF, went to Choiseul.[73] Josselyn would stay on Vella Lavella until October 1943, and Keenan until February 1943. Waddell and Seaton would stay on Choiseul until March 1944.[74]

On Choiseul, Waddell and Seaton found that, while a significant part of the population was supportive or at least neutral, the activities of pro-Japanese villagers from the north-west coast made it difficult to operate. Actions by pro-Japanese locals forced Waddell and Seaton to relocate twice between October 1942 and February 1943, and FERDINAND had two hostile villages bombed.[75] Colonel Marchant, the British Resident Commissioner, immediately intervened after this action and demanded that reprisal-bombing cease immediately. Neither the US Navy nor FERDINAND were keen to stop this sort of activity, and Marchant elevated the matter to the Colonial Office via the Commissioner for the Western Pacific.[76] On 12 February, the Colonial Office formally advised Australia and the United States that it was not permissible for junior officers to order the punitive bombing of British civilians who happened to live in villages in the Solomon Islands.[77]

By February 1943, the matter was settled to most people's satisfaction. The British Administration was not swayed by the arguments for punitive bombing. It would appear that Admiral Halsey also had his doubts because, even before Sir Philip Euen Mitchell had contacted the Colonial Office, he had ordered that no village was to be bombed without his personal authorisation.[78] FERDINAND signalled its parties in the islands telling them of the restrictions and of the need to provide a very strong case so that the Australian naval liaison officer at Vila could get approval for future reprisal raids.[79]

On Guadalcanal itself, the FERDINAND post supporting the US ground forces increased its staff with the arrival of Lieutenant L. Ogilvie, RANVR, and Sub-Lieutenant K. Harding, who took some of the heavy load off Mackenzie and Lieutenant Train.[80] This reinforcement increased the speed with which FERDINAND was able to receive, assess and forward relevant intelligence to the Marine commander on Guadalcanal, MacArthur's GHQ, Halsey's command in the South Pacific, Townsville and Pearl Harbor.

At around this time, the existing FERDINAND parties on Guadalcanal were beginning to wilt. They had been operational for a considerable period of time and now, as the fighting between the Marine defenders at Henderson and the Japanese intensified, they were facing a jungle filled with fleeing locals and large numbers of enemy soldiers. On top of all this, they were within areas subject to bombardment from friendly artillery, warships and aircraft. Lieutenant F.A. Rhodes and Petty Officer Leif Schroeder, who were constantly shifting position, remained in the north-west of the island. On Gold Ridge, the pressure built up on Hay, Andresen and Macfarlane.

In the case of Rhodes and Schroeder, Feldt appears to accept a view he attributes to Mackenzie, that Vandegrift, the Marine Commander on Guadalcanal, had decided that the FERDINAND parties were 'expendables'.[81] To be fair to Vandegrift, he was not responsible for FERDINAND's parties; they were simply co-located within his defensive perimeter and, worse, outside of it. When it became obvious that the coastwatchers needed to be brought in, Vandegrift ordered that no rescue or retrieval missions be launched. Mackenzie ignored this and sent Horton to evacuate Rhodes and Schroeder by boat. Luckily, Horton pulled off this daring rescue without a hitch, and evacuated sixteen people, including Rhodes and Schroeder, crashed Allied aircrew and some Japanese POWs. The action did not go down well with Vandegrift.

In early October 1942, Macfarlane and Andresen made their own way down from Gold Ridge to the Marine position at Lunga. The third member of their party, Hay, stayed and continued to transmit intelligence collected by his local assistants.[82] Feldt attributes Hay's decision to stay to his being too fat to outrun any Japanese patrol they might bump into during the withdrawal to Lunga. The plump Hay maintained his intelligence collection effort on Gold Ridge until after the defeat of the Japanese. When he finally came out of the jungle with his party, which included a Catholic nun, in January 1943 the US officer who met him was stunned at Hay's girth. He did a magnificent job surviving on Guadalcanal from February 1942 until January 1943 and maintaining a constant flow of intelligence throughout that period.[83]

In his 1953 foreword to Martin Clemens' book *Alone on Guadalcanal*, Vandegrift praised Martin Clemens and the other British colonial officials who remained as coastwatchers in the Solomon Islands. He applauded the relationship they had formed with the Solomon Islanders and the loyalty of the latter who, Vandegrift claimed, never betrayed any of the ex-colonial officials or handed over any US personnel to the Japanese.[84] Vandegrift also praised the importance of the intelligence information provided to his division by FERDINAND, stating: 'There were instances when that information and support was a substantial portion of the margin of victory.'[85]

The FERDINAND operations in the British Solomon Islands were the high point of Australia's coastwatch organisation, and were made possible by the mix of British, Australian and wayward European residents of the islands collected by Commander Rupert Long and Lieutenant Commander Eric Feldt to quite rightly sit under the trees and smell the flowers like their mascot, Ferdinand the Bull, who refused to fight. This approach, which eschewed guerrilla operations and sabotage would prove to be a far more successful approach to intelligence collection than all of the special force operations put together. In doing this, the ACNB's coastwatch element of the Admiralty's Reporting Officer system won highly deserved fame as FERDINAND, one of the most successful, if not the most successful, western HUMINT activity of 1939–45.

CHAPTER 23

The Solomons and Pacific Area, 1943

With the defeat of the Japanese push to Port Moresby in late 1942 and the final defeat of the Japanese on Guadalcanal in early February 1943, the Allies in the SWPA and Pacific were now in a position to move to follow-up offensives to drive the Japanese back towards Truk and the Philippines. The war in the Pacific was now moving into its offensive stage, and with this change in strategic outlook came changes in FERDINAND.

Approximately six months after coastwatchers had been withdrawn from New Britain in the face of the Japanese advance, they returned aboard the US submarine USS *Greenling*. The FERDINAND party on the *Greenling* comprised Lieutenant M.H. Wright (SP), RANVR; Captain P.E. Figgis, AIF; a local from the area of Baien, to which the party was heading; Lieutenant H.L. (Les) Williams, AIF; Sergeant Simogun, a local policeman; and three locals, Sanga, Arumei and Sama.[1] Some of the party went ashore on New Britain in the vicinity of Wide Bay on the night of 28–29 February 1943. Once ashore, they made their way to a local village, the home village of the Baien local they had brought with them. The next night, Figgis set off in a canoe to find the *Greenling* and unload approximately one ton of equipment and stores and the rest of the party, including Lieutenant Williams.[2]

Once this was accomplished, the difficulty was getting the beachside locals to supply the manpower to carry these loads into the interior. After a bit of toing and froing, the whole party, its equipment and supplies were carried to a location and the beachside locals released. Over the next four weeks, the party then moved everything to a secluded spot and built a camp.[3]

Lieutenant Wright's party provided sighting information on Japanese barges and submarines that were now being used to ferry equipment to the beleaguered Japanese forces on the southern islands. In order to avoid air attacks, the barges moved by night and hid under the jungle canopy in small inlets and creeks during the day. The submarines offered the ability for underwater transits and could also fit up creeks and hide under the jungle canopy as well. The only countermeasure for this was coastwatcher reports providing precise locations for air attacks. For the next five months, the coastwatchers' observations made even this small level of protection less effective, and a number of these barges and vessels were destroyed because of air attacks from aircraft directed by the coastwatchers.[4]

On 12 July 1943, Lieutenant Commander Pryce-Jones, RANVR, the Deputy Supervising Intelligence Officer on Guadalcanal, sent an appraisal to the DNI outlining the changes needed for coastwatching in the Solomons due to movement of the war northward.[5] The most pressing problem was that the British authorities were now looking to take back control and tasking of their personnel from FERDINAND. The British High Commissioner in Suva was reportedly writing to the Australian prime minister asking for the release of Waddell and Josselyn as soon as their present missions ended. The Resident Commissioner, Colonel Marchant, was planning to send Kennedy, who was currently wounded at Segi, New Georgia, on a long leave. On top of all this, the British civil authorities had appointed Clemens to Kennedy's post as District Officer, New Georgia, and on Rendova, Sub-Lieutenant Horton was evacuated for surgery on a hernia.[6] In light of all this, Pryce-Jones wanted to know if FERDINAND in the Solomons needed to man all of the coastwatch stations or, as an intelligence collector behind enemy lines, only those in the areas still occupied by the Japanese.[7] It was a fair point.

Commander Long replied to Pryce-Jones on 2 August laying out the ACNB's policy for FERDINAND in the Solomons. The first point Long made was that all coastwatch stations that lay within areas occupied and controlled by the US forces were to be handed over to them to man, if they wished to do so. To facilitate this, the ACNB had authorised the handing-over of RAN tele-radios to US forces for their use.[8] This would release remaining FERDINAND personnel for deployment behind enemy lines, which was FERDINAND's sole function, and, if the war moved further and faster north than expected, then the deployment of FERDINAND parties from the Solomons would be authorised onto New Ireland and other islands beyond the Solomons.[9] To assist in this reorganisation, Pryce-Jones was to delegate the management of all coastwatch activity within liberated areas and focus himself on managing FERDINAND activity in enemy-occupied areas.[10]

As this reorganisation was occurring in the Solomons, similar changes were occurring in Australia as the army, supported by GHQ, SWPA moved to pull FERDINAND into the AIB. One of these changes was the closing of FERDINAND's HQ at Townsville.[11] FERDINAND was now changing from an intelligence provider to a reconnaissance organisation, a role that fitted the philosophy of the Australian Army, GHQ, SWPA and the AIB more closely.

This change did not mean that the coastwatchers were not providing significant service. On 30 June 1943, during the landings at Rendova Island, Lieutenant Rhodes won the US Silver Star for his bravery in leading a party of US troops ashore and through a plantation.[12] In the hills above this action, another FERDINAND party was fighting off a large group of retreating Japanese who accidentally came across the observation post.[13]

Coastwatchers were also providing their usual reporting of Japanese air and sea movements, and recovering downed aircrew and sailors from sunken vessels. Henry Josselyn, Robert Firth and A.W.E. Silvester rescued the 160 survivors of the cruiser USS *Helena* who washed up on Vella Lavella Island after the Battle of Kula Gulf.[14]

By September 1943, the only FERDINAND party behind Japanese lines in the Solomons was that led by Waddell and Seaton on Choiseul Island. One member of the party was a local radio operator, Pabula, a graduate of the old radio school at Rabaul, who sent the daily reports on weather and other intelligence while Waddell and Seaton were taking military parties on reconnaissance missions around the island.[15]

Waddell's party, reinforced by Flight Lieutenant E. Spencer, RAAF, conducted a number of missions and fought engagements with Japanese patrols. This party stayed on Choiseul until 2 March 1944, a period of fifteen months.

During this time, it provided intelligence on Japanese barge and vessel movements, enabling the US air forces to inflict substantial damage on the Japanese supply line operated by the Tokyo Express.[16] They also fought a number of engagements with the Japanese, killing a reported hundred or so, assisted the US Marine landings on the island, and directed air attacks on Japanese targets on and around the island.[17]

To meet the requirements for the Torokina landing on Bougainville, FERDINAND prepared three AIB parties, one to land with the troops at Torokina, one to be inserted in the north of the island and one operating in the south. FERDINAND was now working for General MacArthur and GHQ, SWPA.

The experienced Captain E.D. 'Wobbie' Robinson, AIF, led No. 1 Party, the party going to the north of Torokina. No. 2 Party, led by K. Keena, headed to the south.[18] The party landing with the troops on 1 November was led by Flight Lieutenant R.A. 'Robbie' Robinson, RAAF, supported by Sub-Lieutenant R. Stuart and a US Army team comprising Sergeant F. Halverston, Corporal Nash and Private Engler.[19]

These parties departed Brisbane on 14 October for Lunga to report to Pryce-Jones for further training and to join their local carriers and police. They would all be kitted up and provided with semi-automatic M1 carbines and modified webbing.[20] They would be issued their tele-radios, rations for 21 days and other supplies by Pryce-Jones. They were to land at Kunua on Bougainville before moving to their respective area of operations.[21]

The risks they were running were significant. The Japanese had been in these locations for a considerable period, and they had developed their intelligence networks. They had also improved their SIGINT effort and were most certainly reading AIB messages, thanks to intelligence gained from the interrogation of AIB personnel in Timor and other places. There is no doubt that the Japanese SIGINT units were reading FERDINAND's codes.[22]

Hard evidence of how extensively the Japanese had broken these codes came in November 1943, when the intelligence books of the Kira Force were captured. This book held extensive raw intercept from FERDINAND parties operating in the Solomons between April and November 1943. The Japanese knew the names of Read, Mason, Stevenson, Pryce-Jones and others. They knew group sizes and composition, and they knew the areas in which they were operating. They even had the FERDINAND instructions on how to ensure greater communications security through proper procedures. FERDINAND's communications were entirely compromised by early 1943.[23]

Naval Intelligence's evaluation of the captured documents was that they were captured when Read's camp was overrun. The text of the transmissions, however, has an immediacy that only comes from an intercept operator writing down exactly what they are hearing in their headphones.[24] The Naval Intelligence evaluation was wrong.

The role of SIGINT in detecting coastwatch parties via HFDF was not completely lost on FERDINAND. A memorandum of 8 February 1944 from Commander McManus, Supervising Intelligence Officer, North East Area, to the Officer-in-Charge AIB Base at Milne Bay, details a combined FERDINAND–Central Bureau operation to conduct SIGINT operations against Japanese stay-behind parties. FERDINAND and Central Bureau planned to fit the harbour defence motor launch HDML *1321* with specialist W/T equipment and an operator, Sergeant H.A. Dempsey, to detect and plot the positions of these parties.[25]

HDML *1321* would conduct a series of cruises in waters heavily patrolled by Allied forces, so Commander McManus wanted to ensure there was no possible chance of HDML *1321* being sunk by friendly fire. This operation was carried out between February and May 1944, the period when Dempsey served in FERDINAND, according to Eric Feldt's book.[26] It is now not known what findings the SIGINT team on HDML *1321* made or whether it even conducted intercept operations. The suspicion is that its SIGINT team were part of the specialist British communications security group brought in to listen to Allied communications in order to identify poor procedure and to check if ULTRA material was being passed via non-SIGINT systems, as indeed the SRD had been doing.

Even without the Japanese reading messages in real time, the situation facing FERDINAND's parties going into Bougainville was bad. They were told that they would have little chance of surviving on the island for more than three weeks because the locals would betray them. This meant that their mission could not be inserted more than three weeks ahead of the intended landings.[27] Other changes required included the way parties were inserted. In the Solomons, the procedure had been to land all supplies and equipment and place them in a cache. The coastwatcher then went out and negotiated with the local village headmen for the necessary carriers. In

Bougainville, because of the pro-Japanese attitudes of many villages, this would be 'folly'.[28]

At the front, there was increasing criticism from the US Marines, especially 1st Amphibious Marine Force, of FERDINAND's lack of aggression. One reason is that they were not being properly briefed on what FERDINAND did and did not do. The problem had worsened because the Deputy Supervising Intelligence Officer, Pryce-Jones, had stayed on Guadalcanal and not moved forward with his clients.

Pryce-Jones did get involved now, and a stand-off developed between him and Amphibious Marine Force, which escalated when the Chief of Staff, Colonel Thomas, insisted that in future Marine officers would command FERDINAND patrols when Marines were attached. The next such patrol was to be led by Lieutenant Keenan of FERDINAND, and Thomas wanted Keenan to operate under the orders of Lieutenant Colonel James M. Smith during the reconnaissance of Atsinima Bay, Papua New Guinea, in late October.[29]

The complaint was still that FERDINAND was 'not aggressive enough', and the Marines felt they needed to 'work more of our own into it for control purposes'.[30] The Marines were looking for a fight; FERDINAND was not. Lieutenant General A.A. Vandegrift, Commanding General of the First Marine Amphibious Corps, agreed with his Marines.[31] Fortunately, Admiral Halsey, advised by the G2, COMSOUPAC, Colonel F.P. Munson, agreed with FERDINAND.[32]

The Marines remained unhappy. On 16 November Lieutenant Colonel W.F. Coleman, the acting Chief of Staff and C2 of 1st Amphibious, wrote a letter to Lieutenant Colonel Floyd A. Scrow of 3rd Amphibious Force criticising Keenan. Coleman complained that, as expected, the reconnaissance patrol led by Keenan had been 'a bust', as the Australian tele-radios had been soaked by sea water during the landing and rendered useless. Rather embarrassingly, a copy of Coleman's letter found its way into an Australian file, so FERDINAND knew the name of at least one complainer.[33]

The first warning that Pryce-Jones was overreacting was his use of a memorandum of 30 November 1942 in which Hugh Mackenzie, the then Deputy Supervising Intelligence Officer, noted that a report from Colonel Thomas criticised coastwatchers and was defamatory of the British Resident, Lieutenant Colonel Marchant. Mackenzie's memo makes clear, however, that Thomas was reporting the views of the D2, Lieutenant Colonel E.J. Buckley,

US Marines, an officer whose attitude, Mackenzie stressed, 'is not shared by the great majority of US staff officers'.[34]

Mackenzie, Feldt and McManus looked into this case and recommended to Long that Pryce-Jones be recalled. On 4 December, Feldt wrote to Long advising him that the difficulties had arisen mainly because there was no single FERDINAND authority co-located with the Marine HQ. For some reason, Pryce-Jones had remained at Lunga on Guadalcanal, while the most important FERDINAND client, the Commander of Air Operations Solomons (COMAIRSOLS), had moved his HQ to Munda on New Georgia. COMAIRSOLS' requirements were for immediate action to counter air activity reported by coastwatchers. The separation of the two made this impossible, and Pryce-Jones should have moved to Munda. This had also led to a situation where three deputy supervising intelligence officer representatives, call signs PWD, RJH and RAR, were now all sending conflicting requirements and passing traffic that was confusing the coastwatchers in the jungle.[35]

The inquiry advised Long that the failure of Pryce-Jones to remain at the spearhead, now at Munda, was a breach of the written undertaking the RAN had provided to the United States that FERDINAND's deputy supervising intelligence officer would stay with the frontline HQ.[36]

Pryce-Jones's decision to stay at Lunga, which led to multiple FERDINAND sites transmitting identical messages to US commands, provided the Japanese with a SIGINT bonanza, as the same message travelled across different circuits operating at different levels of protection. The FERDINAND codes were already suspect, and there can be little doubt that the habit of sending a message in low-grade codes before re-encrypting them in higher-grade codes, as Marchant's network control station was doing, compromised the cryptography of both FERDINAND and the AIB. Feldt, Mackenzie and McManus were concerned that this was in fact the case.[37]

The inquiry also reported that Pryce-Jones's decision to stay at Lunga was seen by many coastwatchers in the field as being driven more by his wanting to be safe and comfortable than any operational necessity. They felt that Pryce-Jones had let them and FERDINAND down. Some US officers echoed this criticism, expressing surprise that the deputy supervising intelligence officer had not gone to Munda.[38] On the advice of Mackenzie, Feldt and McManus, Macfarlane replaced Pryce-Jones in January 1944.

This takes us north, to New Ireland, where FERDINAND successfully inserted Captain H.J. Murray, O.D. McNicol, Sergeant R.M. Dolby and Corporal R.J. Cream. The party landed successfully, established a secure operating base and began to contact friendly locals. As word spread, however, the Japanese became aware of the party's presence and it had to be withdrawn on 26 November 1943.[39] Personnel from this party subsequently guided US military personnel on reconnaissance patrols onto other islands, including Boang. There, the mission failed because the locals, frightened of being on the losing side, were informing the Japanese and the Australians of each other's positions and activities.[40]

The presence of white men on an island left the locals in an invidious position, and this situation was created every time a FERDINAND or AIB party was inserted. Complicating this were the existing intertribal and village rivalries, especially as people were displaced by pro-Japanese elements taking advantage of the situation to grab land. The result was intertribal wars on Bougainville, New Ireland and New Britain, and in New Guinea as well. This severely reduced the safety of any FERDINAND or AIB party.[41] As we will see, the image of the happy, loyal local resident was a chimera. Happy loyalty was reserved for the strongest power in the local area, depending on how long that power was present and how well it paid.[42] With two out of the three, the Japanese were in the stronger position.

Despite the increasing complexity of the operating environment and the apparent failures, FERDINAND at least got parties away. A US reconnaissance of Nissan Island conducted without coastwatcher support resulted in three killed and the survivors chased into the sea.[43]

By the end of 1943, Rabaul was virtually isolated and the Japanese garrisons, what was left of them, on the various islands no longer presented any threat to Allied forces or plans. The war moved on as US forces careened up the Pacific and planned their return to the Philippines. There was now no role for FERDINAND in the South Pacific Area, and attention in Australia was directed almost exclusively back to the SWPA and Bougainville.

CHAPTER 24

Human Intelligence in the Attack, 1943–45

In New Guinea, with Australian and US forces moving to the offensive in early 1943, FERDINAND was required to supply parties to assist formations advancing up the coast towards New Britain. With the winding-down of the Guadalcanal campaign and the rapid advance of the US Navy north through the Pacific, the work of FERDINAND lessened dramatically. The AIB had by this time firmly taken control of FERDINAND, which was now Section C of the AIB. Feldt's organisation had no defence against the growing demands from GHQ and the US and Australian armies for a more aggressive approach to reconnaissance.

The units of the AIB, FERDINAND and SRD jockeyed for control of intelligence operations with a number of other groups, including ANGAU, and the Australian Army and RAAF observation organisations providing early warnings back to Port Moresby. Under the surface at AIB, there was a strange mix of emotions colouring perceptions of FERDINAND and ANGAU. On the one hand, there was disdain for the civilian mentality that permeated FERDINAND and ANGAU, and on the other jealously that FERDINAND and ANGAU possessed the cream of the experienced field operators in the region. AIB wanted their expertise, but it wanted them to use it as commandos, saboteurs or guerrilla leaders.[1] It was the antithesis of good intelligence collection.

This lack of operators who fully understood the environment and the local people was one of the reasons there was more trouble in New Guinea than in other areas. The truth was that even in 1943, there were large regions of New Guinea where a white man was only a rumour or a legend, and no outsider understood the local inhabitants, their customs or their potential response to trespass. Thus, many of the attacks on AIB parties were not pro-Japanese, but just defensive actions by remote villagers prepared to fight first and talk later with trespassers.[2]

In 1943, ANGAU, which was supposed to handle civilian affairs in New Guinea on behalf of the Australian Army, began to insert itself into intelligence collection behind enemy lines.[3] ANGAU's activities at this time were a good example of what would later be called mission creep, and it caused further ructions within AIB.

AIB, SRD and FERDINAND were also being pressured by a growing number of commanders as more units were fed into the offensive campaigns. These commanders wanted intelligence on their intended areas of operations, areas that the Japanese were busy preparing for defence. The effect of this activity was that by April 1943, as we have seen for other islands, the Japanese in New Guinea no longer simply despatched foot patrols from their bases in the general direction of a suspected FERDINAND or SRD party. Instead, they rapidly deployed numerous patrols at intervals along the coast and moved them in a sweep that drove the FERDINAND and SRD parties deeper into the jungle and away from the possibility of rescue from the sea. Another major Japanese improvement was that they now used local villagers, whose tracking ability was second to none. Another benefit the Japanese derived from using locals was their collection of more accurate information from other locals. Once the local trackers had identified signs of a FERDINAND or AIB party, their local knowledge meant they could predict the routes their quarry would take.

It did not take long for the Japanese to progress from patrols to establishing strong garrisons at Wewak, Ubia, Madang, Rai Coast, Finschhafen and Lae, using them as bases for conducting reconnaissance patrols of the Ramu and Markham valleys.[4] These areas became extremely dangerous for any SRD, FERDINAND or ANGAU party.

In May 1943, Lieutenant George Greathead's party clashed with Japanese patrols near the Lower Ramu and had to withdraw to Bena Bena.[5] Captain L.E.

Ashton's party was chased from the Sepik River towards Wewak and then back to Sepik until flown out by a Catalina that landed on Waskuk Lake on 21 May. In July, locals in the Lumi area south of the Torricellis attacked Lieutenant H.A.J. Freyer's party. This party had been tasked with taking a NEI group, led by Sergeant H.N. Staverman, NEI, part of the way to its area of operations at Hollandia. Staverman and Corporal D.J. Topman, NEI, commanded this Dutch party, with Sergeant Leonard (Len) G. Siffleet, AIF, and two Indonesians, H. Pattiwal and M. Raharing. After crossing the Sepik River, the Dutch party headed off for Hollandia.[6] Freyer's party settled into the area around the Sepik River and sent out carriers to collect as much information as possible.

Staverman's party appears to have been a disaster waiting to happen. Corporal Topman had refused to go on with Staverman, whom he later formally accused of being lazy, arrogant and inexperienced, and, disastrously, of bastardising and humiliating the party's carriers.[7] Other people were saying the same things, including Captain Schroeder, Royal Army Medical Corps, who called Staverman 'clearly irresponsible, lazy and vain'.[8]

According to Topman, Staverman's behaviour resulted in Lieutenant Freyer splitting the party and allowing Staverman to lead his own four-man group to Woma. This party met with disaster. The Japanese killed Staverman and an Indonesian soldier, and Siffleet died in Japanese custody on 24 October 1943 after signalling in early October that Staverman and one of the Indonesian soldiers had been killed.[9] What Feldt had called the 'Boy's Own Annual' attitude to intelligence collection behind enemy lines was proving lethal.

Already by June 1943, the Japanese using local guides, bribes and fear had made the operational environment for any FERDINAND or SRD group extremely hazardous and the increased risk was soon apparent.

As 1943 progressed, there were a series of close contacts with the Japanese. In February, at Maibang near Saidor, on the Rai Coast, Captain B. Fairfax-Ross's party was attacked and three men were killed, including Lieutenant L.J. Bell, RANVR.[10] In March, Captain Lloyd Pursehouse's party was involved in a skirmish with Japanese troops in the mountains west of Finschhafen when Lieutenant Ken McColl, RANVR, exchanged fire with a Japanese patrol after the locals had informed the Japanese of the party's location. They had to be extricated to Bena Bena.[11]

Despite the increasingly aggressive Japanese tactics in New Guinea, the AIB planners did not start thinking more carefully; rather this had the opposite effect. There were many examples of this amateur attitude within AIB. Parties were being inserted into New Guinea without essential equipment like binoculars or watches.[12] One AIB party was even put in with radios that could only function on the naval coastwatch frequency of 6900 kilohertz, for which AIB only had permission until 31 August 1943. This may seem like a small issue, but the presence of the AIB station on the coastwatcher net disrupted the activity of that net.[13]

Unsurprisingly, these schemes originated in the army and envisaged sabotage operations being conducted by the SRD as well as propaganda activities designed and conducted by FELO, and ANGAU-led patrols of twenty to 30 armed locals taking on the Japanese in ambush and counterambush warfare. This was to be supported in the Sepik River area by arming a thousand or so locals with shotguns.[14]

What is still striking about this scheme is the lack of any appreciation of what this would mean for the people of the Sepik River. The army officer who put this proposal did not understand that in any guerrilla war, the Japanese would use brutal tactics and win. What is more startling is that by the time this suggestion was being floated, the AIB's campaign of sabotage, insurrection and intelligence collection in Timor had become a farce. The Japanese had brutally torn the local population apart in what was effectively an area of no tactical or strategic interest. It also ensured that no further intelligence could be derived from the area affected.

Nevertheless, the AIB began preparing its patrols for the Sepik River. Captain W.A. Money and Corporal Monfries from ANGAU were made available because of their local knowledge. Between 18 and 23 May 1943, 9th Operational Group, RAAF, conducted five sorties to drop supplies. The sortie on 18 May to Maimai failed due to bad weather, and the stores were finally dropped there on 20 May. On 21 May, an aircraft landed on Waskuk Lake, Sepik River, and picked up one of the field parties for return to Port Moresby. Two further successful supply drops were conducted on 22 and 23 May to the party at Maimai. The importance of this series of sorties was that, with the exception of the one on 21 May, the aircraft was guided by Lieutenant G.A.V. Stanley, RANVR, who was then able to inform Major J.K. McCarthy, the officer commanding C Section, AIB, of the difficulties involved.[15]

The first of the problems faced by the RAAF crews was the weather, which was bad during the entire period and made worse by the local terrain, in which the high ridges stopped sunlight from burning off the fog, causing the drop zones to remain obscured. Added to the weather, the Japanese airbase at Wewak was just 65 miles (105 kilometres) away from the drop zones, and the Japanese at Aitape, only 40 miles (65 kilometres) from the drop zones, had now probably been equipped with radio DF equipment. As Major McCarthy wrote to the commanding officer of 9th Operational Group, the missions were hazardous, and his implication was that they would become even more so.[16]

Allied planners now prepared to advance in New Guinea, with a plan to capture Lae and Salamaua, and the AIB was asked to assist. This envisaged an amphibious landing of the 9th Australian Division at the mouth of the Basu River and near Malahang, close to Lae. The AIB committed five FERDINAND parties led by G.C. Harris, L. Pursehouse, L.C. Noakes, A. Kirkwall-Smith and W.J. Reid.[17] The AIB passed operational control of these intelligence parties over to Major General G. Wootten's 9th Division, a formation with no experience of conditions in New Guinea, as it had only just arrived in theatre after performing a significant role at the Battle of El Alamein and in the Middle East. The 9th Division's planners prepared the landings using the 8th Army's staff tables for ammunition, supplies and equipment, rather than the tables developed by the US Marines or even the US Army, and they had no idea as to the role of the intelligence parties.[18]

At this critical juncture, the AIB allowed Major McCarthy, the officer-in-charge of FERDINAND in Port Moresby, to be detached to HQ, 6th US Army, which was planning an amphibious landing at Cape Gloucester on the west of New Britain. McCarthy as we have seen above, was extremely familiar with the area, which was his old district. The loss of this experienced officer contributed to the tensions as FERDINAND parties worked to support the 9th Division's operations at Salamaua and Lae, and to the breakdown in the relationship between FERDINAND and the operational staff of the division.

The speed with which offensive operations were being developed was forcing a further dilution of experience on the ground in New Guinea. With McCarthy heavily committed to supporting the 6th US Army, Lieutenant J.H. Paterson, RANVR, and Flight Lieutenant Harold Koch were despatched to Milne Bay to support the Lae–Salamaua landings. Captain B. Fairfax-Ross, who had recently arrived back from sick leave, temporarily took over Port Moresby before being relieved by Lieutenant K. Eglington and Sergeant A. Leydin.

The expansion of offensive operations and the concurrent changes of FERDINAND personnel led to a situation where the organisation was overwhelmed by the demands being placed upon it by operational staffs unversed in intelligence collection. The result was the rapid deployment of parties into areas of operation with which they were completely unfamiliar, and their reticence to seek out and close with the enemy to kill or capture them led to a loss of confidence among the officers of the US Amphibious Force at Cape Gloucester and the 9th Division at Lae–Salamua when the coastwatchers attached to them appeared hesitant to take part in fighting patrols. In his book *The Coastwatchers*, Eric Feldt is frank in his description of inexperienced combat commanders, both Australian and US, attempting to use coastwatchers as forward scouts for fighting patrols. This was not what coastwatchers were trained to do, and neither was it something they were experienced in. It is unsurprising that they felt they were not being used appropriately and that their commanders were not ensuring their safety.[19]

On New Britain, where FERDINAND remained independent and Major McCarthy commanded, the established practices put in place by Feldt at Guadalcanal and in the Solomons were maintained and again proved successful. The FERDINAND parties led groups of technical and operational specialists from the US combat formations on reconnaissance missions at Grass Point, just south of Cape Gloucester and, later in October, at Gasmata. All of these operations were successful. There was no contact with the Japanese, no casualties suffered and the US units were very happy with the support given and the results obtained.

The problem in New Guinea, as Feldt tells it, was that the inexperienced staff of the 9th Division simply threw FERDINAND parties ashore and hoped for the best. It is obvious from the documentary evidence that the members of FERDINAND did not trust the planning or the concept of operations under which they were to operate at either Lae or Salamaua. The coastwatcher parties were unwilling to take anything approaching a risk in such an environment, and it appears they may have staged a bit of a sit-down strike.[20] The situation then descended to a point where the 9th Division no longer wanted FERDINAND involved and FERDINAND's parties wanted no part in the operation. At this point FERDINAND withdrew and the role was taken up by ANGAU.[21]

As the war began to wind down in New Guinea, coastwatchers still had successes. One of these was the capture of Long Island in November 1943 and Rooke Island on 19 November 1943 by the FERDINAND party led by Lieutenant B.G. Hall. The Japanese garrison precipitously evacuated after hearing a landing had occurred. What they didn't know was that it was a landing by Lieutenant Hall's small FERDINAND party, not a landing in force by US troops.[22]

After the 'capture' of Rooke Island, operations against the Japanese on New Britain began on 15 December 1943 with the landing of the 112th Cavalry Regiment at Arawe, to the south-west of Cape Gloucester. This was a preliminary operation intended to block the main Japanese supply line and reinforcement route to Cape Gloucester itself. The main US landings would follow on 26 December at Cape Gloucester, in the vicinity of the Japanese airfields at Poini. Accompanying the troops going ashore would be a FERDINAND party led by L.E. Ashton, whose job was to immediately pass FERDINAND reports to the US commanders on the spot.[23] These reports were primarily air-raid warnings and intelligence on Japanese forces moving to reinforce the Cape Gloucester area.

FERDINAND was required to place three parties onto New Britain, in the areas of Open Bay, Gasmata and Nakanai, by 1 November. Despite this date being five weeks before the intended landing at Arawe, the timings were very tight for parties to make their overland trips, especially to Gasmata, and then establish secure hides, observation posts and establish communications.[24]

The parties being inserted onto New Britain were going onto an island where the Japanese had had their main base in the archipelago for one year and ten months. It was an area they now knew very well. The danger seems to have been downplayed, and whereas FERDINAND had assessed the life expectancy of any party on Bougainville as a maximum of three weeks, they were putting parties onto New Britain five weeks ahead of the proposed landings. All of this boded ill.

The parties involved arrived in two groups. One, the main party, led by Lieutenant M.H. Wright, RANVR, and consisting of Captain P.E. Figgis and Lieutenant H.L. Williams, thirteen other Europeans and 27 locals, was disembarked from a US submarine on the night of 28–29 September 1943 at Cape Orford.[25] Things went wrong from the beginning, when Lieutenant A. McLean, AIF, fell from a ladder on the submarine, injuring his back, and could not continue.[26] More serious was the loss of three of their portable radios, which had not been properly packed and were soaked by sea water. As the radios were the most important equipment on the mission, the commander of the party should have supervised their packing, double-checked by the second-in-command and the despatching staff at FERDINAND. This is utterly astounding and an indicator that standards at FERDINAND were dropping.[27]

With his party ashore, Wright moved inland and established a temporary base camp where others, including Captain Ian Skinner, AIF, joined them. Once all were assembled, Wright broke them into parties destined for Wide Bay on the southern coast, Open Bay on the northern coast, and an area south of Awungi midway between these two bays. Other parties were tasked for Gasmata and Nakanai.

One party, under Captain Figgis, with Lieutenant C.K. Johnston and signaller Corporal A.D. Bliss, remained at Cape Orford. The Wide Bay party under Major A.A. Roberts included Captain Malcolm English, Sergeant J.G. McEvoy and five locals.[28] Captain C.D. Bates, Sergeant J. Gilmore and six locals made up the party to watch the area south of Awungi.[29] The Open Bay party, led by Captain Skinner, included Lieutenant John Stokie, Signaller Matt Foley and five locals. Captain J.J. Murphy with Lieutenant F.A. Barrett and Sergeant L.T.W. Carlson and eight locals led the Gasmata Party. The Nakanai party, led by Wright, included Williams, Sergeant J.W. March, Sergeant P. Simogun, Corporal 'Son' Godamin and fourteen locals.[30]

The six parties departed for their assigned areas in early October, with Wright's party moving on 1 October. As Wright moved up the coastal road that day, reports began to arrive via local messengers that friendly headmen had been arrested and released, and that at least one Japanese patrol was heading in their direction. There were no local carriers available to carry the supplies and equipment as the Japanese had dragooned the local workforce to work on the southern road, their main line of communications to the west of the island. Wright's solution was to call in Beaufighter strikes on the roadworks. These strikes consisted of strafing runs designed to make the workers desert and become available as carriers.[31] It apparently worked.

Murphy's party had to reach Gasmata, which was quite a distance to cover in fourteen days. This forced Murphy to take the quick route via the coast, the area containing the most pro-Japanese population. The risk involved in this was high; in fact, it was extreme. In his book, Eric Feldt describes the decision of Murphy, Barrett and Carlson to take this route as 'above the average in courage'.[32] This above-average courage might be admirable in a soldier in battle, but it is a failing in an intelligence operative. Moreover, Murphy's batteries were dead and he failed to retrieve the replacement batteries sent to him, rendering his radios utterly useless.[33] Murphy's party should have aborted their mission.

The only members of the party who escaped were the local carriers and police, who melted into the jungle and ran for their lives when the Japanese and hostile locals fell upon the party. Lieutenant Barrett and a carrier were killed immediately, then Carlson was killed and Murphy captured.[34]

The capture of Murphy was the biggest blow of all to the operations FERDINAND hoped to carry out on New Britain. Rabaul was the main Japanese base, and Murphy would have been delivered into the experienced hands of the Kempeitai and Tokkeitai. Within a very short time, 'the Japanese extracted a complete account of the coastwatching parties in New Britain from Murphy'.[35]

FERDINAND's parties on New Britain were literally saved by the cavalry. The 112th US Cavalry Combat Team landed at Arawe on 15 December 1943 and this drew all available Japanese forces, including those searching for FERDINAND's parties.

It should not be thought that all of the locals on New Britain were hostile to the Allies. At least seven locals died protecting the FERDINAND parties in late 1943, and many more met untimely and brutal deaths at the hands of the Japanese because of the disruption caused by the presence of FERDINAND parties. One local, an old Malay man named Johannes, had been passing information to the FERDINAND party about which village headmen were friendly and what the Japanese were doing. Somehow, the Japanese got Johannes's name, most likely from Murphy. The Kempeitai arrested and executed Johannes, and then executed his entire family, including his wife, children and grandchildren.[36]

As the campaign on New Britain continued, the mission of the US forces changed. They were no longer charged with the capture of Rabaul, but rather its containment. The campaign now settled down into semi-siege, with FERDINAND's parties and their local supporters dominating the country between the US and Japanese lines. At this point, the role of the FERDINAND parties on New Britain and Bougainville started to morph into something Feldt called, 'a complete reversal of FERDINAND policy'.[37] They were no longer operating as intelligence collectors, but conducting the sabotage and guerrilla warfare to which the AIB and SRD were so addicted. The local population paid the price for this pointless activity, as payback fighting spread among the pro-Allied mountain locals and pro-Japanese coastal locals.

It may appear harsh to call the guerrilla fighting on New Britain pointless, but the fact is that the strategic policy towards Rabaul was now containment, not conquest. The strategic plan was to encircle the Japanese in the area and leave them alone until they surrendered. The hard reality was that the area was no longer of strategic value as the war moved north to the Philippines and the Home Islands of Japan itself. Given this situation, it is hard to see what value the guerrilla fighting on New Britain had.

The last portion of our HUMINT story involving the coastwatchers of FERDINAND brings us back to the work of the AIB at the western end of the archipelago. There, the legitimacy of the FERDINAND parties' concerns was soon confirmed. With the departure of the FERDINAND party from 9th Division, Captain Pursehouse and a sergeant from ANGAU were left under the control of 9th Division for the push from Finschhafen to Sio. On 17 January 1944, Pursehouse led a unit of Australian troops to Sio Mission.[38] At the mission, the troops rested, sending Pursehouse and his sergeant to obtain carriers for their equipment and supplies from Sio Village. Pursehouse was killed and his sergeant wounded. Little wonder that Feldt writes of the coastwatchers accompanying the 7th and 9th Divisions as having little or no confidence in the ability of these formations to use them properly.[39] They were not just being sent on 'adventures', they were being used for jobs others were paid to do.[40]

In May 1944, the Australian Army contemplated mounting operations in the North West Area of Dutch New Guinea to provide time-sensitive reporting of Japanese activities. Until that time, AIB reporting on this area had been by letter back to Melbourne or Brisbane, and from there back to commanders in New Guinea. It was very slow, and while it was acceptable for long-term planning, it was useless for tactical commanders on the ground.[41] It was decided that the answer lay in setting up a network of co-located radio stations in a project called Comonitor.

Comonitor consisted of a control station at Finschhafen, and receiving stations at Hollandia (modern Jayapura), Tadji, Madang, Talasea and Nadzab, servicing all of the important operational commands. To facilitate the exchange and speed of information, the SRD's and SIA's radio stations were to be collocated with the NEI Army stations. This was to be coordinated by Lieutenant Colonel Ind, US Army, and the deputy controller, AIB.[42] The location of the station was to be Inrim Plantation, 7 miles (11 kilometres) west of Lorengau.[43] It proved another disaster.

The Comonitor project failed because the intelligence parties it was to serve were already deployed and operational, and it was being developed far too late in the war in New Guinea to be of any use. The war was now a long way away in the Philippines, on Peleliu and in Burma. Another reason it failed was that the AIB thought someone else was building them ready-made stations they just had to turn up at and man. Finally, no one had expended much thought on how three different high-powered HF stations were going to be able to operate within the ground waves and electrical interference of one another. That this was happening at the end of 1944 demonstrated amazingly poor judgement by the AIB.

It was also in May 1944 that one of the final operations, the landings near Hollandia in West Papua, were planned. This provided the AIB with one last operation for their volunteers who wanted to contribute. Although it was well outside the area for which FERDINAND was responsible, FERDINAND agreed to be part of it, as no Dutch personnel were available following the disaster of the Staverman mission.

The risk entailed in this operation was substantial, because, although FERDINAND's personnel were highly experienced in New Guinea and the Solomons, they were not familiar with West Papua. The intended operation had all the hallmarks of an AIB disaster and none of the characteristics of the more successful FERDINAND operations in the eastern archipelago.

The party selected comprised Captain G.C. (Blue) Harris, leader, with Lieutenant R.B. Webber, the second-in-command, Sergeant R.J. Cream and Privates J.I. Bunning, G. Shortis and P.C. Jeune, Able Seaman J.B. McNicol, RANVR, and Sergeants Yali, Mas and Buka and Private Mariba, all PNG soldiers.[44] Sergeant Lancelot, a Bahasa Indonesian interpreter, was also attached to the party. In support of this party, another led by Captain C.J. Millar was inserted 100 miles (160 kilometres) south of Hollandia in the area of the Idenburg (Taritatu) River to act as a radio relay station for Harris's party.

The planned duration of Harris's operation was fourteen days, with insertion and extraction by submarine. The party embarked on USS *Dace* on

18 March 1944 and began their voyage to their area of operations. They only received the final briefing about the terrain for the area of operations after they boarded the submarine, meaning they had four days to assimilate this vital information.[45]

On 22 March, *Dace* arrived off the landing place and tried to examine the landing area through the periscope to little avail. Harris decided to take a small party, comprising Lancelot, Mas, Shortis and Webber ashore. This put both the party commander, Harris, and the second-in-command, Webber, in the initial reconnaissance group, exposing the mission to the loss of both commanders in one high-risk activity.

The reconnaissance group's rubber raft grounded on a reef they hadn't been able to see through the periscope, and men and equipment were pounded out of the raft and into the sea. They dragged the swamped raft and their sodden selves and equipment 100 metres or so onto the beach. The radio was inoperable, so now they were on an enemy-controlled beach with a ruined raft and no radio. It was at this point that they became aware there were huts with lights in them near the beach.

Harris decided there was no way they could avoid contact with the residents of the huts so they made their presence known, but Harris' instincts told him they were not welcome. He attempted to flash his abort signal back to the *Dace*, but in the meantime someone had decided to disembark the party, and the two rafts were attempting to make landfall, only to suffer the same fate as Harris's raft. One member of the party, Sergeant R.J. Cream, had remained on the *Dace* suffering from malaria.

When they finally got themselves ashore, they found they had two carbines and nine pistols left, the latter being useless in any contact with the Japanese. They had some hand grenades, maps, codes, a medical kit and one week's rations.[46] They decided they would walk to Captain Millar's position on the Idenburg River.

The Japanese fell on them in strength the next morning, using mortars and machine-gun fire. Bunning and Shortis were wounded and subsequently died. Harris, also wounded, was taken alive, tied to a tree and bayoneted to death after a perfunctory interrogation. Sergeant Lancelot stayed in one hiding place for four days before making his way to safety. Jeune and Webber survived and hid, before making their way to the US forces at Hollandia. The PNG soldiers did better. One, Sergeant Yali, walked 120 miles (190 kilometres) to Aitape, where he reported to Lieutenant B. Hall, the ANGAU officer there. All the rest of the party were killed during the fight or later by the Japanese.[47]

Of the eleven men who landed at Hollandia, six died or disappeared, and the entire operation was a disaster, the worst ever suffered by a FERDINAND party. That this occurred in Dutch West Papua is not surprising. That it occurred on an operation under AIB auspices was par for the course. There can also be little doubt that this operation led the ACNB, most likely on Commander Long's recommendation, to sever all ties between the RAN and AIB.

On 6 June 1944, the ACBN informed the army and GHQ that it required the return of all naval officers and ratings, including WRANS, to the control of the ACNB. The list provided to the army included the entire naval contingent of FERDINAND, from Commander J.C.B. McManus, RAN, to Lieutenant Commander Eric Feldt, Lieutenant Commander H.A. Mackenzie, 38 officers and nine WRANS.[48] The fate of Harris's party at Hollandia had been the last straw.

Despite the demise of FERDINAND, the fact remained that this small HUMINT organisation created out of the Admiralty's Reporting Officer system was one of the most effective HUMINT organisations of World War II. FERDINAND's coastwatchers earned from the United States four Distinguished Service Crosses, nine Silver Stars, ten Legion of Merits and one Bronze Star; and from the British four Knight Commanders of St Michael and St George, one Distinguished Service Order, eleven Distinguished Service Crosses, eleven Military Crosses, seven Distinguished Service Medals, five Military Medals, four British Empire Medals, 21 Mentioned in Despatches, four MBEs and two OBEs, a total of 94 significant awards to a unit in which just 407 personnel served between 8 December 1941 and 15 August 1945.[49] Of these, however, 33 were killed and many, many more local inhabitants died or suffered at the hands of the Japanese because of FERDINAND's activities.

FERDINAND's success lay in its strict adherence to simply collecting intelligence and not stirring up trouble by trying to implement a guerrilla war or conduct sabotage operations. The comparison to FERDINAND's approach is the subject of our next chapter, where direct action—sabotage and guerrilla operations—was mixed with intelligence collection, resulting in a series of operations that can only be described as disastrous.

CHAPTER 25

The Kempeitai's Game, 1942-45

The disposition of the Australian ground forces in the islands to Australia's north is a classic example of what you should never do. The forces were distributed in small groupings, with LARK Force at Rabaul, New Britain, and Kavieng, New Ireland, SPARROW Force on Timor and GULL Force at Ambon. These small and isolated forces were never going to do much more than evade capture before surrendering. At Rabaul and Kavieng LARK Force was destroyed so swiftly that it resembled a rout and the Japanese were unable to catch many of the Australian troops before they ran off into the jungle. On Ambon, GULL Force was commanded by Harry Freame's old handler, now Lieutenant Colonel, W.R. Scott, and it was quickly taken prisoner and subjected to a brutal captivity for the remainder of the war. On Timor, SPARROW Force, commanded in the field by Lieutenant Colonel William Leggett, inflicted serious casualties on the Japanese before it too had to surrender the bulk of its strength. Nevertheless, around 300 escaped the Japanese and joined up with 2/2 Independent Company, the one unit to maintain its cohesion, in Portuguese East Timor, where they conducted a guerrilla campaign until the Japanese forced their evacuation in December 1942. It was this that provided a significant boost to the ambitions of those within the SRD and AIB who believed that a successful guerrilla war could be conducted against the Japanese in occupied territory.

2/2 Independent Company began to harass the Japanese who had arrived on Timor, which, as a Portuguese colony, was officially neutral. This neutrality was somewhat lopsided, as the Portuguese administration allowed the Australian force to utilise telephones and postal services to pass messages. Their situation improved further when they finally got an improvised radio working and regained contact with Australian forces in Darwin.

The situation on Timor was one the Japanese would not tolerate for long, and in June 1942 their relationship with the Portuguese administration deteriorated to the point where they cut the communications link to Portugal and lodged a formal complaint about Manuel de Abreu Ferreira de Carvalho's administration of the colony. Finally, their limited patience having evaporated, the Japanese 48th Division, led by Lieutenant General Tsuchihashi Yuitsu, occupied the Portuguese half of Timor and set about suppressing the Australian and Dutch guerrilla units. Tsuchihashi swiftly pushed his forces into the hinterland, took important towns and secured much of the coastline. A significant portion of the 48th Division was then withdrawn to Rabaul in preparation for further advances south through the Solomon Islands ready for the invasion of Fiji and New Caledonia. This operation, although it never eventuated, was seen by the Japanese as more important, because if successful it would have resulted in them cutting off the direct shipping lanes from the west coast of the United States to the east coast of Australia.

The Australian commandos on Timor had now been contained to the areas around their bases, and the Japanese supported by local Timorese began a campaign of destroying them in detail. This resulted in an upsurge of inter-clan and intertribal fighting, as villages used the chaos to settle old scores. Some Timorese even revolted against the Portuguese.

For the Australian commandos, the hard reality was that the Japanese now had 12,000 troops on the island and they were not going to allow a stay-behind party of Australian and Dutch forces to continue operations. As the fighting alienated ever-growing numbers of Timorese, the position of the Australian and Dutch forces became untenable by early 1943.

As the Australian Independent Company was operating on Timor, the AIB was to conduct HUMINT, sabotage and other operations in Japanese-occupied areas. This was in line with the ethos of the SOE and its mission to 'set Europe ablaze'. The success of the 2/2 Independent Company and the survivors of SPARROW in not being captured or destroyed led to the IJA moving more troops onto the island to deal with them and this in turn led to the arrival in September of LANCER Force, 400 men of 2/4 Independent Company. At face value, the situation on Timor looked as if it could lead to the creation of a viable guerrilla war conducted with local support. This attracted the attention of the AIB and the SRD.

In early 1942, two SOE officers, Major G.S. Mott and Major A.E.B. Trappes-Lomax, had arrived in Australia to advise the Australian Army on how to set up a local version of SOE. The outcome was that General Blamey ordered the creation of SOA and the ISD, which later became the SRD, commanded by Major Mott.[1] In June 1942, this organisation was brought under the umbrella of the new AIB, which also oversaw the operations of FELO, the organisation responsible for propaganda in Japanese-occupied areas. The AIB was commanded by the DMI at LHQ, our old friend Colonel C.G. Roberts.

From the very beginning, AIB was double-tasked with obtaining intelligence about the enemy, which is why they form part of our story here, and taking action to weaken the enemy by sabotage and destruction of morale through commando raids and the creation of insurrection, which is not part of our story.[2] As Rupert Long and Eric Feldt at the RAN had already identified, this was a recipe for disaster. As the official history of the SRD notes, in the period from July 1942 to August 1945, the SRD was 'constantly engaged in field operations', but 'between October 1943 and June 1945, all parties in the field were in Japanese hands'.[3] This makes the SRD operations one of the greatest intelligence failures in Australian history, at least as far as we know today.

The first mission undertaken by the SRD was Operation LION, a Dutch affair, led by First Lieutenant H.T. Van Hees. This party consisted of three men and was tasked with proceeding aboard the *Prahu Samoa* to Wotoe near Mailili in the Celebes on 24 June 1942. The party was successfully landed, and it is possible that a weak but unreadable signal from them was detected on 11 July. It was the last time anyone ever heard from them. That the first party to be sent to this area just disappeared did not seem to bother the planners at AIB or the SRD, who proceeded with the WALNUT series of intelligence operations and sent even more men there.

Operation WALNUT I, consisted of two men, Captain C.R. Sheldon, AIF, and N.P. Monsted, a Danish citizen who had lived in the Aroe (Aru) Islands. They were inserted at Dobo on 7 July 1942 to establish an intelligence organisation in the islands. The official SRD history describes Sheldon as a man reputed to be unpopular with the locals. These two men survived until August or September 1942, when they extricated themselves to Thursday Island aboard the lugger *Express*. At Thursday Island, their unexpected arrival led to a hostile reception and they were arrested.[4]

With the failure of WALNUT I and following their release from custody on Thursday Island, Monsted sailed the *Express* to Darwin while Sheldon, along with Lieutenant R.W. Feetum and Sergeant J. McCandlish, was despatched on WALNUT II to join a Dutch official on Penamboela (Penambulai) Island who was in radio contact with Australia. On 8 March, they reported the locals as hostile and the Japanese aware of their presence. They were captured on 12 August 1943, and the Japanese extracted extensive intelligence from them on the organisation and personalities of the AIB, the SRD and their operational methods and equipment. In fact, the Kempeitai built a remarkably accurate profile of the AIB and the SRD from these men. They all died in captivity.[5]

WALNUT III, comprising Monsted, Sergeants J.R. Plumridge and J.H. Dahlberg of the AIF, Sergeant J.A. Bloch, NEI, Mr Mitchell, an Indian, and five Indonesian seamen, sailed from Darwin to the Aroes in the *Express* on 28 January 1943. They reached Djeh Island, just north of Enoe (Enu), on 12 July. They were last heard from on 25 July 1943, after which the Japanese caught and killed all of them.[6]

All three missions to the Aroe Islands had failed, with the loss of thirteen men for no intelligence return for the Allies. The intelligence gleaned by the Japanese was, however, extensive. It is likely they had completely compromised all of the Allied communications and codes used for special operations, and were obtaining intelligence useful against both the SRD in Papua New Guinea and the eastern archipelago and FERDINAND in the Solomons.

Operation MACKEREL, launched from Melbourne on 24 August 1942, was a party of three, Lieutenant G.C.M. Van Arcken, NEI Sergeant Raden Wirjomijardje Iswahjeodi and Seaman 1st Class W.F. Schneau. The party, along with two crewmen from the Dutch submarine *K12*, landed at Radjeg Wesi Baai, Java, on the evening of 14 September 1942. The landing boats capsized, the equipment was lost, and Van Arcken hurt his back. The captain of the *K12* resurfaced on the morning of 15 September in full view of Japanese observation posts to successfully retrieve his crewmen and the rest of the party, and the mission was aborted.[7] MACKEREL was lucky, because they at least survived.

The same could not be said for the small parties and individual agents who attempted to infiltrate Java on the six TIGER operations conducted from 10 November 1942 to 6 August 1943. Of the ten men despatched, one, Sergeant Raden, escaped from Kempeitai custody. The Kempeitai interrogated the rest, no doubt adding to the picture they were building of the AIB. All of these agents, except Raden, were executed. The TIGER operations should have alerted the SRD to the growing sophistication of the Japanese, as they kept TIGER I's radio operational and fed disinformation to the AIB.[8]

During this time, another operation, FLOUNDER, was launched on 18 December 1942 to insert a Dutch party onto Ambon from the US Submarine *Sea Raven*. The Japanese captured all eight members within a week of their insertion on 30 December 1942 and, the evidence suggests, Lieutenant H.F. Nygh RNN and the seven Indonesian members of the NEI military were all beheaded after interrogation.

By early 1943, all twelve SRD operations, LION, the three WALNUT missions, MACKEREL, the six TIGER missions and FLOUNDER had failed, with 34 dead, one hiding on Java, one who was warned off on landing and three recovered on MACKEREL. This is a death rate of 94 per cent for no intelligence return. Every mission had failed, and there were strong indications that the Kempeitai were now operating a double-cross system using the captured equipment and personnel.

All of this should have sent warning signals that the Japanese were an extremely sophisticated opponent, and that no further operations should be launched until a full threat assessment and cost–benefit analysis were completed. Nothing of the sort was done, and the AIB just kept throwing good men to torture and death. In fact, there was little or no oversight of what the AIB and the SRD were doing, and they were not being held answerable to a higher body charged with independently adjudicating whether the activity was worth the cost. If such a body had been in place, it would have shut down all SRD operations immediately.[9]

The failure to conduct a thorough assessment of what was happening was made worse by poor tradecraft. The target area of operations was heavily populated and hostile. No one seems to have considered whether the Javanese and other peoples of the archipelago supported the Dutch. There seems to have been a wilful ignorance of the reality of the politics in the archipelago so that this reality did not stop operations.

On top of this, the series of operations, including MACKEREL and the TIGER missions, consistently used the same landing places. TIGER IV, V and VI were all landed at Pang Pang Baai.[10] On an earlier mission, TIGER II, the practice of revisiting drop-off points almost resulted in the capture of yet another radio operator, his equipment and codebooks as he was about to be landed at the drop-off point used for TIGER I. The landing was aborted only because someone on shore sent a light signal in Dutch warning of danger.[11]

As the SRD was running its missions in the Aroe Islands, Celebes and Java, it concurrently ran a series of operations into Portuguese Timor. These, codenamed LIZARD I, II and III, were intended to support the remnants of the various units, including SPARROW Force, that continued to operate there. There was no initial intention to conduct sabotage operations as part of LIZARD because, as *The Official History of Special Operations Australia* says, there was nothing of value to sabotage on the island.[12] The intention was to run a guerrilla war to tie down Japanese troops.

The interest of the Japanese in Portuguese Timor was limited. The island had no strategic value or resources, and its only real use was as a point from which Allied forces could operate to disrupt Japanese activity on other islands and in the seas around Timor. This may be why the Japanese did not make it a target until 20 February 1942.[13]

Before the arrival of the Japanese military on the island, there were twenty to 30 Japanese who worked for the Japanese Consulate, which had only opened in Dili on October 1941, when Consul Kuroki Tokitaro arrived. There were also Japanese civilians operating the offices of Dai Nippon Airlines and Nan'yo Kohatsu K. K. (the South Seas Development Company).[14] These Japanese civilians had undoubtedly created networks among the Timorese and Indian residents on the island, which may have included Ishag Selam Rafig and his daughter Nora Rafig, who operated Toko Selam (Kupang Stores).[15] This provided the Japanese with the necessary contacts to establish themselves quickly once they occupied the island.

This situation attracted the SRD because, unlike many of the other operations, LIZARD had the major advantage of being able to operate from the safe haven controlled by Australian troops, SPARROW Force, at Mape.

LIZARD I, led by Captain I.S. Wylie, with Captain D.K. Broadhurst and Sergeant J.R.F. Cashman, was inserted from the launch *Kuru* at Suai on 17 July 1942. The safe haven was not as safe as thought, though, as IJN activity soon forced the move of SPARROW from Mape. It was during this move that all of SPARROW's HF radios were sabotaged by unfriendly locals, forcing LIZARD I, now with the only operational HF radio, to accompany SPARROW HQ to Same.[16] As the plans now being discussed for Timor included the evacuation of SPARROW and other elements, LIZARD I decided to extricate itself to Darwin on 17 August 1942. LIZARD I's biggest accomplishment was the establishment of contact with Antonio de Sousa Santos, the Administrator of Fronteira Province, and Dr Carlos Brandau.[17]

LIZARD II, made up of Captain Wylie, Captain Broadhurst, Lieutenant G. Greave and Sergeant Cashman, returned to Timor on 2 September 1942. The party established an operational post at Loi Uno and began caching supplies and arms before contacting the Chef de Poste at Ossu. Contact was then made with Manuel de Jesus Pires, the Administrator of Baucau Province, who had excellent connections within the Portuguese administration. The Japanese were onto LIZARD II within a week of its insertion, and moved a patrol down the Baucau Road in Viqueque District for a few days questioning the locals about LIZARD II's location.[18]

Despite the Japanese attention, LIZARD II, assisted by Pires, was able to establish a network of runners to carry messages, as well as the use of the services of friendly telephone operators to speak to contacts in Dili. They also arranged for the release of a Chinese Nationalist captain and five Chinese soldiers, and rescued a wounded RAAF crewman, Pilot Officer S. Wadey, from Ossu gaol. The intelligence gleaned from all of this was that the Japanese were controlling the Portuguese administration on Timor.

GHQ, SWPA wanted to meet with Pires to talk him into leading an insurrection against the Japanese in San Domingos and Lautém. The idea of raising this insurrection had been generated by a LIZARD II report that the behaviour of the Japanese was alienating the local population, both Portuguese and Timorese, and that arms and other stores were required to arm the potential insurgents. One hundred rifles and 10,000 rounds of ball ammunition were landed at Aliambata for this operation.[19]

The Japanese countered these plans by arming the locals in Dutch Timor and loosing them upon the people of Portuguese Timor. The Japanese also brought in armed men from Alor and Wetar islands for the same purpose. On 1 October 1942, three Portuguese officials and 24 Portuguese colonial soldiers were massacred at Aileu, 25 miles (40 kilometres) from Dili, and the Portuguese Governor, Carvalho, sought to evacuate all Portuguese nationals to Mozambique.[20] By the middle of October, the Portuguese administration had collapsed. For LIZARD II, there was a further blow, the loss of their leader, Captain Wylie, who had to be evacuated on 23 October by HMAS *Vigilant* because of malaria.[21]

By the end of October 1942, LIZARD II estimated that 50,000 Timorese could be raised to fight the Japanese if they were armed. SRD advised LIZARD that this should not be done until a more appropriate time. *The Official History of Special Operations Australia* regards this decision as a tragedy, because it allowed 'a genuinely aroused population to sink back into disgruntled apathy'.[22] This evaluation gives the reader a clear insight into the unreality of SRD thinking. The enemy the SRD faced on Timor was a highly trained and very experienced military force with a reputation for aggression, competence and extreme brutality. They had good air and naval support, and plenty of heavy weapons including artillery. Any uprising would have been quickly put down. The decision not to proceed with this operation was the right one. The idea of 50,000 untrained Timorese going into battle against hardened Japanese troops doesn't bear thinking about, even now.

Despite the questions over what would happen on Timor, the SRD reinforced LIZARD II with three more operatives: Lieutenant J.E. Grimson, W.T. Thomas and Signaller A.K. Smith. These reinforcements brought another 100 rifles with them and some Bren guns. Now LIZARD II had 200 rifles and some light machine guns for their guerrilla army.[23]

At the same time, LIZARD III, with Lieutenant L.W. Ross and Captain R.C. Neave, arrived to collect raw rubber and succeeded in taking away a few tons of rubber to Australia.[24] In response, the Japanese once more moved in strength down the Baucau Road and occupied all of the principal points, driving a mob of refugees before them. On 1 December, HMAS *Armidale* was sunk attempting to bring off more of SPARROW's survivors and Portuguese refugees, consisting of the wives and families of Pires, a man named Don Paulo and some minor local chiefs attached to LIZARD II. The HNLMS *Tjerk Hiddes* finally evacuated this group on the night of 8–9 December. Lieutenant Greave was also evacuated because of ill health.[25]

Around 23 December 1942, the Japanese mortared LIZARD II's main post, killing ten Timorese and forcing the evacuation of the rest of LIZARD II to the secondary post near Hareapa. Now the previously supportive local leaders started changing sides. The Japanese hit more of LIZARD II's posts and began a relentless chase of the survivors in exactly the same way they had driven the FERDINAND parties on New Britain and Bougainville. By 17 January 1943, the Japanese pressure had forced the withdrawal of the bulk of the LANCER Force elements that reinforced SPARROW, the Australian Independent Company, and the break-up of the small guerrilla force set up by LIZARD II. The intelligence network of runners and telephone operators was destroyed by 22 January 1943 with the disappearance of Don Paulo.

Eventually, on 10 February 1943, the remnants of LIZARD along with thirteen volunteers from the now withdrawn LANCER operation and a further seven LANCER men who were found lost in the bush, were evacuated by the submarine USS *Gudgeon*.[26] This withdrawal coincided with an important development in our story, the arrival in Kupang of the 1st Platoon of the 5th Military Police (Kempeitai) commanded by Major Yutani Kiyoshi (Yujiro).[27]

Major Yutani quickly established his HQ in Kupang and sent detachments to Soe in West Timor, Dili and Lautém in East Timor, and a small detachment to Atambua, West Timor.[28] With the arrival of this unit, the Japanese counter-intelligence capability increased dramatically, and the willingness of the local population to support Australian and other Allied operations dropped precipitously. This change was completely missed by the SRD and GHQ, SWPA.

The intelligence group left behind when LIZARD II was pulled out was renamed PORTOLIZARD, and consisted of 60 personnel, mainly regular Timorese soldiers, some Portuguese soldiers and some Nationalist Chinese soldiers. One Australian, Private D. Fittness of LANCER, had been left with PORTOLIZARD because he was too sick to evacuate with LANCER. The second-in-command was Augusto Leal de Matos e Silva, the ex-Chef de Poste at Laga. Communications for this group were the two ATR4 radios left by LIZARD II.[29] Despite Captain Broadhurst having taken the ciphers to Australia with LIZARD II, the PORTOLIZARD party made contact with Australia and began reporting that it was hard-pressed by the Japanese. The radio discipline of PORTOLIZARD appears to have been poor, and they sent a flood of signals to Australia including four in one day.[30] The Japanese

SIGINT organisation would have had little or no trouble locating the radio, and would have been using the captured ciphers from the Java operations to read the content.

The situation on Timor had worsened considerably as the Japanese tightened their grip and the Kempeitai set up their clandestine intelligence networks. They also operated with the same levels of brutality as elsewhere, and kidnapped women for the IJA's brothels and confiscated food. These actions led to severe unrest in the Viqueque area, which was seen as an opportunity by the AIB and SRD. The SRD now planned to send two parties back into Timor,[31] to be led by Portuguese officials in the hope 'that a spirit of competition between the parties would inspire them to achieve excellent results'.[32]

As it happened, the Japanese prevented this idiocy from being put into action by massacring the Western Chief, Dom Alexio, and his family, leaving no friendly contacts alive in the west of the area of operations.[33] That did not mean, however, that the SRD had given up on Timor. They planned to send another party, this one tasked with intelligence collection.

The cover name for this operation was LAGARTO, and it consisted of a party of two Portuguese men, Lieutenant Manuel de Jesus Pires and Patricio Luz, plus one Timorese. LAGARTO landed at the mouth of the Luca River on the night of 1–2 July 1943 and joined up with PORTOLIZARD.[34] During this landing, LAGARTO lost all three of its radios. A signaller from SRD, Sergeant A.J. Ellwood, AIF, then joined them. LAGARTO first arranged by radio for the evacuation of 87 PORTOLIZARD personnel. This evacuation finally occurred on the night of 3–4 August 1943 because the Japanese made it impossible to get the group off any earlier.[35]

The Japanese had no difficulty locating LAGARTO, and pursuing both it and the PORTOLIZARD party hard. On 9 July, 200 Japanese, supported by mortars and machine guns, attacked the party. The men escaped, but in doing so lost most of their equipment, although they saved the radio they inherited from PORTOLIZARD.[36] Japanese mortars attacked them again on 11 July, following which they broke contact and were able to arrange the evacuation of the PORTOLIZARD personnel and camp followers.

The arrival of Ellwood was not a happy event. He had been selected to join LAGARTO because the SRD lacked faith in Pires's leadership, but Pires had worked this out and resented Ellwood's presence.[37] On 5 August, the party was deprived of all its remaining food and stores when a small group sent to recover a cache was surprised by a Japanese patrol. With the Japanese and hostile Timorese now following them, LAGARTO attempted to escape by moving to Manatuto on the north coast. To ensure that the local villagers would not support the Australians, the Japanese chasing LAGARTO publicly tortured and killed all of the chiefs and villagers suspected of having assisted the party.[38] It was a highly effective strategy, and demonstrated the stark reality of trying to build a resistance movement in the face of such an extremely brutal opponent.

LAGARTO's move was ill disciplined, and conflict erupted between Ellwood and Pires. It may have been because of this that Ellwood was commissioned as a lieutenant on 17 September, so that he was of equal rank to Pires.[39] The party was now 34 strong, comprising servants, bearers and camp followers, including the mistresses of Pires and Mateos da Silva, one of whom was pregnant.[40] By 25 September, the Japanese were using tracker dogs and the entire population was too terrified to assist LAGARTO in any way. On 29 September 1943, as it moved along the Baucau Plateau, LAGARTO was ambushed by a large Japanese patrol. On contact, LAGARTO disintegrated, with a number of carriers, including those carrying the radio, cut down and everyone else running for the bush. Most of the personnel from LAGARTO were captured in such a way that it appears that the Japanese wanted them alive. One man, Patricio Luz, escaped and went into hiding. He survived the war.[41]

The Japanese were by now so well informed on SRD procedures they conducted a painstaking search of the area through which LAGARTO had moved following contact. This unearthed Ellwood's notebooks, codes and schedules, which he had, in accordance with SRD procedure, attempted to bury.[42] A Japanese Major General, possibly Tanaka Toru, interviewed all of the captives, particularly Pires and Ellwood, at Kempeitai HQ in Dili, and a major named in the official history as Tanaka but most likely Major Kobayashi, conducted the interrogations, assisted by First Lieutenant Saiki Kasukane and a civilian from the Japanese Consulate.[43]

The Japanese appear to have wanted a trusted radio net established with Australia, and they needed Ellwood and Pires to cooperate in this. The fact that Ellwood survived his captivity and Pires survived until he went insane and died in early 1944 is proof that they were singled out for special treatment. Every other member of LAGARTO died, the majority executed.[44]

In the official history, Pires is blamed for the first compromise of the SRD's cipher, as he handed over the emergency cipher early enough for the Japanese to send their first message to Australia on 6 October 1943. By the time this occurred, however, the Kempeitai had Ellwood's ciphers and signal plan, as well as copious material collected from all of the other botched operations. The fact is that both Pires and Ellwood must have cooperated with the Kempeitai as soon as they were put through processing. Had they not, they would have been beheaded like the rest.

The Kempeitai wanted Ellwood to work his radio set for them, and to do this they had to balance out persuasion with pain before pampering him into compliance. They also needed to ensure that he did what they wanted and did not send any warnings of compromise. This is a hard thing to achieve, but the Kempeitai were very good at it. The fact that Ellwood was kept alive for so long proves that the Kempeitai turned him, but the message logs of the SRD provide the harder proof. Ellwood participated in the Kempeitai's double-cross operation because he had no choice, and if the SRD operators and analysts did not detect that he was compromised, it was not Ellwood's fault. The story that a seriously weakened Ellwood was forced to operate a Morse key with a Japanese operator to guide his hand is not credible.[45] The Kempeitai would have known that the receiving operator would be very familiar with Ellwood's hand,—that is the little quirks each operator has when they key a message. There is no way they would have had his keying ghosted, and the simple fact that Ellwood was not executed and that he survived the war indicates he cooperated.

The turning of intelligence operatives was standard Kempeitai practice. They used the full gamut of techniques, ranging from deprivation to physical abuse and perhaps a little torture, contrasted with moments of kindness, such as cigarettes immediately after capture.[46] What we often overlook is that the Kempeitai were experienced professionals who were practised in all the techniques of winning cooperation. Leaving Ellwood to stew while the expendable members of his group were tortured within his earshot was simply softening him up for his subsequent interrogation. The Kempeitai probably kept Pires alive as a foil for Ellwood, and as a source of intelligence on his family and friends in Timor.

The Kempeitai would have used concurrent questioning of Ellwood and the Portuguese to play on the fears of each prisoner, and they would have used long sessions of repetitive questioning to isolate inconsistencies. Faced with expert interrogators who appeared to have obtained all of the most relevant secrets they had, it is unsurprising that the men of LAGARTO quickly surrendered their remaining secrets.[47]

At some stage, probably as he approached mental exhaustion, the Kempeitai would also have shown Ellwood the extent of the information they had on the AIB and SRD. The shock to his system of finding out that the entire secret organisation was completely compromised would have been devastating. Before this they would have shown all the information they had captured locally, including the full nominal rolls of 2/2 and 2/4 Independent Companies, ciphers, message logs, recent Australian Army lists and documents. They also let him know they had his diary, ciphers and signal plan.[48] Exposing their knowledge of AIB in this way would have removed any rational reason for continued resistance.

With Ellwood's first signal back to Australia, the Kempeitai interrogators would have known they had peeled the onion back to its last layer. Once Ellwood had established routine communication without sending his warning word, they would have known they had him. He was released from close confinement and treated well. His rations improved and he was allowed letters, a magazine a month and given clothing. All of this indicates his Japanese handlers were happy with his performance.[49]

That the SRD did not deduce that LAGARTO had been captured appears to the official historian to be 'incomprehensible',[50] but it's consistent with SRD's management of the earlier operations in the Celebes and on Java. The fact is that the AIB and SRD were untrained in intelligence collection at this level. Their operational need to achieve something overrode the requirement for caution that is characteristic of all effective intelligence work.

The Kempeitai used Ellwood to compromise the security of all future SRD operations in Timor from this time forward, and, as AIB was now sending LAGARTO a flow of information on the conduct of the war everywhere, they were providing the Japanese with a broad insight into Allied operations. By the end of January 1944, the SRD had fallen for the Japanese double-cross so badly that they inserted the COBRA party of Lieutenant J.R.F. Cashman, Sergeant E.J. Liversidge and three Timorese, Paulo da Silva, Sancho da Silva and Cosmo Soares, into the waiting arms of Lieutenant Saiki of the Kempeitai and a company of soldiers who, along with Lieutenant Ellwood, were waiting for them at Dari Bai on 27 or 29 January 1944.[51] COBRA was captured within an hour of its insertion.

The history of COBRA is almost identical to that of LAGARTO, even down to the abysmal tradecraft of the wireless operator, Sergeant Liversidge, who had written down the authenticator for the party being safe, '2926 Slender Silk Key', in a notebook that the Japanese easily found.[52]

The captured party was then taken and subjected to the same treatment as LAGARTO; the leader and radio operators were turned and began working a second trusted radio link to Australia. On 8 February, its radio operator, Lieutenant Cashman, sent his first message to SRD.[53] The Japanese described him as 'an excellent officer' who 'gave personal views as to future Allied Operations'.[54]

As we have seen, SRD was so happy to hear from COBRA that it completely compromised Central Bureau's SIGINT operations, sending a message on 7 March 1944 telling Cashman of the consternation at SRD when they read an 'intercept Jap cipher naming you personally and apparently claiming your capture Jan 29'.[55] Luckily, the Japanese were as complacent as the SRD, and their reaction to the compromise was 'plain unbelief' that the Australians could be reading their unbreakable codes.[56]

After receiving the SIGINT report that COBRA had been captured, the SRD had first begun trying to get the authentication from COBRA it should have obtained at the very beginning. The party was told 'Mother sends loving greetings for twenty-six' and that Paulo's daughter was born on 25 January [a reference to Timorese COBRA member Paulo da Silva].[57] COBRA replied on the same day in message 4, 'PAULO had not yet returned' and thanking SRD for the 'relay of wishes for 26th. Give my love to Mother and Father'.[58] On 26 February, SRD attempted to obtain authentication, sending 'Slender girl sends greetings' and received a reply without the authenticator being repeated. This alone should have told SRD that COBRA was compromised.

Three days later, on 28 February, SRD asked for an acknowledgement of the greetings in the last message 'from this particular girl', who was then described as 'not repeat not the fat repeat fat one', which tipped the Kempeitai as to the significance of the phrase 'Slender girl'. It was then that Cashman sent the authenticator that caused so much relief at SRD that it compromised the SIGINT on 7 March.

Given the clumsy exchange of messages with COBRA, the role played by LAGARTO in getting COBRA ashore on Timor, and the way LAGARTO had gone from being in dire straits to being secure so quickly, it should have been obvious to SRD and AIB that the whole Timor operation was compromised. The truth appears to be that optimism trumped hard analysis, and the scene was set for what the SRD's own official history called 'an operation with no redeeming feature at all'. LAGARTO led to the wretched deaths of nine more Australians, more Portuguese and scores of Timorese.

In early 1944, as the Japanese worked the survivors of LAGARTO and COBRA, the SRD was planning to insert another party, codenamed ADDER, into Timor.

ADDER, consisting of Captain J. Grimson, Sergeant E. Gregg, A. Fernandez, J. Carvalho and Z. Rebelo, went ashore just west of Cape Lai Aco on the night of 21–22 August 1944.[59] Grimson and Gregg were killed in a firefight within hours of landing, Rebelo fell from a cliff and the rest died in captivity.[60] The SRD received no news from ADDER at all. To add insult to injury, they tasked COBRA to find out what had happened. The Kempeitai must have had a good laugh about that.

Subsequent AIB operations in Timor did not run to plan either. Operation SUNBAKER ended in disaster on 17 May 1945 when the aircraft carrying the party crashed near Dili, killing all four members of the party and the crew of the aircraft. Operation SUNABLE ended on 5 July when the party came into contact with the Japanese; its leader, Lieutenant D.M. Williams, was killed and the rest of his party captured during the following week. Operation SUNCOB ended on 17 July with the capture of Captain W.P. Wynne and Sergeant J.B. Lawrence, who were added to the complement of LAGARTO and COBRA in Kempeitai custody.[61]

In May 1945, it seems Central Bureau provided the first hard evidence that the Japanese were controlling the LAGARTO party when Japanese traffic carrying an AIB proforma (questionnaire) provided to LAGARTO was intercepted, decrypted and translated. SRD and AIB were warned:

Have obtained a new translation PROFORMA document picked up by JAPANESE. There is now no doubt what so ever that it was document dropped to LAGARTO repeat LAGARTO on January 19th. View fact challenge parties probably COMPROMISED LAGAROUT and

COBREXIT will have to be replanned. ETD SUNFISH party and self for Darwin today.[62]

The SRD finally proved what was happening on Timor in July 1945, when Operation SUNLAG, led by Captain A.D. Stevenson and consisting of Sergeant R.G. Dawson, AIF, and Celestino dos Anjos, forewarned of the compromise of COBRA and LAGARTO, parachuted into Timor on 29 June, an earlier date than the one supplied to LAGARTO and at a different location. Stevenson sent Celestino to elicit information from relatives in the area and was able to find out that the Japanese knew SUNLAG had arrived on the island.[63]

Stevenson then arranged for a signal to be sent to LAGARTO, telling them that a supply drop was to be made at a drop zone on 1 July. Stevenson moved into an observation post overlooking the proposed drop zone and observed the arrival there of the Japanese and a white man he identified as Ellwood.[64] This was the final proof of LAGARTO's capture, proof that LAGARTO and COBRA had been turned, and proof that the string of disasters—COBRA, ADDER, SUNCOB and SUNABLE—had been engineered by the Kempeitai. Having established that the Japanese had been playing the SRD, Stevenson quickly got permission to evacuate his party from Timor.[65]

By 22 July, SRD Darwin was requesting advice from its higher HQ for assistance in setting policy in relation to the now compromised LAGARTO. This action was prompted because the senior air staff officer in Darwin had refused any further RAAF support in making supply drops after he was told LAGARTO was compromised.

The decision by the RAAF to abandon LAGARTO was not accepted by SRD Darwin and they requested GHQ, General MacArthur, to order the RAAF to continue support to LAGARTO. The reply was, 'Normal signal traffic and maintenance will be kept up ... This is most important.'[66] The rationale was to maintain the illusion that LAGARTO was still trusted, in order to keep the captured members of the missions alive and so that disinformation could then be passed onto the Japanese.[67]

The Timor intelligence operations ended on 12 August 1945, when the Japanese sent a message in the SRD code: 'NIPPON for LMS [Lugger Maintenance Section]. Thanks your assistance for this long while. Hope to see you again. Until then wish your good health. NIPPON Army.'[68]

On 13 August SRD replied:

Your signal received and understood. Thank for your good wishes. Please continue look after our soldiers. Will be good enough inform us of his welfare.[69]

The Official History of Special Operations Australia intimates that the SRD and AIB remained ignorant of the compromise of their parties until they received this message on 12 August, but this is misleading. The SRD had begun to suspect something was wrong at the end of May 1945, when Central Bureau's intercept reported the capture of COBRA. In yet another triumph of hope over reason, the possibility that the operations were compromised was discounted, although it has to be said, not by everyone. The SUNLAG operation was hard proof that everything the SRD had done in Timor and across the eastern part of the archipelago had been a complete waste of time. The whole series of operations stand as a warning against mixing intelligence collection and direct action. And against underestimating an opponent.

AFTERWORD

The premise of this book is that it is not what nations do and say in public that tells us who they really are and what they really want, but what they do and say in secret. In 1901, the new Australian Commonwealth's first actions in the international sphere were not to stand as a loyal member of the British Empire, but to launch an intelligence operation against that Empire in order to protect its self-interest. As former NSW Premier Jack Lang reputedly told a young Paul Keating, self-interest is the only horse that you bet on in any race, because it is the only one really trying to win.[1] Australia's secret action in sending Wilson Le Couteur to the New Hebrides betrays to us what Australia's real attitude towards the British Empire was. Britain was a power that could keep the new nation safe from unknown enemies, but not at the expense of subservience. Australia would make its own way in the world, and if stealing Britain's secrets helped in this, then so be it.

Australia spied on Britain, France, Germany, Russia, Japan, the United States and China, all before the advent of the World War in 1914. This clearly demonstrates that Australia's move towards nationhood was driven by a hard-nosed appreciation of the fact that Australians best protect Australian self-interest. This attitude permeates the story of Australia's secret world of intelligence collection described in this book.

The activities of William Bridges, even sending Charles Hoad to Japan and Manchuria in 1904, are examples of this hard-nosed attitude. So, too, is Atlee Hunt's ad hoc but extensive and pervasive intelligence system extending throughout Australia and the islands, into the heart of Japan, China and even, for a short time, into the United States.

The British Admiralty's Reporting Officer system added to Australian intelligence capabilities by making Australia, through its navy, a member of the world's first broad-ocean surveillance system. It introduced the RAN to the organisation of intelligence collection and to the systemisation of intelligence collation. It even introduced Australia to the use of intelligence in decision-making at the tactical, operational and, to a point, strategic level.

By 1920, Australia had developed its intelligence capabilities to a very high standard, which, while not approaching the sophistication or size of those in either Britain or the Soviet Union, was nonetheless as good as if not better than the intelligence services of the United States at the time. Edmund Piesse's Pacific Branch developed not only as a collector of intelligence, but as an assessor of intelligence that could provide all levels of Australia's government with the considered intelligence necessary for any modern nation-state to fully protect its interests.

The destruction of Piesse's Pacific Branch and Atlee Hunt's intelligence system were not accomplished by Britain or by Australian leaders bending their knee to Britain. They were mainly dismantled by the paltry personal politics of a small man, Billy Hughes, who did not like being embarrassed and who excelled in destroying his opponents wherever he created them. Yet as our story shows, Hughes is not entirely to blame. Piesse gave up the fight during Stanley Bruce's term in office, thus surrendering the real power of the bureaucrat, which is to wait until the time is right.

Australia's intelligence capabilities reverted to the armed services, of which the RAN was the most effective user of intelligence. The SIGINT successes of 1914 and the HUMINT success of the Reporting Officer system and the Wanetta network provided a significant base of experience and knowledge that enabled the creation and maintenance of a small SIGINT capability later developed into the highly successful SIGINT organisations at the Special Intelligence Bureau and Central Bureau. It also enabled the support of the US Navy's FRUMEL, but at FRUMEL the RAN surrendered its independence.

HUMINT was more difficult, and aside from the magnificent success of the RAN's coastwatcher network FERDINAND, it was costly. Harry Freame and the unfortunate members of the SRD sent to torture and death at the hands of the Kempeitai were part of a disastrous waste of life that only provided good intelligence to Japan. It was in HUMINT that the lessons of how to properly conduct intelligence work were underlined, unfortunately in the blood and suffering of the intelligence operatives sent on those appalling missions.

All of this activity provided Australia with the experience and people it needed to create its first formal intelligence organisation, the DSB, in 1947. The most important lesson was that successful intelligence must remain secret and focused on getting the 'inside dope' on the target.

Intelligence collection must be so secret that its successes and failures, but particularly its successes, are never known outside the small group of people with a proven need to know. The purpose of this secrecy is not to exclude the public or even to protect the source, but to ensure that the opponent from whom the secret intelligence has been stolen never becomes aware that their secrets have been discovered. In this lies the real advantage of secret intelligence, for the opponent will continue to act in accordance with their real intentions and attitudes, and remain unaware of the true reason for their failures.

The destruction of Japan's power within ten months of her sneak attacks at Kota Bharu and Hawaii, the reversal of her strategic assumptions on how quickly and strongly the United States would retaliate, and the rapid destruction of her defences in the south-west Pacific were all significantly helped by good intelligence collectors stealing Japan's secrets without her ever knowing.

ACKNOWLEDGEMENTS

No one produces a book alone and it is for this reason that books either start or end with acknowledgements. My acknowledgements start with Frances, my wife, who has lived with this book for over five years and supported me throughout. Another who has been there throughout is my good friend Fred, whose enthusiasm started it all. Less long suffering, but suffering nonetheless, are John Haines and Greg Whiteley, friends who read drafts and provided editing advice. Thankfully, they all still speak to me.

Next, I acknowledge the contributions of two prominent experts in the area of military and intelligence studies, Professor David Horner, Australia's leading military and intelligence historian, and the highly respected intelligence professional, Rear Admiral Paul Becker, USN (Ret). Their advice and kind words enabled me to hone a better book than I otherwise would have. In addition, I would also thank the wonderful generosity of Kate Lance and Sheila Spence in providing advice and photographs for the book.

Also deserving of my thanks are all those who assisted me at the Churchill Archive, Churchill College, Cambridge, UK; National Archives, UK; National Archives, College Park, MD; National Archives, Washington, DC; National Archives of Australia; National Library of Australia; the state libraries of Victoria, Western Australia and Queensland; the Sea Power Centre; and the Australian War Memorial. Finally, my thanks to Elizabeth Weiss and Angela Handley at Allen & Unwin, who, despite not knowing if I was for real, took a gamble to publish this book.

GLOSSARY AND ABBREVIATIONS

ABC	Australian Broadcasting Commission
ACHQ	Area Combined Headquarters
ACNB	Australian Commonwealth Naval Board
ADMI	Assistant Director of Military Intelligence
ADO	Assistant District Officer
AFB	*Allgemeinefunkspruchbuch* (German naval radio codebook)
AIB	Allied Intelligence Bureau
AIF	Australian Imperial Force
ALP	Australian Labor Party
AMF	Australian Military Forces
ANGAU	Australian New Guinea Administrative Unit
ANZAC	Australian and New Zealand Army Corps
ASIO	Australian Security Intelligence Organisation
ASWG	Australian Special Wireless Group
ASWS	Australian Special Wireless Section
AWA	Amalgamated Wireless Australasia Ltd
BSC	British Security Co-ordination
BSIPDF	British Solomon Islands Protectorate Defence Force
CAS	Chief of the Air Staff
CAST	Station CAST, the US Navy's cryptanalytical unit based in the Philippines
CBCS	Commonwealth Bureau of Census and Statistics
CCAS	Commodore Commanding the Australian Squadron
CGS	Chief of the General Staff
CIB	Commonwealth Investigation Branch
CID	Committee of Imperial Defence
C-in-C	Commander-in-Chief
CINCPACFLT	C-in-C, Pacific Fleet
CIU	Communications Intelligence Unit (Melbourne)
CMG	Officer of the Order of St Michael and St George
CNS	Chief of Naval Staff

COIC	Combined Operations and Intelligence Centre
COMAIRSOLS	Commander of Air Operations Solomons
COMSOUPAC	Command, South Pacific
COMSOUWESPACFOR	Command, South West Pacific Forces
COMTASKFOR	Command, Task Force
CPO	Chief Petty Officer
CSS	Captain Superintendent Sydney
CST	Captain Superintendent Training
CTF 31	US Third Fleet's unit 31
DCGS	Deputy Chief of the General Staff
DCNS	Deputy Chief of Naval Staff
DF	direction finding
DFC	Distinguished Flying Cross
DMI	Director of Military Intelligence
DMO&I	Director, Military Operations and Intelligence
DMO&P	Director of Military Operations and Plans
DNI	Director of Naval Intelligence
DNO	District Naval Officer
DSB	Defence Signals Bureau
DSIO	Deputy Supervising Intelligence Officer
DSM	Distinguished Service Medal
ENIGMA	both the German coding machine and the code it produced
FECB	Far East Combined Bureau
FELO	Far Eastern Liaison Office
FERDINAND	codename for the ACNB's coastwatch organisation
FO	Flying Officer
FRUMEL	Fleet Radio Unit Melbourne
FRUPAC	Fleet Radio Unit Pacific (HYPO at Hawaii)
FS	French Ship
GC&CS	Government Code and Cypher School
GHQ	General Headquarters
GOC	General Officer Commanding
HDML	harbour defence motor launch
HF	high-frequency
HFDF	high-frequency direction finding
HIJMS	His Imperial Japanese Majesty's Ship
HIRMS	His Imperial Russian Majesty's Ship
HMAS	His Majesty's Australian Ship
HNLMS	Her Netherlands Majesty's Ship
HQ	headquarters
HUMINT	human intelligence
HVB	*Handelsschiffsverkehrsbuch* (German naval codebook)
HVCCO	handle via COMINT (communications intelligence) channels only
IGN	Imperial German Navy
IJA	Imperial Japanese Army
IJN	Imperial Japanese Navy
ISD	Inter-Allied Services Department
IWIS	Indian Wireless Intelligence Service

JIC	Joint Intelligence Committee (UK)
JPC	Joint Planning Committee
KANA	Japanese Morse
LFDF	low-frequency direction finding
LHQ	Land Headquarters
LMS	Lugger Maintenance Section
LWOP	Leave without pay
MBE	Member of the Order of the British Empire
MFDF	medium-frequency direction finding
MHR	Member of the House of Representatives
MLO	Military Liaison Officer
NEA	North East Area
NEI	Netherlands East Indies
NGA	New Guinea Area
NGF	New Guinea Force
NID	Naval Intelligence Division
NIO	Naval Intelligence Officer
NSA	National Security Agency
OBE	Officer of the Order of the British Empire
PNIC	Pacific Naval Intelligence Centre
product	intelligence reporting derived from SIGINT
QMG	Quartermaster General
RAAF	Royal Australian Air Force
RACHMAF	Rear Admiral Commanding, HM Australian Fleet
RAF	Royal Air Force
RAN	Royal Australian Navy
RANVR	Royal Australian Navy Volunteer Reserve
RAN W/T Service	Royal Australian Navy Wireless Telegraphy Service
RN	Royal Navy
RNR	Royal Navy Reserve
RNZN	Royal New Zealand Navy
RSS	Radio Security Service
sanitisation	process used to hide true source of intelligence
SDA	Special Duty Agencies
Security Service	internal intelligence (UK, also known as MI5)
SIA	Secret Intelligence Australia, Section B of AIB
SIGINT	signals intelligence
SIO	Supervising Intelligence Officer
SIPS	Special Intelligence Personnel Section
SIS	Secret Intelligence Service (UK, also known as MI6)
SKM	*Signalbuch der Kaiserlichen Marine* (German Imperial Navy signal book)
SMS	Seiner Majestät Schiff (His Majesty's Ship)
SNDO	Sub-District Naval Officer
SNO	Senior Naval Officer
SO (I)	Staff Officer (Intelligence)
SOA	Special Operations Australia
SOE	Special Operations Executive (UK)
SRD	Services Reconnaissance Department

SRI	Signal Radio Intelligence
SS	steam ship
SWPA	South West Pacific Area
SY	steam yacht
TA	traffic analysis
take	raw SIGINT intercept
tradecraft	techniques, processes and behaviours used in spying
ULTRA	codename for the intelligence product from high-level diplomatic and strategic SIGINT derived from ENIGMA or other systems
USMC	United States Marine Corps
USN	United States Navy
USS	United States Ship
USSR	Union of Soviet Socialist Republics
WAC	Women's Auxiliary Corps (US)
WEC	Wireless Experimental Centre, India
WRANS	Women's Royal Australian Naval Service
WRNS	Women's Royal Naval Service (UK)
W/T	wireless telegraphy
WU	Wireless Unit, RAAF

NOTES

PREFACE

1 Viscount Palmerston, Speech, Treaty of Adrianople—Charges Against Lord Palmerston, *Hansard*, House of Commons Debates, 1 March 1848, vol. 97, cc66-123, http://hansard. millbanksystems.com/commons/1848/mar/01/treaty-of-adrianople-charges-against, accessed 24 December 2017.

INTRODUCTION

1 *Sydney Morning Herald*, 1 November 1853, p. 2.

2 *Adelaide Observer*, 26 November 1853, p. 6.

3 *Sydney Morning Herald*, 9 November 1853, p. 3.

4 Matthew S. Anderson, *The Eastern Question 1774–1923: A Study in International Relations*, London: Macmillan Press, 1983, p. 129.

5 Peter Overlack, 'Queensland's annexation of Papua: A background to Anglo-German friction', *Journal of the Royal Historical Society of Queensland*, 1978, vol. 10, no. 4, p. 123–38.

6 *Sydney Morning Herald*, 15 September 1883, p. 11.

7 *Sydney Morning Herald*, 4 July 1883, p. 4.

8 *Sydney Morning Herald*, 14 July 1883, p. 7.

9 *Brisbane Courier Mail*, 16 June 1886, p. 5.

10 Neville Meaney, *The Search for Security in the Pacific 1901–1914: A History of Australian Defence and Foreign Policy, 1901–1923*, vol. 1, Sydney: Sydney University Press, 2009, p. 21.

11 *South Australian Register*, 23 July 1889, p. 4.

12 *South Australian Register*, 23 July 1889, p. 4.

13 *South Australian Register*, 23 July 1889, p. 4.

14 Meaney, *The Search for Security in the Pacific*, pp. 33–34.

CHAPTER 1

1 Marginal notes in letter, Wilson Le Couteur to Edmund Barton, 8 February 1901, 'Letter dated 8 Feb 1901—Mr Le Couteur offering his services in connection with the administration of the New Hebrides', BC31404093, NAA: A35, BUNDLE 2/1.

2 'Letter dated July 1901 from Mr James Burns—recommendation of Mr Wilson Le Couteur', BC31404099, NAA: A35, BUNDLE 2/7.

3 Marginal note initialled 'AH' and '9 Feb 1901', letter, W. Le Couteur to E. Barton, 8 February 1901, BC31404093, NAA.

4 'Telegram dated 1 August 1901 from Mr Le Couteur accepting offer of salary', BC31404105, NAA: A35, BUNDLE 2/13.

5 'Telegram dated 5 August 1901 from secretary—travel allowance—Mr Le Couteur', BC31404108, NAA: A35, BUNDLE 2/16.

6 Labour value/cost, 'Six ways to compute the relative value of Australian amounts, 1828 to the present', MeasuringWorth inflation calculator, www.measuringworth.com/australia-compare/relativevalue.php, accessed 14 April 2017.

7 Letter, E. Barton to Sir Critchett Walker, Principal Under Secretary, NSW, Sydney, 17 July 1901, 'Communications—Detective Lyons errand in respect of Mr Le Couteur's intended mission', BC31404102, NAA: A35, BUNDLE 2/10.

8 Letter, W. Le Couteur to E. Barton, 8 February 1901.

9 Letter, W. Le Couteur to E. Barton, 8 February 1901.

10 Letter, W. Le Couteur to E. Barton, 8 February 1901.

11 D.O. Spence, 'Australian naval defence and the 1887 Colonial Conference: Context, policy and reaction', *International Journal of Naval History*, 2007, vol. 6. no. 1, p. 14, www.ijnhonline.org/wp-content/uploads/2012/01/Spence-article-Australian-Naval-Defence.pdf, accessed 23 June 2014.

12 Letter, A. Hunt to W. Le Couteur, 1 August 1901, 'Letter dated 1 Aug 1901 from the Secretary Department of External Affairs to Mr Le Couteur', BC31404104, NAA: A35, BUNDLE 2/12.

13 Telegram, to Atlee Hunt, C. Walker, 24 July 1901, BC31404102, NAA.

14 Letter, A. Hunt to W. Le Couteur, 1 August 1901, p. 1.

15 Letter, A. Hunt to W. Le Couteur, 1 August 1901, pp. 1–3.

16 'Report dated 26 Nov 1901—Mr Le Couteur's trip to the New Hebrides', p. 1, BC31404115, NAA: A35, BUNDLE 2/23.

17 'Report dated 26 Nov 1901', p. 2, BC31404115, NAA.

18 Carton Contrôle 822, CAOM: Rheinhardt, Rapport concernant la vérification du service de M. Aubry Lecomte, Chef du SAI à Nouméa, à l'époque du 28 avril 1902, Marius, Archambault, La Colonisation et le Question Indigene en Nouvelle-Caledonia, Imprimere Girardi—Et Audebert, 1904, p. 52, http://gallica.bnf.fr/ark:/12148/bpt6k5816359q/texteBrut, accessed 30 December 2017; and *Sydney Morning Herald*, 5 March 1901, p. 4.

19 'Report dated 26 Nov 1901', p. 3, BC31404115, NAA.

20 'Report dated 26 Nov 1901', p. 6, BC31404115, NAA.

21 'Report dated 26 Nov 1901', p. 7, BC31404115, NAA.

22 'Report dated 26 Nov 1901', p. 7, BC31404115, NAA.

23 'Report dated 26 Nov 1901', pp. 7–8, BC31404115, NAA.

24 'Report dated 26 Nov 1901', pp. 15–16, BC31404115, NAA.

25 'Report dated 26 Nov 1901', BC31404115, NAA.

CHAPTER 2

1 'Noumea—treatment of secret and confidential reports furnished by Mr Haggard', BC3094409, NAA: A1, 1904/1951; letter, Joseph Chamberlain to E. Barton, via Governor-General Lord Hopetoun, 21 February 1902, 'Petition Noumea—action of British Consul', BC52026, NAA: A8, 1901/124/9.

2 C.D. Coulthard-Clark, *A Heritage of Spirit: A Biography of Sir William Throsby Bridges*, Melbourne: Melbourne University Press, 1979, pp. 43, 57.

3 *Sydney Morning Herald*, 22 March 1892, p. 7.

4 *Sydney Morning Herald*, 25 November 1892, p. 2.

5 Hunt's classified advertisement in the educational section of *Sydney Morning Herald* was still appearing in early 1892. See *Sydney Morning Herald*, 17 January 1891, p. 13, and 23 January 1892, p. 13.

6 R. Fitch, *Commercial Arbitration in the Australian Construction Industry*, Sydney: Federation Press, 1989, pp. 147–48.

7 *South Australian Register*, Adelaide, 19 October 1898, p. 5.

8 *Daily News*, Perth, 20 September 1935, p. 5.

9 Chris Cunneen, 'Steward, Charles Thomas (1865–1920)', *Australian Dictionary of Biography*, National Centre of Biography, Australian National University, adb.anu.edu.au/biography/steward-sir-george-charles-thomas-8657/text15137, published in hardcopy 1990, accessed online 27 April 2014.

10 'Memoirs of Malcolm Lindsay Shepherd', BC4994275, NAA: A1632, 1, Part 2.

11 The introduction of this policy and the anti-Japanese racism of the west coast states of the US caused serious offence in Japan, even in the IJN and is credited with sensitizing the IJN and US Navy to the possibility of a future war between the two. See Evans, D.C. & Peattie, M.R., *Kaigun: Strategy, Tactics, and Technology in the Imperial Japanese Navy 1887–1941*, Naval Institute Press, Annapolis, Maryland, 1997, pp. 110–51.

12 B. Schedvin, *Emissaries of Trade: A History of the Australian Trade Commissioner Service*, Canberra: Commonwealth of Australia, 2008, p. 3.

13 Schedvin, *Emissaries of Trade*, p. 6.

14 Schedvin, *Emissaries of Trade*, p. 7.

15 'Three years in the East: a commercial agent's experiences', *Hawera and Normanby Star*, Hawera, New Zealand, 16 July 1906, p. 6.

16 *The Advertiser*, Adelaide, 10 January 1906, p. 9; *Straits Times*, Singapore, 19 August 1911, p. 16; list of Australian commercial agents, giving J.M. Sinclair's address as 19 Battery Road, Singapore, 'Authority granted to J.B. Suttor, R.B. Levien and J.M. Sinclair to issue letters [to] certain visitors entitling them to Certificates of Exemption', BC14544, NAA: A1, 1912/21372.

17 *The Argus*, Melbourne, 17 January 1906, p. 7; list of Australian commercial agents, giving Sinclair's address in Japan and then, in pencil, the revised or new address in Shanghai, BC14544, NAA.

18 See *The Age*, Melbourne, 12 July 1906, p. 8, for an example of the reporting of comments made by Frederick Jones in Hong Kong and the importance applied to this by Prime Minister Barton. Commonwealth interest is clearly demonstrated by the clippings of this item in the file BC14544, NAA, p. 74.

19 Letter, William Kidston, Premier of Queensland, to Prime Minister, 6 April 1908, BC14544, NAA.

20 Schedvin, *Emissaries of Trade*, pp. 3, 6.

21 J.S. Gregory, 'Morrison, George Ernest (Chinese) (1862–1920)', *Australian Dictionary of Biography*, adb.anu.edu.au/biography/morrison-george-ernest-chinese-7663, accessed 21 November 2016.

22 Letter, J.M. Sinclair to Senator Pearce, Minister for Defence, 23 November 1916, 'Japan. Japanese in the Pacific general', BC177416, NAA: A981, JAP 38, PART 1.

23 P.J. Lloyd, 'The first 100 years of tariffs in Australia: the colonies', Discussion Paper No. 2015-13, ANU Centre for Economic History, November 2015, p. 14, www.cbe.anu.edu.au/researchpapers/ceh/WP201513.pdf.

24 'Three years in the East: a commercial agent's experiences', *Hawera and Normanby Star*, Hawera, New Zealand, 16 July 1906, p. 6.

25 Neville Meaney, *A History of Australian Defence and Foreign Policy, 1901–23*, vol. 2, *Australia and the World Crisis, 1914–1923*, Sydney: Sydney University Press, 2009, p. 90.

26 Letter, Naval Secretary to Secretary, Prime Minister's Department, 3 July 1916, 'Trade in the East. Reports by Mr Suttor', BC48307, NAA: A2, 1918/2416.

27 Letter, J.M. Sinclair, 23 November 1916, BC177416, NAA; memo 15 June 1916, 'Relations of Australia & Japan and Far Eastern and Pacific questions May–Dec. 1918', BC148060, NAA: A2219, EXTERNAL RELATIONS VOLUME 1A; secret report, J.B. Suttor, 26 September 1916, BC177416, NAA; letter, Acting Prime Minister, 6 July 1916, 'Trade in the East. Reports by Mr Suttor', NAA.

28 Memo, 15 June 1916, listed in index on p. 46, detailing Suttor's concerns about being compromised, BC148060, NAA.

29 Letter, J.M. Sinclair to Senator Pearce, Minister for Defence, 23 November 1916, BC177416, NAA.

30 D. Stevens, 'Australian naval defence: selections from the papers and correspondence of Captain W.H.C.S. Thring, 1913–34', in S. Rose (ed.), *The Naval Miscellany*, vol. VII, Aldershot: Navy Records Society, 2008, p. 441.

31 Letter, Sinclair to Pearce, 23 November 1916, BC177416, NAA.

32 Letter, Sinclair to Pearce, 23 November 1916, BC177416, NAA.

CHAPTER 3

1 Chapter XIII, verses 3–4, Sun Tzu, *The Art of War*, trans. Samuel B. Griffith, Sydney: Duncan Baird Publishers, 2005, p. 232.

2 Coulthard-Clark, *A Heritage of Spirit*, p. 43.

3 Coulthard-Clark, *A Heritage of Spirit*, p. 43.

4 B. Bennett, 'Troubled waters: Australian spies in the Pacific', in R. Dixon & N. Birns (eds), *Readings Across the Pacific: Australia–US Intellectual Histories*, Sydney: Sydney University Press, 2010, p. 211.

5 Bennett, 'Troubled waters', p. 211.

6 Letter, Alfred Deakin to Governor-General, 2 March 1904, and letter, Atlee Hunt to Governor-General, 10 March 1904, 'Australian attaché with Japanese Army (Col. J.C. Hoad)', BC422561, NAA: A6661, 1013.

7 Memo, Governor-General to Prime Minister, 24 March 1904, BC422561, NAA.

8 Minute, Secretary, Department of Defence, to GOC, 25 March 1904, 'Colonel Hoad—attachment to Japanese Army', BC426192, NAA: A6006, 1904/12/31; letter, A. Deakin to Governor-General, 28 March 1904, BC422561, NAA.

9 Minute, Secretary, Department of Defence, to GOC, 25 March 1904.

10 N. Meaney, *A History of Australian Defence and Foreign Policy, 1901–23*, vol. 1, *The Search for Security in the Pacific, 1901–1914*, Sydney: Sydney University Press, 2009, p. 72.

11 Minute, Secretary, Department of Defence, to GOC, 25 March 1904.

12 Report by Lieutenant General W. Nicholson, 24 September 1904, BC422561, NAA.

13 Memo, CGS, Hoad, 20 May 1909, 'Lieut JG Fearnley re Japanese espionage and a secret service', BC331612, NAA: MP84/1, 1877/5/5.

14 'General Hutton and Senator Dawson', *Sydney Morning Herald*, 27 August 1904, p. 11; 'Ex-minister's reply—some extraordinary statements—General Hutton accused of "insolence"', *Geelong Advertiser*, 27 August 1904, p. 8.

15 Meaney, *The Search for Security in the Pacific*, pp. 72–75.

16 Longhand records of newspaper reporting, 'Major General Sir John Charles Hoad', BC723334, NAA: A5954, 1923/36.

17 Meaney, *The Search for Security in the Pacific*, p. 72.

18 Meaney, *The Search for Security in the Pacific*, p. 72.
19 BC426192, NAA. This file contains one sheet that was obviously removed from another file that used hole-punch binding. This file contains a marginal note suggesting it is from the file containing Major General Hutton's recommendation that two officers be sent to Japan as attachés, 'Japanese–Russian war GOC recommending 2 Australian permanent officers be sent', BC414644, NAA: B168, 1904/32 PART 3.
20 'Council of defence', *Sydney Morning Herald*, 11 January 1906, p. 7.
21 The Battle of Liaoyang was fought over twelve days 25 August to 5 September 1904 and resulted in 22,922 Japanese dead, wounded and missing, and 19,122 Russian dead, wounded and missing. For Hoad's departure, see 'Colonel Hoad', *Sydney Morning Herald*, 3 November 1904, p. 5.
22 'Reports by Colonel J.G. Head [Hoad] Australian attaché to the Japanese Army during Russo-Japanese war', BC10727179, NAA: P2456, 494/7. Also see W. Perry, 'The military life of Major General Sir John Charles Hoad', *Victorian Historical Magazine*, 1959, vol. XXIX, no. 3, pp. 182–83, in BC662829, NAA: A5954, 1249/22.
23 See K. Kubata, 'The Battle of Tsushima, 1905', June 1980, Naval Historical Society of Australia, www.navyhistory.org.au/the-battle-of-tsushima-1905, accessed 24 November 2016. Russia lost eleven battleships, six cruisers and nine destroyers as well as 4380 killed and 5917 prisoners, including two admirals. The IJN lost three torpedo boats and suffered 117 dead and 583 wounded.
24 P. Oliver, 'Interpreting "Japanese activities" in Australia, 1888–1945', *Journal of the Australian War Memorial*, no. 36, www.awm.gov.au/journal/j36/oliver.asp, accessed 4 March 2017.
25 Geoffrey Serle, 'McCay, Sir James Whiteside (1864–1930)', *Australian Dictionary of Biography*, adb.anu.edu.au/biography/mccay-sir-james-whiteside-7312/text12683, accessed 23 January 2014.
26 For a detailed history of the creation of the Australian Intelligence Corps and the mapping of Australia, see C.D. Coulthard-Clark, *The Citizen General Staff: The Australian Intelligence Corps, 1907–1914*, Canberra: Military Historical Society of Australia, 1976; and *Australia's Military Map Makers: The Royal Australian Survey Corps, 1915–1996*, Melbourne: Oxford University Press, 2000.
27 Review of the results obtained by the Australian Intelligence Corps, 'Formation of Australian Intelligence Corps', BC324142, NAA: MP84/1, 1849/2/13.
28 'Federal affairs. Important military appointments', *The Advertiser*, Adelaide, 21 May 1909, p. 8.
29 Minute 12 July 1909, 'Army administration. Minute dated 16.6.1909 by Colonel W.T. Bridges', BC694183, NAA: A5954 1203/6.
30 Minute, 12 July 1909.
31 *The Argus*, Melbourne, 7 October 1911, p. 19.
32 BC324142, NAA.
33 'Review of the results obtained by the Australian Intelligence Corps', BC325703, NAA: MP84/1, 1902/7/66, p. 4.
34 BC325703, NAA, p. 5.
35 BC325703, NAA, p. 2.
36 BC325703, NAA, p. 2.
37 BC325703, NAA, p. 3.
38 BC325703, NAA, p. 5.
39 BC325703, NAA.

CHAPTER 4

1 Letter, John Fearnley to Senator George Pearce, 17 May 1909, 'Lieut. J.G. Fearnley re Japanese espionage and a secret service', BC331612, NAA: MP84/1, 1877/5/5.
2 Letter, John Fearnley to George Pearce, 17 May 1909, p. 3.
3 Advertisement for Thomas and Madden, *Cairns Post*, 29 September 1888, p. 4.
4 'In the Supreme Court of Queensland', *Brisbane Courier*, 12 April 1902, p. 7.
5 'Notice', *Cairns Post*, 3 July 1889, p. 2. See also 'Thomas and Madden', *Cairns Post*, 16 November 1889, p. 2.
6 'Our neighbours', *The Queenslander*, 12 August 1893, p. 295.
7 *The Queenslander*, 5 February 1898, p. 248.
8 The steamer *Vigilant* is reported assisting after a shipwreck in Lass o' Gowrie. Ashore at Cape Tribulation', *Morning Post*, Cairns, 15 March 1904, p. 2.
9 'Commander Fearnley death at Wahroonga', *Newcastle Morning Herald*, 3 January 1938, p. 4.
10 'Municipality of Cairns, extraordinary election', *Morning Post*, Cairns, 20 September 1901, p. 2.
11 'Cairns Municipal Council', *Morning Post*, Cairns, 9 September 1897.
12 'Cairns Municipal Council', *Morning Post*, Cairns, 9 September 1897.
13 Letter J.G. Fearnley to Senator George Pearce, 17 May 1909, BC331612, NAA; letter J. Fearnley to George Pearce, 17 January 1911, 'Creation of Secret Intelligence Service proposed', BC 451861, NAA: MP84/1, 2021/1/35.
14 'Governor General's Office—correspondence—Japanese activity off the coast of North Queensland', BC941950, NAA: A6662, 1492; letter and report, W.G. Cahill to Chief Secretary, 9 July 1908, 'Japanese in Queensland', BC325203, NAA: MP 84/1, 1877/5/4.
15 Letter, Lord George Horsfall Frodsham, Bishop of North Queensland to Atlee Hunt, 20 May 1909, 'Japanese beche-de-mer boats off the coast of North Queensland', BC5639, NAA: A1, 1909/13685.
16 Oliver, 'Interpreting "Japanese activities" in Australia, 1888–1945'.
17 Letter, John Fearnley to Senator George Pearce, 17 May 1909, p. 4, BC331612, NAA.
18 Letter, John Fearnley to Senator George Pearce, 17 May 1909, BC331612, NAA.
19 Letter, John Fearnley to Senator George Pearce, 17 May 1909, pp. 4–5, BC331612, NAA.
20 Letter, John Fearnley to Senator George Pearce, 17 May 1909, pp. 4–5, BC331612, NAA.
21 Letter, John Fearnley to Senator George Pearce, 17 May 1909, BC331612, NAA.
22 BC10727179, NAA, and see above.
23 Letter, John Fearnley to Senator George Pearce, 17 May 1909, p. 3, BC331612, NAA.
24 Letter, John Fearnley to Senator George Pearce, 17 May 1909, BC331612, NAA.
25 K. Kotani, *Japanese Intelligence in World War II*, trans. Kotani Chiharu, Oxford: Osprey Publishing, 2009, p. ix.
26 'Relations of Australia & Japan', p. 83, BC148060, NAA.
27 'Legislation for protection against espionage [Major Asada suspected Japanese spy]', BC416253, NAA: B197, 1877/5/15.
28 Kotani, *Japanese Intelligence in World War II*, pp. 98–107.
29 Teleprinter message, Department of Defence Coordination to secretaries, Department of the Army and Department of External Affairs, 14 January 1941, 'Major Hashida—visit to Australia', BC170437, NAA: A816, 25/301/176.
30 M. Tsuji, *Singapore: The Japanese Version*, trans. Margaret E. Lake, New York: St Martin's Press, 1960, pp. 29–31, 41–52.
31 Tsuji had a colourful reputation as a dangerous nationalist and, later as a war criminal implicated in planning the Sook Ching Massacre in Singapore in February 1942. Although

it has been claimed that he was 'given a clean slate by Allied War Crimes Investigators' (see 'Singapore fall through Japanese eyes', *The Sun*, Melbourne, 17 October 1960, p. 25), the CIA conducted a full secret investigation into his unexplained disappearance in 1962. This investigation was undertaken for 'scanning by those persons operationally interested in Tsuji'. It is also clear that Tsuji was either part of a CIA operation or the subject of one. The relevant report is stamped with the Nazi War Crimes Disclosure Act exemption for Section 2(b), Methods and Sources (report, Chief of Station to Chief Far East, 8 June 1962, www.cia.gov/library/readingroom/docs/TSUJI%2C%20MASANOBU%20%20%20VOL.%203_0047.pdf, accessed 21 September 2017).

32 Tsuji, *Singapore*, pp. 29–31.
33 The cruiser HIJMS *Ibuki* fomed part of the escort for the First AIF in November 1914.
34 Summary of Japanese activity prepared by Major E.L. Piesse, 30 September 1918, BC148060, NAA.

CHAPTER 5

1 Sun Tzu, *The Art of War*, p. 235.
2 Commonwealth Bureau of Census and Statistics, *Year Book Australia*, no. 1, Melbourne: Commonwealth of Australia, 1908, p. 891; CBCS, *Year Book Australia*, no. 4, Melbourne: Commonwealth of Australia, 1911, pp. 1096–97.
3 Suggested cablegram to Senator Pearce, Senator McGregor, 16 June 1911, 'Designation of the Commonwealth Naval Forces as the RAN', BC394326, NAA: MP1185/9, 559/201/574. Even the name was problematical, as RAN was seen as an 'unfortunate abbreviation'.
4 Letter, Admiralty to Under Secretary of State, Colonial Office, 5 September 1913, 'Establishment of Commonwealth Naval Intelligence Service', BC422481, NAA: A6661, 1357.
5 Letter, Admiralty to the Official Secretary for the Commonwealth of Australia, 8 September 1913, BC422481, NAA.
6 Letter, Admiralty to the Official Secretary for the Commonwealth of Australia, 8 September 1913, BC422481, NAA.
7 Letter, Admiralty to the Official Secretary for the Commonwealth of Australia, 8 September 1913, BC422481, NAA.
8 Addressee list for *RAN Instructions for Naval Intelligence Service*, October 1915, 'Secret intelligence services—army and navy', BC204445, NAA: A1608, B15/1/1.
9 Addressee list for *RAN Instructions for Naval Intelligence Service*, October 1915, BC204445, NAA.
10 Addressee list for *RAN Instructions for Naval Intelligence Service*, October 1915, BC204445, NAA.
11 Stevens, *Australian Naval Defence*, p. 408.
12 Stevens, *Australian Naval Defence*, p. 408.
13 Stevens, *Australian Naval Defence*, p. 410.
14 Letter, William Creswell to Minister, 19 November 1918, 'Honours: granted Captain Walter H.C.S. Thring O.B.E.', BC204197, NAA: A1606, 22/3/181.
15 Letter, William Creswell to Minister, 19 November 1918, BC204197, NAA.
16 *RAN Instructions for Naval Intelligence Service*, October 1915, BC204445, NAA.
17 *RAN Instructions for Naval Intelligence Service*, para. 16, BC204445, NAA.
18 *RAN Instructions for Naval Intelligence Service*, para. 6, BC204445, NAA.
19 *RAN Instructions for Naval Intelligence Service*, para. 19, BC204445, NAA.
20 *RAN Instructions for Naval Intelligence Service*, para. 5, BC204445, NAA.
21 *RAN Instructions for Naval Intelligence Service*, para. 5, BC204445, NAA.

22 *RAN Instructions for Naval Intelligence Service*, para. 10, BC204445, NAA.

23 *RAN Instructions for Naval Intelligence Service*, paras 11, 22, BC204445, NAA.

24 *RAN Instructions for Naval Intelligence Service*, para. 15, BC204445, NAA.

25 Memorandum, Colonial Defence Committee, '"Principles of imperial defence", s.v. "Local defences", et seq., signed by Chancellor, 7 July 1910', in Naval Records Society, *The Collective Naval Defence of Empire, 1900–1940*, Aldershot: Ashgate Publishing, 1997, pp. 130–31.

26 Lord Jellicoe, *Report on Naval Mission to the Commonwealth of Australia (May–August 1919)*, vol. III, Sydney: Government Printer, 1919, p. 210.

27 Jellicoe, *Report on Naval Mission*, vol. III, p. 211.

28 Letter, Minister for the Navy Poynton to Acting Prime Minister, 25 June 1918, BC204445, NAA.

29 Defence, 31 March 1922, in CBCS, *Year Book Australia*, no. 15, Melbourne: Commonwealth of Australia, 1922, p. 928. A further 88,175 personnel were listed as having suffered an illness on active service. Naval casualties are listed in J. Beaumont et al., *Australian Defence: Sources and Statistics*, Australian Centenary History of Defence, vol. VI, Oxford: Oxford University Press, 2001, p. 175. Deaths on active service with the 1st AIF in all theatres in 1914–18, excepting Australia and the Pacific, are listed as 58,339 on p. 277.

CHAPTER 6

1 'Permission to Germans to leave Commonwealth—arrest of German and Austrian reservists', BC 32089, NAA: A1, 1914/24363; 'German and Austrian reservists', BC412959, NAA: B543, W175/1/361.

2 Attribution to Mr W. de Haas, German Trade Commissioner in Australia, in CBCS, *Year Book Australia*, no. 5, Melbourne: Commonwealth of Australia, 1912, Appendix, p. 1244, attribution for figures for the table 'German Exports to the Commonwealth'; de Haas obituary, *Brisbane Courier*, 30 November 1931, p. 10.

3 'De Haas interned at last!', *Mirror of Australia*, Sydney, 27 November 1915, p. 3. The *Mirror of Australia* was particularly virulent in its criticism of the government in allowing de Haas to leave Australia. See *Daily Herald*, Adelaide, 29 November 1915, p. 6 and 'De Haas Scandal', *Mirror of Australia*, Sydney, 6 November 1915, p. 2.

4 'Trade expansion', *Evening News*, Sydney, 24 February 1903, p. 3.

5 'Arrivals', *Australian Star*, Sydney, 23 November 1893, p. 4.

6 *Daily Telegraph*, Sydney, 5 November 1902, p. 3.

7 'Trade expansion', *Evening News*, Sydney, 24 February 1903, p. 3.

8 'German de Haaz [sic] visit Thursday Island and Darwin', BC12184, NAA: A1, 1911/19743; 'Governor General's Office—correspondence De Haaz', BC943548, NAA: A6662, 1866.

9 Letter, Atlee Hunt to Acting Secretary, Department of Defence, 2 October 1911, 'Re visit of German, De Haaz to Thursday Island and Darwin', BC12184, NAA: A1, 1911/19743.

10 'News in brief', *Australian Star*, Sydney, 14 September 1904, p. 1.

11 'Karl Paul Gustav Hentschel—naturalization certificate', BC15655, NAA: A1, 1913/9176.

12 Christopher Andrew, *The Defence of the Realm: The Authorized History of MI5*, London: Allen Lane, 2009, p. 44.

13 'Karl Paul Gustav Hentschel—naturalization certificate', BC15655, NAA.

14 Andrew, *The Defence of the Realm*, p. 44.

15 Andrew, *The Defence of the Realm*, p. 46.

16 Andrew, *The Defence of the Realm*, p. 46.

17 Press cutting from *The Argus*, 13 November 1913, BC15655, NAA.

18 A.W. Jose, *Official History of Australia in the War of 1914–1918*, vol. IX, *The Royal Australian Navy, 1914–1918*, Sydney: Angus & Robertson, 1928, p. 5.

19 Jose, *The Royal Australian Navy*, p. 11.

20 Jose, *The Royal Australian Navy*, p. 10.

21 Signal, 10 August 1914 at 1.06 a.m, marginal notes in red pencil and urgent signal sent at 1530 hours on 10 August 1914, 'Codes found on board German merchant ships on outbreak of War 1914', BC413224, NAA: MP1049/1, 1914/0351.

22 Letter, Secretary, Department of Trade, to Naval Secretary, 3 September 1914, signal, 9 August 1914, and letter, 11 August 1914, BC413224, NAA.

23 Letter and technical report, Captain Clare, Fremantle, to Naval Board, 15 August 1914, BC413224, NAA.

24 Jose, *The Royal Australian Navy*, p. 381.

25 Letter, Secretary, Department of Trade, to Naval Secretary, 3 September 1914, signal, 9 August 1914, and letter, 11 August 1914, BC413224, NAA.

26 'Another German vessel arrested', *Examiner*, Launceston, 14 August 1914, p. 6.

27 Jose, *The Royal Australian Navy*, p. 381.

28 Prisoner of war information, 'PAULSEN Jurgen ex SS Hobart', BC325927, NAA: MP16/1, 1914/2/220.

29 Stevens, *Australian Naval Defence*, p. 459.

30 Signal, ACNB to Admiralty, reporting the capture of two sets of the *Handelsschiffsverkehrsbuch*, 12 September 1914, BC413224, NAA.

31 Signal, ACNB to Admiralty, 12 September 1914, BC413224, NAA.

32 Signal, ACNB to Admiralty, 12 September 1914, BC413224, NAA.

33 Signal, ACNB to all SNOs and DSNOs, 13 August 1914, BC413224, NAA.

34 Letter, Naval Secretary to Commanding Officer, HMAS *Sydney*, 19 August 1914, BC413224, NAA.

35 Letter, Atlee Hunt, Secretary, External Affairs Department, to Naval Secretary, 28 August 1914, and letter, Naval Secretary to Secretary, External Affairs, 28 August 1914, BC413224, NAA.

36 Letter, Atlee Hunt to Naval Secretary, 28 August 1914, and letter, Naval Secretary to Secretary, External Affairs, 28 August 1914, BC413224, NAA.

37 Letter, Atlee Hunt to Naval Secretary, 28 August 1914, and letter, Naval Secretary to Secretary, External Affairs, 28 August 1914, BC413224, NAA.

38 'Vice Admiralty courts: administrative history', NSW State Archives & Records, search. records.nsw.gov.au/agencies/1048, accessed 27 April 2015.

39 Memo, Department of Trade and Customs to Naval Secretary, 3 September 1914, BC413224, NAA.

40 Letter, Gordon H. Castle, Crown Solicitor for the Commonwealth, to Collector of Customs, Sydney, 16 September 1914, BC413224, NAA.

41 Distribution list, BC413224, NAA.

42 Memos, 22, 24 and 29 September 1914, BC413224, NAA.

43 The seizure of codebooks in Australia was soon followed by the seizure of the *Signalbuch der Kaiserlichen Marine* (SKM) from the *Magdeburg* by the Russians on 26 August 1914 and the finding of the GN and VB codes from the destroyer SMS *119* when its safe was captured in the nets of a British trawler on 30 November 1914.

44 Précis outlining the claims of Senior Master Wheatley for recognition for his work through accelerated promotion, 14 December 1926, BC413224, NAA.

45 BC413224, NAA.

CHAPTER 7

1 A. Best, *British Intelligence and the Japanese Challenge in Asia, 1914–1941*, Basingstoke: Palgrave Macmillan, 2002, pp. 27–33.

2 Best, *British Intelligence*, p. 23; Sho Kuwajima, 'Indian mutiny in Singapore, 1915: people who observed the scene and people who heard the news', *New Zealand Journal of Asian Studies*, 2009, vol. 11, no. 1, pp. 375–84.

3 The 5th Indian Light Infantry had a history of mutiny, when it was the East India Company's 42nd Bengal Local Infantry. More than half the soldiers of the unit had joined the Indian Mutiny in 1857. See 'Singapore Mutiny of 1915: a standalone episode not linked to freedom struggle', *Times of India*, 3 August 2014, timesofindia.indiatimes. com/india/Singapore-Mutiny-of-1915-A-standalone-episode-not-linked-to-freedom-strug-gle/articleshow/39563737.cms, accessed 3 May 2015, and Barangkali, 'Singapore memory. The Mutiny of 1915', *Sydney Morning Herald*, 16 January 1936, p. 8.

4 James Clark was one of the most important pearlers in Australia. His connections had enabled him to purchase concessions in the NEI for the exclusive right to work the Aru grounds. The consortiums that Clark led operated up to 135 luggers throughout the Indonesia Archipelago. See S. Mullins, 'James Clark and the Celebes Trading Co.: making an Australian maritime venture in the Netherlands East Indies', *Journal of the Australian Association for Maritime History*, 2002, vol. 24, no. 2, pp. 22–52.

5 'Well-known pearler', *Brisbane Courier*, 24 June 1932, p. 13.

6 See letter, Atlee Hunt to Collector of Customs, Brisbane, 18 November 1903, 'Correspondence relating to application by Wanetta Pearling Company, Thursday Island to Indent Asians', BC5058208, NAA: J3117, 86.

7 'Mail matters at Thursday Island—deputation to Mr Atlee Hunt', *Brisbane Courier*, 11 July 1905, p. 7.

8 'Questions in Parliament', *The Age*, Melbourne, 22 September 1905, p. 8; 'Thursday Island pearlers', *Sydney Morning Herald*, 22 September 1905, p. 6.

9 Letter, Admiral Tudor, C-in-C, China Station, to Secretary, Navy Office, Melbourne, 15 November 1918, 'Naval secret agent', BC3379320, NAA: A11805, B3C/13.

10 Letter, R. Hockings to Commander-in-Chief, China Station, 3 February 1920, 'Recognition of service of assistants to Mr R.W. Hocking for services rendered in c/w his intelligence duties', BC403292, NAA: MP1049, 1920/0230.

11 Memo, Hockings, 3 February 1920, 'Secret intelligence services—army and navy', BC204445, NAA: A1608 B15/1/1.

12 Note attached to letter, 3 February 1920, BC204445, NAA.

13 Note attached to letter, 3 February 1920, BC204445, NAA.

14 Kees van Dijk, *The Netherlands Indies and the Great War, 1914–1918*, Leiden: KITLV Press, 2007, pp. 329–35.

15 Note attached to letter, 3 February 1920, BC204445, NAA.

16 Report to Navy Office, 14 October 1917, 'Mr R Hockings—appointment as secret agent for duty in Netherlands East Indies', BC400547, NAA: MP1049/1, 1916/0224.

17 Sailing orders, ACNB to Captain in Charge, HMAS *Encounter*, 17 July 1915, 'HMAS "Encounter" movements and operations 10th July 1915 to 28th Dec 1917', BC404942, NAA: MP1049/1 1915/0251.

18 Best, *British Intelligence*, p. 24.

19 Memo, Hockings, 3 February 1920, BC204445, NAA: A1608, B15/1/1.

20 'Java news', *Singapore Free Press and Mercantile Advertiser*, 26 September 1917, p. 3.

21 Typewritten report with covering letter, Hockings, 14 October 1917, BC400547, NAA.

22 Letter, Atlee Hunt to Burns Philp and Company, Sydney, 22 October 1913, 'Wireless installation on board SS "Matunga"', BC27540, NAA: A1, 1913/16570.

23 '"Matunga" voyage south August 1914—necessity for secrecy on part of passengers', BC32070, NAA: A1 1914/24248.

24 F.G. Trayes, *Five Months on a German Raider: Being the Adventures of An Englishman Captured by the 'Wolf'*, London: Hedley Bros, 1919, p. 68, Project Gutenberg, archive.org/stream/fivemonthsonager16690gut/16690.txt, accessed 11 May 2014.

25 Letter, R. Hockings to Navy Office, 18 February 1919, BC400547, NAA.

26 Report to Navy Office, 18 February 1919, p. 2, BC400547, NAA.

27 Report to Navy Office, 18 February 1919, p. 2, BC400547, NAA.

28 Cover note attached to report, received 'H', signed by Vice Admiral Sir F.C. Tudor, C-in-C China Station, to Navy Secretary, Melbourne, 15 October 1918, BC400457, NAA.

29 Cover note attached to report received 'H', signed by Vice Admiral Sir F.C. Tudor, C-in-C China Station, to Navy Secretary, Melbourne, 15 October 1918, BC400457, NAA.

30 Memo, Hockings, 3 February 1920, BC204445, NAA.

31 Copy of memo, 23 March 1920, Vice Admiral A.L. Duff to Vice Admiral Tudor, providing details of Hockings' letter of 3 February 1920, 'Arathoon, L', BC1611236, NAA: A11804 1920/871.

32 'Loban Tommy—nationality: Malay—alien registration certificate no. 509 issued 5 February 1917', BC9061946, NAA: BP4/3 MALAY LOBAN T; 'Mingo, Batcho—nationality: Malay—alien registration certificate no. 516 issued 7 February 1917', BC9061978, NAA: BP4/3 MALAY MINGO/B.

33 Copy of letter, Governor-General Lord Forster to Secretary of State for the Colonies, 15 October 1920, BC1611236, NAA.

34 'Domestic occurrences', *Singapore Free Press and Mercantile Advertiser*, 13 April 1932, p. 10. The King made the award of the Order of the British Empire, Membership of the Civil Division, to Lazarus Arathoon on 3 June 1925 for his work as Vice-Consul in Macassar. See *Edinburgh Gazette*, no. 14133, 5 June 1925, p. 636.

35 Letter, Hockings to C-in-C, China Station, 3 February 1920, BC403292, NAA.

36 Enclosure to letter, R. Hockings, 3 February 1920, BC1611236, NAA.

37 Letter, Hockings to C-in-C, China Station, 3 February 1920, BC403292, NAA.

38 Cover note on 'H' report by Vice Admiral Tudor, BC400457, NAA.

39 Telegram, Atlee Hunt, 6 December 1920, BC400457, NAA.

40 Cover note on 'H' report by Vice Admiral Tudor, BC400457, NAA.

41 Telegram, First Naval Member to Navy Office, 7 December 1920, and note of telephone call to Atlee Hunt, BC400457, NAA.

42 Minute, Private Secretary to First Naval Member, 16 December 1920, BC400457, NAA.

CHAPTER 8

1 Best, *British Intelligence*, p. 94.

2 'At Fort Street High School', a report on a gathering at the school attended by a large number of Japanese naval officers and men, and Sir Francis B. Suttor, cousin of John Bligh Suttor, the NSW Consul-General in Kobe, *Sydney Mail*, 30 May 1906, p. 1408; advertisement, *Sydney Morning Herald*, 14 August 1912, p. 18.

3 Meaney, *Australia and the World Crisis 1914–1923*, p. 155.

4 Letter, Premier of Victoria to Prime Minister, 4 October 1916, and attached annex, 'Proposed introduction of study of the Japanese languages into the RANC', BC377013, NAA: MP472/1/0, 5/18/8562.

5 Minute, 12 June 1916, BC377013, NAA.

6 Letter, Minister for Defence to Minister for the Navy, 11 July 1916, BC377013, NAA.

7 Letter, Naval Secretary to Captain Rymer, Naval Attaché in Tokyo, 25 April 1917, BC377013, NAA.

8 Letter, General Powell to Captain Morgan, 14 March 1917, and letter, Captain Morgan to Captain Thring, 26 March 1917, BC377013, NAA.

9 Telegram, from British Ambassador, 6 June 1916, 'Japanese language—visit to Japan of Australian officers for purpose of studying language', BC249671, NAA: A11804, 1924/62.

10 Captain A.M. Cardew, Royal Engineers, was a noted Japanese scholar and a Chinese linguist. He was selected to assist the Indian government in setting up an internal security intelligence system to deal with the Japanese in India. He was also later tasked by the India Office with decrypting Japanese diplomatic telegrams and signals traffic to and from Yunnan in China. It was during this time he was recommended to the Australian government. George Sansom, a member of the Japanese Consular Service (see Best, *British Intelligence*, pp. 18, 31, 45) eventually took up the work in London on the Japanese diplomatic traffic.

11 Telegram, from British Ambassador, 6 June 1916, BC249671, NAA.

12 Best, *British Intelligence*, p. 18.

13 Telegram, from British Ambassador, 6 June 1916, BC249671, NAA.

14 Telegram, from British Ambassador, 6 June 1916, BC249671, NAA.

15 Labour value/cost, 'Six ways to compute the relative value of Australian amounts, 1828 to the present', MeasuringWorth inflation calculator, www.measuringworth.com/australia-compare/relativevalue.php, accessed 15 April 2017.

16 Telegram, Prime Minister, Australia, to British Ambassador, Tokyo, 29 July 1916, BC249671, NAA.

17 Letter, Japanese Consul-General, Sydney, to Secretary, Home and Territories, 20 February 1920, 'Sydney University introduction of Japanese lecturers', BC44526, NAA: A1, 1928/3075; marginal note by James Murdoch on letter, to Captain Morgan, 14 March 1917, BC377013, NAA.

18 Letter, Japanese Consul-General, Sydney, to Secretary, Home and Territories, 20 February 1920, BC44526, NAA.

19 Letter, Commanding Officer, Naval College, to Captain Thring, 18 March 1917, BC377013, NAA.

20 'Photographs and letters from or about Professor Murdoch', BC9024396, NAA: A4311, 774/15.

21 BC44526, NAA.

22 'Training in foreign languages in the RAN', BC377013, NAA.

23 BC44526, NAA.

24 BC44526, NAA.

25 Almost immediately after the death of Professor Murdoch in 1921, the bureaucratic wheels of White Australia began to turn, and an unofficial note was sent to a Mr McManus in Melbourne and a Mr Peters in Sydney to see if Takeko Murdoch, who had been given permanent residency, could be persuaded to leave Australia of her own free will. It would appear the Australian system had not yet developed a fear of the 'disgruntled' officer. James Murdoch, however, was one step ahead of the system and had appointed Captain E.E. Longfield Lloyd as his executor. Lloyd argued that as Okada Rokuo, Takeko's brother, was required for work at Duntroon and they would lose him if Mrs Murdoch was forced to return to Japan, it was necessary that she be allowed to remain in Australia. See unofficial correspondence November and December 1921 in BC44526, NAA. Mrs Murdoch did not accompany her brother Rokuo when he departed

for Japan on the SS *Yesaki Maru* on 29 January 1927. See Letter, Collector of Customs, Sydney, 6 April 1927, BC44526, NAA.

26   BC44526, NAA.

27   Letter, James Murdoch to Eric Nave, 1 September 1920, disclosing his trip with two captains to Japan, BC377013, NAA. See also, Best, *British Intelligence*, p. 94, which lists J. Broadbent and G. Capes, Australian Army, as students on the course.

28   'Recent developments', September 1918, BC148060, NAA.

29   BC44526, NAA. Further evidence for this lies in the clandestine correspondence between Murdoch and Piesse, using the pseudonym H. McRae, Esquire, where a source of intelligence in Japan is referred to as the 'professor'. See letter, 25 January 1919, p. 2, BC9024396, NAA.

30   Helen M. Davies, 'Hunt, Atlee Arthur (1864–1935)', *Australian Dictionary of Biography*, adb.anu.edu.au/biography/hunt-atlee-Arthur-6766/text11699, accessed 15 February 2014.

31   Davies, 'Hunt, Atlee Arthur (1864–1935)'.

32   'Death of Professor Murdoch', *Sydney Morning Herald*, 31 October 1921, p. 10.

33   Letter, Secretary, PM's Department, to Secretary, Home and Territories Department, 21 June 1919, 'Pacific Branch—Prime Minister Dept.—establishment of', BC37705, NAA: A1, 1919/8756.

34   Briefing to Prime Minister—'Objects and duties of Pacific Branch', June 1919, BC37705, NAA.

35   Minutes, 8 May 1919, p. 2, para. 4, '[Hughes Ministry] Prime Minister's copies of Cabinet decisions and papers', BC227934, NAA: A2717, VOLUME 1, FOLDER 4.

36   Meaney, 'Fears and phobias: E.L. Piesse and the problem of Japan 1909–1939', Canberra: National Library of Australia, Occasional Papers Series, no. 1, 1996, pp. 25–28.

37   Meaney, 'Fears and phobias', p. 30.

38   Memo, Malcolm Shepherd, Secretary, Prime Minister's Department, to Official Secretary of the Governor-General, 18 December 1919, 'India—supply of information from intelligence', BC1612778, NAA: A11804, 1922/128.

39   'Governor-General's Office—correspondence—concerning cypher telegrams and other postal arrangements', BC935618, NAA: A6662, 259.

40   Letter, Governor-General of Australia to Viceroy and Governor-General of India, 29 December 1919, BC1612778, NAA.

41   Letter, Viceroy and Governor-General of India to Governor-General of Australia, 13 April 1920, BC1612778, NAA.

42   Letter, Governor-General of Australia to Prime Minister, 14 May 1920, BC1612778, NAA.

43   Letter, Secretary, Prime Minister's Department, to Governor-General, 14 July 1922, BC1612778, NAA.

44   Letter, Governor-General of Australia to Viceroy and Governor-General of India, 29 December 1919, BC1612778, NAA.

45   Letter, Governor-General of Australia to Viceroy and Governor-General of India, 28 July 1922, BC1612778, NAA.

46   Minutes, 20 August 1923, '[Bruce–Page Ministry] Cabinet minutes 12.2.23–7.12.23', BC227945, NAA: A2718, VOLUME 1 PART 1; Meaney, 'N.K., Piesse, Edmund Leolin (1880–1947)', *Australian Dictionary of Biography*, adb.anu.edu.au/biography/piesse-edmund-leolin-8046/text14033, accessed 15 February 2014.

47   Minutes, 20 November 1923, p. 5, BC227945, NAA.

CHAPTER 9

1 Viscount Jellicoe of Scapa, *Report of Admiral of the Fleet, Viscount Jellicoe of Scapa, on Naval Mission to the Commonwealth of Australia (May–Aug. 1919)*, vol. 1, 12 August 1919, p. 1, www.navy.gov.au/sites/default/files/documents/Jellicoe%20of%20Scapa%20 Vol%20I_opt.pdf, accessed 25 June 2014.

2 Jellicoe, *Report of Admiral of the Fleet*, vol. 1, p. 11.

3 G.H. Gill, *Australia in the War of 1939–1945*, vol. II, *Royal Australian Navy 1939–1942*, Canberra: Australian War Memorial, 1957, p. 72.

4 'Naval Representative 40th General Report London', 8 August 1913, p. 3, BC408616, NAA: MP1049/1 1913/0253.

5 Summary of constitution and Australian naval policy, 'Australian Naval Policy', 1926, p. 68, BC735531, NAA: A5954 2378/1.

6 'Australian Naval Policy', p. 68, BC735531, NAA.

7 'Australian Naval Policy', p. 68, BC735531, NAA; minute paper, Second Naval Member to First Naval Member, 15 March 1920, 'A.C. Gregory—Hon. Lieut. RANVR instructions issued for compilation of Naval Intelligence', BC406713, NAA: MP1049/1 1920/0139.

8 'Australian Naval Policy', p. 69, BC735531, NAA.

9 Letter, A.C. Gregory to F. Tickell, 21 February 1912, BC406713, NAA.

10 Letter, Gregory to Tickell, 21 February 1912, BC406713, NAA.

11 Letter, Gregory to Tickell, 21 February 1912, BC406713, NAA.

12 Letter, Gregory to Tickell, 21 February 1912, BC406713, NAA.

13 File note, 30 May 1912, BC406713, NAA.

14 File note 30 May 1912, BC406713, NAA.

15 Letter, Naval Secretary to Naval Representative, London, 21 March 1912, BC406713, NAA.

16 Letter Naval Secretary to Naval Representative, London, 21 March 1912, BC406713, NAA.

17 Letter Naval Secretary to Naval Representative, London, 21 March 1912, BC406713, NAA.

18 A.C. Gregory seems to have had many adventures as a young man. In his letters of application for a commission, he made several claims that could not be substantiated. Among these was that he had been a sub-lieutenant in the RN. In his obituary in the Perth *Sunday Times*, he was credited with serving in the Boer War, the Boxer Rebellion (as a navy lieutenant) and as a prisoner in Vladivostok during the Russo-Japanese War. He was also Mayor of Broome and chairman of the Carnarvon Roads Board for seven years, president of the Broome Pearlers' Association, and rose to the rank of lieutenant commander in the RANVR. See *Sunday Times*, Perth, 27 December 1942, p. 2.

19 J. Bailey, *The White Divers of Broome: The True Story of a Fatal Experiment*, Sydney: Pan Macmillan, 2002, pp. 150–52, and *Sunday Times*, Perth, 27 December 1942, p. 2.

20 D.C.S. Sissons, 'Murakami, Yasukichi (1880–1944)', *Australian Dictionary of Biography*, adb.anu.edu.au/biography/murakami-yasukichi-11201, accessed 25 July 2014.

21 Sissons, 'Murakami, Yasukichi (1880–1944)', *Australian Dictionary of Biography*. Gregory was also the first 'referee' listed by Yasukichi Murakami on his application for a Certificate for Naturalisation in August 1939. See 'Murakami, "Y"—naturalisation', BC79571, NAA: A659 1939/1/12989.

22 Officer's Appointment Form, 25 March 1920, BC406713, NAA.

23 Secret orders, 29 March 1920, and handwritten note, GT to First Naval Member, 31 March 1920, BC406713, NAA.

24 Secret orders, 29 March 1920, and handwritten note, GT to First Naval Member, 31 March 1920, BC406713, NAA.

25 Secret orders, 29 March 1920, and handwritten note, GT to First Naval Member, 31 March 1920, BC406713, NAA.

26 Secret orders, 29 March 1920, BC406713, NAA.

27 Note, GT, 31 March 1920, p. 3, BC406713, NAA.

28 Note, GT, 31 March 1920, p. 3, BC406713, NAA.

29 Gill, *Royal Australian Navy 1939–1942*, p. 72.

30 'Hon. Lt A C Gregory, RANVR, Confidential Intelligence Reports Broome 1920', BC396875, NAA: MP1049/1, 1920/0476; BC406713, NAA.

31 Note, GT, 15 March 1920, p. 4, BC406713, NAA.

32 Reports No. 1, 2 May 1920, and No. 2, 28 May 1920, BC396875, NAA.

33 Minute, 11 June 1920, BC396875, NAA.

34 Minute, 1 July 1920, BC396875, NAA.

35 Minute, Second Naval Member to First Naval Member, 15 March 1920, with marginal note by Cook, 24 March 1920, BC406713, NAA.

36 Minute, 1 July 1920, BC396875, NAA.

37 The RAN and Australian Naval Policy, 'Appendix "A" ', p. 8, BC643877, NAA: A5954 10/6.

38 Note, GT, 15 March 1920, p. 4, BC406713, NAA.

39 Gill, *Royal Australian Navy 1939–1942*, p. 72.

40 'Mr A.C. Gregory, Royal Australian Naval Reserve—suitability for appointment at Broome', BC477331, NAA: MP1049/5, 2021/7/219.

CHAPTER 10

1 C. Andrew, *Secret Service: The Making of the British Intelligence Community*, London: Heinemann, 1985, pp. 259–61.

2 Telegram, Admiralty to Admiral of the Fleet, Viscount Jellicoe, 5 November 1919, JELLICOE PAPERS, Vol. LVII (ff. 260), 1, British Library, Add. MSS 49045.

3 Naval Mission to India and the Dominions, 1919–1920, Enclosure I, p. 6, 3 February 1920, JELLICOE PAPERS, Vol. LVII (ff. 260), 1.

4 *RAN Instructions for Naval Intelligence Services*, 1915, p. 4, 'Secret Intelligence Services', BC204445, NAA: A1608, B15/1/1.

5 Gill, *Royal Australian Navy 1939–1942*, p. 71.

6 NSA, 'The Room 40 compromise', Document Identity: 3978516, released 13 June 2012, www.nsa.gov/news-features/declassified-documents/nsa-60th-timeline/assets/files/1960s/19600101_1960_Doc_3978516_Room40.pdf, accessed 2 May 2016.

7 NSA, 'The Room 40 compromise'.

8 Letter, Admiralty to Under-Secretary of State, Colonial Office, 20 January 1920, 'Singapore Conference', BC398924, NAA: MP1185/8, 1846/4/25.

9 Letter, W.H. Laird Smith, Minister for the Navy, to W.M. Hughes, Prime Minister, 7 January 1921, BC398924, NAA.

10 Nicholas Tracy, *The Collective Naval Defence of Empire, 1900–1940*, Aldershot: Ashgate Publishing and the Naval Records Society, 1997, p. 468.

11 Appendix J, March 1921, p. 1, 'Naval Conference at Penang', BC451771, NAA: B6121, 311J.

12 Appendix J, March 1921, p. 1, BC451771, NAA.

13 Joe Straczek, 'Listening for the empire', Navy, www.navy.gov.au/sites/default/files/documents/Straczek_-_Listening_for_the_Empire.pdf, accessed 15 March 2015.

14 Best, *British Intelligence*, pp. 94–95.

15 Minute, Acting First Naval Member to all ships and stations, 22 June 1921, 'HMA Squadron—Wireless Telegraph "Y" Procedure—Japanese wireless telegraph interception', BC505956, NAA: MP1049/9, 1997/5/196.

16 Minute, Acting First Naval Member to all ships and stations, 22 June 1921, BC505956, NAA.

17 Minute, Acting First Naval Member to all ships and stations, 22 June 1921, BC505956, NAA.

18 Minute, Acting First Naval Member to all ships and stations, 22 June 1921, BC505956, NAA.

19 Minute F. Cresswell, Director, Signal Section, to Head, N Branch, 8 June 1921, BC505956, NAA.

20 Minute, RACHMAF to Secretary, Navy Office, 31 March 1922, BC505956, NAA.

21 Minute, Spurgeon, 1 July 1921, BC505956, NAA.

22 Extract of Secret Docket 21/0641 and Admiralty letter, 5 October 1921, BC505956, NAA.

23 Minute, Secretary, Navy Office, to RACAF, 25 May 1922, BC505956, NAA.

24 Memo to CNS ACNS, 26 March 1924, 'Receipt of letter Prime Minister—concerning visit of HMAS's Brisbane and Marguerite to Vila', BC1330902, NAA: MP138/1, 603/247/158.

25 The story of Eric Nave has been more than adequately covered in the literature of Australia's codebreaking prowess. The best source remains Ian Pfennigwerth's book *A Man of Intelligence: The Life of Captain Eric Nave, Australian Codebreaker Extraordinary* (Sydney: Rosenberg Publishing, 2006), to which readers should direct their attention.

26 Personal Particulars Form, ASIO, 29 June 1949, 'Nave, Theodore Eric', BC7949108, NAA: A6119, 3576; *Kadina and Wallaroo Times*, 6 December 1930, p. 2.

27 BC5332438, NAA. This became a permanent transfer.

28 Letter, E. Nave, 28 November 1918, 'Study of the Japanese Language in Japan (Paymaster Lt E Nave, RAN and Captain G. H. Capes)', BC377013, NAA.

29 Letter, Nave to Commodore Commanding, 21 August 1920, BC377013, NAA.

30 Letter, E. Nave, 15 January 1919, BC377013, NAA.

31 Minute, 18 January 1919, BC377013, NAA.

32 Letter, M. Miyata to Navy Office, 20 March 1919, BC377013, NAA.

33 Minute, 2nd Naval Member, 31 December 1920, BC377013, NAA.

34 Telegram, 16 March 1921, BC377013, NAA.

35 Best, *British Intelligence*, p. 94.

36 Minute, 3 March 1921, BC377013, NAA.

37 'RAAF report by FO AE Hempel on HMAS *Brisbane*', BC1101467, NAA: A9673, 91.

38 'RAAF report by FO EA Mustard, DFC, on HMAS *Adelaide* during RAN Winter Cruise 29 June to 3 August 1923', BC1101463, NAA: A9376, 90; 'RAAF report, Operation of RAAF SEAGULL A9-2 from HMAS *Australia*, 7 October 1932', BC218424, NAA: A9376, 63, Part 1.

39 Best, *British Intelligence*, p. 93.

40 Best, *British Intelligence*, p. 93.

41 Form S.206, report on accountant officers, 26 November 1926, 'Officers (RAN) personal record—Theodore Eric Nave', BC8360031, NAA: A3978, NAVE T E.

42 Best, *British Intelligence*, p. 96.

43 Letter, Major H.A. Corbet, 5th Military District, Perth, to Military Intelligence, Army HQ, Melbourne, 16 July 1924, BC505956, NAA.

44 Minute, F. Cresswell, Director of Signals and Communications, to Head, N, 2 December 1924, BC505956, NAA.

45 Minute, F. Cresswell, Electrical Commander, Signal Division, Naval Staff, to DNI, 21 August 1924, BC505956, NAA.

46 The propagation of radio signals far beyond their origin is one of the most important reasons for Australia's later significance as an intercept site. As Britain fought to intercept German, Italian and Japanese radio communications in Europe, the intercept sites often found themselves in the area beneath the 'skip', whereas the skipping wave bouncing off the ionosphere landed in Australia, where it was more easily intercepted.

47 'Sir Edward Victor Appleton', Electronics Notes, www.electronics-radio.com/articles/history/pioneers/sir-edward-victor-appleton.php, accessed 30 May 2016.

48 Minute, Assistant Chief of Naval Staff to Chief of Naval Staff, 17 January 1924, BC505956, NAA.

49 Letter, Commander F. Cresswell to Assistant Chief of the Naval Staff, 7 July 1926, BC505956, NAA.

50 '1925—first electric recordings of Leopold Stokowski and the Philadelphia Orchestra', The Stokowski Legacy, www.stokowski.org/1925%20First%20Electrical%20Recording%20Stokowski%20-%20Philadelphia.htm, accessed 16 April 2012; D. Morton, *Off the Record: The Technology and Culture of Sound Recording in America*, New Brunswick, New Jersey: Rutgers University Press, 2000, p. 118.

51 S.E. Schoenherr, 'Recording technology history', Audio Engineering Society, www.aes.org/aeshc/docs/recording.technology.history/notes.html, accessed 30 May 2016; 'Application for letters Patent for an invention by the Dictaphone Corporation titled, Improvements in Phonographic Machines', BC4217019, NAA: A627, 752/1926.

52 'Application for letters patent for an invention by the Dictaphone Corporation titled, Improvements in or relating to Machines for the Shaving or Resurfacing Phonograph', BC4205317, NAA: A627, 12665/1928.

53 R. Clark, *Sir Edward Appleton, G.B.E., K.C.B., F.R.S.*, Oxford: Pergamon Press, 1971, p. 42.

54 'Sir Edward Victor Appleton', Electronics Notes.

55 Letter, Alex Flint, Admiralty to C-in-C, China Station, 13 January 1926, forwarded to ACNB in June 1926, BC505956, NAA.

56 Minute, Secretary to Naval Representative, London, 20 January 1924, BC505956, NAA.

57 Letter, T.E. Nave to CSO, HMAS *Sydney*, 14 October 1924, BC505956, NAA.

58 J.H. Straczek, 'The origins and development of Royal Australian Naval signals intelligence', PhD thesis, ADFA, UNSW, pp. 56–63.

59 Memo, to ACNS and CNS DSC, 21 June 1933, 'Establishment of Wireless & Telegraph direction finding stations at Darwin & Rabaul', BC474429, NAA: MP1049/5, 1997/6/20, HFDF.

60 Extract of letter, T.E. Nave, 1 September 1925, BC505956, NAA.

61 Extract of letter, 1 September 1925, BC505956, NAA.

62 Letter, Admiralty to Secretary, Navy Office, Melbourne, 19 November 1 925, BC505956, NAA; minute, Spurgeon, Head of N Branch, to DNI, 30 December 1925, BC505956, NAA; letter, 22 January 1926, to Commodore Commanding HMA Fleet, BC505956, NAA.

63 Letter, Alex Flint, Admiralty, to C-in-C, China Station, 13 January 1926, forwarded to ACNB in June 1926, BC505956, NAA.

64 Best, *British Intelligence*, p. 95.

65 Letter, Alex Flint, Admiralty, to C-in-C, China Station, 13 January 1926, forwarded to ACNB in June 1926, BC505956, NAA.

66 Letter, Alex Flint, Admiralty, to C-in-C, China Station, 13 January 1926, forwarded to ACNB in June 1926, BC505956, NAA.

67 Letter, F. Cresswell to Assistant Chief of the Naval Staff, 7 July 1926, BC505956, NAA.

68 Letter, F. Cresswell to Assistant Chief of the Naval Staff, 7 July 1926, BC505956, NAA.

69 Report on IJN communications organisation by Lt E. Nave, attached to Admiralty letter, 16 June 1926, BC505956, NAA.

70 Straczek, 'The origins and development of Royal Australian Naval signals intelligence', p. 68, fn 51, quoting National Archives, UK, ADM116/6320, Case 6636, M.00423/26, Special W/T Intelligence Abroad, 6 December 1926.

71 Letter, Alex Flint, Admiralty, to ACNB, 16 June 1926, BC505956, NAA.

72 Letter, Alex Flint, Admiralty, to ACNB, 16 June 1926, BC505956, NAA.

73 *The Navy List*, July 1926, p. 60 lists Reginald A. Ball as a Clerk Class III in Naval Branch under Paymaster H. Spurgeon, p. 60.

74 Best, *British Intelligence*, p. 94.

75 Letter, F. Cresswell to Assistant Chief of the Naval Staff, 7 July 1926, BC505956, NAA.

76 Letter, F. Cresswell to Assistant Chief of the Naval Staff, 7 July 1926, BC505956, NAA.

77 Letter, R.A. Ball to F. Cresswell and Acting Chief of the Naval Staff, 17 September 1926, BC505956, NAA.

78 Letter R.A. Ball to F. Cresswell and Acting Chief of the Naval Staff, 17 September 1926, p. 3, BC505956, NAA.

79 Minute, ACNS, Commander H.T. Baillie-Grohman to CNS, 11 March 1927, BC505956, NAA.

80 Minute, F. Cresswell, Director of Signals and Communications, 2 August 1927, BC505956, NAA.

81 Letter, Mr W. Turner, General Manager for the Far East, Reuters Limited, to the Hon. Mr W.T. Southern, Colonial Secretary, Hong Kong, 12 November 1926, 'Japan. Wireless development', BC1607341, NAA: A11804, 1927/74.

82 Letter, L.S. Amery to Lord Stonehaven, 11 February 1927, BC1607341, NAA.

83 Report on Japanese wireless, undated, p. 1, BC1607341, NAA.

84 Report on Japanese wireless, undated, p. 1, BC1607341, NAA.

85 Report on Japanese wireless, undated, pp. 1–4, BC1607341, NAA.

86 Note, 'Short wave W/T trials', BC505956, NAA.

87 Note, 'Short wave W/T trials', BC505956, NAA.

88 Minute, Spurgeon, Head of N Branch, to Baillie-Grohman, 15 June 1927, BC505956, NAA.

89 Minute, Spurgeon, Head of N Branch, to Baillie-Grohman, 15 June 1927, BC505956, NAA.

90 Minute, Baillie-Grohman to Spurgeon, Head of N Branch, 16 June 1927, BC505956, NAA.

91 Note, 'Short wave W/T trials', BC505956, NAA; minute, 'Short wave W/T trials warrant telegraphist', B. Harding to Director, Signals and Communications, 27 July 1927, BC505956, NAA.

92 Note, 'Short wave W/T trials', BC505956, NAA.

93 Minute, 'Short wave W/T trials warrant telegraphist', B. Harding to Director, Signals and Communications, 27 July 1927, BC505956, NAA.

94 Minute, F. Cresswell, Director of Signals and Communications, 2 August 1927, BC505956, NAA.

95 Minute, Acting Secretary, Department of Defence, to First Naval Member, 6 August 1927, BC505956, NAA.

96 Minute, Acting Secretary, Department of Defence, to First Naval Member, 6 August 1927, BC505956, NAA.

97 Minute, Second Naval Member to First Naval Member, 12 September 1927, BC505956, NAA.

98 Letter, Alex Flint, Admiralty to the Secretary, Navy Office, Melbourne, 21 February 1928, BC505956, NAA.

99 Letter, Cresswell to CNS and ACNS, 6 July 1928, BC505956, NAA; draft letter, to Rear Admiral Commanding, HMA Squadron, 8 August 1928, BC505956, NAA.

100 Best, *British Intelligence*, p. 96.

101 Form S.206 report on accountant officers, 26 November 1926, BC8360031, NAA.

CHAPTER 11

1 Letter, Captain H.J. Freakes, 30 September 1930, BC505956, NAA.

2 Report, Rear Admiral W. Chalmers, Commanding HMA Squadron, 4 November 1930, BC505956, NAA; 'HM Australian Squadron—Report of Proceedings, Winter Cruise 1930', BC341732, NAA: MP124/6, 589/202/228.

3 Report, Rear Admiral W. Chalmers, Commanding HMA Squadron, 4 November 1930; BC341732, NAA.

4 'Officers (RAN) personal record—William Edward McLaughlin', BC30675236, NAA: A3978, MCLAUGHLIN W E.

5 Report, Rear Admiral W. Chalmers, 22 May 1931, BC505956, NAA.

6 Quarterly report, 28 March 1932, BC505956, NAA.

7 'BARNES HAROLD JOHN: Service Number—14270', BC4394418, NAA: A6770, BARNES H J.

8 BC4394418, NAA.

9 Letter, Rear Admiral Evans to Captain Superintendent of Training, 11 February 1931, BC505956, NAA.

10 Letter, Commodore Commanding HMA Squadron, 16 July 1931, BC505956, NAA.

11 BC4394418, NAA.

12 BC505956, NAA.

13 CBCS, *Year Book Australia*, no. 26, Canberra: Commonwealth of Australia, 1933, p. 329.

14 Signal 1458, Navy Office to CCAS, CSS and CST, 3 February 1932, BC505956, NAA.

15 Signal 314, CCAS to Navy Board, 4 February 1932, BC505956, NAA.

16 Signal 1458, Navy Office to CCAS, CSS and CST, 3 February 1932, BC505956, NAA.

17 Signal 1458, Navy Office to CCAS, CSS and CST, 3 February 1932, BC505956, NAA; Signal, CCAS to Navy Board, 23 February 1932, BC505956, NAA.

18 File note, F. Cresswell, Director of Signals and Communications, 4 March 1932, BC505956, NAA.

19 Signal 480, Navy Board to CCAS, 29 March 1932, BC505956, NAA.

20 'Japanese squadron', *The Mercury*, Hobart, 14 May 1932, p. 9.

21 Memo, Secretary, Navy Office, to Rear Admiral Commanding HM Australian Squadron, 17 May 1932, BC505956, NAA.

22 'Observations made of the visiting Japanese Training Squadron', BC505956, NAA.

23 Section III, 'Quarterly report of "Y" Procedure reception for quarter ended 30 June 1932', 14 July 1932, BC505956, NAA.

24 'MOST SECRET observations made of the visiting Japanese Training Squadron', BC505956, NAA.

25 'MOST SECRET observations made of the visiting Japanese Training Squadron', BC505956, NAA.

26 BC331612, NAA.

27 National Archives, UK, CAB 53/4, p. 2 (folio 115).

28 'The Far Eastern situation', memo, CNS to CoSSC of the CID, 25 February 1933, p. 2 (folio 115), National Archives, UK, CAB 53/4.

29 Memo, F. Cresswell, DSC, to ACNS and CNS, 21 June 1933, p. 1, BC474429, NAA.

30 Memo, F. Cresswell, DSC, to ACNS and CNS, 21 June 1933, p. 1, BC474429, NAA.

31 Memo, F. Cresswell, DSC, to ACNS and CNS, 21 June 1933, p. 2, BC474429, NAA.

32 Letter, Admiralty to ACNB, 9 September 1933, BC474429, NAA.

33 F.H. Hinsley et al., *British Intelligence in the Second World War*, vol. 1, London: HMSO, 1986, p. 21.

34 Letter, Admiralty to ACNB, 9 September 1933, BC474429, NAA.

35 Extract of report by Chief of Naval Staff on Singapore Conference, January 1934, p. 1, 'Navy—Imperial. Singapore Naval Conference. 1934', BC651792, NAA: A5954, 843/8.

36 'MOST SECRET AMENDMENT NO. 2', 12 June 1934, BC505956, NAA.

37 'MOST SECRET AMENDMENT NO. 2', 12 June 1934, BC505956, NAA.

38 'MOST SECRET AMENDMENT NO. 2', 12 June 1934, BC505956, NAA.

39 Vice Admiral G.F. Hyde. The delegates included Electrical Commander F.G. Cresswell, the staff officer most concerned with 'Y' Procedure and wireless activity; Paymaster Commander J.B. Foley; Commander J. Burnett; and a CPO Writer for secretarial support, led the Australian delegation.

40 A. Meaher, *The Australian Road to Singapore: The Myth of British Betrayal*, Melbourne: Australian Scholarly Publishing, 2010, pp. 142–61.

41 Straczek, 'The origins and development of Royal Australian Naval signals intelligence', p. 89.

42 Extract from report by CNS on Singapore Conference, January 1934, p. 1, BC651792, NAA.

43 Extract from report by CNS on Singapore Conference, January 1934, p. 1, BC651792, NAA.

44 Minute, DSC, 14 March 1934, BC505956, NAA; and extract from report by CNS on Singapore Conference, January 1934, p. 2, BC651792, NAA.

45 Goodman, *The Official History of the Joint Intelligence Committee*, vol. I, *From the Approach of the Second World War to the Suez Crisis*, Abingdon: Routledge, 2014, p. 20.

46 Straczek, 'The origins and development of Royal Australian Naval signals intelligence', p. 91, fn 19.

47 Best, *British Intelligence*, p. 109.

48 Straczek, 'The origins and development of Royal Australian Naval signals intelligence', pp. 91–2.

49 Best, *British Intelligence*, p. 109.

50 BC474429, NAA.

51 The British were deeply involved in obtaining all of the traffic these cables carried, through the good offices of the telegraphic companies operating them. The Chinese, Japanese, Russians and everyone else, except possibly the Americans, were bribing telegraphic company employees to obtain information for them, and the latter were more than happy to oblige, often servicing all sides with the same information. There was no way that 'Y' Procedure material could be safely stored or communicated into and out of Shanghai. As a result, FECB was located in Hong Kong.

52 Extract CID Paper 418-C, BC655420, NAA: A5954, 1961/3.

53 BC4394418, NAA.

54 Straczek, 'The origins and development of Royal Australian Naval signals intelligence', p. 165.

55 Straczek, 'The origins and development of Royal Australian Naval signals intelligence', p. 139.

56 Straczek, 'The origins and development of Royal Australian Naval signals intelligence', p. 139.

57 Photograph of raider, 'Raider: Taken by JH Barnes—Nauru—27 December 1940', BC6431704, NAA: R32, N/15/1417. Other photographs are also at BC6431705, and at BC643101 and BC643102, NAA. See also Gill, *Royal Australian Navy, 1939–1942*, p. 281.

58 M. Smith, *The Emperor's Codes: Bletchley Park and the Breaking of Japan's Secret Ciphers*, London: Bantam Press, 2000, pp. 30–33.

59 Smith, *The Emperor's Codes*, p. 32.

60 Letter, to Minister CNS aboard SS *Marella*, 13 February 1934, BC651792, NAA.

61 Smith, *The Emperor's Codes*, p. 25.

62 Smith, *The Emperor's Codes*, pp. 25–42, and National Security Agency, *Brigadier John Tiltman: A Giant Amongst Cryptanalysts*, Centre for Cryptologic History, Fort Mead, Maryland, 2007. At the time Tiltman was working on IJN-25 and other Japanese codes with Neave he was a GC&CS civilian employee. Tiltman moved between the British Army and GC&CS a number of times during his very long career. His status within the UKUSA SIGINT community is aptly demonstrated by the celebration of his achievements by the National Security Agency in the publication just mentioned. See www.nsa.gov/about/cryptologic-heritage/historical-figures-publications/publications/misc/assets/files/tiltman.pdf.

63 Hinsley et al., *British Intelligence in the Second World War*, p. 53, fn.

64 Hinsley et al., *British Intelligence in the Second World War*, p. 53.

65 'Naval Reserve Training, HM Australian Squadron, Winter Cruise 1939', BC6014642, NAA: MP151/1, 629/213/1880.

66 ACNB minutes, 16 January 1939, 'Naval Board minutes, 1939–1941', BC12205926, NAA: NID 450/0.

67 ACNB minutes, 16 January 1939, BC12205926, NAA.

68 ACNB minutes, 1 December 1939, BC12205926, NAA.

69 See J. Robertson & J. McCarthy, *Australian War Strategy, 1939–1945: A Documentary History*, Brisbane: University of Queensland Press, 1985, pp. 25–37.

CHAPTER 12

1 Letter, Mrs H.E. Freame to Sir Robert Menzies, 30 December 1963, BC563163, NAA.

2 His full name was Wykeham Henry Freame, see 'Freame, Wykeham Henry: SERN 764', BC1994094, NAA: B2455, FREAME W H. He appears to have been called Harry Freame, although he has also been referred to as Henry Freame and Harry Freame-Kobe. I will use Harry Freame throughout.

3 Letter, Mrs H.E. Freame to Sir Robert Menzies, 30 December 1963, BC563163, NAA.

4 Yosha Bunko, Wetherall, W., 'Becoming Japanese in the Meiji Period: Adopted Sons, Incoming Husbands, and Naturalisation', updated 16 July 2014, www.yoshabunko.com/nationality/Naturalization_Meiji.html members.jcom.home.ne.jp/yosha/yr/nationality/Naturalization_Meiji.html, accessed 26 November 2017.

5 members.jcom.home.ne.jp/yosha/yr/nationality/Naturalization_Meiji.html.

6 www.pixnet.co.uk/pixsg/AA-HISTORY/World-War/Goodyear/Goodyear/goodyear-pages/Freame-pages/narrative01.html; and 'Divorce Court ... Freame v. Freame', *Australian Town and Country Journal*, 6 April 1878, p. 14.

7 members.jcom.home.ne.jp/yosha/yr/nationality/Naturalization_Meiji.html.

8 members.jcom.home.ne.jp/yosha/yr/nationality/Naturalization_Meiji.html.

9   members.jcom.home.ne.jp/yosha/yr/nationality/Naturalization_Meiji.html.

10 members.jcom.home.ne.jp/yosha/yr/nationality/Naturalization_Meiji.html. The British Vice-Consul, Joseph Henry Longfield, knew this, but when he became aware of William Freame's bigamy did nothing about it.

11 He also claimed he was born in Canada. See Enlistment Form, p. 1, BC1994094, NAA.

12 members.jcom.home.ne.jp/yosha/yr/nationality/Naturalization_Meiji.html.

13 Letter, 26 February 1916, for allotment of 5/6 per day to 'Mrs Edith Freame, 24 Alfonsues Street, North Ormesby, Yorkshire', to be paid with effect 11 December 1915, BC1994094, NAA.

14 Discussion with his descendent, see John Collins, 'Re: Freames in Somerset and Wiltshire', 13 March 2010, Genealogy.com, genforum.genealogy.com/freame/messages/14.html, accessed 20 May 2014.

15 B. Bennett, 'Traditional myths and problematic heroes: the case of Harry Freame', *Asiatic*, 2010, vol. 4, no. 2, p. 5.

16 Bean, *The Story of Anzac*, p. 241, fn 16.

17 Bean, *The Story of Anzac*, p. 241.

18 Bean, *The Story of Anzac*, pp. 241–44.

19 Bean, *The Story of Anzac*, pp. 241–44.

20 Bean, *The Story of Anzac*, p. 814.

21 Casualty Form, BC1994094, NAA.

22 'Photographs and letters from or about Professor Murdoch', BC9024396, NAA: A4311, 774/15.

23 David Sadleir, 'Lloyd, Eric Edwin Longfield (1890–1957)', *Australian Dictionary of Biography*, adb.anu.edu.au/biography/lloyd-eric-edwin-longfield-10840/text19235, accessed 13 March 2017.

24 Letter, Base Records re Sgt Freame, 5 April 1940, BC1994094, NAA.

25 *Farmer and Settler*, Sydney, 26 May 1916, p. 2; *Sydney Morning Herald*; 29 July 1916, p. 14; *Evening News*, Sydney, 25 April 1922, p. 8; *Dungog Chronicle: Durham and Gloucester Advertiser*, 18 August 1931, p. 2.

26 C.E.W. Bean, *Australia in the War of 1914–1918*, vol. II, *The Story of Anzac: From 4 May 1915 to the Evacuation*, Angus & Robertson, Sydney, 1924, p. 241.

27 NSW government file 19/7034, certificate no. 1916/00445, for orchard land, 2 Bondi Road, Bondi, to Henry Wykeham Freame, 20 November 1916, Soldiers Settlement Miscellaneous File Index, State Archives & Records, NSW, www.records.nsw.gov.au/searchhits_nocopy?id=56&surname=Freame&firstname=&class_of_holding=&land_district=&order=firstname&sort=asc, accessed 21 May 2014.

28 BC9024396, NAA.

29 Letter, Freame to Base Records, Melbourne, 6 January 1920, BC1994094, NAA.

30 'General Birdwood in the north', *Sydney Morning Herald*, 30 April 1920, p. 8.

31 Letter, Mrs H.E. Freame to Sir Robert Menzies, 30 December 1963, BC563163, NAA.

32 Letter, Mrs H.E. Freame to Sir Robert Menzies, 30 December 1963, BC563163, NAA.

33 Minute, Major Scott to Major Powell, 9 October 1940, 'Mr Harry Freame—interpreter Australian Legation to Japan', BC463429, NAA: MP729/6, 15/403/16.

34 'Scott William John Rendal: SERN MAJOR', BC3003941, NAA: B2455, SCOTT WJR. See his other record in 'SCOTT WILLIAM JOHN RENDEL: Service Number—VX71997', BC6071654, NAA: B883, VX71997, SCOTT WJR. Neither record covers the 1919–41 period.

35 C. Hazlehurst, *The Journeys to Cameron's Farm: An Australian Tragedy*, Canberra: ANU Press, 2013, p. 167.

36 Teleprinter message CS.304, 30 August 1940, BC463429, NAA; minute, Major Scott to DMO&I, 9 October 1940.

37 Minute, Major Scott to DMO&I, 9 October 1940, BC463429, NAA.

38 Minute, Major Scott to DMO&I, 9 October 1940, BC463429, NAA.

39 Letter, Minister for the Army to Minister for External Affairs, 30 September 1940, BC463429, NAA.

40 All Friday 13 September 1940: *Daily Telegraph*, Sydney; *The Examiner*, Launceston; 'Personal' *Courier Mail*, Brisbane, p. 4; *The Sun*, Melbourne; *The Argus*, Melbourne, p. 4; *The Mercury*, Hobart, p. 4; *West Australian*, Perth, p. 12; *Sydney Morning Herald*, p. 8; 'Personal', *The Advertiser*, Adelaide, p. 18; 'Crumbs', *Cootamundra Herald*, p. 2. It was also later reported in *Cairns Post*, 4 October 1940, p. 1; *Daily Advertiser*, Wagga Wagga, 1 October 1940, p. 2.

41 Handwritten marginal note beside cutting, *The Sun*, 13 September 1940, BC463429, NAA.

42 Letter, Minister for Army to Minister for External Affairs, 30 September 1940, BC463429, NAA.

43 Secret letter, 30 September 1940, BC463429, NAA.

44 Secret letter, 2 October 1940, BC463429, NAA.

45 Secret letter, 2 October 1940, BC463429, NAA.

46 Secret letter, 2 October 1940, BC463429, NAA.

47 Secret letter, 2 October 1940, BC463429, NAA.

48 Secret letter, 2 October 1940, BC463429, NAA.

49 Handwritten note, 'Freame, Henry Wykeham (Japanese)', BC3314430, NAA: C123, 10067; 'British subject's death demand for inquiry', *The Argus*, Melbourne, 31 July 1940, p. 3.

50 Report, British Consul-General, Seoul, 15 February 1935, 'Japan Espionage—Rev. J.N. Mackenzie', BC177466, NAA: A981, JAP 56.

51 Report, British Consul-General, Seoul, 15 February 1935, BC177466, NAA.

52 Report, British Consul-General, Seoul, 15 February 1935, BC177466, NAA.

53 Kotani, *Japanese Intelligence in World War II*, p. 64.

54 Kotani, *Japanese Intelligence in World War II*, p. 64.

55 Kotani, *Japanese Intelligence in World War II*, p. 65.

56 P. Elphick, *Far Eastern File: The Intelligence War in the Far East, 1930–1945*, London: Hodder & Stoughton, 1997, pp. 250–51; 'Background', *Daily News*, Perth, 31 July 1940, p. 1.

57 Elphick, *Far Eastern File*, p. 250.

58 Elphick, *Far Eastern File*, pp. 250–51; 'Background', *Daily News*, Perth, 31 July 1940, p. 1. Vanya Ringer's brother Michael was also arrested at their family home at Shimonoseki, see 'British subject's death demand for inquiry', *The Argus*, Melbourne, 31 July 1940, p. 3; 'Arrests in Japan—Lord Halifax's statement', *West Australian*, Perth, 31 July 1940, p. 7; 'Japan asked for explanation', *The Advertiser*, Adelaide, 31 July 1940, p. 13.

59 Elphick, *Far Eastern File*, p. 251.

60 Elphick, *Far Eastern File*, p. 188.

61 Elphick, *Far Eastern File*, p. 250; Kotani, *Japanese Intelligence in World War II*, p. 65.

62 'Mr Cox described. "Happy disposition" ', *Sydney Morning Herald*, 31 July 1940, p. 11; 'Mr Melville Cox "Suicide Established" ', *Sydney Morning Herald*, 16 August 1940, p. 7; 'Japan arouses indignation', *The Argus*, Melbourne, 31 July 1940, p. 1; 'British arrests in Japan', *The Argus*, 1 August 1940, p. 3.

63 Handwritten note, 5 August 1941, BC563163, NAA.

64 Mrs Harriett Freame to Col. Longfield Lloyd, 16 June 1941, BC3314430, NAA; letter, Mrs H.E. Freame to Sir Robert Menzies, 30 December 1963, BC563163, NAA.
65 Mrs Harriett Freame to Col. Longfield Lloyd, 16 June 1941, BC3314430, NAA.
66 Report, Dr Ikeda, Y., 20 February 1941, BC563163, NAA.
67 Report, Dr Ikeda, Y., 20 February 1941, BC563163, NAA.
68 See Ikeda's reports in BC563163, NAA. See also letter, Lt G.H.V. Newman, Intelligence Section (Ib), Eastern Command, to G3, Intelligence Section, Eastern Command, 12 June 1941, BC3314430, NAA.
69 Memo, June 1941, BC3314430, NAA.
70 BC3314430, NAA. This file still has three folios exempted public access under paragraphs 33(1)(g) of the *Archives Act 1983*. The masks were applied on 16 July 1998 and appear to be covering details of the medical cause of death. Page 2 of a report by Captain B. Tyrrell follows on one of the masked folios, and is a continuation of a medical report stating 'bladder, and there is nothing tangible to support the allegation of an attempt on Freame's life'. This report seems to have been intended for Colonel Longfield Lloyd.
71 Cable No. 191, Department of External Affairs to Australian Legation in Tokyo, 3 July 1941, BC3314430, NAA.
72 Letter, P.J. Calvin to Secretary, Prime Minister's Department, 18 February 1964, BC563163, NAA.
73 Letter, P.J. Calvin to Secretary, Prime Minister's Department, 18 February 1964, BC563163, NAA.
74 Ministerial briefing note, p. 2, attached to letter, P.J. Calvin to Secretary, Prime Minister's Department, 18 February 1964, BC563163, NAA.
75 Ministerial briefing note, p. 2, BC563163, NAA.

CHAPTER 13

1 Report, 14 October 1943, p. 1 (folio 13), 'Lieut Commander EA Feldt—Coastwatching', BC410697, NAA: B3476, 49.
2 Report, p. 1 (folio 13), 14 October 1943, BC410697, NAA.
3 'FELDT ERIC AUGUSTUS: Date of birth—03 Jan 1899', BC5415638, NAA: A6769, FELDT E A; J.C.H. Gill, 'Commander Eric Augustus Feldt', Navy, www.navy.gov.au/biography/commander-eric-augustus-feldt, accessed 14 October 2016.
4 J.C.H. Gill, 'Commander Eric Augustus Feldt'.
5 BC5415638, NAA.
6 J.C.H. Gill, 'Commander Eric Augustus Feldt'.
7 BC5415638, NAA.
8 Report, 14 October 1943, p. 1 (folio 13), BC410697, NAA.
9 Naval Records Society, 'Memorandum co-operation of dominions in defence. Action required during precautionary period, 4 November 1938', *The Collective Naval Defence of the Empire, 1900–1940*, Aldershot: Ashgate Publishing, 1997, pp. 616–18.
10 Report, 14 October 1943, p. 1 (folio 13), BC410697, NAA.
11 Report, 14 October 1943, p. 1 (folio 13), BC410697, NAA.
12 Report, 14 October 1943, p. 1 (folio 13), BC410697, NAA.
13 Report, 14 October 1943, p. 1 (folio 13), BC410697, NAA.
14 Report, 14 October 1943, p. 1 (folio 13), BC410697, NAA.
15 Report, 14 October 1943, p. 1 (folio 13), BC410697, NAA.
16 Report, 14 October 1943, p. 2 (folio 12), BC410697, NAA.
17 Report, 14 October 1943, p. 2 (folio 12), BC410697, NAA.
18 Report, 14 October 1943, p. 2 (folio 12), BC410697, NAA.

19 Report, 14 October 1943, p. 2 (folio 12), BC410697, NAA.

20 Report, 14 October 1943, p. 2 (folio 12), BC410697, NAA.

21 Report, 14 October 1943, p. 2 (folio 12), BC410697, NAA.

22 Report, 14 October 1943, p. 3 (folio 11), BC410697, NAA.

23 Report, 14 October 1943, p. 2 (folio 12), BC410697, NAA.

24 Report, 14 October 1943, p. 2 (folio 12), BC410697, NAA.

25 Coast reports, Sepik District Staff Officer (Intelligence), Port Moresby, to DNI, 23 January 1940, 'Reports from coastwatchers in New Guinea, New Britain, New Ireland areas', BC411499, NAA: B3476, 37.

26 Report, 14 October 1943, p. 3 (folio 11), BC410697, NAA.

27 Report, 14 October 1943, p. 3 (folio 11), BC410697, NAA.

28 Personal letter, Long to Feldt, 13 January 1940, BC410697, NAA.

29 Personal letter, Long to Feldt, 13 January 1940, BC410697, NAA.

30 Personal letter, Long to Feldt, 13 January 1940, BC410697, NAA.

31 Personal letter, Long to Feldt, 13 January 1940, BC410697, NAA.

32 Testimony of Long, folio 280, 'Files and papers relating to Lieutenant Colonel RFB WAKE', BC1134482, NAA: A7359, BOX4/MS200/23.

33 Lieutenant Colonel Wake was so intent on holding all security and intelligence matters in his own hands that the British SIS representative at the Central Bureau in Brisbane operated clandestinely to avoid Wake's persistent efforts to encroach into SIGINT and SIS matters.

34 Letter, Long to Feldt, 30 July 1940, 'Commander E Feldt—reports—summaries of coast-watching activities', BC508663, NAA: B3476, 49C.

35 Letter Long to Feldt, 30 July 1940, BC508663, NAA.

36 Letter, Feldt to Long, 18 October 1940, BC508663, NAA. The nickname Hereward the Wake was a sarcastic name given to Wake by his fellow officers and refers to the eleventh-century Anglo-Saxon resister to the Norman Conquest England.

37 Report, 14 October 1943, p. 3 (folio 11), BC410697, NAA.

38 Report, 14 October 1943, p. 3 (folio 11), BC410697, NAA.

39 Report, 14 October 1943, p. 3 (folio 11), BC410697, NAA.

40 Report, 14 October 1943, p. 3 (folio 11), BC410697, NAA.

41 Report, 14 October 1943, p. 3 (folio 11), BC410697, NAA.

42 Report, 14 October 1943, p. 4 (folio 10), BC410697, NAA.

43 Report, 14 October 1943, p. 4 (folio 10), BC410697, NAA.

44 Report, 14 October 1943, p. 4 (folio 10), BC410697, NAA.

45 Report, 14 October 1943, p. 5 (folio 9), BC410697, NAA; 'British Phosphate Commission's Steamer Trienza . . .', Australian War Memorial, acc. no. 128076, www.awm.gov.au/collection/128076, accessed 30 October 2016.

46 Report, 14 October 1943, p. 5 (folio 9), BC410697, NAA.

47 Report, 14 October 1943, p. 5 (folio 9), BC410697, NAA.

48 Gill, Royal Australian Navy 1939–1942, p. 423.

49 Gill, Royal Australian Navy 1939–1942, p. 423, fn 7.

50 Report, 14 October 1943, p. 5 (folio 9), BC410697, NAA.

51 Report, 14 October 1943, p. 5 (folio 9), BC410697, NAA; 'British Phosphate Commission's Steamer Trienza . . .', Australian War Memorial.

52 Report, 14 October 1943, p. 5 (folio 9), BC410697, NAA.

53 Report, 14 October 1943, p. 5 (folio 9), BC410697, NAA.

54 Gill, Royal Australian Navy 1939–1942, p. 540.

55 Report, 14 October 1943, p. 6 (folio 8), BC410697, NAA.

56 Report, 14 October 1943, p. 9 (folio 5), BC410697, NAA.

57 Eric Feldt, *The Coastwatchers*, Melbourne: Oxford University Press, 1946, p. 42.

58 Letters, Feldt to 'Cocky', DNI Rupert Long, 31 March 1942 and 7 April 1942, BC508663, NAA. Whale Island is a reference to the rigorous discipline enforced at HMS *Endeavour*, located at Whale Island, a 'stone frigate' shore-based training establishment at Portsmouth in the United Kingdom. Feldt is telling Long he has imposed a strong disciplinary regime on his junior officers, chiefs and ratings.

59 Feldt, *The Coastwatchers*, pp. 410, 412.

60 Letter, Feldt to 'Cocky', DNI Rupert Long, 7 April 1942, BC508663, NAA.

61 Report, p. 7 (folio 7), 14 October 1943, BC410697, NAA.

62 S. Bullard, *Japanese Army Operations in the South Pacific Area: New Britain and Papua Campaigns, 1942–43*, Canberra: Australian War Memorial, 2007, pp. 12–13.

63 Signal, Tulagi to SIO, Townsville, 31 January 1942, BC411499, NAA.

64 Feldt, *The Coastwatchers*, p. 49.

65 Letter, Feldt to Long, 4 February 1942, BC508663, NAA.

66 Letter, to Secretary, External Affairs, Secretary Department of the Navy, 12 February 1942, BC411499, NAA.

67 'Montevideo Maru—serial name list of prisoners of war and internees who perished', NAA: A14143, 1.

68 Report, 14 October 1943, p. 8 (folio 6), BC410697, NAA.

69 Letter, Feldt to Long, 28 January 1942, BC508663, NAA.

70 Memo, DNI to CNS and DCNS, 6 February 1942, BC411499, NAA. The ACNB was aware of the capture of Daymond and Squires on 12 February 1942. See letter, to Secretary, External Affairs, Secretary Department of the Navy, 12 February 1942, BC411499, NAA.

71 Letter, Feldt to Long, 28 January 1942, BC508663, NAA.

72 Feldt, *The Coastwatchers*, p. 57.

73 Letter, Feldt to 'Cocky' Rupert Long, 4 February 1942, BC508663, NAA.

74 Gill, *Royal Australian Navy 1939–1942*, p. 547. A number of coastwatchers were given military rank by the RAAF, which was willing to appoint them without the red tape, medical examinations, interviews and signed documentation demanded by the ACNB and army. Feldt's concerns about the status of his civilian coastwatchers were a credit to him. Harry Freame's case clearly demonstrated how callous the system was.

75 Feldt, *The Coastwatchers*, p. 57. Nelson Tokidoro was a graduate of Nordup Government School at Rabaul, where the Principal, Mr J.H.L. Waterhouse, taught the local students Morse code, radio maintenance and operations. See H. Nelson, 'Bougainville in World War II', in A.J. Regan & H.M. Griffin (eds), *Bougainville Before the Conflict*, Canberra: Pandanus Books, p. 176.

76 As will be seen later, the Japanese were highly competent in SIGINT and had broken the coastwatchers' codes.

77 The Australian New Guinea Administrative Unit (ANGAU) was the military unit established under the Australian Military Board to take over the military government of New Guinea from April 1942 until the end of the war in August 1945.

78 Feldt, *The Coastwatchers*, p. 57.

79 Feldt, *The Coastwatchers*, p. 58.

80 Feldt, *The Coastwatchers*, p. 59.

81 Feldt, *The Coastwatchers*, p. 59.

82 Report, 14 October 1943, p. 8 (folio 6), BC410697, NAA.

83 Feldt, *The Coastwatchers*, p. 59; Gill, *Royal Australian Navy 1939–1942*, p. 547.

84 Gill, *Royal Australian Navy 1939–1942*, p. 547.

85 Gill, *Royal Australian Navy 1939–1942*, p. 548.
86 Gill, *Royal Australian Navy 1939–1942*, p. 548.
87 Feldt, *The Coastwatchers*, p. 60.
88 Feldt, *The Coastwatchers*, p. 60.
89 Report, 14 October 1943, p. 8 (folio 6), BC410697, NAA.
90 Gill, *Royal Australian Navy 1939–1942*, p. 548.
91 Gill, *Royal Australian Navy 1939–1942*, p. 548.
92 Report, 14 October 1943, p. 9 (folio 5), BC410697, NAA.
93 Report, 14 October 1943, p. 9 (folio 5), BC410697, NAA.
94 Gill, *Royal Australian Navy 1942–1945*, p. 6.
95 Gill, *Royal Australian Navy 1942–1945*, p. 6; Feldt, *The Coastwatchers*, p. 47.
96 Feldt, *The Coastwatchers*, pp. 126–27.
97 Gill, *Royal Australian Navy 1942–1945*, p. 7.
98 Bougainville Area, Kieta District, Territory of New Guinea, report by Mr C.I.H. Campbell, 15 February 1943, p. 4, 'Bougainville–Buka area–notes re interrogation of coastwatchers & natives', BC508352, NAA: B3476, 1.
99 Report, 14 October 1943, p. 9 (folio 5), BC410697, NAA. Involvement of IJN Marines is in signal 0631Z/21, SIO, Townsville, to DNI, 21 March 1942, BC411499, NAA.
100 Nelson, 'Bougainville in World War II', p. 198, fn 42.
101 Report, 14 October 1943, p. 9 (folio 5), BC410697, NAA.
102 Report, 14 October 1943, p. 9 (folio 5), BC410697, NAA.
103 Report, 14 October 1943, p. 9 (folio 5), BC410697, NAA.
104 Signal 0642Z/21, SIO, Townsville, to DNI, 21 March 1942, BC411499, NAA.
105 Memo, SOI, Townsville, to DNI, 2 May 1942, 'Ferdinand party—plans and operation', BC436101, NAA: B3476, 174B, shows Read, Page, Mitchell and Mason as all holding appointments as members of the RANVR with the ranks recommended by Feldt in his signal.
106 Memo, SOI, Townsville, to DNI, 2 May 1942, BC436101, NAA; Feldt, *The Coastwatchers*, p. 128.
107 Drummond Thomson was recommended to Long for coastwatching duties by Robert Menzies. See letter, R.G. Menzies to Long, 13 April 1942, 'Ferdinand party establishment—mobilization and transfers', BC411640, NAA: B3476, 174A.
108 Signal 0254Z/30/3, SIO, Townsville, to DNI, 30 March 1942, BC411499, NAA.
109 Feldt, *The Coastwatchers*, p. 126.
110 Nelson, 'Bougainville in World War II', p. 181.
111 Nelson, 'Bougainville in World War II', p. 182.
112 Nelson, 'Bougainville in World War II', p. 183.
113 Letter, Sub-Lt P.E. Mason to Lt Cdr H.A. Mackenzie, 26 March 1943, 'Reports from coastwatchers in the Solomon Islands Area', p. 1, BC410664, NAA: B3476, 37A.
114 Feldt, *The Coastwatchers*, p. 74.
115 Signal 1156Z/25, NB to NOIC, Townsville, 25 March 1942, BC436101, NAA.
116 Signal 0043Z/13, SIO, Townsville, to DNI, 13 June 1942, BC411499, NAA.
117 A.W. Ind, *Secret War Against Japan: The Allied Intelligence Bureau in World War II*, Uncommon Valor Series, 2014, p. 61.
118 'Position of intelligence personnel in enemy occupied territory', p. 1, 'Ferdinand party—plans, operations, distribution, personnel', BC32571389, NAA: B3476, 148 PART 2B.
119 Feldt, *The Coastwatchers*, p. 79. Thirteen bodies were later found buried on Nago. The remains of Con Page, John Talmage, Bill Kyle and Greg Benham were later identified, as were the remains of Page's nemeses, the German 'sailor' Herterich, Father Michael

Murphy from Tabar Island and Father Karl Martin from Ulaputur. The other six bodies have not yet been identified. See Jim Ridges, 'The Japanese invasion of New Ireland 1942', People of the Plaque, www.jje.info/lostlives/exhib/potp/japaneseinvasion.html, accessed 24 October 2016.

120 Feldt, *The Coastwatchers*, p. 84.

121 Signal 0830Z/28, NOIC, Port Moresby, to SIO, Townsville, 28 May 1942, BC411499, NAA.

122 Signal 0700Z/7, COMSOUWESPACFOR to NOIC, Townsville, 7 August 1942, BC411499, NAA.

123 'Debrief of commanding officer of US submarine, S.43', 8 August 1942, BC411499, NAA.

124 'Position of intelligence personnel in enemy occupied territory', p. 1, BC32571389, NAA.

125 Jim Ridges, 'The Japanese invasion of New Ireland 1942'.

CHAPTER 14

1 Kotani, *Japanese Intelligence in World War II*, p. 8.

2 Kotani, *Japanese Intelligence in World War II*, p. 8.

3 Kotani, *Japanese Intelligence in World War II*, p. 1.

4 Kotani, *Japanese Intelligence in World War II*, p. 8.

5 The Tokubetsu Keisatsutai (Tokkeitai), which was much smaller than the Kempetai, was formed by the IJN in order to keep the Kempeitai from interfering in IJN activity or investigating IJN personnel.

6 Strategic Services Unit, '*Japanese Intelligence Service*', Section II, 'Japanese military intelligence in China', Part A, 4 June 1946, p. 1.

7 Strategic Services Unit, '*Japanese Intelligence Service*', Section II, 'Japanese military intelligence in China', 4 June 1946, Part C.6.2.

8 Strategic Services Unit, '*Japanese Intelligence Service*', Section II, 'Japanese military intelligence in China', Part C.6.3.

9 Strategic Services Unit, '*Japanese Intelligence Service*', Section II, 'Japanese military intelligence in China', Part C.6.G.

10 Strategic Services Unit, '*Japanese Intelligence Service*', Section II, 'Japanese military intelligence in China', Part 6.a.

11 Kotani, *Japanese Intelligence in World War II*, p. 8.

12 Strategic Services Unit, '*Japanese Intelligence Service*', Section II, 'Japanese military intelligence in China', Section 6.a.

13 Strategic Services Unit, '*Japanese Intelligence Service*', Section II, 'Japanese military intelligence in China', Section 6.d.

14 Strategic Services Unit, '*Japanese Intelligence Service*', Section II, 'Japanese military intelligence in China', Section 6.d.

15 Memo, SIO NGA to Lt Greathead, 4 August 1943, ' "Ferdinand" parties [coastwatching]', BC410692, NAA: B3476, 174.

16 Letter, Sub-Lt P.E. Mason to Lt Cdr H.A. Mackenzie, 26 March 1943, p. 1, BC410664, NAA.

17 Report, HQ, NGF, ANGAU, to Director, FELO, 11 December 1942, p. 1, 'Field parties, New Guinea, [miscellaneous] Part 1', BC235140, NAA: A3269, C19/A.

18 Report, HQ, NGF, ANGAU, to Director, FELO, 16 December 1942, p. 2, BC235140, NAA.

19 Report, Lt L.F. Howlett, ANGAU, to FELO, 26 January 1943, 16 December 1942, pp. 2–3, BC235140, NAA.

20 Report, Lt L.F. Howlett, ANGAU, to FELO, 26 January 1943, 16 December 1942, p. 2, BC235140, NAA.

21 Report, WO2 J.R.V. Graham, ANGAU, to FELO, 16 December 1942; report, 'Degree of loyalty, sub-divisions Markham', Lt J.S. McLeod, ADO, 13 May 1943, p. 4; report, Lt C. O'Loughlin, October 1943, p. 2, all in BC235140, NAA.

22 Intelligence Report No. 8, 8 July 1945, p. 1, 'AGAS I, copy I [British North Borneo, February—September 1945]', BC235015, NAA: A3269, A1/A, AGAS I, Copy I.

23 Intelligence Report No. 8, 8 July 1945, p. 2, BC235015, NAA.

24 Intelligence Report No. 8, 8 July 1945, p. 3, BC235015, NAA.

25 Strategic Services Unit, 'Japanese Intelligence Service', pp. 47–52, provides an excellent description of Yui Matao's Manwa Company and its intelligence activities funded by retired Vice Admiral Tannawa Toshio and the Japanese military.

26 Intelligence Report No. 8, dated 8 July 1945, p. 5, BC235015, NAA.

27 Intelligence Report No. 8, dated 8 July 1945, p. 4, BC235015, NAA.

28 Intelligence report on New Ireland, Capt. H.J. Murray, AIB, December 1943, p. 2, BC235140, NAA.

29 Report, Mason to Feldt, 26 March 1943, 'Bougainville—party organisation: reports', BC509602, NAA: B3476. 156A.

30 Kotani, *Japanese Intelligence in World War II*, p. 10.

31 'History of Signal Intelligence Service in India and South East Asia Command', 1939–1945', pp. 1–4, BC3199101, NAA: A6923.

32 Strategic Services Unit, 'Japanese Intelligence Service', p. 26.

33 Strategic Services Unit, 'Japanese Intelligence Service', p. 26. Care needs to be taken with this source because, as an English-speaking Filipino working for the IJN, he would be keen to denigrate the Japanese and downplay the success of his own work when being interrogated by US officials.

34 Strategic Services Unit, 'Japanese Intelligence Service', p. 38.

35 Strategic Services Unit, 'Japanese Intelligence Service', p. 26.

36 Strategic Services Unit, 'Japanese Intelligence Service', p. 41.

37 'Special Intelligence', BC3023422, NAA: A6923, SI/1. This file contains the Central Bureau analysis of the Japanese intelligence effort against the AIB. It clearly shows that the entire AIB system, its methods, personnel, organisation and objectives, had been completely compromised by information obtained from captured AIB operatives. This report also underlined the good sense of ensuring that no operative being sent behind enemy lines should know of ULTRA. See Part A of the 'Report Australian Secret Intelligence and Special Operations', 31 August 1945, in this file.

38 'Report Australian Secret Intelligence and Special Operations', Part B, 31 August 1945, BC3023422, NAA.

CHAPTER 15

1 D.M. Horner, *High Command: Australian and Allied Strategy 1939–1945*, Sydney: George Allen & Unwin, 1982, p. 230.

2 W.B. Breuer, *MacArthur's Undercover War: Spies, Saboteurs, Guerrillas, and Secret Missions*, New York: John Wiley & Sons, 1995, pp. 23–24.

3 G. Long, *MacArthur as Military Commander*, London: Angus & Robertson, 1969, p. 87.

4 Statement on behalf of the Treasury in connection with the secret fund established in February 1940, 'Secret Service No. 4 Account', BC134232, NAA: A571, 1946/2511.

5 Allied Intelligence Bureau statement of receipts and expenditure, 1 June 1942–16 January 1946, BC134232, NAA.

6 'Directive governing the organisation, co-ordination and operation of inter-Allied units known as Special Operations, Australian Section, Secret Intelligence Service Australian

Section, Combined Field Intelligence Section and Military Propaganda Section', 6 July 1942, BC134232, NAA.

7   'Directive governing the organisation, co-ordination and operation of inter-Allied units', 6 July 1942, p. 1, BC134232, NAA.

8   'Directive governing the organisation, co-ordination and operation of inter-Allied units', 6 July 1942, p. 1, BC134232, NAA.

9   Letter, Douglas MacArthur to the Rt Hon John Curtin, MP, 8 July 1942, BC134232, NAA.

10 'Directive governing the organisation, co-ordination and operation of inter-Allied units, pp. 1–2, BC134232, NAA.

11 'Directive governing the organisation, co-ordination and operation of inter-Allied units', 6 July 1942, p. 2, BC134232, NAA.

12 'Directive governing the organisation, co-ordination and operation of inter-Allied units', 6 July 1942, p. 3, Distribution, BC134232, NAA.

13 'AIB administrative adjustments', 16 April 1943, p. 1, BC134232, NAA.

14 G. Morgenstern, *Pearl Harbor: The Story of the Secret War*, New York: Devin-Adair Company, 1947, p. 300; R.H. Worth, *Secret Allies in the Pacific: Covert Intelligence and Code Breaking Prior to the Attack on Pearl Harbor*, Jefferson, North Carolina: McFarlane & Company Inc., 2002, pp. 132–42.

15 D.M. Horner, *High Command: Australia and Allied Strategy 1939–1945*, Sydney: George Allen & Unwin, 1982, pp. 365–56.

16 Horner, *High Command*, p. 368.

17 Worth, *Secret Allies in the Pacific*, p. 300.

18 R.J. Aldrich, *Intelligence and the War Against Japan: Britain, America and the Politics of Secret Service*, Cambridge: Cambridge University Press, 2000, p. 127.

19 Aldrich, *Intelligence and the War Against Japan*, p. 129.

20 'AIB administrative adjustments', 16 April 1943, p. 1, BC13423, NAA.

21 'AIB administrative adjustments', 16 April 1943, p. 1, BC134232, NAA.

22 A. Powell, *War by Stealth: Australians and the Allied Intelligence Bureau 1942–1945*, Melbourne: Melbourne University Press, 1996, pp. 215.

23 Powell, *War by Stealth*, p. 346. See also 'Journalist, WREN, and Airways PRO', *The Argus*, Melbourne, 25 May 1946, p. 11. *The Argus* reported that Mrs Eve Walker had been a journalist for the *Daily Mail* before the war and had served in the WRNS in Australia and in New Guinea. In May 1946, she returned to Australia as the only female executive, a public relations officer for British Overseas Airways Corporation (BOAC), to carry out liaison work with Qantas officers with whom she had been 'pen friends' for years. She married Group Captain Clive Alexander Brewster-Joske in Fiji on 24 July 1946 and was widowed on Wednesday 23 April 1947 when her husband fell 80 feet (24 metres) from a window at the Taj Mahal Hotel in Bombay. See 'Former RAAF Officer killed in fall', *Sydney Morning Herald*, 25 April 1947, p. 1. The widowed Eve Brewster continued in journalism, having a story, 'Business kit', about the way Japanese businessmen dressed in Tokyo published in the Australian press. See *Gippsland Times*, 24 January 1949, p. 1; *Border Watch*, 29 January 1949, p. 10; *Kalgoorlie Miner*, 1 February 1949, p. 2.

24 'Journalist, WREN, and Airways PRO', *The Argus*, 25 May 1946, p. 11 and *Sydney Morning Herald*, 22 May 1946, p. 7.

25 Report by Lt Colonel E.A. Airy on 15 August – 8 October 1944 visit, 18 October 1944, p. 7, National Archives, UK, KV 4/453.

26 Supplement, *London Gazette*, 24 January 1941, p. 469.

27 Report by Lt Colonel E.A. Airy, 18 October 1944, p. 6, National Archives, UK, KV 4/453.

28 *Sydney Morning Herald*, 22 May 1946, p. 7.

29 Report by Lt Colonel E.A. Airy, 18 October 1944, p. 6, National Archives, UK, KV 4/453.
30 Report by Lt Colonel E.A. Airy, 18 October 1944, p. 6, National Archives, UK, KV 4/453. A hostile service is any intelligence organisation believed to be conducting collection operations against SIS.
31 See 'Report and recommendations of Alex M. Duncan Esquire, Chief Commissioner of Police, Victoria, upon the organisation of the Security Service of the Commonwealth of Australia, 7 January 1942', 'A.M. Duncan—report on Security Service', BC1110955, NAA: A432; letter, Brigadier Simpson to Attorney-General Evatt, 21 October 1943, folio 35, BC1134482, NAA. This letter dismisses the allegations of shadowing of American officers, emphasising Commander Long's refusal to sign a statement saying he had lost confidence in Wake and the fact that US officers Simpson had spoken to had made no complaints. Despite Simpson's efforts to protect him, Wake was reduced in rank from Lieutenant Colonel to Lieutenant, his substantive rank, by General Blamey and forced to retire from the army. Blamey unsuccessfully tried to get Wake sacked as Deputy Director of the Security Service in Queensland (see letter, General T.A. Blamey to Minister for Army, 5 October 1943, 'Re Lieutenant RFB Wake (retired list)', BC1010436, NAA: MP729/8, 41/431/136).
32 Report by Lt Colonel E.A. Airy, 18 October 1944, p. 6, National Archives, KV 4/453.
33 Signals, Aldridge to CSS, 6 and 9 October 1943, National Archives, HW 52/90; report by Lt Colonel E.A. Airy 18 October 1944, p. 8, National Archives, KV 4/453. An example of the 'cloak and dagger' approach to their work may be a small news item entitled 'Rabaulians to From Ex-Services Branch', The Telegraph, Brisbane, 23 January 1943, p. 2. This article tells anyone who is interested in joining the newly reforming Rabaul branch of the Returned Sailors Soldiers and Airmen's Imperial League of Australia to contact Captain Roy Kendall, RNR, on B6635 or at his residence of Amity, Welby Street, New Farm. This looks like a quiet way of recruiting potential agents for work in New Britain and the islands.
34 Powell, War by Stealth, p. 215.
35 Message, Aldridge to CSS, 9 October 1943, National Archives, UK, HW 52/90. The decision to place the RSS under Alastair Sandford at Central Bureau was made in October 1943 following meetings between Brigadier Aldridge, Indian Army RSS; Brigadier Rogers, DMI (Australia); Kendall and Sandford. This decision was a major source of disharmony between Central Bureau, the Security Service and the army's own Signal Officer in Chief, Brigadier (later Major General) C.H. Simpson.
36 Hinsley et al., British Intelligence in the Second World War, vol. 1, p. 277.
37 Breuer, MacArthur's Undercover War, pp. 64–66.
38 Powell, War by Stealth, p. 21.
39 Powell, War by Stealth, p. 22.
40 'Directive concerning governing the organisation, co-ordination and operation of inter-Allied units', 6 July 1943, BC134232, NAA.
41 'AIB administrative adjustments', 16 April 1943, p. 1, BC134232, NAA.
42 'AIB administrative adjustments', 16 April 1943, p. 1, BC134232, NAA.

CHAPTER 16

1 Hinsley et al., British Intelligence in the Second World War, vol. 1, pp. 22–28.
2 M.S. Goodman, The Official History of the Joint Intelligence Committee, vol. 1, From the Approach of the Second World War to the Suez Crisis, London: Routledge, 2014, p. 11; Hinsley et al., British Intelligence in the Second World War, vol. 1, pp. 36–39.
3 NSA, 'The Room 40 Compromise', DOCID3978516, undated, declassified 13 June 2012. The NSA was still investigating the seriousness of the Hall-Peaslee compromise in the

mid- to late 1950s, and sensitivity was still so high the assessment was classified HVCCO, No Copy, No Dissemination. This assessment essentially blames Vice Admiral Hall for Germany creating and perfecting ENIGMA and all of its variants. The clue to the date of the NSA assessment is the use of references dated 1955.

4   Minute, 'Cryptographic organisation in Australia', Commander Long to DSC, ACNS and CNS, 28 November 1939, 'CGS Branch—Military Intelligence', BC3023506, NAA: A6923, 37/402/425.

5   JPC, First report, 6 August 1940, p. 1, 'Joint operational planning machinery', BC170619, NAA: A816, 31/301/121.

6   JPC, Agendum No. 11, 'Co-ordination and control of intelligence', 18 January 1941, p. 1, BC170619, NAA.

7   Cover letter, 6 January 1942, on draft JPC report (undated), forwarded to DCAS, DCNS, Secretary JPC and HQ Home Forces by Major General Sydney Rowell, DCGS, BC170619, NAA.

8   Minute, CAS to Secretary, Defence Committee, 27 January 1942, BC170619, NAA.

9   Minute, 'Cryptographic organisation in Australia', Commander Long to DSC, ACNS and CNS, 28 November 1939, BC3023506, NAA.

10   Minute, Rear Admiral Colvin, 12 December 1939, Annex A to Defence Committee Agenda No. 2/1940, 12 January 1940, p. 2, 'Cryptographic organisation in Australia', BC6936168, NAA: A7942, Z146.

11   Minute, Rear Admiral Colvin, 12 December 1939, Annex A to Defence Committee Agenda No. 2/1940, 12 January 1940, BC6936168, NAA.

12   Minute, Rear Admiral Colvin, 12 December 1939, Annex A to Defence Committee Agenda No. 2/1940, 12 January 1940, BC6936168, NAA.

13   D. Horner, *Crisis of Command: Australian Generalship and the Japanese Threat, 1941–1943*, Canberra: Australian National University Press, 1978, p. 7, and financial statistics, *Year Book Australia*, no. 32, Canberra: Commonwealth of Australia, 1939, Defence, p. 240.

14   A.B. Lodge, 'Squires, Ernest Ker (1882–1940)', *Australian Dictionary of Biography*, adb. anu.edu.au/biography/squires-ernest-ker-8613/text15045, accessed 3 July 2016.

15   Minute, Lt General E.K. Squires, CGS, to CNS, 16 December 1939, Annex B to Defence Committee Agenda No. 2/1940, 12 January 1940, BC6936168, NAA; and minute CGS to CNS, 16 December 1939, BC3023506, NAA.

16   Minute, Lt General E.K. Squires, CGS, to CNS, 16 December 1939, Annex B to Defence Committee Agenda No. 2/1940, 12 January 1940, BC6936168, NAA.

17   Minute, Rear Admiral Colvin, 12 December 1939, Annex A to Defence Committee Agenda No. 2/1940, 12 January 1940, BC6936168, NAA; and minute, Air Vice Marshal S.J. Goble, CAS, 21 December 1939, Annex B to Defence Committee Agenda No. 2/1940, 12 January 1940, BC6936168, NAA.

18   Minute, 'Defence Committee meeting held Thursday 15 February 1940', BC6936168, NAA.

19   Letter, Prime Minister Menzies to Secretary of State, Dominion Affairs, 11 April 1940, BC6936168, NAA.

20   Letter, Secretary of State for the Dominions, 15 October 1940, BC6936168, NAA.

21   Letter, Secretary of State for the Dominions, 15 October 1940, BC6936168, NAA.

22   Letter, Secretary of State for the Dominions, 15 October 1940, BC6936168, NAA.

23   Minute, 'Defence Committee meeting held Thursday 5 December 1940', BC6936168, NAA.

24   Report, Major Powell, Intelligence Section, Eastern Command, to Intelligence Section, General Staff, Army HQ, Melbourne, 18 October 1940, BC3023506, NAA.

25 Report, Major Powell to Intelligence Section, 18 October 1940, BC3023506, NAA. This letter is mentioned in two recent works on Australia's wartime cryptanalytical effort: D. Dufty, *The Secret Code-Breakers of Central Bureau: How Australia's Signals-Intelligence Network Helped Shorten the Pacific War*, Melbourne: Scribe, 2017, pp. 25–26; C. Collie, *Code Breakers: Inside the Shadow World of Signals Intelligence in Australia's Two Bletchley Parks*, Sydney: Allen & Unwin, 2017, pp. 48–49. Both have wisely not publicised the names of the individuals involved.

26 Pfennigwerth, *Missing Pieces: The Intelligence Jigsaw and RAN Operations from 1939–71*, Canberra: Department of Defence, 2008, p. 24.

27 Pfennigwerth, *A Man of Intelligence*, p. 151.

28 Pfennigwerth, *A Man of Intelligence*, pp. 151–59.

29 Pfennigwerth, *A Man of Intelligence*, pp. 151–59.

30 'Officers of the Cryptographic Section of the Melbourne Communications Intelligence Unit, 1940–1945', p. 1, 'Volume of technical records containing details of codes and cyphers', BC859305, NAA: B5554, WHOLE SERIES.

31 'Officers of the Cryptographic Section of the Melbourne Communications Intelligence Unit, 1940–1945', p. 1, BC859305, NAA. It appears that Keith Miller and Nave had served together aboard HMAS *Brisbane* in 1924. See Department of Defence, *The Navy List*, 1 October 1924, p. 26; 'MILLER KEITH STAFFORD: Date of birth—20 Jan 1904', BC5332031, NAA: A6769, MILLER K S.

32 'Volume of technical records containing details of codes and cyphers', folio 375, BC859305, NAA.

33 'MILLER KEITH STAFFORD: Date of birth—20 Jan 1904', BC5332031, NAA.

34 Notes of conference in ACNB board room, 4 January 1941, p. 1, 'Appreciation of Far Eastern situation—30th Sept. 1940', BC396338, NAA: MP1185/5, 1945/2/6.

35 Notes of conference in ACNB board room, 4 January 1941, p. 5, BC396338, NAA.

36 Disposition is a technical term combining the geographical position of a naval unit with indications of the orientation or behaviour of the unit. The way a unit is operated provides insights into whether it is conducting innocent passage, or potentially hostile or intelligence collection activity.

37 Notes of conference in ACNB board room, 4 January 1941, p. 5, BC396338, NAA.

38 Notes of conference in ACNB board room, 4 January 1941, p. 7, BC396338, NAA.

39 Notes of conference in ACNB board room, 4 January 1941, p. 7, BC396338, NAA.

40 J.F. Straczek, 'The origins and development of Royal Australian Naval signals intelligence', pp. 182–83.

41 Notes on conference, 2 May 1941, p. 1, BC3023506, NAA.

42 Notes on conference, 2 May 1941, p. 1, BC3023506, NAA.

43 Notes on conference, 2 May 1941, p. 1, BC3023506, NAA.

44 Notes on conference, 2 May 1941, p. 1, BC3023506, NAA.

45 'Cryptographic organisation in Australia', DDMI, 8 May 1941, BC3023506, NAA.

46 Minute, CNS to CGS, 15 May 1941, BC3023506, NAA.

47 Letter, GOC, Eastern Command, to Secretary, Military Board, 1 July 1941, BC3023506, NAA.

48 Minute, CNS to CGS, 15 May 1941, BC3023506, NAA.

49 Minute, DMO&I to GOC, Eastern Command, 26 May 1941, BC3023506, NAA.

50 Minute, CGS to Minister for the Army, 3 June 1941, BC3023506, NAA.

51 Minute, CGS to CNS and GOC, Eastern Command, 12 June 1941, BC3023506, NAA.

52 Letter, Vice-Chancellor, University of Sydney, to GOC, Eastern Command, 4 June 1941, BC3023506, NAA.

53 Minute, Private Secretary, Army Minister, to Adjutant General, 14 July 1941, BC3023506, NAA.

54 Handwritten file note, 19 July 1941, BC3023506, NAA.

55 Minute, Secretary, Department of the Army, to Secretary, Military Board, 19 September 1941, BC3023506, NAA.

56 See 'Pearl Harbor review: The Black Chamber', NSA, www.nsa.gov/about/cryptologic-heritage/center-cryptologic-history/pearl-harbor-review/black-chamber.shtml, accessed 25 August 2017.

57 Minute DCGS to Secretary, Department of Army, 4 October 1941, BC3023506, NAA.

58 Minute, 'Defence Committee meeting held Friday 28 November 1941', BC3023506, NAA.

59 Minute, 'Defence Committee meeting held Friday 28 November 1941', BC3023506, NAA.

60 'Volume of technical records containing details of codes and cyphers', folio 375, BC859305, NAA.

61 Letter, Lt Colonel Little to CMI, 24 October 1942, BC859305, NAA; 'Volume of technical records containing details of codes and cyphers', folio 375 and memo, 26 November 1942, BC3023506, NAA.

62 Letter, Mr Archer to Colonel Little, received 24 October 1942, p. 3, BC3023506, NAA; Smith, *The Emperor's Codes*, p. 172; Straczek, 'The origins and development of Royal Australian Naval signals intelligence', p. 209.

CHAPTER 17

1 Telegram 21/108, 19 January 1942, 'War Section—Secret Intelligence Service', BC206045, NAA: A1608, E39/2/1.

2 Telegram 319, 19 February 1942, 'War Records—transfer of American W/T intelligence officers to Australia', BC182723, NAA: A981, WAR 40.

3 Telegram 319, 19 February 1942, BC182723, NAA.

4 Telegram 224, CNS via External Affairs to Naval Attaché, Washington, 23 February 1942, BC182723, NAA.

5 S.A. Maneki, *The Quiet Heroes of the Southwest Pacific Theater: An Oral History of the Men and Women of CBB and FRUMEL*, Fort George G. Mead, Maryland: Center for Cryptologic History, NSA, 2007, p. 5.

6 Foreign Histories Division, *Japan: History of the Imperial General Headquarters*, rev. edn, Monograph No. 45, Fort Leavenworth, Kansas: HQ, US Army, 1959, p. 140.

7 Maneki, *The Quiet Heroes*, p. 56.

8 Maneki, *The Quiet Heroes*, p. 57.

9 Maneki, *The Quiet Heroes*, p. 56.

10 Maneki, *The Quiet Heroes*, p. 56.

11 Maneki, *The Quiet Heroes*, p. 64.

12 Maneki, *The Quiet Heroes*, p. 68.

13 Maneki, *The Quiet Heroes*, p. 62.

14 *Formidable* had been in repair at Norfolk Naval Base in the United States and at Belfast in Northern Ireland since July 1941, and *Indomitable* had just been commissioned and completed her maiden voyage to the West Indies in November 1941. All three main units were still working up their crews, and had all arrived at Colombo since January 1942. Vice Admiral Somerville arrived on board *Formidable* on 24 March and only hoisted his flag on *Warspite* that day. See Naval Historical Branch, Ministry of Defence (Navy), *War with Japan*, vol. II, *Defensive Phase*, London: HMSO, 1995, pp. 120–3.

15 Smith, *The Emperor's Codes*, pp. 128–29.

16 J.R.M. Butler, *History of the Second World War*, vol. III, part II, *Grand Strategy*, London: HMSO], 1964, p. 487. See also J. Pradus, *Combined Fleet Decoded: The Secret History of American Intelligence and the Japanese Navy in World War II*, New York: Random House, 1995, p. 274.

17 Nagumo's delay was due to his hoping he could repeat the success of his Sunday-morning attack on Pearl Harbor by attacking the British in Colombo on Easter Sunday, 5 April, four days later than originally intended.

18 I.W. Toll, *Pacific Crucible: War at Sea in the Pacific, 1941–1942*, New York: W.W. Norton & Co., 2012, pp. 283–96.

19 Toll, *Pacific Crucible*, p. 295.

20 Toll, *Pacific Crucible*, pp. 283–96.

21 Smith, *The Emperor's Codes*, p. 134. MO was thought to be the diagraph for Port Moresby.

22 Smith, *The Emperor's Codes*, p. 134.

23 Prados, *Combined Fleet Decoded*, p. 299.

24 Prados, *Combined Fleet Decoded*, p. 299.

25 Toll, *Pacific Crucible*, p. 293.

26 Prados, *Combined Fleet Decoded*, p. 299.

27 Messages 1, 17 April, 1, 18 April, and 1, 19 April 1942, BC856345, 'FRUMEL records (incomplete) of communications intelligence relating to the Coral Sea Battle', NAA: B5555, 3.

28 Message 3, 9 April 1942, BC856345, NAA.

29 Messages 1, 17 April, 1, 18 April and 1, 19 April 1942, BC856345, NAA.

30 Messages 2, 9 April 1942, and 4, 31 December 1941, BC856345, NAA. It was thus old information.

31 Messages 1, 2, 4 and 7, 27 April 1942, BC856345, NAA.

32 Messages 1, 2, 4 and 7, 27 April 1942, BC856345, NAA.

33 Prados, *Combined Fleet Decoded*, pp. 318–19; Smith, *The Emperor's Codes*, p. 135.

34 Messages 21, 27 and 30, 8 May 1942, BC856345, NAA.

35 Message 30, 8 May 1942, BC856345, NAA.

36 Message 13, 10 May 1942, BC856345, NAA. Following the battles around Java, the commanding officers of IJN ships that had been picked up by the *Akebono Maru* had their messages routed via her call sign.

37 Message 30, 8 May 1942, BC856345, NAA.

38 W.J. Holmes, *Double-edged Secrets: US Naval Intelligence Operations in the Pacific during World War II*, Annapolis, Maryland: US Naval Institute, 1979, p. 86.

39 Prados, *Combined Fleet Decoded*, p. 317.

40 Prados, *Combined Fleet Decoded*, p. 317.

41 Prados, *Combined Fleet Decoded*, pp. 317–18.

42 Prados, *Combined Fleet Decoded*, pp. 318.

43 Message 1, 18 May 1942, 'FRUMEL records (incomplete) of communications intelligence relating to the Midway Battle', BC856346, NAA: B5555, 4.

44 Message 2, 18 May 1942, BC856346, NAA.

45 Message 3, 18 May 1942, BC856346, NAA.

46 Messages 1, 20 May 1942, BC856346, NAA.

47 Message 2, 21 May 1942, BC856346, NAA.

48 Messages 1 and 2, 23 May 1942, BC856346, NAA.

49 Messages 1 and 2, 24 May 1942, BC856346, NAA.

50 Messages 26 and 27 May 1942, BC856346, NAA.

51 Messages 1 and 2, 29 May 1942, BC856346, NAA.

52 Message 2 June 1942, BC856346, NAA.

53 Messages 4 to 8 June 1942, BC856346, NAA.

54 Message 1, 18 June 1942, BC856346, NAA.

55 Foreign Histories Division, *History of the Imperial General Headquarters*, p. 72.

56 Message, 14 June 1942, BC856346, NAA; Foreign Histories Division, *History of the Imperial General Headquarters*, p. 72.

57 Prados, *Combined Fleet Decoded*, p. 359.

58 Toshikazu Ohmae, 'The Battle of Savo Island', in D.C. Evans (ed.), *The Japanese in World War II*, 2nd edn, Annapolis, Maryland: Naval Institute Press, 1986, pp. 222–23.

59 Ohmae, 'The Battle of Savo Island', pp. 222–23; Feldt, *The Coastwatchers*, p. 112.

60 Prados, *Combined Fleet Decoded*, pp. 362–64.

61 Prados, *Combined Fleet Decoded*, pp. 362.

62 Prados, *Combined Fleet Decoded*, pp. 363.

63 Prados, *Combined Fleet Decoded*, pp. 363.

64 Prados, *Combined Fleet Decoded*, pp. 362.

65 Naval Staff Tactical and Staff Duties Division, Historical Section, Admiralty, *Naval Operations in the Campaign for Guadalcanal, August 1942 – February 1943*, Battle Summary No. 21, London: Admiralty, 1949, p. 12.

66 Admiralty, *Naval Operations in the Campaign for Guadalcanal*, p. 12, fn 2.

67 Sanitisation is the alteration of intelligence reports to hide the true source of the information being provided.

68 Captain Bode shot himself on 19 April and died of his wound on 20 April 1943. It appears he learned that he was criticised for his actions at Savo Island in a report by Admiral Hepburn.

69 Prados, *Combined Fleet Decoded*, p. 371.

70 Admiralty, *Naval Operations in the Campaign for Guadalcanal*, p. 33, fn 3.

71 W.J. Holmes, *Double-edged Secrets: Naval Intelligence Operations in the Pacific during World War II*, p. 58; Prados, *Combined Fleet Decoded*, p. 172; J. Winton, *Ultra in the Pacific: How Breaking Japanese Codes and Ciphers Affected Naval Operations Against Japan*, London: Leo Cooper, 1993, pp. 32–33. Gilvin Cooper and his team, all FRUPAC, served on *Enterprise* at Wake Island and on the Doolittle Raid, as well as during the battles of Coral Sea, Midway and the Guadalcanal campaign. By this stage of the war, it appears that FRUPAC was providing mobile SIGINT teams for all carriers on operations.

72 Admiralty, *Naval Operations in the Campaign for Guadalcanal*, p. 37.

73 Admiralty, *Naval Operations in the Campaign for Guadalcanal*, p. 43.

74 Admiralty, *Naval Operations in the Campaign for Guadalcanal*, Appendix E. By comparison, the US Navy lost two battleships damaged, two carriers sunk and two damaged, eight cruisers sunk and eleven damaged, and fifteen destroyers sunk and nine damaged. The United States could easily sustain this level of attrition.

75 Note, Sandford, 21 January 1945, folio 87, 'Australian Military Forces—Central Bureau—administration of', BC3023436, NAA: A6923, 16/6/289.

76 Note, Sandford, 21 January 1945, folio 87, BC3023436, NAA.

77 Letter, Sandford to DMI, 26 January 1945, folio 88, BC3023436, NAA.

CHAPTER 18

1 Minute, to DCGS DMI, 3 March 1942, 'Australian Military Forces—Y Organisation in Australia', BC3023504, NAA: A6923, SI/2.

2 G. Ballard, *On Ultra Active Service: The Story of Australia's Signals Intelligence Operation During World War II*, Melbourne: Spectrum Publications, 1991, p. 142.

3   Ballard, *On Ultra Active Service*, pp. 145–46.
4   Ballard, *On Ultra Active Service*, pp. 145–46.
5   Signal, to ARMINDIA, 23 April 1942, BC3023436, NAA.
6   Minute, to DCGS DMI, 3 March 1942, BC3023504, NAA.
7   Minute, to DCGS DMI, 3 March 1942, BC3023504, NAA.
8   Minute, to DCGS DMI, 3 March 1942, BC3023504, NAA.
9   Minute, to DCGS, 3 March 1942, BC3023504, NAA.
10 Ballard, *On Ultra Active Service*, p. 50.
11 Ballard, *On Ultra Active Service*, p. 136.
12 Ballard, *On Ultra Active Service*, p. 141.
13 Ballard, *On Ultra Active Service*, p. 146.
14 Smith, *The Emperor's Codes*, pp. 80, 119.
15 Ballard, *On Ultra Active Service*, p. 146.
16 Minute, Colonel C.G. Roberts, DMI, 3 March 1942, BC3023504, NAA.
17 Minute, Colonel C.G. Roberts, DMI, 3 March 1942, BC3023504, NAA.
18 Minute, Colonel Roberts, DMI, 3 March 1942, BC3023504, NAA.
19 Copy of 'Notes on the organisation of signals intelligence in Australia and New Zealand', National Archives, UK, HW 52/93; 'Central Bureau Technical Records Part A—Organisation', BC3207624, NAA: B5436, Part A.
20 Minute, to DCGS Colonel C.G. Roberts, DMI, 3 March 1942, BC3023504, NAA.
21 Minutes of 'Y' Committee, 7 April 1942, BC3023504, NAA.
22 Conference minutes, 'Co-ordination of "Y" intelligence', 6 April 1942, BC3023504, NAA.
23 Minute, ADMI to Hirings, 15 April 1942, BC3023504, NAA.
24 Conference minutes, 'Co-ordination of "Y" intelligence', 6 April 1942, BC3023504, NAA.
25 ZYMOTIC 11 of 3/11 for Travis Sandford, sent 2210Z, 3 November 1943, National Archives, UK, HW 52/93.
26 Rough notes on Australia undated, National Archives, UK, HW 52/93.
27 Minutes, 'Y' Committee, 7 April 1942, BC3023504, NAA.
28 Minutes, 'Y' Committee, 10 April 1942, BC3023504, NAA.
29 Minutes, 'Y' Committee, 10 April 1942, BC3023504, NAA.
30 Minutes, 'Y' Committee, 10 April 1942, BC3023504, NAA.
31 Minute, DMI to A Branch, 14 April 1942, BC3023504, NAA.
32 Hinsley et al., *British Intelligence in the Second World War*, vol. 1, p. 219.
33 Hinsley et al., *British Intelligence in the Second World War*, vol. 1, p. 138.
34 Hinsley et al., *British Intelligence in the Second World War*, vol. 1, pp. 571–72.
35 Minutes, 'Y' Committee, 13 May 1942, BC3023504, NAA.
36 Letter, Newman to Sandford, dated in pencil May 1942, BC3023504, NAA.
37 Letter, Newman, 25 July 1942, BC3023504, NAA. Even in his apology, Newman could not help having a dig by pointing out that 'the recent changes of major call signs . . . has been completely flogged out by a well-trained gun's crew of four telegraphist WRANS within 23 hours'. Someone, probably Alastair Sandford, has marked this passage in pencil, BC3023504, NAA.
38 Minutes, 'Y' Committee, 16 June 1942, BC3023504, NAA.
39 Minutes, 'Y' Committee, 16 June 1942, BC3023504, NAA.
40 Board, 'Top Secret ULTRA critique' by Colonel A. Sinkov, Lt Colonel Sandford and Wing Commander H. Roy Booth, RAAF, p. 1, National Archives, UK, HW 52/93; Maneki, *The Quiet Heroes*, p. 1.
41 Another organisation with which Central Bureau maintained an excellent relationship was the Allied Translation and Interpreter Service (ATIS) based in Brisbane. ATIS, led

by Colonel S.F. Mashbir, was charged with conducting interrogations of Japanese POWs and exploiting captured documents. Around 2000 American soldiers of Japanese heritage served in this unit, and it was a vital cog in the intelligence machinery of the SWPA. In early 1942, Mic Sandford had taken personal control of this work before handing it over to the ATIS. See Maneki, *The Quiet Heroes*, p. 28; minutes, 'Y' Committee, 10 April 1942, BC3023504, NAA.

42 E.J. Drea, *MacArthur's ULTRA: Codebreaking and the War Against Japan, 1942–1945*, Lawrence, Kansas: University Press of Kansas, 1992, pp. 9–19. Akin, Sinkov and Sherr were all SIGINT specialists who had worked under William F. Friedman in the 1930s.

43 Minutes, 'Y' Committee, 2 May 1942, BC3023504, NAA.

44 Minutes, 'Y' Committee, 28 May 1942, BC3023504, NAA.

45 Minutes, 'Y' Meeting, 6 July 1942, BC3023504, NAA.

46 Minutes, 'Y' Committee, 4 June 1942, BC3023504, NAA.

47 Minutes, 'Y' Committee, 2 and 31 July 1942, BC3023504, NAA.

48 Minutes, 'Y' Committee, 16 June 1942, BC3023504, NAA.

49 Minute, Signal Officer in Chief to DDMI, 20 August 1942.

50 Minutes, 'Y' Committee, 31 July 1942, BC3023504, NAA.

51 Minutes, 'Y' Committee, 4 June 1942, BC3023504, NAA.

52 Letter, DCGS to QMG, 7 May 1942, BC3023504, NAA.

53 Letter, DMI to ACGS, 18 June 1942, BC3023504, NAA.

54 Minute, Sandford to DMI, 'Raising of further special int, personnel sections', 30 June 1942, BC3023504, NAA; minute, DMI to DMO&P, 8 July 1942, BC3023504, NAA.

55 Maneki, *The Quiet Heroes*, p. 39.

56 Maneki, *The Quiet Heroes*, p. 39.

57 National Archives, UK, HW 52/93; BC3207624, NAA.

CHAPTER 19

1 Maneki, *The Quiet Heroes*, pp. 57, 90.

2 GC&CS was reading the Machine, Fuji, LA and X ciphers, and Delhi was reading Fuji, LA and X. See letter, Brigadier J.P.T. O'Brien, Office of DMI, India, to Lt Colonel Rogers, DMI Australia, 15 May 1943, BC3023506, NAA.

3 Hinsley et al., *British Intelligence in the Second World War*, vol. 2, fn, p. 79.

4 '"C" daily ULTRA file for Prime Minister', National Archives, UK, HW 1/420.

5 Hinsley et al., *British Intelligence in the Second World War*, vol. 3, part 1, p. 515.

6 Hinsley et al., *British Intelligence in the Second World War*, vol. 3, part 2, pp. 787–92.

7 Letter, Archer to Colonel Little, received 24 October 1942, BC3023506, NAA.

8 Memorandum, Fabian to Commander McCollum, 29 January 1943, US Archives, A1/27, 5500/1 FRUMEL (Fleet Radio Unit Melbourne) Security, NAI6230486, Declassification Authority 003012.

9 Memorandum, Fabian to Commander McCollum, 29 January 1943, US Archives, A1/27, 5500/1.

10 Letter, Archer to Colonel Little, received 24 October 1942, BC3023506, NAA. The impetus for Archer's letter was a remark made by Lt Colonel Little to Professor Trendall that the work 'might be shifted to the north'.

11 Letter, Archer to Colonel Little, received 24 October 1942, BC3023506, NAA.

12 Letter, Archer to Colonel Little, received 24 October 1942, p. 2, BC3023506, NAA.

13 Letter, Lt Colonel Little to DMI, 24 October 1942, p. 2, BC3023506, NAA.

14 Letter, Lt Colonel Little to DMI, 24 October 1942, p. 2, BC3023506, NAA.

15 Memorandum, Fabian to Commander McCollum, 29 January 1943, US Archives, A1/27, 5500/1.

16 Letter, 6 October 1943, Admiral King to C-in-C, Pacific Fleet, US Archives, A7/2, CINCPAC FILES 1943 (SECRET), Censorship, NAI6077910, Declassification Authority NND745002.

17 Letter, Commander Allied Naval Forces, South West Pacific to Allied Naval Activities, Monterey Building, 15 June 1942 [SIC] 1943, US Archives, A1/27, 5500/1 FRUMEL (Fleet Radio Unit, Melbourne, Australia) SECURITY, NAI6230486, Declassification Authority 003012.

18 Letter, Lt Colonel Little to DMI, 24 October 1942, p. 2, BC3023506, NAA.

19 For the best description of how extensively Soviet intelligence had penetrated Australian governmental, scientific and academic institutions see D. Horner, *The Spy Catchers: The Official History of ASIO 1949–1963*, Sydney: Allen & Unwin, 2014, pp. 23–91. See also unpublished research J. Fahey, 'Spies, traitors and unfortunates', which lists 214 Australians identified by Operation VENONA, the successful postwar SIGINT attack on NKGB one-time pad coded messages, and from the A6119 series of ASIO files held at NAA, particularly those detailing observation and surveillance reports on identified or suspected NKGB officials.

20 Letter, Dennison to Travis, 10 December 1942, National Archives, UK, HW 52/93.

21 Letter, Dennison to Travis, 10 December 1942, National Archives, UK, HW 52/93.

22 Letter, Dennison to Travis, 10 December 1942, National Archives, UK, HW 52/93.

23 Letter, Dennison to Travis, 10 December 1942, National Archives, UK, HW 52/93.

24 Message CXG 437, Major General Dewing to C, paragraph 8, 13 March 1943, National Archives, UK, HW 52/93.

25 Letter DDMI, Lt Colonel Little, to DMI, AHQ, Wellington, 27 January 1943, folio 345, BC3023506, NAA; letter, Lt Colonel Little to DMI, 1 February 1943, folio 347, BC3023506, NAA.

26 Letter, DDMI to DMI, AHQ, 27 January 1943, folio 345, BC3023506, NAA; letter, Lt Colonel Little to DMI, 1 February 1943, folio 347, BC3023506, NAA.

27 Letter, Sir Ronald Cross, British High Commissioner, to John Curtin, Prime Minister, 5 January 1943, 'Wireless stations carrying intercepted enemy traffic', BC171228, NAA: A816, 48/302/64.

28 Signal, BRILIST Melbourne to War Office, 30 March 1943, National Archives, UK, HW 52/93.

29 Letter, DDMI, Lt Colonel Little, to DMI, AHQ, Wellington, 27 January 1943, folio 345, BC3023506, NAA; letter, Lt Colonel Little to DMI, 1 February 1943, folio 347, BC3023506, NAA.

30 Letter, Lt Colonel Little to Brigadier J.P.T. O'Brien, Office of DMI, 9 April 1943, BC3023506, NAA.

31 Letter, Brigadier J.P.T. O'Brien, Office of DMI, India, to Brigadier Rogers, DMI Australia, 15 May 1943, BC3023506, NAA.

32 Letter, Brigadier J.P.T. O'Brien, Office of DMI, India, to Lt Colonel Rogers, DMI Australia, 15 May 1943, BC3023506, NAA.

33 Letter, Lt Colonel Sandford to ADMI, Lt Colonel Little, 16 July 1943, folios 266, 265, BC3023506, NAA.

34 Memo, Williams to DD (6) and Waterfield, 28 April 1943, National Archives, UK, HW 52/93.

35 Memo, Williams to DD (6) and Waterfield, 28 April 1943, National Archives, UK, HW 52/93.

36 Memo, Williams to DD (6) and Waterfield, 28 April 1943, National Archives, UK, HW 52/93.

37 Signal, War Office to CGS, New Zealand, 19 July 1943, National Archives, UK, HW 52/93.

38 Signal, War Office to CGS, New Zealand, 19 July 1943, National Archives, UK, HW 52/93. This signal leaves little doubt that London and Washington regarded Alastair Sandford as Australia's representative for 'Y' matters, and that Australia was being included in high-level policy decisions affecting Japanese 'Y' matters. It is proof Australia had been brought inside the tent. The fact that Australia was not informed of the discussions between New Zealand and Britain but that the British advised the New Zealand CGS to speak directly to Australia via Sandford, while keeping London advised, shows that Central Bureau, and particularly Alastair Sandford, were held in high regard in London and Washington, even if the Australian government was not.

39 Minutes, meeting held at Bletchley Park, 10 May 1943, National Archives, UK, HW 52/93; signal, War Office to CGS New Zealand, 19 July 1943, National Archives, UK, HW 52/93.

40 Memo, Williams to Sandford, 10 May 1943, National Archives, UK, HW 52/93.

41 Memo, Williams to Sandford, 10 May 1943, National Archives, UK, HW 52/93.

42 Notes, 'Wireless intercept ("Y") in the field, 32/Wireless/717 (SD!)', 26 May 1943, BC3023504, NAA.

43 Notes, 'Wireless intercept ("Y") in the field, 32/Wireless/717 (SD!)', 26 May 1943, pp. 1–2, BC3023504, NAA.

44 Notes, 'Wireless intercept ("Y") in the field, 32/Wireless/717 (SD!)', 26 May 1943, p. 7, BC3023504, NAA.

45 Notes, 'Wireless intercept ("Y") in the field, 32/Wireless/717 (SD!)', 26 May 1943, p. 7, BC3023504, NAA.

46 Winston Churchill was the only official who had untrammelled access to SIGINT. It worked with Churchill because he was a very sophisticated consumer of intelligence.

47 Notes, 'Wireless intercept ("Y") in the field, 32/Wireless/717 (SD!)', 26 May 1943, p. 7, BC3023504, NAA.

48 Letter, CGS to Major General Dewing, British MLO, Australia, 16 June 1943; letter, Consul Graves to Lt Colonel Little, 10 June 1943; letter, CGS, Lt General Northcott to Colonel Hodgson, External Affairs, 14 June 1943, all in BC3023506, NAA.

49 Letters, CGS, General Dewing, Graves, Little, Northcott and Hodgson, June 1943, BC3023506, NAA.

50 Letter, CGS to Major General Dewing, British MLO, Australia, 16 June 1943, BC3023506, NAA.

51 Letter, CGS to Major General Dewing, British MLO, Australia, 16 June 1943, BC3023506, NAA.

52 ' "Y" organisation in Australia and New Zealand', 3 January 1944, National Archives, UK, HW 52/93.

53 Letter, Lt Colonel Little to DMI, 24 October 1942, p. 2, BC3023506, NAA.

54 Letter, DMI to Lt Colonel Little, 10 April 1943, p. 2, BC3023506, NAA.

55 Letter, DMI to Lt Colonel Little, 10 April 1943, p. 2, BC3023506, NAA.

56 Letter, DMI to Lt Colonel Little, 10 April 1943, p. 2, BC3023506, NAA.

57 Letter, DMI to Lt Colonel Little, 10 April 1943, p. 2, BC3023506, NAA.

58 Letter, Sandford to Lt Colonel Little, 3 February 1944, BC3023506, NAA.

59 Letter, Sandford to Lt Colonel Little, 3 February 1944; letter, DMI to ADMI, LHQ, 29 March 1944; letter, ADMI to DMI, GHQ, New Zealand, 12 April 1944; letter to DNI, ADMI, 22 April 1944, all in BC3023506, NAA. All of this correspondence forbids any

Australian or New Zealand officers or officials to show or even speak of the existence of the Washington diplomatic précis to any Allied officer at all.

60 Letter, Sandford to Lt Colonel Little, 3 February 1944, BC3023506, NAA.
61 Notes of meeting, 21 January 1944, folio 63, BC3023436, NAA.
62 Notes of meeting, 21 January 1944, folio 63, BC3023436, NAA.
63 Notes of meeting, 21 January 1944, folio 63, BC3023436, NAA.
64 Notes of meeting, 21 January 1944, folio 63, BC3023436, NAA.

CHAPTER 20

1 Letter, Sandford to Little, 14 December 1944, 'Australian Military Forces—[Rogers] Director of Military Intelligence—DMI—Central Bureau', BC3023441, NAA: A6923, SI/8.
2 Letter, Sandford to Little, 14 December 1944, BC3023441, NAA.
3 Letter, Sandford to Little, 14 December 1944, BC3023441, NAA.
4 Letter, Sandford to Little, 14 December 1944, BC3023441, NAA.
5 Letter, Sandford to Little, 14 December 1944, BC3023441, NAA.
6 Teleprinter message No. 1539, 12 August 1940, 'Japan & Australia Intercepted Messages from Japanese Consul-General', BC170257, NAA: A816/19, 304/420.
7 Teleprinter message No. 1539, 12 August 1940, BC170257, NAA.
8 Teleprinter message No. 1539, 12 August 1940, BC170257, NAA.
9 Teleprinter message, Secretary, Prime Minister's Department to Secretary, Department of Defence Co-ordination, 29 September 1939, BC170257, NAA.
10 Marginal note mentioning Captain Foley as having handled the CNS's copy on Circulation Advice, 30 September 1939, BC170257, NAA.
11 Cover Sheet signed by relevant officers and officials, BC170257, NAA.
12 Hasluck, *Diplomatic Witness: Australian Foreign Affairs 1941–1947*, Melbourne: Melbourne University Press, 1980, p. 4.
13 Hasluck, *Diplomatic Witness*, pp. 2–6.
14 Hasluck, *Diplomatic Witness*, p. 4.il
15 Telegrams, M.84, Menzies to Fadden, 26 April 1941 and M.86, Menzies to Fadden, 26 April 1941, '[Personal papers of Prime Minister Menzies] Mr Menzies: M's [cables re war situation, defence supplies etc.]', BC257498, NAA: CP290/9, 13; 'Military advice to government', *Sydney Morning Herald*, 23 April 1941, p. 11.
16 File note, 16 September 1941, 'Intelligence organisation in Australia', National Archives, UK, KV 4/453.
17 File note, 16 September 1941, National Archives, UK, KV 4/453.
18 Signal, '"Y" Board matters', Sandford to Chairman, 'Y' Board, 29 July 1943, National Archives, UK, HW 52/93.
19 Message, 'C' to Dewing, 23 February 1943, National Archives, UK, HW 52/93.
20 Message, 'C' to Dewing, 23 February 1943, National Archives, UK, HW 52/93.
21 Hinsley et al., *British Intelligence in the Second World War*, vol. 2, fn p. 79.
22 Message, 'C' to Dewing to C, 23 February 1943, National Archives, UK, HW 52/93.
23 Signals CXG 435, 436, 437, Dewing to 'C', 15 March 1943, National Archives, UK, HW 52/93.
24 Signals CXG 435, 436, 437, Dewing to 'C', 15 March 1943, National Archives, UK, HW 52/93.
25 Signal, BRILIST Melbourne, 30 March 1943, National Archives, UK, HW 52/93.
26 Signal, BRILIST Melbourne, 30 March 1943, National Archives, UK, HW 52/93.
27 Signal, BRILIST Melbourne, 30 March 1943, National Archives, UK, HW 52/93.

28 Signal 226, Merry to GC&CS, 16 June 1943, National Archives, UK, HW 52/93.
29 Signal 226, Merry to GC&CS, 16 June 1943, National Archives, UK, HW 52/93.
30 Signal CXG 613, Sandford to 'C' as Chairman of 'Y' Board and Director of GC&CS, 29 July 1943, National Archives, UK, HW 52/93.
31 Signal CXG 613, 29 July 1943, National Archives, UK, HW 52/93.
32 Signal CXG 613, 29 July 1943, National Archives, UK, HW 52/93.
33 Signal 655, to Chairman 'Y' Board, 5 September 1943, National Archives, UK, HW 52/93.
34 Signal SJ 195, CSS to Brisbane, National Archives, UK, HW 52/93.
35 Letter, A. Sandford to DMI, 2 April 1945, BC3023441, NAA; Best, *British Intelligence*, p. 171.
36 Kotani, *Japanese Intelligence in World War II*, pp. 20–1.
37 Kotani, *Japanese Intelligence in World War II*, pp. 20–1.
38 Aldrich, *Intelligence and the War Against Japan*, p. 249.
39 Kotani, *Japanese Intelligence in World War II*, pp. 20–1; signal, MBJ 30965, Decrypt of message No. 79, Tokyo to Menado, Manila, 29 August 1944, BC3023441 NAA.
40 Kotani, *Japanese Intelligence in World War II*, p. 21.
41 Signal, MBJ 30965, 19 December 1944, BC3023441, NAA.
42 COBRA Messages In, Message No. 6, DTG 1005Z/6/3, '[Tanimbar, Timor, Lesser Sunda, Java—] COBRA [messages] in [Timor]', BC235162, NAA: A3269, D3/E.
43 COBRA Messages Out, Message No. 10, DTG 1500L/7/3, '[Tanimbar, Timor, Lesser Sunda, Java—] COBRA [messages] out [Timor]', BC235161, NAA: A3269, D3/F.
44 COBRA Messages Out, Message No. 10, DTG 1500L/7/3, BC235161, NAA.
45 COBRA Messages In, messages 6 and 8 with marginal note 'shown to C-in-C 15/3', BC235162, NAA.
46 ULTRA reports, p. 11, BC3023422, NAA.
47 ULTRA reports, p. 5, BC3023422, NAA.
48 Letter, Sandford to Little, 14 December 1944, BC3023441, NAA.
49 'The official history of the operations and administration of Special Operations—Australia', p. 37, BC235327, NAA: A3269, 08/A.
50 Message MBJ 30601, 12 December, and 'Resume of significant and interesting items SWAP', 13 December 1944, BC3023441, NAA.
51 Signal, MBJ 30028A, 25 November 1944, BC3023441, NAA.
52 Signal, MBJ 30028A, 25 November 1944, BC3023441, NAA; letter, Sandford to Little, 19 December 1944, BC3023441, NAA.
53 Signal, MBJ 30028A, 25 November 1944, BC3023441, NAA.
54 Letter, Sandford to Little, 19 December 1944, BC3023441, NAA.
55 Letter, Sandford to Little, 19 December 1944, BC3023441, NAA.
56 Signal, GCCS 6982 DTG011827Z, February 1945, BC3023441, NAA.
57 Letter, Sandford to Little, 25 December 1944, BC3023441, NAA.
58 Signal, MBJ 31258, 25 December 1944, BC3023441, NAA.
59 Signal, UBJ 2201, 25 January 1945, BC3023441, NAA.
60 Letter, Sandford to DMI, 25 January 1945, BC3023441, NAA.
61 Signal, UBJ 2201 (BC3023441, NAA) provided the details of the D Intelligence Operation as being SIGINT Chungking. This information was sent by Tokyo to commands throughout South-East Asia in signal 79, 29 August 1944, BC3023441, NAA.
62 Letter, ADMI to DG Security, 3 February 1945, and briefing note for C-in-C, 7 February 1945, BC3023441, NAA.
63 Signal, MIS 568, 2 April 1943, BC3023441, NAA.
64 Signal, TOPSEC 2019, 2 February 1945, BC3023441, NAA.

65 Kotani, *Japanese Intelligence in World War II*, pp. 36–37, 109.

66 Kotani, *Japanese Intelligence in World War II*, pp. 36–37, 109.

67 Kotani, *Japanese Intelligence in World War II*, pp. 36–37, 109.

68 Signal, GCCS 6982 DTG011827Z, February 1945, BC3023441, NAA.

69 File notes, ADMI re telephone call with DG Security, CGS and others, 5 February 1945, BC3023441, NAA.

70 Letter, Sandford to Little, 2 February 1945, BC3023441, NAA.

71 Letter, Sandford to Little, 2 February 1945, BC3023441, NAA.

72 Letter, Blamey to DG Security, 25 January 1945, BC3023441, NAA.

73 Report on meeting of Squadron Leader Burley and Brigadier Simpson, 1 February 1945, BC3023441, NAA.

74 Report on meeting of Burley and Simpson, 1 February 1945, BC3023441, NAA.

75 Report on meeting of Burley and Simpson, 1 February 1945, BC3023441, NAA.

76 Report on meeting of Burley and Simpson, 1 February 1945, BC3023441, NAA.

77 Report on meeting of Burley and Simpson, 1 February 1945, BC3023441, NAA.

78 Report on meeting of Burley and Simpson, 1 February 1945, BC3023441, NAA.

79 Report on meeting of Burley and Simpson, 1 February 1945, BC3023441, NAA.

80 Letter, Blamey to DG Security, 19 February 1945, BC3023441, NAA.

81 Signal, Winterbotham, in letter, Sandford to Little, 20 February 1945, BC3023441, NAA.

CHAPTER 21

1 Letter, Lt Colonel A.W. Sandford, to Lt Colonel Little, ADMI, 3 December 1943, with margin note, Lt Colonel Little, DDMI, to Professor Trendall, asking for statistics on Japanese diplomatic traffic, BC3023504, NAA. See also, minute, Sandford to Trendall, folio 157, BC3023504, NAA.

2 Letter, Sandford to Little, 3 December 1943; letter, Professor Trendall to Little, 6 December 1943; letter, Little to Sandford, 6 December 1943, all in BC3023504, NAA.

3 Letter, Professor Trendall to Sandford (?), 6 December 1943, BC3023504, NAA.

4 Minute, 'Diplomatic interception', Sandford to Trendall, undated, BC3023504, NAA. What is interesting about this minute is that the ADMI is now an information addressee, meaning that either Sandford has been given DIRLAUTH (Direct Liaison Authority) with Trendall's section or Sandford is now the Commanding Officer for Trendall's unit.

5 Letter, Little to Sandford, 6 December 1943, BC3023504, NAA.

6 Memo, Sandford to Webb, 12 April 1944, 'Australian Military Forces', BC3023487, NAA: A6923, SI/10.

7 Signal, GC&CS to CBB, 19 April 1944, BC3023487, NAA.

8 Signal, GC&CS to CBB, 18 April 1944, BC3023487, NAA.

9 Meeting of 5 August 1944, 'Decisions of Signal Intelligence Board on signal intelligence in Japan', National Archives, UK, HW 67/17.

10 Letter, British High Commissioner, Sir Ronald Cross, to Prime Minister John Curtin, 25 August 1942, BC171228, NAA. This file is a good example of the Australian government's poor security awareness, as the overall file is classified SECRET by Australia while it contains information classified at the much higher MOST SECRET and ULTRA levels.

11 Letter, Sir Ronald Cross to John Curtin, 25 August 1942, BC171228, NAA.

12 Letter, Sir Ronald Cross to John Curtin, 25 August 1942, BC171228, NAA.

13 Letter, Secretary, Department of Air, to H. Farrands, Department of Defence, 22 September 1942, BC171228, NAA.

14 Letter, Macandle, Department of the Navy, to Secretary, Department of Defence, 13 October 1942, BC171228, NAA.

15 Agendum No. 147/1942, 'Overseas network of wireless stations', 14 October 1942, BC171228, NAA.

16 Minute, 'Establishment for Central Bureau', 25 September 1942, BC3023436, NAA.

17 Memo, Secretary, Department of Defence Co-ordination, to the Minister, 22 October 1942, BC171228, NAA.

18 'Australia: Demi-official letter, General R.H. Dewing to Chief of Imperial General Staff', 2 June 1944, National Archives, UK, WO 106/4847.

19 Letter, Sir Fredrick Shedden to Secretary, Prime Minister's Department, 18 November 1942, BC171228, NAA.

20 Letter, Prime Minister to British High Commissioner, 24 November 1942, BC171228, NAA.

21 Letter, Sir Ronald Cross to John Curtin, 5 January 1943, BC171228, NAA.

22 Letter, Secretary of Defence to Defence Communications Committee, 15 January 1943, and report and decision of this committee, 22 January 1943, BC171228, NAA.

23 Letter, Fanning, Director-General, PMG Department, to Fredrick Shedden, Secretary, Department of Defence, 14 June 1943, BC171228, NAA.

24 Defence Committee Agendum No. 59/1944, 3 April 1944, BC171228, NAA.

25 Letter, Secretary, Department of Air, to Secretary, Department of Defence, 15 August 1944, BC171228, NAA.

26 10,206 Australians died in the SWPA between 1942 and 1945: 5770 army, 1094 RAN and 3342 RAAF. See 'Remembering the war in New Guinea', Australian War Memorial, ajrp.awm.gov.au/ajrp/remember.nsf/Web-Printer/58EBD6D993E15CE8CA256D05002 671FD?OpenDocument, accessed 2 October 2016. US losses were approximately 10,690, including 6790 marines and army personnel, approximately 1500 sailors in the battles of Java Sea and the Coral Sea, and 2400 USAAF aircrew in theatre. These figures do not count US Navy losses on submarines or vessels sunk during the Battle of Leyte Gulf or on other actions until late 1944.

27 War Cabinet Agendum 505/45, Signed by General Northcott, 15 May 1945, BC166599.

28 Minutes, meeting of Technical Sub-committee, 28 July 1944, National Archives, UK, HW 67/17.

29 Letter, Sandford to ADMI, 29 January 1945, BC3023504, NAA.

30 Letter, Sandford to ADMI, 29 January 1945, BC3023504, NAA.

31 Letter, Sandford to ADMI, 29 January 1945, and attachment (folios 187–89), BC3023504, NAA.

32 Letter, Little to Sandford, 5 February 1945, BC3023504, NAA.

33 War Cabinet Agendum 205/45, Copy 39, 16 May 1945, BC3023504, NAA.

34 War Cabinet minute, Appendix A to War Cabinet Agendum No. 205/45, 16 May 1945, BC3023504, NAA.

35 Report by CGS, Appendix B, War Cabinet Agendum No. 205/45, 15 May 1945, BC3023504, NAA.

36 Report by CGS, Appendix B, War Cabinet Agendum No. 205/45, 15 May 1945, BC3023504, NAA.

37 Folio 230, BC3023504, NAA.

38 Cover letter, amendment to WE 111/80M/G—Central Bureau—Intelligence Corps, 30 June 1945, 'Central Bureau—Intelligence Corps, war establishment', BC7764659, NAA: A10857, 111/80M.

39 Cover letter, amendment to WE 111/80M/G—Central Bureau—Intelligence Corps, 30 June 1945, BC7764659, NAA; Letter to DMI, 27 April 1945, BC7764659, NAA.

40 Amendment to WE of Central Bureau, 28 January 1945, BC7764659, NAA.

41   Minute, 'Re: Canadian Special W/T Group—accommodation', Lt Colonel Searl for QMG, 23 January 1945, with margin note; Little, 2 February, and minute, 'Royal Canadian Signal Personnel on Loan to AMF'; Brigadier F.R. Brunton for Adjutant-General (folio 70), 'Australian Military Forces—Canadian Special W/T', BC3023573, NAA: A6923, 16/6/502.

42   Minutes, meeting, March 1944, National Archives, UK, HW 67/17.

43   Minutes, meeting, March 1944, National Archives, UK, HW 67/17.

44   Minutes, meetings, 5 August and 17 August 1944, National Archives, UK, HW 67/17.

45   Minutes, meeting, 8 August 1944, National Archives, UK, HW 67/17.

46   Minutes, meeting, 8 August 1944, National Archives, UK, HW 67/17.

47   Letter, Sandford to DMI, 15 August 1945, BC3023504, NAA; Signal, Sandford to LANDFORCES, for DMI, 13 October 1945, BC3023504, NAA.

48   Letter, Sandford to DMI, 15 August 1945, BC3023504, NAA.

49   Signal, GCCS, to ZON103, CBB 269, and SLK 095 DTG 130930I, October 1945, BC3023504, NAA.

50   Notes on conference held 29 November 1945, called to decide disposal of Central Bureau records and other matters, pending determination of postwar policy, BC3023504, NAA.

51   'SANDFORD ALASTAIR WALLACE: Service Number—SX11231', BC6389615, NAA: B883, SX11231.

52   BC6389615, NAA.

53   BC6389615, NAA.

54   BC6389615, NAA.

55   'Proposed awards of US Decorations to Lt Col. A.W. Sandford and Maj. S.R.J. Clarke, AMF and to W/Cdr H.R. Booth', BC273037, NAA: A816, 66/301/232.

CHAPTER 22

1   Foreign Histories Division, *History of the Imperial General Headquarters*, p. 72.

2   Foreign Histories Division, *History of the Imperial General Headquarters*, p. 72.

3   'Offensive operations against Rabaul and surrounding strategic areas', in Bullard, *Japanese Army Operations in the South Pacific Area*, p. 4.

4   Foreign Histories Division, *History of the Imperial General Headquarters*, p. 72.

5   Foreign Histories Division, *History of the Imperial General Headquarters*, p. 73.

6   Foreign Histories Division, *History of the Imperial General Headquarters*, p. 74.

7   Foreign Histories Division, *History of the Imperial General Headquarters*, p. 72.

8   Foreign Histories Division, *History of the Imperial General Headquarters*, pp. 82, 97.

9   Minutes of conference, 16 April 1942, BC411640, NAA.

10   Minutes of conference, 16 April 1942, BC411640, NAA.

11   Letter, DNI Rupert Long to Feldt, 10 September 1942, for the outline plan to defeat the army's efforts to control FERDINAND, BC508663, NAA.

12   Feldt, *The Coastwatchers*, p. 100.

13   Feldt, *The Coastwatchers*, pp. 100–1.

14   'Big Man' was used to denote chieftains or tribal leaders in the islands.

15   Report, Mason to Feldt, 26 March 1943, BC509602, NAA.

16   W. Lord, *Lonely Vigil: Coast Watchers of the Solomons*, London: Allen Lane, 1978, p. 9.

17   Ken Wright, 'Read, Mason, Tashiro and the Bougainville mystery', PNGAA, 2009, www.pngaa.net/Library/Bougainville.htm, accessed 27 March 2017.

18   Ken Wright, 'Read, Mason, Tashiro and the Bougainville mystery'.

19   Feldt, *The Coastwatchers*, p. 261.

20   Signal, 0835Z/28, SIO, Port Moresby, to CSWP SIO, Townsville, 28 January 1943, 'Ferdinand party—plans, operations distribution and personnel—Section 1—Solomons

and Bougainville', BC32571390, NAA: B3476, 148 PART 2A; letter, Sub-Lt P.E. Mason to Lt Cdr H.A. Mackenzie, 26 March 1943, p. 2, BC410664, NAA. Mason's letter intimates that Ebery's death was not an accidental drowning, while Feldt says he drowned crossing the river (see Feldt, *The Coastwatchers*, p. 261). See also, report, W J. Read, 28 April 1943, in the same file. It is most likely that Ebery was deliberately killed because he was slowing down the Japanese party too much.

21 Letter, Sub-Lt P.E. Mason to Lt. Cdr H.A. Mackenzie, 26 March 1943, p. 1, BC410664, NAA.

22 Feldt, *The Coastwatchers*, p. 269.

23 Feldt, *The Coastwatchers*, p. 269.

24 Feldt, *The Coastwatchers*, p. 266.

25 Feldt, *The Coastwatchers*, pp. 268–69.

26 Feldt, *The Coastwatchers*, p. 269.

27 Letter, Colonel C.G. Roberts, Controller AIB, 15 April 1943, BC32571390, NAA.

28 Feldt, *The Coastwatchers*, p. 270; letter, Colonel C.G. Roberts, Controller AIB, 15 April 1943, BC32571390, NAA. In his letter, Roberts says 50. Because of Roberts' remoteness from the action, it is likely Feldt's number is the more accurate. It is also notable that Feldt's book, while it can be stylistically annoying, is accurate when compared with the files.

29 Feldt, *The Coastwatchers*, p. 270; letter, Colonel C.G. Roberts, Controller AIB, 15 April 1943, BC32571390, NAA.

30 Feldt, *The Coastwatchers*, p. 271.

31 Feldt, *The Coastwatchers*, p. 272.

32 Feldt, *The Coastwatchers*, p. 273.

33 Feldt, *The Coastwatchers*, pp. 273–74.

34 Feldt, *The Coastwatchers*, p. 274.

35 Feldt, *The Coastwatchers*, p. 274.

36 Feldt, *The Coastwatchers*, p. 275.

37 Feldt, *The Coastwatchers*, p. 283.

38 Feldt, *The Coastwatchers*, p. 283.

39 Signal 100238, CTF 31 to COMSOUPAC, 11 July 1943, BC32571390, NAA.

40 This explains why Fijian troops operated in this part of the South Pacific. See Feldt, *The Coastwatchers*, p. 305.

41 Feldt, *The Coastwatchers*, p. 107.

42 Gill, *Royal Australian Navy 1939–1942*, p. 72.

43 Feldt, *The Coastwatchers*, p. 108.

44 Feldt, *The Coastwatchers*, p. 33.

45 A. Kirk-Greene, *Glimpses of Empire: A Corona Anthology*, London: I.B. Taurus, 2001, p. 226.

46 Gill, *Royal Australian Navy 1942–1945*, p. 123.

47 Ruby Boye-Jones's honorary rank meant that, unlike her male counterparts, she was unpaid for her service. This action appears discriminatory, but within the circumstances is understandable. The first problem was the Australian government's ban on female service personnel serving in dangerous postings. If Boye-Jones had been appointed to a paid position, it is likely that pressure would have been brought to bear to have her returned to Australia in line with government policy. As the holder of an honorary appointment, this did not apply. The other issue was that the main reason for the appointment of FERDINAND civilians to military positions was that their families would not otherwise receive compensation in the case of their death or wounding. This did not apply to Boye-Jones, as she was living with her husband and he was receiving his salary throughout.

48 A. Powell, 'Boye-Jones, Ruby Olive (1891–1990)', *Australian Dictionary of Biography*, adb. anu.edu.au/biography/boye-jones-ruby-olive-12242, accessed 24 October 2016.

49 Letter, DNI to DSIO, Guadalcanal, 1 May 1943, BC436101, NAA.

50 Kirk-Greene, *Glimpses of Empire*, p. 226.

51 Kirk-Greene, *Glimpses of Empire*, p. 226 and Feldt, *The Coastwatchers*, pp. 106–110.

52 Kirk-Greene, *Glimpses of Empire*, p. 226.

53 Kirk-Greene, *Glimpses of Empire*, p. 226.

54 Kirk-Greene, *Glimpses of Empire*, p. 226.

55 Re-encrypting low-grade messages into a higher-level code, if true, was a highly risky one. It provided the Japanese SIGINT organisations with duplicate messages in easily broken codes and higher-grade codes. This is a major contravention of communications security, and can only indicate that the SIGINT authorities in London and Washington were not directly involved in Communications Security (COMSEC) at this stage of the war in the SWPA and Solomons.

56 Kirk-Greene, *Glimpses of Empire*, p. 226.

57 Kirk-Greene, *Glimpses of Empire*, p. 226.

58 Kirk-Greene, *Glimpses of Empire*, p. 227.

59 Gill, *Royal Australian Navy 1942–1945*, p. 123.

60 Gill, *Royal Australian Navy 1942–1945*, p. 123.

61 Gill, *Royal Australian Navy 1942–1945*, p. 137.

62 Feldt, *The Coastwatchers*, p. 112.

63 'Coastwatchers', Solomon Islands Historical Encyclopaedia 1893–1978, www.solomonencyclopaedia.net/biogs/E000068b.htm, accessed 28 March 2017.

64 Feldt, *The Coastwatchers*, pp. 152–53.

65 Feldt, *The Coastwatchers*, p. 159.

66 Feldt, *The Coastwatchers*, p. 159.

67 Feldt, *The Coastwatchers*, p. 160.

68 Feldt, *The Coastwatchers*, p. 160.

69 Prados, *Combined Fleet Decoded*, p. 363.

70 Letter, DNI Rupert Long to Feldt, 1 September 1942, BC508663, NAA.

71 Letter, Feldt to 'Cocky', DNI Rupert Long, 4 October 1942, BC508663, NAA.

72 Letter, DNI Rupert Long to Feldt, 12 October 1942, BC508663, NAA.

73 Feldt, *The Coastwatchers*, p. 161.

74 Feldt, *The Coastwatchers*, pp. 160, 388, 391, 398.

75 Signal 0835Z/28, Deputy SIO, Guadalcanal, to DNI and SIO, Townsville, 7 February 1943, BC32571390, NAA.

76 Signal 0835Z/28, 7 February 1943, BC32571390, NAA.

77 Signal 0445Z/12, High Commissioner Pacific to Secretary of State for the Colonies, 12 February 1943, BC411499, NAA. In New Guinea, punitive bombing was being used to deter indigenous villages cooperating with the Japanese. See 'Intelligence report for July 1943', A/Lt A.C. Ewing, 2 August 1943, p. 3, BC235140, NAA, for an example of the reasoning.

78 Signal 0445Z/12, 12 February 1943, BC411499, NAA.

79 Signal 0057Z/9, Australian NLO Vila to DNI Melbourne, 9 February 1943, BC32571390, NAA.

80 Feldt, *The Coastwatchers*, p. 155.

81 Feldt, *The Coastwatchers*, p. 155.

82 Feldt, *The Coastwatchers*, p. 156.

83 Feldt, *The Coastwatchers*, p. 388.

84 M.W. Clemens, 'Foreword', *Alone on Guadalcanal: A Coastwatcher's Story*, Bluejacket Books, Naval Institute Press, Annapolis, Maryland, 2004, p. i.

85 Clemens, 'Foreword', *Alone on Guadalcanal*, p. ii.

CHAPTER 23

1 Feldt, *The Coastwatchers*, p. 316; Ken Wright, 'Organisation of coastwatching in the New Guinea WW 2', September 2009, Naval Historical Society of Australia, www.navy-history.org.au/organisation-of-coastwatching-in-the-new-guinea-ww-2/3, accessed 27 November 2017.

2 Feldt, *The Coastwatchers*, p. 318, and Ken Wright, 'Organisation of coastwatching in the New Guinea WW 2'.

3 Feldt, *The Coastwatchers*, pp. 318–19.

4 Feldt, *The Coastwatchers*, p. 320.

5 Memo, DSIO Guadalcanal to DNI, 12 July 1943, BC32571390, NAA.

6 Memo, DSIO Guadalcanal to DNI, 12 July 1943, BC32571390, NAA.

7 Memo, DSIO Guadalcanal to DNI, 12 July 1943, BC32571390, NAA.

8 Memo, DNI to DSIO Guadalcanal, 2 August 1943, BC32571390, NAA.

9 Memo, DNI to DSIO Guadalcanal, 2 August 1943, BC32571390, NAA.

10 Memo, DNI to DSIO Guadalcanal, 2 August 1943, BC32571390, NAA.

11 Memo, SIO NEA to DNI, 16 August 1943, BC32571390, NAA.

12 Feldt, *The Coastwatchers*, p. 290.

13 Feldt, *The Coastwatchers*, p. 291.

14 Feldt, *The Coastwatchers*, p. 294.

15 Feldt, *The Coastwatchers*, p. 297.

16 Feldt, *The Coastwatchers*, p. 300.

17 Feldt, *The Coastwatchers*, pp. 298–99.

18 Orders, 'AIB intelligence collection parties on Bougainville', SIO NEA to Captain Robinson, AIF, and Lt Keenan, RANVR, 13 October 1943, BC32571390, NAA.

19 Feldt, *The Coastwatchers*, pp. 301–302.

20 Translation of captured Japanese documents, Kira Force, April–November 1943, BC32571390, NAA.

21 Orders, 'AIB intelligence collection parties on Bougainville', SIO NEA to Captain Robinson, AIF, and Lt Keenan, RANVR, 13 October 1943, BC32571390, NAA.

22 'Report on suspected compromise of BULL code cards number 04 and 68', likely August 1943, BC32571390, NAA.

23 Translation of captured Japanese documents, Kira Force, April–November 1943, BC32571390, NAA.

24 Handwritten minute, 28 March 1944, read by DNI Long on same day, BC32571390, NAA.

25 Memo, SIO NEA to OiC AIB Base, Milne Bay, 8 February 1944, BC32571390, NAA.

26 Feldt, *The Coastwatchers*, p. 400.

27 Orders, 'AIB intelligence collection parties on Bougainville', SIO NEA to Captain Robinson, AIF, and Lt Keenan, RANVR, 13 October 1943, BC32571390, NAA.

28 Memo, DSIO Lunga to DNI, 7 September 1943, BC32571390, NAA.

29 Orders, Office of Commanding General, First Marine Amphibious Corps, to Lt Colonel James Smith, 22 October 1943, BC32571390, NAA.

30 Memo, Lt Mackenzie, Noumea, to DNI and SIO Townsville, detailing parts of a report, 'Major [sic] Thomas, USMC, to G2 Amphibious Corps HQ, Noumea', 20 November 1943, BC32571390, NAA.

31 Memo, DSIO Lunga to Chief of Staff, 1st Marine Amphibious Force, 29 October 1943, BC32571390, NAA.
32 Letter, Assistant SIO NEA to SIO NEA, 30 October 1943, BC32571390, NAA.
33 Letter, Colonel W.F. Coleman to Lt Cole, BC32571390, NAA.
34 Letter, Mackenzie to DNI, 20 November 1942, BC32571390, NAA.
35 Letter, signed Mackenzie, to DNI, 4 December 1941, BC32571390, NAA. This letter is signed by Mackenzie but has the tone and style of one of Feldt's letters. It is also addressed to 'Cocky', Long's old naval college nickname only seen on letters from Feldt. This is Feldt's letter, but added to and signed by Mackenzie
36 Letter, signed Mackenzie, to DNI, 4 December 1941, BC32571390, NAA.
37 Letter, signed Mackenzie, to DNI, 4 December 1941, BC32571390, NAA.
38 Letter, signed Mackenzie, to DNI, 4 December 1941, BC32571390, NAA.
39 Feldt, *The Coastwatchers*, p. 310.
40 Feldt, *The Coastwatchers*, p. 310.
41 Report, SIO, NEA (FERDINAND), to Deputy Controller AIB, 16 June 1944, BC411640, NAA.
42 Report, SIO, Townsville (Feldt), to NOIC, Townsville, 16 May 1942, BC411640, NAA.
43 Feldt, *The Coastwatchers*, p. 310.

CHAPTER 24

1 'Report on Madang and Wewak Situation', J.K. McCarthy, 15 February 1943, BC410692, NAA.
2 Report, Lt Greathead to Major J.K. McCarthy, 11 April 1943, p. 1, BC410692, NAA.
3 'Report on Madang and Wewak Situation', J.K. McCarthy, 15 February 1943, BC410692, NAA.
4 Memo, SIO NGA to Lt Greathead, 4 August 1943, BC410692, NAA.
5 D. Dexter, *The New Guinea Offensives*, Canberra: Australian War Memorial, 1961, p. 257.
6 Report by 2589, Corporal Topman, NEI Armed Forces, undated, BC410692, NAA.
7 Report by 2589, Corporal Topman, NEI Armed Forces, undated, BC410692, NAA.
8 Report by Major J.K. McCarthy, 20 May 1943, BC410692, NAA.
9 Report by Major J.K. McCarthy, 20 May 1943, BC410692, NAA; Dexter, *The New Guinea Offensives*, p. 260.
10 Dexter, *The New Guinea Offensives*, p. 257.
11 Dexter, *The New Guinea Offensives*, p. 257.
12 Minute, 'Supply Drop for Greathead party', to SIO Townsville OC Section C, Port Moresby, 12 April 1943, BC410692, NAA; letter, SIO Townsville to OiC, C Section, AIB, Port Moresby, 16 April 1943, BC410692, NAA.
13 Letter, Brooky to SIO, 9 November 1943, BC411640, NAA.
14 Minute, OiC NEA to Paymaster Commander J.C.R. Proud, 22 April 1943, and attached brief, 23 April 1943, BC410692, NAA.
15 Letter, to CO, 9th Operational Group, RAAF, from, C Section, AIB, 28 May 1943, BC410692, NAA.
16 Letter, to CO, 9th Operational Group, RAAF, from, C Section, AIB, 28 May 1943, BC410692, NAA.
17 This included Major General Wootten ordering his men to carry ten days' rations (Dexter, *The New Guinea Offensives*, p. 274). It should also be remembered that MacArthur and his staff were concerned at the paucity of detail in the Australian planning (see Dexter, *The New Guinea Offensives*, pp. 281–83).
18 Dexter, *The New Guinea Offensives*, p. 274.

19   Feldt, *The Coastwatchers*, p. 331.
20   Feldt, *The Coastwatchers*, p. 331.
21   Feldt, *The Coastwatchers*, p. 332.
22   Feldt, *The Coastwatchers*, pp. 334–36.
23   Feldt, *The Coastwatchers*, p. 346.
24   Feldt, *The Coastwatchers*, p. 342.
25   Feldt, *The Coastwatchers*, p. 341.
26   Feldt, *The Coastwatchers*, p. 341.
27   Feldt, *The Coastwatchers*, p. 345.
28   Feldt, *The Coastwatchers*, p. 346.
29   Feldt, *The Coastwatchers*, p. 346.
30   Feldt, *The Coastwatchers*, p. 342.
31   Feldt, *The Coastwatchers*, p. 344.
32   Feldt, *The Coastwatchers*, p. 344.
33   Feldt, *The Coastwatchers*, p. 344.
34   Feldt, *The Coastwatchers*, p. 345.
35   Feldt, *The Coastwatchers*, p. 345.
36   Feldt, *The Coastwatchers*, p. 345.
37   Feldt, *The Coastwatchers*, p. 350.
38   Dexter, *The New Guinea Offensives*, p. 736.
39   Feldt, *The Coastwatchers*, pp. 331–32.
40   Feldt, *The Coastwatchers*, pp. 331–2.
41   'Analysis of COMONITOR PROJECT—May–October 1944', Lt F.W. Harwood, RANVR, around end of October 1944, BC32571390, NAA.
42   'Analysis of COMONITOR PROJECT', BC32571390, NAA.
43   'Analysis of COMONITOR PROJECT', BC32571390, NAA.
44   Feldt, *The Coastwatchers*, p. 365.
45   Feldt, *The Coastwatchers*, p. 365.
46   Feldt, *The Coastwatchers*, p. 367.
47   Feldt, *The Coastwatchers*, p. 372.
48   Memo, B.F. Fellers to G1 to G2, GHQ, SWPA, 6 June 1944, BC436101, NAA.
49   Feldt, *The Coastwatchers*, pp. 387–408.

CHAPTER 25

1   Given the ever-changing nomenclature, the ISD will be referred to as the SRD throughout.
2   G.M. Long, *Australia in the War of 1939–1945*, vol. VII, *The Final Campaigns*, 1st edn, Canberra: Australian War Memorial, 1963, p. 617.
3   'The official history of the operations and administration of Special Operations—Australia', Timor-Lesser Sundas–Java Area, p. 1, BC235326, NAA: A3269, O8/B.
4   'Official history of . . . Special Operations—Australia', p. 8, BC235326, NAA.
5   'Official history of . . . Special Operations—Australia', BC235326, NAA.
6   'Official history of . . . Special Operations—Australia', p. 9, BC235326, NAA. In addition, letter, Carl Monsted to Secretary, Department of Immigration, 1 May 1946 ('MONSTED CARL ANTHON—born 4 September 1889—Danish', BC3055999, NAA: A435, 1946/4/3284) tells of death of his nephew, N.P. Monsted, on active service with AIB. See 'PLUMRIDGE JAMES RUPERT—VX86704 AIF; Year of Death—1943', buried Amboina, BC21517228, NAA: A8231, 29/PLUMRIDGE JAMES RUPERT; 'DAHLBERG JOHN HERBERT—VX35092 AIF; Year of death—1943', buried Amboina, NAA: A8231, 9/DAHLBERG JOHN HERBERT.

7 'Official history of . . . Special Operations—Australia', p. 3, BC235326, NAA.
8 'Official history of . . . Special Operations—Australia', BC235326, pp. 2–6, BC235326, NAA.
9 'Official history of . . . Special Operations—Australia', p. 4, BC235326, NAA.
10 'Official history of . . . Special Operations—Australia', p. 4, BC235326, NAA.
11 'Official history of . . . Special Operations—Australia', p. 4, BC235326, NAA.
12 'Official history of . . . Special Operations—Australia', p. 12, BC235326, NAA.
13 Ken'ichi Goto et al. (eds), *Materials on East Timor during World War II*, Forum for Historical Documents on East Timor during the Japanese Occupation Period, Tokyo: Ryukel Shyosha, 2008, p. 26.
14 Goto, *Materials on East Timor*, p. 24.
15 S.G. Farram, 'Timor Koepang to Timor NTT: a political history of West Timor, 1901–1967', PhD Thesis, Charles Darwin University, 2004, p. 172.
16 'Official history of . . . Special Operations—Australia', p. 13, BC235326, NAA.
17 'Official history of . . . Special Operations—Australia', p. 13 BC235326, NAA.
18 'Official history of . . . Special Operations—Australia', p. 14, BC235326, NAA.
19 'Official history of . . . Special Operations—Australia', p. 14, BC235326, NAA.
20 'Official history of . . . Special Operations—Australia', p. 15, BC235326, NAA.
21 'Official history of . . . Special Operations—Australia', p. 15, BC235326, NAA.
22 'Official history of . . . Special Operations—Australia', p. 16, BC235326, NAA.
23 'Official history of . . . Special Operations—Australia', p. 17, BC235326, NAA.
24 'Official history of . . . Special Operations—Australia', p. 17, BC235326, NAA.
25 'Official history of . . . Special Operations—Australia', p. 17, BC235326, NAA.
26 'Official history of . . . Special Operations—Australia', pp. 12–13, BC235326, NAA.
27 Major Yutani would later be charged with the murder of Corporal J.H. Armstrong, TX3282, AIF, and Gunner Martin of the Royal Artillery at Kupang on 12 June 1943. See D. Lockwood, 'Japs on murder charges', *Courier Mail*, Brisbane, 16 April 1946, p. 3.
28 Goto, *Materials on East Timor*, p. 27.
29 'Official history of . . . Special Operations—Australia', p. 20, BC235326, NAA and E.P. Chamberlain, *Forgotten Men: Timorese in Special Operations during World War II*, Point Lonsdale, Victoria: Ernest Chamberlain, 2010, p. 18, at www.scribd.com/doc/29688334/Forgotten-Men-Timorese-in-Special-Operations-during-World-War-II#scribd, accessed 15 August 2015.
30 'Official history of . . . Special Operations—Australia', p. 20, BC235326, NAA.
31 'Official history of . . . Special Operations—Australia', p. 20, BC235326, NAA.
32 'Official history of . . . Special Operations—Australia', p. 20, BC235326, NAA.
33 'Official history of . . . Special Operations—Australia', p. 23, BC235326, NAA.
34 'Official history of . . . Special Operations—Australia', p. 28, BC235326, NAA.
35 'Official history of . . . Special Operations—Australia', p. 21, BC235326, NAA.
36 'Official history of . . . Special Operations—Australia', p. 24, BC235326, NAA.
37 'Official history of . . . Special Operations—Australia', p. 25, BC235326, NAA.
38 'Official history of . . . Special Operations—Australia', p. 25, BC235326, NAA.
39 'ELLWOOD ALFRED JAMES: Service Number—VX67548: Date of birth—16 Dec 1921', BC6072067, NAA: B883, VX67548.
40 'Official history of . . . Special Operations—Australia', p. 25, BC235326, NAA.
41 'Official history of . . . Special Operations—Australia', pp. 26–29, BC235326, NAA.
42 'Official history of . . . Special Operations—Australia', p. 41, BC235326, NAA.
43 'Official history of . . . Special Operations—Australia', pp. 29, 40. The name of the major given at the 1946 trial of Saiki by the defendants was Kobayashi. There is no mention of a Major Tanaka.

44 'Official history of . . . Special Operations—Australia', pp. 33–34, BC235326, NAA.
45 'Official history of . . . Special Operations—Australia', p. 30, BC235326, NAA.
46 'Official history of . . . Special Operations—Australia', p. 29, BC235326, NAA.
47 'Official history of . . . Special Operations—Australia', pp. 42–33, BC235326, NAA.
48 'Official history of . . . Special Operations—Australia', p. 30, BC235326, NAA.
49 'Official history of . . . Special Operations—Australia', p. 31, BC235326, NAA.
50 'Official history of . . . Special Operations—Australia', p. 31, BC235326, NAA.
51 Letter, 10 December 1943, 'Tanimbar, Timor, Lesser Sunda, Java, COBRA messages', BC235160, NAA: A3269, D3/G. This file lists the supplies dropped to the Japanese, including 1000 cigarettes and 150 tins of fine-cut tobacco on 21 January 1944. The landing date is given as 29 January in the summary and 27 January in the text of the history (see 'Official history of . . . Special Operations—Australia', p. 98 [document p. 35], BC235327, NAA).
52 T. Hall & L. Silver, *The Heroes of Rimau: Unravelling the Mystery of One of World War II's Most Daring Raids*, London: Leo Cooper, 1991, pp. 232–33.
53 Message 1, Desp.1120Z/8/2, 'Tanimbar, Timor, Lesser Sunda, Java—COBRA Messages In', BC235162, NAA: A3269, D3/E.
54 'Special Intelligence', p. 8, BC3023422, NAA.
55 Message, 10 1500L, 7 March 1944, 'Tanimbar, Timor, Lesser Sunda, Java—COBRA, Messages Out', BC235161, NAA: A3269, D3/F.
56 'Official history of . . . Special Operations—Australia', p. 98 (document p. 37), BC235327, NAA.
57 COBRA message out, 5, despatched 1630Z, 23 February 1944, p. 108, BC235161, NAA.
58 COBRA message in, 4, 25 February 1944, p. 115, BC235162, NAA.
59 'Official history of . . . Special Operations—Australia', p. 41, BC235327, NAA.
60 Chamberlain, *Forgotten Men*, p. 25.
61 Chamberlain, *Forgotten Men*, pp. 25–33.
62 Signal, Brisbane to Morotai, LMS and Melbourne, 240620 MAY (?) 45, 'Tanimbar, Timor, Lesser Sunda, Java—LAGARTO, Part 1', BC235169, NAA: A3269, D4/A.
63 'Official history of . . . Special Operations—Australia', p. 58, BC235327, NAA.
64 'Official history of . . . Special Operations—Australia', p. 58, BC235327, NAA.
65 'Official history of . . . Special Operations—Australia', p. 58, BC235327, NAA.
66 Signal, Morotai to SRD Darwin ML 82, 050705Z JUL 45, folio 338, BC235169, NAA.
67 Signals, Morotai to Darwin ML97, 131300/7/45; Darwin to Morotai LM 226; and Melbourne LZ715, 290415Z JUL 45, folio 342, all in BC235169, NAA.
68 Signal, LAGARTO to LMS, 121140Z, AUG 45, folio 149, BC235169, NAA.
69 Signal, SRD to LAGARTO, 130618Z, AUG 45, folio 150, BC235169, NAA.

AFTERWORD

1 J. Edwards, *Keating: The Inside Story*, Ringwood, Victoria: Penguin Books, 1996, p. 62.

BIBLIOGRAPHY

National Archives of Australia (NAA)
With NAA files, the barcode (BC) provides the fastest and most accurate route to the actual file and, as a result, is included in all references to these files.

A1, 1904/1037, BC2001
A1, 1904/1951, BC3094409
A1, 1909/13685, BC5639
A1, 1911/19743, BC12184
A1, 1912/8306, BC13137
A1, 1912/21372, BC14544
A1, 1913/9176, BC15655
A1, 1913/16570, BC27540
A1, 1914/24248, BC32070
A1, 1916/29032, BC35253
A1, 1920/7685, BC38683
A1, 1923/8359, BC43185
A1, 1928/3075, BC44526
A2, 1918/2416, BC48307
A8, 1901/124/9, BC52026
A35, BUNDLE 2/1, BC31404093
A35 BUNDLE 2/6, BC31404098
A35, BUNDLE 2/7, BC31404099
A35, BUNDLE 2/10, BC31404102
A35, BUNDLE 2/12, BC31404104
A35, BUNDLE 2/23, BC31404115
A231, 1941/TOKYO, BC209946
A373, 2100, BC65374
A373, 4522B, BC65442
A432, 1940/153, BC72858
A433, 1942/2/2815, BC209208
A457, 306/5/14, BC83768

A461, D346/1/1, BC1889600
A627, 752/1926, BC4217019
A627, 12665/1928, BC4205317
A816, 19/306/158, BC170305
A816, 31/301/21, BC170613
A816, 44/301/9, BC171096
A816, 48/302/64, BC171228
A816/19, 304/420, BC170257
A981, CHIN 96, BC173578
A981/4, FAR 22, BC176222
A981, JAP 31, BC177410
A981, JAP 38 PART 1, BC177416
A981 JAP 56, BC177466
A981, WAR 40, BC182723
A1606, 22/3/181, BC204197
A1608, B15/1/1, BC204445
A1608, E39/2/1, BC206045
A1608, G39/2/1, BC206047
A1608, S39/2/3, BC274835
A1632, 1, BC4994275
A1838, 1255/43 BC563163
A2219, BC148060
A2585, 1939/1941/REFERENCE COPY, BC12205926
A2718, BC227945
A2863, 1920/22, BC3139189
A3269, C19/A, BC235140

A3269, D3/E, BC235162
A3269, D3/F, BC235161
A3269, D3/G, BC235160
A3269, D4/A, BC235169
A3269, D4/G, BC235168
A3269, H7, BC235285
A3269, O8/A, BC235327
A3269, O8/B, BC235326
A3269, Q1/A, BC235338
A3269, Q7/A, BC235346
A3269, Q8/B, BC1942544
A3978, BC8360031
A3978, MCLAUGHLIN W E, BC30675236
A4144, 741/1944, BC237695
A4311, 774/15, BC9024396
A571, 1946/2511, BC134232
A5954, 427/3, BC648984
A5954, 428/3, BC649030
A5954, 431/10, BC674385
A5954, 843/8, BC651792
A5954, 1203/6, BC694183
A5954, 1248/34, BC696622
A5954, 1923/36, BC723334
A5954, 1961/3, BC655420
A5954, 2378/1, BC735531
A6006, 1904/12/31, BC426192
A6769, BC5216358
A6769, BC5331964
A6661, 1013, BC422561
A6661, 1357, BC422481
A6662, 259, BC935618
A6662, 1492, BC941950
A6769, BC5332031
A6769, BC5332438
A6769, FELDT E.A., BC5415638
A6770, BC4394418
A6923, SI/1, BC3023422
A6923, SI/2, BC3023504
A6923, SI/3, BC3023454
A6923, SI/8, BC3023441
A6923, SI/10, BC3023487
A6923, 16/6/289, BC3023436
A6923,16/6/502, BC3023573
A6923, 37/401/425, BC3023506
A6923, 37/402/425, BC3023506
A6963, 16/6/289, BC3023436
A7942, Z146, BC6936168
A8510, 190/1, BC228711
A8908, 7A, BC4727814

A8908, 7B, BC30091097
A9376, 90, BC1101463
A9673, 91, BC1101467
A10857, 111/80M, BC7764659
A11804, 1916/65, BC248994
A11804, 1920/871, BC1611236
A11804, 1922/128, BC1612778
A11804, 1924/62, BC249671
A11804, 1925/178, BC1617419
A11804, 1926/501, BC1618651
A11804, 1927/74, BC1607341
A14143, 1, BC31720999
B168, 1904/32, BC414644
B197, 1877/5/15, BC416253
B2455, BC7017947
B2455, BC8030333
B3476, 1, BC508352
B3476, 37, BC411499
B3476, 37A, BC410664
B3476, 49, BC410697
B3476, 49C, BC508663
B3476, 148PART 2A, BC32571390
B3476, 148 PART 2B, BC32571389
B3476, 174, BC410692
B3476, 174A, BC411640
B3476, 174B, BC436101
B6121, 311J, BC451771
B2455, SERN 764, BC1994089
B883, BC5631545
B884, N60119, BC5601022
B5554, WHOLE SERIES, BC859305
B5555, 3, FRUMEL, BC856345
B5555, 4, FRUMEL, BC856346
BP4/3 MALAY, BC9061946
BP4/3 MALAY MINGO/B, BC9061978
C123, 10067, BC3314430
C1580, 124, BC8430839
CP290/9, 1, BC257486
CP290/9, 8, BC257493
CP290/9, 13, BC257498
MP 84/1, 1877/5/4/, BC325203
MP/84/1, 1877/5/5, BC331612
MP84/1, 1849/2/13, BC324142
MP138/1, 603/247/158, BC1330902
MP472/1/0, 5/18/8562, BC377013
MP729/6, 15/403/16, BC463429
MP729/8, 41/431/136, BC1010436
MP742/1, 175/1/81, BC392061
MP1049/1, 1913/0253, BC408616

MP1049/1, 1914/0351, BC413224
MP1049/1, 1915/0251, BC404942
MP1049/1, 1916/0224, BC403292
MP1049/1, 1920/0139, BC406713
MP1049/1, BC400631
MP1049/5, 1877/13/152, BC402939
MP1049/9, 1997/5/196, BC505956
MP1049/5, 1997/6/20, BC474429

MP1049/9, 1997/5/196, BC25868
MP1185/8, 1846/4/25, BC398924
MP1185/8, 1945/2/6, BC396338
MP1185/9, 559/201/574, BC394326
MP2456, 494/7, BC10727179
MT1487/1, BC6044592
P617, 534/1/18, BC530493

The National Archives, UK

ADM 116/6320
CAB 18/8A
CAB 24/4/23
CAB 24/34/9
CAB 24/44/51
CAB 24/206/39
CAB 24/212/23
CAB 24/215/27
CAB 24/229/4
CAB 24/239
CAB 53/4
CAB 62/23/18
CAB 65/1/27
CAB 65/1/32
CAB 65/2/2
CAB 65/7/39
CAB 65/30/9
CAB 66/10/1
CAB 66/18/21
CAB 66/24/21
CAB 66/24/30
CAB 67/3/55

CAB 101/249/9
FO 881/10025
FO 954/4
HO 144/1727/278967
HW 1/420
HW 52/80
HW 52/90
HW 52/93
HW 53
HW 62/17
HW 67/17
HW 80
HW 43/4
PREM 1 310
PREM 3 145/3
PREM 3 151/2
PREM 3 159/10
PREM 3 167/2
PREM 3 206/2
PREM 4 50/7a
WG 110/2/48
WO 106/3389

National Archives, USA

A1/27, 5500/1 FRUMEL (Fleet Radio Unit, Melbourne, Australia) SECURITY, NAI6230486, Declassification Authority 003012

A7/2 CINCPAC FILES 1943 (SECRET) CENSORSHIP, NAI6077910, Declassification Authority NND745002

A8/1 CINCPAC FILES 1943 (SECRET) INTELLIGENCE SYSTEMS, CENTERS, NAI6077912, Declassification Authority NND745002

A8/37, (Detached Enclosure) Report of Japanese Kiska Radars, NAI 6079417, NND745002

A8/EF13 CINCPAC FILES 1942 (SECRET) INTELLIGENCE INFORMATION BRITAIN, NAI 6077917, Declassification Authority, NND745002

A61215, Memorandum for Mr Friedman, declassified and approved for release by NSA on 01-30-2014 pursuant to E.O. 13526, undated

A65434, MAGIC—FAR EAST SUMMARY No. 194, 30 September 1944, declassified by NSA on 25 April 2014 pursuant to Executive Order 13526

DOCID: 3978516, 'The Room 40 compromise', declassified and approved for release by NSA on 06-13-2012 pursuant to E.O. 13526

I. D. Special Analysis Report #1, 'Covernames in diplomatic traffic', prepared by ASA I.D., 30 August 1947

NSA, 'The Room 40 compromise', classified HVCCO, No Copy, No Dissemination, DOCID3978516, undated, declassified 13 June 2012, www.nsa.gov/news-features/declassified-documents/nsa-60th-timeline/assets/files/1960s/19600101_1960_Doc_3978516_Room40.pdf, accessed 2 May 2016

Pearl Harbor review: The Black Chamber', NSA, www.nsa.gov/about/cryptologic-heritage/center-cryptologic-history/pearl-harbor-review/agreement.shtml, accessed 26 July 2016

'William F. Friedman Letter: to Mr. Leo Rosen, Invitation to Join the National Security Agency Scientific Advisory Board (NSASAB)', at archive.org/stream/41787259082626 - page/n0/mode/2up, accessed 26 July 2016

Family archives

JELLICOE PAPERS, vol. LVII (ff. 260). 1. ff. 1–3, 1918–1920, British Library
Mr Richard Mawhood, email correspondence, 2016

Official Publications, Australia

Australian Bureau of Statistics (earlier, Commonwealth Bureau of Census and Statistics), *Year Book Australia*

ACNB, *Navy List*

Bean, C.E.W., *Australia in the War of 1914–1918*, vol. II, *The Story of Anzac: From 4 May 1915 to the Evacuation*, Sydney: Angus & Robertson, 1924

Commonwealth of Australia, Statutory Rules 1939, no. 87, National Security (General) Regulations, Regulation 26, (1), (a), (b) and (c)

Dexter, D., *The New Guinea Offensives*, Canberra: Australian War Memorial, 1961

House of Representatives, Hansard

Hasluck, P., *Australia in the War of 1939–1945*, Series 4, Civil, vol. 2, *The Government and the People 1942–1945*, Canberra: Australian War Memorial, 1970

Gill, G.H., *Australia in the War of 1939–1945*, Series 2, Navy, vol. 1, *Royal Australian Navy 1939–1942*, Canberra: Australian War Memorial, 1957

Gill, G.H., *Australia in the War of 1939–1945*, Series 2, Navy, vol. 2, *Royal Australian Navy 1942–1945*, Canberra: Australian War Memorial, 1968

Horner, D.M., *The Spy Catchers: The Official History of ASIO, 1949–1963*, Sydney: Allen & Unwin, 2014

Jellicoe of Scapa, Viscount, *Report of Admiral of the Fleet, Viscount Jellicoe of Scapa, on Naval Mission to the Commonwealth of Australia (May–August 1919)*

Jose, A.W., *Official History of Australia in the War of 1914–1918*, vol. IX, *The Royal Australian Navy, 1914–1918*, Sydney: Angus & Robertson, 1928

Long, G., *Australia in the War of 1939–1945*, Series 1, Army, vol. 1, *To Benghazi*, Canberra: Australian War Memorial, 1961

Wigmore, L., *Australia in the War of 1939–1945*, Series 1, Army, vol. 4, *The Japanese Thrust*, Canberra: Australian War Memorial, 1966

Official Histories, UK

Historical Section, Naval Staff Tactical and Staff Duties Division, Admiralty, *Naval Operations in the Campaign for Guadalcanal, August 1942 – February 1943*, Battle Summary No. 21, London: Admiralty, 1949

Andrew, C., *The Defence of the Realm: The Authorized History of MI5*, London: Allen Lane, 2009

Central Statistical Office, *Statistical Digest of the War*, London: HMSO and Longmans, Green and Co., 1951

Butler, J.R.M., *History of the Second World War*, vol. III, part II, *Grand Strategy*, London: HMSO, 1964

Edinburgh Gazette, Edinburgh

Goodman, M.S., *The Official History of the Joint Intelligence Committee*, vol. I, *From the Approach of the Second World War to the Suez Crisis*, Abingdon, Oxford: Routledge, 2014

Hinsley, F.H., Thomas, E.E., Ransom, C.F.G. & Knight, R.C., *British Intelligence in the Second World War*, vol. 1, London: HMSO, 1979

Hinsley, F.H., Thomas, E.E., Ransom, C.F.G. & Knight, R.C., *British Intelligence in the Second World War*, vol. 2, London: HMSO, 1981

Hinsley, F.H., Thomas, E.E., Simpkins, C.A. & Ransom, C.F.G., *British Intelligence in the Second World War*, vol. 3, part 2, 1988

Hinsley, F.H. & Simkins, C.A.G., *British Intelligence in the Second World War*, vol. 4, *Security and Counter-Intelligence*, New York: Cambridge University Press, 1990

London Gazette, London

Ministry of Defence (Navy), Naval Historical Branch, *War with Japan*, London: HMSO, 1995

Woodburn Kirby, S., *Singapore: The Chain of Disaster*, London: Cassell, 1971

Woodburn Kirby, S., *The War Against Japan*, vols I, II, III, IV, London: HMSO, 1957–65

Official Histories, USA

Borrmann, D.A., Kvetkas, W.T., Brown, C.V., Flatley, M.J. & Hunt, R., *The History of Traffic Analysis: World War I – Vietnam*, Fort George G. Mead, Maryland: Center for Cryptologic History, National Security Agency, 2013

Central Intelligence Agency, 'Japanese intelligence organisations in China', Section II, Japanese Military Intelligence, 4 June 1946

Foreign Histories Division, HQ, US Army, Japan, *History of the Imperial General Headquarters*, rev. edn, Monograph No. 45, Fort Leavenworth, Kansas: Army Section, 1959

Ishiwara, H., Azuma, S. & Chiyoshi, S., *Army Operations in China, December 1941 – December 1943*, Japanese Monograph No. 71, Tokyo: Headquarters, USA Forces Far East and Eighth US Army (Rear), Department of the Army, 1956

Maneki, S.A., *The Quiet Heroes of the Southwest Pacific Theater: An Oral History of the Men and Women of CBB and FRUMEL*, Fort George G. Mead, Maryland: Center for Cryptologic History, NSA, 2007

Parker, F.D., *A Priceless Advantage: US Navy Communications Intelligence and the Battles of Coral Sea, Midway and the Aleutians*, Fort George G. Mead, Maryland: Center for Cryptologic History, NSA, 1993

Rumsfeld, D.H., 'News transcript: DoD news briefing—Secretary Rumsfeld and Gen. Myers', 12 February 2002, US Department of Defense, www.defense.gov/transcripts/transcript.aspx?transcriptid=2636, accessed 1 March 2015

Australian Official Government Online

Air Force HQ, 'Australia's voice loud and clear in the global F-35 test team', 24 April 2013, RAAF, www.airforce.gov.au/News/50-Years-of-the-Air-Force-Intelligence-Specialisation/?RAAF-P0RQKJqVLxdErtezXtr/VS0m9eScdWdo, accessed 19 June 2016

British Phosphate Commission's Steamer *Trienza . . .*', Australian War Memorial, acc. no. 128076, www.awm.gov.au/collection/128076, accessed 30 October 2016

'Bomber Command', Department of Veterans' Affairs, May 2012, www.dva.gov.au/sites/default/files/files/about%20dva/media-centre/media-backgrounder/Bomber_Command.pdf, accessed 13 August 2016

'Commander Eric Augustus Feldt', Navy, www.navy.gov.au/biography/commander-eric-augustus-feldt, accessed 14 October 2016

Department of Defence Science and Technology, Anticipating Tomorrow's Defence Needs: A Century of Australian Defence Science, Canberra: Commonwealth of Australia, 2007, www.dst.defence.gov.au/sites/default/files/publications/documents/Anticipating-tomorrows-defence-needs.pdf

Fenton, Damien, 'Remembering the war in New Guinea: how many died?', Australian War Memorial, ajrp.awm.gov.au/ajrp/remember.nsf/Web-Printer/58EBD6D993E15CE8CA25 6D05002671FD?OpenDocument, accessed 2 October 2016

'History', Australian Signals Directorate, Department of Defence, www.asd.gov.au/about/history.htm, accessed 26 September 2016

Index to Inward Passenger Lists to Victoria, 1852–1924, VPRS 944, Public Record Office Victoria, access.prov.vic.gov.au/public/component/daPublicBaseContainer?component=daViewSeries&entityId=944

Kubata, K., 'The Battle of Tsushima, 1905', June 1980, Naval Historical Society of Australia, www.navyhistory.org.au/the-battle-of-tsushima-1905, accessed 24 November 2016

Lot 674, Canadian Memorial Cross, G.V.R. (1051391 Pte H.N. Bills), 'Long Service medals from the collection formed by John Tamplin', Dix Noonan Webb, London, www.dnw.co.uk/auction-archive/special-collections/lot.php?specialcollection_id=57&lot_id=67264, accessed 26 December 2015

'Montevideo Maru—serial name list of prisoners of war and internees who perished', BC31720999, NAA: A14143, 1, 2 November 2012, recordsearch.naa.gov.au/SearchNRetrieve/Interface/DetailsReports/SeriesDetail.aspx?series_no=A14143, accessed 27 November 2017

NSW government file 19/7034, certificate no. 1916/00445, for orchard land, 2 Bondi Road, Bondi, to Henry Wykeham Freame, 20 November 1916, Soldiers Settlement Miscellaneous File Index, State Archives & Records, NSW, www.records.nsw.gov.au/searchhits_nocopy?id=56&surname=Freame&firstname=&class_of_holding=&land_district=&order=firstname&sort=asc, accessed 21 May 2014

Straczek, J., 'Listening for the empire', Navy, www.navy.gov.au/sites/default/files/documents/Straczek_-_Listening_for_the_Empire.pdf, accessed 15 March 2015

'Vice Admiralty courts: administrative history', NSW Archives & Records, search.records.nsw.gov.au/agencies/1048, accessed 27 April 2015

Viscount Jellicoe of Scapa, *Report of Admiral of the Fleet, Viscount Jellicoe of Scapa, on Naval Mission to the Commonwealth of Australia (May–Aug. 1919)*, vol. 1, 12 August 1919, p. 1, www.navy.gov.au/sites/default/files/documents/Jellicoe%20of%20Scapa%20Vol%20I_opt.pdf, accessed 25 June 2014

www.records.nsw.gov.au/searchhits_nocopy?id=56&surname=Freame&firstname=&class_of_holding=&land_district=&order=firstname&sort=asc, accessed 21 May 2014

www.yoshabunko.com/nationality/Naturalization_Meiji.html

Newspapers

Unless specifically mentioned, all newspapers quoted were accessed through the Trove database maintained by the National Library of Australia at trove.nla.gov.au.

The Advertiser, Adelaide
The Age, Melbourne
The Argus, Melbourne
Barrier Miner, Broken Hill

Brisbane Courier, Brisbane
Canberra Times, Canberra
Cootamundra Herald, Cootamundra
Cumberland Argus and Fruitgrowers Advocate, Parramatta
Courier Mail, Brisbane
Daily Advertiser, Wagga Wagga
Daily News, Perth
Dubbo Liberal, Dubbo
Cairns Post, Cairns
Dungog Chronicle, Dungog
Durham and Gloucester Advertiser, Durham, New South Wales
Evening News, Sydney
The Examiner, Launceston
Farmer and Settler, Sydney
Geelong Advertiser, Geelong
The Guardian, London
Hawera and Normanby Star, Hawera, New Zealand
Kadina and Wallaroo Times, Kadina, South Australia
Macquarie Advocate, Port Macquarie
The Mercury, Hobart
Newcastle Morning Herald, Newcastle
The Queenslander, Brisbane
Singapore Free Press and Mercantile Advertiser, Singapore
South Australian Register, Adelaide
Straits Times, Singapore, http://www.straitstimes.com/tags/national-archives-of-singapore
The Sun, Melbourne
Sunday Times, Perth
Sydney Mail, Sydney
Sydney Morning Herald, Sydney
The Telegraph, Sydney
Times of India, http://timesofindia.indiatimes.com/india
West Australian, Perth

Autobiographies
Churchill, W.S., *History of the Second World War*, Boston, Massachusetts: Houghton Mifflin Company, 1949
Hasluck, P., *Diplomatic Witness: Australian Foreign Affairs 1941–1947*, Melbourne: Melbourne University Press, 1980
Menzies, Robert, *Afternoon Light*, Melbourne: Penguin, 1970
Percival, A.E., *The War in Malaya*, London: Eyre & Spottiswood, 1949
Spencer Chapman, F., *The Jungle is Neutral*, London: Chatto & Windus, 1948
Tedder, A., *With Prejudice: The War Memoirs of Marshal of the Royal Air Force, Lord Tedder G.C.B.*, London: Cassell, 1966
Yasutaro, Soga, *Life Behind Barbed Wire: The World War II Internment Memoirs of Hasai'i Issei*, Honolulu: University of Hawaii Press, 2008

Australian Dictionary of Biography
Beddie, B. 'Pearce, Sir George Foster (1870–1952)', *Australian Dictionary of Biography*, National Centre of Biography, Australian National University, adb.anu.edu.au/biography/pearce-sir-george-foster-7996, accessed 24 January 2014

Cunneen, C., 'Steward, Sir George Charles Thomas (1865–1920)', *Australian Dictionary of Biography*, National Centre of Biography, Australian National University, http://adb.anu. edu.au/biography/steward-sir-george-charles-thomas-8657/text15137, accessed online 27 April 2014

Davies, Helen M., 'Hunt, Atlee Arthur (1864–1935)', adb.anu.edu.au/biography/hunt-atlee-Arthur-6766/text11699, accessed 15 February 2014

Fitzhardinge, L.F., 'Hughes, William Morris (Billy) (1862–1952)', adb.anu.edu.au/biography/hughes-william-morris-billy-6761, accessed 15 February 2014

Gregory, J.S., 'Morrison, George Ernest (Chinese) (1862–1920)', adb.anu.edu.au/biography/morrison-george-ernest-chinese-7663, accessed 21 November 2016

Haldane, R., 'Duncan, Alexander Mitchell (1888–1965)', adb.anu.edu.au/biography/duncan-alexander-mitchell-10062, accessed 1 January 2016

Lamont, R., 'Thring, Walter Hugh Charles Samuel (1873–1949)', adb.anu.edu.au/biography/thring-walter-hugh-charles-samuel-8804, accessed 23 June 2014

Lodge, A.B., 'Squires, Ernest Ker (1882–1940)', adb.anu.edu.au/biography/squires-ernest-ker-8613/text15045, published first in hardcopy 1990, accessed 3 July 2016

Meaney, N.K., 'Piesse, Edmund Leolin (1880–1947)', adb.anu.edu.au/biography/piesse-edmund-leolin-8046/text14033, accessed 15 February 2014

Moore, A. 'Scott, William John (1888–1956)', adb.anu.edu.au/biography/scott-william-john-8373, accessed 2 January 2016

Powell, A., 'Boye-Jones, Ruby Olive (1891–1990)', adb.anu.edu.au/biography/boye-jones-ruby-olive-12242, accessed 24 October 2016

Serle, G., 'McCay, Sir James Whiteside (1864–1930)', adb.anu.edu.au/biography/mccay-sir-james-whiteside-7312, accessed 23 January 2014

Sissons, D.C.S., 'Murakami, Yasukichi (1880–1944)', adb.anu.edu.au/biography/murakami-yasukichi-11201, accessed 25 July 2014

Biographies

Booker, M., *The Great Professional: A Study of W.M. Hughes*, Sydney: McGraw Hill, 1980

Coulthard-Clark, C.D., *A Heritage of Spirit: A Biography of Major-General William Throsby Bridges*, Melbourne: Melbourne University Press, 1979

Edwards, J., *Keating: The Inside Story*, Melbourne: Penguin, 1996

Pfennigwerth, I., *A Man of Intelligence: The Life of Captain Eric Nave, Australian Codebreaker Extraordinary*, Sydney: Rosenberg, 2006

Unpublished research

Fahey, J., 'Britain 1939–1945: the economic cost of strategic bombing', PhD thesis, University of Sydney, 2004

Fahey, J., 'Warriors not warlords: Australian economic, social and industrial conduct 1939–1945', unpublished essay

Farram, S.G., 'Timor Koepang to Timor NTT: a political history of West Timor, 1901–1967', PhD thesis, Charles Darwin University, 2004

Horner, D.M., 'Australia and Allied strategy in the Pacific 1941–1946', PhD thesis, Australian National University, October 1980

Rajkai Zsombor Tibor, 'The Timurid Empire and Ming China: theories and approaches concerning the relations of the two empires', Doktori Disszertáció, Eötvös Loránd Tudományegyetem, Nyelvtudományok Doctoral School, 2007, at doktori.btk.elte.hu/hist/rajkai/diss.pdf, accessed 2 September 2010

Shimazu, Naoko, 'The racial equality proposal at the 1919 Paris Peace Conference: Japanese motivations and Anglo-American responses', PhD thesis, Magdalen College, University of Oxford, Hilary Term, 1995

Straczek, J.H., 'The origins and development of Royal Australian Naval Signals Intelligence in an era of imperial defence 1914–1945', PhD thesis, University of New South Wales, 2008

Articles

Aldrich, R.J., 'Britain's Secret Intelligence Service in Asia during the Second World War', *Modern Asian Studies*, 1998, vol. 32, no. 1, pp. 179–217

Bennett, B., 'Traditional myths and problematic heroes: the case of Harry Freame', *Asiatic*, 2010, vol. 4, no. 2, pp. 1–13

——, 'Troubled waters: Australian spies in the Pacific—glimpses from the early twentieth century', in Dixon, R. & Birns, N. (eds), *Readings Across the Pacific: Australia–US Intellectual Histories*, Sydney: Sydney University Press, 2010, pp. 209–23

Boghardt, T., 'America's secret vanguard: US Army Intelligence operations in Germany, 1944–47', *Studies in Intelligence*, 2013, vol. 57, no. 2, pp. 1–18

Chen, Ta-Yuan, 'Japan and the birth of Takao's Fisheries in Nanyo 1895–1945', Working Paper No. 139, Asia Research Centre, Murdoch University, November 2006, 25 pp.

Ingersoll, R.G., 'Motley and monarch', *North American Review*, 1885, vol. 141, no. 349, pp. 528–32

Kuwajima, Sho, 'Indian mutiny in Singapore, 1915: people who observed the scene and people who heard the news', *New Zealand Journal of Asian Studies*, 2009, vol. 11, no. 1, pp. 375–84

Lloyd, P.J., 'The first 100 years of tariffs in Australia: the colonies', Discussion Paper No. 2015-13, ANU Centre for Economic History, November 2015, 38 pp.

Meaney, N., 'Troubled waters: Australian spies in the Pacific—glimpses from the early twentieth century', in Dixon, R. & Birns, N. (eds), *Reading Across the Pacific: Australia-US Intellectual Histories*, Sydney: Sydney University Press, 2010

Nelson, H., 'Bougainville in World War II', in Regan, A. & Griffen, H. (eds.), *Bougainville Before the Conflict*, ANU eView, Canberra: Australian National University, 2015

Oliver, P. 'Interpreting "Japanese Activities" in Australia, 1888–1945', *Journal of the Australian War Memorial*, 2002, no. 36, www.awm.gov.au/journal/j36/oliver.asp, accessed 8 August 2015

Spence, D.O., 'Australian naval defence and the 1887 Colonial Conference: context, policy and reaction', *International Journal of Naval History*, 2007, vol. 6. no. 1, www.ijnhonline. org/wp-content/uploads/2012/01/Spence-article-Australian-Naval-Defence.pdf, accessed 23 June 2014

Stevens, D., 'Australian naval defence: selections from the papers and correspondence of Captain W.H.C.S. Thring, 1913–34', in Rose, S. (ed.), *The Naval Miscellany*, vol. VII, Aldershot: Navy Records Society, 2008

Stuart, R., 'Was the RCN ever the third largest navy?', *Canadian Naval Review*, vol. 5, no. 3, 2009, pp. 4–9

Touwen-Bouwsma, E., 'Japanese policy towards the Chinese on Java, 1942–1945: a preliminary outline', in Kratoska, P.H.E. (ed.), *Southeast Asian Minorities in the Wartime Japanese Empire*, Abingdon: Routledge-Curzon, 2002, pp. 55–64

Tsu Yun Hui, 'Japanese in Singapore and Japan's southward expansionism, 1860–1945: historical notes for Under Another Sun', Asian Educational Media Service, www.aems. illinois.edu/mpg/sun/tsu.html, accessed 2 September 2010

Books: Primary Accounts

Ballard, G., *On Ultra Active Service: The Story of Australia's Signals Intelligence Operations During World War II*, Melbourne: Spectrum Publications, 1991

Churchill, W., *History of the Second World War*, vol. II, *Their Finest Hour*, Boston, Massachusetts: Houghton Mifflin, 1949

Clemens, M.W., *Alone on Guadalcanal: A Coastwatcher's Story*, Annapolis, Maryland: Naval Institute Press, 2004

Falt, O.K. & Kujala, A. (eds), *Rakka Ryusui: Colonel Akashi's Report on His Secret Cooperation with the Russian Revolutionary Parties during the Russo-Japanese War*, Helsinki: Societas Historica Finlandiae, 1988

Feldt, E., *The Coast Watchers*, Melbourne: Oxford University Press, 1946

Goto Ken'ichi et al. (eds), *Materials on East Timor during World War II*, Forum for Historical Documents on East Timor during the Japanese Occupation Period, Tokyo: Ryukel Shyosha, 2008

Ind, A.W., *Secret War Against Japan: The Allied Intelligence Bureau in World War II*, Uncommon Valor Series, 2014 (first published New York: MacKay, 1958)

Mitrokhin, V. & Andrew, C., *The Mitrokhin Archive: The KGB in Europe and the West*, London: Allen Lane, 1999

Stockings, C.A.J., *The Making and Breaking of the Post-Federation Australian Army, 1901–09*, Canberra: Land Warfare Studies Centre, 2007

Trayes, F.G., *Five Months on a German Raider: Being the Adventures of an Englishman Captured by the 'Wolf'*, London: Hedley Bros, 1919, at archive.org/stream/ fivemonthsonager16690gut/16690.txt, accessed 11 May 2014

Tsuji, Masanobu, *Singapore The Japanese Version*, trans. M.E. Lake, Sydney: Ure Smith, 1960

Wyett, J., *Staff Wallah at the Fall of Singapore*, Sydney: Allen & Unwin, 1996

Books: Secondary Sources

Aldridge, R.J., *Intelligence and the War Against Japan: Britain, America and the Politics of Secret Service*, Cambridge: Cambridge University Press, 2000

Andrew, C., *For the President's Eyes Only: Secret Intelligence and the American Presidency from Washington to Bush*, London: HarperCollins, 1996

——, *Secret Service: The Making of the British Intelligence Community*, London: Heinemann, 1985

—— (ed.), *Codebreaking and Signals Intelligence*, London: Frank Cass, 1986

Ashton, T.S., *An Economic History of England: The 18th Century*, London: Methuen and Co., 1966

Bailey, J., *The White Divers of Broome: The True Story of a Fatal Experiment*, Sydney: Pan Macmillan, 2002

Ball, D. & Horner, D., *Breaking the Codes: Australia's KGB Network*, Sydney: Allen & Unwin, 1998

Beaumont, J., Joshi, V., Somford, J., Blair, D. & Pratten, G., *Australian Centenary History of Defence*, vol. VI, *Australian Defence: Sources and Statistics*, Melbourne: Oxford University Press, 2001

Bennett, B., *The Spying Game: An Australian Angle*, Melbourne: Australian Scholarly Publishing, 2009

Best, A., *British Intelligence and the Japanese Challenge in Asia, 1914–1941*, Basingstoke: Palgrave Macmillan, 2002

Black, J., *British Foreign Policy in an Age of Revolutions, 1783–1793*, Cambridge: Cambridge University Press, 1994

Breuer, W.B., *MacArthur's Undercover War: Spies, Saboteurs, Guerrilla's, and Secret Missions*, New York: John Wiley & Sons, 1995

Bullard, S., *Japanese Army Operations in the South Pacific Area: New Britain and Papua Campaigns, 1942–43*, Canberra: Australian War Memorial, 2007

Cave Brown, A., *The Secret Servant: The Life of Sir Stewart Menzies, Churchill's Spymaster*, Sphere Books, London, 1987

Clemens, M.W., *Alone on Guadalcanal: A Coastwatcher's Story*, Annapolis, Maryland: Naval Institute Press, 2004

Collie, C., *Code Breakers: Inside the Shadow World of Signals Intelligence in Australia's Two Bletchley Parks*, Sydney: Allen & Unwin, 2017

Donovan, P. & Mack, J., *Code Breaking in the Pacific*, Cham, Switzerland: Springer, 2014

Drea, E.J., *MacArthur's ULTRA: Codebreaking and the War Against Japan, 1942–1945*, Lawrence, Kansas: University Press of Kansas, 1992

Dufty, D., *The Secret Code-Breakers of Central Bureau: How Australia's Signals-Intelligence Network Helped Win the Pacific War*, Melbourne: Scribe, 2017

Dull, P.S., *A Battle History of the IJN (1941–1945)*, Annapolis, Maryland: Naval Institute Press, 2007

Elphick, P., *Far Eastern Intelligence: The Intelligence War in the Far East, 1930–1945*, London: Hodder & Stoughton, 1997

Evans, D.C. (ed.), *The Japanese Navy in World War II: In the Words of Former Japanese Naval Officers*, 2nd edn, Annapolis, Maryland: Naval Institute Press, 1986

—— & Peattie, M.R., *Kaigun: Strategy, Tactics, and Technology in the Imperial Japanese Navy 1887–1941*, Annapolis, Maryland: Naval Institute Press, 1997

Frost, A., *Convicts and Empire: A Naval Question, 1776–1811*, Melbourne: Melbourne University Press, 1995

Goldstein, D.M. & Dillon, K.V., *The Pacific War Papers: Japanese Documents of World War II*, Dulles, Virginia: Potomac Books Inc., 2004

Griffen-Foley, B., *Changing Stations: The Story of Australian Commercial Radio*, Sydney: UNSW Press, 2009

Harrell, P., *Sowing the Seeds of Change: Chinese Students, Japanese Teachers, 1895–1905*, Stanford, California: Stanford University Press, 1992

Hall, T. & Silver, L., *The Heroes of Rimau: Unravelling the Mystery of One of World War II's Most Daring Raids*, London: Leo Cooper, 1991

Henderson, A., *Joseph Lyons: The People's Prime Minister*, Sydney: NewSouth Publishing, 2011

Hitler, A., *Mein Kampf*, trans. R. Manheim, London: Pimlico, 1992

Höhne, H., *Canaris*, London: Secker & Warburg, 1976

Holmes, W.J., *Double-edged Secrets: Naval Intelligence Operations in the Pacific during World War II*, Annapolis, Maryland: Naval Institute Press, 1979

Horne, A., *To Lose a Battle: France 1940*, London: Penguin, 1982

Horner, D.M., *High Command: Australia and Allied Strategy 1939–1945*, Sydney: George Allen & Unwin, 1982

——, *Crisis of Command: Australian Generalship and the Japanese Threat, 1941–1943*, Canberra: Australian National University Press, 1978

Jansen, Marius B., *The Japanese and Sun Yat-Sen*, Stanford, California: Stanford University Press, 1979

Johnson, C., *Australians Awarded: A Concise Guide to Military and Civilian Decorations, Medals and other Awards to Australians from 1815 to 2007 with Their Valuation*, Sydney: Renniks Publishing, 2008

Johnson, W.J., *The Pacific Campaign in World War II: From Pearl Harbor to Guadalcanal*, Abingdon: Routledge, 2006

Kahn, D., *The Code-Breakers: The Comprehensive History of Secret Communications from Ancient Times to the Internet*, New York: Scribner, 1996

Kirk-Greene, A., *Glimpses of Empire: A Corona Anthology*, London: I.B. Taurus and Co., 2001

Kotani, K., *Japanese Intelligence in World War II*, trans. C. Kotani, Osprey Publishing, Oxford, 2009

Kratoska, P.H., *The Japanese Occupation of Malaya: A Social and Economic History*, London: Hurst, 1998

Lance, K., *Redbill: From Pearls to Peace—The Life and Times of a Remarkable Lugger*, Fremantle: Fremantle Arts Centre Press, 2004

Larrabee, E., *Commander in Chief: Franklin Delano Roosevelt, His Lieutenants, and Their War*, New York: Touchstone Books, 1988

Leaf, M. & Lawson, R., *The Story of Ferdinand*, New York: Viking Press, 1936

Legg, F., *The Gordon Bennett Story: From Gallipoli to Singapore*, Sydney: Angus & Robertson, 1965

Lodge, B., *Lavarack: Rival General*, Sydney: Allen & Unwin, 1998

Long, G., *MacArthur as Military Commander*, Sydney: Angus & Robertson, 1969

Lord, W., *Lonely Vigil: Coastwatchers of the Solomons*, Allen Lane, London, 1978

Machiavelli, N., *The Prince*, trans. W.K. Marriott, London: Everyman's Library, 1992

Maffeo, S.E., *US Navy Codebreakers, Linguists, and Intelligence Officers Against Japan, 1910–1941: A Biographical Dictionary*, Lanham, Maryland: Rowman & Littlefield, 2016

Meaher, A., *The Australian Road to Singapore: The Myth of British Betrayal*, Melbourne: Australian Scholarly Publishing, 2010

Meaney, N., *A History of Australian Defence and Foreign Policy 1901–23*, vol. 1, *The Search for Security in the Pacific, 1901–1914*, Sydney: Sydney University Press, 2009

——, *A History of Australian Defence and Foreign Policy 1901–23*, vol. 2, *Australia and the World Crisis, 1914–1923*, vol. 2, Sydney: Sydney University Press, 2009

——, *Fears and Phobias: E.L. Piesse and the Problem of Japan 1909–1939*, Occasional Papers Series Number 1, Canberra: National Library of Australia, 1996

Mercado, S.C., *The Shadow Warriors of Nakano: A History of the IJA's Elite Intelligence School*, Washington, DC: Brassey's Inc., 2002

Morgenstern, G., *Pearl Harbor: The Story of the Secret War*, New York: Devin-Adair Company, 1947

Morton, D., *Off the Record: The Technology and Culture of Sound Recording in America*, New Brunswick, New Jersey: Rutgers University Press, 2000

Naval Records Society, *The Collective Naval Defence of the Empire 1900–1940*, Aldershot: Ashgate Publishing, 1997

Netherlands Information Bureau, *Ten Years of Japanese Burrowing in the Netherlands East Indies: Official Report of the Netherland East Indies Government on Japanese Subversive Activities in the Archipelago During the Last Decade*, New York: Netherlands Information Bureau, 1942

Ong, Chit Chung, *Operation Matador, World War II: Britain's Attempt to Foil the Japanese Invasion of Malaya and Singapore*, Singapore: Marshall Cavendish Editions, 2011

Owen, D., *Anti-submarine Warfare: An Illustrated History*, Barnsley: Seaforth Publishing, 2007

Pfennigwerth, I., *Missing Pieces: The Intelligence Jigsaw and RAN Operations, 1939–71*, Canberra: Department of Defence, 2008

Powell, A., *War by Stealth: Australians and the Allied Intelligence Bureau, 1942–1945*, Melbourne: Melbourne University Press, 1996

Prados, J., *Combined Fleet Decoded: The Secret History of American Intelligence and the Japanese Navy in World War II*, New York: Random House, 1995

Prange, G.W., *At Dawn We Slept: The Untold Story of Pearl Harbor*, New York: McGraw Hill, 1981

Regan, A.J. & Griffen, H.M., *Bougainville Before the Conflict*, Canberra: ANU eBooks, Australian National University, 2015

Reid, A., *The Blood of the People: Revolution and the End of Traditional Rule in Northern Sumatra*, Singapore: NUS Press, National University of Singapore, 2014

Ricks, T.E., *The Generals: American Military Command from World War II to Today*, New York: Penguin Press, 2012

Roberts, A., *Masters and Commanders: How Roosevelt, Churchill, Marshall and Alanbrooke Won the War in the West*, London: Allen Lane, 2008

Robertson, J. & McCarthy, J., *Australian War Strategy 1939–1945: A Documentary History*, Brisbane: University of Queensland Press, 1985

Ross, A.T., *Armed and Ready: The Internal Industrial Development and Defence of Australia 1900–1945*, Turton & Armstrong, Sydney, 1995

Russell, B., Rempel, R.A. & Haslam, B., *Uncertain Paths to Freedom: Russia and China, 1919–1922*, London: Routledge, 2000

Schedvin, B., *Emissaries of Trade: A History of the Australian Trade Commissioner Service*, Canberra: Commonwealth of Australia, 2008

Shiraishi, S. & Shiraishi, T., *The Japanese in Colonial Southeast Asia*, Ithaca, New York: Cornell Press, 1993

Singh, S., *The Code Book: The Secret History of Codes and Code-Breaking*, London: Fourth Estate, 1999

Smith, M., *The Emperor's Codes: Bletchley Park and the Breaking of Japan's Secret Ciphers*, London: Bantam Press, 2000

Stockings, C.A.J., *The Making and Breaking of the Post-Federation Australian Army, 1901–09*, Canberra: Land Warfare Studies Centre, 2007

Sun Tzu, *The Art of War: The New Illustrated Edition*, trans. Samuel B. Griffith, Sydney: Duncan Baird Publishers, 2005

Tracy, N., *Collective Naval Defence of the Empire, 1900–1940*, Aldershot: Ashgate Publishing and the Naval Records Society, 1997

van Dijk, Kees, *The Netherlands Indies and the Great War, 1914–1918*, Leiden: KITLV Press, 2007

Wilkinson, N.J., *Secrecy and the Media: The Official History of the UK's D-Notice*, London: Routledge, 2009

Winton, J., *Ultra in the Pacific: How Breaking Japanese Codes and Ciphers Affected Naval Operations Against Japan*, London: Leo Cooper, 1993

Wood, W., *North Sea Fishers and Fighters*, London: Keegan Paul, Trench, Trübner & Co., 1911

Worth, R.H., *Secret Allies in the Pacific: Covert Intelligence and Code Breaking Prior to the Attack on Pearl Harbor*, Jefferson, North Carolina: McFarlane & Company Inc., 2002

Wurth, B., *1942: Australia's Greatest Peril*, Sydney: Pan Macmillan, 2008

Other online publications

Chamberlain, E.P., *Forgotten Men: Timorese in Special Operations during World War II*, monograph Point Lonsdale: Ernest Chamberlain, 2010, at www.scribd.com/doc/ 29688334/Forgotten-Men-Timorese-in-Special-Operations-during- World-War-II - scribd, accessed 15 August 2015

'Coastwatchers', Solomon Islands Historical Encyclopaedia 1893–1978, www. solomonencyclopaedia.net/biogs/E000068b.htm, accessed 28 March 2017

Ridges, Jim, 'The Japanese invasion of New Ireland 1942', People of the Plaque, www.jje.info/ lostlives/exhib/potp/japaneseinvasion.html, accessed 24 October 2016

Schoenherr, S.E., 'Recording technology history', International Audio Engineering Society, www.aes.org/aeshc/docs/recording.technology.history/notes.html, accessed 30 May 2016

'Sir Edward Victor Appleton', Electronics Notes, www.electronics-radio.com/articles/history/ pioneers/sir-edward-victor-appleton.php, accessed 30 May 2016

'Six ways to compute the relative value of Australian amounts, 1828 to the present', MeasuringWorth inflation calculator, www.measuringworth.com/australiacompare, accessed 14 April 2017

'Sydney University Union War Service Record, Ballantyne Simpson, William', 1916–19, Beyond 1914: The University of Sydney and the Great War, 2002–14, beyond1914.sydney. edu.au/media/cache/image_gallery/media/files/0001-jpg-37162.jpg, accessed 1 October 2016

'The Church of St Luke, Preston, in the County of Lancashire: Baptisms at St Luke in the Town of Preston, Baptisms recorded in the Register for the years 1859–1871', Lancashire Online Parish Clerks, www.lan-opc.org.uk/Preston/Preston/stluke/baptisms_1859-1871. html, accessed 27 November 2016

Wright, Ken, 'Read, Mason, Tashiro and the Bougainville mystery', PNGAA, 2009, www. pngaa.net/Library/Bougainville.htm, accessed 26 October 2016

www.bchg.org.au/index.php/en/people/individuals/a-f/66-john-fearnley, accessed 27 November 2016

INDEX

Note: Entries are filed word-by-word. All ranks, titles and honorifics are ignored in filing, as are leading articles and prepositions. Page numbers in *italics* refer to figures.